KING'S COLLEGE LONDON

MEDIEVAL STUDIES

VIII

King's College London
Centre for Late Antique and Medieval Studies

Director: Roy Wisbey

KING'S COLLEGE LONDON MEDIEVAL STUDIES

A CATALOGUE OF NAMES OF PERSONS IN THE GERMAN COURT EPICS

An Examination of the Literary Sources and
Dissemination, together with Notes on the Etymologies
of the More Important Names

by

FRANK W. CHANDLER

Edited with an Introduction and an Appendix
by

MARTIN H. JONES

King's College London

Centre for Late Antique and Medieval Studies

1992

ISSN 0953-217X

ISBN 0 9513085 7 2

British Library Cataloguing in Publication Data

Chandler, Frank W.
Catalogue of Names of Persons in the German Court epics: An
Examination of the literary Sources and Dissemination,
Together with Notes on the Etymologies of the More Important
Names. - (King's College London Medieval Studies Series,
ISSN 0953-217X)
I. Title. II. Jones, Martin H. III. Series
831.209

ISBN 0-9513085-7-2

Printed on

Acid-free long life paper

by

Short Run Press

Exeter

1992

CONTENTS

ACKNOWLEDGEMENTS

Mrs Hazel Chandler warmly welcomed the proposal to publish the thesis of her late husband, and the editor owes a special debt of gratitude to her for graciously granting permission to proceed. Mr W.G. Simpson, the University Librarian, and the staff of the Thesis Department of the University of London Library provided valuable assistance at the outset of the project, and Professor Roy Wisbey, Director of the Centre for Late Antique and Medieval Studies at King's College, ensured its progress by making available a grant from the Centre's funds to finance the retyping of the thesis on disk preparatory to the work of editing. Thanks are due also to the Editorial Board of King's College London Medieval Studies, and in particular to the Executive Editor, David Hook, for supporting the undertaking and accepting the volume for inclusion in their series. Computing facilities were provided by the Department of German, while the technical expertise required to master the finer points of preparing camera-ready copy was supplied by David Powell of the King's College Computing Centre, whose patient assistance it is a particular pleasure to acknowledge.

Department of German
King's College London

INTRODUCTION

The catalogue of personal names in the German court epics which is published here for the first time was compiled by the late Frank W. Chandler and submitted as his thesis for the M.A. degree of the University of London in May 1936. The catalogue comprises more than five and a half thousand names, including variants, drawn from sixty-one sources. The abstract which accompanies the thesis describes the scope of the study in the following terms:

'The Thesis consists of a complete list of names of persons who are mentioned in the German Court Epics, arranged in alphabetical order. The term "Court Epic" has been interpreted as widely as possible, embracing all poems which are of sufficient length to be called epics, from the fragments of *Graf Rudolf* to the fifteenth-century *Lorengel*, provided that such poems treat in some way or other with knights and their deeds. Although they cannot all be said to come within this definition, for the sake of greater completeness all versions of the *Alexanderlied* (excluding that of Lampreht) and all versions of the Trojan legend have been included.'

Conceptions of what constitutes courtly literature have changed since the 1930s, and the compiler of today might differ from Mr Chandler in deeming such terms of reference generous enough to take in not only Pfaffe Lamprecht's *Alexander*, but also Pfaffe Konrad's *Rolandslied* and some other reflexes of the Old French *chanson de geste* traditions concerning Charlemagne and Roland which likewise have not found a place here. There are, however, few further omissions to necessitate qualification of the claim that the catalogue provides coverage of that large body of longer verse narratives composed in German between the twelfth and fifteenth centuries which may be described as courtly and chivalric. Thus, in addition to the histories of Alexander and the versions of the Trojan legend that are specifically mentioned above, the sources include most notably the Arthurian, Grail, and Tristan romances, Heinrich von Veldeke's *Eneide*, the so-called romances of love and adventure, adaptations of parts of the Guillaume d'Orange cycle of *chansons de geste*, Ulrich von Liechtenstein's *Frauendienst*, and a number of courtly *Mären*. In its range, which encompasses several distinct narrative traditions in their entirety and a range of genres, the catalogue is without parallel in the German field.

The original thesis does not describe in detail the construction of the entries for the names listed in the catalogue, but the following observations, based on the experience of editing the text, will give users some guidance as to what it has to offer.

The names in the catalogue are ordered alphabetically in accordance with the principles set out in the next section 'The Arrangement of the Catalogue'. Names of identical form referring to different persons are distinguished by numbering (e.g. Heinrîch (1), Heinrîch (2), etc.). Where variants of a name occur, one form – usually the commonest, the best known, or the one appearing in the text in which the person of that name most prominently figures – is chosen as the headword for the main entry, and the variants (excluding those which differ from the 'standard' form only by the presence or absence of a final -*e* or -*s*) are listed in the appropriate alphabetical position with a cross-reference to the main entry. The use of the circumflex accent to indicate long vowels follows the practice of the editions cited; this may result in the inconsistent presentation of a name if it occurs in editions differing in this respect.

Each entry includes references to the text(s) in which the person of that name is to be found. The references are coded in such a way as to enable the user to ascertain not only the verse in which the name first occurs in a text, but also at what point the person first appears or is first mentioned by the author or by another character, if either of these does not coincide with the first naming. The information provided by this system of coding (for details of which, see 'The Arrangement of the Catalogue') is a particular strength of the catalogue, distinguishing it from the lists of names appended to the text in many editions, which indicate only the point(s) of naming.[1]

The information provided about the persons listed varies from case to case but may include any of the following:

- Titles, cognomens, and epithets occurring in the text(s). These are enclosed in single quotation marks and are usually placed immediately after the headword; titles are presented in normalized MHG.

- Brief details serving to identify biblical and historical persons where these are referred to or occur in a text or texts.

- Relationships to other characters in the work(s) – relatives, spouse, lover, lord, friends, etc.

- A brief description of the role that the person plays in the work(s) in which he or she occurs. In order to avoid repetition, cross-references are often made to other entries.

- Occurrences of the same person in works of other literatures, especially such as are actual or possible sources of the German works concerned. The form of the name and/or the role of the person in the other literature(s) may be noted.

- Consideration of the etymology of the name where this has been the subject of debate, with summaries of the views of the major commentators.

It will be apparent from the above account that the catalogue compiled by Mr Chandler consists of a great deal more than a list of names and references, useful as that would be in itself. As is implied in the work's subtitle, which is taken over from the original thesis, it includes information which can facilitate several kinds of literary enquiry. This makes the work comparable in conception to G.D. West's indexes of proper names in French Arthurian

---

[1] Also recorded are instances in which characters are mentioned or appear in a work but are not actually named, the description of the role that they play, their title, their family relationships, etc. serving as the means of identification. See, for example, the entries for Dalidâ and Îsolt (1).

literature and George T. Gillespie's catalogue of personal names in German heroic literature,[2] but whereas these excellent reference works are generally available and widely used, the catalogue of names in the German court epics has remained little known, being accessible in readily usable form only in the original typescript held by the University of London Library and a copy lodged at the University's Institute of Germanic Studies.[3] This is all the more regrettable in that readers of medieval German literature, unlike their counterparts in French, are not well served with reference works dealing with personal names.[4] Such aids as are available for German are concerned almost exclusively with individual works, above all those of Wolfram von Eschenbach, which have received comprehensive treatment in publications by Werner Schröder and Charles E. Passage.[5] For numerous works, on the other hand, nothing more is available than a list of names appended to the edition, and in some cases not even that. Among published studies, only the catalogue of George Gillespie extends beyond the confines of a single work or author to survey a whole literary tradition, providing a full account of the characters' literary appearances.[6] The advantages of such a holistic approach are particularly obvious in treating German heroic literature, where the original audiences of any individual work may be presumed to have been familiar with the characters' wider role in the tradition, but they are scarcely any less self-evident when dealing with courtly and chivalric works, for questions of one author's influence on another and of audiences' prior acquaintance with literary figures arise already at an early stage in the development of that body of literature and its constituent traditions.

---

2   G.D. West, *An Index of Proper Names in French Arthurian Verse Romances, 1150–1300*, University of Toronto Romance Series, 15 (Toronto, 1969); G.D. West, *An Index of Proper Names in French Arthurian Prose Romances*, University of Toronto Romance Series, 35 (Toronto, 1978); George T. Gillespie, *A Catalogue of Persons named in German Heroic Literature* (Oxford, 1973).

3   The condition of the original typescript does not permit satisfactory photocopies of the whole text to be made, and the only form in which copies have been made available by the University Library is on microfiches.

4   The position is surveyed by Kurt Gärtner, 'Vorschläge zur provisorischen Erschließung der Namen mittelhochdeutscher Texte', in *Namen in deutschen literarischen Texten des Mittelalters. Vorträge: Symposion Kiel, 9.–12.9.1987*, ed. by Friedhelm Debus and Horst Pütz, Kieler Beiträge zur deutschen Sprachgeschichte, 12 (Neumünster, 1989), pp. 147–60, see esp. pp. 147–50. Gärtner includes a brief description and appreciation of Chandler's thesis. Since Gärtner's account was written, there has been completed a lexicon of names in *Der Jüngere Titurel*: Klaus Zatloukal, 'Die Eigennamen im *Jüngeren Titurel*' (unpublished habilitation dissertation, University of Vienna, 1987). Announced for publication in 1992 is Werner Schröder, *Die Namen im 'Trojanerkrieg' Konrads von Würzburg*, Veröffentlichungen der Akademie der Wissenschaften und der Literatur, Mainz, Abhandlungen der Geistes- und sozialwissenschaftlichen Klasse, 1992,3 (Stuttgart: Franz Steiner Verlag). For French literary names there are available, in addition to West's Indexes, notably the studies by E. Langlois and L.-F. Flutre.

5   *The Middle High German Poem of Willehalm by Wolfram of Eschenbach*, transl. by Charles E. Passage (New York, 1977), pp. 318–404: List of 434 Proper Names in *Willehalm*; *Wolfram von Eschenbach: 'Willehalm'*, ed. by Werner Schröder (Berlin/New York, 1978), pp. 617–63: Register B. Die Namen; Werner Schröder, *Die Namen im 'Parzival' und im 'Titurel' Wolframs von Eschenbach* (Berlin/New York, 1982); Charles E. Passage, *Titurel: Wolfram of Eschenbach. Translation and Studies* (New York, 1984), pp. 157–220: List of 57 Proper Names in Wolfram's *Titurel*.

6   Professor Gillespie's work too began life in studies for a higher degree (doctorate) of the University of London, under the direction of Professor Frederick Norman at King's College. This was some years after the completion of Mr Chandler's thesis.

There is at least one project currently being undertaken which promises to place the study of names in medieval German literature on the comprehensive and secure footing that it requires. This is the compilation of a lexicon of literary names in medieval German texts (Old and Middle High German) which is proceeding at the University of Kiel.[7] The scale of this project is, however, such that it will, it seems, be many years before this highly desirable research tool is generally available.[8] In the situation in which scholarship finds itself at present it is recognized that it is expedient to make the best possible use of the resources which are already in existence,[9] and it is in this spirit that the decision was taken to publish Mr Chandler's catalogue of names.

It was clear from the outset that, in preparing the work for publication, a thoroughgoing revision of the entire text of the catalogue should not be undertaken: the appearance of the volume would have been very considerably delayed in return for gains which were of uncertain value, spot checks having confirmed the conscientiousness with which the work had in general been done in the first place. Nor was it felt necessary to substitute more recent editions of the texts examined, where they exist, for those originally used, since verse numbering rarely differs significantly from one edition to the next and most potential users of the catalogue will have access to libraries holding the editions to which reference is made. The text appears, therefore, essentially as in the original typescript. This means that certain perceptions, widely held at the time of composition but no longer subscribed to, remain. These include literary judgements which, where they are not the individual view of the compiler, reflect the state of scholarship at the time. Furthermore, and most strikingly, references to the texts are as a rule listed in an order conforming to a view of the chronology of their composition which is in certain respects not that of today. This is evident above all in the presentation of works of the Arthurian tradition. Readers may refer to the entry for Artûs for details of the (approximate) chronology which was employed.

While the text is reproduced essentially in unaltered form, it would have been no service either to the memory of the original compiler or to users of the catalogue to have left uncorrected such errors and omissions as were detected in preparing the text for publication, or to refrain from making certain changes in the interests of efficient presentation.

---

7   For a description of this project, see Friedhelm Debus,'Über ein entstehendes Lexikon der literarischen Namen in deutschen Texten des Mittelalters', in *Namen in deutschen literarischen Texten des Mittelalters* (as note 4 above), pp. 271–86; see also the contribution by Horst Pütz on technical aspects of the project in the same volume.

8   See the judgement of Kurt Gärtner in the essay referred to in note 4 above: 'Da in absehbarer Zeit weder ein umfassendes mhd. Namenwörterbuch zu erwarten ist noch ein neues großes mhd. Wörterbuch, in dem vermutlich die Namen ebenso ausgespart sein würden wie im neuen "Althochdeutschen Wörterbuch", bleibt die Situation dessen, der lexikographischen Rat sucht, auf Jahre hinaus unbefriedigend' (p.151).

9   See the hope expressed by Werner Schröder in *Die Namen im 'Parzival' und im 'Titurel'* (as in note 5 above), p. XXVIII, and the considerations which led Kurt Gärtner, in the essay already cited, to propose the creation of a 'Namenfindebuch' which would facilitate use of the name lists which have already been published.

Accordingly, corrections and other editorial interventions have been undertaken (and, where appropriate, marked) as follows:

- The entries in the Bibliography have been revised to conform as far as possible to modern standards of reference. Some items which originally appeared only in the footnotes have been added to the Bibliography, making it a consolidated record of the literature consulted.

- Footnote references to primary and secondary literature have been abbreviated to include in general only the author's name and the relevant pages, full details of each item being recoverable from the Bibliography.

- Obvious typing errors and solecisms have been corrected; some archaisms have been replaced; and minor adjustments have been made in verse references where they would help to locate the persons referred to more directly. Such changes are not marked.

- In the few instances where references to specific texts had been omitted, these have been supplied, the whole reference – the abbreviated title and the verse number – being enclosed in square brackets, e.g. [GT 5672].

- In cases where the verse reference was noticed to be inaccurate, this has been corrected and has alone been enclosed in square brackets, e.g. W [nm8,2].

- Where, in the body of an entry, it was thought helpful to add a verse reference to pinpoint the passage being discussed, this also has been placed in square brackets.

- Where a new entry has been made, the headword is preceded by an asterisk. Such entries serve chiefly to register variants of names which are already recorded elsewhere, and they consist of a cross-reference to the main entry (see e.g. *Ylmot). The works of Wolfram von Eschenbach are referred to in the editions of Albert Leitzmann, and some names appear in the catalogue in a form which may not be readily identifiable by all users with the form which they have in the more widely read sixth edition of the complete works of Wolfram by Karl Lachmann (Berlin/Leipzig, 1926, frequently reprinted) or in the edition of *Willehalm* by Werner Schröder (Berlin/New York,1978); in such instances a new entry has been made, with the Lachmann or Schröder form as the headword, preceded by an asterisk, and a cross-reference to the existing entry (see e.g. *Kahenîs (2) and *Castable). In the very few instances detected of a name having been overlooked altogether, this has been supplied and the headword of the new entry is similarly preceded by an asterisk, e.g. *Sar.

- Where the substance of an entry has been altered in any way, either to correct a factual error or to incorporate additional information, this has been indicated at the end of the entry by an obelus enclosed in square brackets [†].

- For the most part the amendments which had to be made in the substance of entries concerned matters of detail and could be readily accommodated within the existing text. There were, however, a number of instances of a more complex nature which deserved some comment, and these are dealt with in an appendix to be found at the end of the volume; the relevant entries in the catalogue refer the reader to this appendix.

Working on the catalogue over a period of some time has been an instructive experience, not the least part of it being the reminder of what earlier generations of scholars were able to achieve without access to technical aids which the compiler of today would think indispensable. Close reading of the texts and methodical procedures, even if they involved nothing more sophisticated in the nature of hardware than index cards, could yield impressive results. The material gathered in this way is rich in possibilities. The entries for individual names may be found to establish new connections, extending in unsuspected directions the range of texts in which a character appears, and thus may help in the construction of a fuller picture of that character's literary existence and of the continuities of the literary tradition. Individual authors can be seen to display a personal signature in their preference for names of a certain formational type or of a particular origin. Clusters of names emerge as distinctive for specific kinds of subject, irrespective of the authors dealing with them. Cumulatively, the entries convey an impression of the diversity of the names and, already implicit in them but reinforced by the summaries of action, of the themes which characterize this literature and which show how wide were the boundaries of the imaginative and intellectual world with which it made courtly and chivalric society familiar. In the fullness of time this catalogue will no doubt be superseded by the fruits of more extensive projects undertaken in circumstances more propitious than those of 1936; in the meantime, it is hoped that its publication, though delayed by more than half a century, will help to further the study of a corpus of texts which continues to occupy a central place in our interest in the medieval phase of the history of German literature.

THE ARRANGEMENT OF THE CATALOGUE

The arrangement of the names in the catalogue is alphabetical, subject to the following modifications:

F, Pf, Ph	are treated throughout as identical with V;
Y	is treated as identical with I;
I	between vowels and initially before a vowel is treated as identical with J;
C	before *e* and *i* is treated as identical with Z; in all other positions, as identical with K.

Long vowels are indicated by use of the circumflex accent in accordance with the practice of the editions cited; vowel length has no effect on the alphabetical arrangement of the names.
Variants of a person's name are not noted when they differ from the form used as the headword in the main entry only by the presence or absence of final *-e* or *-s*. The inflexional *-n* is omitted throughout.

References to the works in which a name occurs are coded in accordance with the following scheme:

m	precedes the number of the line in which a character is first mentioned, either by the author or by another character, before being named (or, under certain circumstances, without being named in the work in question);
a	precedes the number of the line in which a character first appears;
n	precedes the number of the line in which a character is first named, having previously appeared or been mentioned;
nm	precedes the number of the line in which a character's name is mentioned for the first time;
no letter	precedes the number of the line in which a character, not previously mentioned, is named immediately on appearance.

Where all references in respect of a particular name are 'nm', this is placed *before* the first reference only.

Editorial interventions are marked in the following ways:

[ ]	enclose references which have been supplied or corrected;
*	precedes the headword of a new entry;
[†]	is placed at the end of an entry whose substance has been altered.

(Further information on corrections and editorial interventions is given in the Introduction.)

THE SOURCES
EDITIONS AND ABBREVIATIONS*

A   *Alexander.* Rudolf von Ems, *Alexander*, ed. by V. Junk (Leipzig, 1928–29)

AM   *Abor und das Meerweib.* (Meyer-Benfey, pp. 188–91)

AP   *Athis und Prophilias.* (Kraus, 2nd edn)
           Fragments: A, Ab, Ac, Ad, Ae, A*, A**, B, C, C*, D, E, F

Blan   *Blanschandin.* (Meyer-Benfey, pp. 164–74)
           Fragments: I, II, III

C   *Crône.* Heinrich von dem Türlîn, *Diu Crône*, ed. by G.H.F. Scholl (Stuttgart, 1852)

Crane   *Crane.* Berthold von Holle, *Demantin, Crane, Darifant*, ed. by K. Bartsch (Nürnberg, 1858)

Dar   *Darifant.* See *Crane.*

DB   *Daniel von dem Blühenden Tal.* Der Stricker, *Daniel von dem Blühenden Tal*, ed. by G. Rosenhagen (Breslau, 1894)

Dem   *Demantin.* Berthold von Holle, *Demantin*, ed. by K. Bartsch (Tübingen, 1875)

E   *Erec.* Hartmann von Aue, *Erec – Iwein*, ed. by H. Naumann and H. Steinger (Leipzig, 1933)

Ed   *Eneide.* Heinrich von Veldeke, *Eneide*, ed. by O. Behaghel (Heilbronn, 1882)

Edol   *Edolanz.* (Meyer-Benfey, pp. 154–59)

Eng   *Engelhard.* Konrad von Würzburg, *Engelhard*, ed. by P. Gereke (Halle, 1912)

ET   Eilhart's *Tristrant.* Eilhart von Oberge, *Tristrant*, ed. by F. Lichtenstein (Straßburg, 1877)

FB   *Flore und Blanscheflur.* Konrad Fleck, *Flore und Blanscheflur*, ed. by E. Sommer (Quedlinburg/Leipzig, 1846)

FD   *Frauendienst.* Ulrich von Liechtenstein, *Frauendienst*, ed. by R. Bechstein (Leipzig, 1888)

FS   *Friedrich von Schwaben. Friedrich von Schwaben*, ed. by M.H. Jellinek (Berlin, 1904)

G   *Garel.* Der Pleier, *Garel von dem blüenden Tal*, ed. by M. Walz (Freiburg im Breisgau, 1892)

GM   *Gauriel von Muntabel. Gauriel von Muntabel*, ed. by F. Khull (Graz, 1885)

GR   *Graf Rudolf.* (Kraus, 1st edn, pp. 54–71)
           Fragments: A–K and α, αb, β, βb, γ, γb, δ, δb

GT   *Gottweiger Trojanerkrieg. Der Gottweiger Trojanerkrieg*, ed. by A. Koppitz (Berlin, 1926)

---

*   For full details of the editions used, see Bibliography, pp. xxiff.

HK	Heinrich von Kempten. Konrad von Würzburg, *Kleinere Dichtungen*, ed. by E. Schröder (Berlin, 1924), vol. I, pp. 41–68
HT	Heinrich's *Tristan*. Heinrich von Freiberg, *Tristan*, ed. by R. Bechstein (Leipzig, 1877)
I	*Iwein*. Hartmann von Aue, *Erec – Iwein*, ed. by H. Naumann and H. Steinger (Leipzig, 1933)
JT	*Der Jüngere Titurel*. Albrecht, *Der Jüngere Titurel*, ed. by K.A. Hahn (Quedlinburg/Leipzig, 1842)
KT	*Königstochter von Frankreich*. Hans von Bühel, *Königstochter von Frankreich*, ed. by J.F.L.T. Merzdorf (Oldenburg, 1867)
L	*Lanzelet*. Ulrich von Zatzikhoven, *Lanzelet*, ed. by K.A. Hahn (Frankfurt, 1845)
Ll	*Lorengel*. *Lorengel*, ed. by E. Steinmeyer (*ZfdA*, 15 (1872), 181–244) (MS W). The Kolmarer MS (MS K) readings are given as Lesarten to *Ll*.
Loh	*Lohengrin*. *Lohengrin*, ed. by H. Rückert (Quedlinburg/Leipzig, 1858)
LT	*Liet von Troye*. Herbort von Fritslâr, *Liet von Troye*, ed. by G.K. Frommann (Quedlinburg/Leipzig, 1837)
M	*Meleranz*. Der Pleier, *Meleranz*, ed. by K. Bartsch (Stuttgart, 1861)
MA	*Manuel und Amande*. (Meyer-Benfey, pp. 160–63)
MB	*Mai und Beaflor*. *Mai und Beaflor*, ed. by A.J. Vollmer (Leipzig, 1848)
MC	*Moriz von Craon*. *Zwei altdeutsche Rittermæren. Moriz von Craon. Peter von Staufenberg*, ed. by E. Schröder, 3rd edn (Berlin, 1920)
Mer	*Merlin*. Albrecht von Scharfenberg, *Merlin und Seifrid de Ardemont*, ed. by F. Panzer (Tübingen, 1902)
Mtl	*Der Mantel*. Heinrich von dem Türlîn, *Der Mantel*, ed. by O. Warnatsch (Breslau, 1883)
NRFB	*Das niederrheinische Flore und Blanscheflur*. *Floyris*, ed. by E. Steinmeyer (*ZfdA*, 21 (1877), 307–31)
P	*Parzival*. Wolfram von Eschenbach, *Parzival*, ed. by A. Leitzmann (Halle (Saale)) Books I–VI, 3rd edn, 1928 Books VII–XI, 2nd edn, 1926 Books XII–XVI, 1st edn, 1903
PM	*Partonopier und Meliur*. Konrad von Würzburg, *Partonopier und Meliur*, ed. by K. Bartsch (Vienna, 1871)
Port	*Portimunt*. (Kraus, 2nd edn, pp. 162–67)
PS	*Peter von Staufenberg*. *Zwei altdeutsche Rittermæren. Moriz von Craon. Peter von Staufenberg*, ed. by E. Schröder, 3rd edn (Berlin, 1920)
R	*Rennewart* (Nabburger Fragments). Ulrich von Türheim, *Rennewart, deutsches Gedicht des 13. Jahrhunderts. Nabburger Bruchstücke*, ed. by K. Roth (Regensburg, 1856) Fragments: Eingang zu Blatt I (= Eing. I), Blatt I (= Bl. I), Fortsetzung I (=

Forts. I), Eingang zu Blatt II (= Eing. II), Blatt II (= Bl. II), Blatt III (= Bl. III), Fortsetzung II (= Forts. II)

RB   *Reinfrid von Braunschweig. Reinfrid von Braunschweig*, ed. by K. Bartsch (Tübingen, 1871)

RP   *Rapoltsteiner Parzifal.* Claus Wisse and Philipp Colin, *Parzifal*, ed. by K. Schorbach (Straßburg, 1888)

RW   Rudolf's *Willehalm.* Rudolf von Ems, *Willehalm von Orlens*, ed. by V. Junk (Berlin, 1905)

S   *Segremors.* (Meyer-Benfey pp.175–87)
       Fragments: I^a, I^b, II, III

SA   Seifrit's *Alexander.* Seifrit, *Alexander*, ed. by P. Gereke (Berlin, 1932)

Sey   *Seifrid de Ardemont.* Albrecht von Scharfenberg, *Merlin und Seifrid de Ardemont*, ed. by F. Panzer (Tübingen, 1902)

T   *Titurel.* Wolfram von Eschenbach, *Titurel*, ed. by A. Leitzmann, 2nd edn (Halle (Saale), 1926)

TF   *Tandareis und Flordibel.* Der Pleier, *Tandareis und Flordibel*, ed. by F. Khull (Graz, 1885)

Tirol   *Tirol.* (Meyer-Benfey pp. 149–53)
       Fragments: A–H

TK   *Der Trojanische Krieg.* Konrad von Würzburg, *Der Trojanische Krieg*, ed. by A. von Keller (Stuttgart, 1858)

Tn   *Tristan.* Gottfried von Straßburg, *Tristan*, ed. by R. Bechstein, 4th edn (Leipzig, 1923)

UA   Ulrich's *Alexander.* Ulrich von Eschenbach, *Alexander*, ed. by W. Toischer (Tübingen, 1888)

UT   Ulrich's *Tristan.* Ulrich von Türheim, *Tristan*, ed. by E. von Groote, in *Tristan von Meister Gotfrit von Straszburg mit der Fortsetzung des Meisters Ulrich von Turheim* (Berlin, 1821)

UW   Ulrich's *Willehalm.* Ulrich von dem Türlin, *Willehalm*, ed. by S. Singer (Prague, 1893)

W   *Willehalm.* Wolfram von Eschenbach, *Willehalm*, ed. by A. Leitzmann, 2nd edn (Halle (Saale), 1926–28)

WA   *Wernigeroder Alexander. Der Große Alexander aus der Wernigeroder Handschrift*, ed. by G. Guth (Berlin, 1908)

Wigl   *Wigalois.* Wirnt von Gravenberg, *Wigalois*, ed. by J.M.N. Kapteyn (Bonn, 1926)

Wigm   *Wigamur.* F.H. von der Hagen and J.G. Büsching, *Deutsche Gedichte des Mittelalters*, I, (Berlin, 1808), and Kraus, 2nd edn, pp. 109–61

WO   *Wilhalm von Österreich.* Johann von Würzburg, *Wilhelm von Österreich*, ed. by E. Regel (Berlin, 1906)

WW   *Wilhelm von Wenden*. Ulrich von Eschenbach, *Wilhelm von Wenden*, ed. by W. Toischer (Prague, 1876)

BIBLIOGRAPHY

1. ABBREVIATIONS

Bibl.d.ges.dt.Nat.-Lit.	Bibliothek der gesamten deutschen National-Literatur von der ältesten bis auf die neuere Zeit
CFMA	Les Classiques Français du Moyen Age
DDM	Deutsche Dichtungen des Mittelalters
DTM	Deutsche Texte des Mittelalters
Germ.	*Germania. Vierteljahresschrift für deutsche Altertumskunde*
PBB	*Beiträge zur Geschichte der deutschen Sprache und Literatur*
QF	Quellen und Forschungen zur Sprach- und Kulturgeschichte der germanischen Völker
SATF	Société des Anciens Textes Français
StLV	Bibliothek des Stuttgarter Litterarischen Vereins
ZfdA	*Zeitschrift für deutsches Altertum und deutsche Literatur*
ZffSL	*Zeitschrift für französische Sprache und Literatur*
ZfromPh	*Zeitschrift für romanische Philologie*

2. EDITIONS AND SECONDARY LITERATURE

Abor und das Meerweib. See Meyer-Benfey, pp. 188–91.

Albrecht, *Der Jüngere Titurel*, ed. by K.A. Hahn, Bibl.d.ges.dt.Nat.-Lit., 24 (Quedlinburg/Leipzig, 1842)

Albrecht von Scharfenberg, *Merlin und Seifrid de Ardemont*, ed. by F. Panzer, StLV, 227, (Tübingen, 1902)

Alexander und Antiloie. See Haupt and Hoffman, I, pp. 250–66.

Aliscans, ed. by F. Guessard (Paris, 1870)

———— ed. by E. Wienbeck, W. Hartnacke, P. Rasch (Halle (Saale), 1903)

Amis and Amiloun, ed. by E. Kölbing, Altenglische Bibliothek, 2 (Heilbronn, 1884)

Amis et Amiles, ed. by K. Hofmann (Erlangen, 1882)

Arrianus, *Reliqua Arriani et Scriptorum de Rebus Alexandri M. Fragmenta*, ed. by C. Müller (Paris, 1846)

Athis et Prophilias, Li Romanz d', ed. by A. Hilka, Gesellschaft für romanische Literatur, 29 and 40, 2 vols (Dresden, 1912–16)

Athis und Prophilias. See Kraus, 2nd edn, pp. 63–82.

Bächtold, J., *Der Lanzelet des Ulrich von Zatzikhoven* (Frauenfeld, 1870)

Bacon, S.A., *The Source of Wolfram's 'Willehalm'*, Sprache und Dichtung, 4 (Tübingen, 1910)

Baist, G., 'Oliverus daemon', *ZfromPh*, 18 (1894), 274–76

Bartsch, K. [= Bartsch (1)], 'Über Christian's von Troies und Hartmann's von Aue Erec und Enide', *Germ.*, 7 (1862), 141–85

Bartsch, K. [= Bartsch (2)], 'Die Eigennamen in Wolframs *Parzival* und *Titurel*', in Karl Bartsch, *Germanistische Studien*, vol. II (Vienna, 1875), pp. 114–59

Bataille Loquifer I, La, ed. by J. Runeberg (Helsinki, 1913)

Bauer, 'Zur Namenforschung', *Germ.*, 18 (1873), 214–15

Bédier, J., *Les Légendes Épiques*, 2nd edn, 4 vols (Paris, 1914–21)

Benoît de Sainte-Maure, *Le Roman de Troie*, ed. by L. Constans, SATF, 6 vols. (Paris, 1904–12)

Berthold von Holle, *Demantin, Crane, Darifant*, ed. by K. Bartsch (Nürnberg, 1858)

———— *Demantin*, ed. by K. Bartsch, StLV, 123 (Tübingen, 1875)

———— *Crane*, ed. by W. Müller, *ZfdA*, 1 (1841), 57–95

———— *Darifant*, in *Symbolae ad Literaturam Teutonicam antiquiorem*, ed. by E. Nyerup (Copenhagen, 1787), col. 83–92

Bethmann, J., *Untersuchungen über die mittelhochdeutsche Dichtung vom Grafen Rudolf*, Palaestra, XXX (Berlin, 1904)

Birlinger, A., 'Beiträge zur Kunde mittelalterlicher Personennamen aus mittelrheinischen Urkunden', *ZfdA*, 32 (1888), 128–37

Blanschandin. See Meyer-Benfey, pp. 164–74.

Braune, W., *Althochdeutsches Lesebuch*, 9th edn (Halle (Saale), 1928)

Bruce, J.D. [= Bruce (1)], *The Evolution of Arthurian Romance from the Beginnings down to the Year 1300*, Hesperia, Ergänzungsreihe, 8–9, 2nd edn, 2 vols (Göttingen, 1928)

Bruce, J.D. [= Bruce (2)], 'Arthuriana', *Romanic Review*, 3 (1912), 173–93

Brugger, E. [= Brugger (1)], 'Ein Beitrag zur arthurischen Namenforschung: Alain de Gomeret', in *Aus romanischen Sprachen und Literaturen: Festschrift Heinrich Morf* (Halle (Saale), 1905), pp. 53–96

Brugger, E. [= Brugger (2)], 'Beiträge zur Erklärung der arthurischen Geographie. II: Gorre', *ZffSL*, 28 (1905), 1–71

Callisthenes. See Pseudo-Callisthenes.

Chançun de Willame, La, ed. by E.S. Tyler (New York, 1919)

Chancun de Willame, La (Chiswick Press, London, 1903)

Chestre, Thomas, *Launfal*, in *Ancient Engleish Metrical Romanceës*, ed. by J. Ritson, 3 vols (London, 1802), I, pp. 170–215

Chevalier à l'Épée, Le, ed. by E.C. Armstrong (Baltimore, 1900)

Chevalier au Cygne et de Godefroid de Bouillon, La Chanson du, ed. by C. Hippeau (Paris, 1874)

Chrestien de Troyes, *Erec und Enide*, ed. by W. Foerster, Romanische Bibliothek, 13, 2nd edn (Halle (Saale), 1909)

—— *Der Löwenritter (Yvain)*, ed. by W. Foerster, *Christian von Troyes sämtliche erhaltene Werke*, vol. 2 (Halle (Saale), 1887)

—— *Der Karrenritter (Lancelot)*, ed. by W. Foerster, *Christian von Troyes sämtliche erhaltene Werke*, vol. 4 (Halle (Saale), 1899)

—— *Der Percevalroman (Li Contes del Graal)*, ed. by A. Hilka, *Christian von Troyes sämtliche erhaltene Werke*, vol. 5 (Halle (Saale), 1932)

Collatio Alexandri cum Dindimo, rege Bragmanorum, per litteras facta. See Valerius, pp. 170–89.

Comparetti, D., *Vergil in the Middle Ages*, 2nd edn (London, 1908)

Cross, T.P. and Nitze, W.A., *Lancelot and Guenevere* (Chicago, 1930)

Curtius Rufus, Q., *Historiarum Alexandri Magni Macedonis Libri qui supersunt*, ed. by E. Hedicke (Leipzig, 1908)

Dares Phrygius, *De Excidio Troiae Historia*, ed. by F. Meister (Leipzig, 1873)

Deutsches Heldenbuch, 5 vols
    I, ed. by O. Jänicke (Berlin, 1866)
    II, ed. by E. Martin (Berlin, 1866)
    III, ed. by A. Amelung and O. Jänicke (Berlin, 1871)
    IV, ed. by A. Amelung and O. Jänicke (Berlin, 1873)
    V, ed. by J. Jupitza (Berlin, 1870)

Dictys Cretensis, *Ephemeridos Belli Troiani*, ed. by F. Meister (Leipzig, 1872)

Du Cange, C. D., *Glossarium mediae et infimae latinitatis*, 7 vols (Paris, 1840–50)

Dunger, H., *Die Sage vom trojanischen Kriege* (Leipzig, 1869)

Edolanz. See Meyer-Benfey, pp. 154–59.

Ehrismann, G., *Geschichte der deutschen Literatur bis zum Ausgang des Mittelalters*, 4 vols (Munich, 1918–35)

Eilhart von Oberge, *Tristrant*, ed. by F. Lichtenstein, QF, 19 (Straßburg, 1877)

Elster, E., 'Beiträge zur Kritik des Lohengrin', *PBB*, 10 (1885), 81–194

Encyclopaedia Britannica, 14th edn (London/New York, 1929)

Eneas, ed. by J.-J. Salverda de Grave, CFMA, 44 and 62, 2 vols (Paris, 1925–29)

Entwistle, W.J., *The Arthurian Legend in the Literatures of the Spanish Peninsula* (London/Toronto, 1925)

Epistola Alexandri ad Aristotelem, magistrum suum, de itinere suo et de situ Indiae. See Valerius, pp. 190–221.

Ersch, J.S. and Gruber, J.G., *Allgemeine Encyklopädie der Wissenschaften und Künste*, Sektion II, Theil 37 (Leipzig, 1885)

Expeditio Alexandri. See Arrianus.

Fleck, Konrad, *Flore und Blanscheflur*, ed. by E. Sommer, Bibl.d.ges.dt.Nat.-Lit., 12 (Quedlinburg/Leipzig, 1846)

Floyris, ed. by E. Steinmeyer, *ZfdA*, 21 (1877), 307–31

Förstemann, E., *Altdeutsches Namenbuch*, 2 vols
    Vol. I, 2nd edn (Bonn, 1900)
    Vol. II, 3rd edn (Bonn, 1913–16)

Freymond, E. [= Freymond (1)], 'Beiträge zur Kenntnis der altfranzösischen Artusromane in Prosa', *ZffSL*, 17 (1895), 1–128

Freymond, E. [= Freymond (2)], 'Artus' Kampf mit dem Katzenungetüm', in *Beiträge zur romanischen Philologie: Festgabe für Gustav Gröber* (Halle (Saale), 1899), pp. 311–96

Friedrich von Schwaben, ed. by M.H. Jellinek, DTM, 1 (Berlin, 1904)

Füetrer, Ulrich, *Prosaroman von Lanzelot*, ed. by A. Peter, StLV, 175 (Tübingen, 1885)

Gauriel von Muntabel, ed. by F. Khull (Graz, 1885)

Geoffrey of Monmouth, *Histories of the Kings of Britain* (London/Toronto, 1928)

Geoffrey of Monmouth, *The Historia Regum Britanniae*, ed. by A. Griscom (London/New York/Toronto, 1929)

Gerbert de Montreuil, *La Continuation de Perceval*, ed. by M. Williams (Paris, 1922)

Godefroy, F., *Dictionnaire de l'ancienne langue française*, 10 vols (Paris, 1880–1902)

Golther, W. [= Golther (1)], *Parzival und der Gral* (Stuttgart, 1925)

Golther, W. [= Golther (2)], *Tristan und Isolde* (Leipzig, 1907)

Golther, W. [= Golther (3)], *Die deutsche Dichtung im Mittelalter*, Epochen der deutschen Literatur, 1 (Stuttgart, 1922)

Gottfried von Straßburg, *Tristan und Isolde*, transl. by W. Hertz (Stuttgart, 1877)

————— *Tristan*, ed. by R. Bechstein, Deutsche Classiker des Mittelalters, 7–8, 4th edn, 2 vols (Leipzig, 1923)

Gottweiger Trojanerkrieg, Der, ed. by A. Koppitz, DTM, 29 (Berlin, 1926)

G.P. See Paris, G.

Graf Rudolf. See Kraus, 1st edn, pp. 54–71.

Greif, W., *Die mittelalterlichen Bearbeitungen der Trojanersage*, Ausgaben und Abhandlungen aus dem Gebiete der romanischen Philologie, 61 (Marburg, 1886)

Griffin, N.E., *Dares and Dictys* (Baltimore, 1907)

Grimm, J., 'Tyrol und Fridebrant', *ZfdA*, 1 (1841), 7–20

Grimm, J., 'Über eine Urkunde des XII. Jahrhunderts', in Jacob Grimm, *Kleinere Schriften*, vol. II (Berlin, 1865), pp. 333–65

Grimm, W., 'Bruchstücke aus einem Gedicht von Assundin', in *Archiv für Geschichte und Alterthumskunde Westphalens*, ed. by P. Wigand (Lemgo, 1829)

Große Alexander aus der Wernigeroder Handschrift, Der, ed. by G. Guth, DTM, 13 (Berlin, 1908)

Gualterus, M. Philippus, *Alexandreis*, ed. by F.A.W. Mueldener (Leipzig, 1863)

Hagen, F.H. von der, *Gesammtabenteuer*, 3 vols (Stuttgart/Tübingen, 1850)

Hagen, F.H. von der, *Minnesinger*, parts 1–4 (Leipzig, 1838)

Hans von Bühel, *Königstochter von Frankreich*, ed. by J.F.L.T. Merzdorf (Oldenburg, 1867)

Hartmann von Aue, *Erec – Iwein*, ed. by H. Naumann and H. Steinger, Deutsche Literatur, Reihe 3: Höfische Dichtung, 3 (Leipzig, 1933)

Haupt, M. and Hoffmann, H., *Altdeutsche Blätter*, 2 vols (Leipzig, 1836–40)

Heinrich von Freiberg, *Tristan*, ed. by R. Bechstein, DDM, 5 (Leipzig, 1877)

Heinrich von Neustadt, *Apollonius*, ed. by J. Strobl (Vienna, 1875)

――― *Apollonius von Tyrland*, ed. by S. Singer, DTM, 7 (Berlin, 1906)

Heinrich von dem Türlîn, *Diu Crône*, ed. by G.H.F. Scholl, StLV, 27 (Stuttgart, 1852)

――― *Der Mantel*, ed. by O. Warnatsch, Germanistische Abhandlungen, 2 (Breslau, 1883)

Heinrich von Veldeke, *Eneide*, ed. by O. Behaghel (Heilbronn, 1882)

Heinrichs, R., *Die Lohengrin-Dichtung und ihre Deutung*, Frankfurter Zeitgemässe Broschüren, 24 (Hamm i.W., 1905)

Herbort von Fritslâr, *Liet von Troye*, ed. by G.K. Frommann, Bibl.d.ges.dt.Nat.-Lit., 5 (Quedlinburg/Leipzig, 1837)

Hertz, W., *Aristoteles in den Alexanderdichtungen des Mittelalters*, Abhandlungen der Philosophisch-Philologischen Classe der Königlichen Bayerischen Akademie der Wissenschaften, 29 (München, 1892)

Historia Scholastica. See Petrus Comestor.

Hofstäter, F.F., *Altdeutsche Gedichte aus den Zeiten der Tafelrunde*, 2 parts (Vienna, 1811)

Homer, *Iliad*, ed. by T.W. Allen, 3 vols (Oxford, 1931)

――― *Iliad*, ed. by A.T. Murray, 2 vols (London/New York, 1924–25)

――― *Odyssey*, ed. by A.T. Murray, 2 vols (London/New York, 1919)

Hyginus, *Fabulae*, ed. by M. Schmidt (Jena, 1872)

Hystory herzen Tristrants und der schenen Ysalden, Die (Augsburg, 1498)

International Standard Bible Encyclopaedia, ed. by J. Orr, 5 vols (Chicago, 1930)

Johann von Würzburg, *Wilhelm von Österreich*, ed. by E. Regel, DTM, 3 (Berlin, 1906)

Joseph, E., 'Dares Phrygius als Quelle für die Briseida-Episode im Roman de Troie des Benoit de Sainte-More', *ZfromPh*, 8 (1884), 117–19

Kölbing, E., 'Zur Überlieferung und Quelle des mittelenglischen Gedichtes: Lybeaus Disconus', *Englische Studien*, 1 (1877), 121–69

Konrad, Pfaffe, *Das Rolandslied*, ed. by C. Wesle, Rheinische Beiträge und Hülfsbücher zur germanischen Philologie und Volkskunde, 15 (Bonn, 1928)

Konrad von Würzburg, *Kleinere Dichtungen*, ed. by E. Schröder, 3 vols (Berlin, 1924–26)

——— *Partonopier und Meliur*, ed. by K. Bartsch (Vienna, 1871)

——— *Der Trojanische Krieg*, ed. by A. von Keller, StLV, 44 (Stuttgart, 1858)

——— *Engelhard*, ed. by P. Gereke (Halle (Saale), 1912)

Kraus, C. von, *Mittelhochdeutsches Übungsbuch*, Germanische Bibliothek, I. Sammlung, III. Reihe, 2ter Band, 1st edn (Heidelberg, 1912), 2nd edn (Heidelberg, 1926)

Kreuzfahrt des Landgrafen Ludwigs des Frommen von Thüringen, Die, ed. by H. Naumann, Monumenta Germaniae Historica, Deutsche Chroniken, IV, 2 (Berlin, 1923)

Lamprecht, Pfaffe, *Alexanderlied*, ed. and transl. by R.E. Ottmann (Halle (Saale), [n.d.])

——— *Alexander*, ed. by K. Kinzel, Germanistische Handbibliothek, 6 (Halle (Saale), 1884)

Lancelot, Roman van, ed. by W.J.A. Jonckbloet, 2 parts ('s-Gravenhage, 1846–49)

Langlois, E., *Table des noms propres de toute nature compris dans les chansons de geste imprimées* (Paris, 1904)

Lempriere, J., *Classical Dictionary*, 4th edn (London, 1843)

Leo, Archipresbyter, *Der Alexanderroman*, ed. by F. Pfister, Sammlung mittellateinischer Texte, 6 (Heidelberg, 1913)

Lexer, M., *Mittelhochdeutsches Handwörterbuch*, 3 vols (Leipzig, 1872–78)

Libeaus Desconus, ed. by M. Kaluza, Altenglische Bibliothek, 5 (Leipzig, 1890)

Lohengrin, ed. by H. Rückert, Bibl.d.ges.dt.Nat.-Lit., 36 (Quedlinburg/Leipzig, 1858)

Lorengel, ed. by E. Steinmeyer, *ZfdA*, 15 (1872), 181–244

Löseth, E., *Le Roman en Prose de Tristan, le Roman de Palamède et la compilation de Rusticien de Pise*, Bibliothèque de l'École des Hautes Études, fasc. 82 (Paris, 1891)

Lot, F., [= Lot (1)], 'Le Roi Hoël de Kerahès', *Romania*, 29 (1900), 380–402

Lot, F., [= Lot (2)], *Étude sur le Lancelot en prose*, Bibliothèque de l'École des Hautes Études, fasc. 226 (Paris, 1918)

Lot, F., [= Lot (3)], 'Celtica', *Romania*, 24 (1895), 321–38

Lucanus, M. Annaeus, *Pharsalia*, ed. by C.E. Haskins (London, 1887)

Lucas, C.T.L., *Über den Krieg von Wartburg*, Historische und literärische Abhandlungen der königlichen deutschen Gesellschaft zu Königsberg, 4te Sammlung, 2te Abtheilung (Köningsberg, 1838)

Madden, Sir F., *Syr Gawayne* (London, 1839)

Mai und Beaflor, ed. by A.J. Vollmer, Dichtungen des deutschen Mittelalters, 7 (Leipzig, 1848)

Malory, Sir Thomas, *Le Morte d'Arthur*, 2 vols (London/Toronto, 1906)

———— *Le Morte Darthur*, ed. by H.O. Sommer, 3 vols (London, 1889–91)

Manuel und Amande. See Meyer-Benfey, pp. 160–63.

Marie de France, *Die Lais der Marie de France*, ed. by K. Warncke, 3rd edn (Halle (Saale), 1925)

Martin, E. [= Martin (1)], *Wolframs von Eschenbach Parzival und Titurel, Zweiter Teil: Kommentar*, Germanistische Handbibliothek, 9, ii (Halle (Saale), 1903)

Martin, E. [= Martin (2)], *Zur Gralsage*, QF, 42 (Straßburg, 1880)

Meier, J., 'Studien zur Sprach- und Litteraturgeschichte der Rheinlande', *PBB*, 16 (1892), 64–114

Merlin, ed. by G. Paris and J. Ulrich, SATF, 2 vols (Paris, 1886)

Methodius. See Pseudo-Methodius.

Meyer-Benfey, H., *Mittelhochdeutsche Übungsstücke*, 1st edn (Halle (Saale), 1909)

Morien, transl. by J.L. Weston, Arthurian Romances, 4 (London, 1901)

Moriz von Craon. See *Zwei altdeutsche Rittermæren*.

Muspilli. See Braune.

Ovid, *Metamorphoses*, ed. by F.J. Miller, 2 vols (London/New York, 1916)

Paiens de Maisières, *La Mule sanz Frain*, ed. by R.T. Hill (Baltimore, 1911)

Panzer, F. [= Panzer (1)], *Lohengrinstudien* (Halle (Saale), 1894)

Panzer, F. [= Panzer (2)], 'Personennamen aus dem höfischen Epos in Baiern', in *Philologische Studien: Festgabe für Eduard Sievers* (Halle (Saale), 1896), pp. 205–20

Paris, G. [= Paris (1)], 'Lancelot du Lac. II: Le *Conte de la Charrette*', *Romania*, 12 (1883), 459–534

Paris, G. ("G.P.") [= Paris (2)], 'Périodiques', *Romania*, 4 (1875), 148–50

Paris, G. [= Paris (3)], 'Romans en vers du cycle de la Table Ronde', in *Histoire littéraire de la France, ouvrage commencé par des religieux bénédictins de la congrégation de Saint-Maur et continué par des membres de l'Institut*, 30, Académie des Inscriptions et Belles-Lettres (Paris, 1888), pp. 1–270

Perceval le Gallois, ou le Conte du Graal, ed. by Ch. Potvin, Société des Bibliophiles Belges, 21, 6 vols (Mons, 1866–71)

Perlesvaus: Le Haut Livre du Graal, ed. by W.A. Nitze and T.A. Jenkins (Chicago, 1932)

Peter von Staufenberg. See *Zwei altdeutsche Rittermæren*.

Petrus Comestor, *Historia Scholastica*, J.P. Migne, Patrologiae Cursus Completus, Series Latina, 198 (Paris, 1855), pp. 1050–1722

Pleier, Der, *Garel von dem blüenden Tal*, ed. by M. Walz (Freiburg im Breisgau, 1892)

———— *Meleranz*, ed. by K. Bartsch, StLV, 60 (Stuttgart, 1861)

———— *Tandareis und Flordibel*, ed. by F. Khull (Graz, 1885)

Portimunt. See Kraus, 2nd edn, pp. 162–67.

Potvin. See *Perceval le Gallois*.

Pseudo-Callisthenes. See Arrianus.

Pseudo-Methodius, *Revelationes*, Bibliotheca Veterum Patrum, 3 (Coloniae Agrippinae, 1618), p. 363

La Quest del Saint Graal, ed. by A. Pauphilet (Paris, 1923)

Ranke, F., *Tristan und Isold*, Bücher des Mittelalters (Munich, 1925)

Raoul (le Trouvère), *Messire Gauvain, ou la Vengeance de Raguidel*, ed. by C. Hippeau (Paris, 1862)

Raoul de Houdenc, *Meraugis de Portlesguez*, ed. by M. Friedwagner (Halle (Saale), 1897)

Reinfrid von Braunschweig, ed. by K. Bartsch, StLV, 109 (Tübingen, 1871)

Renaut de Beaujeu, *Le Bel Inconnu*, ed. by G.P. Williams, CFMA, 38 (Paris, 1929)

Richey, M.F. [= Richey (1)], *Schionatulander and Sigune* (London, [n.d.])

Richey, M.F. [= Richey (2)], *Gahmuret Anschevin* (Oxford, 1923)

Richey, M.F. [= Richey (3)], *The Story of Parzival and the Graal* (Oxford, 1935)

Richter, W., *Der Lanzelet des Ulrich von Zazikhoven*, Deutsche Forschungen, 27 (Frankfurt am Main, 1934)

Rischin, C.H., *Bruchstücke von Konrad Flecks Floire und Blanscheflûr*, Germanistische Bibliothek, 4 (Heidelberg, 1913)

Robert de Borron, *Le Roman de l'Estoire dou Graal*, ed. by W.A. Nitze (Paris, 1927)

Robertson, J.G., *A History of German Literature*, 2nd edn (Edinburgh/London, 1931)

Rother, ed. by Jan de Vries, Germanische Bibliothek, II, 13 (Heidelberg, 1922)

Rudolf von Ems, *Willehalm von Orlens*, ed. by V. Junk, DTM, 2 (Berlin, 1905)

——— *Alexander*, ed. by V. Junk, StLV, 272 and 274, 2 vols (Leipzig, 1928–29)

Runeberg, J., *Études sur la Geste Rainouart* (Helsinki, 1905)

Sachse, 'Über den Ritter Kei, Truchsess des Königs Artus', *Archiv für das Studium der neueren Sprachen und Literaturen*, 29 (1861), 165–82

Sanct Brandan: Ein lateinischer und drei deutsche Texte, ed. by C. Schröder (Erlangen, 1871)

San-Marte, *Über Wolfram's von Eschenbach Rittergedicht Willehalm von Orange*, Bibl.d.ges.dt.Nat.-Lit., II, 5 (Quedlinburg/Leipzig, 1871)

——— See also Schulz, A.

Sarrazin, G., *Wigamur: Eine litterarhistorische Untersuchung*, QF, 35 (Straßburg, 1879)

Schneider, H., *Heldendichtung, Geistlichendichtung, Ritterdichtung*, Geschichte der deutschen Literatur, 1, ed. by A. Köster and J. Petersen (Heidelberg, 1925)

Schultz, A., *Das höfische Leben zur Zeit der Minnesinger*, 2nd edn, 2 vols (Leipzig, 1889)

Schulz, A. [= Schulz, 'Eigennamen'], 'Über die Eigennamen im *Parzival* des Wolfram von Eschenbach', *Germ.*, 2 (1857), 385–409

———— See also San-Marte.

Segremors. See Meyer-Benfey, pp. 175–87.

Seifrit, *Alexander*, ed. by P. Gereke, DTM, 36 (Berlin, 1932)

Singer, S. [= Singer (1)], *Wolframs Stil und der Stoff des Parzival*, Sitzungsberichte der Kaiserlichen Akademie der Wissenschaften in Wien, Philosophisch-Historische Klasse, 180, No. 4 (Vienna, 1916)

Singer, S. [= Singer (2)], *Wolframs 'Willehalm'* (Bern, 1918)

Der Singerkriec uf Wartburc, ed. by L. Ettmüller (Ilmenau, 1830)

Sir Gawain and the Green Knight, ed. by J.R.R. Tolkien and E.V. Gordon (Oxford, 1925)

Solinus, C. Julius, *Collectanea Rerum Memorabilium*, ed. by Th. Mommsen (Berlin, 1895)

Sommer, H.O., *The Structure of Le Livre d'Artus* (London/Paris, 1914)

Statius, *Achilleid*, ed. by J.H. Mozley (London/New York, 1928)

Strauch, P., 'Bruchstücke mittelhochdeutscher Gedichte, III: Ein Herbortfragment', *ZfdA*, 21 (1877), 203–06

Stricker, Der, *Daniel von dem Blühenden Tal*, ed. by G. Rosenhagen, Germanistische Abhandlungen, 9 (Breslau, 1894)

Thornton Romances: Perceval, Isumbras, Eglamour, and Degrevant, ed. by J.O. Halliwell, Camden Society, 30 (London, 1844)

Tirol. See Meyer-Benfey, pp. 149–53.

Toischer, W., 'Ueber die Alexandreis Ulrichs von Eschenbach', Sitzungsberichte der Kaiserlichen Akademie der Wissenschaften in Wien, Philosophisch-historische Klasse, 97, No. 2 (Vienna, 1881), pp. 311–408

Þiðriks saga af Bern, ed. by H. Bertelsen, Samfund til Udgivelse af gammel nordisk Litteratur, 34, 2 vols (Copenhagen, 1905–11)

Ulrich von Eschenbach, *Alexander*, ed. by W. Toischer, StLV, 183 (Tübingen, 1888)

———— *Wilhelm von Wenden*, ed. by W. Toischer, Bibliothek der mittelhochdeutschen Litteratur in Boehmen, 1 (Prague, 1876)

Ulrich von Liechtenstein, *Der Frowen Buoch*, ed. by K. Lachmann (Berlin, 1841)

———— *Frauendienst*, ed. by R. Bechstein, DDM, 6–7, 2 vols (Leipzig, 1888)

Ulrich von Türheim, *Tristan*, ed. by E. von Groote, in *Tristan von Meister Gotfrit von Straszburg mit der Fortsetzung des Meisters Ulrich von Turheim* (Berlin, 1821)

———— *Rennewart, deutsches Gedicht des 13. Jahrhunderts. Nabburger Bruchstücke*, ed. by K. Roth (Regensburg, 1856)

Ulrich von dem Türlin, *Willehalm*, ed. by S. Singer (Prague, 1893)

Ulrich von Zatzikhoven, *Lanzelet*, ed. by K.A. Hahn (Frankfurt am Main, 1845)

Universal Encyclopedia, newly revised edition (London, [n.d.])

Valerius, Julius, *Res Gestae Alexandri macedonis*, ed. by B. Kuebler (Leipzig, 1888)

Virgilius Maro, P., *Opera*, ed. by O. Ribbeck (Leipzig, 1872)

Verfasserlexikon, Die deutsche Literatur des Mittelalters, ed. by W. Stammler and K. Langosch, 1st edn, 5 vols (Berlin, 1933–55)

Vogt, F., *Geschichte der mittelhochdeutschen Literatur: I. Teil*, Grundriß der deutschen Literaturgeschichte, 2, i (Berlin/Leipzig, 1922)

Vulgate Version of the Arthurian Romances, ed. by H.O. Sommer, 7 vols and Index (Washington, 1908–16)

Wace, *Le Roman de Brut*, ed. by Le Roux de Lincy, 2 vols (Rouen, 1836–38)

Walshe, M. O'C., 'Travel Description in Middle High German Arthurian Epics' (unpublished M.A. thesis, University of London, 1935)

Wartburgkrieg. See *Singerkriec uf Wartburc*.

Weston, J.L. [= Weston (1)], *The Legend of Sir Gawain* (London, 1897)

Weston, J.L. [= Weston (2)], *The Legend of Sir Lancelot du Lac* (London, 1901)

Weston, J.L. [= Weston (3)], *Sir Gawain and the Lady of Lys*, Arthurian Romances, 7 (London, 1907)

Weston, J.L. [= Weston (4)], 'The Relation of the *Perlesvaus* to the Cyclic Romances', *Romania*, 51 (1925), 348–62

Wigamur, ed. by F.H. von der Hagen and J.G. Büsching, in *Deutsche Gedichte des Mittelalters*, I (Berlin, 1808)

Willelmus Malmesbiriensis, *Gesta Regum Anglorum atque Historia Novella*, 2 vols (London, 1840)

Wirnt von Gravenberg, *Wigalois*, ed. by J.M.N. Kapteyn, Rheinische Beiträge und Hülfsbücher zur Germanischen Philologie und Volkskunde, 9 (Bonn, 1926)

Wisse, Claus and Colin, Philipp, *Parzifal*, ed. by K. Schorbach, Elsässische Litteraturdenkmäler aus dem XIV–XVII. Jahrhundert, 5 (Straßburg, 1888)

Wolf, F., 'Über Raoul de Houdenc und insbesondere seinen Roman Meraugis de Portlesguez', Denkschriften der Kaiserlichen Akademie der Wissenschaften, Philosophisch-historische Classe, 14 (Vienna, 1865), pp. 153–98

Wolfram von Eschenbach, *Die Amberger Parcifal-Fragmente und ihre Berliner und Aspersdorfer Ergänzungen*, ed. by A. Beck (Amberg, 1902)

———— *Parzival*, transl. by W. Hertz, 2nd edn (Stuttgart, 1898)

———— *Parzival*, ed. by A. Leitzmann
Books I–VI, 3rd edn (Halle (Saale), 1928)
Books VII–XI, 2nd edn (Halle (Saale), 1926)
Books XII–XVI, 1st edn (Halle (Saale), 1903)

———— *Parzival und Titurel*, ed. by E. Martin, Germanistische Handbibliothek, 9, i-ii, 2 vols (Halle (Saale), 1900–03)

———— *Titurel*, ed. by A. Leitzmann, 2nd edn (Halle (Saale), 1926)

———— *Willehalm*, ed. by A. Leitzmann, 2nd edn, 2 vols (Halle (Saale), 1926–28)

Ywain and Gawain, in *Ancient Engleish Metrical Romanceës*, ed. by J. Ritson, 3 vols (London, 1802), I, pp. 1–169

Zahn, J. von, 'Über steiermärkische Taufnamen', *Mittheilungen des Historischen Vereines für Steiermark*, 29 (Graz, 1881), 3–56

Zarncke, F., *Der Priester Johannes* (Erste Abhandlung), Abhandlungen der Philosophisch-historischen Klasse der Königlichen Sächsischen Gesellschaft der Wissenschaften, 7 (Leipzig, 1879)

Zimmer, H., review of G. Paris, 'Romans en vers du cycle de la Table Ronde' [see Paris (3)], in *Göttingische gelehrte Anzeigen* (1890), pp. 785–832

Zingerle, I.V., 'Die Personennamen Tirols in Beziehung auf deutsche Sage und Literaturgeschichte', *Germ.*, 1 (1856), 290–95

Zingerle, O., *Die Quellen zum Alexander des Rudolf von Ems*, Germanistische Abhandlungen, 4 (Breslau, 1885)

Zwei altdeutsche Rittermæren. Moriz von Craon. Peter von Staufenberg, ed. by E. Schröder, 3rd edn (Berlin, 1920)

A

Aamanz (< OF Amans (?), a common name for persons.) A. is called the Second Gawein, owing to his resemblance to Gawein. A. is pursuing Gîgamec, who has slain his brother, when he is stopped by Zedoêch, whom he defeats; he is about to kill Zedoêch, when he is challenged and overcome by Gawein. Gawein leaves A. to Zedoêch and Gîgamec, who treacherously slay him and cut off his head. Gîgamec takes the head to Arthur's court, where he causes great consternation by pretending that it is Gawein who has been slain. – *C* a16502f. n16516ff. [†]

Aanzim brother of Samaidîe (q.v.). A. acts as host to Gawein after the latter's visit to the court of Vrou Sælde. – *C* 15949ff.

Aaron biblical, brother of Moses. – nm *JT* 535,1; *UA* 11453; *RB* 13107

Abacus According to *JT*, A. is the name of an ancient mathematician. It is actually the name of an early device for computation, but it is possible that the author of *JT* thought that the word was derived from the name of the inventor. (Cf. Algorismus.) – *JT* nm2009,5

Abarinse see Gabarîns

Abas son of Bêlûn. The name does not occur in any of Ulrich's known sources. – *UA* nm6975

Abastuleis 'der von Turkanie', a warrior in Akarîn's army against Ipomidôn. – *JT* nm3111,3f.

Abdalôminus chosen by the people to wear the crown of Sîdônje, which was given to Ephestiôn to dispose of. A. occurs in Curtius Rufus. – *A* 8406ff.

Abdenagon see Asarîas

Abegal see Abigal

Abel biblical, son of Adam. – nm [*P* 464,17]; [*W* 51,30]; *A* 17009; *JT* 171,5; *PM* 952; *UA* 11217; *GT* 23005; *WO* 6152; *RP* 637,39

Abell see Abel

Abîâ biblical (Abijah), king of Judah, son and successor of Rehoboam. – *A* nm16289

Abigal oppresses Penielle, who sends to Agâmennon's court for a champion. Paris, who undertakes the mission, slays A. – *GT* m7305ff. n8617 a8983f.

Abygall, Abygel, Abigell see Abigal

Abirôn (1) biblical (Abiram), see Dathân. – *RB* nm15820

Abiron (2) giant whom Ajax (1), during his search for Achilles, finds molesting a maiden, Antonne. Ajax kills him. – *GT* a15403 n15429

Abisso see Bessus

Abner biblical, cousin of Saul. According to *UA*, A. was slain by David, but historically, although he was an enemy of David's, he was slain by Joab. – *UA* nm11557f.

Abolan leader of the wild men, whom Eleander attacks and kills, when he is searching for Amalita. – *GT* 20220

Abor a knight who, too badly wounded to bear his armour, falls asleep by the side of a rejuvenating spring, where he is found by a *Meerweib*, who heals him and takes him home to her castle. She gives him roots which enable him to understand the language of the birds, and a bathrobe which ensures him against wounds. After six weeks he must leave her, as her husband is returning. Here the fragment breaks off. – *AM* a1 n101

Abore, Abort see Albort

Abraham biblical. – nm *A* 175; *JT* 172,5; *TKf* 49835; *UA* 1127; *RB* 27079; *WA* 1

1

Abrioris 'von Brunemuns', knight whose lion is killed by Parzivâl in his search for the white hart. Parzivâl then meets A. and defeats him. In Potvin, *Perceval le Gallois*, A. is called Abrioris à Briemes. – *RP* a341,8f. n342,14

Absalôn biblical, son of David. – nm *E* 2817; *P* 796,8; *LT* 11228; *DB* 7537; *W* 355,16; *UA* 11597

Absolôn (1) MHG poet. In *A* Rudolf von Ems refers to him as his friend, whilst in *RW* he is said to have written a poem on the life and death of Friedrich Barbarossa. – nm *A* 3249; *RW* 2209

*Absolôn (2) see Absalôn

Absterne 'künec von Palerne', standard bearer for Bilas in the first battle against Athis. In the OF version he is called Abïerne. – *AP* C,79

Abûlites 'burcgrâve von Sûsîs', formerly a vassal of Dârîus; he surrendered to Alexander without fighting. In Curtius Rufus and *Expeditio Alexandri*. – *A* 13441

Adâm (1) biblical, the first man. – nm *Ed* 13420; *P* 82,2; *Tn* 12615; *W* 62,2; *A* 17001; *G* 16508; *UW* 5,27; *Dem* 7469; *JT* 2075; *PM* 8885; *TK* 2172; *UA* 230; *WW* 3038; *RB* 10877; *GT* 2075; *RP* 624,34; *FS* 2977; *SA* 58

Adam (2) 'grâve von Selanden', fights for Jofrit (1) against Willehalm (3). Killed by Fierliun. – *RW* 486

Adân (1) 'vürste von Âlârîe', a knight who is defeated by Rôaz, who compels A. to act as his gate-keeper. A. fights for Wigalois against Lîon and kills Galopêar. He is the grandfather of Marîne. – *Wigl* a7090 n7840f.

Adan (2) see Adâm (1)

Adanz (1) (Schulz derived the name from OF *adans*, 'adoring',[1] whereas Martin suggests < OF Adans, Adam.[2] (Cf. Mazadân.)) A. is the father of Gandîn and cousin to Utepandragûn. It is interesting to note that there is an uncle of Arthur's in the 15th-century MS No. 99 of the prose *Tristan* named Ardans.[3] – *P* nm56,8f.

Adanz (2) wove in Ghent a rich cloth worn by Blandukors. – *C* nm6857

Adârîas 'vürste', in charge of one of Alexander's armies. A. is apparently an invention of Rudolf, as he does not occur in any of the sources. – *A* 13403

Ade daughter of Patricjus von den Bîgen; she gives herself to Lanzelet, who becomes lord of her lands after he has killed her uncle, Lînier. A. accompanies Lanzelet to Lôt's tourney, but allows herself to be led away from him by Diepalt, her brother, after Lanzelet has been overcome by the magic of Mâbûz. – *L* a1444 n1538

Adrastus (1) 'künec von Eurôpâ', father-in-law to Polînices, he is killed in the battle between Polînices and Ethiocles, and in *Ed* is seen by Ênêâs when the latter visits Hades. – *Ed* 3313; *UA* nm3140

Adrastus (2) 'von Sicilien', in Trojan army against the Greeks. A. does not occur in Homer, but is in Dares, Dictys, and Benoît. – *LT* 3980

Adrastus (3) 'von Colabiâ', in Trojan army against the Greeks. A. occurs only in *TK* but is probably the same as Adrastus (2). – *TK* 24824f.

Adrastus (4) messenger sent by Pirrus to obtain news of Acastus. This character is an invention of Herbort. – *LT* 17833ff

---

1   Schulz, 'Eigennamen', p. 397.
2   Martin (1), p. 64, to 56,9.
3   Löseth, p. 199.

Adrîagnê   It is clear from *TK* that this name represents Ariadne, the lover of Theseus.[4] – nm *C* 11580f.; *TK* 22142f.

Adriachnes   see Adrîagnê

Agalôn   see Aggalôn

Agâmennon   brother of Menelaus and father of Helen (in *GT*) and Orestes. *LT* keeps very close to the account given by Dictys and Benoît. The command of the Greek army is taken from A. and given to Palimedes, but later restored, as in Homer. On his return from Troy, A. is slain by Clitemnestre, his wife, and Egistus. The differences in *TK* are in detail only, but the account of the slaying of the hart by A. and the subsequent propitiation of Diana by the sacrifice of Iphigene is added. *GT* shows more obviously the influence of the Arthurian legends. A., whose wife is named Florand, holds a tourney, at which the young Paris is present, and later engages in battle with Matribulus. Paris is knighted by A. for his services in this battle. A second great tourney is held to celebrate the engagement of Helen to Menelaus. A. does nothing of note in the war against Troy, and afterwards returns home with Helen, whom he will not permit to marry. He fights and kills Bevar, who insists on marrying Helen, but later many of his men are killed and he himself is put to flight by Segromans, who takes Helen to Persia and marries her. A. is killed in a subsequent battle with Segromans in an endeavour to recover Helen. He is succeeded by his son, Menon. In *Ed*, A. is seen by Ênêâs, when the latter is visiting Hades. – *Ed* 3346; *LT* 2799; *C* nm11595; *TK* 23448ff.; *RB* nm19948; *GT* 2903

Agar (1)   comrade of Girabob. He is captured by Rudolf and hanged before the city of Ascalun. Bethmann considers this name to be the same as Agorlôt, both deriving from OF Aigar.[5] – *GR* δb,14f.

Agar (2)   biblical (Hagar), slave to Sarah, Abraham's wife. Owing to Sarah's barrenness, A. was taken by Abraham, and by him had Ismahêl. This passage is misinterpreted by Junk in his index to *A*, where she is stated to be Jacob's wife. – *A* nm17219

Agariton   see Agraton

Agariz   a knight who attends the tourney held by Leigamar in the service of Aram. – *C* 18175 [†]

Agarrain   comrade of Girabob. He is captured by Rudolf and hanged before the city of Ascalun. (According to Bethmann, this is the same name as Agorlîn (q.v.),[6] Bartsch explaining the form in *Crane* by its having come down to Berthold von Holle through oral tradition. Bartsch also joins W. Grimm in holding the name to be the same as Akarîn (q.v.),[7] but Bethmann thinks the difference is so great that a common origin is doubtful.) – *GR* δb,14f. [†]

Agatôn (1)   placed by Alexander in command of Babylon, and later (20327) one of the men commanded by Alexander to kill Parmênîôn. A. occurs in Curtius Rufus and *Expeditio Alexandri*. – *A* 13363f.

Agaton (2)   a knight in the Trojan army, he is slain by Ajax (1). A. occurs, as Agathon, in Dictys. – *TKf* 43220ff.

Agavus   a knight in the Trojan army, he is slain by Ajax (1). A. occurs in Dictys. – *TKf* 43220ff.

---

4   *TK* 22142ff.: 'Des ist geziuc Esipfilê / unde Adrîagnê diu maget, / die bêde wurden ouch gejaget / ze leides ungewinne / dur eines gastes minne, / der si verlâzen hæte.'
5   Bethmann, p. 169, note.
6   Bethmann, p. 169, note.
7   Berthold von Holle, *Demantin, Crane, Darifant*, ed. by K. Bartsch, pp. xxxiif.

3

Agboys 'künec', father of Segromans. – *GT* nm24155

Agemennon, Agemonen, Agemonne see Agâmennon

Agenor founder of Tyre. Mentioned also in Curtius Rufus, *Expeditio Alexandri*, and Gualterus. – nm *A* 9396; *UA* 9206f.

Agerlin see Agorlîn

Aggalôn 'künec', in the Greek army against the Trojans. This character is an invention of Konrad. – *TK* 25510

Agyax see Ajax (1)

Âgilôn in army of Dârîus, he is killed by Parmênîôn at Issôn. A. occurs in Gualterus. – *UA* 8145

Agyr 'von Elisan', a knight in the service of Wigamur. He announces to Atroclas the arrival of Wigamur to marry Dulcefluor. – *Wigm* 4385

Agyris wife of Candaulus, she is abducted by Schoieranz and recovered by Alexander. The story is told in Leo, where she bears the name Marpissa. – *UA* m19775 n19806 a23325

Agirres see Agirtes

Agirtes an expert trumpeter. He accompanies Ulixes, when the latter goes to fetch Achilles to Troy, and his fanfares are the deciding factor in awakening Achilles' martial spirit. A. was taken over from the *Achilleis* of Statius. – *TK* 27514ff.

Aglay see Agly

Agly daughter of Agrant and lover of Wildhalm (q.v.) – *WO* a594ff. n610f.; *FS* nm4827

Aglofals a knight of the Round Table and brother of Parzivâl. A. plays an important part in the OF romances, particularly in the Vulgate Cycle, but he is unknown in German literature, which was completely under the influence of the genealogy introduced by Wolfram, until he appears in *RP*, which at this point is a translation of the Manessier continuation of Chrestien's *Perceval*. In the Dutch *Roman van Lancelot*, A. is the father of an illegitimate black knight, Moriaen, whose history and appearance strongly resemble those of Feirefîz. – *RP* nm626,43

Agmonen, Agmonnen, Agomennon, Agommnon see Agâmennon

Agorlîn 'van Osterrîche'. (For the derivation of this name, see Agarrain.) A. takes service with Gayol and Agorlôt under the kaiser. A. is given the name of 'Valke' by Acheloyde, and accompanies her to Ungerlant after her marriage to Gayol. Fired by the appearance of a knight, whom Gayol has overcome, A. sets out to practise knight-errantry. He attacks Gayol, who has changed his armour, but they recognise each other before either of them is hurt. A. falls in love with Sêkurîe and after the defeat of Acurteis he returns with her to Austria and marries her. – *Crane* a50 n116 [†]

Agorlôt 'von Beiern'. (See Agar (1).) A. takes service under the kaiser with Agorlîn and Gayol. He is given the name of 'Stare' by Acheloyde. – *Crane* a50 n117

Agors see Strangedorz

Agoss a warrior who is killed fighting for Matribulus. – *GT* 3470

Agrant 'künec von Zyzya', father of Agly. A. is friendly to Liupolt von Osterrich but is opposed to the marriage of Wildhalm and Agly. He leads a great army against Crispin, when he learns of Agly's marriage to Wildhalm and the part which Crispin played in arranging the marriage. He loses the battle, is captured by Wildhalm, and turns Christian. – *WO* a316 n467

Agrapens see Agravains

Agrasyn 'von Euefandt', ally of Paltriot against Atroclas. – *Wigm* 3648ff.

Agraton 'von Saragos', kills Condiflor's husband and tries to force her to marry him. Condiflor sends to Arthur's court for assistance, and Seyfrid, who undertakes the mission, succeeds in defeating A. – *Sey* m82,6 a172,1f. n184,1

Agravains brother of Gawein and knight of the Round Table. A. is consistently represented as the worst of Gawein's brothers. He is proud and pitiless and his only redeeming features are his courage and skill in fighting. In *Mtl* he is called 'li orguelleus' and is sent with Keiî to fetch the ladies of Arthur's court to try on the cloak of chastity. In *RP*, where he is called Agravens, Agrefen, and Agrapens, he bears the epithet 'mit der herten hende' and is also called 'der hochvertige'. He assists Arthur against Bruns von Mielant and is present at the tourney held by Ris. In the OF *La Mort le Roi Artu* (Vulgate Cycle), as also in Malory, A., as leader of the conspiracy to betray Lancelot's association with Ginovêr, is the ultimate cause of the breaking up of the fellowship of the Round Table. – *Mtl* m629 a653; *RP* 22,27 [†]

Agravens see Agravains

Agraffin 'von Pudande', a warrior in Akarîn's army against Ipomidôn. – *JT* nm3137,5

Agrefen see Agravains

Agrimanz 'markîs', a warrior in the Trojan army against the Greeks. This character was invented by Konrad. – *TK* 30225

Agrimont 'der von' (*JT*), see Ypadens

Agrippa Alexander bequeathed Media to him. A. does not occur in any other version of the Alexander history. – *SA* nm8493

Agros see Strangedorz

Agrovals see Aglofals

Agulant brother of Lippatreiz; a warrior in the Greek army against the Trojans, he is slain by Perseus (1). A. does not occur in any of the sources of *TK*. – *TK* 33546f.

Agumennôn see Agâmennon

Aguses see Angwisiez

Aigax, Aigiax see Ajax (1)

Aimon nephew of Bilas, for whom he fought against Athis, Gayte being entrusted to him during the battle before Rome. In the OF version he is called Amanz. – *AP* A**,16

Ajax (1) son of Thelamon and Esîonâ, and therefore nephew of Priam. In *LT* he has two sons, Antides and Eustates. In *LT* and *TK* he takes part in the battle against the Trojans and (in *LT*) slays Paris; he is found murdered after a quarrel with Ulixes as to who should possess the Palladium. This version of the story of A.'s death follows the account given by Dictys and Benoît, which agrees neither with the Greek legendary version, in which he commits suicide, nor with the account in Dares, in which he dies of wounds received during his fight with Paris. As always, the account in *GT* is very corrupt. A. is the brother of Medea and Hercules. He is badly wounded during a sortie by the Trojans, but healed by Medea, who is fetched to Troy by Hercules. A. accompanies Ulixes to fetch Achilles and on his return is defeated in single combat by Hector. His death follows Greek legend; he quarrels with Ulixes as to who shall have Achilles' shield and commits suicide when this is awarded to Ulixes. In *Ed*, A. is seen by Ênêâs in Hades.– *Ed* 3347; *LT* 3009; *TK* 23806; *UA* nm18457; *GT* 10612ff. [†]

Ajax (2) 'Oilêus', a warrior in the Greek army against the Trojans. A. is prominent in all the versions of the Trojan legend, and in the Greek legend, as also in Dictys, he is drowned on the way home to Greece, owing to his violation of the temple of Minerva during the sack of Troy. – *LT* 3001; *TKf* 40938

5

Ajax (3) called 'der dritte', in the Greek army against the Trojans. A. is an invention of Herbort. – *LT* 3377

Ajax (4) 'de Curtin', brother of Landorye. He pursues Ursyan to Agâmennon's court and kills him. – *GT* nm4163 a4242ff.

Ajax (5) 'von Demonîe', called 'der kleine'. In the Greek army against the Trojans. Probably identical with Ajax (2), who otherwise does not appear in Konrad's poem. – *TK* 23827

Aiaz see Ajax (1). This form of the name is derived from the OF form, Aïaus, used throughout by Benoît.

Akarîn (1) (Considered by Bartsch to have been taken over from *Aliscans*.[8] See also Agarrain.) His name is not mentioned in *P*, where he is called 'der bâruc von Baldac' (Bagdad). Gahmuret hears that the *bâruc* is the greatest lord on earth, and enters his service against Pompêjus and Ipomidôn, from whom the *bâruc* had taken Ninivê. It is in a second battle for A. against these two that Gahmuret is killed. The story is repeated in *JT*, but a third battle is added, in which Schîonatulander and many knights of the Round Table take part and Pompêjus and Ipomidôn are finally defeated. In *UA*, 'der bâruch Ackerîn' takes the oath of allegiance to Alexander on the death of Dârîus. The anachronism is obvious. In *JT*, A. has two sons, Kardibulunen and Pardrigun. His wife is named Klarissilie. – *P* m13,16f. al4,5; *T* 40,2; [*W* 45,16]; *JT* a667,3 n782,1; *UA* 17149; *RB* m16597ff. [†]

Akarîn (2) 'künec von Marroch', relative of Akarîn (1). A. is one of the group of 15 Saracen kings who attack Willehalm (1) at the end of the first battle at Alischanz. A. is wounded by Willehalm in that encounter. He is among the besiegers of Orange and fights in the second battle. [See Appendix (9).] In imitation of the battle in *W*, he is taken over into *Loh*, where he fights for the heathens against the Christians and is killed by Lohengrîn. – *W* m71,22 a72,17f. n73,19; *Loh* 4819 [†]

Acastus father of Thetis; he imprisons his son-in-law, Peleus, but in turn is captured by Pirrus, when the latter returns from Troy, and is compelled to release Peleus. He has two sons, Manalippus and Plastines. This story is told in Dictys and Benoît, and a king of this name is mentioned by Ulixes in the *Odyssey*, without, however, any indication as to who he is. – *LT* nm17825 a18026

Akerîn see Akarîn (1) and (2)

Achalmus 'von Indiâ', a warrior in the Trojan army against the Greeks. This character is an invention of Konrad. – *TK* 24938f.

Achamas brother of Demophon. A. is a Greek warrior. After the fall of Troy, he marries Dimena. A. does not occur in Homer, but appears as Acamus in Dares and as Acamas in Benoît. – *LT* 16361 [†]

Achanayss a maiden, who is rescued from the violence of Malagriss by Paris, when the latter is on his way to India. She appears also (16995f.) as a messenger from Acharon recalling Passirius. – *GT* a7422ff. n7555

Achanaysz see Achanayss

Achanes a descendant of Jupiter. This name does not occur in any of the known sources to *UA*. – *UA* nm6990

Achap biblical (Ahab), correctly described in *A* as a king of Israel. In *UA* he is said to have possessed a vineyard which was taken from him by the king, Nabôt. This is the exact

---

8   Bartsch (2), p. 131.

opposite of the story as told in I Kings 21, where Ahab is the king and Naboth the owner of the vineyard. – nm *A* 16363; *UA* 11654ff.

Acharon 'künec von India', he sent Passirius with eleven dwarfs to Agâmennon to assist at the siege of Troy. – *GT* nm14342

Achas biblical (Ahaz), king of Judah. – nm *A* 16314; *UA* 11754

*Achaz see Achas

Achel 'künec von Tenemark', assisted the Greek army at the siege of Troy. A. is not in any other version of the legend. – *TK* 23916

Acheleyde see Acheloyde

Achelies see Achilles

Acheloyde (< Ἀχελωΐς, a siren[9]), daughter of the kaiser under whom Gayol and his friends take service. She falls in love with Gayol, and, for some reason which, owing to a gap in the MS, we do not know, she and her friend, Achûte, give to Gayol and his companions the names of birds. A. keeps her love a secret from her father until Gayol is falsely reported to be slain. A tourney is held, the victor to marry A. The winner is the King of Ungerlant, who is thought to be Assundîn, a married man, and the choice of a husband is left to A., who chooses Gayol. The kaiser is very angry until Assundîn reveals Gayol's true identity, when the marriage duly takes place. – *Crane* 133f.

Achilant a leader in Bêâmunt's army at Antrîûn. – *Dem* nm9880 a10956

Achyles see Achilles

Achillas 'von Galâciâ', a messenger sent by Dârîus to Alexander on the death of Carafilîe. He is a soldier in Dârîus's army, but does not appear in any of the sources to *UA*. – *UA* 10571ff.

Achilles son of Thetis and Peleus. His boyhood and youth are told in *TK*, where Konrad follows the *Achilleis* of Statius very closely. The only addition which Konrad permits himself is that, whilst A. is a baby under the care of Cheiron, he has a lioness as foster-mother. His training under Cheiron, his invulnerable skin, the effort which Thetis makes to preserve his life by hiding him, disguised as a woman at the court of Licomedes, and his love-match with Dêîdamîe, who has Pirrus by him, are all exactly as in Statius. *LT*, following Benoît, who in turn follows Dares, introduces A. as one of the princes who decide on the war with Troy, and he takes part in the siege from the beginning. In both *LT* and *TK*, to prove his love for Pollixena, he refrains from fighting for a time, but the heavy losses of the Greeks prove too much for him and he joins the battle, killing Troilus. At the command of Hecuba, he and Antilocus are lured into a temple at Troy under a promise of seeing Pollixena there, and are treacherously slain by Paris and twenty knights. In *GT* the Greeks learn from Medea that Achilles is necessary for victory and that he is at Licomedes' court disguised as a maiden. Ulixes, in the guise of a merchant, entices A. onto his ship and then sets sail for Troy. The death of Patroclus causes A. to challenge Hector, whom he eventually kills. Paris challenges him in revenge and slays him. Pollixena sets his head on a lance, a deed which Pirrus avenges by slaying her when Troy is sacked. In *Ed*, A. is seen by Ênêâs in Hades. – *Ed* 3346; *LT* 2839; *FB* nm1630; *TK* a5780 n5796; *UA* nm1302; *RB* nm16426; *GT* nm14943ff. a16372; *GM* nm3561

Achimanîs standard-bearer to Achilles. Not in any other version of the Trojan legend. – *TK* 30860ff.

Achor biblical, the Israelite, put to death for stealing gold during the sack of Jericho. The biblical form of the name is Achan, but it occurs in Gualterus as Achor. – *UA* nm11470

---

9 Berthold von Holle, *Demantin, Crane, Darifant*, ed. by K. Bartsch, p. xxxiii.

Achûte friend of Acheloyde, she appears at the beginning of the third fragment of the poem in conversation with Acheloyde. She marries Satrî. – *Crane* 138ff.

Accapador 'künec von Capadiâ', a warrior in the Greek army against the Trojans. A. does not appear in Homer, but the name occurs in Benoît as a variant of Agapenor, who appears in both Dictys and Dares as 'Arcadiae imperator'. – *TK* 23898

Ackaron 'vürste ûz Barbasone', present at a tourney held by Arthur. – *JT* 2055,1f.

Ackerin see Akarîn (1)

Ackratanie, Ackraton 'der von' (*JT*), see Kalebitor

Ackrin see Akarîn (1)

Ackrison 'von Tharsis und Arminzidole', a knight in Ipomidôn's army against Akarîn. – *JT* m3264,4ff. n3268,5

Ackusirie father of Ebusar. A. was buried in the same tomb as his son, Ebusar, and his grandson, Secureis. – *JT* 4827,1 [†]

Aclamet a maiden sent to fetch Gawein from Blandukors to Amurfinâ. Later at Arthur's court she unsuccessfully tries on Giranphiel's glove of chastity. She is the *amie* of Aumagwîn. – *C* a7673ff. n8322

Aclervis see Gylorette

Acrîsius son of Abas and father of Dâne. In the Greek legend he is accidentally killed by his grandson, Perseus. – *UA* nm6977

Actorides father of Dorilum, he is killed fighting for Alexander at Issôn. The name rests on a misunderstanding of Gualterus, where the name of one person, which is used in the accusative case, is 'Actoridum Dorilum'. – *UA* 8235

Akuleis 'von Ache', a scout in Akarîn's army against Ipomidôn. He carried a mirror to oppose the basilisk carried by Ledibudantz. – *JT* a3851,1f. n3863,1

Acurteis husband of Plansofeide; he is called 'der von Schoufe' and 'der Schoufer'. A. is brother-in-law to Sêkurîe, and takes her and her brother's lands after the death of their father. Gayol slays him in single combat and restores their lands to them. – *Crane* m2078 an3842

Accedille sister of Utepandragûn; she brings Arthur news of the captured Sangîve. A. is almost certainly an invention of the author of *JT*, the name being formed in imitation of Sekundille. (See also Enfeidas.) – *JT* 2433,1

Accidant 'von Olmodent', a warrior in Ipomidôn's army against Akarîn. – *JT* 3217,6

Alacrînis Alexander's nurse. So in Valerius and in Pseudo-Callisthenes. – *A* 1361

Alamassare a warrior in Ipomidôn's army against Akarîn. – *JT* 3216,2

Alamîs 'herzoge von Satarchjonte'. (According to Martin, Hagen suggests < Apalaei (var. Apamei), a name which occurs in Solinus.[10]) In *P* he is stated to have been defeated by Feirefîz, and *JT* places the scene of that defeat in a tourney held to decide who shall marry Sekundille, which was won by Feirefîz. – *P* nm770,16; *JT* 5278,1f.

Alan 'künec von Irlant', brother-in-law to Kaiver. Attends the tourney at Kurnoy, where he arrives after Willehalm has departed. He attacks Sävine (11808ff.), and ignores Amelot's message calling him to account. Amelot collects an army and, proceeding against A., completely routs the latter's forces. – *RW* nm8407 a8788ff.

Alardins 'vomme Se', a knight who loves Gyngeniers, who does not return his love. He fights Kardors as the latter is riding to Arthur's court with his sister and, after wounding him, rides away with Gyngeniers. He is challenged by Karadot, who defeats him but spares his life, and the three knights swear eternal friendship. He falls in love with Gyngenor,

---

10 Martin (1), p. 504, to 770,16.

whom he sees at the tourney held by Ris, and marries her. A.'s sister is called 'die von dem Pavelun'. A. occurs as Alardins del lac in Potvin and is probably the same Alardyn (of the Isles) who is killed by Gawein in Malory (III,vi). – *RP* a59,29 n60,2

Alardinz see Alardins

Alacîe a maiden, see Phenstis. – *RB* nm25294

Albân see Albânus

Albânus a bishop brought by Willehalm from Norway to carry out the baptism of the converts of Bohemia. – *WW* 7742f.

Albaflore In *Sey* she is the daughter of Flordibintze, and one of four ladies imprisoned by Klinschor and released when Seyfrid slays Amphigulor. The character is evidently taken from *JT*, where she occurs as the wife of Flordibintze. – *JT* 5704,2; *Sey* m27,6 a44,2 n65,1

Albazona daughter of Joseranns (q.v.). – *Sey* a336,1 n344,6

Alber 'von Arnsteine' (Alber = Adelber, Athalbero, according to Förstemann.[11]) A. jousted with Ulrich von Liechtenstein under the name of Segremors, during Ulrich's *Artusfahrt*. – *FD* 1439,2f.

Alberosen 'küneginne', loved by Feirefiz before he gained Sekundille. – *JT* 5295,1f.

Albertus Magnus see Albreht (1)

Albewîn (< MHG *alp*, 'elf' + *wine*, 'friend'.) A. is a dwarf king who had been defeated by Purdân. When Gârel kills Purdân, he swears fealty to Gârel, to whom he gives a magic ring and sword. Wearing *tarnkappen*, A. and three comrades help Gârel in his fight with the sea-monster by stealing the latter's petrifying shield. It is quite evident from his actions and character that A. is based on the dwarf Albrîch in the *Nibelungenlied*, although his name is that of the famous king of the Lombards, Alboin. – *G* a6364 n6815

Albîân chaplain to Elsam (see Sondelban). – *Loh* 354f.; *Ll* (MS K) 4,4f.

Albiûn 'küneginne'; she entertains Tandareis at her house at La Salvatsch Montân, when he loses himself one day whilst out riding. The following day Tandareis fights and defeats a knight, Kuriôn, who has been oppressing A. – *TF* a8570 n8590

Albort 'von Gerunge', a knight who was present at a tourney held by Arthur. He is later killed in the service of Schîonatulander against Ipomidôn. – *JT* 2029,3f.

Albreht (1) (Albertus Magnus) In *UA* he is called the bishop of Köln, but although he spent much of his life in Cologne, he was never bishop there but was for a time bishop of Regensburg. The book which is referred to in *UA* is his *Philosophorum maximi de mineralibus libri quinque*.[12] – *Mer* nm36,5; *UA* nm24275ff.

Albreht (2) author of *Der Jüngere Titurel*. – *JT* nm5883,1f.

Albreht (3) 'von Hayerloch-Hohenberch', the overlord of Johann von Würzburg, the author of *WO*. – *WO* nm13234ff.

Albreht (4) 'von Kemenât', MHG poet, author of a poem, *Goldemar*, of which a few fragments have come down to us. – *A* nm3252; *RW* nm2244f.

Albreht (5) 'bischof von Metze', slain by the king of Durkâny in the battle against the heathens. – *Loh* 4153

Albreht (6) 'von Nuzperc', present at the tourney attended by Ulrich von Liechtenstein at Friesach. – *FD* 196,7

Albreht (7) 'von Scharffenberg', author of *Merlin* and *Seifrid de Ardemont*. – *Sey* nm518,4; *Mer* nm10,5f

---

11 See Ulrich von Liechtenstein, *Frauendienst*, ed. by R. Bechstein, II, p. 186.
12 Toischer, p. 392.

Albreht (8) 'grâve von Tyrol', present at the tourney attended by Ulrich von Liechtenstein at Friesach. – *FD* 188,6

Albrecht see Albreht (7)

Albrich 'von Bizenze' (Albrich de Besançon). Author of an OF poem on Alexander, translated by Pfaffe Lampreht. Der Stricker claims to have got the story of *DB* from A. – *DB* nm7

Aldamas son of Arnolt (4); he fights for Partonopier against the Soldan. – *PM* 18802ff.

Aldîn 'vürste', a heathen in the army of Sornagiur against Partonopier, by whom he was killed. – *PM* 3600

Aleander see Eleander

Alemandîn sister of Pirithous; she marries Prophilias at the request of her brother when he is dying. (See Athis.) So also in the French version. – *AP* nmF,51 aF,133

Alexander (1) 'der grôze', Emperor of Macedonia. The best account of A.'s earlier years is found in *A*. Wondrous signs and portents accompany the birth of the future Emperor, who, in spite of his small stature, distinguishes himself at a very early age, both in his studies under the guidance of Aristôtiles and in his physical qualities. He unwittingly kills his own father, Nectanabus, whom he pushes over the battlements. A.'s first military success is against Nikolâus, whilst he shows his determination by insisting on the restoration of his mother, Olimpias, who has been displaced in Philipp's favour by Cleôpatra, and by sending the tribute-collectors from Dârîus away empty-handed. On the death of Philipp at the hands of Pâusânîâ, A. is made king, and he immediately sets out on an expedition of conquest, in which he is uniformly successful, taking many towns, including Athens and a number in Africa. Dârîus (3), who has watched his success, at first with scorn and later with anxiety, eventually sends an army against him, under Mennôn (1), who is defeated, as is also Amontâ. A. visits Dârîus's court in the guise of his own messenger, but unduly draws attention to himself, is recognized, and barely manages to escape safely back to his own army. The engagement with Dârîus's main army follows, and Dârîus, who is wounded and his army routed, flees, leaving his mother, Sisigambis (see Rodone), his wife, his daughter, Rôsâne (see Roxane), and his son in Alexander's power. The siege of Tyre, which lasts for 56 weeks before the city eventually falls, is followed by a visit to Jerusalem which brings about a transformation in A.'s character, and instead of being a purposeless conqueror, he now assumes the character of the scourge of God, doing the will of God against the unbelievers. After further conquests in Egypt and the founding of Alexandria, a second battle takes place with Dârîus, in which the latter is again defeated and is slain by Bessus (q.v.). In accordance with his promise to the dying Dârîus, A. marries Rôsâne, and is made king of Persia, but immediately sets out again on his expedition. He meets the Amazon queen, Tâlistrîâ, and crushes a conspiracy to murder him and put Philôtas in his place. The army suffers from a shortage of water during the march to capture Bessus, and a soldier (see Cephilus), who has managed to find a little, brings it to A. in a helmet. A. refuses, however, to enjoy that which is denied to his soldiers, and throws the water away. Bessus is about to be betrayed to A. when Rudolf's poem breaks off.

Up to this point, the history is substantially the same as that in *UA*, in which A. is frequently called 'der Pelliur', and which goes on to describe his campaign against Porrus, whom A. himself captures after a fierce fight. He visits Candacis (q.v.), and then attacks the city of Sûdrâcas, where he himself climbs over the wall to take the city. He is severely wounded but is saved by the arrival of three of his warriors (see Aristôn) and eventually of the remainder of his army. His character in *UA* is less noble than in *A*, and his ambition leads him to explore the sea and the air, and to lead an expedition to demand tribute from

10

Paradise, where Elîas gives him a stone and bids him to go and discover its meaning. No weight, however heavy, can weigh down the stone in a balance, but a handful of earth is sufficient. From this allegory A. learns the transience of his earthly successes.

An *Anhang* to *UA* describes the siege of Trîtôniâ, a town which defends itself by magic, until, under the advice of Aristôtiles, A. succeeds by kindness where force had failed. The action takes place between the second battle with Dârîus and the latter's death.

There are two other histories of A. among the MHG epics. Both *SA* and *WA* contain most of the above episodes, in slightly different order, and with small omissions and additions, the most important of which are as follows. In *SA* and *WA* he encounters at one point a Basilisk, which petrifies men with its glance. A. kills it by carrying a mirror before him, and the Basilisk, seeing itself, is slain by its own glance. *WA* omits all reference to the journey to Paradise and the visit to Candacis, but adds a few details, such as A.'s demand for a tribute of twelve philosophers from the people of Athens, and an incident where he learns from a talking tree when he is to die.

In *RP*, A. is called 'von Alier', a surname which, according to Potvin,[13] was first given to him in the Middle Ages by Lambert li tors in his *Roman d'Alixandre*, where, after telling of a victory during his youth on the plains of Aliers, he says: 'de coi ot li sornom'.

The medieval poets derived their knowledge of the life of Alexander mainly from the account by Curtius Rufus, which is based on the *Expeditio Alexandri*, and that of Julius Valerius, the source of which is the account by Pseudo-Callisthenes. Influential medieval accounts were the *Alexandreis* of Gualterus and the *Historia de Proeliis* of Leo. An OF poem by Albrich de Besançon, which survives only in a few fragments, was translated into MHG by Lampreht, on whose account, however, the other MHG versions do not appear to be in the slightest degree dependent.

– *E* nm2821; *P* nm773,21ff.; *MC* nm94; *C* nm11578; *A* m41f. n72 a1231; *FD* nm Büchlein III,146; *JT* nm3076,1; *Eng* nm838; *TK* nm13808; *UA* m706f. a1158 n1212; *HT* nm4514; *RB* nm15159; *GT* nm16272; *RP* nm72,37; *SA* nm15f. a553f.; *WA* nm51 a265f.

Alexander (2)   the name under which Paris is almost always referred to in the Greek and Latin versions of the Trojan history. It occurs in only one instance in the MHG versions, when Paris assumes the name as a disguise during his stay at the court of Menelaus preparatory to abducting Helen. – *TK* 20664f.

Alexander (3)   is sent, together with his brother Philipp, by Arabadille to avenge the death of Secureis on Schîonatulander. They both attack the latter together, but he defeats them. One of the brothers is referred to as 'der uz kaukasas', but there is no indication as to which brother is intended. They would appear to have been invented by the author of *JT* on the example of Alexander the Great and his father, Philipp. – *JT* a4677,6 n4778,1f.

Alexander (4)   husband of Sûrdâmûr and father of Cligés. A. was known to Wolfram or his source from Chrestien's poem, *Cligés*. – *P* nm586,26f.

Alexander (5)   'von Assim', a leader in Akarîn's army against Ipomidôn. – *JT* 3105,1

Alexander (6)   'von Pergalt', son of Retân and nephew of Gilân, he is imprisoned by Eskilabôn, and released when the latter is defeated by Gârel. A. fights in Gârel's army against Ehkunat and subsequently marries Flordiâne. – *G* nm2489ff. a3532

Alexander (7)   son of Purrel, he fights on the side of Terramêr against Willehalm[1] in the second battle at Alischanz. Singer considers him to be an invention of Wolfram.[14] – *W* a358,25 n427,8

---

[13]   *Perceval le Gallois*, III, p. 153, note.
[14]   Singer (2), p. 121.

Alexander (8)   Roman Emperor (Alexander Severus), AD 205–235. A. was murdered in the neighbourhood of Mainz. – *WW* nm7832

Alexandir   fought for Bilas against Athis. So also in the OF version. – *AP* C,6

Algorismus   considered by the author of *JT* to be the name of an ancient mathematician. It was actually the name used in the Middle Ages for arithmetic involving the use of Indo-Arabic numerals, but it was a common belief at that time that the word was derived from the name of the Indian king Algor.[15] In point of fact the word is a corruption of the territorial name (Al Khwarizmi) of the Arab mathematician, Abu Ja'far Mohammed Ben Musa Al Khwarizmi,[16] who is almost certainly the person intended in *JT*. (Cf. Abacus.) – *JT* nm2009,4

Algusier   'von Parliente', a warrior in Akarîn's army against Ipomidôn. – *JT* 3193,1

Alyant   'künec', also called 'künec von A.' Prompted by his love of Elene, A. fights for Agrant in the battle at Firmin and is killed by Wildhalm. – *WO* 7784ff. [†]

Aliart   'ûz Flander', present at a tourney held by Arthur. – *JT* 2065,2

Alîe   *amie* of Gerant. – *Dem* m4696 n4880

Aliers (1)   'grâve' (OF Alier, the name being a corruption of Maheloas, according to Brugger[17]). A. is oppressing 'vrou von Narisôn', the lady who finds Iwein in his madness and cures him. Iwein leads her army against A., whom he forces to surrender to her. A. is called Alier in Chrestien's *Yvain* and Alers in the ME *Ywain and Gawain*. – *I* nm3407ff. a3704f.

Aliers (2)   'grave von Kret', unhorsed by Seyfrid at the tourney held by Duzisamor. – *Sey* 373,6ff.

Alikarnasus   a Persian; he surrendered to Alexander. A. does not appear in any of the sources to *A*. – *A* nm5874

Alimus, Âlîn   see Alinus

Alinus   'künec von Cumenîe', son of Ascalaphus, in the Greek army against the Trojans. A. does not occur in Homer, but appears in Dares as Almenus (and Ialmenus) and in Benoît, where he is killed by Hector. – *LT* 3317; *TK* 23786

Alîs   a heathen, he has killed Turkîs, whose death Markabrê attempts to avenge. A. beats him off with the assistance of Supplicius and Anshelm (1) and then returns with the two latter to Arnolt's castle. – *PM* 19046ff.

Alyse   see Alîze (2)

Alius   son of Arnolt (4); he fights for Partonopier against the Soldan. – *PM* 18802ff.

Alîze (1)   sister of Hardîs and wife of Lembekîn, the 'herzoge von Brabant'. A. was formerly the lover of Kailet, who however did not marry her, and this insult was the cause of the enmity between him and Hardîs. Martin has drawn attention to the fact that this name is borne by the Duchess of Brabant in the OF *Chevalier au Cygne*,[18] the OF counterpart to the Lohengrîn legend. (See Elsam.) – *P* nm67,26

Alîze (2)   daughter of Lôis; she materially assists Willehalm in obtaining aid from Lôis by reconciling Willehalm with her mother. She is in love with the kitchen-boy, Rennewart, and kisses him when he leaves to go with Willehalm to Alischanz. The sequel is told in the OF *Bataille Loquifer*, where they are married and A. dies giving birth to a young giant, Malfer. This incident is also mentioned in *RB*. The name Alyze (= Alice), popularised

---

15   *Encyclopædia Britannica*, I, p. 622.
16   *The Universal Encyclopedia*, I, p. 271.
17   Brugger (2), pp. 60f.
18   Martin (1), p. 75, to 67,26.

possibly by Wolfram from *W*, is recorded by Panzer as appearing in Bavarian documents of the 14th and 15th centuries.[19] – *W* a148,18 n154,2; *UW* 266,8; *RB* nm23369

Alcamus, Alchamîs see Alchamus

Alchamus 'von Falede', a warrior in the Trojan army against the Greeks. The name occurs in Benoît as a variant of Thalamus de Valadès. – *LT* 4020; *TK* 29742ff.

Alchimeliar 'markîs von Klamîe', a warrior in the Trojan army against the Greeks. This character does not occur in any of the sources of *TK*. – *TK* 24878ff.

Alcmêne mother of Hercules. Probably taken by Konrad from Ovid's *Metamorphoses* IX. – *TK* nm14477ff.

Alleander see Eleander

Allecto one of the Furies (Alecto in Greek mythology). – *LT* nm16404

Almadian son of Priam and half-brother to Hector. A. is in the Trojan army against the Greeks. So in Benoît. – *LT* a4808 n4832

Almazare one of Ither's knights. A. is killed in the battle between Akarîn and Ipomidôn. – *JT* 3462,1f.

Almirate a warrior in Ipomidôn's army against Akarîn. – *JT* 3259,1

Almon slain in the battle between Akarîn and Ipomidôn. – *JT* 4186,1

Alogries 'von Tangulor', slain by Daries whilst fighting for Akarîn against Ipomidôn. Tangulor (q.v.) is also (3465,6) taken to be the name of a warrior. – *JT* nm3113,1 a3465,6

Aloguries see Alogries

Aloyso see Aloysse

Aloysse wife of Thedalus. – *GT* 2492ff.

Alom knight of the Round Table; he is unhorsed by Daniel. A knight of the Round Table named Ales (var. Alon) occurs in the Vulgate *Merlin* and the *Livre d'Artus*, but it is doubtful if this is more than a coincidence, as there are no other instances of correspondence in the names in these works. – *DB* 249

Alophîe probably the *amie* of the *Vogt* of Fandorîch's castle, who is killed by Firganant. The name occurs only once, in the battle-cry of the *Vogt*, but in this poem the battle-cries of all the knights consist of the names of their ladies, with only one exception. – *Dem* nm6730

Alreste see Areste

Althessor a wild man; takes Seyfrid to Ardemont after he has escaped from the griffon. – *Sey* a438,6 n440,3

Alfenor comrade of Ulixes; he abducted the sister of Polifemes, who, however, regained her after the slaughter of a large number of the Greeks under Ulixes. A. occurs as Alphenor in Dictys and Benoît, but he does not appear in the *Odyssey*. – *LT* nm17589

Alpheolan 'von Schottan', husband of Landorye. A. is killed by Paris during the tourney held when the latter is made knight. – *GT* 3973ff.

Alphunsus (Petrus Alphonsi), author of the *Disciplina Clericalis*. – *UA* nm27233

Alceon father of Nausica. Ulixes passes through his land on the return from Troy, and A. gives him some knights to assist him in freeing Penelope from her lovers. A. occurs as Alcinous in the *Odyssey* and Dictys, and Alcenon in Benoît. – *LT* 17755ff.

Alciân a Frenchman, one of the leaders in Bêâmunt's army at Antriun. – *Dem* nm9843 a10905

Alcîdes another name for Hercules. The young Alexander is compared to him. – *UA* nm1308

---

19 Panzer (2), p. 217.

Alzippus he taught music to the young Alexander. So also in Valerius and Pseudo-Callisthenes. – *A* 1364

Amakûn a warrior in the Greek army against the Trojans; he is slain by Troilus. A. appears to be an invention of Konrad. – *TK* 31602

Amalye see Amely

Amalita wife of Eleander; she is abducted by Hannor, but won back by Eleander. – *GT* 19813ff.

Aman (1) a warrior in Dârîus's army. This name does not appear in any of the sources of *UA*. – *UA* nm12243

Aman (2) biblical (Haman), he tried to encompass the death of Mordecai (Esther 3). – *UA* nm11804

Amande (1) a maiden at Agâmennon's court; she helps to entertain the victorious Nectarus. – *GT* 6083

Amande (2) wife of Manuel (q.v.). – *MA* 43

Amander (1) a knight at Arthur's court when Êrec returns with Ênîte. This name does not occur in Chrestien's *Erec*. – *E* 1690

Amander (2) *amie* of Prinel (q.v.). – *UW* nm255,18f.

Amangon 'künec von Logers', he dishonoured the maidens who lived in his land. Owing to his sin, the crops failed and his land became poor, and the court of the Rich Fisher, which was in it, disappeared. A. occurs in the *Elucidation*, a prologue which was added to Chrestien's *Perceval*. – *RP* Prologue nm67ff. [†]

Amanit 'von Flagenal', brought Arâbel a mirror, in which she could see all that was happening for 100 miles around. – *UW* nm125,7ff.

Amantrîs (1) 'der werden Kerlingære voget', in the Greek army against the Trojans. This character is an invention of Konrad. – *TK* 23948

Amantrîs (2) in the Trojan army against the Greeks. Greif considers that this character is the same as Amantrîs (1), and that Konrad became confused.[20] – *TK* 29868

Amâsîas biblical (Amaziah), king of Judah. – *A* nm16298

Amasiol a warrior in Akarîn's army against Ipomidôn. – *JT* nm3094,3

Amaspartîns 'von Schipelpjonte'. (In one MS the name has been altered to Arimaspis. The one-eyed Arimaspen is mentioned by Solinus (86,5), and Hagen sees in Schipelpjonte a corruption of Cyclops, the 'gentem Cyclopum' being mentioned by Solinus (50,12).[21]) A. is overcome in a joust by Feirefiz in *P*. In *JT*, where he is called Aspramatinse von Zippelant, the scene of this defeat is laid at the tourney held between the wooers of Sekundille. – *P* nm770,6; *JT* 5259,1

Amator 'künec von Jerusalen', present at the tourney held at Solia. – *WO* 15706f.

Ambigâl 'grâve von Sâlîe', he fought for Wigalois against Lîon. – *Wigl* nm10115 a10410ff.

Ambiôn 'von Tenabrî', in Dârîus's army against Alexander. This name does not appear to be in any of the sources to *UA*. – *UA* 10959

Ambrâ 'künec', he flees when his city is captured by Alexander in *UA*. In *SA*, where he is called Ambyras, he is king of the town of Polus antarticus, which is captured and destroyed by Alexander. Ambira occurs in Orosius III,19 (11), and in Leo (MS S).[22] – *UA* 22962; *SA* 6179f.

Ambrî biblical (Amri), king of Israel. – *A* nm16360

---

[20] Greif, p. 114.

[21] See Martin (1), p. 503, to 770,6.

[22] O. Zingerle, p. 64.

Ambryas see Ambrâ

Ambrius 'von Tîre', slain by Hector when fighting for the Greek army against the Trojans. A. does not occur in any of the sources to *TK*. – *TK* 31310

Ambrosius (St. Ambrose), the Father of the Church, AD c.340–397. – *SA* nm47 [†]

Ambross 'vürste von Indien', one of Bevar's army, who tries to make peace before the battle between Bevar and Agâmennon. – *GT* 23795

Amely daughter of Rainher. A. loves Willehalm (4) (q.v.), and pines away when he is lost to her. She refuses to marry Avenis, and her constancy is rewarded when Sävene learns her story. In *JT* she occurs as one of the ladies at Arthur's court. – *RW* m83f. a3718ff. n3746; *JT* 1777,3; *RB* nm15300; *FS* nm1535

Amelot 'künec von Norwac', son-in-law of Coradis, father of Duzabel (2). Willehalm (4) strikes his encampment soon after leaving the English court and is there cured of his wound. A. takes Willehalm to Norway with him, where he fights battles with Witechin and Alan, in both of which Willehalm distinguishes himself. When he learns Willehalm's identity, he reveals that his own father's sister was Willehalm's maternal grandmother. – *RW* nm10042f. a10166

Amênâ mother of Lârîe; she is absent from Korntîn at the time Roaz is devastating the country, but is still alive and present at the wedding of Wigalois and Lârîe. – *Wigl* m3751 a8825f. n8851

Amênîdas a Persian, formerly scribe to Dârîus; Alexander makes him 'herzoge von Evergêten'. A. occurs in Curtius Rufus as Amedines. – *A* 20723ff.

Amerellus see Amerillus

Amerillus brother of Picorye and husband of Vernande; he entertains Picorye and Hector after the latter's fight with Waradach. – *GT* nm12656f. a12692

Amerilus see Amerillus

Amerclîe 'diu lange', one of the ladies at Arthur's court who unsuccessfully try to drink out of the cup of chastity sent by Priure. – *C* 1608

Amigdalûr castellan to Priam; he is slain by the Greeks. This character is an invention of Konrad. – *TK* 24824f.

Amicare see Aminkas

Amich Alexander bequeathed to him Segredia. A. does not appear in any of the other histories of Alexander. – *SA* nm8524

Amilot see Amelot

Aminactis see Aternantes

Aminal, Aminall see Amivall

Aminkas (Bartsch sees in this name another form of the name Amintas < Greek Amyntas,[23] and Martin points out that Amyntae (genitive of Amyntas) occurs in Solinus (65,10; 66,1).[24]) In *P*, where he is called 'rois von Sotofeititôn', he is said to have been defeated by Feirefîz. In *JT* he is called Amicare von Larifotikone, and the scene of the defeat is laid at the tourney held by Sekundille to decide which of her wooers she shall marry. – *P* nm770,17; *JT* 5279,1f.

Aminctas 'grâve', a warrior in Alexander's army. Alexander left him Patriânôs. A. is apparently an invention of Ulrich (suggested by Amintas?). – *UA* 4707

Amintas (1) a prominent leader in Alexander's army; he captured many towns and slew Mâzâzes. A. was concerned in the conspiracy of Dimnus to slay Alexander, but was

---

23 Bartsch (2), p. 155.
24 Martin (1), p. 502, to 770,17.

15

pardoned together with his brother Polemôn. A. occurs in *Expeditio Alexandri*, Curtius Rufus, and Gualterus. Although there is no similarity in detail, it is possible that the name served as a model for Aminctas. – *A* 6994

Amintas (2) 'von Linzeste', a leader in Alexander's army. He occurs in Curtius Rufus. – *A* 13413

Aminus (1) see Emimor

Aminus (2) see Antinus

Âmîre 'künec von Lîbîâ', killed by Lîôn, who abducts A.'s wife Lîamêre. – *Wigl* nm9814f. a9946f.

Amirillus see Amerillus

Âmîs one of the heathens besieging Oransche. A. occurs in the OF *Aliscans* as Amis de Cordes. – *W* 98,13

Amivall a young Greek; he accompanies Ajax, Ulixes, and Hercules in their quest for Achilles, and plays a prominent part in the fighting which takes place on the way. He is killed by Paris outside Troy. – *GT* 15171f.

Ammeras a warrior in Ipomidôn's army against Akarîn. – *JT* 3216,4

Ammilôt the son of Ehkunat's cousin. He is in charge of the advance army which fights the first battle with Gârel. A. is badly wounded in single combat with Gârel, but is saved by his men. He is placed in charge of Ehkunat's land, when the latter has to go to Arthur's court to submit himself as captive. – *G* 13696ff.

Ammoreon he arrives at Tanian to avenge his father, who was slain by Minos. Jason fights and kills him. – *GT* 21877ff.

Ammusse see Antinus

Amolita, Amolitte see Amalita

Amolos see Amolot

Amolot cousin of Paltriot and nephew of Atroclas; he buys the land of Deleferant from Pannt and dies intestate, thus causing the quarrel for succession between Paltriot and Atroclas. – *Wigm* nm3482

Amôn (1) the Egyptian god, whose form Nectanabus takes when he lies with Olimpias. A. constantly advises Alexander in dreams, when he is in difficulties. A. is mentioned in all the histories of Alexander. – *A* nm701 a4107f.; *R* nm Eing. I,85; *JT* nm3357,5; *UA* nm9770; *SA* m324 n337 a2331; *WA* nm174 a764f.

Amôn (2) biblical, king of Judah (II Kings 21). *A* nm16322

Amontâ 'vürste von Persia'. In *WA*, which follows the account in Leo, A. is the first of Dârius's commanders to attack Alexander. His army is wiped out, and A. just escapes to tell Dârius about Alexander's terrible army. In *A* the first of Dârius's commanders to attack Alexander is Memnôn (see Mennôn (1)), but in all other particulars the story of A. is told, except that he is here 'herzoge von Arâbîa'. – *A* 4651f.; *WA* 1373f.

Amor (1) son of Venus and brother of Cupid. – nm *Ed* 9911; *Wigl* 831; *P* [478,30]; *W* 24,5; *Dem* 5056; *JT* 1730,6; *M* 670; *PM* 20724; *Mer* 182,6; *UA* 6204; *W* 684; *FS* 6748

Amor (2) see Emimor

Amorantt owner of the castle, Byabe; he was killed by Hercules during the latter's search for Achilles. – *GT* 15854

Amôrêus 'künec', captured by Eresdes. A. does not occur in Pseudo-Methodius, from which this passage in *A* appears to have been taken. – *A* nm17164

Amsor 'der marke herre von Prurine', present at a tourney held by Arthur. – *JT* 2040,5

Amunall see Amivall

Amur (1) a knight who, jealous of the way in which Hector is honoured in Bagdad, challenges him and is killed. – *GT* a819 n952

Amûr (2) see Amor (1)

Amurât 'von Turtûse', father of Duzabel (1) and husband of Klârîne (2); he fights for Gârel against Ehkunat. – *G* nm5884f. a6943

Amurelle wife of Blandukors (q.v.). – *C* 6926

Amurfinâ elder daughter of Laniure. On the death of her father, A. seizes a magic bridle, which enables its possessor to govern the land, and her sister, Sgoidamûr, goes to Arthur's court to find a champion to help her to win the bridle, which is hers by rights. A. sends Aclamet to find Gawein to fight for her, and when he arrives, they fall in love. Gawein is given a drink to make him forget who he is, but he recovers his memory after fifteen days and leaves without fighting for A. Gawein is later sent by Sgoidamûr to recover the bridle, which, in spite of the temporary opposition of A.'s maternal uncle, Gansguoter, he succeeds in doing, and finally marries A. (See Gawein, for a consideration of the story as a version of the OF poem, *La Mule sanz Frain.*) – *C* m7698 n7796 a8125

Amurfinê see Amurfinâ

Ampfidamas a Trojan; he conspires with Ênêâs to betray Troy to the Greeks. This name does not occur in Dictys, Dares or Benoît, but it is mentioned in Homer, where it is that of a Greek. – *TKf* 46830

Amphigulor a giant; he is slain by Seyfrid, who releases the ladies whom A. was guarding. – *Sey* m28,4 a33,4 n46,7

Amphicôn Alexander bequeathed to him Greater Syria. A. does not occur in any of the other histories of Alexander. – *UA* nm27003

Amfileus in the Greek army against the Trojans; he is slain by Hector. This character is an invention of Konrad. – *TK* 30611ff.

Amphilicôn a warrior in Dârîus's army; he is slain by Crâtherus at Issôn. So also in Gualterus. An Amphilochus is mentioned in *Expeditio Alexandri* II, 5 (9). – *UA* 8059

Ampfimach (1) 'von Cariâ', a warrior in the Trojan army against the Greeks, by whom he is slain. In Dictys, where he is called Amphimacus, his slayer is Ajax. He does not occur in Benoît or any of the other versions of the legend. – *TKf* 44050

Ampfimach (2) see Amphimachus (2)

Amfimachus (1) 'von Lîciâ'. (Identical with Phimacus?) A warrior in the Trojan army against the Greeks. A. does not occur in any other version of the legend. – *TK* 24812ff.

Amphimachus (2) youngest son of Priam. The conspirators, in the name of the Greeks, demanded his renunciation of all claims to the throne of Troy. So in Dares and Benoît. A. does not occur in Homer or Dictys. – *LT* 15033; *TKf* 46627

Amphimachus (3) a warrior in the Greek army against the Trojans. He is slain by Hector. A. occurs in Dares and Benoît, in both of which he is slain by Ênêâs. His fate is not stated in *TK*. – *LT* 3384; *TK* 23814

Amphimacus see Amphimachus (2) and (3)

Amphiôn a former king of Thebes, husband of Niôbês. A. is mentioned in Leo, where he is called Anfiones. – *UA* nm2771

Amphioras 'vürste', killed in the battle between Polînices and Ethiocles. In *Ed*, A. is seen by Ênêâs in Hades. – *Ed* 3316; *UA* nm3165

Amphiorâus see Amphioras

Amphius see Amphus

Amphlîse (1) 'küneginne der Franzoiser'. (Schulz derived the name from OF *afflis*, 'afflicted',[25] a view with which Bartsch disagrees, preferring the form in *JT* to that in *P*, and deriving Anfolise from OF *Affolie*, 'mortally in love'.[26] Gaston Paris points out that Anfelise would be a well-known name, as it occurs in the popular romance *Foulque de Candie*,[27] a view which is supported by Singer[28] and Martin[29]. The last-named, in considering the possibility of identifying Gahmuret with Fulco, who was king of Jerusalem AD 1131–1143,[30] points out that Anfelise could be a derivation of Amalasuinth, through the transformation of the German pet-name forms Amalizza, Amblizza, under the influence of the Latin *felix*. From Amalsuinth is derived the corrupt form Melisuinth, which, as Melisande, is the name of Fulco's wife. In *Foulque de Candie*, Anfelise, the daughter of a heathen prince, gives herself to Fulco.) Gahmuret had been A.'s knight, and when the king of France dies, she sends him an offer of marriage, which he refuses, as he has now fallen in love with Herzeloide. In *T* and *JT*, A. has at her court the young Schîonatulander, whom she lends to Gahmuret, when the latter goes to Akarîn. – *P* m12,11 n76,6f.; *T* 37,3ff.; *JT* 664,5ff.

Amflîse (2) daughter of Jernîs (see Lernîs); one of the maidens who tend the Graal. A. carries the silver knives in the Graal procession. – *P* a232,12ff. n806,18ff.

Amfortas the Graal King. (Schulz suggested a connection with OF *enfertume*, 'illness', and *enfers*, 'ill',[31] and most scholars adhere more or less closely to this etymology. Bartsch considered it a derivation from OF *enfertés*, 'infirmitatus',[32] to which Gaston Paris objects, on the grounds that the word suggested by Bartsch has never existed.[33] Martin is of the opinion that the name comes from the Latin *infirmitas*,[34] a view which Singer rejects, without giving a reason or an alternative explanation.[35] Bruce considers it derived from OF *enfertez*, 'infirmity', with the common variant of *an-*, *am-* for initial *en-*.[36]) In *P*, Parzivâl first sees A. fishing in a boat. He directs Parzivâl to the Graal castle, where Parzivâl discovers that the fisher is the Graal King. He has been wounded in the groin, owing to his having been guilty of an unchaste love towards Orgelûse (the personification of worldly vanity) in his youth. He can neither stand nor lie down, until such time as his predestined successor as Graal King shall come to the Graal Castle and ask a question of sympathy . A. will then be released from his sufferings. His father, Frimutel, is already dead, but his grandfather, Titurel, lives still, a very old man, kept alive only by gazing at the Graal. Parzivâl fails to ask the question on this occasion and prolongs A.'s sufferings for more than four and a half years. Up to this point, the story is substantially that of Chrestien's *Perceval*, in which, however, A. is not named. The latter poem does not reach as far as the conclusion of *P*, where Parzivâl asks the question on his second visit to the

---

25 Schulz, 'Eigennamen', p. 392.
26 Bartsch (2), p. 138.
27 Paris (2), p. 149.
28 Singer (1), p. 61.
29 Martin (1), pp. 83f., to 76,7.
30 Martin (1), pp. XLff.
31 Schulz, 'Eigennamen', p. 391.
32 Bartsch (2), p. 140.
33 Paris (2), p. 149.
34 Martin (1), p. 362, to 472,22.
35 Singer (1), p. 90.
36 Bruce (1), I, p. 317, note 9.

Graal castle. A. is then transformed into a man of extreme beauty, his suffering ceases, and he lives on.

The symbol of the Graal King as a fisher is evidently older than Chrestien's poem, as it appears in Robert de Boron's *Joseph*, a poem of a somewhat later date it is true, but uninfluenced by *Perceval*. In *Joseph*, Bron, the brother of Joseph of Arimathea, is commanded by God to catch a fish, which he places next to the Graal, on the occasion that the powers of the latter are first made known to the Graal company, and he is thenceforth referred to as the Rich Fisher or the Good Fisher. In *L'Estoire del Saint Graal* (Vulgate Cycle), the honour of being the first *rich pecheor* is carried over to Bron's twelfth son, Alain li gros, who catches a fish to feed the sinners in Joseph's Graal company, as the Graal will only feed those who are without sin. This fish, like the five loaves and two fishes in Luke 9, is sufficient to feed the company and yet leave more than the original fish. For this, Alain was called the Rich Fisher, and all the Graal Kings after him were given the same title.[37]

In those MHG epics which go back to French originals, A. is not named. He is referred to as 'der arme vischære' in *C*, which appears to be quite independent of *P*, and as 'der riche Vischer', 'der arme Vischer', and 'der Vischer' in *RP*, which simply translates Chrestien's continuators, but which makes a somewhat belated effort to bring the poem into line with Wolfram by bringing in the name A. towards the end. All references to A. by name can be traced back directly to Wolfram.

Such a reference is the episode in *JT*, where A., a young man still in the prime of life, leads a band of Graal knights at a tourney held by Arthur. It is at this tourney that he sees and falls in love with the beautiful Orgelûse, who is married immediately after the close of the tourney to Zidegast.

– *P* a225,8 n251,16; *W* nm99,29; *T* nm9,3; *C* m14001; *UW* nm200,6; *JT* m310,5 n463,5 a1724,3f.; *RB* nm143; *RP* m Prol.113f. a3,11 n506,21; *FS* nm4821 [†]

Amfotêr 'vürste', in charge of Alexander's navy in the Hellespont. He is attacked by Aristômenes but is saved by the arrival of reinforcements from Macedonia. Later he assists Hegelôch at Kîun. So also in Curtius Rufus; in *Expeditio Alexandri* he is represented as being a son of Alexander. – *A* 5067

Amphus 'von Istris', he attacks Paris for the sake of his armour, just after Paris leaves Ribalin. Paris kills A. and one of his companions and puts the other to flight. – *GT* a2311ff. n2327

Anachêl 'künec von Engellant', he fights for the Greeks against the Trojans and is slain by Panthelamon. This character is an invention of Konrad. – *TK* 23924f.

Anamor had been slain with the sword which Venus gives Paris. – *GT* nm2160

Ananîas biblical, comrade of Daniel. In *UA* he is called Sydrach (= Shadrach, the name given to him by the Babylonians) – nm *A* 15443; *JT* 71,1ff.; *UA* 1086

Anaximenes tutor in rhetoric to the young Alexander. A. intends to plead with Alexander to save Athens from destruction, but Alexander swears to do the opposite of what he requests, and A. saves Athens by pleading with Alexander to destroy it. This story is told in Valerius and in Leo (MS S). Rudolf did not recognize in the Naximeneâ, which appeared in the MS of Leo which he used, a variation of A. and included both these names in his list of Alexander's tutors. – *A* 1355

---

37 *L'Estoire del Saint Graal*, in *Vulgate Version of the Arthurian Romances*, I, pp. 251f.:
'Car il lapelerent le riche pecheor. & pour lamor que nostre sires li monstra en cele iournee furent tout cil puis apele riche pescheor qui seruirent del saint graal.'

Andeclis 'vrouwe', her *ami* had been slain by Îaphîne. His death is avenged by Gawein. – *C* nm 9007

Anderoch see Androchus

Andevagus see Andrômachus

Andyalt a knight who pursues Dêmantîn and Sirgamôte. He is unhorsed by Dêmantîn. – *Dem* 4113

Andîân a knight, unhorsed by Dêmantîn at the tourney held by Bêâmunt. – *Dem* 763

Andifoie 'vrouwe', *amie* of Ertgêr. – *Dem* nm9128f.

Andifôr 'von Krêchinlant', *ami* of Delasîe; he is defeated by Dêmantîn in single combat in the battle between Eghart and Dêmantîn. – *Dem* 5422f.

Andolŷâ 'vrouwe', she is maid to Pheradzoye and acts the part of Lûnete by encouraging Pheradzoye to fulfil the custom of the castle and marry Dêmantîn, who has defeated her husband, Pandulet. – *Dem* 3390f.

Andolt master of the hunt at Arthur's court. – *JT* 4803,1

Andrastus see Adrastus (3)

Andrêas see Jordanich

Andrimachâ see Andromache

Andrîôn he pursues Firganant after the latter has slain the *Vogt* of Fandorîch's castle. A. is also killed by Firganant. – *Dem* 6803

Androines see Androcheus

Androcheus a knight who fights for Athis and Prophilias against Bilas. In the OF poem he is called Androgëon. – *AP* A*,102

Androchus a warrior in Alexander's army; he takes part in the raid made by Symachus on Porrus's army. A. is killed by Porrus. – *UA* 19535

Andromachâ see Andromache

Andromache wife of Hector. In *LT*, as in Dictys, she accompanies Pirrus back to Greece after the fall of Troy. So also in Benoît. In *TK* (13266) she is one of the three daughters of Priam, but later (37676) she is correctly called Hector's wife. A. accompanies Priam when he goes to the Greek camp to beg for the body of Hector. In *TK* it is Pollixena who is given to Pirrus after the sack of Troy, and the fate of A. (as in Dares) is not mentioned. – *LT* 9207; *TK* m13254 n13266 a37676

Andrômachus placed by Alexander over Judah, when that land had been conquered. In *A* he is burned alive by the Samarîten, against whom Alexander sends a punitive expedition. A. occurs in *Expeditio Alexandri* and in Curtius Rufus. – *A* nm10665ff.; *SA* 1974ff.; *WA* 1038f.

Andromato see Andrômachus

Andrônîcus he fought with Erîgûus for Alexander against Sartibarzânes. A. occurs in *Expeditio Alexandri* and Curtius Rufus. – *A* 20708

Anêpolis a Persian prince who had been sent to Philipp's court as collector for the tribute which was paid to Dârîus. He recognizes Alexander when the latter visits Dârîus's court disguised as his own messenger. In *SA* the name has become corrupted to Antiopolis. A. occurs in Leo. – *A* a2768 n6541; *SA* 2533f.

Angaras 'von Karamphî', brother of Seimeret. Gawein had slain his brother some years before in a tourney. This brother's name was Dahamorht. Learning that Gawein is in the castle with Seimeret, A. attacks him, and Gawein, who is unarmed, has to defend himself with a chess-board and retires with Seimeret to the tower where the attack continues. It is eventually stopped by the arrival of A.'s father, who reminds his son of the sacred duty of hospitality, and peace is made. This story is obviously the Antikonîe episode of *P* decked out with new names, only the cause of the fight being different (but Vergulaht has challenged Gawein because of his supposed guilt in killing his father). Like Vergulaht, A. makes Gawein undertake to search for the Graal for one year. Meeting Gawein just after the latter has seen the Graal, A. returns with him to Arthur's court, where he is made a knight of the Round Table. – *C* 18823ff.

Angelburg daughter of Mompolier. By censuring her step-mother, Flanea, for her loose conduct, A. incurs her hatred, and Flanea conspires with a magician, Jeroparg, who contrives to fix on A. the guilt of sending her father blind. A. and her two maidens, Salme and Malmelona, are changed into harts, and roam in the woods during the day but turn back to maidens at night. They will only be released from the spell if a prince lies in chastity with A. for thirty nights out of a year without seeing her face. Fridrich (3) has almost done this when he sees her face, and A. and her companions are changed into doves and fly to a spring, where they become maidens only when they bathe. Fridrich finds them here, and after concealing their clothes, compels them to make the necessary promise to be his wife. He chooses A. and then discloses his identity. The maidens now having permanently regained human form, Fridrich marries A., who dies after nine years of married life. –
FS a122f. n220

Angenîs 'künec von Iserterre', he is an ally of Ehkunat against Arthur. He is killed in the battle between Ehkunat and Gârel. – *G* m380 n11807 a12687ff.

Angênor see Agenor

Angeras see Angaras

Angilûn 'von Belinat'. Whilst fighting for Terramêr against Lôîs, A. is killed by Willehalm (1). – *UW* 45,7ff.

Anginon 'künec', attended a tourney held by Arthur. – *C* 593

Angiron 'von Irlant', attended a tourney held by Arthur. – *C* 594

Angnîe mother of Claudîn – *TF* nm10724 a11717

Angorant 'der von' (*Crane*), see Satri

Angsir 'von Slaloi', he is mentioned by Gawein as having been present at a tourney held some years before by Arthur. – *C* nm22645

Angurs 'künec', a heathen who fights against Uter and Pandragun. He is killed by the former, against whom he had planned treachery. – *Mer* 77,6

Anguschias see Angwisiez

Angwisiez 'künec von Schotten', in *E* he is one of the five young kings who come to the wedding of Êrec and Ênîte. Two of the other young kings are his two sons, Côî and Goafilroet. A. is first mentioned in Geoffrey of Monmouth, where he appears as 'Anguselus rex Albaniae quae nunc Scotia dicitur'. In Chrestien's *Erec* he is called Anguisiaus, but he does not appear in the corresponding list in *C* (2291ff.). From Chrestien he is taken over into Gautier's continuation of *Perceval* (var. Aguisiés, which accounts for the variant form, Aguses, in *RP*; elsewhere in *RP* (513,18) he is called Anguschias). In Gautier, and therefore in *RP*, he takes part in the tourney held by Arthur at Orgelus and is present at Arthur's court when Bagumades fights Keiî. A. plays a prominent part in the Vulgate Cycle among the knights who fight for Arthur, but he is never credited with individual adventures. A. appears to correspond to Malory's Agwysaunce (in I,14 etc.), not to Anguysshe, king of Ireland, although Malory himself confuses them (V,2) and calls the latter king of Scotland. In the Dutch *Roman van Lancelot* he is called Anguisel van

Scollant, and an obviously home-made etymology is appended: 'Anguisel . . . die hiet Angelus in Latijn'.[38] – *E* 1973; *RP* 473,5

Anias 'der von' (*JT*), see Rodoltzen

Animal see Amivall

Anchardassîn 'atmerât', a heathen, brother-in-law of Gêrfridolt. A. is killed by Heinrîch (1) in the battle against the Christians. – *Loh* m4228 an4807f.

Anchilles see Achilles

Anchîses father of Ênêâs; he appears in *Ed* as a spirit, warning Ênêâs against approaching difficulties. Ênêâs meets him in Hades, where A. foretells the descendants of Ênêâs down to Romulus. A. occurs in all versions of the fall of Troy, and in *LT* is one of the conspirators to betray the city. His relationship to Ênêâs is ignored by the MHG romances apart from *Ed*. – *Ed* a2546f. n2648; *LT* 14987; *TKf* nm41632

Ankî see Oukîn [See Appendix (7).]

Anmorion see Ammoreon

Anna (1) biblical (Hannah), mother of Samuel. – *RB* m13082f. n13094

Anna (2) wife of Joachim (1) and mother of the Virgin Mary. According to *RB*, Joachim was driven out of the temple because of the barrenness of A., who was subsequently made fruitful by God. This story is not told in the Bible, neither is A. mentioned there, but that this story was current in the Middle Ages is evident from a reference by Konrad von Würzburg to Joachim and Anna as the parents of Mary.[39] – *UA* nm11504; *RB* nm13002

Anna (3) sister of Dîdô; she acts as Dîdô's *confidante*. – *Ed* 1450f.

Anne (1) 'küneginne von Lamparten', daughter of Jordanich. – *Loh* a6225 n6390

Anne (2) see Anna (2)

Annomel, Annopel see Onopel

Annôr 'küneginne von Averre'. (Schulz identified the name with OF *Anor*, 'fief',[40] and Martin points out that this name is common in OF poems and documents.[41] Bartsch considers it an abbreviation of OF Eleonore, Provençal form Lianor, and suggests that Wolfram considered *Li* as the definite article (cf. Orilus < 'li Orgueilleus').[42] This Eleonore he considers to have been the beautiful wife of Henry II, who was much celebrated by the French and German poets. Singer points out that the daughters of Ebrac in Wace's *Brut* (1598ff.) include two named Galaes and Anor, and he sees in these the origin of Gâlôes and Annôr.[43]) A. was the *amie* of Gâlôes and died of grief when the latter was killed in a joust. The name, Anfolê, which she bears in *G* rests on a misunderstanding of *P* 91,16: 'ouwî, künegîn fôle' ('Alas, foolish queen'). There is, in Malory, a Lady Annoure who, failing to gain Arthur's love, tries treacherously to slay him, but the resemblance does not go deeper than the name. – *P* m81,1f. n346,15f.

Anopel see Onopel

Anoxius he is consulted by Agâmennon as to a suitable reward for Paris. – *GT* 3724

Ansgavîn brother of Salmanîde (q.v.); he is captured by Gawein. – *C* m7395 a7434ff. n7520

Ansgîe 'von Îlern', mother of Amurfinâ and Sgoidamur, and sister of Gansguoter. – *C* nm13563ff.

---

38 *Lancelot, Roman van*, Part 2, Book IV, vv. 9708–10 (p. 252).
39 F. von der Hagen, *Minnesinger*, III, p. 339.
40 Schulz, 'Eigennamen', p. 400.
41 Martin (1), p. 289, to 346,16.
42 Bartsch (2), p. 137.
43 Singer (1), pp. 59f.

Ansgü a knight; he is sent by Lohenîs to ride after Gawein on the latter's horse and kill him. Gawein defeats A. and recovers his horse. A. corresponds exactly to Lischois Gwelljus in *P*, and like the latter is given as captive to the ferryman instead of Gawein's horse. – *C* a20161f. n20185

Anshelm (1) name assumed on baptism by Fursîn (2). – *PM* 10228

Anshelm (2) 'von Poitouwe', son of Hûc (2), he is killed by Purrel, whilst fighting against Terramêr in the second battle at Alischanz. Singer is of the opinion that this character appeared in the MS of *Aliscans* used by Wolfram.[44] – *W* 428,27

Ansins 'künec', one of the seven judges at Meliûr's tourney. – *PM* a13476 n13487

Anschevin 'der' (*Loh*), see Lohengrîn

Anschevîne 'der' (*T*), see Gahmuret

Anschewîn 'der' (*Dem*), see Feirefîz

Anschoes knight who attends the tourney held by Leigamar in the service of Aram. – *C* 18164

Ansors see Ansins

Ansusîn a knight killed by Dêmantîn in the battle against Eghart. – *Dem* 5272

Antanôr 'der verswigen', present at Arthur's court. In *P* he will not speak until Kunnewâre has smiled. When she smiles at Parzivâl and is struck by Keiî for doing so, A. opens his mouth and prophesies Keiî's punishment at the hands of Parzivâl. In Chrestien's *Perceval* A. is the unnamed court fool (Culîanz in *C*), and he is not dumb. Most critics agree that A. was named by Wolfram in imitation of Anthenor in *Ed*,[45] a view with which Singer disagrees.[46] – *P* 152,23

Antecrist see Anticrist

Antenor 'grâve', he is sent by Priam to the Greeks, to demand the return of Esîonâ. The scornful treatment he receives causes Priam to decide to attack the Greeks, the occasion being utilized by Paris to fetch Helen. With his two sons, Polidamas and Glaucon, A. fights for the Trojans during the siege of Troy and he is the leader of the conspiracy to betray Troy to the Greeks (see Ênêâs). In *Ed*, A. is seen by Ênêâs in Hades. A. occurs in all versions of the Trojan legend. – *Ed* 3326; *LT* 1916ff.; *TK* 17964ff.

Anterchrist see Anticrist

Antesâl a knight in Bêâmunt's army; he is wounded by Ortamîn. – *Dem* 10738

Anthart 'grâve von Pocîant', father of Dolyfân. A. is in the army against Dêmantîn. – *Dem* nm5153 a10794

Anthenor see Antenor

Anthêus (Antæus) the son of Neptune and Terra, who is squeezed to death by Hercules. – *UA* nm9937

Anthilion 'phallenzgrâve von Salmonîe', in the Greek army against the Trojans; he is slain, after a fierce fight, by Paris. A. is an invention of Konrad. – *TK* 32976

Anthimach see Antimach

Anthimôdes a warrior in Dârîus's army, he is killed by Krâterus at Issôn. A. does not appear in any other history of Alexander. – *UA* 8072f.

Anthisass a vassal of Gamorett. He and his son, Hostras, assist Gamorett in his battle against the Greeks. – [*GT* 5672]

Anthomus see Anthônius (1)

---

[44] Singer (2), p. 122.

[45] Golther (1), p. 152.

[46] Singer (1), p. 61.

Anthona see Anthonye

Anthonax a Trojan, brother of Meloantz (2). – *GT* nm22768

Anthonye a maiden who informs Orgaloyse of the arrival of Nectarus at the court of Agâmennon. – *GT* 4767

Anthônius (1) natural son of Priam; he fights in the Trojan army against the Greeks. A. appears to have been invented by Benoît. – *LT* a4768f. n4777; *TK* 30370f.

Anthonius (2) a knight who fights for Athis against Bilas. So also in the OF version. – *AP* C,18

Anthonjê (1) sister of Arthur; she married the king of Grîtenlant, by whom she had a son, Gahariet. This is the only mention of such a sister of Arthur, but it seems possible that this is a confused memory of Gawein's sister, Sûrdâmûr, whose husband in Chrestien's *Cligés* was Emperor of Greece. – *M* nm127ff.

Anthônje (2) see Anthônius (1)

Antides son of Ajax (1) and Glauca. A. occurs in Benoît as Eantidès. – *LT* nm16899ff. [†]

Antidotus vassal of Gamorett, for whom he fights against the Greeks. – *GT* 5674

Antigênis 'vürste', leader in Alexander's army. A. occurs in *Expeditio Alexandri* and Curtius Rufus. – *A* 13406

Antigôn see Antigonus

Antigonus a prominent leader in Alexander's army; he occurs in all the histories of Alexander. In *UA*, as in Leo and Lampreht, Alexander pretends to be A. when he visits Candacis. In *WA* he calls himself Antiochus (1) (q.v.). – *A* 8590; *UA* 4721

Antikonîe (Schulz thought that the name was derived from OF *entiers conue*, 'she who is recognized as honest'.[47] Martin, on the other hand, thinks it likely that it came from an OF romance with classical names,[48] and Singer names the OF *Roman de Thèbes* as the source.[49]) A. is the sister of Vergulaht and niece of Gahmuret. Gawein, who has to appear at Vergulaht's court, finds her alone in the castle. He evinces signs of passion which are seen by a courtier, and Gawein is attacked. He defends himself and A. in a tower, until the attack is eventually stopped by Kingrimursel, who has tacitly guaranteed him safety at Vergulaht's court. Gawein is compelled, as punishment, to search for the Graal for a year. The story is told fully in Chrestien's *Perceval*, but A. is not named. It is repeated with different names (except that of Gawein) in *C* (see Seimeret). It seems possible that this story is also the source of the episode of Gylorette (q.v.). In *TF*, A. has married Dulcemâr and is the mother of the hero of the romance, Tandareis. She appears also at Arthur's court in *JT*. – *P* m402,21 an404,22f.; *JT* 1611,6; *TF* nm226 a1507

Antikotê 'künec', a former owner of Arofel's sword; he passed it on to Esserê. This character rests on a misunderstanding by Wolfram of *Aliscans*, 11713[2]: 'Salatrez, li rois d'antiquité'. – *W* nm77,26

Anticrist (the Antichrist). – nm *GR* Cb,9; *MC* 886; *A* 17558; *RB* 19560; *SA* 4293

Antikunie see Antikonîe

Antilôis a dwarf king whom Alexander meets whilst out hunting. A. takes Alexander and shows him his court and promises to come whenever Alexander calls him. He comes later to Alexander's court, visible only to Alexander, and buffets the soldiers, causing considerable confusion. A short poem of about 500 verses, which has been preserved in a paper MS of uncertain date (partly also in a parchment MS of the 14th century), appears to

---

47   Schulz, 'Eigennamen', p. 400.
48   Martin (1), p. 322, to 404,23.
49   Singer (1), pp. 104ff.

represent an older form of the story, the point of which has been lost in *UA*. In this poem, called *Alexander und Antiloie*, A., in accordance with his promise to Alexander, buffets only those around the Emperor who are not to be trusted, thus showing him those upon whom he can rely. – *UA* a18971 n19121

Antiloch see Antilocus

Antilocus son of Nestor; he fights in the Greek army against the Trojans. In *LT*, which follows Dares through Benoît, in which latter he is called Antilogus, A. accompanies Achilles into the temple at Troy to see Pollixena and is there slain with him. In *TKf*, as in Dictys, A. is slain in battle by Mennon (2) before the death of Achilles, who goes alone into the temple. A. occurs in Homer. – *LT* 12938f. *TKf* 40949

Antimach father of two Trojans who are stoned to death by the Greeks because A. had recommended treachery to the Greek messengers when they arrived in his land. In Homer it is against Menelaus himself that the treachery is planned, but in Dictys, from where the account in *TKf* is taken, the names of the Greeks are not mentioned. – *TKf* nm45583

Antimus, Antimusz, Antinnus see Antinus

Antinus husband of Contulo, father of Antonne and cousin of Thetis; he gives hospitality to Ulixes and his companions during their search for Achilles, and then accompanies them. He is killed by Hector before Troy. – *GT* m15500 an15544

Antiochius see Antiochus (1)

Antiochus (1) In *SA* Alexander bequeathed Syria to him. In *WA* he is confused with Antigonus and is said to be one of the chief of Alexander's leaders. Alexander pretends to be A. when he visits Candacis. A. occurs in *Expeditio Alexandri* and is mentioned in Valerius as the father of Amyntas. – *SA* nm8489; *WA* 4725ff.

Antiochus (2) brother-in-law of Augustus (Mark Antony). – *UA* nm14660f.

Antiochus (3) (Antiochus Epiphanes), against whom the Maccabees revolted. – *JT* nm3075,4; *RB* nm15914

Antiochus (4) Dârîus instructs A. and Prîmus (q.v.) to capture Alexander. In *SA*, A. is called Anttilogus, a form which is somewhat nearer the original name in Leo, Antilochos. – *A* 4438ff.; *SA* 2206ff.

Antiopolis see Anêpolis

Antipalar a warrior in the Greek army against the Trojans; he challenges Hector, who kills him. – *GT* a18585 n18597

Antipater 'vürste', he is, in all versions of the Alexander-history with the exception of *A*, which does not reach this point, behind the murder of Alexander, which is carried out by his two sons, Cassander and Jullas (see Jobas). In *WA* he only has one son, Cassander, whilst Jobas is his brother. A. is trusted by Alexander, who leaves him in command of Macedonia whilst he is away campaigning. – *A* 3386; *SA* 8203ff.; *WA* 5997f.

Antipins Karadins 'künec', who, it is related, once held a tourney at Castle Orgelus (see Orgelus). A. is not named in the Mons MS of Gautier's continuation of *Perceval*, from which the story is taken. – *RP* nm466,3ff.

Antipolar see Antipalar

Antipus (1) 'von Lide', also called 'Cantipus von Lize' (which occurs in Benoît as a variant reading of Elide). A. fights in the Greek army against the Trojans and is slain by Hector. So also in Dares, where he is called Antiphus ex Elide. In Homer his fate is not recounted. – *LT* 3383

Antipus (2) a warrior in the Trojan army against the Greeks, he is slain by Ajax (1). A. does not occur in Benoît, but the story is told in Dictys, where he is named Antiphonus. He occurs in Homer as Antiphonos. – *TKf* 43220ff.

25

Antîs 'von Pulle', he slew Dêmantîn's father. – *Dem* nm4477

Antisus a vassal of Gamorett; he fights for him against the Greeks. – *GT* 5669

Antonîe sister of Kandaljôn; she releases Tandareis from her brother's prison and keeps him a prisoner in her *kemenâte* for a year. She permits him to attend Arthur's tourney at Sabins but he has to promise to return. His rescue is subsequently made known to Kandaljôn, and when Tandareis is restored to Flordibel, A., who has loved him in vain, is married to Bêâkurs. – *TF* a11206 n13273

Antonne a maiden, daughter of Antinus; she is rescued by Ajax (1) from the clutches of the giant Abiron (2). She takes the heroes, who are searching for Achilles, to her father's house. – *GT* a15399ff. n15481

Antor father of Keiî and foster-father of Arthur. In the OF romances the spelling of this name varies, though the form Auctor (from which comes Malory's Ector) seems to be more usual than Antor. A., although mentioned, is not named in Geoffrey of Monmouth. (See Yttra.) – *Mer* 237,6

Antowe see Antonne

Antrêd see Antrêt

Antrêt (< OF Audret, with misreading of 'n' for 'u'?) A. occurs only in the gleeman versions of the Tristan legend, and in the earliest of these he is called Andrez (Beroul fragments). In *ET* he is the son of Marke's sister and the leader of Tristan's opponents at Marke's court. He tries constantly to betray Tristan but never quite succeeds. In both *UT* and *HT* he is maltreated by Tristan when the latter comes to Marke's court disguised as a fool, and in the former, seeing Tristan and Îsôt lying together, he realises the true identity of the fool and gives the alarm. – *ET* 3156f.; *UT* 1222f.; *HT* 4475

Anttilogus see Antiochus (4)

Antumus, Antunus see Antinus

Anfelis standard-bearer to Hector. A. is an invention of Konrad. – *TK* 30846ff.

Anfimachus see Amphimachus (3)

Anfimacus see Amphimachus (2) and (3)

Anfiole 'küneginne', *amie* of Arbidol. – *JT* 1316,1ff.

Anfissân 'von Ephasê', also called 'von Schotten', counsellor to Bêâmunt; he accompanies her to Antrîûn. – *Dem* nm9668f. a10583

Anfliese see Amphlîse (1)

Anfoies a knight present at the tourney held by Leigamar; A. is under the command of Lorez. – *C* 18150

Anfolê (1) wife of Avenis, sister of Klârîne (3) and mother of Laudamîe and Anfolê (2). She derives her name from that of her daughter. – *G* nm7357

Anfolê (2) daughter of Avenis and Anfolê (1), and sister of Laudamîe; she is identical with Annôr (q.v.). – *G* nm7360ff.

Anfoleise, Anfolise, Anforeise see Amphlîse (1)

Anfortas see Amfortas

Anfroihin he tries to abduct Isazanz but is frustrated by Gawein. – *C* nm9013ff.

Anphus see Amphus

Anzansnûse wife of Riwalîn (2). – *C* 6721

Ancipater see Antipater

Anziflor brother of Turkoit; he is captured and imprisoned by Schandamur; he is released when Seyfrid kills the latter. – *Sey* nm218,1 a248,6

Apatrîs see Aspatrîs

Apelles a famous painter who lived at the time of Philipp and Alexander. In *UA* he paints the panels in the tomb of Carafilîe. – *UA* 11118

Apôbêtus one of the conspirators with Dimnus against the life of Alexander. So also in Curtius Rufus, where he is called Aphobetus. – *A* nm18889

Apolisz killed with the sword which Venus gives Paris. – *GT* nm2160

Apoll, Apollius see Apollô

Apollô the sun-god in Greek mythology; he appears at the wedding of Thetis and Pêleus in *TK*. – *Tn* nm4868f.; *LT* nm3462; *W* nm17,20; *A* nm3406; *R* nm Eing. 1,85; *UW* nm43,30; *JT* nm2800,6; *PM* nm10138; *TK* 944; *MB* nm118,15; *Loh* nm4237; *UA* nm387; *WW* nm2448; *RB* nm16399; *SA* nm2437; *WO* nm609

Apollodôrus in Alexander's army. (See Mênêtas.) A. occurs in *Expeditio Alexandri* and Curtius Rufus. – *A* 13377

Apollônides a warrior under Farnâbâzus at Kîun; he is captured by Hegelôch (1). So also in *Expeditio Alexandri* and Curtius Rufus. – *A* 9524ff.

Apollônîus given by Alexander the task of collecting tribute from Egypt and bringing it to Alexandria. So also in *Expeditio Alexandri*, Curtius Rufus, and Lampreht. – *A* 10632

Appatrîs see Aspatrîs

Appell, Appolle see Apollô

Appollinart squire to Graf Rudolf. – *GR* Ab,4f.

Apt 'Jacob', MHG poet. The author of *RB* refers to him as a contemporary and mentions a poem by him called 'der Ritter unterm Zuber'. – *RB* nm15222

Aquitain see Melôt

Arab 'künec', 'li nains' (i.e. the dwarf), he attended a tourney held by Arthur. – *C* 597

Arabadille wife of Secureis and mother of Sekundille; she sends two knights, Alexander and Philipp, to avenge the death of her husband on Schîonatulander, who overcomes them. A. dies of a broken heart. Her name is evidently invented to provide the latter half of Secundille, just as that of Secureis provides the first half, this being a favourite trick of the author of *JT* (cf. Titurel). – *JT* nm2934,1 a4810,1

Arabastine 'uz Valturmie', 'der ûz' (*JT*), see Senabor (1)

Arâbel the pre-baptismal name of Gîburc (q.v.). In the OF *chansons de geste* she is called Orable and in the *Chancun de Willame* she appears to have given her name to the mother of Rennewart and herself, who is called Oriabel. – *W* 7,27; *UW* nm6,14; *FS* nm1387

Arabie 'künec von' (*JT*), see Zôrôastêr

Araboysin 'diu' (*UW*), see Gîburc

Arabs a Persian knight who is wounded by Alexander at Gaza. This name rests on a misunderstanding of Dictys, IIII, 6 (15), where an 'Arabs quidam Darei miles' occurs at Gaza. – *A* 10251

Araclium a knight in Arthur's army against Marroch. – *Wigm* 3237

Aram 'herzoge von', he brings a company of knights to Leigamar's tourney. – *C* 18161f.

Arap 'von Orlerise', a warrior in Ipomidôn's army against Akarîn. – *JT* 3261,3

Arbasones see Narbâsones

Arben 'vrouwe', present at Arthur's court. A. is included in a list of ladies, between the names of Itonjê and Kundrîe (2) (= Bêne or Arnîve?). – *JT* 1612,3

Arbesselet see Arbessulet

Arbessulet a leader in Akarîn's army against Ipomidôn. – *JT* 3114,1

Arbidale eldest daughter of Parzivâl and Kondwîrâmûrs; she is placed in charge of the Graal (see Elyze (1)). – *JT* a5917,1 n6027,1

27

Arbidol nephew of Orilus and Lehelîn, and *ami* of Anfiole; he is accidentally slain by Schîonatulander in a joust. His death is the original cause of the enmity between Orilus and Schîonatulander which eventually results in the death of the latter. – *JT* a1313,1ff. n1318,6

Arbidone, Arbidunol see Arbidol

Arbosorans 'von Sizily', he jousts with Seyfrid and is unhorsed. They proceed together to Duzisamor's tourney, where Seyfrid, who wins her as the prize in the tourney, gives her to A. – *Sey* a361,4 n362,6

Ardall consulted by Agâmennon as to what reward he should give Paris. – *GT* 3726

Ardân 'künec von Riuelanze', he is badly wounded whilst fighting for Ehkunat against Arthur. Ehkunat sees this and attacks Gârel, who struck the blow. Gârel captures him and later captures A. also. – *G* m373 n11800 a12701

Ardebileis see Ardibileis

Ardente 'der von' (*JT*), see Todan

Arderoch a knight at Arthur's court when Êrec returns with Ênîte. A. does not appear in Chrestien's *Erec*, but it is doubtful whether the addition is to be attributed to Hartmann or to later interpolators. – *E* 1690

Ardessurel 'von Sires', a warrior in Akarîn's army against Ipomidôn. – *JT* nm3126,5

Ardibileis 'von Nubrande', nephew of Akarîn and brother of Ardolise. A. is a commander in Akarîn's army against Ipomidôn. – *JT* 3182,1ff.

Ardibuntze 'von Zifarie', a warrior in Akarîn's army against Ipomidôn. – *JT* 3197,3ff.

Ardilet 'von Lordesse', a warrior in Akarîn's army against Ipomidôn. – *JT* nm3625,3

Ardimole 'von Ungrudies', a warrior in Ipomidôn's army against Akarîn. – *JT* 3231,4

Ardolise 'von Tanarche', also called 'von Kananarke', nephew of Akarîn and brother of Ardibileis. A. is a commander in Akarîn's army against Ipomidôn. – *JT* 3183,1f.

Arebois 'küneginne von' (*UW*), see Gîburc

Ares father of Tor; he never appears in the MHG epics in person. The first mention of A. occurs in Chrestien's *Erec*, v. 1728: 'Et Torz li fiz le roi Arés', which in *C* (2320) became distorted to: 'Und des küneges sun Silâres'. In *RP* the variant reading 'Heres' also occurs. In the Vulgate Cycle, A. is only mentioned on a very few occasions as the father of Tor, but in the *Huth-Merlin* he appears as a cowherd who brings his putative son to Arthur's court so that he can be made a knight. Here Merlin reveals that the real father of Tor is Pellinore, the father of Perceval. In all the OF romances the name is Arés, but in Malory, where the *Huth-Merlin* story is repeated, the name has become altered throughout to Aryes (by a rough association with the Latin *aries*, 'ram'?). – nm *E* 1515; *C* 2320; *RP* 45,3

Areste daughter of Akarîn and wife of Arisuleis. A. is also called Alreste. – *JT* nm3173,5

Arestemeiz 'künec', a warrior in Terramêr's army in the second battle at Alischanz. A. does not occur in the OF versions, but Singer sees in the name a possible confused memory of Aristés[50] (see Hastê). – *W* 423,1

Arêtes a warrior in Alexander's army. A. occurs also in *Expeditio Alexandri* and Curtius Rufus. – *A* 12336

Arêthas 'von Syriâ', a warrior in Dârîus's army, he is killed by Alexander at Issôn. A. does not occur in any of the sources of *UA*. – *UA* 7855f.

Argraspites a commander in Alexander's army against Dârîus. A. occurs in Curtius Rufus as Argyraspides. – *A* 11963

Argunis 'von Marchine', a warrior in Akarîn's army against Ipomidôn. – *JT* nm3138,5

---

[50] Singer (2), p. 120.

Argus he constructed the boat in which Jason sailed to fetch the Golden Fleece. So also in Dares and Benoît. – *LT* 273; *TK* 6840

Argusille wife of Barille and mother of Titurison. – *JT* nm109,1

Arialt 'grâve von Provenzal', unhorsed by Willehalm (4) in the *vesperîe* before the tourney at Komarzi, and taken captive by Elymant at the tourney at Poys. – *RW* nm6182 a6417ff.

Arides 'von Cafalun'. When the devil in the form of Kondwîrâmûrs comes to tempt Parzivâl, he says that he has come to enlist Parzivâl's assistance against A. (called here Calides), who has been oppressing him. When, a little later, Kondwîrâmûrs actually does send for Parzivâl, she gives the name of her oppressor correctly. In the Manessier continuation of *Perceval*, A. is called Aridès de Cavalon; the variant form of Calides in *RP* may possibly be the result of some confusion with Calidès de la Marche (see Talides). – *RP* nm744,31 a769,22

Arideus brother of Alexander and one of the chief of his princes. Alexander bequeathed to him the land of Pelepnensen. A. occurs in Leo. – *SA* 8427f.

Aridol see Arbidol

Aridus see Arideus

Ariguleis 'von Ieresse', a warrior in Akarîn's army against Ipomidôn. – *JT* nm3127,6

Aricheide Alexander bequeathed to him Mesopotan. – *SA* nm8533f.

Arichilone 'von Archilune', a warrior in Akarîn's army against Ipomidôn. – *JT* nm3178,4

Ariolus one of Alexander's learned men, who interprets certain of Alexander's dreams for him and explains the significance of the supernatural birth which precedes the Emperor's death. The name rests on a misunderstanding of certain passages in Leo, where Alexander consults the *ariolus* (i.e. soothsayer). In the absence of capital letters at the commencement of proper names, a practice which was common in the Middle Ages, the noun was thought to be the name of the person. – *A* 8877ff.; *UA* 23594; *WA* 5952f.

Aripuleis 'von Sarrassol', son of Pitagaras, a warrior in Akarîn's army against Ipomidôn. – *JT* 3196,1ff.

Arisayim see Arisaim

Arisaim the *ami* of Pfandimoi (q.v.); A. is rescued by Dêmantîn from the prison, in which he had been kept by Kanphyant. – *Dem* m2387ff. n2577 a2692

Arisidol 'von Ierande', a warrior in Akarîn's army against Ipomidôn. – *JT* 3126,6f.

Arisius a graceless descendant of Romulus. Koppitz, in his index to *GT*, thinks that Arius, the celebrated founder of Arianism, is probably intended. – *GT* nm25111ff.

Aristander one of Alexander's learned men, who interprets various dreams for him. A. occurs in *Expeditio Alexandri*, Curtius Rufus, and Gualterus. – *A* 8975ff.; *UA* 10095f.

Aristêmonês see Aristômenes

Aristes (1) one of Alexander's soothsayers. A. does not occur in any other version of the Alexander-history, but Toischer has pointed out that in the *Philosophorum maximi de mineralibus libri quinque* of Albertus Magnus, the following passage occurs: 'et de hoc mentionem dicitur Aristoteles fecisse in libro de natura serpentum'.[51] According to Toischer, Aristotle's name was undoubtedly written with an abbreviation, which was not recognized by Ulrich, who made from it the name of a new soothsayer. – *UA* 26186

Aristes (2) a knight, son of Saladres; he attacked and was defeated by Parzivâl. So also in Manessier, from which this part of *RP* is taken. – *RP* a842,6 n844,45

Aristôgitôn 'vürste', in Dârîus's army; he was captured by Alexander. A. occurs in *Expeditio Alexandri* and Curtius Rufus. – *A* 7627

---

51 Toischer, pp. 392f.

29

Aristômêdes 'vürste von Tessâlje', one of the leaders in Dârîus's army. So also in *Expeditio Alexandri* and Curtius Rufus. – *A* 6927ff.

Aristômenes In *A* he attacks Amfôter, but his force is routed by the fleet from Macedonia. So in Curtius Rufus and Gualterus. In *UA*, where he is called Aristêmonês, he is 'vürste von Crêtês' and a relative of Dârîus. He also has an *amie*, Tabrôn. – *A* 8608; *UA* 11971

Aristôn a warrior in Alexander's army against Porrus; he saves Alexander's life at Sûdrâcas by climbing over the wall and defending him until the arrival of his army. So in Curtius Rufus and Gualterus. – *UA* 19666

Aristonâ 'burcgrâve von Pêônje', a warrior in Alexander's army. A. met the attack of Satrôpates and killed him. So also in *Expeditio Alexandri* and Curtius Rufus. – *A* 11071f.

Aristônîcus 'herzoge von Medimnêâ', he worried the Macedonians with piracy. Not having heard of the capture of Farnâbâzus at Kîun, he came to visit him and was captured. Alexander, when he heard of the death of Andrômachus, ordered A. to be killed. A. occurs in *Expeditio Alexandri* and Curtius Rufus. – *A* 9590

Aristotel see Aristôtiles

Aristôtiles Alexander's tutor and mentor in later life. A. is generally represented as remaining behind in Macedonia whilst Alexander is campaigning, and sending him advice by letter, whilst Alexander in return keeps A. fully informed as to his conquests. Of the MHG versions, only in *SA* does A. accompany Alexander on his travels, in the course of which he shows Alexander how to overcome the basilisk by means of a mirror. This story must, however, have been current in Germany long before, as it is referred to in *JT*,[52] which was written about eighty years before *SA*. A popular medieval legend shows A. in love with a woman whom he allows to saddle him and ride him like a horse. This legend is referred to in *RB*, where the woman is called Silarin (q.v.). – *A* nm82 a1379ff.; *JT* nm99,5; *Loh* nm115; *UA* a1263 n1289; *RB* nm15183; *WO* nm14315; *SA* nm45 a6707; *WA* 293

Aristotilis see Aristôtiles

Arisuleis 'von Sardine', husband of Areste, a leader in Akarîn's army against Ipomidôn. – *JT* 3173,1ff.

Arisun 'der starke', killed fighting for Akarîn against Ipomidôn. – *JT* 3459,5

Arîûn a vassal of Schaffilûn; he comes to take the oath of allegiance to Wigalois on his enthronement. A. fights for Wigalois against Lîon. – *Wigl* a9080ff. n10098

Arjôbarzanes a commander in Dârîus's army in the second battle against Alexander. A., with an army of Persians, offers some resistance after the battle, but his army is routed and he himself flees to Persipolis, where he is killed by Krâterus. A. appears in *Expeditio Alexandri* and Curtius Rufus. – *A* 11655

Archâbatus a relative of Dârîus, for whom he fights against Alexander. A. does not occur in any other version of the Alexander-history. – *UA* 15877

Archais see Archibeis

Archandibeis 'von Lardubose', a warrior in Akarîn's army against Ipomidôn. – *JT* nm3141,4ff.

Archanî father of Pharôs; A. is not mentioned in any of the sources of *UA*. – *UA* nm12011

Archaxerses see Artâxerses

Archeinor 'herzoge von Nouriênte'. (Bartsch sees in this name a form of the Greek name, Archenor,[53] whilst Martin quotes a doubtful suggestion by Hagen, who points out the

---

[52] *JT* 3933,5.
[53] Bartsch (2), p. 156.

similarity of this name with two words, which are, however, well separated, in Pliny (8,81): 'Anthi . . . (tra)nare'.[54] Feirefîz relates that he defeated A. in a joust. – *P* nm770,25

Archeis see Archibeis

Archelaus (1) 'künec von Boêzîe', brother of Prôthênor; he fights for the Greeks against the Trojans. A. occurs also in Benoît. – *LT* 3312ff.; *TK* 23790

Archelâus (2) 'grâve', he is left by Alexander as prefect with Abûlites. So in *Expeditio Alexandri* and Curtius Rufus. – *A* 13493f.

Archibeis 'von Remichare', also called Archais and Archeis; he is wounded by Kailet whilst fighting for Ipomidôn against Akarîn. – *JT* nm3233,1 a3671,1

Archies Alexander bequeathed to him the Pilases. – *SA* nm8531f.

Archikoleis 'von Andervîle', steward to Meie; he accompanied Meie when he went to Rome. – *MB* 208,16

Archilogus (1) 'künec', he is slain by Hector, whilst fighting for the Greeks against the Trojans. So also in Benoît. – *TK* 39840

Archilogus (2) son of Theseus von Therasche; he fights for the Trojans against the Greeks. This character was taken by Benoît from Dares, where he is called Archelochus e Thracia. The territorial name given to A. in *TK*, viz. 'von Grossiâ', appears to be a corrupt form of Thracia. An Archelochos occurs in Homer, but he is there the son of Antenor. – *LT* 4064; *TK* 24892

Archilôcram Alexander bequeathed Mesopotâmia to him. A. does not occur in any other version of the Alexander-history. – *UA* nm27043

Arkûn 'von Lûnatel', a warrior who fought for Lôîs against Terramêr. – *UW* 46,13

Arl 'der von' (*Loh*), see Gêrvrit

Arl 'künec von' (*UW*), see Pirre

Arl 'küneginne von' (*UW*), see Kyburg (1)

Arlot 'von Lordibise', a warrior in Akarîn's army against Ipomidôn. – *JT* nm3639,1f.

Armessulans a warrior in Akarîn's army against Ipomidôn. – *JT* nm3127,7

Arminolt 'vürste von Norwegen', he kills Osann's father and mother, and intends to violate her, when he is challenged and defeated by Fridrich (3). This is the first recorded adventure of Fridrich in his search for the spring, where he is to find Angelburg. – *FS* m1881f. a1982f. n1989

Arminzidole 'der von' (*JT*), see Ackrison

Armiones see Ermiona

Arnalt 'von Gerunden', son of Heimrîch (1) and brother to Willehalm (1). The wife of the justice whom Willehalm kills appeals to A. for revenge, and although he agrees with Willehalm and blames the townsfolk for asking a knight for toll, he is compelled to follow and challenge Willehalm. After he has been unhorsed, the brothers recognize each other, and A., learning Willehalm's plight, returns to the town to collect his men to assist Willehalm. In *UW* he is depicted as an ally of Lôîs against Terramêr. In the OF *chansons de geste* of the Guillaume d'Orange cycle he is called Hernaut. – *W* a5,16f. n6,27; *UW* m4,14 a21,1 n24,1

Arnîve see Îgerne

Arnolt (1) a trusted friend of Reinfrid von Braunschweig. Reinfrid placed Yrkâne in his care whilst he was warring in the Holy Land. – *RB* m14370 an14381ff.

Arnolt (2) 'herzoge', called 'der Beier herre'; he fought for Karl in the battle against the Hungarians. – *Loh* 2921

---

54 Martin (1), p. 504, to 770,25.

Arnolt (3) 'von Havenerpurc', brother of Gotfrit (2). A. jousted with Ulrich von Liechtenstein during the latter's *Venusfahrt*. – *FD* 616,1

Arnolt (4) 'von Malbriûn', counsellor to Meliûr; he suggests the holding of the tourney. When Partonopier is attacked by the Soldan, he brings his five sons, and together they bear the brunt of the opening battle. – *PM* nm11562ff. a14062

Arnolt (5) 'der Fuhs', helped Konrad to write *PM*. – *PM* nm214f.

Arnost a knight in Sornagiur's army; he is slain by Partonopier. – *PM* 3622ff.

Arnûs 'künec', one of the seven judges at Meliûr's tourney. – *PM* a13476 n13491

Aron see Aaron

Aropatîn 'von Gamfassâsache', leader of Terramêr's sixth army in the second battle at Alischanz. Of the OF *chansons de geste* A. occurs only in *Aliscans*, where he is called Alipantin. – *W* 348,2

Arofel 'künec von Persîâ', brother of Terramêr and uncle of Gîburc. He is also maternal uncle to Libilûn. A. is placed in command of Terramêr's ten sons and is killed by Willehalm at the first battle at Alischanz. In *Aliscans* he is named Aerofle. – *W* 9,22; *FD* nm1410,7; *JT* nm3639,6; *RB* nm16756

Aroffel see Arofel

Arpon 'von Sicilien', in the Trojan army against the Greeks. A. occurs in Benoît as Ampon (var. Apon). – *LT* 3980

Arragûn 'künec von' (*P* and *JT*), see Schafillôr

Arragun 'künec von' (*RW*), see Gilbert

Arrant 'licont', a knight present at a tourney held by Arthur. – *JT* 1991,2

Arras a Trojan who slays Kamille (1). He is a coward but manages to take Kamille off her guard and slays her with a javelin. He is seen by Carpîde, who attacks and kills him. In the OF *Eneas* he is called Arranz, and in Virgil, Arruns. – *Ed* 9046

Arsâmes 'sâtrâpas von Sicilia'. When A. learned that Alexander's army was approaching, he laid waste the land so that they were unable to find food. So also in Curtius Rufus. – *A* 5622f.

Artabânus a former king of Persia, who, according to *A*, reigned between Xerses (1) and Artâxerses (1). There appears to be no historical justification for this character. – *A* nm15717

Artâbâzus 'vürste', father of Ilîôn. A. remains faithful to Dârîus to the end and barely escapes with his life, when Bessus and his companions turn traitor. When, after the death of Dârîus, A. surrenders to Alexander, he is an old man of 95 years, but nevertheless he fights against Sârtibarzânes. Alexander makes him king of Bactrîâ. A. occurs in *Expeditio Alexandri*, Curtius Rufus, and Gualterus. – *A* nm7614ff. a14306

Artanna wife of Marcus (1). She heals Paris after his maltreatment at the hands of Gamorett. – *GT* 6341ff.

Artaus see Artûs

Artaxerses (1) a former king of Persia. He bore the surname Longimanus, which is given as the name of a separate person in *A*. – *A* nm15718

Artaxerses (2) 'künec von Persîâ' (historically Artaxerses III). A. attackes Egypt, causing Nectanabus to flee to Macedonia. In *A*, Ochus is given as an alternative name for A. – *A* 182ff.; *SA* 101ff.; *WA* 106f. [†]

Arthur see Artûs

Artûs king of Britain, son of Utepandragûn and Îgerne, and father of Lôhût. (Bruce shows that the name is Roman, occurring as Artorius in Tacitus and Juvenal.[55] The form of the name which was used exclusively by the MHG poets is the *cas sujet* of the name as it appeared in the OF romances.) Bruce gives reasonable proof that A. was an historical figure, probably a Romanized Celt, or a man of Roman descent who attained leadership of the Celts during the wars against the Anglo-Saxons.[56] Chronicles recount that A. was instrumental in winning the battle of Mons Badonis, but the first authentic mention of him was made by Nennius when he re-edited the *Historia Brittonum*, a work originally written in 679. The legend of A. was firmly established by 1131, as is testified by a treatise by Hermann of Tournai,[57] whilst evidence of its growth is supplied by William of Malmesbury's *Gesta Regum Anglorum* (1125), and, above all, by Geoffrey of Monmouth's *Historia Regum Brittaniae* (*c.* 1137), in which the supernatural element is brought into prominence. Geoffrey's history was widely diffused by a rimed paraphrase, called *Brut*, written by the Anglo-Norman poet, Wace, in 1155.

The first of the extant romances proper is the *Erec* of Chrestien de Troyes (*c.* 1150–60). Other evidence of the spread of A.'s popularity, such as the frequent occurrence of the names Artusius and Galvanus (Gawein) in Italy *c.* 1100,[58] and the bas-relief on the architrave of the cathedral at Modena,[59] is of too uncertain a nature to carry much weight.[60]

The following is a summary of the part played by A. in the various MHG epics, arranged in approximate chronological order. [See Introduction.]

ET	Marke sends Tristan on an embassy to A.'s court as a pretext for getting him away for some time. A. arranges a hunt and spends the night with Marke, Tristan using the opportunity to see Îsolt (2).
L	Passive rôle. He permits Êrec and Gawein to be handed over to Malduc (see Maldwîz) as the latter's reward for rescuing Ginovêr.
E	A. kills the white hart at a hunt, the prize for which feat is a kiss from the prettiest lady present. He takes it from Ênîte. His sister Feimorgân is mentioned.
I	A. undertakes, with his knights, the adventure of the spring (see Îwein (1)). A. himself does not joust.
Wigl	Passive rôle.
Mtl	A. refuses to eat until an adventure is heard of. It is almost mid-day before a squire arrives with the cloak of chastity.
P	A. is away searching for Sangîve and Arnîve (see Îgerne) when his father is at Herzeloide's tourney. His rôle is passive until he busies himself with bringing about the reconciliation between Gawein and Gramoflanz, for which he is largely responsible.
DB	A. is required by Matûr to submit to the latter's overlordship. A. attacks Matûr with his army and proves a valiant fighter, killing Matûr himself. The

---

55 Bruce (1), I, pp. 3ff.; for further suggested etymologies, see p. 4, note 4.
56 Bruce (1), I, pp. 3ff.
57 Bruce (1), I, p. 10.
58 Weston (1), p. 8.
59 A good description of this is given in Cross and Nitze, pp. 22ff.
60 Bruce (1), I, pp. 12 and 14ff.

fight goes on for three days, and on the fourth day A.'s side wins by a trick. On the day of Daniel's wedding, A. is captured by an old man with strong arms, who retains him until Daniel manages to capture the old man with his invisible net.

C The story is told of how A.'s father died when A. was six years old. A. became king, was married, and at the age of 21 was made a knight. He holds a great tourney at the opening of *C*. One day he returns from a hunt, and is warming himself before the fire when Ginovêr taunts him with a knight, who, for love of her, is riding about, clad only in his shirt. A. sets out to find the knight, Gasosîn, and a fierce fight is left undecided, as Gasosîn, who has no armour, learns A.'s identity just before his shield is hacked to pieces. A combat is arranged for six weeks later, but a reconciliation is brought about just before the fight, and Ginovêr is left to decide with whom she will go. She elects to remain with Arthur.

MA The marriage of Manuel and Amande takes place at A.'s court (see below).

Wigm A. holds a tourney to dispose of the crown of Deleprosat, and he himself takes part. At the request of Ysope, he leads an army against her oppressor, Marroch, whom he himself kills, being wounded by Offratin.

G Ehkunat challenges him to battle, because Utepandragûn slew Ehkunat's father. The fight does not take place, as Gârel defeats Ehkunat beforehand.

JT A. attends Schîonatulander's *swertleite* and later holds a great tourney, in the course of which the inscription on the leash of Ehkunat's hound is read. On the return of Schîonatulander from the East, A. assists him in the battle against Orilus and is himself challenged by the Emperor of Rome, Lucius, who demands A.'s submission or abdication on the grounds of his illegitimate birth (see Utepandragûn). A. leads his army against Lucius, whom he himself kills.[61]

M A. has three sisters, Antonjê, Seifê (see Sangîve), and Olimpîâ, the mother of Meleranz. A reference is made to A.'s custom of never sitting down to breakfast without first hearing of an adventure. For the rest, his rôle is passive.

TF Passive rôle

Sey Passive rôle

Mer An account is given of his boyhood with his foster-father, Antor, and his foster-brother, Keiî, how he draws the sword from the stone in the churchyard and is proclaimed king, and marries Ginovêr. All this is almost identical with the account in *L'Estoire de Merlin* (Vulgate Cycle) and in Malory.

Loh The sound of the bell attached to the hawk which Elsam catches rings loudly at Arthur's court, where the Graal is kept. At Keiî's suggestion three maidens enter the Graal temple and read the message of the Graal. Elsam's need of a champion is thus made known, and A., amongst others, offers himself, until it is made known that Lohengrîn has been specified by the Graal.

HT A. arranges a hunt as in *ET*

---

61 This episode is of considerable importance, as, although it occurs in Geoffrey, Wace, and the *Estoire de Merlin* (where he is called Luces), this is the only reference to Lucius in the MHG epics. In view of this, it is difficult to see how Bruce (Bruce (1), II, p. 299) can say: 'The author uses Wolfram's *Parzival* and *Titurel*, but no French romance.'

GM	When Gauriel arrives at Arthur's court and overthrows the best knights of the Round Table, A. puts on his armour and wishes to fight, but Gauriel refuses, as he considers himself unworthy to fight A.
RP	A. wages a successful war against Bruns (1), and later leads a band of knights to the rescue of Gifles, but he himself does not joust. He is attacked by Catras, who is defeated, and A. then holds a tourney before the Castle Orgelus, which is attended by Parzivâl in disguise.
Ll	As in *Loh.* In MS K it is A. who suggests that the Graal message should be read, not Keiî as in *Loh* and *Ll.*

As can be seen from the above summary, A. is the central figure, around which the action takes place, whilst his own rôle, as in the bulk of Arthurian literature, is essentially passive. This was evidently realised by the author of the *Torec* episode in the Dutch *Lancelot.* In this story, A. is a very powerful jouster, and after heavily unhorsing Parzivâl, Lanzelet, and Gawein, he vows never to fight again. In a scene very much like that in *GM*, he breaks his vow, however, to joust with Torec (the hero of the poem!), whom he unhorses.

None of the MHG epics (excluding Füetrer's compendium) tells the story of Arthur's death in battle against Mordred, but in *MA* he is said to have suffered through a fish which took the shape of a cat.[62] Freymond shows that by this is meant the Cath Palug[63] (see also Keiî). The same suggestion that Arthur met his death fighting the cat is contained in the OF *Romanz des Franceis*, by André.[64] This cat, A.'s battle with which is described in *L'Estoire de Merlin* (Vulgate Cycle) and in the *Livre d'Artus* and Malory is, in the Welsh triads, fished out of the sea.

In *La Mort le Roi Artu* (Vulgate Cycle) and in Malory, A. is borne away mortally wounded to Avalon, where, as the legend has it, he waits for the hour of his country's need, when he will return.[65]

During the 13th century a legend, mentioned by Gervasius of Tilbury in England, and by Cäsarius von Heisterbach in Germany, grew up, that A. was waiting with his knights in Mount Etna, the mountain of the Sibyl.[66] His court in Etna is mentioned in the *Wartburgkrieg*, where Juno and Felicia are added to his company.

– *ET* nm3876f. a5024; *L* nm1264 a1354; *E* 1095ff.; *I* nm5 a31; *Wigl* 145ff.; *Mtl* nm29 a62; *P* nm66,3 a148,29; *Tn* nm16865; *DB* 33; *W* nm356,8; *C* 163ff.; *A* nm20670; *RW* nm2235; *Edol* nm A,111; *MA* nm57 a88; *Wigm* 31ff.; *FD* nm1416,7; *G* a14 n37; *JT* nm930,5 a1101,3ff.; *M* nm112f. a2053ff.; *TF* nm178 a198; *Sey* nm11,1ff. a63,3; *Mer* m233,5 a237,1f. n240,4; *Loh* nm232 a377; *HT* nm1213 a1970; *RB* nm158; *GM* nm19 a419; *WO* nm16988; *RP* nm Prol.133 a16,40f.; *FS* nm4811; *Ll* nm1,7 a27,1 (MS K) 7,7 [†]

Arundîs a knight, whom the wounded knight, who gives Dêmantîn news of Sirgamôte in the wood, claims to have unhorsed. – *Dem* nm2943ff.

Arfaxât (1) a king of the Medes and a contemporary of Nâbuchodônosor, by whom he was defeated. – *RB* nm26722

---

62 *MA* 156ff.: 'ein visch wurde uf gerizzen/ Des der kunic sere engalt,/ als ein katze gestalt.'

63 Freymond (2), pp. 327ff.

64 Freymond (2), pp. 327ff.

65 *MA* 142ff.: 'Die do lebten an der zit,/ die heten alle den strit,/ Er queme wider als er wolte', and *I* (12ff.): 'des hânt die wârheit/ sîne lantliute:/ sî jehent er lebe noch hiute'.

66 Golther (1), p. 246.

Arfaxât (2)   builder of Ecbâtanâ, the chief city of Mêdîâ. – *A* nm14231

Arpfenan   a dwarf in the service of Waradach; he is slain by Hector at Troy. – *GT* a12368ff.
n12498

Arfidantz   'burcgrâve von Kamfoleis', also called Affridantze; he is present at a tourney held
by Arthur. – *JT* 2007,3

Arfiklant   'künec', brother of Turkant; he is slain by Willehalm (1) during the first battle at
Alischanz. A. occurs elsewhere only in MS M of the OF *Aliscans* (471ª); in the other MSS
this character is called Claradut, etc., but in MS M, Arfulant. – *W* 29,1

Arxes   a former king of Persia (Arsēs), son of Artâxerses (2). – *A* nm15730

Arzêpolis   one of the conspirators with Dimnus against the life of Alexander. A. occurs in
Curtius Rufus as Archepolis. – *A* nm18891

Arciarxes   Alexander bequeathed to him Agres, Sicedres, and the Parapetimines. A. is not
mentioned in any of the other histories of Alexander. – *UA* nm27026f.

Asâ   biblical, king of Judah (I Kings 15). – *A* nm16290

Asahel   biblical, brother of Joab; he was slain by Abner. – *UA* nm11555

Asach   'von Joppitê', his death in the battle against the Greeks is lamented by the Trojans but
not described. A. is slain in Dictys, where he is named Arsacus and is a natural son of
Priam. – *TKf* nm43405

Asarîas   comrade of Daniel (Azariah). A. is also referred to by his Babylonian name,
Abdenagon (= Abednego). – nm *A* 15444; *JT* 71,1ff.; *UA* 1086

Asya   'künec von' (*WO*), see Melyemodan

Asius (1)   son of Climant and brother of Ecubâ (3); he is slain by Ajax (1), whilst fighting for
the Trojans against the Greeks. So also in Dictys. A. occurs in Homer, but his fate is not
given. – *TKf* 44030f.

Asius (2)   'von Sestô', a warrior in the Trojan army; he is captured by the Greeks and slain.
So also in Dictys. – *Tkf* 40510

Ascalaph   see Ascalaphus

Ascalaphus   'künec von Cumenîe', father of Alinus and (in *TK*) brother of Jamêne; he fights
in the Greek army against the Trojans. In *GT*, A. is badly wounded in single combat with
Paris and is healed by Medea. He then attacks Hector, who kills him. A. occurs in Homer,
Dares (as Ascalaphus ex Orchomeno), and Benoît. – *LT* 3318; *TK* 23786; *GT* a18176ff.
n18195

Ascalinor   'von Cloramîr', in the Greek army against the Trojans; he is slain by Paris. A. is
an invention of Konrad. – *TK* 33684

Ascalôn   'künec', husband of Laudîne. A. is the lord of a magic spring in the forest of
Breziliân (Broceliande), and when any knight is so bold as to pour water from the spring on
to a near-by stone, A. issues forth to challenge him. In this way he defeats Kalogreant but
is himself defeated and killed by Îwein (1), who subsequently marries Laudîne and becomes
lord of the spring. In Chrestien's *Yvain*, A. is called Esclados le Ros. In *JT*, as Ascalone
von Precilie (Breziliân), he is present at a tourney held by Arthur. His name is also
(1610,6) used as a place-name in Laudine von Ascalon. – *I* m694f. a1000ff. n2274; *C*
m1347; *JT* 1747,2

Askalôn   'künec von' (*W*), see Glôrîôn (2)

Ascalosius   see Ascalofius

Ascalofius   father of Machaon and Polidarius (1); he fights in the Greek army against the
Trojans. In Homer he is called Asklepios, in Dares and Dictys, Aesculapius, and in Benoît,
Esculape. – *LT* nm3364 a4908ff.

Ascalûn 'burcgrâve von Troie', a warrior in the Trojan army against the Greeks. This character is an invention of Konrad. – *TK* 31350

Ascalun 'künec von' (*JT*), see Kingrisîn

Askalûn 'künec von' (*P*), see Vergulaht

Ascânjus son of Ênêâs, also called Jûlus. A. acts throughout *Ed* as Ênêâs's right-hand man. He slays a tame hart belonging to Tŷrus, and thus gives Turnus his first pretext for attacking Ênêâs. A. occurs in the OF *Eneas* and in Virgil. – *Ed* nm760ff a824

Aschalafer, Aschalafus see Ascalaphus

Aschalonê 'von Syriâ', nephew of Laamez; he is unhorsed by Mitarz at the tourney held by Leigamar. – *C* 18055f.

Aschalophus see Ascalaphus

Aschos 'von Horchan',[67] a knight who, with twelve others, attacks Thedalus, after Paris had left the latter's service. Paris sees the attack, however, and rescues Thedalus, killing all the attackers. – *GT* a3222 n3265

Ascolone, Ascone see Ascalôn

Ascurant A fight is mentioned, which appears to have taken place between Gawein and A. in a cave. – *C* nm6124f.

Aspatrîs 'von Nubîe', a heathen king who did great feats of arms at the tourney held by Meliûr. A. fights for the Soldan against Partonopier and engages in single combat with Walther (1). After a hard fight, one thousand of A.'s men arrive to assist him, but although he is a heathen, he scorns to use them and allows Walther to go free. – *PM* 14476ff.

Aspinogres see Espinogres

Aspjol 'von Tîmant', a relative of Lanzelet, whose entry into Genewîs he helps to prepare. – *L* 8260ff.

Aspramatinse see Amaspartîns

Asprat 'von Schipolonte' (for the territorial name, cf. Amaspartîns), a warrior in Ipomidôn's army against Akarîn. – *JT* nm3220,4

Asprîân a giant who occurs in the MHG poem *König Rother*. – *RB* nm25266

Assandrus (1) brother of Egyal; he is killed fighting for her against the army under Dyomedes. A. appears to be one of the few characters invented by Herbort. – *LT* 17231f.

Assandrus (2) he gave Crispus news of Peleus. A. occurs also in Dictys and Benoît. – *LT* 17842

Assibor brother of Barille. – *JT* m104,1 n105,5

Assiles a giant, brother of Baingranz; he lays waste the land belonging to Flôis, who sends to Arthur for help. Gawein, who undertakes the mission, overcomes A.'s henchman, Galaas, then defeats A.'s army and kills A. – *C* m5469ff. n5520 a10025ff.

Assilier 'von Clinobare', a warrior in Ipomidôn's army against Akarîn. – *JT* 3231,1

Assiponte 'von Elmondare', a warrior in Akarîn's army against Ipomidôn. – *JT* nm3134,1

Asspynogres see Espinogres

Assundîn Dassir's right-hand man, and afterwards marshal to Gayol. A. wounds Gayol, when the latter is a child, and by the scar, he recognizes Gayol, when the latter comes to

---

67 The passage in which A. is named is undoubtedly corrupt, v. 3264ff. reading as follows: 'Da ich geritten für den wald/ Was, Aschos von Horchan,/ Die ritten mich mit zwölffen an.' Koppitz (*GT*, to 3265) suggests, therefore, either the alteration of 'von' to 'und', in which case Horchan would be the name of a knight, or the emendation of v. 3266 to read: 'Der reit mich selbzwölfte an'. The latter reading is to be preferred, since, as Koppitz indicates, v. 3222 states that there are only twelve attackers in all.

claim his kingdom, which A.has been controlling for him. At the tourney for Acheloyde, A. plays the part of king, until Gayol has been chosen as husband by Acheloyde, when the real situation is revealed. Whilst Gayol is on his quest against Acurteis, A. again looks after his land for him. A. marries Gayol's mother, the widow of Dassir. – *Crane* m667 a709 n720

Assuntîn   father of Firganant. – *Dem* nm6744

Astalabus   killed whilst fighting for Matribulus against Agâmennon. – *GT* 3469

Astar   'von Sencepunt', also called 'von Nibrodoltze', a warrior in Ipomidôn's army against Akarîn. – *JT* nm3241,5

Astacê   'von Persîâ', Dârîus's commander in Egypt. This character appears to have been invented by Rudolf. – *A* 10416

Asteropêus   a warrior in the Trojan army; he is wounded by Achilles. In Dictys, as in Homer, he is eventually slain by Achilles. A. does not occur in Benoît. – *TKf* 43264ff.

Astirot   according to *P*, one of the fallen angels. Golther identifies A. with Astarte, the Semitic goddess, who was also the principal female deity of the Phoenicians and who appeared as a male devil in the popular plays of the Middle Ages.[68] – *P* nm463,10

Astor (1)   'künec', present at the fight between Parzivâl and Agors (see Strangedorz). (The same as Astor (2)?) – *JT* 5635,1ff

Astor (2)   'herzoge von Lanverunz', a knight in the army which Poidikonjunz leads against Lipaôt in *P*. In *JT* he is present at a tourney held by Arthur, being called on his first appearance 'Ducastor, vürste ûz Lavariuntze'. According to Bartsch, Astor was a common name in the south of France,[69] whilst Martin points out that Estor occurs in the Breton legends.[70] – *P* nm343,22 a358,23; *JT* 1998,4

Astor (3)   'cuns von Pamfatîs', he is stated to have been defeated by Feirefîz. Martin shows that the name Aster occurs in Solinus (62,14); he refers also to Hagen's suggestion that the name should read Castor, who, as the brother of Pollux, is mentioned frequently in Solinus.[71] – *P* nm770,26

Astririsel   'von Purmidac', a warrior in Ipomidôn's army against Akarîn. – *JT* 3218,1

Astrolis   a vassal of Gamorett, brother of Belion; he fights for Gamorett against the Greeks. – *GT* 5665

Astulôn   a relative of Arnolt (4); he fights with him for Partonopier against the Soldan. – *PM* 20623

Aswerro   see Aswerus (1)

Aswerus (1)   king of Persia (Ahasuerus), usually identified with Xerses (1). In *UA* a reference is made to his marriage to Esther, whilst in *JT* he is stated to be the son of Karfidûn and the ancestral head of Akarîn's family. According to *SA*, A. was a former king of India and the builder of the palace in which Porrus dwelt. – nm *JT* 2829,5; *UA* 11801; *RB* 24950; *SA* 4811

Aswerus (2)   king of Persia; this name is incorrectly given in *A* for Artaxerses II. – *A* nm15724

Atamûn   a warrior in the Greek army against the Trojans. This character appears to have been invented by Konrad. – *TK* 34286

Atanâgoras   'von Persîâ', under the command of Farnâbâzus at Kîun; he is captured by Hegelôch. So also in Curtius Rufus, where he is named Athenagoras. – *A* 9524ff.

---

68   Golther (1), p. 214.
69   Bartsch (2), p. 148.
70   Martin (1), p. 287, to 343,22.
71   Martin (1), p. 504, to 770,26.

Aternantes son of Hector; in *TKf*, where he is called Aminactis, he is stated to be the elder son. Dares and Dictys have the correct Virgilian form, Astyanax, which Benoît has distorted into Asternatès (var. Aternantès). In Benoît, A. is the younger son of Hector. – *LT* nm9649f.; *TKf* 41001ff.

Âthamas a Trojan who is seen by Ênêâs during the latter's visit to Hades. A. does not occur in the OF *Eneas. – Ed* 3327

Athanatâ (< θάνατος, 'death'; therefore 'the Immortal'?) a Roman lady, of whom Virgil, according to medieval legend, became enamoured. Refusing to accede to his desires, she reveals Virgil's passion to her husband and at his suggestion arranges a midnight tryst with her would-be lover. A basket is lowered to draw him up to her bedroom window, but it is only half raised, and Virgil is left to spend the night hanging in the basket half-way between the ground and the window and to provide an amusing spectacle for the eyes of the mocking Romans the next morning. Virgil, who was far better known as a magician than as a poet in the Middle Ages, takes his revenge in a manner which is peculiarly medieval in its indelicacy. Although the legend was a very popular one, the woman is hardly ever named. According to F. von der Hagen, the name Athanata does not occur anywhere else in this connection,[72] and she is unnamed in the extract from *Jansen Enenkels Weltbuch*,[73] in which the story is told, and in the *Fabel* of Hans Sachs, *Der Filiüs* (i.e. Virgilius) *im korb. – RB* nm15177

Athen 'herzoge von' (*LT*), see Menesteus

Athis an Athenian lord who is married to Cardionese, whom he abandons to his friend Prophilias, when he learns that the latter is dying for her. A. wanders out into the world, and at a chance meeting in Rome, Prophilias fails to recognize A., who feels that life is now worthless and, seeing a man murdered, takes upon himself the guilt in order to court death. Prophilias, who recognizes A. and believes him to be the murderer, says that he himself did the crime. The position is cleared up by the discovery of the real murderer, and A. meets, and falls in love with, Prophilias's sister, Gayte, who reciprocates his passion, but who has been promised to Bilas, a powerful king who is approaching with a large army to claim her. Bilas refuses to forego his claim, and a battle takes place, in which he is defeated and Gayte, who has been given to him in accordance with the promise, is recovered. A. marries her, and after some time A. and Prophilias, together with their wives, return to Athens. Whilst they are there, Pirithous, a prince who has fallen in love with Gayte, embroils them in a war with Thelamon, who is at first defeated, but who returns with Bilas as his chief ally. Pirithous is killed in the ensuing battle, and Cardionese, who hears incorrectly that it is Prophilias who is dead, dies of grief. At the request of the dying Pirithous, his sister, Alemandîn marries Prophilias. This is the story as told in the OF romance by Alexandre, who used an oriental legend, which appears in the *Disciplina Clericalis* of Alphonsus, and who himself supplied the Gayte love story and the battle scenes.[74]

Of the MHG poem, which was a by no means slavish translation of the OF romance, only the following fragments remain:

A	A. takes upon himself the blame for the murder and is arrested.
Ab – Ad	Prophilias confesses to the murder.
Ae	A. and Prophilias are free.
A*	Gayte's love for A. is declared. Preparations for the battle with Bilas.

---

72 F. von der Hagen, *Gesammtabenteuer*, III, pp. cxlf.
73 F. von der Hagen, *Gesammtabenteuer*, III, pp. 509ff.
74 Vogt, pp. 195f.

A**, B, C	Battle before Rome.
C* and D	Marriage of A. and Gayte.
E	Battle with Bilas and Thelamon before Athens.
F	Death of Pirithous (who is not named), and the highly poetical lament (not in the OF) of Theseus over his son.

– AP [aA,1] [nA,45]

Atilus see Attalus

Atis see Athis

Atîzies a warrior in Dârîus's army; he is killed by Alexander. So also in *Expeditio Alexandri* and Curtius Rufus. *– A* 7487

Atlas the giant who, in Greek mythology, was compelled to bear the universe on his shoulders. *– RB* nm25285

Atrides brother of Agâmennon; he brings an army against the Trojans and is killed in single combat by Paris. The name is really a patronymic, meaning 'son of Atreus', the Atridæ being Agâmennon and Menelaus. A. is not used in *GT* as a synonym for Menelaus, however, as the latter appears as a separate character. *– GT* 4865

Atridos see Atrides

Atrisidol 'von Latriset', a warrior in Akarîn's army against Ipomidôn. *– JT* 3123,5

Atriss he is consulted by Agâmennon as to a reward for Paris. *– GT* 3723

Atrites see Atrides

Atroclas 'künec von Rerat', uncle of Amolot; he is fighting Paltriot for the land of Deleferant. Wigamur offers himself as champion, but just as he is about to fight Paltriot, his relationship to the latter is discovered, and the quarrel is patched up. Wigamur marries Atroclas's daughter, Dulcefluor, and together they rule Deleferant. *– Wigm* nm3467f. a3564

Atroclos, Atroclosz see Atroclas

Atropos 'vrouwe', the eldest of the three Fates in Greek mythology. *–* nm *C* 293; *UA* 3740

Attalus a commander in Alexander's army. According to *A*, A. married Philôtas's sister, and there was a certain amount of enmity between him and Alexander. A. occurs in *Expeditio Alexandri* and Curtius Rufus. *– A* 12014; *UA* 19597

Attaras see Attarras

Attarras marshal at Alexander's court; he arrested Philôtas, when the latter was charged with plotting against Alexander's life. So also in Curtius Rufus, where he is named Atarrhias. *– A* 19018f.

Attribuson 'von Jesse', a warrior in Akarîn's army against Ipomidôn. *– JT* nm3101,1

Attroclas, Attroclasz see Atroclas

Auguintester a knight (?); Keiî, in a mocking speech to Ginovêr, when she returns to Arthur's court after having been rescued by Gawein from Gasosîn, says that, without armour, she has overcome four knights since yesterday: Gotegrin, A., Gasosîn and Gawein. The first and last two are justified, as they have all been hurt fighting for possession of her, but this is the only mention of A., nor is there any unnamed character to whom the reference could apply. *– C* nm12490

Augustinus (St. Augustine). *SA* refers to his immortal writings, from which it is clear that the reference is to the Father of the Church, the bishop of Hippo, AD 354–430. *– SA* nm47

Augustus (1) the first Roman Emperor. (See also Octavian.) *–* nm *Ed* 13397ff.; *L* 4763; *UA* 14657f. [†]

Augustus (2) the name which, according to Gêrfridolt, is adopted by Heinrîch (1) as Holy Roman Emperor. *– Loh* nm4523

Aucumedon a warrior in the Greek army against the Trojans. This character appears to have been invented by the continuator of *TK*. – *TKf* 41119

Aumagwîn 'der rôte', a knight who is present when Êrec returns to Arthur's court with Ênîte in *E*. In *C*, where he is the *ami* of Aclamet, he accompanies Arthur in his quest for Gasosîn, by whom he is unhorsed. A. also spills Priure's cup of chastity. The earliest known reference to A. is in Chrestien's *Erec*, where he is called Amauguins, a form which is fairly well preserved in the Aumagwîn of *C*, but which was distorted into Maunis in *E*. – *E* 1659; *C* 2317

Aureliant 'künec von Jerusalêm', a knight in the Trojan army against the Greeks. A. is evidently the invention of Konrad. – *TK* 24918f.

Aurelio brother of Utepandragûn, who, according to Geoffrey of Monmouth, preceded Utepandragûn as king of the Britons. His full name in Geoffrey is Aurelius Ambrosius, under which name he became known to French literature through Wace's *Brut*. (Cf. Moygines (2).) – *JT* nm4606,2

Aurorâ wife of Tîton and mother of Mennon (2). A. is referred to in *Tn* as the mother of Leda. In Dictys she is the same as in *TKf*, the mother of Mennon and wife of Tîton. – nm *Tn* 8270; *TKf* 42615

Ausones a warrior in Dârîus's army; he fled with Dârîus from the battle against Alexander. So also in Gualterus. – *UA* 8568f.

Avalac see Evaleth

Avanus brother of Elena; he fights with Paris against Matribulus. – *GT* 3478f.

Avarôz 'künec von Centrun', a heathen who is killed by Rulf in the battle against the Christians. – *Loh* a4241 n4458

Avenîs (1) husband of Anfolê (1), father of Laudamîe and Anfolê (2). – *G* nm7355 [†]

Avenis (2) 'künec von Yspanie', he has been betrothed by Rainher to Amely. The latter is abducted by Willehalm (4), and A. rides with an army in pursuit. He is unhorsed by Willehalm in the ensuing battle, and his leg is broken. When he sees that Amely does not want him but is in love with Willehalm, he nobly renounces all claim to her. His daughter, who is not named, marries the son of Willehalm and Amely. – *RW* 7220ff.

Avenol 'von Cardall', a knight who has slain more than one thousand knights at his spring. Paris lifts a fish out of the water, and a dense fog arises. He throws the fish back, and the fog clears and the birds sing more sweetly than before. Then comes A., who attacks Paris, and is killed by him. The whole episode is obviously an imitation of the Ascalôn (q.v.) episode in *I*. – *GT* a9884f. n9899

Avenor a knight who challenges Segromans at Agâmennon's court and is killed by him. – *GT* a24088 n24103

Avenos see Avenor

Aventînus son of Hercûles; he is a knight in Turnus's army. A. occurs in the OF *Eneas* and in Virgil. – *Ed* 5046f.

Averre 'küneginne von' (*P*), see Annôr

Avia a knight in the Trojan army against the Greeks. – *GT* 22716

Afinamus (1) 'herzoge von Amantasîn'. (Bartsch suggested < Greek ἐπίνομος,[75] but Martin's conjecture seems more likely, viz., that the name comes from Amphinomus, the name of a famous runner, who is mentioned in Solinus (51,2).[76]) A. is stated to have been defeated by Feirefîz. – *P* nm770,30

---

[75] Bartsch (2), p. 156.
[76] Martin (1), p. 505, to 770,3.

Afinamus (2) 'von Klitiers', a knight in the service of Gramoflanz; he comes with Brandelidelîn and Bernout to stop the fight between Gramoflanz and Parzivâl. – *P* 707,2

Avinor father of Venus. – *GT* nm2159

Avicenna see Avicenne

Avicenne the Arabian philosopher and physician. – nm *JT* 1755,5; *WO* 11959

Afrus 'künec', captured by Eresdes. A. does not appear in the passage in Pseudo-Methodius from which this portion of *A* was taken. – *A* nm17166

Affer a warrior in Dârîus's army; he was slain by Alexander at Erbela. So also in Gualterus. – *UA* 13919

Affibla 'delet', a knight who is present at Arthur's court, when Êrec returns with Ênîte. This name does not occur in Chrestien's *Erec*, but whether it was in the original list of knights given by Hartmann, or was added by an interpolator, it is impossible to say definitely. Martin has drawn attention to the similarity between this name and Kardefablêt (q.v.).[77] – *E* 1689

Affridantze see Arfidantz

Affrosydones 'von lant Campill', *muome* of Eydes; she stole the latter's inheritance, a spring. She was championed by Dyartorforgrannt, who fought Eydes' champion, Wigamur. Wigamur defeated Dyartorforgrannt and compelled A. to return to Eydes the spring and the accompanying land. – *Wigm* m1585f. an1780f.

Affrosodanes see Affrosydones

Azary see Asarîas

Azet a knight who attends Leigamar's tourney in the service of Aram. A. is captured by Gawein. – *C* 18170

Azinde a knight who attends Leigamar's tourney in the service of Aram. – *C* 18163

Azzadac steward to Amênâ, in whose charge the latter leaves the castle of Roimunt. A. jousts with Wigalois, when the latter first arrives at Roimunt, but the fight is not carried to a decision. He later fights for Wigalois against Lîôn. – *Wigl* a3888f. n8852f.

---

[77] Martin (1), p. 305, to 376,15.

B

Baal   see Belî (1)
Baasâ   biblical (Baasha), king of Israel. – *A* nm16358
Babilon   'der von' (*WO*), see Melehalin
Bademagun   a knight who, in *RP*, is unhorsed by Parzivâl at a tourney. In the OF romances,
B. plays a prominent part as king of Gorre and father of Meleagant (see Meljakanz). He is
consistently represented as a just and courteous knight in spite of the character borne by his
son. In Chrestien's *Conte de la Charrette*, B. holds a tourney to decide the ultimate fate of
Ginovêr, when the protagonists are Lancelot and Meleagant. In *La Vengeance de
Raguidel*, he plays an exactly similar part in an episode which, from the occurrence of his
name, is obviously a copy of the *Conte de la Charrette*, the protagonists being Gawein and
Druidan, who however is not B.'s son. They are fighting for Gawein's *amie*, Ydain. B. is
slain by Gawein in *Les Aventures del Saint Graal*.
In Manessier (Potvin's edition), B. is called Bandemagus, and a similar form occurs in the
Dutch *Lancelot*. Chrestien's continuator in the *Conte de la Charrette* places B.'s kingdom
in Bade (= Bath), and Gaston Paris inclines to the view that the connection was original,[1]
but Lot holds that the town was suggested by the name, and supports his theory by pointing
to the fact that B. already has one kingdom, viz. Gorre.[2]
It is generally agreed that Poidikonjunz, 'künec von Gors', who appears in *P* as an ally of
Meljanz against Lipaôt, is identical with B.[3] Like B., his son is Meljakanz (= Meleagant).
The most notable opposer of this theory is Bartsch,[4] who tries to derive the latter half of
the name from *d'Iconiun*, 'of Iconium', a town which was well-known to the Crusaders,
and which certainly does appear in Hartmann (*Erec* 2007) as Conne. The first part of the
name in question, *Poy*, Bartsch thinks reminiscent of Boydurant (q.v.). Poidikonjunz is
mentioned in *TF*, and appears in *JT*, where he takes part in a tourney held by Arthur. He
seems to be identical with Kumuns, 'künec von Pore', also called Kuniuntz and Rois der
Kuniun (= Poidikonjunz ?), who (5635,1) witnesses the fight between Parzivâl and Agors.
Brugger identifies B. also with Bagumades (q.v.). – *P* nm343,21 a358,26; *JT* 1998,2; *TF*
nm11090; *RP* 814,13
Bâgistân   'von Babilonje', brings news to Alexander of the treacherous action of Bessus
towards Dârîus. So also in *Expeditio Alexandri* and Curtius Rufus. – *A* 14688
Bâgôfanes   'von Persîâ', chamberlain to Dârîus; he welcomes the victorious Alexander into
Babylon. B. occurs also in Curtius Rufus. – *A* 13241
Bagumades   a knight who is found by Parzivâl during his quest for the Graal, hanging upside
down from a tree. He had been attacked by Keiî and three other knights, who, after they
had overcome him, hung him up in the tree. Parzivâl releases him, and he goes to Arthur's
court, where he challenges Keiî to single combat and defeats him. He is persuaded by
Arthur to spare Keiî's life. Brugger contends that B. is identical with Bademagun (q.v.),
basing his opinion largely on an episode in an unpublished part of the Pseudo-Robert
continuation of *Merlin*, in which Bandemagus (= Bademagus) is found hanging from a tree

---

1   Paris (1), p. 513.
2   Lot (3), p. 332.
3   Golther (1), p. 170.
4   Bartsch (2), p. 148.

exactly as is B.[5] Brugger is uncertain which form was the original one and derives Bagumades from Bangus + Madus (= Madoc),[6] and Bademagun from Baduc + Mangon (= Amangon, a knight in *Meraugis de Portlesguez*).[7] It must, however, be admitted that a metathesis such as is postulated by Brugger's theory works both ways, and the similarity in the names may have caused the episode in the one romance to have been transferred to the other. The presence of Manessier's form Bandemagus in the *Merlin*-continuation mentioned above may possibly denote a knowledge of the former on the part of the author of the latter. – *RP* a506,31 n507,33

*Bahsigweiz see Passigweiz (1)

Baingranz 'von Ainsgalt', brother of Assiles; he imprisons Gawein, Lanzelet, Keiî, and Kalogreant in a mountain, and they each have to fight a knight in order to regain their freedom. Gawein fights and defeats B. – *C* nm26510 a26914

Bachidis 'von Perciâ', a warrior in Dârîus's army against Alexander. B. does not appear in any of the sources to *UA*. – *UA* 10937

Bâchus the Greek and Roman god of wine and fertility (Bacchus). It seems probable that this is the god intended by the Bâkûn of *UW*. In *TK*, B. is present at the wedding of Thetis and Peleus. – *UW* nm90,9; *TK* 986

Bâkûn see Bâchus

Balaise 'künec von der Wilde', a commander on the side of the heathens in the final battle against the Christians. – *WO* 16444

Balacrus a warrior in Alexander's army; he drove Hidarnes out of the town of Milête. So also in *Expeditio Alexandri* and Curtius Rufus. – *A* 9492

Balban see Gawein

Baldac 'bâruc von' (*P*), see Akarîn

Baldac 'vogt von' (*W*), see Terramêr

Baldewin (1) nephew of Terramêr; he is present at the latter's court, when Malfer captures Fansaserat. – *R* Eing. I,44

Baldewin (2) 'grâve', carries the declaration of war from Witechin to Amelot. – *RW* 10536

Baldewine an ally of Fridebrant and Tirol. – *Tirol* C,12

Baldrioth see Paltriot

Bâligân uncle of Terramêr and father-in-law to Purrel; we learn from *W* that he was slain by Karl (1). In *UW* he appears as the opponent of Lôîs and is instrumental in capturing Willehalm. In *JT* he is the son of Jermidol and brother of Kanabeus, making him uncle to Terramêr. B. occurs as Baligant in the OF *Chanson de Roland*, where his death at the hands of Karl is recounted, as it is also in Konrad's *Rolandslied*, where he is called Paligan, the form of the name which appears in *UW* and *RB*. – *W* nm108,12; *UW* nm11,26ff. a32,10; *JT* nm2835,7f.; *RB* nm16156 [†]

Balifeit 'von Torkîs', a friend of Darifant. The fragment opens with his marriage to Lôcêdîan and his coronation as king of Torkîs the following morning. – *Dar* a1 n33

Balon 'von Mirmidisse', a warrior in Ipomidôn's army against Akarîn. – *JT* 3263,2

Baltasân see Balthasar (2)

Balthasar (1) biblical (Belshazzar). His death at the hands of Cyrus and Dârîus (1) is referred to in *UA*, where he is also (7709ff.) called the son of Evilmôradac. In *SA* he is called Walthesar. – nm *UA* 914f.; *RB* 26758; *SA* 3233

---

5   Brugger (2), pp. 11f.
6   Brugger (2), p. 12.
7   Brugger (2), pp. 12f.

Balthasar (2) biblical, called in *JT* 'von Sabba', one of the three Magi who came to worship the Christ-child. – nm *W* 307,9; *JT* 5475,1ff.

Bamundêr 'ein Wale', a knight who is unhorsed by Dêmantîn at Bêâmunt's tourney. – *Dem* 788f.

Bandarap brother of Gâmeranz, also called Sandarap. B. attacks Gawein with Gâmeranz (q.v.) and is killed. – *C* m5963 a6262 n6449

Banderous see Brandes

Barasilangander a warrior in Ipomidôn's army against Akarîn. – *JT* nm3230,3

Baravartt see Barfartt

Barberîe 'künec von' (*W*), see Kursaus

Barbidele 'küneginne', she was loved by Feirefîz, before the latter obtained Sekundille. – *JT* 5296,1

Bardigries son of Secureis. – *JT* nm2951,5

Bardigris see Pardrigun

Bargaltt see Pargaltt

Bargis son of Purrel; he flees with Terramêr from the second battle at Alischanz. B. occurs in MSS M and e of *Aliscans*, v. 6800: 'Li fil Borrel Bargis'. – *W* a358,25 n427,9

Bargungenden 'von Iermalie', a warrior who is killed whilst fighting for Ipomidôn against Akarîn. His slayer is Îthêr. – *JT* 4183,6

Baridach a warrior in Dârîus's army; he is slain by Alexander at Erbela. This character was apparently invented by Ulrich. – *UA* 13955

Barigaltt see Pargaltt

Barille, Barillus see Parille (1)

Baris see Parîs

Barlaâm a hermit who converts the Indian prince, Jôsaphât, to Christianity. This legend is the subject of a poem, *Barlaam und Josaphat*, written by Rudolf von Ems. – nm *A* 3284; *RW* 15641

Barlam see Barlaâm

Barrast see Warrast

Bartholomêus (St. Bartholomew). His day, August 24, is referred to. – *FD* nm1700,2

Bâruc 'von Baldac' (*P*), see Akarîn

Barufartt see Barfartt

Baruz a knight in the service of Lorez; he is present at the tourney held by Leigamar. Baruc 'li noirs' is the name of a knight who is defeated by Segremors in the *Livre d'Artus*.[8] – *C* 18148

Barfartt a giant, brother of Maroltt (q.v.); he is killed by Paris. – *GT* m11322 an11346

Barzentes 'grâve', he was with Bessus and his companions, when they killed Dârîus. B. fled and his army joined Alexander. So also in *Expeditio Alexandri* and Curtius Rufus, where he is called Barzaentes. – *A* 18732f.

Barcinier a knight who is present at Arthur's court, when Êrec returns with Ênîte. This name does not appear in Chrestien's *Erec*. – *E* 1679

Basan 'künec von' (*WO*), see Og

Basiphe wife of Minos (q.v.) and the mother of the Minotaurus. She is a bad woman and is slain by Minos as being the cause of his losing Meierra and Fedra through Jason. – *GT* 21551ff.

---

8   Published with the romances of the Vulgate Cycle in *Vulgate Version of the Arthurian Romances*, vol. VII.

*Bassigweiz   see Passigweiz (1)

Batewain   'fil roy Cabcaflir', a knight at Arthur's court, when Êrec returns with Ênîte. B. does not occur in Chrestien's *Erec*, neither is there any apparent connection between B. and the Bawdewyn (= Banin), son of Gracien de Trebes, who appears in most of the romances of the Vulgate Cycle. – *E* 1674

Batris   a maiden attendant on Agley. – *WO* 9933

Bauban   see Gawein

Baulas   see Talas

Beachut   'der junge', a knight present at a tourney held by Arthur. It seems probable that this name is a variant of Bêâkurs (q.v.). – *JT* 1987,1

Beakuns   see Behantîns

Bêâkurs   (= handsome figure),[9] brother of Gawein. B. is unknown to literature outside the MHG romances, which have copied him from *P*. Wolfram, who appears to have invented this character, refers to him as being, with Parzivâl, the most handsome knight who ever lived. B. is not credited with any particular adventures in the MHG romances, appearing always in a minor part. He is mentioned in *M*, where he is called Bêâtus, assists Arthur against Ehkunat in *G*, and against Tandareis in *TF*, whilst in *JT*, where he is named Bealtors (also Beachut (q.v.)?), he is present at a tourney held by Arthur. In *TF* he marries Antonîe. – *P* nm39,25 a323,1; *G* 17670f.; *JT* 1773,4; *M* nm151; *TF* 1693

Bêals (1)   'herzoge von Morark', also called 'von Gerunde'; he is an ally of Lôîs against Terramêr. – *UW* 36,19

Beâls (2)   see Pant (1)

Bealtors   see Bêâkurs

Beamunt (1)   'grâve von', he kills a man at a tourney and retires penitent from the field. He is very worried and remorseful that night, and when Mauricius (3) appears all bloody at his bedside, he thinks it is the devil. He flees, hurts his shin, and faints, giving Mauricius the opportunity to lie with his wife. – *MC* 899f.

Beamunt (2)   'grævinne von', wife of Beamunt (1) and lover of Mauricius (3) (q.v.). – *MC* nm263ff. a524ff.

Bêâmunt (3)   'herzoginne von Brabant', she is sent by the queen of England to Dêmantîn's country with a sparrow-hawk, which is to be the prize in a tourney. Whoever wins the prize is to fight Firganant, who wishes to marry B. Dêmantîn wins the tourney and also defeats Firganant but is so impressed by the latter's courage and nobility that he gives B. to him. When later Firganant goes to assist Dêmantîn, B. collects an army and takes it to Antrîûn, assists Fandorîch, and arrives in time to assist Dêmantîn and Firganant in the final battle. – *Dem* a207f. n216

Bêamunt   'grâve von' (*UW*), see Hoygier

Bearosi   see Bearosine

Bearosine   daughter of Fansaserat, who offers her to Malfer, if the latter will spare his life, but Malfer refuses the offer. According to Roth, B. eventually marries Passigweiz (1).[10] – *R* m Eing. I,101f. n Bl. I,48 a Bl. II,109ff.

Beaterse   'vrouwe', attendant on Irmingart, whom she accompanies on her flight to Constantinople and from thence to Arras. – *GR* E,15f.

Bêâtrîs (1)   wife of Arnolt (4). – *PM* 20496

---

9   Wolfram himself explains this etymology in *P*, when he says (187,22f.) of Kondwîrâmûrs: 'diu truoc den rehten bêâ curs: / der name ist tiuschen schœner lîp.'

10   Ulrich von Türheim, *Rennewart*, p. 17, note 13.

Beatris (2)   see Beaterse

Beatrise 'küneginne', wife of Rainher and mother of Amely. – *RW* m3305f. a3660f. n3690

Bêâtus   see Bêâkurs

Bêâveis 'burcgrâve von' (*W*), see Kiûn (1)

Bêaflôr daughter of Teljôn and Sâbîe (1); she is brought up by Rôbôâl and Benignâ. She guards herself against her father's incestuous desires and, to escape him, puts to sea in a small boat. She arrives at Greece, where Meie is *grâve*, falls in love with him and eventually marries him. Whilst her husband is away fighting for his uncle in Spain, she is saved by Kornêljus (q.v.) from death, but owing to the machinations of Elîacha (q.v.), she is again cast adrift and is carried by the wind to Rôbôâl. B. remains hidden with Rôbôâl until Meie arrives to obtain absolution from the Pope for the supposed death of B., when Rôbôâl, who happens to meet Meie's messenger, invites Meie to his house and a general reconciliation takes place. This story is re-told in *KT* in a more prosaic setting. No names are given, but B. is the daughter of the king of France, Meie is the king of England, and his enemy is the king of Scotland. – *MB* a5,22f. n7,4

Bêâflûrs wife of Pansâmûrs and mother of Lîahturteltart. – *P* nm87,27 [†]

Bedevart 'grâve von Cluris', slain by Troilus, whilst fighting for the Greeks against the Trojans. The name does not appear in any of the other versions of the Trojan legend and was evidently invented by Konrad. – *TK* 31592

Beduwiers a knight of the Round Table; he appears in *RP* as one of the knights present at the tourney held by Ris. The MS used by the authors of *RP* was evidently a better one than that now at Mons (published by Potvin), in which B. appears as Degevier. In *C* he is one of the knights who spill Priure's cup of chastity. The name, which is here taken from Chrestien's *Erec* (1735), beginning: 'Ne Bedoiiers . . .' (MS P: 'Ne bedoins'), has become distorted to Nebedons. B. first appears in Geoffrey of Monmouth (X,9), where, as Bedevere the Butler, he is slain in the battle against Lucius. According to Gaston Paris,[11] B. is identical with Lodoer, the knight who, in the OF *lai, Tyolet*, is the first to make an attempt to obtain the stag's foot (cf. Keiî in the episode in *C*). – *C* 2323; *RP* 81,21

Behalim sister of Mahardî, she is saved from the clutches of Reimambram by Gawein. – *C* 8577ff.

Behantîns 'grâve von Kalomidente'. (Martin, quoting Hagen, derives the name from Byzantio, mentioned by Solinus (20,1), with intercange of *h* and *z*.[12]) B. is included in the list of knights whom Feirefiz says he has beaten. In *JT*, where the name is distorted to Beakuns von Salabiden, the scene of this defeat is placed at the tourney held by Sekundille among her wooers. – *P* nm770,2; *JT* 5250,5ff

Beygamur   see Wigamur

Bejolâre wife of 'grâve von Lêodarz', mother of Bejolarz and sister of Morâl. – *Wigl* nm8718

Bejolarz son of 'grâve von Lêodarz'; he accompanies his uncle, Morâl, to inform Lârîe of the success of Wigalois. B. later fights for Wigalois against Liôn. – *Wigl* 8714ff.

Bel (1) 'künec von Alexandria', a knight who fights on the side of the heathens in the final battle against the Christians. – *WO* 16348f.

Bêl (2)   see Belî (1)

Beladant 'von Pockadanie', a warrior in Akarîn's army against Ipomidôn. – *JT* nm3141,1

---

11   Paris (3), p. 115.
12   Martin (1), p. 502, to 770,1.

Beladigant 'herzoge von Zône', comes to Arthur's court to be made a knight. He marries Sandinôse. – *DB* a8008f. n8026

Belakâne 'küneginne von Zazamanc'. (Bartsch attempts to derive this name from *bela cana*, the Provençal form of the OF *bele cane*, 'beautiful cane', in reference to her slenderness,[13] a derivation which Gaston Paris considers to be impossible.[14] Golther draws attention to the similarity of an Arabian feminine name, Balqîz, Belqîz.[15] B.'s land, Zazamanc, has been identified with Garamantae, a North African tribe mentioned in Solinus.[16]) B., who is a Moorish queen, refuses to give her love to Îsenhart until he has proved himself worthy of it. He therefore rides out, unarmed, in search of adventure, and is slain by one of B.'s men. Vridebrant, who believes that B. deliberately sent Îsenhart to his death, comes with a large army to avenge him, but has to return to Scotland, leaving his allies to besiege Patelamunt, the capital of Zazamanc. Gahmuret arrives at the town by chance, defeats in single combat the leaders of the besieging army, and marries B. After a while, tired of inactivity, he steals away from her and goes to Seville. B. bears a son, Feirefîz, and then, according to *P* (750,24), she dies of a broken heart. In *JT* she is said to marry Razalîc, who looks after the education of the young Feirefîz. B. is apparently the prototype of Palmina, a Moorish queen, who, in *Apollonius von Tyrland*, marries Apollonius and by him has a pied son. –*P* nm16,7 a20,30; *T* nm37,1; *UW* nm74,18; *JT* 664,1f.; *UA* nm9880; *RB* m15278

Belamîs a knight of the Round Table; he is unhorsed by Daniel (1). B. marries vrou vom Trüeben Berge. – *DB* 250

Belankane see Belakâne

Bêlêâre wife of Morâl; she is found weeping by Wigalois, who learns that a dragon has gone off with Morâl. Wigalois kills the dragon and, in return for saving Morâl's life, is nursed back to health by B. – *Wigl* a4869f. n9042

Belestigweiz 'künec von' (*W*), see Goliam

Bêlet one of the fallen angels. According to Golther,[17] this is the name of a Phoenician god, of whom he thinks Wolfram must have heard or read somewhere. (Cf. Astirot and Belzimôn.) – *P* nm463,11

Belgalgan 'küneginne von' (*WO*), see Crispin

Belî (1) a Babylonian god, also called Baal and Bêl. – nm *A* 16642; *UA* 11863

Bêlî (2) see Bêlus

Belianz 'li rus' (i.e. the red), brother of Gâmeranz (q.v.). B. attacks Gawein with his brothers and is killed. A knight, Belias, 'li vermeil Chevalier', is mentioned as the brother of Agravadain in *L'Estoire de Merlin* (Vulgate Cycle). – *C* m5963 a6262 n6478

Belicâne see Belakâne

Belin 'künec von Waschuni', a knight captured by Willehalm (4) at Komarzi. B. is also present at the tourney held near Kurnoy. –*RW* nm6174f. a6652

Belion brother of Astrolis and vassal of Gamorett, for whom he fights against the Greeks. – *GT* 5668

Bêliur a warrior in Dârîus's army. B. does not occur in any of the sources to *UA*. – *UA* 15777

---

13 Bartsch (2), p. 138.
14 Paris (2), p. 149.
15 Golther (1), p. 140.
16 Richey (2), p. 7.
17 Golther (1), p. 214.

Belloys 'burcgrâve von Scharters', he is killed by Jofrit (1), whilst fighting for Willehalm (3). – *RW* 531f.

Belni 'vrouwe von Dânois', a lady who spills Priure's cup of chastity at Arthur's court. – *C* 1604

Bêlûn son of Cefalus. This name does not occur in any of the sources to *UA*. – *UA* nm6973

Bêlus father of Nînus, and a former king of Babylon. – nm *A* 15665; *UA* 895

Belfant a maiden attendant upon Agly. Being pure, she is chosen (18871ff.) to assist in the capture of the unicorn which Wildhalm is hunting when he is murdered. B. is with Wildhalm when he dies. – *WO* 9934

Belffomors 'von Engelanndt', a knight who sent Arthur the horse which he gives to Wigamur. – *Wigm* nm2333

Belzimôn according to *P*, one of the fallen angels. Golther points out that this is the name of a Phoenician deity, of whom, he thinks, Wolfram must have read somewhere. (Cf. Astirot and Bêlet.)[18] – *P* nm463,10

Bênâdap biblical (Benhadad), king of Syria. – *A* nm16364

Benalas 'küneginne von Belinar', daughter of Dûzanga. – *UW* a70,18f. n94,14

Bêne (1) wife of Willehalm (2) (q.v.) and mother of Boizlabe and Dânus. Willehalm leaves her in a Bohemian town with a widow. B. refuses several offers of marriage, when she has become famous by her beauty, and on the death of the Duke of Bohemia, she is chosen as Duchess. She never gives up hope of seeing Willehalm, and she orders all pilgrims to be well cared for and to be brought to her. In this way Willehalm is eventually brought before her, and they are re-united. B. is also (2216) called Vrouwe Guote. – *WW* a67f. n3725

Bêne (2) daughter of Plipalinot (see Inpripalenôt); she waits on Gawein, whilst he is staying with her father, and acts as messenger between him and Gramoflanz afterwards. The name occurs in *JT*, where B. has become confused with Kundrîe (2), as Lôt (1) is said to be grieving over the loss of Sangive, Itonjê, and Bêne, who have been abducted by Klinschor. B. is generally agreed to be the creation of Wolfram, Golther explaining the name as a pet-name form of Benedicta.[19] Bartsch thought that the name might possibly have arisen from a misunderstanding of Chrestien's *Perceval* (8977); Gawein says to the knight of the ferry: 'que beneois soit vostre osteus'.[20] Such an explanation seems to provide an argument against the existence of Kîot, in whom Bartsch firmly believed, since a Provençal poet could hardly be expected so completely to have misunderstood the French original, and if Wolfram was capable of creating such a character as B., who is in some ways one of the most perfect of female portraits, for which *P* is famous, it was quite possible for him to have created the remainder of the additions to Chrestien. – *P* a549,1 a550,25; *JT* nm4587,5

Benedige see Penylle (1)

Benedictus (Pope Benedictus VIII). – *Loh* nm7561

Benelopê see Penelope

Benemias 'von Raguleis', one of the knights captured by Eskilabôn and released by Gârel. B. fights for Gârel against Ehkunat. – *G* 4838

Benignâ wife of Rôbôâl (q.v.). – *MB* nm16,9ff. a16,36

Benîvel 'ein Schotten', the first knight to joust with Engelhart after the latter has been made a knight. B. is unhorsed by Engelhart in the *vesperîe* before the tourney at Normandie. – *Eng* 2494ff.

---

[18] Golther (1), p. 214.
[19] Golther (1), p. 184.
[20] Bartsch (2), p. 150.

49

Benjamin biblical, youngest son of Jacob. – *A* nm16263

Benolit wife of Bertram (2). – *UW* a272,15 n273,10

Benukardis see Kardeis

Bêonet 'herzoge von Portigâl', brother-in-law of Zukander; he is an ally of Lôîs against Terramêr. – *UW* 36,17

Bergtal 'der wîbe trôst', a knight slain by Firganant. – *Dem* 6885ff.

Berhte 'mit dem fuoze', daughter of Flôre and Blanscheflur (2). B. appears in the OF *chansons de geste* as Bertha with the Big Foot and is the daughter of Count Charibert of Laon, the wife of Pepin, and the mother of Charlemagne. – *FB* nm307ff. a7861ff.

Berhtolt (1) 'herzoge von Nieman', a knight on the side of the Christian army in the final battle against the heathens. – *WO* 16565ff.

Berhtolt (2) 'der Rebestoc', a knight who jousts with Ulrich von Liechtenstein during the latter's *Venusfahrt*. – *FD* 924,4f.

Berhtolt (3) abbot of St. Gall; he fights on the side of the Christians in the final battle against the heathens. – *WO* 16672ff.

Berhtolt (4) 'von Herbolzheim', MHG poet. – *A* nm15774

Berhtram (1) see Bertrams (1)

Berhtram (2) see Bertrams (2)

Beriete daughter of Olivier (2). – *RW* 7180ff.

Berichel 'von Trisfatilân', also (9906) called 'von Marroch', a commander in Bêâmunt's army at Antrîûn. On the journey to Antrîûn, he unhorses Tefilant, who leads him to Fandorîch. – *Dem* nm9673 a10250f.

Berlin (1) 'von Bulgarie', a knight on the side of the Christians in the final battle against the heathens. – *WO* 17164

Berlîn (2) a squire whom Tydomîe sends with gifts to Meleranz on the day the latter is made a knight. Tydomîe also sends B. to ascertain the truth of the report that Meleranz is on his way to champion her against Libers (1). – *M* a2738ff. n10555

Bernant 'grâve', father of Elye and grandfather of Willehalm (4). B.'s death is reported in 15000f. – *RW* nm193 a7002f.

Bernart (1) 'grâve von Hollant', a knight who is captured at the tourney held at Komarzi. – *RW* nm6207f. a6683

Bernart (2) 'von Brûbant', son of Heimrîch (1) and brother of Willehalm (1). B. is also the father of Bertrams (2). He fights for Willehalm against Terramêr at Alischanz, and in *UW* he appears as an ally of Lôîs against Terramêr. B. appears in the OF *chansons de geste* of the Guillaume d'Orange cycle, including the *Chancun de Willame*. – *W* a5,16f. n6,27; *UW* m4,14f. a21,1 n23,1

Bernat see Bernart (2)

Bernhard see Bernart (1)

Bernhart (1) 'grâve', suggests to the Amiral that he should forgive Flôre and Blanscheflûr (2). The corresponding character in *FB* is not named. – *NRFB* 273; *FB* a6782

Bernhart (2) (St. Bernard, AD 1090–1153) – *WW* nm2828

Bernhart (3) 'von Kärnden', his quarrel with Heinrîch von Ysterîch was the cause of the tourney at Friesach. – *FD* m177,3ff. n188,1f.

Bernhart (4) 'von Treven', a knight who jousts with Ulrich von Liechtenstein during the latter's *Venusfahrt*. – *FD* 616,5

Bernhart (5) see Bernart (2)

Bernout 'von Riviers' (the Romance or Netherland form of the High German name Bernolt < OHG *bero*, 'bear').[21] B. is the son of Nârant and is a knight in the service of Gramoflanz. – *P* 682,17f.

Berole 'der von' (*JT*), see Forumar

Bersabê biblical (Bathsheba), former wife of Uriah, and mother of Solomon by David. – *UA* nm11567

Bertholt 'von Emmerberg',[22] a knight who jousts with Ulrich von Liechtenstein during the latter's *Venusfahrt*. – *FD* 721,8f.

Bertolt 'von Holle', MHG poet, and author of *Crane*, *Dem* and *Dar*. – nm *Crane* 2144; *Dem* 1

Bertrams (1) 'von Berbester', son of Heimrîch (1) and brother of Willehalm (1); he fights for the latter at Alischanz. In *UW*, where he has a wife, Benolit, B. is often called 'der pfalnzgrâve', a title which belongs to Bertrams (2). In the OF *chansons de geste*, B. is called Garin. – *W* a5,16 n6,22; *UW* m4,14f. a21,1 n23,1

Bertrams (2) 'der phalenzgrâve', son of Bernart (2) and standard-bearer (93,17f.) to Willehalm. He and seven others are captured by Halzebier as they are going to the rescue of Vîvîans. They are later (416,9) liberated by Rennewart. B. appears as Willehalm's standard-bearer in *UW*, where his title of 'phalenzgrâve' is transferred to Bertrams (1), and it is only by his office that he is to be differentiated from Willehalm's brother. B. occurs in the OF *chansons de geste* of the Guillaume d'Orange cycle, including the earliest known *chanson*, the *Chancun de Willame*. – *W* 13,15ff.; *UW* 53,18 [†]

Bessus a commander in Dârîus's army. The best account of the deeds of B. is to be found in *A*, where he is called 'herzoge von Bactrîân'. In this version, B. advises Dârîus to attempt the second battle against Alexander, and when Dârîus is defeated, B. and Narbâsones turn traitor and enchain Dârîus (as in MS S of Leo) in golden chains. Their army is attacked by Alexander, and they slay Dârîus. B. flees to Bactrîâ, where he is later pursued by Alexander. The poem breaks off just as B. is about to become the victim of a conspiracy on the part of Spitâmenes to deliver him over to Alexander. In *UA*, Dârîus is said to have raised B. and Narbâsones from very humble positions, and their ingratitude is all the more striking. Alexander gets them into his power by promising to pay the murderers what they deserve, and they, expecting to receive Dârîus's lands, give themselves up and are slain. *SA* gives a slight variation of the final scene. Alexander promises to make the murderers the highest men in Persia, and when he discovers who they are, redeems his promise by hanging them on a gallows fifty yards high. B. occurs in all histories of Alexander. The forms of the name in *SA* are Abisso and Liso; the latter – as also Fyses, the form in *WA* – seems to be a corruption of the form in Leo, Bysso (Bysân in Lampreht). – *A* 10088ff.; *UA* m15912 an15949; *SA* 3588ff.; *WA* a2705 n2719 [†]

Bêtis 'von Persîâ', the commander of Dârîus's army at Gazâ. He wounds Alexander with a spear but is captured when the town falls. B. is dragged through the city by wild horses and then killed. He occurs also in Curtius Rufus. – *A* 10178

Bevar 'künec von Schotten', he sends Marke (3) and Ericius to woo Helen for him on her return from Troy. Agâmennon refuses to countenance suitors, and B. declares war on him. B. is killed in the resultant battle, and his army defeated. – *GT* 23253ff.

---

21 Bartsch (2), p. 154, and Martin (1), p. 462, to 682,18.
22 The territorial name of B. is not given in the text of *FD*, but is completed by Bechstein in his note to 722,1.

Bêcias a giant, brother of Pandarus (1) (q.v.); he is slain by Turnus. B. occurs in the OF *Eneas* as Bicias, and in Virgil as Bitias. – *Ed* 7096ff.

Biblîs daughter of Miletus; she falls in love with her own brother, Caunus, who refuses to accede to her incestuous desires. B. cries herself to death and is transformed into a spring. The story is told in Ovid's *Metamorphoses*. – nm *Tn* 17196; *FB* 2434

Biduwer, Biduwiers see Beduwiers

Bigamê 'grâve von', brother of Sorgarit; he is present at the tourney held by Leigamar, where he and his brother are unhorsed by Gawein and Quoikos. – *C* 18134

Bilas 'künec von Bile', he is betrothed to Gayte, and, refusing to give her up, he is attacked by Athis (q.v.). In the OF romance, B. is pictured as haughty and arrogant, but it is probable that his character has been softened in *AP*, as he is referred to (A**,1) as 'der hobische kunig'. – *AP* nmA*,7 aA**,1

Bîlêî 'künec von Antipodes', king of the dwarfs and brother of Brîans (2); he is one of the five old kings who attend the wedding of Êrec and Ênîte. B. brings with him two other rulers of dwarf-land, Grigoras and Glecidolân, who are also included among the five old kings. In *C*, where he is one of the knights who spill Priure's cup of chastity, he is called Wilis (also Bilis) von Dantipades. Both references originate in Chrestien's *Erec* (1994): 'Bilis, li rois d'Antipodés'. – *E* 2087; *C* 2341

Bilis see Bîlêî

Bilisibol see Blisibole

Bilwer a heathen god. – *WO* nm5364

Biôn a knight in Alexander's army against Dârîus. B. occurs also in Curtius Rufus. – *A* 12051

Bisias 'von Damascone', a commander in Ipomidôn's army against Akarîn. – *JT* 3234,1

Bissurus apparently a commander, who had taken Babylon (for Akarîn ?). – *JT* nm3106,6

Biterolf MHG poet who, according to *A*, wrote a poem on Alexander. B. is one of the poets in the *Wartburgkrieg* (XII). – nm *A* 15789; *Loh* 224

Byworans a knight who is present at the tourney which Arthur holds for Deleprosat. – *Wigm* 2199

Blandukors husband of Amurelle and father of Sgaipegaz; his son is held as hostage by the giant, Assiles. The presence of any knight coming to B.'s castle is made known by a horn which blows automatically. Gawein spends the night with B. during his quest for Assiles. – *C* a6828 n6908

Blankeflûr see Blanscheflûr (1)

Blancheflurs see Blanscheflûr (2)

Blanlis 'vrouwe', one of the ladies who spill Priure's cup of chastity at Arthur's court. – *C* 1590

Blanschandin 'vürste', the hero of a romance which has come down to us in three fragments. I: B. hears of chivalry from his tutor and burns to leave his father's court and to fight. That night he steals away from the court, leaving his father and mother. II: B. rescues a maiden, who is being beaten by a knight, and kills the knight. III: B. leaves the sorrowing *amie* of a knight he has just slain and arrives at a river. A knight on the other side bids him not to try to cross that night but to seek shelter, and on the morrow they will meet and fight. – *Blan* aI,1 nI,90

Blanschemore 'von Kurnuwale', mother of Espinogres. B. founds a chapel, and after she has been slain by her own son, a hand comes out from behind the altar and slays one knight every night. Parzivâl sees the hand but is not harmed by it. In the Mons MS of Manessier,

B. is at first called Brangemor but later (40217), more correctly, Blancemorne. –
RP nm621,37f.

Blanschefliur, Blanschefluor see Blancheflûr (1)

Blancheflûr (1) (< OF *blanche flour*, 'white flower, lily'[23]), sister of Marke (1), she falls in
love with Riwalîn (1), who is staying at Marke's court. Visiting Riwalîn while he lies in
bed wounded after a tourney, she lies with him and conceives Tristan. When Riwalîn
recovers and returns to his own land, she accompanies him. In the gleeman version of the
Tristan legend, exemplified in *ET*, she dies in the boat on the journey, and the babe,
Tristrant, is cut out of her body. This feature has been refined in the courtly version (*Tn*),
where she marries Riwalîn, who is killed before the birth of Tristan. B. dies in child-birth.
The name appears occasionally in documents of the 13th and 14th centruries, but whether
through the influence of the Tristan legend or of *FB* (see Blancheflûr (2)), it is impossible
to decide. – *ET* 83ff.; *Tn* 629ff.; *UT* m2451; *TK* nm2310; *HT* m271 n6416

Blancheflûr (2) lover of Flôre (q.v.). B. is the daughter of a Christian woman, who is
captured by Fênix (2) after the death of her husband but before the birth of B. – *NRFB* nm3
a180; *FB* m120ff. n298 a582f.; *A* nm3243; *RW* nm2223; *FS* nm1523

Blancheflûr (3) 'von Gâl', *amie* of Parzivâl; she is one of the ladies at Arthur's court who
spill Priure's cup of chastity. It is clear that Heinrich has gone direct to Chrestien's
Perceval for this character. Parzivâl's *amie* (Kondwîrâmûrs (q.v.) in *P*) is called
Blanchefleur in *Perceval*, and the night which she and Parzivâl spend together and with
which Keiî taunts her when she spills the cup of chastity is not as innocent in Chrestien's
poem as Wolfram has made it. – *C* 1545

Blanschiflûr see Blancheflûr (1)

Blanschol 'vrouwe', one of the ladies at Arthur's court who spill Priure's cup of chastity. –
C 1607

Blant 'grâve von Alverne', a knight who attends a tourney held by Arthur. – *C* 601

Blantsefluor see Blancheflûr (2)

Blanzamant a knight who is unhorsed by Phoriân. – *Dem* 1701

Blavi 'der von' (*UW*), see Gerart

Bleheris a knight who is present at the tourney between Ris and Cadoalans. B. occurs in the
Mons MS of the Pseudo-Gautier continuation of *Perceval*, but it seems probable that the
word is a form of Blîobleherîn. – *RP* 81,33

Bleiden 'vrouwe', one of the ladies at Arthur's court who spill Priure's cup of chastity. –
C 1590

Bleis 'grâve von' (*PM*), see Partonopier

Blende 'vrouwe', one of the ladies at Arthur's court who spill Priure's cup of chastity. A
maiden, named Benigne (var. Blenined) de Glocedon, is rescued by Boort from being
drowned by four knights in the *Livre de Lancelot del Lac* (Vulgate Cycle), but there is
nothing to identify her with B. – *C* 1619

Blêos see Blîobleherîn

Blerios a knight at Arthur's court, when Êrec returns with Ênîte. B. does not appear in the
corresponding list of knights in Chrestiens's *Erec*, and Singer is of the opinion that it is a
later interpolation in Hartmann's list, suggested by Blîobleherîn.[24] – *E* 1666

---

23 Gottfried von Straßburg, *Tristan und Isolde*, transl. by Hertz, p. 547.
24 Singer (1), p. 60.

Bligger 'von Steinach', MHG poet, author of *Der Umbehanc*. – nm *Tn* 4690; *A* 3207; *RW* 2197

Blickêr see Bligger

Blîobleherîn (Martin draws attention to the similarity of this name to the first part of Bliocadrans,[25] the name given to Parzivâl's father in the *Bliocadran Prologue*, added to Chrestien's *Perceval* in the early 13th century.) In *E* he is present at Arthur's court, when Êrec returns with Ênîte. In *C*, which, like *E*, draws on Chrestien's *Erec*, he is called Blêos von Blirîers; he spills Priure's cup of chastity. In *I*, where he is said to have been unhorsed by Meljaganz when the latter is abducting Ginovêr, he is called Plîoplihêrî, and the name appears in the same form in *P*, where he is said to have been unhorsed by Orilus. In the prologue to *RP* he is called Plyopliris (< Blihos Bliheris in v. 162 of the *Elucidation* prologue to Chrestien's *Perceval*) and is one of the band of knights, composed of the illegitimate sons of Amangon (q.v.) and the maidens of his land, which Arthur's knights meet when they come to search for the Graal castle; in the ensuing battle B. is captured and then sent to Arthur's court. B. appears also in tournaments in *Wigm*, as Phyoplerin (var. Piolplerin), and in *JT*, as Pliporie von Iorapant. (See also Bleheris.) He plays a prominent part in the OF prose *Tristan* (Loseth's analysis), and after the death of Lancelot he becomes a hermit. – *E* 1651; *I* nm4705; *P* nm134,28; *C* 2304; *Wigm* 2064; *JT* 2045,1; *RP* nm Prologue, 179ff. [†]

Blisibole 'künec von Ierepars', a knight who is present at a tourney held by Arthur. – *JT* 2042,1

Boetes 'von Botina', a warrior in the Trojan army against the Greeks. He occurs in Benoît as Boëtès. – *LT* 4030

Boecius (Boethius) the Roman philosopher and author. – *SA* nm46

Bogudaht 'grâve von Pranzilê', a knight included in the list of those overcome by Parzivâl. – *P* nm772,18

Bohedân 'künec von Schipelpunte'. (Singer considers this name to be identical with Boidant, a common OF name for Saracens, which occurs in other *chansons de geste* of the Guillaume d'Orange cycle (*Les Narbonnais* and *Li Covenans Vivien*).[26] Singer thinks that Boidant probably stood in Wolfram's MS of *Aliscans*. Boidant does actually occur as a variant of Salmuant (which, however, appears in *W*, as Samirant), in MS m of *Aliscans* (v. 5447).) B. is one of the kings who assist in arming Terramêr, before the second battle at Alischanz. – *W* 356,29

*Bohereiz see Pohereiz

Boydurant a knight who is unhorsed by Êrec at the tourney given to celebrate the latter's wedding. B. does not appear in Chrestien's *Erec*, but it seems quite certain that the original of B. is Chrestien's Rainduranz, who is likewise unhorsed by Erec at the tourney. – *E* 2693

Boizlabe son of Bêne (1) and Willehalm (2) and twin brother of Dânus. The two boys are born in a forest and are sold by Willehalm to merchants, who, in turn, sell them to two separate poor families. As young men they learn of their unknown parentage, are cast adrift and meet each other, without knowing of the relationship between them. They are treated well by Hônestus but leave him to seek their parents. They reach extreme depths of poverty and eventually become robbers in Bohemia, the land over which Bêne rules. She is

---

25 Martin (1), p. 134, to 134,28.
26 Singer (2), p. 107.

persuaded by Willehalm to try to reform them by kindness, and she gives them posts at court. Their identity is soon discovered. – *WW* m1085f. a1945f. n6218

Bocubel   see Brôcûbêlus

Bol   'von Ardibieden', he gave Schîonatulander the lance he is carrying when he is killed by Orilus. B. had given a similar lance to Kolatriande. – *JT* nm5010,4

Bolitars   'von Kahafiezze', called 'der brune', a knight in Akarîn's army against Ipomidôn. – *JT* a2130,1f. n3200,1

Bôlôn   a warrior in Alexander's army. B. appears in Curtius Rufus. – *A* 10815f.

Bônafeide   *amie* of Harturam. – *Crane* m2714 n2751

Bondonîl   husband of Kanfinôn. – *UW* nm83,7ff.

Bonîant   a knight, who is unhorsed by Dêmantîn at Bêâmunt's tourney. – *Dem* 753

Bonifait   nephew of Rudolf; he accompanies Irmingart to Constantinople and cares for her until the arrival of Rudolf. On the homeward journey, B. undertakes to keep watch for the first night. He is attacked by robbers, all of whom he fights together, rather than awaken Rudolf, but he is slain after he has killed five of the robbers. Rudolf wakes up and kills the rest of the robbers. – *GR* γb13

Bonifant (1)   see Bonifacie

Bonifant (2)   'von Arragun', father of Elyzabel. – *JT* nm124,5

Bonifant (3)   brother of Dêmartôn, he is a commander in Bêâmunt's army at Antriûn. – *Dem* nm9926f. a11020

Bonifacie   'bischof', dedicates the monastery which is built for Sigûne. This character is undoubtedly intended to be the historical bishop Boniface (AD 680–755), the Anglo-Saxon missionary who converted Germany to Christianity. – *JT* 5464,1

Boors   see Boort

Boort   'von Gannes'. A prominent knight of the Round Table in the OF romances, B. occurs in MHG literature only in *RP* (also as Boors). He sees his brother, Lyonel, being led away to his death by six knights. B.'s sense of chivalry compels him to abandon Lyonel to his fate and go to the rescue of a maiden, who is being molested by another knight. B. receives false news of the death of his brother, whom he then meets and who wants to fight him for having failed to effect a rescue, but B. refuses. He is trampled to the ground by Lyonel's horse but still refuses to fight his own brother, and Kalogreant, who comes to his rescue, is slain by Lyonel. His death makes B. decide to fight, but just as they are about to start, a cloud descends between them. They accept the significance of the intervention and take Kalogreant to a hermitage, where he is buried. In the Vulgate *Lancelot* (and also in the 15th-century prose *Lancelot* of Ulrich Füetrer), B. and Lyonel are the sons of Bohort of Gannes (or Gaunes), the brother of Ban (see Pant (1)), and are therefore cousins to Lancelot. The story of the brothers' quarrel is first told in *Les Aventures del Saint Graal* (Vulgate Cycle) and is repeated in Malory. In the Vulgate version, B. is one of the three knights (the other two are Galahad (see Galaal) and Perceval) who are pure enough to see the Graal. B. has vowed eternal chastity and is only once tricked into breaking this vow. Of the knights who are granted a glimpse of the Graal, he is the only one who returns to Arthur's court. – *RP* nm791,24f. a791,35ff. [†]

Booz   'von Raap', biblical (Boaz), the husbandman who gave Ruth employment and later married her. – *UA* nm11489

Bope   'von Busenberc', a knight who was brought by Hadmâr (1) to joust with Ulrich von Liechtenstein, when the latter was tired. B. was defeated. – *FD* 892,6

Bordin   'von Ormalariezze', a warrior who is mentioned by Akuleis. It is probable that he is in Akarîn's army against Ipomidôn. – *JT* nm3867,1ff.

Borîolus 'von Larigiâ', also called (37800) 'von Ilarîe', a warrior in the Greek army against the Trojans. B. was invented by Konrad. – *TK* 23880

Borse 'der ander', also called 'der Risenburgære' (Borse II. von Riesenburg), the patron to whom the *Anhang* to *UA* is dedicated. – *UA* nm Anhang, 124f.

Böse 'der schöne', a knight, who first appears in Chrestien's *Erec* (1696), as li Biaus Coarz. Hartmann did not recognize that Coarz was not a name, and when he included this character among the list of knights who are present at Arthur's court, when Êrec returns with Ênîte, he called him 'li bels Côharz'. As 'der schöne Zage', B. is one of the knights present at the tourney between Ris and Cadoalans in *RP*. The next time he appears in *RP*, he is called 'der schöne Böse', a translation of Gautier's le beau Mauvais, a name he has acquired by reason of his reluctance to fight. He is defeated by Parzivâl during the quest of the latter for the head of the white hart and is sent to Arthur's court. Later he falls in with Parzivâl again, and they travel together for five years, during which time B. will fight only with the greatest reluctance. When he does fight, however, he exhibits extraordinary skill and courage. Parzivâl scorns his peace-loving ways, but finally re-names him 'der schöne Kuene' on account of his great deeds, when at last he does fight. A variation of this story is told in *Perlesvaus*, where li Coartz Chevaliers suddenly turns brave during a fight with Roberes in the presence of Parzivâl (they are together only for one day); B. is later mortally wounded by the tyrant Aristor. – *E* 1633; *RP* 81,26f.

Bozorgorgias a warrior in Dârîus's army against Alexander. B. does not appear in any of the sources to *UA*. – *UA* 10933

Brabant 'herzoge von' (*P*), see Lembekîn

Bradins 'von Garcionte', a warrior in Ipomidôn's army against Akarîn. – *JT* nm3221,1

Brainons see Prauerâûs

Bran, Brandalis see Brandelis

Brandân (St. Brendan) an Irish saint, AD 484–577. – nm *MC* 884; *Loh* 93; *Ll* 3,9

Brandelidelîn 'künec von Punturteis', uncle to Gramoflanz; he is unhorsed by Gahmuret at the tourney held by Herzeloide. In *JT*, 'Ponturteise mit Brandelideline' fight for Orilus against Schîonatulander. According to Martin, this name would correspond to the OF Brandalis (see Brandelis) or to Brandis des Illes (see Briens).[27] – *P* nm67,16f. a74,21; *JT* 4471,1f.

Brandelin see Brandelis

Brandelis also called 'Bran von Lis'; son of Ydier (2) and brother of Meljanz de Lis and Gylorette. B. returns home to find that Gawein has taken the virginity of Gylorette and has slain his father. He wants to fight Gawein, but the latter pleads his wounds, and it is agreed that wherever they next meet, the fight shall take place. They meet at B.'s castle, while Arthur is on his way to rescue Gifles, and a long and fierce fight is eventually stopped by the intervention of Gylorette with her son by Gawein, Gingelens (see Wigalois). The story is also told in the ME romance, *Jeaste of Syr Gawayne*, where B. is called Brandles. This is the only name which remotely resembles the names in Pseudo-Gautier, which would seem rather to indicate that the story has crystallized around B. and his antagonism to Gawein. B. occurs also in the Vulgate *Lancelot*, and a Brandalus (var. Brandillis) appears in *Perlesvaus* as one of Parzivâl's eleven uncles. (See also Brandelidelîn.) – *RP* m36,2 an39,13 [†]

Brandes 'grâve von Doleceste', a knight who attends the wedding of Êrec and Ênîte. As Banderous de Linis, he is one of the knights in *C*, who spill Priure's cup of chastity. Both

---

27 Martin (1), p. 75, to 67,17.

forms of the name originate in Chrestien's *Erec* (1935), where he is named Brandes de Leocestre. – *E* 1906; *C* 2328

Brandigan grandfather of Gawein. – *RP* nm500,43

Brandigân 'künec von' (*P*), see Klâmidê

Brandilogus 'markîs von Clîre', a knight who is slain by Hector, whilst fighting for the Greeks against the Trojans. This character was invented by Konrad. – *TK* 31308

Brangæne, Brangâne see Brangêne

Brangebart 'küneginne', a fairy who married Gingemors, by whom she had a son, Brangemor. (See Gingemors, for a consideration of this story as a version of the OF *lai*, *Guingamor*.) – *RP* nm310,33

Brangelis father of Wis. In the Mons MS of Pseudo-Gautier, B. is called Baudigant. – *RP* nm240,28

Brangemor son of Gingemors and a fairy, Brangebart; he is slain by a knight and arrives in a boat at Arthur's court, drawn by a swan, with the point of the lance still in his heart. Gaheries inadvertently withdraws the lance-point and has to undertake the quest, viz. avenge the murder, which he succeeds in doing. This episode bears a striking similarity to the opening scene in *La Vengeance de Raguidel*. – *RP* a288,39f. n310,29

Brangêne maiden attendant on Îsolt (2); in *Tn* she is also her cousin; she persuades Îsolt to spare Tristan's life, when his identity is discovered as he lies wounded at the Irish court, after slaying the dragon. The love-potion is given by Îsolt (1) into her care, to give to Marke and Îsolt on their wedding night. The guilt she feels at having imperfectly guarded the potion compels her to consent to spend the night with Marke on his wedding night, so that Îsolt's loss of virginity shall not be discovered. She contrives to escape the death which Îsolt plans to prevent her from revealing this deceit, and thenceforth she is Îsolt's closest friend and *confidante*. When Îsolt is in the *Minnegrotte* with Tristan, B. remains at Marke's court, but on Îsolt's return, her sense of guilt for the whole tragic love-match compels her to make every effort to facilitate meetings between the lovers. According to Golther, the name and origin of B. have never been satisfactorily explained.[28] He considers the original form of the name to have been Brangain or Brangvain; in Thomas it occurs as Bringvain. Hertz points out that the Kymric Brangwen (= beautiful throat) is the name of the wife of the Irish prince, Martholouch (see Môrolt), and he draws attention to the fact that in *Tn*, B. is a relative of Môrolt.[29] – *ET* 1772; *Tn* 9321; *UT* 1183; *HT* 4426ff. [†]

Branîe 'vrouwe von der hôhen montanîe', sister of Isel; she is one of the ladies at Arthur's court who spill Priure's cup of chastity. – *C* 1618

Brantrivier (Martin is of the opinion that the latter half of this name is the same as the territorial name of Bernout, both being identical with the English family name, Rivers.[30]) In *E*, B. is one of the knights present at Arthur's court when Êrec returns with Ênîte, and in *C* he appears among the list of knights who spill Priure's cup of chastity. B. does not occur in the corresponding list in Chrestien's *Erec*, from which the lists of knights in *E* and *C* were taken (cf. also Lanfal). Unless interpolations have been made from *C* into *E*, or vice versa, a possibility which is very remote in view of the great dissimilarity between the forms of the same names in the two lists, it is clear that the list in Chrestien must at one time have been fuller than that given in the extant MSS of *Erec*. – *E* 1678; *C* 2303

---

28 Golther (2), p. 29 and note 1.
29 Gottfried von Straßburg, *Tristan und Isolde*, transl. by Hertz, p. 587.
30 Martin (1), p. 463, to 682,18.

Bremasur 'künec', a knight on the side of the heathens in the final battle against the Christians. – *WO* 16459

Brians (1) a knight who attends the tourney held by Leigamar in the service of Aram. – *C* 18163

Brîans (2) 'künec von Antipodes', brother of Bîlêî; he is one of the five old kings who come to the wedding of Êrec and Ênîte. Although his brother is a dwarf, B. is the tallest man alive. In *C* he is one of the knights who spill Priure's cup of chastity. B. occurs in Chrestien's *Erec* [1996] as Briën. – *E* 2088; *C* 2342 [†]

Brîen (1) a knight who is present at Arthur's court in *E*, when Êrec returns with Ênîte. In *C* he is one of the knights who spill Priure's cup of chastity. The origin of both references is Chrestien's *Erec* (1705), where he is called Briien. – *E* 1640; *C* 2299

Brîen (2) a knight who slew his brother, Lâmêr, for his fine armour. Kapteyn, in his index to *Wigl*, considers B. to be identical with Brîên (1). – *Wigl* nm6069

Brîen (3) 'lingo mathel', a knight who is present at Arthur's court, when Êrec returns with Ênîte. A knight named Breons occurs in Chrestien's *Erec* (1745) in a passage which is generally considered to be a later interpolation. Singer is of the opinion that B. is a later interpolation in *E*, based on Brîên (1).[31] – *E* 1668

Briens 'von der inselen', a knight who is present at the tourney held by Arthur at Orgelus. B. is first mentioned in Chrestien's *Erec* (6730), where he is called Bruianz des Illes (MSS B and P: brianz). He occurs as Brianz des Illes in the Montpellier MS of Gautier, and in *Perlesvaus*, where he is a traitor to Arthur and the mortal enemy of Lancelot. He is also probably the same person as Branduz (var. Brandis) des Illes, the owner of the castle, Dolereuse Garde, which Lancelot frees from enchantment by defeating Brandus in the Vulgate *Lancelot* and *Le Livre d'Artus*. Brandis (see Brandelidelîn) is thought by Martin to be probably the 'Rex insularum', who occurs in chronicles as a Norwegian prince on the Isle of Man.[32] B. also occurs in the OF romance, *Li Chevaliers as Deus Espees*,[33] where he treacherously attacks Gawein. Miss J.L. Weston suggests that B. may be identical with the historical enemy of Stephen of Blois, viz. Brian of Wallingford, who was known as Brian de Insula.[34] – *RP* 473,8 [†]

Brickus (Schulz thought this name to be identical with Bryt of *Brut Tysilio*, and Brutus of Geoffrey of Monmouth (I,3).[35] Bartsch considers the possibility of its derivation from the Provençal Bricos, 'the Unhappy', but inclines towards the explanation of Schulz.[36] Martin derives it from Britus,[37] a view which Golther does not accept without a query.[38]) B. is the son of Mazadân and the brother of Lazaliez. – *P* nm56,12ff.

Brinus a knight who is wounded by Absterne, whilst fighting for Athis against Bilas. B. does not occur in the OF version. – *AP* C,103

Brios 'von dem gebogenen walde', he entertained Parzivâl, whilst the latter was on his quest, and told him the history of Karmedit and Orgelus. In Gautier he is called Brios de la Foriest Arsée. – *RP* a456,44f. n457,34

---

31 Singer (1), p. 60.
32 Martin (1), p 75, to 67,17.
33 Bruce (1), II, p. 231.
34 Weston (4), p.362.
35 Schulz, 'Eigennamen', p. 395.
36 Bartsch (2), p. 145.
37 Martin (1), p. 64, to 56,16.
38 Golther (1), p. 141.

Brîsaz 'künec', one of the knights at Arthur's court who spill Priure's cup of chastity. – *C* 1890

Brîsêîdâ first mentioned in Homer's *Iliad*, where she is a slave who is taken from Achilles by Agâmennon and is thus the cause of the breach between these two princes, which results in Achilles' decision to refrain from fighting. Dares includes B. among the Greeks and describes her beauty, but he says nothing more about her. She is not mentioned in Dictys. From the meagre material which he found in Dares, Benoît invented one of the most famous love stories of the Middle Ages. He makes B. the daughter of the traitor Kalcas and the *amie* of Troilus. She is compelled by the Trojans to leave Troy and join her father with the Greeks, and her somewhat frivolous behaviour towards Diomedes, who falls in love with her, causes a hatred between him and Troilus which culminates in the death of the latter at the hands of Achilles. *LT* follows closely the story as told in Benoît, but the reference to B. as the *amie* of Achilles in *RB* shows a knowledge of the Homeric version. Boccaccio found the story of B. and Troilus in Benoît or one of his successors, and, owing perhaps to some confusion with Chriseis, another slave who plays a part in the same episode in Homer, he calls her Griseida in *Filostrato*. Through Boccaccio the story reached English literature (Chaucer, Caxton, and Shakespeare) as Troilus and Cressida.[39] – *LT* nm8144ff. a8331; *RB* nm24548

Brises 'von Pedason', father of Ypodomia; he hanged himself when Pedason was taken by Achilles. B. is called Briseus in Homer and Dictys, and Brisès in Benoît. – *LT* nm16660

Brôcûbêlus son of Mazêus, a warrior in Alexander's army, he confirms to Alexander the report of the betrayal of Dârîus by Bessus. B. occurs in Curtius Rufus, as Brochubelus, and in Gualterus. In *UA* he is called Bocubel. – *A* 14761; *UA* 16503

Brubanie 'der uz' (*JT*), see Lembekîn

Brun 'Senpitê' (OF Bruns sanz Pitié). This name frequently occurs in the OF romances and appears for the first time in Chrestien's *Erec* (1715), although none of the known MSS preserves the name in its correct form, the usual form being a variant of Brun de Piciez. That the correct form must have appeared in Chrestien's poem is almost certain from the reference in *C*, where, as Sempitebruns, he is one of the knights at Arthur's court who spill Priure's cup of chastity, the whole list of knights in *C* being a reproduction of Chrestien's list in *Erec*. B. does not occur in the corresponding list of knights in *E*. He occurs in *Mtl*, and again in *C*, where, as Bruner Sempitê [24653], he takes part in another chastity test, this time of Giranphiel's glove, and he is mentioned in *RP* as the *ami* of the Graal maiden, who refers to him as Bruns one erbermekeit. In the OF romances, where he is usually called Brehus sanz Pitié, he is, as his name implies, a bad knight. He plays a part in most of the romances of the Vulgate Cycle, and occurs in the prose *Tristan* (Löseth's analysis), where he is characterized by his treachery, particularly towards maidens. – *Mtl* 887; *C* 2305; *RP* m446,30f. n447,6f.

Brunecke 'ein Franken', on the side of the Christians in the final battle against the heathens. – *WO* 16745ff.

Bruns (1) 'von Mielant', he is attacked by Arthur for refusing to do homage at the wedding of the latter's two nieces, Clarate and Tanete. In Pseudo-Gautier he is called Bruns de Branlant, and as such appears in several of the OF romances, including the *Livre d'Artus*, where, instead of being the lord of Branlant, he is seneschal to Lore (q.v.). B. is called de Mïelant in MS R of Pseudo-Gautier. – *RP* 20,40

---

39 *Encyclopædia Britannica*, III, p. 414.

Bruns (2) 'von dem plon', he abducts a maiden, who is rescued by Gawein, when the latter defeats B. B. occurs in Gautier as Bruns de la Lande. – *RP* m563,41 a565,16 n569,25

Budîn 'herre von der marke', a knight in Alexander's army against Dârîus. B. was apparently invented by Ulrich. – *UA* 4712f.

***Buer** see Bûr

Büheler 'der' (Hans von Bühel), author of *KT*. – *KT* nm1236

Buktzinos a dwarf, Jerome's chief counsellor; he brings to Fridrich (3) the news that a daughter has been born to Jerome. – *FS* a2922 n2948

Bûlaz see Pûlaz

Buobe, Buov, *Buove see Buovun

Buovun son of Heimrîch (1) and brother of Willehalm (1), for whom he fights at Alischanz. In *UW* he is an ally of Lôis against Terramêr. He occurs in most of the OF *chansons de geste*, including the very early *Chancun de Willame*, where he is at first brother-in-law to Willehalm and father to Vivien (see Vîvîans), and later is referred to as Willehalm's brother. – *W* a5,16f. n6,24; *UW* m4,14f. a21,1 n25,1

Bûr 'künec von Siglimessâ', one of the group of 15 Saracen kings who attack Willehalm (1) at the end of the first battle at Alischanz. B. is wounded or killed by Willehalm in that encounter. [See Appendix (9).] This name may have appeared in the MS of *Aliscans* used by Wolfram, but there is no justification for it in the extant MSS. San-Marte thought that it was a corrupt form of Corboclez,[40] but this seems more likely to have been the original of Korsudê (q.v.). – *W* m71,22 a72,17f. n74,15 [†]

Burchart (= Burchardus, Count of Melun, Corbie and Vendome, who lived in the 10th century ?) B. slew the Count of Flanders, whose name (not given in *UA*) is stated to be Louis in Gualterus (VIII, 168ff.). Gualterus refers to the incident as though it was well-known and compares B. with Philôtas. – *UA* nm18365

Buroîn 'herzoge von dem Wîzen sê', tutor of Diepalt. – *L* nm 2790

Bursett a knight who takes part in the tourney held by Arthur for Deleprosat. – *Wigm* 2057

---

40 San-Marte, p. 57.

C

(see under K or Z)

D

Dahamorht brother of Angaras (q.v.), he was slain at a tourney by Gawein. – *C* m18839ff. n22652ff.

Dayron see Dinodaron

Dalbuneis 'der More', a knight who had been unhorsed by Hiutegêr. – *JT* nm3308,3

Dalidâ biblical (Delilah), the woman who betrayed Samson to the Philistines. – *UA* m11480f.; *RB* nm15167

Dalkors see Delekors

Damor a natural son of Priam; he fights for the Trojans against the Greeks. D. occurs elsewhere only in Benoît, where he is called Nez d'Amors. – *LT* a4808 n4837

Dâne daughter of Acrisius and mother of Perseus by Jupiter, who visited her in a shower of gold. In Greek mythology she is called Danaë. – *UA* nm6981

Danias a knight who joins in the search for Parzivâl. In Gautier he is called Daniaus, who, however, can hardly be identified with Daniel (1). – *RP* 526,8

Daniel (1) 'von dem Blüenden Tal', an unknown knight who comes to Arthur's court, where he jousts with and defeats a succession of knights of the Round Table, headed, as usual, by Keiî. D. follows Matûr's messenger, when the latter leaves Arthur's court after delivering his challenge. He meets vrouwe von dem Trüeben Berge, whom he frees from the oppression of Jurân, and then frees the grâve von dem Liehten Brunnen (q.v.) from the giants. He then joins Arthur and his army against Matûr. An unusual feature of this romance is that it is not the hero, but Arthur, who fights and defeats the overweening challenger in single combat. The next night D. steals away to find the grâve von dem Liehten Brunnen, who had disappeared into a castle, and, by defeating the grâve von der Grüenen Ouwe (q.v.), and the latter's oppressor, he rescues his friend and returns at dawn to assist Arthur in the ensuing fight with Matûr's men. He then marries Danîse, but on the day of his wedding Arthur is abducted by a very strong old man. With the help of Sandinôse (q.v.) and her net, D. succeeds in capturing Arthur's abductor and releases not only Arthur, but also Parzivâl, who had tried to rescue the king. D. occurs in *GM* as 'D. von Plüental', where he is one of the knights at Arthur's court. – *DB* 160ff.; *RW* nm2233; *GM* (MS D) 38577 (MS I) 3867; *FS* nm4819

Daniel (2) biblical. – nm *A* 9814; *JT* 2518,4; *Loh* 116; *UA* 23; *RB* 8462; *FS* 2905; *SA* 1932; *WA* 1009

Danîse wife of Matûr. On the death of her husband, she marries Daniel (1). Although D. marries one of her late husband's foes a few days after his death, her case does not quite provide a parallel to that of Laudîne, since it is not the actual slayer of her husband (who is slain by Arthur) whom she marries. – *DB* m5810f. a5897 n7568f.

Dânus son of Bêne (1) and Willehalm (2) and twin brother of Boizlabe (q.v.). – *WW* m1085f. a1945f. n7545

Dardân see Dardanus

Dardanus father of Trôa, and founder of Troy. D. was an ancestor of Ênêâs. He is mentioned in the OF *Eneas* and Virgil. – *Ed* nm61

Darêl vassal of Schaffilûn; he comes to take the oath of allegiance to Wigalois at the latter's enthronement. He fights for Wigalois against Lîon. – *Wigl* a9080ff. n10098

Dares the alleged author of a Latin account of the siege of Troy, which was supposed to have been written by a Trojan at the time of the war. There is no doubt that the work is a spurious one, although a Dares, a Trojan priest, does occur in Homer's *Iliad* (IX, 9 and

27). D. is mentioned by Benoît, who used his account freely, but Konrad introduces him into the story as an uncle of Hecuba. – *LT* nm53; *MC* nm37; *TK* nm296 a12392ff.

Darîel (1) see Lernîs

Dariel (2) see Daries (1)

Daries (1) 'von Orledune', also called 'von Orlendune', a commander in Ipomidôn's army against Akarîn. – *JT* 3210,1

Dâries (2) entertains Flôre when the latter arrives at the city of the Amiral, and suggests methods by which Flôre could enter the tower in which Blanscheflûr is imprisoned. – *NRFB* 11; *FB* m3604f. a3652 n3998

Darion a warrior in the Greek army against the Trojans. He is called Dorion in *TK*, which more accurately represents Benoît's form, Dorius. In Dares he is called Diores, MSS G and L, Dorius, and in Homer, Diores. – *LT* 3335f. *TK* 23814

Dârîus (1) a former king of Persia and son of Idaspis (Darius I), who invaded Babylon with Cyrus. – nm *A* 15711; *UA* 904

Dârîus (2) 'qui et Nôtus', a former king of Persia (Darius II, surnamed Nothos). D. was historically the father of Sisigambis. –*A* nm15723

Dârîus (3) 'keiser von Persîâ', the chief enemy of Alexander (Darius III). D. first meets with the opposition of Alexander when he sends the customary tribute collectors to Philipp's court. They are sent back empty-handed and with a defiant answer from Alexander. The remainder of D.'s existence is occupied with war and preparations for war with Alexander, of whose ability he is at first scornful. In most accounts there are only two battles, the first at Issôn, where D. is defeated, and his mother, wife and daughter are captured, and the second at Erbela, where he is again defeated, and betrayed by Bessus and Narbâsones. In *WA* his death takes place before a battle at the hands of Färtes, Fysus, and Oriaber. The usual version is that D. dies in Alexander's arms, where a reconciliation takes place between the two foes and D. makes Alexander promise to marry his daughter, Roxane. D.'s mother is sometimes called Rodone and sometimes Sisigambis. His wife is named only in *UA*, where she is called Carafilîe, and his brother, Oxîatres, occurs in *A*. –*L* nm4761; *A* 2756f.; *UA* nm1364 a5414; *RB* nm19941; *SA* 1039ff.; *WA* nm87 a 509ff.

Darius (4) 'von Matrius', also called 'von Matrisande', a warrior who is killed by Môrolt whilst fighting for Ipomidôn against Akarîn. – *JT* nm3235,6 a3675,6

Darius (5) 'künec von Media', he sends a maiden as messenger to Persit, because the latter makes a practice of killing all messengers, and D. thinks that he would spare the life of a maiden. Persit orders her to be taken away and killed, but she is rescued by Wildhalm. For chronological reasons D. cannot be identified with either of the kings of Persia, but it is probable that the name was suggested by them. – *WO* nm4498f.

Darifant the hero of a MHG romance which has come down to us only in two fragments. In the first, D. is present at the wedding of his friend, Balifeit, whom he leaves, accompanied by a fairy, to rescue Effardîe. In the second fragment, D. meets with and fights Offiart, his battle-cry being Fiolêde, the name of his *amie*. He defeats Offiart but spares him, and conforms to the custom of the land and spends the night there. Here the second fragment breaks off. – *Dar* 91

Darchôs Alexander bequeathed to him Pelâosôs. D. does not occur in any other history of Alexander. –*UA* nm27042

Dassir 'künec von Ungerlant', father of Gayol; he dies whilst the latter is away from court. – *Crane* m35ff. n908

Dâtaphernes a warrior engaged in the conspiracy with Spitâmenes against Bessus. So also in *Expeditio Alexandri* and Curtius Rufus. – *A* 21564ff.

Dathân biblical, an Israelite who, with Abiram (see Abirôn (1)) and others, disputed the leadership of Moses and Aaron in the wilderness. They were swallowed up with their families by the earth. – *RB* nm15820

Daunus father of Turnus. This name has the same form in Virgil but appears as Daumus in the OF *Eneas*. It seems probable, however, that the MS used by Heinrich had the correct form. – *Ed* nm7738

Davalon 'li fiers', a knight at Arthur's court who spills Priure's cup of chastity. The name rests on a misunderstanding of Chrestien's *Erec* (1955): 'De l'Isle d'Avalon fu sire'. (See Gwinganiers.) – *C* 2334

David see Dâvît (1)

Daphyr 'von Nagrahyr', a knight in Paltriot's army against Atroclas. – *Wigm* 3677

Dâvît (1) biblical (David). – nm *E* 5562; *P* 796,8; *W* 355,13; *A* 8797; *G* 408; *UW* (MSS B and D) 111,11¹⁰; *JT* 199,5; *PM* 8897; *TK* 2168; *UA* 19; *WW* 2806; *RB* 18913

Dâvît (2) 'von Tintaguel', called (in *E*) 'von Luntaguel'; a knight who, in *E*, is one of those who come to the wedding of Êrec and Ênîte, and, in *C*, is present at Arthur's court and spills Priure's cup of chastity. D. occurs in Chrestien's *Erec* (1959). – *E* 1935; *C* 2335

Dafnes (Daphne) the daughter of a river god; she was turned into a laurel, when she prayed to be delivered from Apollo, who was chasing her. – *C* nm11593

Dêân 'grâve', a knight who is unhorsed by Dêmantîn in the battle against Eghart. – *Dem* 5416f.

Dêbora daughter of Eve. D. is not a biblical character but is mentioned as a daughter of Eve in Pseudo-Methodius. – *A* nm17010

Dedamia see Deidamîa

Dedelus a magician, father of Parklise, to whom he taught the secrets of magic. It seems quite certain that the legendary Greek inventor, Daedalus, is intended. – *WO* nm10861ff.

Deidamîa daughter of Licomedes and lover of Achilles (q.v.), by whom she has Pirrus. The story of her love for Achilles is told in Statius. – *LT* m13848; *C* nm11589; *TK* nm13900ff. a14601f.; *RB* nm22580f.; *GT* 16372ff.

Dêîdamîe see Deidamîa

Deyrant a knight who is badly wounded by Florandâmîs, who is permitting him to bleed to death. Firganant overcomes Florandâmîs and compels him to give D. medical attention. – *Dem* m7779 a8144ff. n8180

Deiphebus son of Priam; he fights for the Trojans against the Greeks. In *LT*, as in Benoît and Dares, D. is slain by Palimedes, whilst the account in *TK* follows more closely the story as told by Dictys. It is related in the continuation to Konrad's poem that, after the death of Paris, D. took Helen, and when Troy fell, Menelaus had his limbs cut off one by one and then had him put to death. D. occurs in Homer as Deiphobos, and in the Latin versions as Deiphobus. – *LT* nm1664ff. a2223; *MC* nm21; *TK* nm13254ff. a18968

Delabander see Orilus

Delasîe *amie* of Andifôr, who, like all the other knights in *Dem*, uses her name as his battle-cry. – *Dem* nm5441

Delekors a knight at Arthur's court who is unhorsed by Tristan. The episode is repeated by Heinrich in *HT*, where he is called Dalkors. – *ET* 5059ff.; *HT* a2019 n2030

Delemorsz a scout in Paltriot's army against Atroclas. – *Wigm* 3692

Delŷâ a maiden attendant on Sirgamôte; she helps her to escape with Dêmantîn from Eghart. – *Dem* 3696

Delymors see Delemorsz

Delmitten a knight at Arthur's court. – *Wigm* 2510

Delogroisie see Zidegast

Delon natural son of Priam; he fights for the Trojans against the Greeks. In *TK* he is called Dolunt, and he occurs in Benoît as Delons (var. Dolon) and in Hyginus as Dolon. – *LT* a4768f. n4779; *TK* 30374

Delonîs 'künec', a warrior in the Greek army against the Trojans. This character was invented by Konrad. – *TK* 30680ff.

Delofin wife of Sinofel and mother of Syrodamen; she comes to court after the latter has been pardoned. – *FS* m3134 an7836ff.

Dêmantîn 'von Antrîûn', he falls in love with Sirgamôte whilst she is still very young, and her father, Meliân, refuses to consider him as a suitor. He wins Bêâmunt in a tourney but gives her to Firganant, and then defeats Phoriân (q.v.). He helps Pfandimoi to regain her lover and is told about Pheradzoye by a wounded knight in a wood. But he also has news of Sirgamôte and is going to seek her, when a maiden taunts him with being afraid to undertake the Pheradzoye adventure. He returns and kills Pandulet, and lives with Pheradzoye (q.v.) for six months, at the end of which time he makes his way to Sirgamôte, whom he reaches on the day of her wedding to Eghart, whom her father is compelling her to marry. Sirgamôte and D. flee together, and although they are followed by many knights, D. unhorses them all, and they arrive safely at Antrîûn, where they are married. Meliân and Eghart follow, and a long siege takes place. Firganant arrives to help D. but fights with him for some time before his battle-cry reveals his identity to D. The arrival of Bêâmunt with her army turns the tide, and, Meliân and Eghart both being captured, a peaceful recognition of the marriage of the two lovers is obtained. Meliân gives up his throne in favour of his daughter and D., who become king and queen of Greece. – *Dem* a73f. n189

Dêmartôn 'von Schotten', brother of Bonifant (3) and chief counsellor of Bêâmunt. He is a commander in her army at Antrîûn. – *Dem* 9617

Demesticus lover of Pillis (q.v.). – *RB* nm24553

Demestius a philosopher (= Domitius?). According to *WO*, D. wrote a book entitled *De Anima*. – *WO* nm15123

Dêmêtrîus (1) a warrior in Alexander's army and one of the conspirators with Dimnus against the life of Alexander. – *A* nm 18885; *UA* 4681

Dêmêtrîus (2) one of the philosophers to whom Alexander listens after Athens has surrendered. D. seems to correspond to Demades in Valerius and Leo, as a Demetrius does not appear among the philosophers in any of the histories of Alexander. The alteration in the name may have been suggested by Dêmêtrîus (1) or possibly by Demetrius Phalereus, the Attic orator and philosopher and some-time governor of Athens. – *A* 3817

Demetrius (3) see Demetron

Demetron brother of Matribais; he is captured by Akarîn whilst fighting for Ipomidôn in the battle in which Gahmuret meets his death. – *JT* 812,5ff.

Demefrön mentioned as an example of a brave warrior. – *Wigm* nm3424

Dêmôkritus (Democritus) the Greek philosopher. – *A* nm17681

Demostenes a Greek philosopher; he is one of the rhetoricians who debate whether or not Athens shall surrender to Alexander. In *A* and in *UA*, in which he is the military commander of Athens, he takes the same attitude as in MS S of Leo,[1] that is to say, he advises against the surrender. In *WA* he puts the case for and against and leaves it to the people to decide. They surrender. The main group of MSS of Leo follow Valerius in

---

[1] O. Zingerle, p. 57.

making D. speak in favour of surrendering, but this is not followed by any of the MHG versions. – *A* 3653; *UA* 2480; *WA* 1672

Dêmosthenâ, Dêmosthenes, Demostinis see Demostenes

Demophon brother of Achamas, a warrior in the Greek army against the Trojans. After the sack of Troy he is married to Ethra (1). In Greek legend D. is the lover of Phyllis (see Phillis). He occurs in Dares as Demophoon, son of Theseus, and in Benoît, but he does not occur in Homer. – *LT* 16362; *TK* m2318ff. [†]

Derafeit 'künec', husband of Odassie; he is a commander in Bêâmunt's army at Antrîûn. – *Dem* nm9716 a11110

Deselmiur wife of Kardêuz. – *M* nm3581

Desiderius king of the Lombards, whose daughter Karl (1) married, and who afterwards became his enemy. D. is only mentioned in MS D of *UW*, where his name may have been taken from the *Kaiserchronik*, in which he occurs (14857). – *UW* nm (MS D) 12,226-8

Dessân 'burcgrâve', a knight who is slain by Dêmantîn at a tourney. – *Dem* 5723

Deute 'künec von Ammiravel', a warrior in Akarîn's army against Ipomidôn. – *JT* 3881,3f.

Dêphân 'von Kalîe', a knight who pursues Dêmantîn and Sirgamôte as they are escaping from Eghart. He jousts with Dêmantîn and is killed by him. – *Dem* 4195

Decipeneus 'künec von Manfriûl', a warrior in the Greek army against the Trojans. This character was invented by Konrad. – *TK* 23890

Decius the Roman Emperor, who died AD 215. According to *GT*, D. was descended from Romulus and was driven out of Rome by Diocletian (see Dioclecinus), who, however, was not born until thirty years after the death of D. – *GT* nm25103

Diadorforgrant see Dyartorforgrannt

Dîâna the goddess of hunting. In *TK* she is present at the wedding of Thetis and Pêleus, and later the story is told of how she demands sacrifice from the Greeks for a hart which is slain by Agâmennon, and how she relents at the last minute and snatches the doomed Iphigene away in a cloud. – *Ed* nm1794; *LT* nm3601; *TK* 1078; *UA* nm2802; *RB* nm16415; *SA* nm2934

Dîanîra wife of Hercules. The story of her abduction by Hercules, and the way in which she was the innocent cause of his death, is told in Ovid's *Metamorphoses* IX, where she is called Deïanira. – *TK* nm21430f.

Dyartorforgrannt 'von Triasoltrifertrant', a knight who is severely wounded by Wigamur whilst championing Affrosydones against the claims of Eydes, whom Wigamur is championing. – *Wigm* 1784ff.

Diâspes a warrior in Dârîus's army; he is killed by Eumenidôn at Issôn. D. occurs elsewhere only in Gualterus. – *UA* 8157

Diatorforgrant see Dyartorforgrannt

Dîden 'grâve von Litenant', an ally of Lôîs against Terramêr. D. is also (212,11) called Tŷde. – *UW* 39,13

Didimus see Dindimus

Dîdô 'küneginne von Kartâgô', she is driven from Tyre by her brother, who had slain her husband, Sichêus. She founds Kartâgô, and when Ênêâs arrives at her shores, she falls in love with him. Ênêâs is compelled by the gods to continue his voyage, and D., heartbroken at his departure, kills herself with the sword he leaves behind. This is substantially the same story as is found in Virgil and the OF *Eneas*. – *Ed* nm288 a455; *E* nm7558; *Wigl* nm2720; *P* nm399,14; *Tn* nm17198ff.; *MC* nm1152; *C* nm530; *FB* nm2434; *A* nm8742; *RB* nm3211

Didones see Dodines

Diebalt 'von Gahgunie', a knight who is unhorsed by Olivier at the tourney at Poys. – *RW* 7228

Diens a knight who fights for Bilas against Athis. D. occurs in the OF version as Drïens. – *AP* C,7

Diepalt brother of Ade; he attends Lôt's tourney as squire to Lanzelet. – *L* 2780

Diepolt 'margrâve von Voheburc', a knight who is present at the tourney held at Friesach. – *FD* 188,2

Diepreht a burgher of Esslingen, who, according to *WO* (13254ff.), wrote many romances, one of which was used by Johann for *WO*. – *WO* nm9098

Dieterich 'von Brâbant', he goes to the court of Fruot with his double, Engelhart (q.v.). D. is recalled to Brâbant on the death of his father. – *Eng* a446f n618

Diether (1) nephew of Salmurte; he accompanies Arthur to the assistance of Isope. – *Wigm* 2846

Diether (2) 'ûz Ungerlant', he occurs in MS K of *Ll* only, as squire to Lohengrîn. In *Loh* the squire is called Kyir, and in *Ll*, Neithart. – *Ll* (MS K) 36,5f.

Dietherich 'grâve', son of Perrin; he is in attendance on Gillelm in the tourney at Komarzi. He is also called Dirrich, Tyrric and Tierrich, and attends the tournaments held at Poys and Kurnoy. – *RW* 5942ff.

Dietmâr (1) 'von Liehtenstein', brother of Ulrich von Liechtenstein; he is present at the tournaments held at Friesach and Kornneuburg and fights as Gawein on Ulrich's side during the latter's *Artusfahrt*. – *FD* 181,3

Dietmâr (2) 'von Mûre', a knight who jousts with Ulrich von Liechtenstein during the latter's *Artusfahrt*. – *FD* 1427,5

Dietmâr (3) 'von Potensteine', a knight who attends the tourney held at Friesach. – *FD* 191,8

Dietmâr (4) 'von Schœnenkirchen', a knight who welcomes Ulrich von Liechtenstein to Neustadt during the latter's *Artusfahrt*. – *FD* 1485,3

Dietmâr (5) 'von Styr', a knight who is present at the tourney held at Friesach and who later (666,3f) jousts with Ulrich von Liechtenstein during the latter's *Venusfahrt*. – *FD* 196,2

Dietrich (1) 'von Basel an dem Orte', called by Konrad 'der werde singer'; he assisted Konrad with the writing of *TK*. – *TK* nm245f.

Dietrîch (2) 'von Bern' (Theodoric the Great), the famous king of the Ostrogoths and hero of a number of MHG heroic poems. – *ET* nm5973; *A* nm20668; *Loh* nm573; *Ll* nm7,2; *Ll* (MS K) m32,3

Dietrîch (3) 'von Buches', a knight who attends the tourney held at Friesach. – *FD* 303,1

Dietrîch (4) 'schenke von Dobrach', a knight who welcomes Ulrich von Liechtenstein to Neustadt during his *Artusfahrt*. – *FD* 1483,3

Dietrîch (5) 'von Smidâ', a knight who is unhorsed by der von Lüentz during Ulrich von Liechtenstein's *Artusfahrt*. – *FD* 1554ff.

Dictys the alleged author of a diary supposed to have been written by a Greek warrior during the war at Troy. Herbort, who is simply quoting Benoît, mentions D., whom he calls Ytis, but it is evident that he made no personal use of this account. – *LT* nm14938

Dillibande 'von Atzagouch', a warrior in Akarîn's army against Ipomidôn. – *JT* nm3142,1ff.

Dimena maiden attendant on Cassandra; she is married after the fall of Troy to Achamas. The correct form of her name is Clymena, and she occurs as such in Benoît, Dictys, and Homer. – *LT* 16358

Dimitter a warrior in Alexander's army during the siege of Trîtôniâ. D. does not appear in any of the sources to *UA*. – *UA* Anhang, 660ff.

Dimnus a warrior in Alexander's army, he conspires with others to kill Alexander and make Philôtas king in his place. In *A*, which follows Curtius Rufus and Gualterus, he betrays the conspiracy by trying to enlist the support of Nicômachus, who reports the matter to Zêbalîn, through whom it reaches Alexander, and the conspirators are stoned to death. The account in *UA* differs slightly, as D. is the brother of Nicômachus and confesses direct to Zêbalîn. He commits suicide when the conspiracy reaches the ears of Alexander. In *UA* he is called Dîmus. – *A* 18814; *UA* 2547

Dîmôn a warrior in Dârîus's army, he is killed by Parmênîôn during the battle at Issôn. D. occurs elsewhere only in Gualterus, where he is called Dimus. – *UA* 8085ff.

Dimothenes 'von Tripe', standard-bearer to Bilas in the battle against Athis. D. does not occur in the OF version. – *AP* C,81

Dymszogar 'küneginne', she holds a tourney at which she herself is the prize. The victor is Wigamur, who, however, does not accept her. She was to find a husband, because she is being oppressed by Gamgrinot, but no account is given of whether she manages eventually to free herself of her oppressor. D. is also called Dinifogar and Nyfrogar. – *Wigm* nm4673 a4896

Dîmus see Dimnus

Dinasdanreis see Dinasdanres

Dinasdanres a knight whom Gawein meets as he is on his way to take up the fight with Gynganbertil (see Kingrimursel), as arranged in *P*. Gawein and D. start to fight, but the contest is held over until the next time they meet. This proves to be at the place where Gawein is to fight Gynganbertil, and he agrees to fight them both together, the fight being averted at the last minute, however, by the arrival of Arthur, who marries his two nieces, Tanete and Clarate, to Gawein's two opponents. This story is told in the Montpellier MS of Pseudo-Gautier, where D. is called Dinadares.[2] The name appears to have been suggested by the town of Dinadaron, which is mentioned in the Mons MS at about the same place and which occurs in Chrestien's *Perceval* (2732) as Dinasdaron, the town in Wales at which Arthur holds his court. (See also Tinas.) In Gerbert's continuation to *Perceval*, the name has become distorted (3978) to Dysnadarés, a form which is strikingly similar to the name of a Saxon king, Disnadaron, who occurs in *Le Livre d'Artus*. – *RP* a8,42 n11,3

Dindimus 'künec von Brâgmânâ', his land is skirted by Alexander during his campaigns. In *WA*, where he is named Didimus, he carries on a correspondence with Alexander, in which he tries to convince the latter of the futility of his triumphs. The correspondence in Latin between D. and Alexander is preserved in several medieval MSS under the title of *Collatio Alexandri cum Dindimo, rege Bragmanorum, per litteras facta*. – *UA* nm22395 a22410; *WA* 4104ff.

Dînîse see Dionîsius

Dinisodres son of Saladres, with whom he and his brothers attack Parzivâl, who defeats them all. D. is called Dinisordres in the Mons MS of Manessier, and Dinosodre in the Montpellier MS. – *RP* a842,6 n844,41

Dinifogar see Dymszogar

Dinodaron natural son of Priam; he fights for the Trojans against the Greeks. He is also called Donosdaron in *TK*, and Dayron in *LT*, all three forms deriving from Benoît's Dinas

---

2   *Perceval le Gallois*, III, p. 84, note.

Danon, which in the opinion of Greif originated in Democoon, a name which appears in Hyginus.[3] – *LT* a4768f. n4783; *TK* 30368

Diôgenî (Diogenes the Cynic). – *C* nm3158

Dioclecinus Roman Emperor (Diocletian), AD 245–313. In *GT* he is said to have driven Decius (q.v.) from Rome. – *GT* nm25108

Diomedea daughter of Forbante; she is taken by Achilles, when he slays her father. D. occurs in Homer, Dictys, and Benoît. – *LT* nm16646f.

Dyomedes a warrior in the Greek army against the Trojans. In *LT*, which follows the account in Benoît, D. falls in love with Brîsêîdâ (q.v.) and brings her back from Troy with him. Egyal, his wife, learning of this, meets D. with an army and drives him away. He returns to Troy, where he obtains the support of Ênêâs, and Egyal, realising that she cannot fight them both, permits him to return. He is not the lover of Brîsêîdâ in Homer, Dares or Dictys, but in the last-named he is repelled by Egyal on his return from Troy. In *TK*, as in Statius, D. accompanies Ulixes, when the latter goes to fetch Achilles to the war. – *LT* 2840; *TK* 23839; *UA* nm18464ff.

Dionise (1) a knight who fights for Athis against Bilas. So also in the OF version. – *AP* A*,112

Dîonîse (2) see Dionîsius

Dionîsius (St. Denis) the patron saint of France. – nm *Tn* 8066; *W* 330,20; *UA* 14436

Diores a natural son of Priam; he is slain by Ulixes whilst fighting for the Trojans against the Greeks. – *TKf* 43154

Dirrich see Dietherich

Dirtes the person who, according to *C*, arranged to murder Agâmennon. Historically the murder was carried out by Clitemnestre and Egistus; Heinrich seems to be confusing the former with Dirce (this spelling appears in MS V), the wife of Lycus, and persecutor of Antiope. – *C* nm11594

Discordia the malevolent goddess who, not invited to the wedding of Thetis and Pêleus, sends an apple, which is to be given to the most beautiful woman present. Paris, who is the judge, awards the prize to Venus, who rewards him with Helen, thus causing the war between the Greeks and the Trojans. In *TK*, D. comes to the wedding to hand over the apple in person, whilst in *GT* she merely accompanies Terius, when the latter visits Paris to give him the apple and warn him of the approaching visit of the goddesses. – *TK* 1250ff.; *UA* nm4891; *GT* 1787ff.

Distordia see Discordia

Dythalt a knight who is unhorsed by Dêmantîn whilst he is riding with his *amie*. He leaves her and swears she will not hear from him again until he has overcome ten knights. – *Dem* nm4402f.

Diunâ a maiden attendant on Senebalŷn's wife. – *UW* 207,16

Diunalt a maiden attendant on Gîburc. She accompanies Willehalm and Gîburc on their flight from Tîbalt (1). – *UW* 131,28

Do father of Gifles. D. never appears as a character, and his name only occurs in conjunction with that of his son. The first mention of D. that is recorded is in Chrestien's *Erec* (1729): 'Girflez li fiz Do', which appears in *E* as 'fil Dou Giloles'. It is generally accepted that D., as the father of Gifles, is identical with Wolfram's Îdœl (Idele in *JT*), the father of Jofreit (see Gifles). In the OF prose *Tristan* (Löseth's analysis) D. is said to be the son of Arés. – *E* nm1663; *P* nm277,4; *JT* nm1976,5; *RP* nm44,46 [†]

---

3   Greif, pp. 26ff.

Dôas see Thoas

Dobatîn 'von Erasôt', 'marschal' to Bêâmunt. – *Dem* a10051 n10158

Dôdermunt *amie* of Carifêgis. On his defeat, she has to hand over his parrot to Acheloyde. – *Crane* nm3543 a3606

Dodinas a name given to Gingelens (see Wigalois), owing to his recklessness. According to the authors of *RP*, this name means 'little fool', but it occurs neither in the Mons MS of Pseudo-Gautier, where he is called Yoniaus, nor in the prose version of 1530, where he is called Lyoncel. – *RP* 281,7

Dodineas, Dodineaz see Dodines

Dodines a knight of the Round Table; he is usually called 'der wilde', although none of the extant romances provide any justification for this epithet. His adventures consist solely of being unhorsed by other knights, usually the hero of the romance in which he occurs. D. is probably identical with Sodines and is first mentioned in Chrestien's *Erec* [1700]. – *L* 7098; *E* 1637; *I* 87; *Wigl* 458; *P* nm271,13; *C* 2296; *JT* 2344,1; *TF* 2205f.; *Sey* 56,7; *GM* 1242; *RP* 526,4

Dodinias see Dodines

Dodontôn 'vürste von Mêdâ', a warrior in Dârîus's army; he is killed by Ptolômêus (2) during the battle at Issôn. D. does not occur in any of the sources to *UA*. – *UA* 7932f.

Does see Do

Doglas see Duglas

Dolamîdes a warrior in the Greek army against the Trojans. This character was invented by Konrad. – *TK* 25766f.

Dolyfân 'von Crêchinlant', son of Anthart; he fights in the Greek army against Dêmantîn, who unhorses him. – *Dem* 5152

Dolodageles natural son of Priam; he fights in the Trojan army against the Greeks. D. appears to have been invented by Benoît, who calls him Goluz d'Agluz. – *LT* a4808 n4833

Dolon a scout in the Trojan army against the Greeks. In *LT*, which follows Benoît and Dares, he meets Ulixes and Dyomedes, as they are coming to the Trojan camp at night. In Dictys, as also in Homer, the account is slightly different, as he is sent out exploring by Hector and meets Ulixes and Dyomedes, who kill him. D. is one of the traitors who betray Troy in *TKf*. – *LT* 8008ff.; *TKf* 46832

Dolostalus, Dolostolus, Dolotalus see Doroschalcus

Dolunt see Delon

Donion the engineer who built the fortress of Ilion for Priam. This name, which appears only in *LT*, has been explained by Bartsch as a misunderstanding by Herbort of Benoît's 'li mestre donjons', which Herbort translated as 'maister Donjon'.[4] – *LT* 1796

Donosdaron see Dinodaron

Dôpant 'von Assie', a knight who is killed whilst fighting in Eghart's army against Dêmantîn. – *Dem* nm5402

Dorastes 'von Cariâ', a warrior in the Trojan army who is slain by the Greeks. In Dictys, where he is slain by Ajax (1), he is called Nastes, a name which appears as Nesteus in Benoît. – *TKf* 44050

Dorilaus a knight who fights for Bilas against Athis. D. occurs also in the OF version. – *AP* C,7

Dorilum son of Actorides (q.v.), a warrior in Alexander's army who is killed by Negûsar during the battle at Issôn. – *UA* 8236

---

4   Bartsch (1), p. 183.

Dorion (1)   a warrior in the Greek army against the Trojans; he is slain by Hector in *TK*. In *LT*, where he is called Dormus on his first appearance, but later (5303) Doriun, his fate is not given. D. appears to have been invented by Benoît, who calls him Dorius (var. Dorion) and in whose account he is likewise slain by Hector. – *LT* 4878; *TK* 30611ff.

Dorion (2)   see Darion

*Doriun   see Dorion (1)

Dormus   see Dorion (1)

Doroschalcus   a natural son of Priam; he is slain by Achilles whilst fighting for the Trojans against the Greeks. In *LT* he is also called Roscalcus, on the occasion of his first appearance only, whilst in *TK* he appears as Dolostalus, Dolostolus and Dolotalus. In Benoît he is named Doroscalcus, which, according to Greif, is probably derived from the Doryclus of Hyginus.[5] D.'s mother is stated in *LT* to be Mahtines. – *LT* a4768 n4785; *TK* 30378

Dos, Dou   see Do

Doun   'von Aglen', a knight who is a member of the party which accompanies Arthur to the rescue of Gifles. In Pseudo-Gautier he is called Doon de Glai, Doon being a form of Do, the name of Gifles' father, but there is no justification for identifying the two characters. – *RP* 179,18

Drances   a knight in the service of Lâtin, to whom he recommends that Ênêâs and Turnus be allowed to fight in single combat for Lavînia. D. is alluded to in *P*, where he is called Tranzes. – *Ed* 8528; *P* nm419,13 [†]

Drasbarun   a scout in Marroch's army; he is overcome by Gawein. – *Wigm* a2880ff. n2894

Drasbraun   see Drasbarun

Driapisbiâ   brother of Eritâ; he is slain whilst fighting for the Trojans against the Greeks. In Dictys this is the name of two men, Dryops and Bias, both of whom are killed, as is D., by Idomeneus. MS G of Dictys has the two names written as one, viz. Dryaspisbia. – *TKf* [43182]

Driopaz   'von Felundagas', a knight in Marroch's army against Arthur. – *Wigm* 3213

Dropides   'vürste', a warrior in Dârîus's army; he is captured by Alexander. So also in *Expeditio Alexandri* and Curtius Rufus. – *A* 7631

Drusliep   'von Heimenburc', a knight who welcomes Ulrich von Liechtenstein to Neustadt during his *Artusfahrt*. – *FD* 1484,1f.

Duglas   natural son of Priam; he fights in the Trojan army against the Greeks. He occurs in *TK*, as Doglas, but no mention is made of his relationship to Priam. Benoît, who appears to have invented this character, calls him Doglas also. – *LT* a4808 n4835; *TK* 30000ff.

Ducastor   see Astor (2)

Dulcâmûr   wife of Medeamanz; she is with Carafilîe when the latter is captured by Alexander. This character appears to have been invented by Ulrich. – *UA* nm4016ff. a8777ff.

Dulzamîs   a knight who is overcome by Phorîân. – *Dem* 1725

Dulzasîn   'von Massidôn', a young commander in Bêâmunt's army against Melîân and Eghart at Antriûn. – *Dem* nm7871ff. a10954

Dulcemâr   'künec von Tandarnas', father of Tandareis, husband of Antikonîe, and uncle of Ginovêr. – *TF* m199 n225 a1500

Dulceflor   see Dulceflûr (1)

---

5   Greif, pp. 26ff.

Dulcefluor daughter of Atroclas; she marries Wigamur and becomes queen of Deleferant. She is later abducted by Lympondrigon, and is rescued by Wigamur and her father. – *Wigm* m3898 n3913 a4449

Dulceflûr (1) daughter of Gediens; she is being oppressed by Verangôz, who has killed her father. She sends to Arthur's court for help, but the messenger meets Meleranz on the way, and the latter returns with the messenger to D. He defeats and kills Verangôz, and she eventually marries Libers (1). D. is a relative of Tydomîe, who marries Meleranz. – *M* m4845 n4879 a7399ff.

Dulceflur (2) see Dulcefluor

Dulcicors *amie* of Segremors. – *UW* nm256,4

Dulciweygar son of Dulcefluor and Wigamur. This name, as Hertz has pointed out,[6] is simply composed of the first half of each of the names of D.'s parents, Wigamur being spelt Weygamur in *Wigm*. – *Wigm* 6096f.

Durans 'von Toris', a knight who unhorsed many other knights in the field outside Arthur's court. This is the only time that this name is mentioned, and the passage in *JT* reads as though D. were accompanying Schîonatulander in his search for the hound,[7] but there is no previous hint that Schîonatulander has companions. – *JT* 1324,5

Duritus uncle of Dârîus; he was placed over Persia by Alexander after the death of Dârîus. D. occurs as Duriti in Leo. – *A* 15253; *SA* 4008ff.; *WA* 2974ff.

Duricius, Düricius see Duritus

Durkiôn a giant, brother of Margôn (1) and Uliân; he is killed by Tandareis, whilst guarding the way to his master, Karedôz. – *TF* m5302 n5434 a5722f.

Duscanie 'herzoge von' (*JT*), see Kârub

Duzabel (1) daughter of Amurât and Klârîne; she is captured by Fidegart, who holds her prisoner until she is released by Gârel. D. marries Klârîs (1). – *G* 5880ff.

Duzabel (2) daughter of Amelot; she withdraws the splinter from the wound of Willehalm (4). She falls in love with him, but when it transpires that he is her cousin, she has to give up all hope of him and eventually marries Witechin. – *RW* nm10052f. a10118ff.

Dûzanga mother of Benalas. – *UW* nm94,17

Dûzet niece of Mîle; she marries Mamurtanit. – *UW* nm294,8 a302,21f.

Duzisamor a maiden who is the prize in a tourney. She is won by Seyfrid, who gives her to Arbosorans. – *Sey* m365,5f. n368,4 a377,4

---

6 Gottfried von Straßburg, *Tristan und Isolde*, transl. by Hertz, p. 532.

7 *Der Jüngere Titurel*, 1324,5ff: 'Durans von toris und trakvnt von yspanie / Vnd der von graswaldane mit tiost hie valten manige vf die planie.'

E

Êbê (Hebe) in Greek mythology she was the goddess of youth and cup-bearer to the gods before Ganymede. – *UA* nm4861

Eberhart 'herzoge von Swâben', a knight who kills Hachaberc whilst fighting for the Christians against the heathens. – *Loh* 4134ff.

Ebolantz see Edolanz

Ebrân a knight who welcomes Ulrich von Liechtenstein to Neustadt during his *Artusfahrt.* – *FD* 1481,5

Ebrol 'grâve von Morie', a knight who is present at Arthur's tourney. – *JT* 2017,1

Ebruîn 'herzoge', a knight who is slain whilst fighting for the Trojans against the Greeks. This character was invented by Konrad. – *TK* 36316

Ebusar son of Ackusirie and father of Secureis, with whom he is buried in the same tomb. – *JT* 4827,5f.

Edbart 'grâve', a knight in the service of Dêmantîn. – *Dem* 5323ff.

Edelantz see Edolanz

Edîmus a warrior in Dârîus's army and a relative of Cyrus; he is killed by Nicânor (1) during the battle at Issôn. E. does not occur in any of the other histories of Alexander and appears to have been invented by Ulrich. – *UA* 8181f.

Edippus see Oedippus

Edissôn 'von Lanzesardîn', a knight who is included in the list of those whom Feirefîz states he has overcome. In *JT*, where he is called 'von Ladurbodine', E. is one of the suitors of Sekundille and takes part in the tourney for her hand. Martin has pointed out the similarity of this name to the Essedones, an Asiatic tribe mentioned in Solinus (84,15ff).[1] – *P* nm770,22; *JT* 5281,1

Editons Gawein recalls how he defeated E., after the latter had led Segremors astray and then left him after he had been captured by a monstrous woman. In MS V, E. is called Edysson, but there is no justification for identifying him with Edissôn. – *C* nm9041ff.

Ediffrisol 'künec von' (*JT*), see Ediffrison

Ediffrison 'von Lacridare', also called 'der ûz Larchidare', and 'künec von Ediffrisol', a warrior in Ipomidôn's army against Akarîn. – *JT* 3231,2f.

Edolans, Edolantz see Edolanz

Edolanz a knight, he is the hero of an epic which has come down to us only in two fragments. At the beginning of Fragment A, E. is fighting a giant to save a queen, and Gawein is a spectator. E. wins, and he and Gawein go off together to look for adventure, but, meeting with none, they decide to part company. E. meets a dwarf, who tells him of a terrible knight in the neighbourhood who lets no knight return alive. In Fragment B, E. is fighting for a town against the heathens who are invading it, and largely through his efforts the invaders are beaten off. Finally, in another, not consecutive, part of the same fragment, E. defeats the 'pontschurn' (for whom he was fighting in the above town) in single combat before Arthur and his knights, and the sparrow-hawk is given to Grysalet. E. occurs also in *JT*, where he takes part in a tourney held by Arthur and later fights against Orilus for Schîonatulander. He is also one of the knights at Arthur's court in *GM*. – *Edol* aA,1 nA,27; *JT* 2077,3; *GM* (MS D) 38579

Êdron see Esdras (1)

---

1   Martin (1), p. 504, to 770,22.

Eeneas see Ênêâs (1)

Egelolf referred to by the author of *JT* as being a more fitting butt for his critics than he himself. It seems possible that this is the same as Egenolt (for Egenolf), the author of *PS*, whose name is probably recorded as Egelolf already in AD 1273.[2] – nm *JT* 3545,3; *PS* 1174

Egenoê see Oenône

Egenolt see Egelolf

Eghart 'künec von Antioch', from whom Sirgamôte is stolen by Dêmantîn. He and the father of Sirgamôte come with an army to Antrîûn to recover her. E. is captured by Dêmantîn and has to resign his claim on Sirgamôte. – *Dem* m2956 a3999 n4935

Egyal wife of Dyomedes (q.v.). The story is told in Benoît, and in Dictys, where she is called Aegiale. – *LT* 17201

Egistus lover of Clitemnestre and murderer of Agâmennon (q.v.). He is slain by Orestes. – *LT* 17255f.; *TKf* nm49546f. a49618f.

Egkart see Eghart

Egri see Engrî

Ehkunaht see Ehkunat

Ehkunat (Singer derives this name from the OF Esquinart or Eschinet, a common name for Saracens.[3]) E. is brother to Mahaute, and we learn from *P* that he killed Kingrisîn. In *T*, where he is also called Ehkunat de Salvâsche Flôrîen (151,1) and Ehkunaver von Bluomederwilde (152,4), he wins the hand of Klauditte (2), who sends him the hound which is to prove the death of Schîonatulander. (For the epithets given to him in *T*, cf. Eskilabôn.) In *G* he is called Ekunaver von Kanadic, the territorial name of Klauditte, and he declares war on Arthur because Utepandragûn had killed his father (l. 307, not named). Gârel anticipates the battle with an army of his own and personally captures E., who is led to Arthur and afterwards reconciled with him. In *Wigm* two brothers of Kanedic (not named) are present at the tourney held by Dymszogar, whilst in *JT*, E. is present at Schîonatulander's *swertleite*. Martin does not think that the character who kills Kingrisîn is identical with the *ami* of Klauditte.[4] [See Appendix (10).]– *P* nm178,18f. a503,16; *T* nm42,1; *Wigm* 4746; *G* m299 an477ff.; *JT* nm671,1f. a1098,1f.; *RB* nm20164 [†]

Ehkunaver see Ehkunat

Ehmereiz 'künec von Arabi und Todjerne', son of Tîbalt and Gîburc; he fights for Terramêr against Willehalm (1) in both the battles at Alischanz. At the end of the first battle he is one of the group of 15 Saracen kings who attack Willehalm, but Willehalm refuses to engage him in combat because he is Gîburc's son (74,26ff.). [See Appendix (9).] E. appears only in certain MSS of *UW*, but in *R* he is present at Terramêr's court and is friendly to Malfer, although his father is still at enmity with him. The form of the name in *FS* is the same as that in *UW*, viz. Emereys, whilst in *R* he is called Heimereis (var. Hemereis). E. occurs in the OF *Aliscans* as Esmeré d'Odierne. – *W* 28,25; *R* Eing. II,30; *UW* (MSS B and D) 42,3; *FS* nm1427 [†]

Eydeys see Eydes

Eydes 'von dem Synbein (= *sinweln*, 'round') Berg', a maiden whose inheritance is stolen by her *muome*, Affrosydones, who has procured a champion, Dyartorforgrannt. Wigamur fights for E., defeating Dyartorforgrannt and restoring E.'s inheritance to her, but he

---

2 *Verfasserlexikon*, I, col. 507f.
3 Singer (1), p. 111.
4 Martin (1), p. 174, to 178,19.

. refuses her proffered hand on the grounds that he is ignorant of his own parentage. – *Wigm* a1526 n1564

Eigunt a maiden attendant on Gîburc; she flees with Willehalm and Gîburc when they escape from Tîbalt. – *UW* 132,17

Eilhart 'von Hôbergin', author of *ET.* – *ET* nm9466

Eist 'der von' (Dietmâr von Aist), MHG poet. – *C* nm2438f.

Eckatell (Hecate) in Greek mythology, the goddess of magic; she was conjured up by Medea to assist in the rejuvenation of Êson. – *TK* nm10528

Ekke see Êrec

Eckehart (1) 'von Dobringen', a knight whose name Ulrich gives as a guarantor that he has obtained the matter of his history of Alexander from the bishop of Salzburg. – *UA* nm27620

Eckehart (2) 'von Tanne', a knight who is present at the tourney held at Friesach. – *FD* 196,3

Ekkehart (3) 'Posche', a knight who welcomes Ulrich von Liechtenstein to Neustadt during his *Artusfahrt.* – *FD* 1483,1

Ekken the hero of a poem, *Der Wallære*, by Heinrîch von Lînouwe. – *RW* nm2227

Ector (1) see Hector (1) and (2)

Ektor (2) 'von Salenîe', a warrior who is slain whilst fighting for Terramêr against Willehalm (1) in the second battle at Alischanz. E. occurs as Ector de Salorie in *Aliscans* and is one of the protagonists in the 14th-century French poem, *Baudouin de Sebourc.* – *W* 353,1

Ecuba (1) mother of Ekubâ (2) and Frigureis. Her name was obviously an invention of Albreht, based on that of her daughter, who is named in *P*. According to *JT*, the name means 'heidenisch tvgende'. – *JT* nm3152,2

Ekubâ (2) 'küneginne von Janfûse', also called 'die heidenîn von Janfûse', a relative of Feirefiz (his 'muoter muomen tohter'); she is present at the ill-fated banquet in *P*, which is interrupted firstly by Kundrîe (1) and then by Kingrimursel. The fact that they have the same territorial name has caused the author of *JT* to make her the sister of Frigureis (see Fristines), and he has given them a mother, Ecuba (1). E. does not occur in Chrestien's *Perceval*, and Golther is of the opinion that she was invented by Wolfram to provide a little more detail for the character of Feirefiz.[5] Martin suggests that the source of the name might have been Solinus (71,6), where 'Hecubae sepulcrum' occurs,[6] whilst Singer contents himself with a denial that the name was taken from *Ed*.[7] – *P* a314,16 n336,1; *JT* nm3152,3ff.

Ecubâ (3) wife of Priam; she dreams (in *TK* and *GT*), shortly before the birth of Paris, that she is delivered of a firebrand, and when she learns the meaning of the dream, and Paris is born, she sends him away to be killed. E. is responsible for the death of Achilles by causing him to be lured into a temple and there slain, and when Troy falls, the Greeks, in *LT* and *GT*, as also in Benoît, take their revenge and kill her. In *TKf*, which follows Dictys, she is given to Ulixes as his share in the spoils of war. – *Ed* nm794; *LT* 1689; *TK* 336ff.; *GT* 1

Ekubert a warrior in the Greek army against the Trojans, he is wounded by Antenor. This character was invented by Konrad. – *TK* 33394ff.

Ekunar, Ekunât, Ekunaver see Ehkunat

Elâ biblical (Elah), king of Israel. – *A* nm16358

---

5   Golther (1), p. 143.
6   Martin (1), p. 279, to 336,1.
7   Singer (1), p. 61.

Elæte a maiden attendant on Gauriel's *amie*. This character is obviously based on Lûnete, whom she resembles, however, only in a limited degree. – *GM* 2838

Êlamîe 'küneginne von Tŷrô'; a horse, which was presented to E. by the king of Ireland, is forcibly taken from her by Hojir. The latter is slain by Wigalois, who recovers the horse. E. brings an army to fight for Wigalois against Lîôn. – *Wigl* a2356 n9126

Êlân a warrior in Dârîus's army; he is killed by Parmênîôn whilst fighting against Alexander at Issôn. – *UA* 8145

Elander see Eleander

Elar 'von Alakose', a warrior in Akarîn's army against Ipomidôn. – *JT* nm3095,1

Elbart 'von Berbester', a knight who is present at a tourney held by Arthur. – *JT* 2029,6

Eleander 'von Gabaache', a knight who arrives at the shores of Troy in a boat, asleep, and with his head resting in the lap of his wife, Amalita. He censures Agâmennon for his judgment against Ajax (1) in favour of Ulixes and slays 1500 of Agâmennon's men who attack him. E. then travels after Ulixes, whom he slays together with his wife, Penelope. He returns to his own land to find it devastated, and Amalita abducted by Hannor. He goes in search of her, overcoming and killing in the course of his quest Abolan and Galantte's *ami*, Magonogrin. After he has also slain Livian, he arrives at Hannor's castle and slays him and his retinue, whilst they are out hunting. He dresses in Hannor's armour and thus gains entry to the castle, where he is attacked by Rubel, whom he defeats. A further fight, with Gaball, takes place before E., with the friendly help of Passirius, finally arrives safely back at Gabaache. – *GT* 19803ff.

Eleyse see Lîâze

Elemant see Elymant

Elemîn nephew of Tarcôn; he is slain whilst fighting for Ênêâs against Kamille (1). This character does not occur in the OF *Eneas* and appears to have been invented by Heinrich. – *Ed* 9012ff.

Elena the wife of Menelaus; her abduction was the cause of the war between the Greeks and the Trojans. In most versions of the Trojan legend, as in *LT*, E.'s rôle is purely passive, but in *TKf* a grim incident is added from the account in Dictys, which does not accord with her character elsewhere. When Ênêâs and Antenor are conspiring to betray Troy to the Greeks, E. persuades them to try to placate Menelaus, and she murders her three sons by Paris – Sunom, Caratît, and Idoneus – as an earnest of her repentance. As usual, the story in *GT* differs widely from all other versions. Paris is at her father's court before she is married to Menelaus, and she gradually falls in love with him but permits herself to be betrothed by her father, Agâmennon, to Menelaus during the absence of Paris. She is abducted by Paris on his return, and after the fall of Troy, she returns home with Agâmennon, who will not permit any suitors. Bevar, who tries to obtain her by force, is killed in the resultant battle, but she is eventually abducted by Segromans, to whom she finally becomes a dutiful wife. In *Tn*, E. is referred to by her cognomen, Tintarides, derived from the name of her stepfather, Tyndareus (cf. Tindarîus). – *Ed* nm30; *Tn* m8271; *LT* m2209 n2402 a2466; *C* nm526; *FB* nm1684; *Port* nm21; *M* nm589; *TK* nm313f. a19635ff.; *RB* nm9236; *GT* nm2143ff. a2963; *GM* nm3563; *WO* nm3603 [†]

Elene 'küneginne von Athene', *amie* of Alyant, a knight who fights for Agrant and is slain by Wildhalm. – *WO* nm7791

Êlenor a Trojan, relative of Lîcus (q.v.); he is slain by Turnus. So also in the OF *Eneas*, and in Virgil, where he is called Helenor. – *Ed* 6964ff.

Elenus son of Priam; he is wise and has the power of foreseeing events. In all versions of the Trojan legend, he foretells the disastrous consequences of Paris's abduction of Helen and

76

speaks strongly against the journey. In *TKf* he takes an active part in the betrayal of Troy, whose doom he realises is sealed. E. occurs, usually as Helenus, in all versions of the legend. – *LT* nm1664ff. a2231; *MC* nm21; *TK* 1093ff.

Ely biblical, the high priest at the time of Samuel. – nm *UA* 11514; *RB* 13100

Elyadus a knight, son of Elydus; he entertains Parzivâl and 'der schön Unerkante' (see Wigalois). So also in Gautier's continuation of *Perceval*, where he is called Eliadeus. – *RP* a369,18 n370,6

Elîachâ mother of Meie; she is at first friendly to Bêaflôr, but she is opposed to Meie's marriage to her. She substitutes false letters for the news of the birth of Schoiflôrîs, and for Meie's reply, which she replaces by a command to kill Bêaflôr and the child. Her treachery is discovered when Meie returns, and he kills her with his sword. – *MB* m57,27ff. a58,7 n69,9

Elîachim 'künec von Kartâge', nephew of Laomedon, for whom he fights in the first battle between the Trojans and the Greeks. He is slain (in *TK* by Pollux). In *LT* he is called Eliacus, both forms originating in Benoît's Eliachim. – *LT* 1490; *TK* 12074f.

Eliacus see Elîachim

Elian see Clîan

Eliander see Eleander

Elîas biblical (Elijah). In *UA*, E. is said to be the old man who gives Alexander the miraculous stone at the gates of Paradise. He is represented as sitting with Ênoch guarding the gates of Heaven, an idea which was quite common in the Middle Ages,[8] but which was introduced only by Ulrich into the Alexander legend. The old man appears in the *Iter ad Paradisum*, from which this incident originated, but he is not named here or in Lampreht, who also includes the episode in his *Alexanderlied*. – *W* nm218,18; *A* nm16374; *JT* nm4692,1; *UA* nm11695 a24502; *RB* nm13055

Elyasip high priest in Jerusalem, and father of Judas (3). This name appears to have been invented by Ulrich. – *UA* nm17741

Elyafres a knight at Arthur's court. E. is in love with Iseve, and on the first few nights after her marriage to Karode, he substitutes enchanted animals for Iseve and lies with her himself. They have a son, Karadot, who eventually becomes a knight at Arthur's court, but who thinks that his father is Karode. One day, E., who is a magician, arrives at Arthur's court and announces that he will permit his head to be struck off, if the knight who does so will agree to suffer the same thing after a year (cf. Gansguoter). Karadot is the only knight brave enough to accept the challenge, but E. merely puts the severed head back on and rides away. He returns after a year, but instead of claiming his penalty, he tells Karadot the secret of his parentage, and the latter is so horrified that he tells Karode, who shuts Iseve in a tower, where she is visited by E. E. takes his revenge on Karadot by fastening a serpent to his arm. In the Mons MS of Pseudo-Gautier, E. is called Gahariés, but he appears as Eliaures in the prose edition of 1530. – *RP* 46,7

Eliden a knight who is unhorsed by Dêmantîn, when they meet in a wood just before the latter finds Sirgamôte. – *Dem* a3164f. n4039

Elidîâ a maiden who has been transformed by an enchantment into a serpent. Lanzelet, who hears of her, seeks her and frees her from the enchantment by kissing her on the mouth.

---

8 E. appears as guarding the gate of Paradise alone against the Antichrist in *Muspilli* (37ff.), and together with Ênoch in the MHG poem *Von Sente Brandan* (in *Sanct Brandan*, ed. by C. Schröder), 530ff.: 'der der pforten warte:/ daz was der herr Enouch./ uns saget daz bûch ouch/ daz under dem burgetore/ saz der herre Helîas'. E.'s name also occurs in conjunction with that of Ênoch in the above references in *W* and *JT*.

This is, of course, the well-known folk-lore motif of the *fier baiser*, and gives a further proof, if one be necessary, of the chaotic conglomeration of independent episodes of which *L* is composed, since in the original version the hero would certainly marry the maiden whom he has thus freed from enchantment, an outcome which is neglected in *L*, even though Lanzelet does not object to a plurality of marriages. – *L* m7846 n7990 a7888 (as serpent) a7938 (as maiden)

Elydus father of Elyadus. In Gautier's continuation of *Perceval*, he is called Elideus. – *RP* nm370,6

Eyle also called Ylie, daughter of Bernant, wife of Willehalm (3), and mother of Willehalm (4). She dies with grief when she hears of the death of her husband. – *RW* 189ff.

Elîes 'von Landuz', one of the knights at Arthur's court who spill Priure's cup of chastity. This name is derived from Chrestien's *Erec* (1705), where he is called Esliz (var. Elis), and from the same source comes Êsus, a knight who is present at Arthur's court when Êrec returns with Ênîte in *E*. E. occurs also as Eslis in Gerbert's continuation of *Perceval* (3960), and in the *Torec* episode in the Dutch *Roman van Lancelot* as Eslijs, one of a list of knights present at a tourney (I, 26487ff.). (Cf. also Elis (1).) – *E* 1639; *C* 2298

Elichar brother of Efianes, a warrior in the Trojan army against the Greeks. This character was invented by Konrad. – *TK* 36314

Êlim a warrior in Alexander's army; he is killed by Negûsar whilst fighting against Dârîus at Issôn. This character appears to have been invented by Ulrich. – *UA* 8231

Elymant 'künec von Portegâl', a knight who takes part, with varying fortunes, at the tournaments held at Komarzi, Poys, and Kurnoy. – *RW* nm6180f. a6547ff.

Elimâr (1) 'herzoge von Argentîn', husband of Klârîne (3) and father of Klârîs; he is slain by Purdân when the latter captures Klârîs (1). – *G* m5872ff. n6184f.

Elimâr (2) standard-bearer to Gârel (1); he is slain whilst fighting for the latter against Ehkunat. His slayer is Rubert (1). – *G* 14799ff.

Elimas a knight who attends the tourney held by Leigamar. – *C* 18126f.

Elimor 'von Niffenlant', a knight who is present at a tourney held by Arthur. – *JT* 1975,6

Elyna see Elena

Elinôt (1) a knight who snatches up and carries the banner of Anferre (Gârel's land), which had fallen when Elimâr (2) was slain. It is quite clear that this is not the same character as Elinôt (2), Arthur's son (see Lohût). – *G* 15858

Elinôt (2) see Lohût

Elyos (1) 'von Archiente', a warrior in Ipomidôn's army against Akarîn. E. is also called Eliosim von Archiundie. – *JT* 3216,1

Elyoss (2) 'von Tennabry', nephew of Agâmennon; he slays Pirrus, because the latter strangled Pollixena. – *GT* 23175

Elis (1) 'der Calescen sun', a knight who is present at the tourney held by Arthur before Orgelus. In the Mons MS of Gautier, E. is called Elis li fius à le Galette. (Identical with Elîes?) – *RP* 472,43

Elis (2) 'von Climon', a knight who is present at Arthur's court and who spills Priure's cup of chastity. This name rests on a misunderstanding of Chrestien's *Erec* (1938): 'Qui cuens estoit de Clivelon'. (See Margue Gormon.) – *C* 2330

Elise wife of Jofrit (1) and foster-mother of Willehalm (4); she dies one year after Willehalm's marriage. – *RW* 2593

Êlisêus biblical (Elisha). – nm *A* 16394; *UA* 11696

Eliphat 'von Egyptô', a warrior in Dârîus's army who is killed by Alexander at Erbelâ. The name occurs in Gualterus as Eliphas. – *UA* 11989

Elizabant 'von der wilden monte', a warrior in Akarîn's army against Ipomidôn. – *JT* nm3134,3ff.

Elyzabel daughter of Bonifant (2) and wife of Titurisone. Her name was probably invented by the author of *JT* to provide his etymology for the name of her son, Titurel (q.v.). – *JT* 124,3

Elizabet (1) see Elizabeth

Elyzabet (2) see Elsam

Elizabeth biblical, mother of John the Baptist. – nm *JT* 2505,4; *WW* 2958; *RB* 13046

Elyze (1) daughter of Parzivâl; she tends the Graal and reads its message concerning Elsam to her brother, Lohengrîn. In *Ll* she is called Isilia. (Cf. Arbidale.) – *Loh* nm457 a477; *Ll* nm23,7f.; *Ll* (MS K) nm15,7 a19,7

Elicê (2) 'diu schöne von', a lady present at Arthur's court who spills Priure's cup of chastity. – *C* 1618

Elchanâ biblical (Elkanah), father of Samuel. – *RB* nm13092f.

Ellander see Eleander

Ellânîcas a commander in Alexander's army. So also in *Expeditio Alexandri* and Curtius Rufus, where he is called Hellanicus. – *A* 13418

Elleiander see Eleander

Elsam 'von Brabant', a maiden whose father dies, leaving her in the care of Friderîch (2), who tries to compel her to marry him against her will. She finds a hawk with a golden bell, the sound of which resounds in Arthur's court and causes them to send a champion, Lohengrîn, to her. After Lohengrîn has defeated Friderîch, he marries E., and they live happily until she insists on knowing his parentage, when the union is broken up. In *Loh* the name occurs also as Elsâny. In *Ll* she is called Isilie, and in *Ll* (MS K), Else Pravades. – *P* m824,2; *JT* a5918,7; *Loh* 301; *Ll* nm3,5 a4,7; *Ll* (MS K) a1,10 n9,1 [†]

Elsâny, Else see Elsam

Emânuel biblical, name by which Isaiah refers to Christ. – *UA* nm11752

Emargalûn a warrior in the Greek army; he is slain by Priam whilst fighting for the Greeks against the Trojans. This character was invented by Konrad. – *TK* 34284f.

Emblîe daughter of Emil and *amie* of Lohenîs (1) (q.v.). – *C* a19351ff. n19554

Embrons 'künec von Alimec', one of the group of 15 Saracen kings who attack Willehalm (1) at the end of the first battle at Alischanz. E. is wounded or killed by Willehalm in that encounter. [See Appendix (9).] E. occurs elsewhere only in the OF *Aliscans*, where he is called Ebrons (var. Embrons). – *W* m71,22 a72,17f. n74,24 [†]

Emelius 'grâve von Tygerlant' (in *TK*), a warrior in the Greek army against the Trojans. In *LT* he is called Emilius, whilst in *TKf* his name is spelt Eumelus and Eumelius. E. occurs in Benoît as Emelius, in Dares and Dictys as Eumelus, and in Homer as Eumelos. It is thus obvious that Herbort and Konrad took the name from Benoît, whilst the author of *TKf* used Dictys (or Dares) direct. – *LT* 5617; *TK* 23846f.

Emelcus a warrior in the Trojan army against the Greeks. This character appears to have been invented by Herbort, as it does not appear in any of the known sources to *LT*. – *LT* 5795

Êmenidis 'künec'; his son (not named?[9]) attends a tourney held by Arthur. – *C* nm600

Emereys see Ehmereiz

---

9 It is not possible to tell from the passage in *C*, which reads (599ff.): 'Von dem grüenen wert Flôis, / Fil li rois Êmenidis, / Von Alverne grâve Blant', whether E.'s son is Flôis or Blant, or neither. (On the probability of this passage's being a translation from French, see Noirs.)

Emerit a knight who attends the tourney held by Leigamar in the service of Aram. – *C* 18164

Emidalûs a sentinel in the service of the Soldan, he is slain by Partonopier. – *PM* 20998ff.

Emil 'künec', father of Emblîe. – *C* nm19562

Emilius (1) natural son of Priam; he is slain by Antilocus whilst fighting for the Trojans against the Greeks. E. does not occur in any of the sources to *LT*, and the name was evidently invented by Herbort, who admits (4813ff.) that there are three sons whose names he does not know. – *LT* m4808 an12950

Emilius (2) see Emelius

Emimor 'künec', overlord of Zacheria, marries Meierra. – *GT* m22280f. n22297 a22389

Eminêus a god who is present at the marriage of Thetis and Pêleus. – *TK* 994

Eminor, Eminoss see Emimor

Emolus see Eumîliô

Emosz a warrior in the Greek army against the Trojans. He tries to dissuade Achilles from challenging Hector to single combat. – *GT* 18916ff.

Emulôn a warrior in Dârîus's army; he is slain by Alexander during the battle at Erbela. This character appears to have been invented by Ulrich. – *UA* 13941

Emulus see Eumîliô

Enachus a warrior in Porrus's army. He is slain by Alexander. This name rests on a misunderstanding of Gualterus, where it is a part of one name, Enachides Hiulcon (see Julkôn). – *UA* 19654

Enalde *amie* of Zirell (q.v.). – *GT* 8191

Endekrist see Anticrist

Endelit 'von Lundis', a knight who attends a tourney held by Arthur. – *C* 612

Ênêâs (1) he accompanies Paris, when the latter goes to Greece to fetch Helen, and then fights for the Trojans in the war against the Greeks. He and some of the other princes, notably Antenor, suggest to Priam that they should restore Helen to the Greeks when the prospect of a Trojan victory seems hopeless, but Priam treats their suggestion with such scorn that they arrange to betray Troy to the Greeks to get their revenge. After the fall of Troy, E. is forbidden by the Greeks to remain in the city, because he tried to hide Pollixena, contrary to his pact with the Greeks, by which he was not to hinder them in any way. This version of the story is substantially the same in Benoît, Dictys, and Dares. In *GT* he is the brother of Nestor and lies hidden in Creta after he has betrayed Troy. Romulus sends his servant Remus to him here, and together they attack Menon, who completely routs them. They flee to Italy and found Rome. A more accurate version of the history of E. after the fall of Troy is to be found in *Ed*, which is a close translation of the OF *Eneas*, a poem which is based on Virgil's *Aeneid*. In *Ed* his mother is Venus (as in Homer) and he is therefore the brother of Cupid. After the destruction of Troy, he arrives with his army at Lîbie, where he is welcomed by Dîdô, who falls in love with him. The gods command him to continue his journey, and Dîdô kills herself when he leaves. E. descends into Hades with Sibille (1), and taking the right-hand path to the Elysian Fields, he finds his father, Anchises, who reveals to him the future glory of his descendants. Returning from Hades, E. goes with his army to Italy, where they acquaint the king, Lâtîn, of their arrival, and proceed to build themselves a fort. Lâtîn promises E. his daughter, Lavînia, and a kingdom, but Turnus, to whom Lâtîn had formerly promised her, collects an army and fights a great battle with E. E. procures help just in time from Evander and is able to arrange a peace. A further battle takes place outside Laurente, and in spite of the part played by Kamille (1) and her maiden warriors, E. is again successful. It is eventually arranged that the possession of Lavînia and of the kingdom shall be decided by single combat between Turnus and E. (who, by now, has seen and fallen in love with Lavînia). Just before the fight starts, however, one of Turnus's men attacks and kills one of the Trojans. In the ensuing battle, E., who fights without armour, is wounded and carried off the field. He is soon healed, however, and the single combat eventually takes place, in accordance with the customary rules of knighthood. Turnus is killed, and E. marries Lavînia, and they have a son, Silvius. – *Ed* nm37 a67; *E* nm 7553; *Wigl* nm2717; *P* nm399,12; *LT* 2365ff.; *MC* nm50; *C* nm531ff.; *A* nm17777; *JT* nm84,4; *M* nm592; *TK* 19428; *RB* nm3213; *GT* 13265; *FS* nm4830

Ênêâs (2) son of Silvjas Ênjas and a descendant of Ênêâs (1). – *Ed* nm3664f.

Enelyacas a king who, according to *LT*, was compelled by Achilles to conduct the Greeks to Troy. This name occurs only in a passage where the Greeks are recalling the deeds of Achilles. Already Frommann realised that this name originated in the name of the king Cilicas, who occurs in Dictys,[10] but as Benoît had not been discovered at the time he published *LT*, he was completely mystified to account for the corruption of the name and particulars which appears in the latter work. In Dictys, Cilicas is attacked by Achilles, but Benoît, taking Cilicas to be the name of a country, imagined that Achilles led his army to this land.[11] – *LT* nm16653f.

Engelbreht 'von Strâzburc', a knight who jousts with Ulrich von Liechtenstein during the latter's *Venusfahrt*. – *FD* 634,8f.

Engelhart 'ûz Burgundenrîche', one of ten brothers, he sets out for the court of King Fruot, meeting on the way his double, Dieterich, who accompanies him. They become very popular, and Fruot's daughter, Engeltrût, who falls in love with them both, eventually chooses E. because of the resemblance in their names. Dieterich has to return to Brabant on the death of his father, and Engeltrût promises E. her love when he has become renowned for his valour. Fruot makes him a knight, and he attends a tourney at Normandie, from which he returns covered with glory. He enjoys the favours promised him by Engeltrût, but the meeting of the two lovers is observed by Ritschier, who accuses him before Fruot. E. undertakes to prove his innocence in single combat, and, stealing away to Dieterich, takes his place, whilst his friend returns to fight the accuser. Since, as far as Dieterich is concerned, there has been no intercourse with Engeltrût, right is triumphant and Ritschier defeated (cf. the similar verbal quibble in the ordeal episode in *Tristan*). Dieterich, who is thought to be E., is then married to Engeltrût and lives with her, outwardly her husband, until he is able again to change places with E., who has meanwhile been living in chastity with Dieterich's wife. On the death of Fruot, E. becomes king, and he and Engeltrût have two children. One day, however, Dieterich is struck with leprosy and learns that his only cure is a bath in the blood of E.'s two children. Shunned by his own people, he goes to E. for sympathy and is well cared for, until one day E. learns the only cure for his friend. He sacrifices his children, and Dieterich, bathing in their blood, becomes well, whilst the children are, by a miracle, again restored to health. This story is a fairly close reproduction of the well-known OF legend of *Ami et Amilis*, which first appears in OF literature in an *Epistola* by a monk, Raoul de Tourtier, who was writing in Latin at

---

10 Herbort von Fritslâr, *Liet von Troye*, p. 329, to 16654.
11 Dictys (II, 17) reads: 'Achilles . . . Cilicas aggreditur', which Benoît translates (26857): 'En Cilicas (MS L: Celyas) conduist sa gent' (Achilles being the subject understood). Herbort, who read 'En Cilicas' as one word, thought that this name was the subject of 'conduist', and thus arrives at the following translation (16653ff.): 'Wir genvzzë es alle gemeine/ Daz enelyacas/ Vnser geleite her was/ Ez wer im liep oder leit.'

the end of the 11th century, and which forms the subject of a Latin poem, *Vita sanctorum Amici et Amelii carissimorum*, which appeared early in the 12th century.[12] Konrad has changed all the names, E. corresponding to Amilis, and Dieterich to Ami, whilst in the French versions, even the earliest, the king is Karl (1), i.e. Charlemagne, and his daughter, Belissant. The legend of a pair of devoted friends is, of course, familiar from classical literature and may be compared, in MHG literature, with the story of *AP* (see Athis). – *Eng* a228ff. n260

Engelram 'von Strâzpurc', a knight who jousts with Ulrich von Liechtenstein during his *Venusfahrt*. – *FD* 634,4f.

Engelschalc 'von Künegesbrunne', a knight who warns Ulrich von Liechtenstein of the anger of Hadmâr (1). He also takes part in the tourney at Kornneuburg. – *FD* 880,3ff.

Engelschalch see Engelschalc

Engeltrût daughter of Fruot and *amie* of Engelhart (q.v.). In the account by Raoul she is called Beliardis, in the OF *Amis et Amiles*, Belissans, and in the ME *Amis and Amiloun*, Belisaunt. – *Eng* a853f. n876

Engis a knight who is unhorsed by Absterne whilst fighting for Athis against Bilas. E. does not occur in the OF version. – *AP* C,96

Engrewein see Agravains

Engrî a knight who attends Leigamar's tourney in the company of Heimet. – *C* 18140

Enibreis 'von Trale', a warrior in Ipomidôn's army against Akarîn. – *JT* nm3241,6

Ênîte (According to Schulz, this name is derived by Ellis Jones from the Welsh *enid*, 'woodlark', and by Owen from the Welsh *enydd*, 'the seat of the intellect'.[13]) E. is the daughter of Coralus and Karsinefîte and becomes the wife of Êrec (q.v.). She occurs in several of the MHG romances but is throughout an entirely colourless figure, portrayed without a gleam of characterization. It is impossible to say what part E. played in the fragmentary *Mtl*, but it is interesting to notice that, although it does not fit perfectly, she achieves by far the best result with the mantle of chastity. She first appears in literature as the heroine in Chrestien's *Erec*. – *L* 6098; *E* a308ff. n431; *I* nm2791ff.; *Wigl* nm6308; *Mtl* 956; *P* nm143,29; *C* 1361; *FD* nm1169,6; *JT* 1610,1; *TF* nm10781f.; *GM* nm2895

Encalegon see Ucalegon

Ênoch biblical, he guards the gates of Paradise with Elîas (q.v.). – *W* nm218,18; *A* nm17563; *JT* nm4692,1; *UA* a24522f. n24559

Enôs 'von Elamîe', a warrior in Dârîus's army; he is killed by Philôtas during the battle at Erbela. So also in Gualterus. – *UA* 12029

Enschelades a giant. This is evidently an attempt to represent a name out of Greek mythology, apparently that of one of the Titans. – *RB* nm25284

Entekrist see Anticrist

Entreferich with Tenebroc (q.v.) and two other knights, the leader of the side opposed to Gawein in the tourney held to celebrate the marriage of Êrec. These two names rest on a misunderstanding of Chrestien's *Erec* (2131), where he gives 'Antre Evroïc et Tenebroc' (between York and Edinburgh (?)) as the venue for the tourney. – *E* 2231

Enfeidas 'eine götinne', sister of Utepandragûn, 'küneginne von Avalôn'. Gawein meets her, and she tells him of his forthcoming encounter with Angaras. (Cf. Accedille.) Whether this name was invented by Heinrich or whether it appeared in the OF source, it is not possible to say, but it would seem possible that either MHG *fei* or OF *feie*, 'fairy', is the basis on which the name was constructed. To the name of a fairy, the addition of the

---

12 Bédier, II, pp. 178ff.
13 Schulz, 'Eigennamen', p. 397.

territorial name von Avalôn (the Celtic Elysium) would be natural and might have been done by Heinrich in imitation of Hartmann (see Gwinganiers), or it might have occurred thus in the source of this episode in *C*. – *C* a18712 n18726

Enforbius see Euforbes

Enfrîe a knight who attends Leigamar's tourney in the service of Lorez. – *C* 18148

Eolis a king in whose land Ulixes meets Circe. So also in Benoît, and in Dictys and the Odyssey, where he is called Aeolus. – *LT* nm17622

Epistroples see Epistropus (1)

Epistropus (1) 'von Botina', a warrior in the Trojan army against the Greeks. E., who is called Epistroples in *TK*, occurs in Benoît as Epistrot (var. Epistropilis), in Dares and Dictys as Epistrophus, and Homer as Epistrophos. – *LT* 4030; *TK* 24992

Epistropus (2) 'von Focidis', twin brother of Cedius. In *LT*, as in Benoît, he is slain by Hector whilst fighting for the Greeks against the Trojans. *TK*, in which he is called Epistros von Defôte, follows Dictys, and there is no mention of his death, which, however, is recorded at the hands of Hector in Dares. E. is called Epistroz (var. Epistrophus) in Benoît, and Epistrophus in Dares and Dictys, whilst in Homer he occurs as Epistrophos. – *LT* 3324ff. *TK* 23798

Epistros see Epistropus (2)

Epius a Greek carpenter who made the wooden horse by which the Greeks were able to enter Troy. E. occurs in Benoît, Dictys, and Virgil. The horse is, of course, not mentioned in Homer, but a Greek warrior Epeios appears. – *LT* 15929; *TKf* 47782

Eppe 'grâve', a knight who is present at a tourney held by Arthur. – *JT* 2012,1

Epureis 'von Prisse', a warrior in Ipomidôn's army against Akarîn. – *JT* 3367,2

Equinot 'fil cont Haterel', a knight who is present at Arthur's court when Êrec returns with Ênîte. E. does not occur in the corresponding list in Chrestien's *Erec*. – *E* 1669

Erâklîus 'oder Erkules', a Greek emperor (AD 610–641). E. is the hero of an OF poem by Gautier d'Arras, *Eracle*,[14] which was translated into MHG by a certain Otto, who called his poem *Eraclius*. Wolfram also gives the alternative Latin form of the name. – *P* nm773,21f.

Eralapins see Translapîns

Erbol 'von Iurisolt' (or 'Ivrisolt'[15]), a warrior in Akarîn's army against Ipomidôn. – *JT* nm3638,1ff.

Eregg see Êrec

Êrec (According to Zimmer, this is a Normanic name,[16] but Bruce asserts that it is a form of the Celtic name Weroc.[17]) E. is the son of Lac and the hero of the earliest Arthurian romance which has come down to us, the poem by Chrestien which bears his name and which was translated into MHG by Hartmann.

E. is a young knight who is insulted by Îdêr and his dwarf, Maledicur, in the presence of Ginovêr. He follows Îdêr and is given shelter for the night by an impoverished nobleman, Coralus, whose daughter, Ênîte, is proclaimed by E. to be the most beautiful maiden present at a tourney for a sparrow-hawk on the following day. E.'s opponent is Îdêr, who is defeated and, with Maledicur, sent to Arthur's court. E. returns the next day with Ênîte, whom he weds. He distinguishes himself at the tourney held to celebrate his marriage, but afterwards, in the delights of married life at Karnant, he neglects the duties of knighthood,

---

14 Vogt, p.198.
15 In Hahn's edition of *JT*, E.'s territorial name is printed 'ivrisolt'.
16 Zimmer, p. 830.
17 Bruce (1), I, p. 109.

until the murmuring of his courtiers is accidentally brought to his notice by Ênîte. E. sets out to seek adventure, making his wife ride before him and forbidding her to speak a word unless addressed. By breaking this command, she enables him to be prepared for and to overcome numerous robber knights. He also meets with Guivreiz, whom he defeats only with the greatest difficulty. E. is cured of his wounds at Arthur's court but leaves again after a short rest. His wounds burst open again when he rescues Cadoc from two giants, and he is found by Oringles, who, believing him to be dead, tries to force Ênîte to marry him. Her cries awaken E., who rescues her, and, being at last convinced of the reality of her love for him, is reconciled with her. A further adventure, the defeat of Mabônagrîn and the restoration of eighty widowed ladies to society, has to be achieved, before E., on the death of Lac, finally returns with Ênîte to reign in Karnant.

E.'s adventures in the other MHG romances are all of the usual type for a knight of the Round Table. In *L* he is said to have slain Malduc's father (see Maldwiz) and is delivered up to Malduc as the latter's reward for his assistance in the recovery of Ginovêr. In *GM* he gives the newly married Gauriel advice against *verligen*, that over-indulgence in uxoriousness to the exclusion of knightly exercises which had been the cause of his own unhappiness. For the rest, he assists Arthur against his enemies in *TF*, *DB*, and *G*, whilst he is present at tourneys held by Arthur in *Wigm* and in *JT*, where he is called 'her ekke' and 'herek'. In *Wigl* he attends the hero's wedding and fights for him against Lîôn. Although E. was such a popular figure in MHG literature, he is hardly mentioned in the remainder of the OF romances and, apart from Chrestien's poem, is never a prominent figure. His name is not mentioned once in the whole of the Vulgate Cycle.

– *L* 2264; *E* 2; *I* nm2791f.; *Wigl* 9567ff.; *Mtl* 956; *P* nm134,6; *DB* 984; *C* 847f.; *RW* nm2177; *Wigm* 2198; *FD* nm1169,6; *G* nm4835 a17675f.; *JT* 1939,3; *TF* 1692; *GM* nm845 a1288; *FS* nm4817 [†]

Erech, Ereck see Êrec

Eresdes son of Cûsiresdes. E. is mentioned in Pseudo-Methodius, where he is called Elisdes.
– *A* nm17158

Erressulas see Erosse

Ergôn a knight in the Greek army which is besieging Dêmantîn at Antrîûn. – *Dem* 10742f.

Erigena daughter of Clitemnestre and Egistus and half-sister to Orestes. She hangs herself when Orestes slays her parents. So also in Dictys and Benoît, where she is called Erigona.
– *LT* 17507f.

Erîgûus a commander in Alexander's army; he leads the force against the faithless Sârtibarzânes, who offers to settle the conflict by single combat. E. slays him, and his army surrenders. So also in *Expeditio Alexandri* and Curtius Rufus, where he is called Erigyius.
– *A* 17599

Erictô (Erichtho) the hideous witch of Thessaly, described in the *Pharsalia* of Lucanus (VI, 508ff.). – *E* nm5217

Eritâ brother of Driapisbiâ; he is slain by Idomenêus whilst fighting for the Trojans against the Greeks. E. occurs in Dictys, where he is a son of Priam and is slain by Ulixes. –
TKf 43183

Erifân 'von Denemarke', a commander in Bêâmunt's army at Antrîûn. – *Dem* nm9850f. a10908

Ericius 'von Hemor', a knight who is sent by Bevar with a cortège of 12 maidens to woo Helen. He is refused and declares war on Agâmennon. – *GT* 23403ff.

Erchengêr 'von Landesêr', a knight who, under the name of Ywein, jousts with Ulrich von Liechtenstein during the latter's *Artusfahrt*. – *FD* 1437,1f.

Erkuleduntze 'von Orledarie', a warrior in Akarîn's army against Ipomidôn. – *JT* 3197,3ff.

Erkules (1) see Hercules

Erkules (2) see Erâklîus

Ermagoras natural son of Priam. He fights in the Trojan army against the Greeks. This name occurs in the same form in Benoît, and is believed by Greif to be derived from the Evagoras of Hyginus.[18] – *LT* a4808 n4824

Ermedantz 'von Laridune', a warrior in Akarîn's army against Ipomidôn. – *JT* nm3178,1ff.

Ermenrîch (Ermanarich) King of the Ostro-Goths. – nm *P* 421,27; *W* 384,21

Ermiona daughter of Menelaus and Helen; she marries Orestes. She is abducted by Pirrus but rescued by Orestes, who slays the former. This is the story as told in Dictys and copied by Benoît and *LT*. In *TK* (she is called Armiones in *TKf*) Menelaus promises her to Pirrus when he is trying to persuade Licomedes and Deidamîa to permit Pirrus to come to Troy. She occurs a second time (*TKf* 49244ff.), but there is no mention of a marriage with Orestes. E. is one of the characters in the *Odyssey*. – *LT* 17516f.; *TK* a20782 n44488ff.

Ermolâus 'von Kriechen', a young Greek of noble family who shoots a hart which Alexander wants to shoot. Alexander strikes him with a staff, and E. cries. Calistenes, his tutor, bids him act like a man, and Alexander, construing this as a counsel that he should take his revenge, has them both put to death. So also in *Expeditio Alexandri*, Curtius Rufus, and Gualterus. – *UA* 18918

*Ernalt see Arnalt

Ernest see Ernst

Ernst 'herzoge', hero of the popular gleeman's epic which bears his name. – nm *UA* 25102; *RB* 21057f.

Erolas 'von Orfilune', nephew of Lehelîn; he is killed whilst fighting for Schîonatulander against Ipomidôn. His death is one of the reaons why his uncle, Orilus, nurses an implacable hatred of Schîonatulander. – *JT* nm4171,1

Erosse 'von Sigdebunt', a warrior in Ipomidôn's army against Akarîn. E. is also called Eressulas. – *JT* 3368,3

Ertgêr 'von Dassilân', *ami* of Andifoie. Dêmantîn had killed his father. He jousts with Firganant at Antrîun, and when captured, reveals that he is not a hired knight, but is simply riding in search of adventure, and is equally willing to fight for Dêmantîn, in whose service he soon distinguishes himself. – *Dem* a9118f. n9127

Erthgêr see Ertgêr

*Erfiklant see Arfiklant

Êsaû biblical, son of Isaac and brother of Jacob. – *UA* nm11303

Esdra biblical, he repulsed the Babylonians (= Ezra ?). – *UA* nm11818

Esdras (1) natural son of Priam; he fights for the Trojans against the Greeks. E. is called Êdron in *TK*, and Esdron in Benoît. – *LT* a4768f. n4776; *TK* 30367

Esdras (2) 'von Greste', also called 'von Agreste', and in *TK* 'von Grossiâ' and Estras. E. is a warrior in the Trojan army against the Greeks. He appears to have been invented by Benoît. – *LT* 4069f.; *TK* 29993

Esêalt 'der lange', a knight of Arthur's court who accompanies Lanzelet when the latter goes to rescue Êrec and Gawein from Malduc (see Maldwîz). According to Lot, this is the same person as Galehalt, who plays a similar part in the OF version, the name being derived from (G)alehalt, with *l* misread as *h*.[19] – *L* a7531 n7544

Eselig, Esilg see Elyze (1)

---

18 Greif, pp. 26ff.
19 Lot (2), p. 168, note 1.

Esîonâ daughter of Laomedon; she is taken back to Greece by Thelamon to be his concubine after the defeat of the Trojans in the first battle against the Greeks. It is the insult which is thus offered to the Trojans which is the initial cause of the enmity between the two peoples. E. is the mother of Ajax (1) by Thelamon. She is not known to Homer, but occurs in Dares, Dictys, and Benoît. E.'s name occurs as Chiona in *LT*. – *LT* 1607f.; *TK* 12960ff. [†]

Esipfilê (Hypsipyle) daughter of Thoas, king of Lemnos. E. was wooed and then abandoned by Jason, by whom she had twins. – *TK* nm22142

Esipholus a warrior in Alexander's army at the battle of Erbela, where he was slain by Enôs. This character appears to have been invented by Ulrich. – *UA* 13378

Eskelabôn 'künec von Sêres', he is slain by Vîvîans whilst fighting for Terramêr against Willehalm (1). He is the brother of Galafrê. This name rests on a misunderstanding of *Aliscans* (358), where 'Esclavon' was misread as the name of a person. – *W* 26,25

Eschalus 'vürste', placed by Alexander in charge of Alexandria. So also in *Expeditio Alexandri* and Curtius Rufus, where he is called Aeschylus. – *A* 10621f.

Eschibach 'der von' (*RW*), see Wolfram

Eschilus see Eschinus

Eschinus a philosopher in Athens. In *A* and *UA*, as in Valerius and MS S of Leo, E. advises the Athenians not to fight Alexander, whilst in *WA*, as in the majority of the MSS of Leo, he advises them not to surrender. He is called Eskilus in *A*, and Eschilus in *WA*, but Eschinus in *UA*, where he is 'burcgrâve von Athêniâ'. In Pseudo-Callisthenes and Valerius he is named Aeschines, a form which Gualterus uses and from which the form in *UA* is no doubt derived, whilst in Leo he is called Eschillis, possibly owing to some confusion with Aeschylus, an error which Junk in his Index to *A* seems to share. – *A* 3662f; *UA* 2565; *WA* 1666f.

Eskilabôn 'von der schoenen Wilde', a knight who, for the love of Klârischanze, guards a flower garden. Any knight who plucks a flower has to fight him and, if defeated, take a wreath to Klârischanze. He defeats 500 knights in this way and requires but one more victory to win his lady. Frîâns (see Ûrjans) is defeated but does not keep his oath to go to Klârischanze. When E. comes to claim his lady, he is repulsed as untruthful and retires to his garden, where he imprisons any knights that he overcomes. Flôrîs (2) and Alexander (6) are among the captives, all of whom are released when E. is defeated by Gârel. E. afterwards brings a large army to assist Gârel against Ehkunat. It is obvious that the character of E. is an imitation and combination of Gramoflanz and Ehkunat. – *G* nm2498 a3440

Eskilus see Eschinus

Êson brother of Peleas and father of Jason. In *TK* he undergoes a successful operation for rejuvenation at the hands of Medea. E. occurs in Dares and Benoît, where his name is spelt Aeson. – *LT* 118ff.; *TK* m6532 n10251 a10288

Esoras 'herzoge von Aggaron', a warrior in the Trojan army against the Greeks. This character was invented by Konrad. – *TK* 24922

Espinogres a knight who joins in the search for Parzivâl. E., who is also called Aspinogres and Asspynogres, is the son of Blanschemore and uncle of Partinias. The name has the same form in Gautier, but occurs as Spynagrose in the ME poem, *Gologros and Gawane*. A Saxon king of this name (var. Pinogres) occurs in *L'Estoire de Merlin* (Vulgate Cycle) and in the *Livre d'Artus*. – *RP* 526,8

Essechiel see Ezechîel

Essemerel 'von Mekka', also called Essemfrel, nephew of Akarîn, in whose army he is a commander in the battle against Ipomidôn. – *JT* 3129,1f.

Essemfrel see Essemerel

Esserê 'der emerâl', he gave Arofel his sword, which had originally belonged to Pantanor. This corresponds to *Aliscans*, where E. is called l'amiré Aceré, a Saracen of this name occurring in the OF *chanson de geste, Prise d'Orange*. Wolfram, however, introduces him into the second battle at Alischanz, where he is slain by Rennewart, who gives his horse to Kibelîns. Singer has shown that the origin of this appearance is *Aliscans* (5537), where an Amirant Estiflé (in most MSS: Estele) is slain by Rennewart, who gives his horse to Bertrams (2).[20] – *W* nm77,27 a417,29

Esserel a warrior in Akarîn's army against Ipomidôn. – *JT* nm3171,5

Estylant 'künec von' (*RW*), see Gierrart

Estor half-brother of Lanzelet, he meets and fights with Parzivâl. They both lie badly wounded on the ground, when an angel appears and carries the Graal round them, when they are immediately healed. In Manessier he is called Ector, a knight who plays a prominent part in the romances of the Vulgate Cycle, particularly the *Livre de Lancelot del Lac*, where we learn that he is the son of Ban (see Pant (1)), begotten on the wife of the Sire de Marès. E. was apparently confused on occasion with Tors, who is often called Estorz, and this fact, together with the fact that they are both of illegitimate birth, led Brugger to identify them as one and the same character.[21] – *RP* 822,29ff.

Estorz see Tors

Estras see Esdras (2)

Estravagaot a knight who is present at Arthur's court when Êrec returns with Ênîte. E. does not occur in Chrestien's *Erec*, and appears to be an attempt to reproduce the name of the city Estrangoire (var. Estrangot). This view is shared by Brugger.[22] – *E* 1686

Estreus a warrior in the Trojan army against the Greeks. This character was invented by Konrad. – *TK* 29928

Êsus see Elîes

Ethardet counsellor to Bêâmunt. – *Dem* 9711

Etherhêm a knight who jousts with Dêmantîn. – *Dem* 5752

Ethiocles son of Oedippus and brother of Polinices. In Greek mythology he is called Eteocles. – nm *C* 15541ff.; *UA* 3007ff.

Ethra (1) a maiden attendant on Cassandra; she is given to Demophon at the fall of Troy. E. is not mentioned in Dares, but occurs in Benoît, in Dictys, as Aethra, and in Homer, where she is called Aithre. (See Ethrâ (2).) – *LT* 16359

Ethrâ (2) a maiden attendant upon Helen, whilst the latter is still in Greece. It is she who informs Helen of Paris's love for her. It is probable that this character is a copy of Ethra (1). – *TK* nm21970

Etiocles see Ethiocles

Etzel (Attila) the famous king of the Huns. – nm *W* 384,20; *Ll* 1,2

Eudis see Eydes

Eudochiôn a warrior in Dârîus's army; he is wounded by Eumenidôn during the battle at Issôn. E. occurs elsewhere only in Gualterus. – *UA* 8157

Euctêmôn one of the prisoners who had been maimed by Dârîus and who are released by Alexander. Alexander gives them a land of their own where they can stay at peace. So

---

20   Singer (2), p. 120.
21   Brugger (1), p. 84.
22   Brugger (2), p.70, note 131.

also in Curtius Rufus and Gualterus. In *UA*, where he is called Euticiôn, E. advises his comrades to accept this offer of Alexander's. – *A* 13997; *UA* 15513

Eumelius, Eumelus see Emelius

Eumenides one of the four toll-collectors (see Gâmeranz) who attack Gawein. Seeing his three brothers dead and realising that he himself is defeated, E. puts an end to his own life by falling on his sword. – *C* m5963 a6262 n6449

Eumenidôn a warrior in Alexander's army. This character appears to have been invented by Gualterus, in whose account he first appears. – *UA* 8157f.

Eumîliô marshal to Alexander; in *A*, he conquers Italy, whilst Alexander is occupied with the campaign around Athens. E. does not occur in *UA*, but in all other versions he accompanies Alexander as far as the frozen river and minds his horses whilst the emperor goes in disguise to the court of Dârîus. In *SA*, E. is called Emolus and Emulus. Of the Latin verions, E. occurs in Valerius, Pseudo-Callisthenes, and Leo. – *A* 3412; *SA* 2355ff.; *WA* 2352ff. [†]

Eunuchus 'von Kypre', a warrior in the Greek army against the Trojans. E. occurs in Benoît as Cuneüs de Cipe (var. Euneus de chipre). – *LT* 4933

Eurialus (1) 'künec', a warrior in the Greek army against the Trojans. So also in Benoît, Dares, and Dictys. E. is called Urielus in *TK*. – *LT* 2841; *TK* 30680ff. [†]

Euriâlus (2) a Trojan in Ênêâs's army. He and his friend Nisus make a sortie one night and kill hundreds of the warriors in Turnus's army, who are lying in a drunken sleep. On the return to the Trojan camp they meet Volzân, who pursues them with a band of knights and kills them both. So in the OF *Eneas* and in Virgil, where he is called Euryalus. – *Ed* 6540f.

Euriolus see Eurialus (1)

Euripilus (1) 'von Mêsiâ', son of Telêfus and grandson of Priam. E. joins the Trojan army after the arrival of Pirrus at Troy and is slain by him in battle. So also in Dictys. – *TKf* 44660f.

Euripilus (2) 'künec von Yrcanige', also called 'künec von Orcanie' (*LT* 10239), a warrior who, as in Benoît, is killed whilst fighting for the Greeks against the Trojans. E. occurs also in Dares and Dictys, where his death is not mentioned. – *LT* 3380; *TK* 23870

Euritus father of Îolê. So in Ovid's *Metamorphoses* IX. – *TK* nm38192f.

Eurôpâ a maiden who, in Greek mythology, was abducted by Zeus in the guise of a white bull. – *UA* nm3981

Eusimacus 'von Lide', a warrior in the Greek army against the Trojans. E. does not occur in any of the other versions of the Trojan legend. – *LT* 4918ff.

Eustachîus 'sante', who, according to *A*, became a Christian after having been a heathen. (Identical with Eustathius, the commentator on Homer, who died AD 1198? There is, however, no suggestion in connection with Eustathius that he was once a heathen.) – *A* nm3289

Eustates son of Ajax (1) and Themisa. E. is mentioned in Benoît and Dictys, where he is called Eurisacis. – *LT* nm16899ff.

Euticiôn see Euctêmôn

Eufebius see Euforbes

Eufemes 'von Lauconie', also called (6845) 'von Calcedonie'; he is slain by Achilles whilst fighting for the Trojans against the Greeks. So also in Benoît, and in Dares and Dictys, where he is called Euphemus e Ciconia; he occurs also in Homer as Euphemos of Kikonia. – *LT* 3995ff.

Eufêstiô Alexander's closest friend and comrade. He is depicted in *UA* as young and small, but strong and brave. In *A*, where he is called Ephestiôn, Alexander gives him the crown of

Sîdônje to dispose of as he wishes, and he gives it to Abdalôminus. E. appears to have been invented by Gualterus, who calls him Hephaestio. – *A* 7721f.; *UA* 7477f. [†]

Eufimacus a warrior in the Greek army against the Trojans. He is in the service of Ajax (1). E. does not appear in any of the other versions of the legend. – *LT* 3335ff.

Euforbes a prophet, and, according to Dares and Benoît, where he is called Euphorbus and Eüforbius respectively, he is the father of Panthus and foretells the fall of Troy. *LT* follows this, except that in this version he is the tutor of Panthus and foretells the fall of Troy through Paris fifty years before the latter sets out to fetch Helen. *TK*, in which E. is called Eufebius, follows Dares in making him the father of Panthus, and says that he was a hundred years old when he died. In Homer he is the son of Panthoös and has no prophetic gifts, but takes part in the war with the Greeks. Dictys and *TKf* follow this version, and in the former he is slain by Menelaus and Ajax (2), whilst in the latter (43381) his death is lamented but not described. – *LT* nm2299; *TK* m19247 n19254 [†]

Eufreide 'grâve', placed in charge of Meie's kingdom jointly with Kornêljus (q.v.). – *MB* 62,10ff.

Êvâ see Êve

Evalet see Evaleth

Evaleth 'künec in Grosz Priton', he welcomes Joseph of Arimathia, when the latter comes to Britain. Joseph helps him to defeat Tholomer, and E. becomes a Christian, assuming the name of Mordelas (q.v.). This is the story as told in *Mer*, but in the *Estoire del Saint Graal*, in which the story is originally told, his land is Sarraz, a city near Jerusalem. – *Mer* nm156,6; *RP* nm614,29

Êvander (1) an old friend of Anchises, to whom Ênêâs applies for help against Turnus. E. sends an army in which is his son Pallas (2). So also in the OF *Eneas* and Virgil. – *Ed* nm5850ff. a6029ff.

Evander (2) natural son of Priam; he is captured by Ajax (1) whilst fighting for the Trojans against the Greeks. – *TKf* 40520

Evas father of Gayte and Prophilias. So also in the OF version. – *AP* aA^d,17 nm[A^e,38]

Evax 'künec von Arabîâ', an Arabian king of the first century who had a very great knowledge of medicine and who wrote a book on the power of jewels for the Emperor Tiberius. – nm *L* 8528ff.; *JT* 4838,5f.

Êve the first woman. – *P* nm463,19; *Tn* nm17952; *W* nm62,2ff.; *A* nm17003; *UW* nm3,12; *Dem* nm7468; *JT* nm2491,1; *PM* m9322; *Loh* nm3700; *UA* nm113; *WW* nm2790; *RB* nm10877; *WO* nm14391; *RP* nm67,37; *FS* nm2977

Ephestiôn see Eufêstiô

Êvilmôradac biblical (Evil-Merodach), king of Babylon (d. 560 BC). – *UA* nm7691f.

Efrâim biblical, name-father of one of the tribes of Israel. – *A* nm10030

Efranes brother of Elichar, he is slain whilst fighting for the Trojans against the Greeks. This character was invented by Konrad. – *TK* 36314f.

Efroi brother of Pelde, a knight who is present at the tourney held by Leigamar. – *C* 18049

Effardîe a maiden whom Darifant is on his way to champion. – *Dar* nm157

Effeidas see Enfeidas

Effigenniâ see Iphigenie

Effimenîs 'herzoge', a warrior who is slain by Ulixes whilst fighting for the Trojans in the opening battle of the war against the Greeks. This character was invented by Konrad. – *TK* 25556

Ewsebius (Eusebius Pamphili) a Latin author. – *SA* nm10

Exâtreus see Oxîatres

Exersus   see Xerses (1)

Ezdeiz   a knight who is present at the tourney held by Leigamar. – *C* 11384

Ezêchiâ   biblical (Hezekiah), king of Judah. – nm *A* 16316; *UA* 11709

Ezechîel   biblical, the OT prophet. – nm *RB* 13434; *SA* 4238

Ecidon   'von Avaritze', a warrior in Ipomidôn's army against Akarîn. – *JT* 3259,6

Ezzerîas   'künec von Falturnye', a warrior in Gêrfridolt's army; he is trampled to death by the Christian army. – *Loh* 5663ff.

F

(see under V)

G

Gabal see Gaball

Gaball a giant in the service of Hannor. He attacks Eleander, who kills him. – *GT* 21143ff.

Gaban see Gawein

Gabarîns 'cuns von Assigarzjonte'. (Bartsch suggests the derivation of the name from the Provençal Gabaret,[1] but Martin undoubtedly points to the true source when he shows that the name occurs as Gabbaram (var. Gabarium) in Solinus (21,22).[2]) G. is one of the knights in the list of those whom Feirefîz says he has defeated. In *JT*, where he is called Abarinse von Assigarciunde, he takes part in the tourney held by Sekundille to decide which of her wooers she shall marry. – *P* nm770,9; *JT* 5265,1f.

Gabenîs an old knight who rebukes Parzivâl for riding in armour on Good Friday (var. Kahenîs). – *P* a446,10 n457,11 [†]

Gabin see Gawein

Gabrîêl the archangel. – nm *UW* (MS B and D) 111,9f; *JT* 5470,5; *Loh* 1249; *WW* 2796; *FS* 7503

Gabwein see Gawein

Gagyol see Gayol (2)

Gahardyz see Kardeiz (2)

Gahares a knight who is present at Arthur's court when der schöne Böse arrives to give himself up after being defeated by Parzivâl. He is called Carahés in the Mons MS of Gautier and is possibly identical with Gaheres, a knight who occurs in *RP* (525,33) and who appears in Gautier as Gahieris. – *RP* 391,16

Gaharet, Gahariet see Gaherîez

Gaheres see Gahares

Gaheries see Gaherîez

Gaherîez brother of Gawein. G. first appears in Chrestien's *Erec* (1725), where two knights are mentioned: 'Gaherïez et Keus d'Estraus'. This verse has become distorted in *C* to Galeres von Destrauz, a knight who spills Priure's cup of chastity. In *E* the name takes the same form as in Chrestien, but in *P*, where he is Gawein's cousin, he is called Gaherjê, a form which is copied in *M* (var. Gaharet), where he is the son of Anthonjê (1) and the king of Grîtenlant. In *RP*, G. is called Gaheries and, as in Pseudo-Gautier, he is Gawein's brother and is overcome by a dwarf in a beautiful garden. He has to vow to return at the end of a year and fight to the death. He accidentally withdraws the truncheon of the lance from the body of Brangemor (q.v.) and with it returns and slays the dwarf. G., who occurs in most of the OF romances and in Malory, is in all versions the best of Gawein's brothers. Following *La Mort le Roi Artu* (Vulgate Cycle), Füetrer relates how G. is accidentally slain by Lanzelet, when the latter is fighting against the knights of the Round Table.[3] (See also Karjet.) – *E* 1658; *P* nm664,30; *C* 2315; *M* nm156f. a2391; *RP* 90,3 [†]

Gaherjêt see Gaherîez

Gahillet a knight at Arthur's court when Êrec returns with Ênîte. G. does not occur in Chrestien's *Erec*. He is thought by some scholars to be the source of Wolfram's Kailet (q.v.). – *E* 1672

---

1 Bartsch (2), p. 150.
2 Martin (1), p. 503, to 770,9.
3 Hofstäter, I, p. 247.

Gahmuret (Schulz saw in this name an OF name composed of *game*, 'jewel', and *amorous*, 'amorous', i.e. 'jewel of love', the whole being a misunderstanding of a Celtic name derived from the Welsh *camgred*, 'heresy', or *camgredwr*, 'heretic', a reference to G.'s heretical marriage to Belakâne.[4] Such an etymology has no support in modern times, however, most scholars being of the opinion that the name is a form of Gomoret, the territorial name of Ban (see Pant (1)) in *E*.[5] Bartsch identifies it with the OHG name Gamarit[6] (< OHG *gaman, gaudium*?[7]). Hertz points out that the MS readings Gamuret and Gagmuret correspond to the OF Gaumeret, a name which occurs in the 13th-century poem *Atre Perillous*.[8] Hertz also points out that it is possible for the name to be a diminutive of Gamor,[9] but this name only occurs in an English poem of a later date. Panzer asserts that G. is a common German name, appearing already in the 8th century in a document of the Monastery of Lorsch, and gives examples of its occurrence in Bavaria in 1237 and 1247; according to Panzer, this name was particularly common in the 14th and 15th centuries.[10] He is unable to agree that it is a form of Gomoret, a view which Singer shares.[11] In Freymond's analysis of the fragmentary OF *Livre d'Artus*,[12] Segremors plays a part in an adventure which Brugger parallels with the G.-Belakâne episode in *P*,[13] and partly for this reason he derives the name of G. from the diminutive of Segremors, viz. Sagremoret, which he translates as 'the young Segremors'.[14])

G. is the younger son of Gandîn, and on the death of his father, he is left penniless. In spite of the generous offer of his brother Gâlôes (1), he prefers to seek fame and fortune in the world and enters the service of Akarîn, for whom he distinguishes himself in the wars against Pompêjus and Ipomidôn. Leaving Akarîn, he comes to Zazamanc, where he frees the Moorish queen, Belakâne, from her enemies and marries her. He soon tires of inactivity, however, and steals away, leaving his wife with child. A little later, G. falls in love with Herzeloide, whose hand he wins at a tourney. Comforting himself with the thought that Belakâne is a heathen, he marries Herzeloide but soon learns that Akarîn is again in need of his help. G. meets his death in the campaign, and the broken-hearted Herzeloide retires into solitude with her son Parzivâl, who is born shortly after the death of his father. Belakâne's child, Feirefîz, is born pied, half black, half white, exactly as is Moriaen, the illegitimate son of Parzivâl's brother, Agloval, in the Dutch *Lancelot*. It seems possible that Wolfram knew this story and transferred it from Parzivâl's brother to his father. Beyond stating that he is dead, Chrestien tells us nothing of importance about Parzivâl's father in his *Perceval*. Apart from the etymological considerations detailed above, there is no trace of a character such as G. before Wolfram. He has nothing in common with Alain, the father of Parzivâl in *Perlesvaus*, nor with Pellinore, who is his father in the Vulgate Cycle and in Malory. In Gerbert's continuation of *Perceval* (3072), Parzivâl's father is called Gales li Caus. G. is certainly the source of the episode in

4   Schulz, 'Eigennamen', p. 400.
5   Bruce (1), I, p. 314, and Martin (1), p. 16 to 5,23.
6   Bartsch (2), p. 138.
7   Förstemann, I, col. 59.
8   Wolfram von Eschenbach, *Parzival*, transl. by W. Hertz, p. 469.
9   Wolfram von Eschenbach, *Parzival*, transl. by W. Hertz, p. 469.
10 Panzer (2), pp. 211f.
11 Singer (1), pp. 63f.
12 Freymond (1), pp. 112f.
13 Brugger (1), pp. 59ff.
14 Brugger (1), p. 63

Apollonius von Tyrland, where the hero leaves his white wife, Diomena, for the Moorish queen Palmina, with whom he has a pied son, Garamant. Of the other MHG poems, G. only appears in *JT*, where the story of *P* is re-told, and in *Wigm*, where he takes part in the tourney held by Arthur for Deleprosat and in the tourney held by Dymszogar. – *P* 5,22f.; *Wigl* nm8244; *W* nm73,22f.; *T* nm27,2 a39,1; *RW* nm7826; *Tirol* nmD,9; *Wigm* 2057; *G* nm4179; *UW* nm76,10; *JT* nm651,3 a664,1f.; *TF* nm2081; *MB* nm159,15; *Loh* nm7099; *UA* nm3388; *RB* nm15281; *WO* nm12295

Gaylet see Kailet

Gaîn see Keiî

Gaiol (1) 'Gruwin', a heathen. G. is a comrade of Girabob, with whom he is slain by Rudolf during the siege of Ascalun. Grimm thought G. identical with Gayol (2), and expressed the view that Berthold von Holle translated Gruwin as Crane, mixing it up with the OF *grus*, *grue*, 'crane'.[15] Bethmann points out that such a theory postulates a French original of Berthold's poem, as he would hardly have translated a word already in the German.[16] – *GR* δb,14f.

Gayol (2) son of Dassir von Ungerlant. G. leaves his father's court at an early age and takes service with his two friends, Agorlîn and Agorlôt, under the kaiser. G. gains the love of the kaiser's daughter, Acheloyde, and she and her friend, Achute, give the three friends pseudonyms (presumably in order to be able to talk about them more freely). G. they call 'Crane'. When the tourney for Acheloyde's hand is announced, G. leaves the court in order to prepare himself, and meeting Assundîn (q.v.), he discloses his identity but insists that Assundîn shall continue to be king of Ungerlant for the present. At the tourney, G. dresses in the king's armour and is declared the victor. But the knight in that armour is thought to be Assundîn, a married man, and Acheloyde is therefore given a free choice of husband. She chooses G., who is posing now as Assundîn's marshal, and he thereupon discloses his true identity. Sêkurîe arrives during the wedding celebrations and is given leave to choose any knight to champion her against Acurteis. She chooses G. and he has to leave Acheloyde and accompany Sêkurîe. On the way he defeats a number of knights and sends them to do homage to his wife. He is later joined by Agorlîn, and defeats and kills Acurteis. He then returns to Acheloyde in Ungerlant, where he thenceforth reigns. – *Crane* 50ff.

Gayte sister of Prophilias, she marries Athis (q.v.). – *AP* mA^e,25 aA*,1 nA*,63

Gachmuret see Gahmuret

Galaal a knight who assists Arthur against Bruns (1). This is none other than the most famous of all the Arthurian knights, Galahad, as is clear from the Mons MS of Pseudo-Gautier, where he is called Galahad. (The name does not appear in the Montpellier MS.) In the OF Vulgate Cycle and in Malory, G. is the son of Lancelot and the daughter of Pelles and displaces Parzivâl as the knight who achieves the Graal quest. The story is retold by Füetrer, where G. is called Galat.[17] – *RP* 22,32

Galaas a knight who has to fight the hostages due to Assiles, the giant who is G.'s master. This name occurs in the Vulgate Cycle as a variant of Galahad, but G. cannot be identified with Galaal. – *C* nm5488

Galades 'vrouwe von Canelle', one of the ladies at Arthur's court who spill Priure's cup of chastity. – *C* 1613

---

15 See Bethmann, p. 169, note.
16 Bethmann, p. 169, note.
17 Hofstäter, II, pp. 200ff.

Galagandreiz 'von Môreiz'. Lanzelet spends the night at G.'s house and is visited by his daughter, with whom he lies. Lanzelet is challenged the next morning by G., whom he kills. (Identical with Galogandres?) – *L* m723 n734 a780

Galaganteis, Galagaundris see Galogandres

Galahies a knight who assists Arthur against Bruns (1). – *RP* 22,31

Galaidâ sister of Leimas and *amie* of Keiî. G. is unable even to hold Priure's cup of chastity, much to the discomfiture of Keiî, who has been deriding those who have spilt the cup. G. is also (23893) called Calaidâ. – *C* 1436ff.

Galamîde 'ein rîche fei', sister of Gasosîn. – *C* nm10499

Galandertas marshal of Trefferîn (Dulceflûr's land). G. assists Meleranz against Verangôz's men. – *M* a8481 n8556f.

Galangatis see Galogandres

Galangelle 'von Clumester', a giant who is slain by Gawein. – *C* nm9003

Galantte a beautiful woman whom Eleander sees on his search for Amelita. Eleander has to fight her *ami*, Magonogrin, whom he kills, and G., seeing the latter dead, falls dead by his side. – *GT* a20251 n20272

Galarantis see Galogandres

Galat 'vrouwe', one of the ladies at Arthur's court who spill Priure's cup of chastity. – *C* 1620

Galathîs 'von Orient', a relative of Aspatrîs, he fights for the Soldan against Partonopier and wounds Arnolt (4). He is slain by Walther (1). – *PM* 20698ff.

Galafrê brother of Eskelabôn. He is slain by Vîvîans whilst fighting for Terramêr against Willehalm (1). In *Aliscans* he is called Galafer (var. Agolafre). – *W* 26,30

Galeres see Gaherîez

Gâles see Galez

Galesche father or mother of Elis (1). G. is only mentioned in conjunction with Elis, who is called on the first occasion 'der Calescen sun' (translating Gautier's 'Elis li fius à le Galette' (29149) and on the second occasion as 'der Galeschen sun' (*RP* 525,37) (translating Gautier's 'li fius à la Galesce' (31369)). Calescen is the name of a knight who plays a prominent part in the Vulgate Cycle, whilst a knight named Galescin occurs in the OF prose *Tristan* (Löseth's analysis). Galesche is also the feminine form of the OF *galois*, 'Welsh', which may account for the feminine definite article in Gautier 31369 (see above). – *RP* nm472,43

Galez 'der kale', a knight at Arthur's court when Êrec returns with Ênîte. G. appears in Chrestien's *Erec* (1726) as Gales li chaus (i.e. the bald), the name occurring in *C* as Gâles (var. Kâles) Lithauz (var. Lischas). He is one of the knights who spill Priure's cup of chastity, and is also unhorsed by Gasosîn. His *amie* in *C* is named Filleduoch. G. occurs in lists of knights in the *Estoire de Merlin* and in the *Livre de Lancelot del Lac* (Vulgate Cycle). – *E* 1659; *C* 2316

Galîag son of the grâve von Mîlîag. He rides by the side of Gymêle when Tristan is lying in wait with Kaedîn to observe the passing of Îsolt (2). – *ET* 6471

Galyantis see Galogandres

Galien (1) 'von Kurnewale', one of five knights who attack Gawein and Agravains. G. is slain by Gawein. In Manessier he is called Galiains. – *RP* a718,1 n720,6

Galyen (2) a relative of Gafyens. In Manessier he is called Galiien. – *RP* nm777,36

Galienus (Claudius Galenus) the Greek physician. – *JT* nm1755,5

Gâlôes (1)   (Schulz derived this name from the OF *gallois*, 'gallant',[18] whilst Singer believes
it to be a form of Galaes, who, with Anor, is one of the daughters of Ebrac in Wace's
Brut.[19])   G. first occurs in MHG literature in *E*, where it is the result of a wrong translation
by Hartmann of Chrestien's *Erec* (1738): Galegantins li Galois, a knight who is present at
Arthur's court when Êrec returns with Ênîte. Hartmann changed this name into that of two
knights, Galagaundris and G. It is probable that Wolfram took the name from *E*. In *P* he is
Gahmuret's brother and is slain by Orilus in a joust. His *amie* is named Annôr. All other
corrupt forms of the name which appear can be traced back to Wolfram. – *E* 1662; *P* a6,2
n80,14; *G* nm4181; *JT* nm3807,1f.; *TF* nm2082; *UA* nm9879 [†]

Gâlôes (2)   'ein Franzois' (= Galois?). A warrior in Alexander's army. This character was
invented by Ulrich. – *UA* 4748

Galogander   see Galogandres

Galogandres   a knight who is present at Arthur's court when Êrec returns with Ênîte in *E*,
where G. is called Galagaundris. G. is first mentioned in Chrestien's *Erec* (1738) as
Galegantins li Galois, from which is derived Galarantis li Gâleis, a knight who spills Priure's
cup of chastity in *C*. In *P*, where he is one of the commanders in Klâmîde's army, he is
called 'herzoge von Gippones', and this mention in *P* is no doubt the origin of his
appearance in *JT* at a tourney held by Arthur. G. occurs, spelt in various ways, in *RP*,
where he is present at the tourney held by Ris and takes part in the rescue of Gifles. – *E*
1662; *P* 205,9; *C* 2326; *JT* 1991,1; *RP* 81,21 [†]

Galoyss   squire to Pictagines. – *GT* 10378

Galopamur   a knight who is present at Arthur's court when Êrec returns with Ênîte. G. does
not occur in the corresponding list of knights in Chretien's *Erec*. – *E* 1676

Galopêar   'herzoge', he fights for Lîon against Wigalois and kills Marîne. He is himself slain
by Adân (1). – *Wigl* 11026f.

Galther   'von Avenis', a knight who is on the side of the Christians in the final battle against
the heathens. – *WO* 17081

Galthêrus   see Walther (2)

Galusideis (1)   'von Grikulanie', a warrior in Akarîn's army against Ipomidôn. – *JT* 3124,1ff.

Galusideis (2)   'von Korasen', a warrior in Akarîn's army against Ipomidôn. – *JT* nm3095,5

Galvân   a knight who is sent with 400 men by Ehkunat to occupy the fort vacated by
Malserôn. Gârel is already in possession when he arrives, and a pitched battle takes place
in which G. is slain by Gârel. – *G* nm12812 a12829

Galferat   'vürste'. Owing to the fragmentary nature of this poem it is impossible to decide
what part G. plays. – *Tirol* B,3

Galves   see Gâlôes (1)

Galfier   'vürste von Nubŷâ', a courtier who speaks in favour of immediate punishment
without trial for Flôre and Blanscheflûr when they are caught by the Amiral. – *FB* 6628f.

Galwes   see Gâlôes

Gamaet   a knight of the Round Table who is mentioned by Talides. In Manessier, G. is
called Cahariet. – *RP* nm655,18

Gamareth   see Gamorett

Gamas   'künec von' (*Loh*), see Hachaberc

Gamelarot   son of Fansaserat, he comes to Terramêr's court to plead for his father's life. He
becomes a Christian. In *JT*, G. is a commander in Akarîn's army against Ipomidôn. –
R nm Eing. I,92 a Bl. I,98; *JT* 3139,1

---

18   Schulz, 'Eigennamen', p. 400.
19   Singer (1), pp. 59f.

Gamelerot, Gamelorat see Gamelarot

Gamêr vassal of Schaffilûn. G. takes the oath of fealty to Wigalois on the latter's enthronement and fights for him aginst Liôn. – *Wigl* a9080ff. n10098

Gâmeranz one of four brothers who attack anyone who stays the night in the castle of Riwalîn (2). They attack Gawein, who kills them all. – *C* m5963 a6262 n6284

Gamereth see Gamorett

Gamgrinot a heathen who is oppressing Dymszogar (q.v.), who holds a tourney to find a husband to protect her and her land. – *Wigm* nm5053f.

Gamile see Gamylle

Gamylle 'künec von Zaloan', brother of Minos. He avenges the disgrace of his nieces, Fedra and Meierra, by slaying Jason at Troy. – *GT* 22535ff.

Gamis an old man who is given by Agrant to Liupolt as a companion. – *WO* 468ff.

Gamoret see Gahmuret

Gamoreth see Gamorett

Gamorett brother of Trifon. G. brings a large army to avenge the death of his brother on the Greeks, but is defeated and flees. He lies in ambush with 10,000 men, and when Paris rides by, almost unarmed, they capture him and take him to Yberne, where they leave him, naked and tied to a tree. – *GT* 5648f.

Gamorith see Gamorett

Gamur 'der Sarrazîn', a knight who is mentioned by Gawein as having been present at a tourney held some years before by Arthur. – *C* nm22646

Gamuret see Gahmuret

Ganatulander see Schîonatulander

Gandalûz (1) 'grâve von Schampâne', slain by Tedalûn whilst fighting for Willehalm (1) against Terramêr. According to Singer, Wolfram took this name over from Gandilûz in *P*.[20] – *W* 366,16ff. [†]

Gandaluz (2) see Gandelus

Gandelus (Bartsch suggests < Provençal *gandir*, 'to flee', and *lutz*, 'light'.[21]) G. is one of the knights in *E* who are present at Arthur's court when Êrec returns with Ênîte. In *P*, where he is called Gandilûz, he is represented as still a young lad, performing the duties of squire to Gawein, whilst in *C*, where he is called Gandaluz, he is one of the knights at Arthur's court who spill Priure's cup of chastity. The first reference to G. is contained in Chrestien's *Erec*. – *E* 1638; *P* 429,20; *C* 2297 [†]

Gandêr 'der alte', father of Gêrant. G. pursues Dêmantîn and Sirgamôte as they are escaping from Eghart's court, and is unhorsed by the former. – *Dem* 4257

Gandilûz see Gandelus

Gandîn (1) (Bartsch thinks that this name, or a similar form of it, stood in Kîôt, and that the similarity in their names suggested the connection with the town, Gandîne, to Wolfram (498,25ff.).[22] Golther, on the other hand, regards the town as being the sole source of this name.[23]) G. is the husband of Schôette and the father of Gâlôes, Gahmuret, Lamîre, and Flûrdâmûrs. All references to him are derived from *P*. – *P* m5,25 n8,19; *T* 82,2; *Wigm* nm3208; *G* nm4177; *JT* nm726,3; *Loh* nm7098 [†]

Gandîn (2) an Irish nobleman who arrives at Marke's court, and is promised any reward he cares to name for playing his rote. He demands Îsolt (2), who is given to him. When

---

20 Singer (2), p. 109.
21 Bartsch (2), p. 142.
22 Bartsch (2), p. 135.
23 Golther (1), p. 181.

97

Tristan, who has been out hunting, returns, he recovers Îsolt, gaining access to G.'s tent disguised as a harpist. – *Tn* 13110ff.

Gangier 'von Neranden', brother of Scos. G. is a knight who is present at Arthur's court when Êrec returns with Ênîte. There is no knight with this or a similar name in Chrestien's *Erec*. – *E* 1681

Ganimêde in Greek mythology cup-bearer to the gods. – *UA* nm4851

Gansguoter 'von Michelolde', uncle of Amurfinâ and Sgoidamur. G. accompanied Îgerne, when the latter secretly left her husband, and he built for her the Castle Marvellous, called Salîe in *C*. The origin of G., as of his counterpart in *P*, Klinschor, is to be found in Chrestien's reference to 'un sages clers d'astrenomie', and he is consequently referred to (*C* 13025) as 'ein pfaffe wol gelêrt'. Klinschor's character rests on a misunderstanding of a statement by Chrestien (see Klinschor), a mistake which Heinrich did not make, so that the whole character of G. is nobler than that of Klinschor. As his knowledge of astronomy implies, G. is a magician, and when Gawein arrives at his castle to recover Sgoidamur's bridle, he is permitted to strike off G.'s head, which the magician simply picks up and puts back on again. In return, G. tests Gawein's courage by pretending twice to cut off the latter's head, but Gawein does not flinch. This is, of course, none other than the story of the well-known ME poem of *Sir Gawain and the Green Knight*, the motif being repeated also in *RP* (see Elyafres). Later (*C* 28405ff.) Gawein meets G.'s sister, who is unnamed. – *C* m8306ff. a13007ff. n13034f.

Gantitiers see Gues

Gaoles see Gâlôes

Gardibor 'von Saigatine', a warrior in Akarîn's army against Ipomidôn. – *JT* nm3625,2

Gardubose 'von Jochris', called 'der swartze', a warrior in Ipomidôn's army against Akarîn. – *JT* nm3233,5

Garedeas see Karadot

Gârel (1) brother of Gawein. G. is mentioned in *P*, where he is said to be Gawein's cousin and is stated to have been captured in a brush with the knights of Lôgrois as Arthur is on his way to witness the fight between Gawein and Gramoflanz. In Chrestien's *Perceval*, G. is Gawein's brother (spelt Garies, Garaes, and Guerhes), and as such he occurs frequently in the Vulgate Cycle. In the *Livre de Lancelot del Lac* he appears in a very unfavourable light, offering violence to a lady, whilst in the *Mort le Roi Artu* he takes part in the conspiracy to betray Lancelot, who accidentally slays him. In *RP*, G. assists Arthur against Bruns (1), where he is called Gerschiers (Guerrehès in Potvin), and later (*RP* 525,28) he appears as one of the knights who take part in the search for Parzivâl. On this occasion he is called Gyseres (Garahiés in Potvin). G. occurs in *E* as one of the knights at Arthur's court when Êrec returns with Ênîte, but he does not appear in the corresponding list in Chrestien's *Erec* and may be a later interpolation taken from *P*. In Malory he is called Gareth, whilst in the Vulgate Cycle his name is usually spelt Guerrehès. (See also Gârel (2).) – *E* 1650; *P* nm664,30; *RP* 22,26

Gârel (2) son of Meleranz and Lammîre (1). G. is educated at Arthur's court and returns there just after Meljaganz has abducted Ginovêr. He hears the challenge delivered by Karabîn and goes to spy out the land of Kanadic. He has adventures with Gilân, Eskilabôn, and Purdân, and frees Laudamîe, whom he marries, from a sea-monster, Vulgân, which carries a petrifying shield. G. then collects a huge army and leads it against Ehkunat, who is defeated and captured and taken to Arthur. On his return journey to Laudamîe, G. arranges numerous marriages between those whom he has helped. (Cf. *TF* for the general outline of the story.) A knight named Karel is present at Arthur's court in *TF* and *GM*, and after making due allowances for the greater popularity of Wolfram's work, it seems more probable that G., the hero of a poem of a recent date,[24] is the knight referred to. In *TF*, moreover, Karel is 'muomen sun' to Antikonîe, a relationship which is impossible to the cousin or brother of Gawein. G. is called 'von dem blüenden Tal', but this appears to be merely in imitation of Daniel (1) and has no significance in the poem. – *G* a94f. n115; *TF* 1697; *GM* (MS I) 3861 (MS D) 3857[10]

Gârel (3) 'künec', a knight who is mentioned in *P* as having thrown a lion from the palace at Nantes. From the same source we learn that G. also fetched a knife which caused him suffering in a marble pillar. We have no further knowledge of the adventure to which Wolfram is alluding, but it seems to bear a superficial resemblance to an adventure undergone by Boort, when he visits the Perilous Palace and there slays a lion and is wounded by a lance in the Vulgate Lancelot. (Cf. also Gawein's visit to the Schastel Marveile in *P*.) Martin is of the opinion that G. is the same character as the 'künec von Mirmidône', an old knight who is kept a prisoner by Rôaz, who makes him act as door-keeper.[25] G. is slain by Wigalois as the latter is effecting an entry into the castle. – *P* nm583,12; *Wigl* a7090 n8625ff.

Gareles see Caroes

Gârez 'von Lîbîâ', cousin of Lâr and father of Lîamêre. – *Wigl* nm9874ff.

Gariell 'von Payerlant', oppressor of Thedalus. He is slain by Paris. – *GT* 2577ff.

Garîôle wife of Nampêtenîs (q.v.). In the OF prose *Tristan* she is called Gargeolain, which Singer thinks is possibly an oblique case of Gargeole.[26] *UT* has Cassie, a form which, according to Golther, was copied by Heinrich in *HT*.[27] – *ET* 7872f.; *UT* m2858 n2877 a2972; *HT* nm5753ff. a5849f.

Garlîn 'künec von Galore', father of Ginovêr and Gotegrîn. In the Vulgate Cycle, Ginovêr's father is Leodegan. – *C* nm590

Garmoreth see Gamorett

Garredoin a knight who is present at Arthur's court when Êrec returns with Ênîte. This name does not appear in the corresponding list of knights in Chrestien's *Erec*, and Singer is of the opinion that it is a later interpolation based on Garedeas.[28] – *E* 1666

Garriel see Gariell

Garsalas 'des herzogen sun von Genelogen lant', *ami* of Trischans. G. is a knight who is defeated by Parzivâl. The name is spelt the same way in Gautier, and Brugger[29] identifies him with the Hontzlake of Malory, tracing the name through its various stages of Ganselas > Ganslas > Onslac > Hontzlake. (See also Garschiloie.) – *RP* a425,34ff. n430,13

Garsidis 'künec von Kamarîe', father of Tydomîe. G. dies young, followed shortly afterwards by his wife, Lambore, who dies of a broken heart. – *M* nm7675f.

Garschiloie 'vrouwe von Gruonlant'. (Schulz derived this name from OF *garce*, 'young girl, virgin', and *loi*, 'law'.[30] Bartsch thinks it was taken by Wolfram from *ET*, where, in the Heidelberg MS and the prose version, Garîôle appears as Gardiloie.[31] Golther accepts this

---

24 *G* was written *circa* 1260, *TF circa* 1280, and *GM circa* 1305, whilst *P* was certainly completed by *circa* 1210.
25 Martin (1), p. 420, to 583,12.
26 Singer (1), p. 61.
27 Golther (2), p. 96.
28 Singer (1), p. 60.
29 Brugger (2), p. 18.
30 Schulz, 'Eigennamen', p. 392.
31 Bartsch (2), p. 126.

view,[32] which is opposed by Singer, who thinks the likeness is coincidental only.[33] Martin draws attention to the Spanish name Garcilaso,[34] whilst Brugger thinks that it is derived from Garsalas (q.v.) de Guenelande, Wolfram mistaking the father's name for the name of the girl.[35]) G. is one of the maidens who tend the Graal. In *JT* she is said to be the daughter of the king of India, and is chosen to succeed Repanse de Schoie as bearer of the Graal. – *P* nm255,9 a806,14; *JT* 5915,2

Gartes see Carnîz

Garvilune 'herzoge von Terrimare', a knight who is present at a tourney held by Arthur. – *JT* 2039,1

Gaskâne 'künec von' (*P*), see Hardîs

Gaschier 'von Normandie'. (Schulz suggested < OF *gagier*, 'saisir, engager', or from the noun *gagier*, 'gagement, promesse'.[36] Bartsch sees in it the Provençal *gagier, gatgier*, 'pledge',[37] whilst Martin favours the view that it comes from the OF name Gauchier, Walter.[38] Golther considers that the name still awaits a satisfactory explanation.[39]) G. is a member of the army besieging Patelamunt. He is defeated by Gahmuret and sent back to his army to prevent the Scots from taking any further part in the fight. He is present at the tourney held by Arthur in *JT*. – *P* nm25,13f. a38,16f.; *JT* 1986,2

Gaskôn 'künec von' (*P*), see Hardîs

Gasosîn 'von Strangot', a knight who is present at Arthur's court when Êrec returns with Ênîte. He occurs in Chrestien's *Erec* [1710] as Garravains (MS E: Gasoras) d'Estrangot. In *C*, where he is called Gasozein de Dragôz, he rides in mid-winter, clad only in his shirt, to prove his love for Ginovêr, who taunts Arthur with this fact. The latter goes to look for G., who unhorses Arthur's three companions and cedes only to Arthur when he learns who he is. G. claims to have been Ginovêr's first *ami* and contends that she still loves him. It is left to Ginovêr to decide which she wants, and she chooses Arthur. G. later rescues Ginovêr from Gotegrîn but immediately evinces designs upon her honour, which are prevented only by the timely arrival of Gawein, who severely wounds him after a fierce fight. G. occurs in most of the romances of the Vulgate Cycle and is the villain in the *Vengeance de Raguidel*. Brugger points out that Gosangos abducts Ginovêr in exactly the same way as G. in the *Estoire de Merlin* (Vulgate Cycle), and considers that the similarity in the names led to a confusion of the deed (cf. Bagumades).[40] – *E* 1647; *C* m3395ff. a3694 n4775

Gasozein see Gasosîn

Gastablê 'künec von Kômîs', one of the group of 15 Saracen kings who attack Willehalm (1) at the end of the first battle at Alischanz. G. is wounded or killed by Willehalm in that encounter. [See Appendix (9).] G. occurs in *Aliscans* as Gasteblé, rois de Sarragosse, and appears also in *Li Covenans Vivien* and in the *Chancun de Willame* as Wanibled. – *W* m71,22 a72,17f. n74,5 [†]

Gasterne 'küneginne von', *muome* of Tydomîe. – *M* nm3924f.

---

32 Golther (1), p. 158.
33 Singer (1), p. 61.
34 Martin (1), p. 232, to 255,9.
35 Brugger (2), p. 18.
36 Schulz, 'Eigennamen', p. 404.
37 Bartsch (2), p. 137.
38 Martin (1), p. 36, to 25,14.
39 Golther (1), p. 141.
40 Brugger (2), pp. 42f.

Gatschier see Gaschier

Gatschiloe see Garschiloie

Gaudîers 'von Tuluse', a knight who is captured by Halzebier when he is going to the rescue of Vîvîans. G. is, however, omitted from the list of knights who are released by Rennewart, although the list (416,10) includes Hûwes, whose capture has not been mentioned. In *UW*, where he is called Gautiers, G. assists Lôîs against Terramêr. G. occurs in all of the OF *chansons de geste* of the Guillaume d'Orange cycle. – *W* 15,3; *UW* 46,1

Gaudîn (1) 'de Montein', a knight who is captured by Gawein at the tourney held to celebrate Êrec's wedding. So also in Chrestien's *Erec*. – *E* 2752ff.

Gaudîn (2) 'von Spangenlant', a knight who attends Meliûr's tourney with Partonopier. G. also helps the latter in his battle against the Soldan. – *PM* a13090 n13178

Gaudîn (3) 'der brûne', a knight who is captured by Halzebier when he is going to the rescue of Vîvîans. He is later released by Rennewart. In *UW* he assists Lôîs against Terramêr. G. occurs in *Aliscans* and a number of other *chansons de geste* of the Guillaume d'Orange cycle. – *W* 15,1; *UW* 46,1

Gaudine see Gandîn (1)

Gaueros 'von Rabedic', a knight who is present at Arthur's court when Êrec returns with Ênîte. In *C*, where he is called Cauterous von Solaz, he is one of the knights who spill Priure's cup of chastity. Both references to G. originate in Chrestien's *Erec* (1721), where he is called Caverons (var. Cauerrons) de Robendic (see Rebedinch). – *E* 1654; *C* 2310

Gaumerans see Gresmurs

Gaumeranz see Gâmeranz

Gauriel 'von Muntabel', also called 'der ritter mit dem bock'. G. loses the favour of his lady, a fairy, through boasting of her to a mortal woman (cf. Seyfrid). He learns that to regain her love he must take three of Arthur's bravest knights captive to her land. He pitches a tent outside Arthur's court, unhorses many of the knights, and takes captive Gawein, Walban, and Îwein (1), the last named after a fierce fight in which Îwein's lion and G.'s buck both take part and are killed. Êrec goes with G. and his captives and after overcoming many dragons and giants they eventually reach G.'s *amie*, and the two are reconciled. After they are married, G. obtains leave to go to Arthur's court for a year (cf. *I*), at the end of which period his wife arrives at the court. – *GM* a33ff. n1012

Gautiers see Gaudîers

Gafyens a knight who steals Dodines' *amie*. Parzivâl rescues her and compels G. to surrender himself to Arthur. In the Mons MS of Manessier, G. is called Gaulïien. – *RP* a757,16 n777,35

Gaviol a merchant who is sent by Tristan to fetch Îsolt (2) to heal his poisoned wound. – *UT* 3301ff.

Gaffirdir 'künec von Agrippe', standard-bearer to the heathen army under Gêrfridolt. G. is captured when the heathen army is put to flight. – *Loh* 4951ff.

Gâwân see Gawein

Gâwânides 'lifort', son of Wigalois and Larîe. – *Wigl* a11626ff. n11639

Gawein (Geoffrey of Monmouth calls him Walgainus, Walguainus. This name seems to be derived from the OF form, Gauvain,[41] rather than from the Welsh, Gwalchmei.[42])
G. appears in Geoffrey as a brave knight who distinguishes himself in the battle against

---

[41] Bruce (1), I, p. 21, note.

[42] Hertz quotes Rhys as deriving this name from Kymric *gwalch*, 'falcon', i.e. *Gwalchmei* 'Mayfalcon' (Wolfram von Eschenbach, *Parzival*, transl. by W. Hertz, p. 512).

Lucius and who is killed whilst fighting for Arthur against Mordred. Some sort of legend had, no doubt, already crystallized around his name by the time Chrestien wrote *Erec*, as, although he does nothing of note in this poem, he is enumerated as the bravest of the knights.[43] In *Cliges* and *Yvain*, as also in *Perceval*, Chrestien uses him as a touchstone of the hero's prowess, a capacity in which he appears in a number of the MHG romances. G. engages in undecided fights with the hero of the romance in *I, L, DB, HT*, and, of course, *P*; in all except *L* the combatants are ignorant of the identity of their opponent, and the fight is stopped as soon as this is revealed.

In Chrestien's *Perceval* and *Conte de la Charrette*, G. appears in a light scarcely inferior to that of the hero, and this is the rôle which he plays in nearly all of the MHG epics, the fashion being probably set by *I* and *P*. In the latter poem, where he is called Gâwân, his part is not only secondary to that of the hero, but is also contrasted with it. Valiant and courteous and skilful as he is, his character lacks the depth which characterizes Parzivâl, and in the facility with which he falls in love Miss Weston sees the ultimate cause of the degradation of his character which is so marked in the OF prose romances.[44]

In *P* he is challenged by Kingrimursel on behalf of Vergulaht, who wishes to avenge the death of his father, who, he thinks, was killed by G. On his way to accept the challenge, G. is persuaded by Obilôt (q.v.) to fight for Lipaôt. At Vergulaht's court he makes advances to the latter's sister, Antikonîe, which place him in a dangerous position, from which he escapes only with difficulty. He undertakes to search for the Graal, and during the quest he meets and falls in love with Orgelûse (q.v.), whose advances Parzivâl had scorned. He successfully withstands the dangers of the Schastel Marveile and eventually marries Orgelûse. The continuation is told in *RP*,[45] where he visits the Graal Castle but fails to join together the two pieces of the Graal sword; he then goes to fight Vergulaht's champion, Kingrimursel, but the fight is averted at the last minute by Arthur. G. then finds Gylorette in a tent and begets on her a son, Gingelens. He is challenged by Gylorette's brother, Brandelis (q.v.), but in consideration of G.'s weak state (he has been wounded in the war between Arthur and Bruns (1)), it is agreed that they shall fight whenever they next meet. This proves to be when Arthur is taking a band of knights to the rescue of Gifles, and a fierce fight is stopped by Gylorette, who holds G.'s son between the combatants. (This episode is the subject of the ME poem, *Jeaste of Syr Gawayne*.[46])

Another version of the birth of Gawein's son is told in *Wigl* (which appears to come from a common source with the OF *Li Biaus Descouneus*; from this latter poem comes the ME *Libeaus Desconus*). In this poem, G. is defeated by Jôram (2), who takes him back to his land, where G. marries Jôram's niece, Flôrîe (2), and by her has Wigalois. G. leaves his wife to return to Arthur's court, but without a certain magic girdle he is unable to find his way back. In only two MHG epics is G. defeated in single combat, by Jôram in *Wigl* and by Gauriel in *GM*.

Heinrich has made him the hero of *C*, a poem which is certainly not a translation of one OF poem but seems to be a combination of several. G. is riding to the assistance of Flôis, when, after defeating four knights at the castle of Riwalin (2), he is led by Aclamet to Amurfinâ, who gives him a drink of forgetfulness, so that he stays with her until the effects of the potion wear off. In the meantime he sleeps in the same bed as Amurfinâ, whose chastity is,

---

43   *Erec*,1691f.: 'Devant toz les buens chevaliers / Doit estre Gauvains li premiers.'
44   Weston (1), p. 10.
45   In this poem occurs the feature that Gawein's strength waxes and wanes with the sun (cf. Lanzelet).
46   Madden, pp. 207ff.

however, guarded by a sword which hangs over the bed and which wounds G. when he attempts to violate her (this episode occurs in the OF *Le Chevalier à l'Epée*). After fifteen days, G. leaves Amurfinâ and fights successively Reimambram, Galaas, and Assiles. On his way back to Arthur's court he rescues Ginovêr from Gasosîn, but is severely wounded and lies ill for months. He has hardly recovered when Sgoidamûr arrives at the court in search of a champion who will recover the bridle of her mule from Amurfinâ. After the failure of Keiî, G. undertakes this adventure, which leads him through a fearful valley, past savage monsters, and over a perilous bridge (cf. Parzivâl's passage over a perilous bridge with a bridle etc. given to him by the Graal maiden in *RP*). At the castle of Gansguoter (q.v.), he has to prove his courage and prowess; he is invited to cut off Gansguoter's head on the condition that he will submit to having his own cut off on the following day. Three times does the magician pretend to deal the blow to strike off G.'s head, but G. does not flinch. (Cf. *Gawain and the Green Knight, La Mule sanz Frain*, and Karadot in *RP*. Miss Weston has paralleled this incident with Cuchulinn's adventure in *Fled Bricrend*.[47]) After other trials at Gansguoter's castle, G. finds Amurfinâ, whom he brings back to Arthur's court and marries. The bridle is restored to Sgoidamûr. (This adventure is obviously based on the OF *La Mule sanz Frain* (told also in the Dutch *Lancelot*), whilst a similar story is told in Marie de France's *lai, Tyolet*. Miss Weston points out the close similarity which this story bears to the journey of Cuchulinn to win Emer, the daughter of the magician, Forgall.[48]) As Arthur and his knights are on their way to a tourney, G. wanders off on his own and spends the night in the Graal Castle, which vanishes in the morning. He is misdirected by Giramphiel and has to kill a dragon, and then, with the aid of Seimerac, he overcomes the magician, Laamorz, after which he pays a symbolic visit to the court of Vrou Sælde and her son, Heil. He then goes to Leigamar's tourney, and from here onwards the story is that of Chrestien's *Perceval*, only the names being altered, up to the point where Gramoflanz marries Itonjê. G. then leaves Arthur's court to take his revenge on Giramphiel and Fimbeus, after which he again visits the Graal Castle, and asks the question regarding the meaning of the wonders which he sees and thus breaks the spell. The Castle vanishes, leaving only the maidens who were tending the Graal.

In the OF prose romances (excluding *Perlesvaus*), G.'s character becomes worse and worse as Lanzelet displaces him as the most brilliant of the knights at Arthur's court. In the MHG epics, however, he retains his position throughout. Already in *ET*, G. is called Walwân, and his name appears in this form in *E* and *L* (also Wâlwein), but in *GM*, Walwan is taken to be a separate knight (see Walwân (2)). In *Sey* he is called Gaban, in *Ll* Gabin, whilst in *Wigm* appear: Gabwein (2708), Balban (2460), Gaban (2797), and Walban (3233), all of whom are probably identical with G. In *JT* the form Bauban appears.
– *ET* 5026f.; *L* 2311f.; *E* 1152; *I* 73; *Wigl* 343; *Mtl* 421; *P* nm66,15 a221,7; *DB* 254f.; *W* nm403,20; *C* nm701 a860ff.; *S* I,18; *Edol* A,11; *Wigm* 2708; *FD* nm1520,1; *G* 74; *JT* a1353,1 n1773,4; *M* nm151 a2391; *TF* 598; *Sey* nm5,1f. a52,5; *Loh* nm459; *UA* nm14670; *HT* a1692 n1847; *RB* nm8931; *GM* nm848 a1288; *RP* nm Prol.183 a1,1; *FS* nm4817; *Ll* 42,1 (MS K) 13,1 [†]

Gawen see Gawein
Gawîn (1)   father of Henec. G. is not mentioned in Chrestien's *Erec*. – *E* nm1671
Gawin (2), **Gawon** see Gawein
Gebert   'grâve von Artaiz', a knight who fights on the side of the Christians in the final battle against the heathens. – *WO* 17006f.

---

47   Weston (1), p. 93.
48   Weston (1), p. 29.

Gêdêôn biblical (Gideon), the Hebrew judge and warrior. – nm *A* 17268; *UW* 276,31; *JT* 2511,4; *UA* 7167; *RB* 15843

Gediens 'von Karedonas und Trefferîn', father of Dulceflûr (1). G. is slain by Verangôz, who then oppresses Dulceflûr. – *M* m4852 n7149

Gehires see Guivreiz

Geldipant 'künec', a knight who is slain by Gauriel and his companions. – *GM* 3760

Geloars brother of Hiutegêr, he fights for Orilus against Schîonatulander. – *JT* 4470,5

Gelpher 'Überwalt', a knight who is overcome by Lohengrîn in the battle between Karl (1) and the Hungarians. – *Loh* 2751

Gemelle 'künec von' (*WO*), see Meluchpat and Firmonis [†]

Gemyelder a knight who takes part in the battle between Atroclas and Paltriot. – *Wigm* 3738

Gemoreth see Gamorett

Genalî 'der von' (*UW*), see Zukander

Gener 'vrouwe von Kartîs', sister of Humildîs. G. assists Gawein across a torrent by freezing the water. In return she extracts a promise from him that he will do whatever she asks him. She is not, however, mentioned again in the romance. – *C* a14458 n14557

Gengemôr a knight of the Round Table who is unhorsed by Daniel (1). (Identical with Wigamur?) – *DB* 248

Genteflûr sister of Guivreiz, she heals Êrec's wounds. Guivreiz has two sisters in Chrestien, neither of whom is named. (Cf. Schenteflûrs.) – *E* a7207ff. n7787

Gentis a knight who attends Leigamar's tourney in the service of Aram. – *C* 18175

Gentrilurs 'der ûz' (*JT*), see Schenteflûrs

Genzian 'vrouwe', married by Seyfrid to the host who gives him shelter at Ardemont. – *Sey* 515,3ff.

Geometras a skilled magician who, in *Ed*, made the tomb of Kamille (1), whilst in *P*, where he is called Jêômetras, he is said to have constructed the magic pillar in the Schastel Marveile through which one could see the surrounding country. – *Ed* nm9404; *P* nm589,14 [†]

Geôn a warrior who is slain by Alexander whilst fighting for Dârîus at Erbela. So also in Gualterus, where his father is a Moor and his mother comes from a race of giants. Toischer has pointed out that in *UA*, G. is a combination of Feirefiz and Rennewart,[49] with a huge club, great speed, and parti-coloured skin (he is called (*UA* 13269) 'der ungefüege vêch gevar', and we are told (12074) 'wîz und swarz was der gevar'). – *UA* 12073

Georg (St. George) the patron saint of chivalry. G. was martyred on account of his opposition to the anti-christian policy of Diocletian, and was a Cappadocian by birth. It is probable, therefore, that it is G. who is intended when reference is made in *JT* to Ieori, who converted Cappadocia to Christianity. G. also seems to be intended in a reference to sente Jurie in *AP*, who is the only person who could save a doomed knight in battle;[50] this reference does not occur in the OF version. – nm *AP* A**,76; *FD* 460,6; *JT* 4746,1; *Mer* 17,6; *Sey* 470,7

Georie see Georg

Gêrant *ami* of Alîe and son of Gandêr, he is released by Dêmantîn when the latter kills Kanphyant. – *Dem* m4690 a4870 n4909

Gêrart 'von Blavî', a knight who is captured by Halzebier whilst he is endeavouring to rescue Vîvîans, and is later released by Rennewart. In *UW* he is also referred to as 'der von

---

49 Toischer, p. 356.

50 *AP* A**,76ff.: 'Do were sente Jurien/ Helfe not da gewesin/ Daz her were genesin', a rôle peculiarly appropriate for the patron saint of chivalry.

Blavi'. G. occurs in most of the OF *chansons de geste* of the Guillaume d'Orange cycle and in *Aliscans* is called Girars de Blaives. – *W* 13,15f.; *UW* a211,28 n323,11

Gerbolt a knight who accompanies Parzivâl after he leaves Gloris. – *JT* 5673,1

Gerhart (1) 'der guote', hero of a poem of that name by Rudolf von Ems. – nm *A* 3281; *RW* 15633

Gerhart (2) 'von Riviers', a knight who wishes to marry Sabîe (2). He attacks her father's castle each year and has slain her brother Kilpert, and he is about to attack once more, when Gârel appears as champion of Sabîe. Gârel unhorses and captures G., who later fights for his conqueror in the battle against Ehkunat, in which he is wounded by Helpherîch, whom he succeeds in capturing. – *G* nm1016 a1417

Gêrhart (3) see Gêrart

Gerion 'künec von Navarre', a knight who is unhorsed by Willehalm (4) at the tourney at Komarzi and also in the *vesperîe* before the tourney at Poys. – *RW* nm6186f. a6667

Germanz 'künec', one of the seven judges at Meliûr's tourney. – *PM* a13476 n13486

Gernomantz see Gurnemanz

Gerolt 'vürste von Schwauben', a knight who begged Karl (1) to be allowed to be the first of his knights to go into battle. Karl granted him and his descendants this privilege for ever. This character appears to have been invented by the author of *FS*, as the name does not occur in Langlois,[51] neither is there a person of this name in the MHG *Rolandslied*. – *FS* nm5741

Gerschiers see Gârel (1)

Gertrude 'sant', sister of Karl (1), died AD 659. – *E* nm4021

Gerunde 'grâve von' (*UW*), see Willekîn (1)

Gêrvalch chamberlain to Bêâmunt. – *Dem* a10066f. n10093

Gêrfridolt 'künec von Affrica'. G. leads a heathen army against Jôhan (4) and Jordanich. Heinrich (1) and Lohengrîn come to the aid of the Christians, and a great battle is fought, in which G. is badly wounded by Lohengrîn. He manages to make his escape, and his defeated army follows him. – *Loh* 4224

Gêrvrit 'künec von Arl', a knight who fights in the Christian army against Gêrfridolt. – *Loh* a3495 n4149

Gesparis 'künec von Jerichô', a knight who is slain by Prûn (1) whilst fighting for the heathens against the Christians. – *Loh* a4364 n4383

Geuarn 'von Dudel', a knight who takes part in the tourney held by Arthur for the crown of Deleprosat. – *Wigm* 2097f.

Gêûn 'von Turîe', apparently one of the ladies who help to bring up the young Lanzelet. Richter points out that the MSS vary in their spelling of G., and draws the conclusion that the passage was not understood by the writers.[52] By references to ll. 3273 and 4426f., he shows that the word intended by Ulrich is 'saben von Turîe' or 'Turkîe', 'saben' being a particularly fine kind of linen and clothes made from it. – *L* nm375

Gewellis litschoie see Lischois Gwelljus

*Gibelin see Kibelîns

Gîbert (1) 'künec von Sizilje', husband of Îblis. G. finds Klinschor in the arms of Îblis and has him rendered impotent. Singer, who uses the form Ibert, considers G. identical with Iweret (q.v.).[53] – *P* nm656,25f.

---

51 E. Langlois, *Tables des noms propres de toute nature compris dans les chansons de geste imprimées* (Paris, 1904).

52 Richter, p. 82.

53 Singer (1), pp. 116f.

Gîbert (2) son of Heimrich (1). He fights for Willehalm (1) in the second battle at Alischanz, and in *UW* he assists Lôîs against Terramêr. In the OF *chansons de geste*, G. is called Guibert d'Andernas and is thus identical with Schilbert (1) (q.v.). [See Appendix (4).] G. is, in the OF versions, the youngest of Heimrich's sons, and in *Les Narbonnais* Heimrich says that for that reason he will leave him all his land, but in *Guibert d'Andernas* he also is disinherited. – *W* a5,16f. n6,29; *UW* m4,14f. a21,1 n23,1 [†]

*Giblin see Kibelîns

Gîbôez 'der schahteliur von Kler', a warrior in Terramêr's army. G. is unhorsed whilst scouting and is later wounded by Rennewart in battle. Singer is of the opinion that G. is identical with Gîbûê (q.v.).[54] – *W* a333,16 n365,1

Gîbûê 'künec', slain in battle by Rennewart whilst fighting for Terramêr. In the opinion of Singer, G. is identical with Gîbôez (q.v.). – *W* 442,24

Gîburc daughter of Terramêr and wife of Willehalm (1) (q.v.). Before being baptised, she was called Arâbel and was the wife of Tîbalt, by whom she had a son, Ehmereiz. It is to recover G. that Terramêr is fighting Willehalm, but her belief in her new faith is so strong that she defends the castle alone whilst Willehalm has gone to seek aid. In the OF *chansons de geste* she is called Guibourc. – *W* 7,27ff.; *UW* m4,18 a58,16 n59,31; *R* nm Bl. II,128ff.; *JT* nm5929,4; *RB* nm9242; *FS* nm1402

Gielewast see Merlin (2)

Gierrart 'künec von Estylant', a knight who is wounded and captured by Willehalm (4) outside the town of Galverne whilst he is fighting for Witechin against Amelot. – *RW* nm10638f. a10740f.

Gîgamec a knight who is being pursued by Aamanz, whose brother G. has slain. The pursuit is interrupted by Zedoêch, who is defeated by Aamanz. Gawein arrives in time to prevent Aamanz from killing Zedoêch, but after defeating Aamanz, he leaves him in the hands of G. and Zedoêch, who treacherously cut off his head, which G. takes to Arthur's court, where he swears that it is the head of Gawein whom he has defeated in single combat. – *C* 16500

Gilâm see Gilân

Gilân 'herzoge von Swâles', a friend of Tristan. G. is the owner of a marvellous dog, Petitcriu, which Tristan obtains for Îsolt (2) by killing the giant Urgân, who has been oppressing G. G. occurs also in *G*, where he is called 'Gîlân (also Gilâm) von Gâles', and is defeated by Gârel, whom he takes to his brother-in-law, Retân, for whom Gârel promises to fight Eskilabôn. G. at the same time overcomes three of the latter's knights. He later acts as commander in Gârel's army against Ehkunat. – *Tn* 15773ff.; *G* a2150 n2194; *HT* nm3968

Gilbert 'künec von Airagun', a knight who is unhorsed by Willehalm (4) at the tourney at Komarzi. G. is also captured by Dietherich's men at the tourney at Poys, and takes part in the tourney held near Kurnoy. – *RW* nm6123 a6366ff.

Gilbertus a learned man. (= St. Gilbert, the founder of the monastic order of the Gilbertines?). – *Mer* nm36,7

Gilgen 'sante'. It is clear from the form in Gautier that the reference here is to St. Julien. – *RP* nm475,12

Gylien lant 'grâve von sant' (*RW*), see Wide

Gilimâr 'der wîse stumme', a knight who extends hospitality to Lanzelet and his comrades on their return from Plurîs. – *L* a6575 n6597

Gillamur 'künec von Waleis', nephew of Coradis. G. assists Amelot against Witechin. – *RW* 10838ff.

---

[54] Singer (2), p. 103.

106

Gillebert 'grâve von Clerimanz', a knight who is slain by Hector whilst fighting for the Greek army against the Trojans. This character was invented by Konrad. – *TK* 31289

Gillehelm see Gillelm

Gillelm 'von Francrîche', a knight who is present at the tournaments which are held at Komarzi, Poys, and near Kurnoy. – *RW* 5932ff.

Gillem see Gillelm

Giloles see Gifles

Gylorette sister of Brandelis (q.v.), she lies voluntarily with Gawein in her tent and by him has Gingelens (see Wigalois). The episode is described at the beginning of Pseudo-Gautier, and then retold (completely inaccurately) by Gawein some time later. On the first occasion, G. is called (*RP* 43,30) Aclervis, a name which rests on a misunderstanding of Pseudo-Gautier (12391): 'sa seror au cler vis'. When Gawein re-tells the story, he calls her G. (Glorìète in Pseudo-Gautier). – *RP* a35,22 n255,12

Gilot king of Jerusalem. G. is at first the overlord of Graf Rudolf, but later, owing to a quarrel which is not preserved in the extant fragments, he becomes Rudolf's opponent. – *GR* aBb,4 nFb,9

Gilstram 'künec', the first of the heathen kings to open Crispin's tourney. G. is unhorsed by Wildhalm. G. occurs in *P* (9,12) as the name of a land. – *WO* 14788

Gilules see Gifles

Gîmazet a knight who attends the tourney held by Leigamar in the service of Aram. – *C* 18168

Gymeanus natural son of Priam who fights for the Trojans against the Greeks. G. occurs in Benoît as Bruns de Gimel, the origin of which, according to Greif, is probably Brissonius, a name which appears in Hyginus.[55] – *LT* a4808 n4830

Gymêle 'von der Schitrîêle', a maiden attendant on Îsolt (2). She inspires the love of Kaedîn, who wishes to spend the night with her. She deceives him, however, by putting a magic pillow under his head which sends him to sleep immediately. The story is told in *ET*, in *UT*, where she is called Kamele, and in *HT*, where she is named Kamelîne von der Scheteliure. In a reference which is made to her in *P*, she is called 'G. von Monte Ribêle'. (Identical with Gimîle?) – *ET* a6454 n6469; *P* nm573,14f.; *UT* 1183; *HT* 4422ff.

Gimîle 'vrouwe', one of the ladies present at Arthur's court who spill Priure's cup of chastity. Since Îsolt is also present, it seems probable that G. is identical with Gymêle (q.v.). – *C* 1606

Gimoers see Gwinganiers

Ginabels a knight of the Round Table who joins in the search for Parzivâl. In Gautier he is called Guirabres. – *RP* 526,1

Gynganbertil, Ginganbertin see Kingrimursel

Gingelens see Wigalois

Gingemors father of Brangemor and husband of the fairy, Brangebart. In Pseudo-Gautier, G. is called Guingamuer, who is undoubtedly identical with Guingamor, the hero of the *lai* by Marie de France which bears his name, and who was likewise the husband of a fairy. There is, however, in Marie's *lai* no reference to a son, nor has the action any connection with Arthur's court. (See also Gwinganiers and Wigamur.) – *RP* nm312,29

Gyngeniers sister of Kardors. G. is loved by Alardins (q.v.), whose affection she does not return. She eventually marries Karadot (q.v.). In the Mons MS of Pseudo-Gautier she is called Guimer. – *RP* 59,1f.

Gyngenirs see Gyngeniers

---

55 Greif, pp. 26ff.

Gyngenor a maiden, the daughter of Itonjê and Gramoflanz. Ris and Cadoalans hold a tourney to decide which is to have her to wife, but at the tourney she sees and falls in love with Alardins, whom she marries. In the Mons MS of Pseudo-Gautier she is called Guinor, and in the Montpellier MS, Guigenor. In both she is the daughter of Gawein's sister, Clarissant. – *RP* a75,28f. n77,36

Gingenors see Gingemors

Gingrisine see Kingrisîn

Gynniers see Gyngeniers

Ginovêr (This name appears as Ganhumara and Guanhumara in Geoffrey of Monmouth, the Kymric form being Gwenhwyvar or Gwenhwyfar.[56] Schulz prefers the former form of the Kymric, which he translates as 'the Lady of the Vast Extension'.[57] The OF forms which occur are Ganièvre and Guenièvre, but, according to Hertz, it is from the Italian Ginevra that the MHG form, Ginovêr, is derived.[58])

For the most part, G., like most of the women in the MHG court epics (Wolfram's female characters are the only exceptions), is colourless and completely lacking in characterization. Interest in G. is, therefore, centred on two main points: her abduction, and her infidelity to Arthur. The second feature, which lends to her character all the distinction it possesses, is completely unknown to MHG literature, leaving only (with the possible exception of her rôle in *C*) a passive figure.

The oldest recorded account of G.'s abduction is that in Caradoc's *Vita Gildae*, in which she is abducted by Melwas (see Meljaganz) and rescued by Arthur. Chrestien's *Conte de la Charrette*, which was written only about a decade later, shows Lanzelet firmly established as rescuer and lover of the queen. Chrestien summarizes this story in *Yvain*, but Hartmann, in *I*, ignores Lanzelet completely. G.'s abduction is the theme of the bas-reliefs on the architrave of the Modena Cathedral, but in the castle with her is Malduc (see below), whilst one of the apparent rescuers is Îdêr, a knight who, in the OF romance *Yder*, is suspected by Arthur of being G.'s lover. Versions of the abduction story, with Meljaganz as the abductor, appear in *I*, *C*, and *G*. In *L* the abductor is Valerîn, and G. is rescued by the magic arts of Malduc (see Maldwîz).

C is the only one of the MHG romances in which there is any tangible characterization of G. She taunts Arthur with the fact that Gasosîn is riding in mid-winter, clad only in his shirt, to prove his love for her. When she is confronted with the choice of Gasosîn or Arthur, she elects to stay with the latter; but when later she is abducted by Gasosîn, she does not appear to condemn his unchaste advances as wholeheartedly as the circumstances would seem to require. Nor does she successfully stand the chastity tests, of the cloak in *Mtl*, of Priure's cup and Giramphiel's glove in *C*. Only in these two poems, both incidentally by the same author, does any suspicion attach to G. regarding her infidelity to Arthur in MHG literature. The story of G.'s infidelity is first met with in Geoffrey of Monmouth, where she enters into a voluntary union with Mordred. Wace, of course, followed Geoffrey, but with the advent of Lanzelet into Arthurian literature, G.'s voluntary compliance with Mordred's desires became a thing of the past. In *MA*, G. is portrayed as a perfect example of pure womanly love and fidelity, and she dies of a broken heart after waiting for the return of Arthur from Avalon for eleven years after his death.

– *L* m1277 an2276f.; *E* a14 n5100; *I* a59; *Wigl* a222 n514; *Mtl* a137 n208; *P* nm143,22 a149,2; *DB* 8064f.; *C* m424 an551; *MA* m163; *Wigm* a2549; *G* a55 n19460; *UW* m255,21;

---

56 Wolfram von Eschenbach, *Parzival*, transl. by W. Hertz, p. 495.
57 Schulz, 'Eigennamen', p. 395.
58 Wolfram von Eschenbach, *Parzival*, transl. by W. Hertz, p. 495.

JT a1416,1 n1763,1; *M* a2049 n2801; *TF* a205 n234; *Sey* a260,5f.; *Mer* a261,5 n267,5; *Loh* a421; *GM* a459; *RP* nm36,38f. a55,4; *Ll* a26,1 (MS K) a13,1

Ginses a knight who is captured by Gawein at the tourney held to celebrate Êrec's marriage. G. occurs in Chrestien's *Erec* [2226] as Guincel, and in *C*, where he is present at Arthur's court and spills Priure's cup of chastity, as Quînas (MS V: Guinas). – *E* 2752f.; *C* 2344

Gîot a messenger sent by Lanzelet to Genewîs to announce his coming. – *L* 8154

Gipones see Gipponeis

Gipponeis 'künec von Ukkerlant', a knight present at a tourney held by Arthur. Gippones occurs in *P* (205,10) as the territorial name of Galogandres, whilst Ukerlant (*P* 205,14) is the territorial name of Nârant. – *JT* 1990,6f.

Girabob a heathen commander in Halap's army. – *GR* δ,18

Giramphiel see Giranphiel

Girant 'von Purdel', a knight who is killed by Purrel whilst fighting for Willehalm (1) at the second battle at Alischanz. G. occurs in the OF *Aliscans* and in the *Chancun de Willame* as Girart de Bordel. – *W* 428,25f.

Giranphiel 'ein rîchiu fei'. G. and her sister made a magic girdle which renders the wearer incapable of suffering defeat. Gawein, at the command of Ginovêr, obtains it from Fimbeus, for whom it was made, and Ginovêr gives it to Gasosîn. Gawein stays at G.'s castle, not knowing who she is, and she, to avenge Fimbeus, tells Gawein that there is a small dragon in the neighbourhood, but the latter finds, when he comes to kill it, that it is a huge monster. He succeeds, however, in killing it, though not without great difficulty. G. later sends a glove of chastity to Arthur's court, which renders invisible the right half of the body of the chaste who wear it. All the ladies try it on, but none succeeds in becoming completely invisible on the right-hand side. A knight then arrives from G. with the other glove, and succeeds by a trick in obtaining from Gawein the stone on which the efficacy of the magic girdle depends. Gawein immediately goes to G.'s castle, where he defeats Fimbeus and obtains the girdle and gloves. – *C* nm4885 a15023

Gyrart see Gierrart

Gîremelanz see Gramoflanz

Girot (1) 'grâve', a knight who tries to compel Mundirosa to marry him. Seyfrid appears on the scene just in time to fight for Mundirosa, and kills G. – *Sey* m443,5 an468,1

Girot (2) see Kyrot

Girrat see Gierrart

Gysel sister of Heinrich (2), she marries Steffan. – *Loh* nm7541f.

Gyselbreht 'der Lutringe', cousin of Elsam. G. marries the daughter of Heinrich (1) and fights with Lohengrîn against the heathens. – *Loh* a729 n2591

Gyseres see Gârel (1)

Gypfelt see Gifles

Gifleiz 'grâve', a knight who fights for Willehalm (1) against Terramêr in the second battle at Alischanz. He jousts with Sînagûn. Singer is of the opinion that Wolfram took this name from *Erec*.[59] – *W* 369,27f.

Gifles 'li fils Do', a knight who is present at Arthur's court when Êrec returns with Ênîte. He is first mentioned in Chrestien's *Erec* [1729], where he is called Girflez li fiz Do, which, in Hartmann's *Erec*, is distorted to 'fil Dou Giloles', whilst in *C*, where he is one of the knights at Arthur's court and spills Priure's cup of chastity, he is called Gofrei. In *RP* the name appears as Gypfelt, Giflet, and Gifles, and he assists Arthur against Bruns (1), and is present at the tourney held by Ris. He is also imprisoned in Schastel Orgelus, for which he

---

[59] Singer (2), pp. 109f.

undertakes to search in Chrestien's *Perceval*, and from which he is rescued by Arthur and his knights.

Most scholars are agreed that G. is identical with Jofreit fiz Îdœl, who appears in *P*,[60] and Miss Weston points out that Jofreit is said by Arthur to have been captured by the knights of Logrois (in the service of Orgeluse), whilst in Gautier he is imprisoned in Schastel Orgelluse. Bartsch agrees that G. and Jofreit are probably the same person,[61] and holds that Wolfram did not attempt to reproduce Gifles, but substituted Jofreit, the Normanic form of Jeoffroi, 'sicherlich Guiot folgend'.[62] From the form Gofrei which appears in *C*, it would seem possible that some of the MSS may have made the alteration already in the OF. In *JT* the name occurs as Iofret fis Idele (1976,5: 'iofret fisidele').

Richter identified G. also with Guivreiz (q.v.), but by asserting that the latter was unknown to Wolfram, he denied, in effect, the identification of G. with Jofreit.[63] G. plays an important part in the OF romances, and is the last to be with the dying Arthur, who gives him his sword to cast back into the lake. – *E* 1663; *P* 277,4; *C* 2321; [*JT* 1976,5;] *RP* 44,45f. [†]

Giflet see Gifles

Givreiz see Guivreiz

Giwanet (< OF Yonet? Cf. Îwânet.) G. is a squire who is sent by Flôis to get help from Arthur. He meets Gawein, who sets off to succour Flôis. – *C* 5638ff.

Gkakotholes see Glockotheles

Gladensch a knight of the Round Table who was brought up in a forest. He is one of those who join in the search for Parzivâl. In Gautier, G. is called Gladouains, and he also occurs in the Vulgate *Lancelot*, where his death is avenged by Lanzelet. – *RP* 525,28

Glais 'künec'. A tourney is announced, but not described, in which G. and Riwalîn (3) are the protagonists. – *C* nm3208ff.

Glackotheles, Glakotelsfloir, Glacotesflorir see Glockotheles

*Glangodoans see Grangodoans

Glancon see Glaucus (1)

Glauca mother of Antides by Ajax (1). So also in Benoît. – *LT* nm16902

Glaucon a warrior in the Trojan army against the Greeks. In *LT* he is called 'künec von Syze' and is the brother of Sarpedon and father of Fion, whilst in *TK* he is called Glaukûn von Lîciâ. He appears in Benoît as Glaucus de Lize, in Dares as Glaucus e Lycia, and in Homer as Glaucus of Likia, where he is cousin to Sarpedon. In Benoît he is said to have been slain by the Greeks, and is therefore probably the Glaucus who, in Dictys and in *TKf* (43220ff.), is slain by Ajax (1). – *LT* 3989; *TK* 29714f.

Glaukûn see Glaucon

Glaucus (1) son of Antenor. G. fights in the Trojan army against the Greeks and is slain by Pirrus in *LT* and Benoît, whilst in *TKf* and Dictys he is slain by Agâmennon. G. does not occur in Homer. – *LT* 14841; *TKf* 43071

Glaucus (2) a warrior in Alexander's army against Porrus. So also in Gualterus, to whom the name may have been suggested by Glaucus Aetolus, who occurs in Dârîus's army in *Expeditio Alexandri*. – *UA* 19683

Glaucus (3) see Glaucon

---

60 Golther (1), p. 192.
61 Bartsch (2), p. 118.
62 Bartsch (2), p. 135.
63 Richter, p. 100.

Gletechleflors a knight who is present at the tourney held by Arthur for the crown of Deleprosat. – *Wigm* 2079

Glecidolân one of the rulers of dwarf-land who accompany Bîlêî to Êrec's wedding. This name appears in Chrestien's *Erec* [2005] as Glecidalan, and occurs in *C* as Glotigaran, where he is one of the knights who spill Priure's cup of chastity. – *E* 2112; *C* 2343

Gligoras see Grigoras

Glôbâris the governor of Persîpolis, which he surrendered to Alexander. So also in Curtius Rufus, where he is called Gobaris. – *A* 14131

Glockotheles 'Floyr', the first knight to meet Wigamur after the latter has found his suit of armour. They fight, and G. is overcome. – *Wigm* 555

Gloramatis 'von Persia', a commander in Akarîn's army against Ipomidôn. The name appears also as Cloramatis and Gloromatis. – *JT* nm3069,1 [†]

Glorasmeis 'von Rabs', an old knight who thought he was going to die and therefore gave his sword to Schîonatulander. G. did not die then, however, and regretted parting with his sword. – *JT* nm3482,5

Gloraxidus 'von Amatiste' (also 'von Amantiste'). A commander in Akarîn's army against Ipomidôn. – *JT* 3146,1

Gloriamantine see Gloramatis

Glorian a warrior in Akarîn's army against Ipomidôn. G. is the father of Gloramatis. – *JT* nm3071,4

Glôrîax son of Terramêr, for whom he fights against Willehalm (1) at Alischanz. G., who appears as Clariäus in *Aliscans*, occurs in most of the *chansons de geste* of the Guillaume d'Orange cycle. – *W* a29,18f. n32,15

Glôrîôn (1) 'künec', a warrior who is slain by Vîvîans whilst fighting for Terramêr at Alischanz. So also in the OF *Aliscans*. – *W* 27,6

Glôrîôn (2) 'künec von Askalon', a warrior who fights under the command of Aropatîn for Terramêr in the second battle at Alischanz. G. does not occur in *Aliscans* and is probably an imitation by Wolfram of Glôrîôn (1). – *W* 348,27f. [†]

Gloris husband of Pardiscale, from whom she was stolen by Klinschor. After the rescue of his wife by Parzivâl, G. entertains the latter at his castle for a short while. – *JT* m5538,1ff. n5549,1 a5563,6

Glorisibais 'von Satrois', a warrior in Akarîn's army against Ipomidôn. – *JT* 3123,3f.

Gloromatis see Gloramatis

Glotigaran see Glecidolân

Goafilroet son of Angwisiez, with whom he attends the wedding of Êrec. In Chrestien's *Erec* (1972) G. is called Cadret. – *E* 1976

Gobal see Gaball

Godeles natural son of Priam. G. fights in the Trojan army against the Greeks. In Benoît he is called Hugodelez (var. Godeles (9895)). – *LT* a4808 n4834

Godefrit 'von Swavenlant', counsellor to the kaiser, and the first person whom Gayol and his friends meet on joining the kaiser's court. – *Crane* 49ff.

Godonas 'von Terrandes', a knight who is defeated and killed by Meleranz after a hard fight. G. was a brave fighter, but cruel, and kept 600 captured knights and 400 captured women doing rough work for him. They were released by Meleranz, who succeeded G. as king of the land. – *M* nm4469 a5832

Gog biblical, referred to in *UA* as the name of a king of the tenth tribe of Israel. In Ezekiel 38, G. is called the chief prince of Meshech and Tubal. G. is referred to in *SA* as the name of a land. – *UA* nm20903

Gogaris see Gorgaris

Goldemâr 'kaiserliches getwerc', the protagonist in the MHG poem which bears his name. G. abducts a maiden, who is recovered by Dietrich von Bern. – *RB* nm25274

Gôlîam 'künec von Belestigweiz', a warrior who is killed by Rennewart whilst fighting for Terramêr at Alischanz. A warrior called 'der von Palestigweise' occurs in *JT* (3621,1), but his name is not given. G. occurs in *Aliscans* as Golias de Balesguez, and in the *Chancun de Willame*. – *W* a423,2 n432,22 [†]

Golias biblical (Goliath), the Philistine giant who was slain by David. – nm *E* 5564; *G* 410; *JT* 2881,5; *UA* 11537; *RB* 7734

***Gollîam** see Gôlîam

Golodîas according to *UA*, he was left in Jerusalem by Nâbuchodônosor after the latter had taken most of the Israelites to Babylon. – *UA* nm1026

Gôorz see Gurnemanz

Gorbedin 'Porsidanden', a warrior in Ipomidôn's army against Akarîn. – *JT* 3320,1

Gorgaris a knight who abducts Malolehat. The latter is rescued by her brother, Marguns, who imprisons G. for seven years. G. occurs (spelt in the same way) in Manessier. – *RP* nm700,34ff. a701,13

Gorgatân a warrior who is compelled by Amintas (1) to join Alexander. So also in Curtius Rufus, where he is called Gorgidas. – *A* nm20145

Gorgîas a warrior who is compelled by Amintas (1) to join Alexander. So also in *Expeditio Alexandri* and Curtius Rufus. – *A* nm20144

Gorgone son of Saladres, with whom he attacks Gawein. G. is defeated. In the Mons MS of Manessier, G. is called Gogonne, whilst in the Montpellier MS he is named Corgone. – *RP* a842,6 n844,45

Gorhant 'künec', he comes with an army from his land near Ganjas (Ganges) to fight for Terramêr. His men have horn skins and fight on foot with steel clubs, with which they cause great havoc among the French knights. Of the OF *chansons de geste*, G. occurs only in *Aliscans*. – *W* 35,10f.

Gôrîax 'künec von Kordubin', one of the group of 15 Saracen kings who attack Willehalm (1) at the end of the first battle at Alischanz. G. is wounded or killed by Willehalm in that encounter. [See Appendix (9).] G. occurs in *Aliscans* as Ariaus. – *W* m71,22 a72,17f. n74,9 [†]

Gormigdalus 'herzoge von Entalîe', a warrior in the Greek army against the Trojans. This character was invented by Konrad. – *TK* 31836

Gornemanz, Gornomanz Côorz see Gurnemanz

Gors 'künec von' (*P*), see Bademagun

Gossengos a knight who fights for Arthur against Bruns (1). So also in Pseudo-Gautier. G. also occurs in Gerbert's continuation to *Perceval* and the *Livre d'Artus*. In *L'Estoire de Merlin* (Vulgate Cycle) G. abducts Ginovêr in the same way as does Gasosîn in *C*. Brugger considers that the similarity in the names caused a confusion of the deeds of the two, who could not be one and the same, as both names occur in *L'Estoire de Merlin*.[64] – *RP* 22,29

Gotegrîn 'grâve von Galôre', son of Garlîn and brother of Ginovêr. In *C*, G. is disgusted with his sister's behaviour with regard to Gasosîn (q.v.), and abducts her. He is about to slay her to redeem the honour of his family, when Gasosîn comes that way, and wounding G. severely, rides away with Ginovêr. G. occurs in Chrestien's *Erec* [1943] as Godegrains, the name appearing in *E* as Gundregoas, one of the knights who come to Êrec's wedding.

---

[64] Brugger (2), pp. 42f.

In neither version of *Erec* is any suggestion made that G. is a relative of Ginovêr. – *E* 1918; *C* 589

Gotehart (1) grandfather of Elsam, and king of England. – *Loh* m741 n1494

Gotehart (2) son of Gotehart (1), a knight who is present at the fight between Lohengrîn and Friderîch (2). – *Loh* nm165ff. a1642

Gothardelen 'der getriuwe', a knight who is present at Arthur's court when Êrec returns with Ênîte. G. does not occur in the corresponding list in Chrestien's *Erec*. – *E* 1680

Gotfrit (1) 'von Havenerpurc', brother of Arnolt (3), a knight who jousts with Ulrich von Liechtenstein during the latter's *Venusfahrt*. – *FD* 615,7

Gotfrit (2) 'von Hohenloch', a MHG poet who is unknown apart from this reference. – *RW* nm2239

Gotfrit (3) 'von Strâzburc', the well-known MHG poet, author of *Tn*. – nm *A* 3153f.; *UT* 4; *RW* 2185; *HT* 15; *GM* 29; *WO* 2063f.

Gotfrit (4) 'von Tozenpach', cousin of Sîfrit (5), a knight who jousts with Ulrich von Liechtenstein during the latter's *Venusfahrt*. Ulrich also says that G. composed *Minnelieder* (886,8), of which, however, there is no trace today. – *FD* 272,2

Gouns Wueste brother of Amfortas and father of the maiden who bears the Graal. G. was treacherously slain by Partinias, and the sword with which he was killed broke in two, becoming the Graal sword, which can be joined together again only by the rightful successor to Amfortas as Graal king. G. is called Goon Desert in Manessier (55249), who evidently invented the story to introduce a little originality into his continuation of the legend. – *RP* nm616,15

Gofrei see Gifles

Gradoans a knight who is present at Arthur's court and spills Priure's cup of chastity. G. appears in Chrestien's *Erec* [1727] as Gornevains (MS A: Gordeuains). (See also Grangodoans.) – *C* 2319

Grahardois 'der' (*JT*), see Schîonatulander

Grahart 'der' (*WO*), see Schîonatulander

Grâlant the hero of the Breton *lai*, *Graelent*, the story of which is similar to that of Marie de France's *lai*, *Lanval* (q.v.). G. is also the hero of a version of *Herzemære*, a story by Konrad von Würzburg, in which the hero's heart is cooked and set before his *amie* by her husband. Hertz is of the opinion that the lay which Tristan sings is the former story,[65] but it is clear from the reference in *C* that the latter version was known in Germany at about the time Gottfried was writing *Tn*.[66] – nm *Tn* 3583ff.; *C* 11564

Gralars 'von Graliduse', a warrior in Ipomidôn's army against Akarîn. – *JT* 3262,3

Gram a knight at Arthur's court. He is one of those who spill Priure's cup of chastity. G. occurs in Chrestien's *Erec* [1727] as Grains. (See also Grangodoans.) – *C* 2318

Gramaflan, Gramaflantz, Gramolanz see Gramoflanz

Gramoflanz a knight who guards an orchard and jousts with any knight who dares to pluck a sprig from the trees. He has slain Zidegast, the husband of Orgelûse, who sends Gawein to pluck a flower in the hope that he will avenge the death of Zidegast. G., who formerly loved Orgelûse but is now in love with Itonjê, prides himself on never fighting with just one man at a time and initially declines to fight Gawein. When he learns, however, that his adversary is Gawein, the son of Lôt, who killed G.'s father Îrôt, he quickly arranges a day for a combat to take place. G. jousts with Parzivâl, thinking that he is Gawein, and is so

---

65 Gottfried von Straßburg, *Tristan und Isolde*, transl. by. W. Hertz, p. 562.

66 The reference in *C* occurs in the middle of an enumeration of tragedies which had caused great grief (11564): 'Und dô man Grâlanden sot'. (See also Gresmurs.)

badly wounded that the fight with the latter has to be postponed for a day. In the meantime Arthur succeeds in settling the feud, and the fight is abandoned. G. marries Itonjê, and (in *RP*) they have a daughter, Gyngenor. In Chrestien's *Perceval*, G. is called Guiromelans, often preceded by the definite article 'li' (so in the *Livre d'Artus*), which is the origin of the form 'der Schyromelans' in *RP*, although later, when referred to in conjunction with Itonjê (77,40), he is called Gramaflan; the name occurs in *RP* also in the form Gramolanz. Bartsch suggests, somewhat diffidently, an etymology of Chrestien's form from OF *guirlande*, 'garland', and *melans* < *meller, mesler*, 'to fight', i.e. 'he who fights for the garland'.[67] G. occurs as an ally of Arthur in *G* and *TF*, as well as in *RP*, where he assists him against Bruns (1), whilst the story as told in *P* is repeated in *C*, where he is called Gîremelanz. – *P* nm[445,23] a604,7ff.; *C* a21492; *G* 17665; *JT* 2154,5; *TF* 1694; *Sey* nm5,7; *UA* nm3428; *RB* nm17378; *RP* 22,2 [†]

Grangodoans a knight at Arthur's court when Êrec returns with Ênîte. This name is a combination of the names of two knights who appear in Chrestien's list in *Erec* [1727], Grains and Gornevains (var. Gordeuains), which appear in *C* as Gram and Gradoans (q.v.). That Heinrich used *E* appears certain, however, from the fact that G. appears in *C* as Greingradoan, a knight who reproves Keiî for his mockery of the ladies who spill Priure's cup. G. does not appear in the list of knights in *C* which corresponds to the lists in Chrestien's *Erec* and in *E*. – *E* 1660; *C* 1464 [†]

Grâswaldâne 'vürste ûz' (*JT*), see Schîonatulander

Graswalden 'der ûz' (*JT*), see Schîonatulander

Graphant a knight who pursues Dêmantîn and Sirgamôte as they are escaping from Eghart and who is unhorsed by Dêmantîn. – *Dem* 4075

Graveas 'künec', a relative of Agly. G. is the leader of the band which murders Wildhalm, and he himself throws the poisoned spear which causes the latter's death. Although mortally wounded, Wildhalm succeeds in slaying G. before he dies. – *WO* 18999

Graciens see Gracius

Gracius a knight who fights for Athis against Bilas. G. does not occur in the OF version. – *AP* A*,102

Gregorius 'bâbest' (Pope Gregory V). – *Loh* nm7455

Greingradoan see Grangodoans

Greins a knight who accompanies Heimet to the tourney held by Leigamar. – *C* 18140

Gresmurs 'fîne Posterne', brother of Gimoers (see Gwinganiers). G. attends the wedding of Erec. He occurs in Chrestien's *Erec* [1952] as Graislemiers de Fine Posterne, and in *C*, where he is one of the knights at Arthur's court who spill Priure's cup of chastity, as Gaumerans. Both Miss Weston[68] and Brugger[69] identify G. with Grâlant (q.v.), and Brugger considers that G. and Gimoers (Guingomar in OF) were made brothers because of the similarity in the termination of their names.[70] – *E* 1928, *C* 2332

Gressamant a knight of the Round Table who is unhorsed by Daniel (1). – *DB* 246

Grêûsâ 'von Thêbân', *amie* of Jason (q.v.). In Greek legend she is called Creusa. – *TK* 11204ff.

Grigoras a ruler of dwarf-land who accompanies Bîlêî to the wedding of Êrec. So also in Chrestien's *Erec* [2005]. In *C*, where he is one of the knights who spill Priure's cup of chastity, G. is called Gligoras. – *E* 2112; *C* 2343

---

67 Bartsch (2), p. 121.
68 Weston (1), p. 65.
69 Brugger (2), p. 12, note 20.
70 Brugger (2), p. 12, note 20

Grigors see Grîgorz

Grîgorz 'künec von Ipotente', nephew of Klâmidê. In *JT*, where the form Grigors occurs, he is present at the tourney held by Arthur. – *P* nm210,8; *JT* 1990,2 [†]

Grimme a giant from whom Dietrich von Bern is said to have obtained his helmet. G. occurs in the *Eckenlied* and *Sigenot*. – *RB* nm25268

Grymoalt a knight who has been defeated by Gawein, who has to take his place as the consort of the fairy, Karmente. – *S* nmIII,228

Grymuas nephew of Marroch, for whom he acts as a scout in the battle against Arthur. He is overcome by Unarck. – *Wigm* a2880ff. n2892

Grymuras see Grymuas

Grysalet a maiden to whom the sparrow-hawk, which is won by Edolanz, is given. – *Edol* B,242

Griffâne 'künec von' (*W*), see Poidjus

Grôhier 'künec von Nomadjentesîn', a warrior who assists in the arming of Terramêr in the second battle at Alischanz. G. is not mentioned in *Aliscans* at this point, but in another place (5192) Gohier (= Grôhier) occurs. (Cf. Krôhier.) [See Appendix (1).] – *W* 356,3f.

Gronosis a knight who is present at Arthur's court and spills Priure's cup of chastity. G. is omitted from the list of knights in *E*, or occurs in an unrecognizable form, but since he occurs in Chrestien's *Erec* (1740) as the son of Keiî, he would correspond in *E* to Lernfras. – *C* 2327

Grüenen Ouwe 'grâve von der', father of Sandinôse (q.v.). A knight comes to G.'s land and hypnotizes everyone with his voice. He bathes weekly in the blood of males, and G., under the spell of his voice, has to bring him a supply from the outside world. The grâve von dem Liehten Brunnen follows G. into his castle and is captured in an invisible net. Daniel (1) defeats but spares G., and enters the castle, where he is caught in the invisible net by Sandinôse, who releases him immediately. Daniel slays the hypnotizer, and releases all the prisoners who have been collected for his bath that day, and breaks the spell for the others. – *DB* a2444f. n[5122f.]

Grundalis 'künec', one of the seven judges at the tourney held by Meliûr. – *PM* a13476 n13490

Grüninger the name of the printer of *KT*. – *KT* nm8256

Guelguezins 'herzoge von dem Hôhen bois', a knight who attends Êrec's wedding. G. occurs in Chrestien's *Erec* (1961) as Guergesins, li dus de Haut Bois, whilst in *C*, where he is one of the knights at Arthur's court who spill Priure's cup of chastity, he is called Gwirnesis li isnel (= 'der Schnelle'). – *E* 1936; *C* 2336

Gues 'von Strauz', a knight who is present at Arthur's court when Êrec returns with Ênîte. This name is derived from Chrestien's *Erec* (1725), where he is called Keus d'Estraus. The form of the name which appears in *E* may possibly have been influenced by Chrestien's Grus (MS V: Granderies), a knight who appears in the same position in Chrestien's list [1716], as does G. in Hartmann's. Grus occurs in *C* as Gantitiers von Jastuns, a knight who spills Priure's cup of chastity. (See also Gaherîez.) – *E* 1653; *C* 2306

Guetelîn see Günetlîn

Guivreiz 'künec über Îrlant', also called 'le pitîz', because he is short, though broad and very strong. G. fights with Êrec, and the latter wins but spares G.'s life, and they become friends. Whilst Êrec is still weak from his wounds after his rescue of Ênîte from Oringles, G. again jousts with him, not knowing who he is, and this time unhorses him. As soon as the identity of his opponent is discovered, G. makes amends for his breach of friendship by his hospitality. G. occurs also as Gîvreiz, one of the knights at Arthur's court, in *L*, whilst in *RP*, where he is called 'Gehires der kleine' (Guiviers in Gautier), he is one of the knights who take part in the search for Parzivâl. G., who appears for the first time in Chrestien's *Erec*, where he is named Guivrez, is identified by Richter with Gifles (q.v.).[71] – *L* 6017; *E* m4279 a4321 n4476f.; *RP* 525,44

Gundaker 'von Starkenberc', a knight who is present at the tourney held at Friesach. – *FD* 196,5

Gundacker (1) 'von Stîr', brother of Dietmâr (5), a knight who is present at the tourney at Friesach and who later jousts with Ulrich von Liechtenstein during the latter's *Venusfahrt.* – *FD* 196,1

Gundacker (2) 'von Vrowenstein', a knight who jousts with Ulrich von Liechtenstein during the latter's *Venusfahrt.* – *FD* 628,3

Gundemâr 'von Clârebrunn', an abbot attendant on Elsam. – *Loh* a741f. n807

Gunderlach 'von dem rotten Turm', a knight who fights for Paltriot against Atroclas. – *Wigm* 3953

Gundregoas see Gotegrîn

Gundrey, Gundrie see Kundrîe (2)

Gundrueis 'von Gundernale', a warrior in Akarîn's army against Ipomidôn. – *JT* nm3179,3f.

Gunete, Günetel, Gunetîn see Günetlîn

Günetlîn squire to Meleranz. – *M* 9295

Guntel see Günetlîn

Gunther the famous king of the Burgundians in the *Nibelungenlied.* – *P* nm420,27

Guote 'der schöne', a knight who is present at the tourney held by Ris and Cadoalans. – *RP* 81,31

Guote 'vrouwe' (*WW*), see Bêne (1)

Gûrâz 'herzoge', husband of Sŷbille (2) (q.v.). – *FB* 1372

Gurdimalander 'künec von Manziflôr', a warrior who is slain by Achilles whilst fighting for the Trojans against the Greeks. This character was invented by Konrad. – *TK* 32538

Gurmûn a king who came from Africa and conquered Ireland, compelling, according to *Tn*, Îsolt (1) to marry him. Their daughter is Îsolt (2). G. is an historical figure and was introduced into the Tristan legend by Thomas, who found the name in Wace, where it is taken from Geoffrey of Monmouth (XI, 8).[72] – *ET* m358 a1163; *Tn* nm5883ff. a7154

Gurnemantz see Gurnemanz

Gurnemanz (Bartsch suggests < OF *guernir*, 'to warn', < *warnen*, or < German *Warinman* > OF *guerneman*.) G. is called 'de Grâharz' and is the father of three sons, Schenteflûrs, Laskoit, and Gurzgrî, all of whom are dead, and of Lîâze. The most important account of G. is to be found in *P*, where he is present at Herzeloide's tourney, and later initiates the young Parzivâl into the laws of chivalry. During the course of this instruction, he tells Parzivâl to avoid asking lots of questions. Following this advice, Parzivâl fails to ask the question of sympathy which is trembling on his lips in the Graal Castle, and thus prolongs the suffering of Amfortas. G. first occurs in Chrestien's *Erec* [1695], where he is called Gornemant de Gohort, and occurs in *E* as Gornemanz von Grôharz, one of the knights present at Arthur's court when Êrec returns with Ênîte. In *L* he is called Gurnemanz, and holds a tourney with Lôt (4) as his opponent. The references in *T*, *JT*, and *Sey* are dependent on *P*, whilst in *C*, where he attends a tourney held by Arthur, he is called Gornomanz Côorz, Gôorz von Cornomant, and Goorz von Goromant. It is perhaps significant that Chrestien has the form with *Gorn-* as the stem, as have *E* and *C*, whilst *L*, *P*

---

[71] Richter, pp. 99ff.
[72] Golther (2), p. 142.

and those dependent on *P* have *Gurn-* as the stem. – *L* nm2628ff. a2826; *E* 1632; *P* 68,22; *T* nm41,2; *C* 607; *JT* 670,3; *Sey* 65,5ff. [†]

Gurûn the hero of a lay which is sung by Tristan. According to Hertz, G. occurs as Guirun in a Breton story, the theme of which is that of Konrad von Würzburg's *Herzemaere*.[73] – *Tn* nm3523f.

Gurzegrin see Gurzgrî

Gurzgrî son of Gurnemanz and husband of Mahaute. G. is killed by Mabônagrîn in attempting the adventure of Schoidelakurt, and his mother dies of grief. He leaves behind him two sons, Gandilûz and Schîonatulander. – *P* m175,16 n178,15; *T* nm41,4; *JT* nm670,6 [†]

Gurzigrine, Gurzcgrin see Gurzgrî

Gutshart see Gutschart

Gutschart 'künec von Liflanden', an ally of Witechin against Amelot. G. is unhorsed and captured by Willehalm (4) in the battle at Galverne. – *RW* nm10640f. a10746

Gwalther see Walther (2)

Gwî, Gwîgâlois see Wigalois

Gwigrimanz (1) 'der Burgunjois', a knight who is killed or captured whilst fighting for Willehalm (1) at Alischanz. He occurs in *UW* as an ally of Lôîs against Terramêr. Of the OF *chansons de geste*, G. occurs in *Aliscans* only, as Guinemans (MSS B and C). – *W* 14,20; *UW* 46,6 [†]

Gwigrimanz (2) 'ein gast von Britânî', a warrior who is slain by Medeamanz whilst fighting for Alexander against Dârîus at Issôn. This character appears to have been invented by Ulrich. – *UA* 4737

Gwillams see Willehalm (1)

Gwimant 'von Gereit', a knight of the Round Table who is unhorsed by Daniel (1). – *DB* 243

Gwinganiers a knight who spills Priure's cup of chastity at Arthur's court. In *E* he is called Gimoers and is the brother of Gresmurs (q.v.), as also in Chrestien's *Erec* [1954], where he is called Guingomars. G. is the hero of a *lai* by Marie de France, *Guingamor*, in which he lives with a fairy for three hundred years which pass like a day. Chrestien identified the fairy with Morgan (see Feimorgan), and hence called G.'s land Avalon, the Celtic Isles of the Blest. – *E* 1930; *C* 2333

Gwirnesis see Guelguezins

---

[73] Gottfried von Straßburg, *Tristan und Isolde*, transl. by W. Hertz, p. 561.

H

Hademâr see Hadmâr (1)

Hadmâr (1) 'von Küenringe', a knight who jousts with and wounds Ulrich von Liechtenstein at the tourney held at Friesach. He brings Bope to fight with Ulrich during the latter's Venusfahrt. – *FD* 197,1

Hadmâr (2) 'von Schœnenberc', a knight who takes part in the tourney held at Friesach. – *FD* 198,4

Hâel a knight who is unhorsed by Dêmantîn. – *Dem* 5835ff.

Hagenouwe see Reinmâr

Hâgis driven by Alexander out of Lacedemonia, he attacks Macedonia but is killed by Antipater and his army is routed. So also in *Expeditio Alexandri* and Curtius Rufus, where he is called Agis. – *A* 8665

Hainrich (1) son of Hainrich (5) and brother of Fridrich (3). H. marries Malmelona and fights for Fridrich against Mompolier. – *FS* m16 a31 n5040

Hainrich (2) 'kaiser' (Heinrich VII). – *WO* nm16889

Hainrich (3) son of Friderich (3) and Angelburg. – *FS* 7061ff.

Hainrich (4) 'bischof von Kostentz'. H. fights on the side of the Christians in the final battle against the heathens. – *WO* 16669

Hainrich (5) 'von Swäben', a good prince who dies at the age of 106 years, leaving behind three sons, Ruoprecht, Hainrich (1), and Fridrich (3). – *FS* 5ff.

Hachaberc 'künec von Gamas', a knight who is slain by Eberhart whilst fighting for the heathens against the Christians. – *Loh* a4373 n4459

Halap a heathen king, father of Irmingart. H. is at first Graf Rudolf's opponent, and later his commander. Ehrismann has pointed out that this name is really that of the town in which H. was Sultan, being the MHG form of Aleppo, which occurs as Hallap in the MHG chronicle poem *Landgraf Ludwigs Kreuzfahrt*, and in *P*.[1] – *GR* mBb,2 aδ,15f. nEb,6

Haltzbier 'künec von Turkanas', a warrior in the heathen army in the final battle against the Christians. The name appears to have been copied from Halzebier. – *WO* 16353

Haltzibor 'von Halzibant', a warrior in Akarîn's army against Ipomidôn. – *JT* nm3137,7

Halzebier 'künec von Falfundê', a kinsman of Terramêr and one of his chief allies against Willehalm (1). In the first battle at Alischanz he takes eight Christian knights prisoner, whilst in the second he kills Hûnas and is himself slain by the other seven captives, who have been liberated by Rennewart. In *UW* he assists Terramêr against Lôis and is wounded whilst trying to capture Willehalm. H., who is called Hauchebier in the OF *chansons de geste*, is slain by Rennewart in *Aliscans*, and appears also in *Li Covenans Viviens* and *Prise d'Orange*. – *W* 9,22f.; *UW* 42,3 [†]

Halcibier see Halzebier

Hammôn, Hâmôn see Amon

Hamor see Hannor

Hanibâl the Carthaginian enemy of Rome. – *RB* nm19954

Hannor 'künec von Prandigan'. H. abducts Amalita and is pursued by her husband, Eleander (q.v.), who kills H. whilst he is out hunting. – *GT* nm20129f. a20621f.

Harbungeliezze 'künec von Disine', a warrior in Ipomidôn's army against Akarîn. – *JT* nm3217,2

---

[1] Ehrismann, II, 2, i, p. 59.

118

Hardies see Hardîs

Hardîs (Schulz suggested that this name is derived from OF *hardi, hardiesse*, 'bold',[2] a view which Martin also adopts.[3] Singer identifies H. with Kurâus.[4]) H. is called 'künec von Gaskâne' and 'künec von Gaskôn', and is unhorsed by Gahmuret at the tourney held by Herzeloide. He is at enmity with Kailet because of the latter's treatment of H.'s sister, Alîze (1). In *JT* he fights for Schîonatulander and is mortally wounded in the battle by Daries. – *P* m48,10 n65,5 a72,24f.; *JT* 2597,5

Hardifius 'von Agardas'. (< OF *hardi*, 'bold', and *fius*, 'son'?) H. is a knight who attends the tourney held by Leigamar. – *C* 18126f.

Hardîz see Hardîs

Hardîz, Lays see Lays

Harolt uncle to Orilus, for whom he fights against Schîonatulander. – *JT* 4481,5

Haropîn 'künec', father of Klîboris. H. fights for Terramêr against Willehalm (1). Harpin appears as a variant form of Turpiûn (q.v.) in *Aliscans*, whilst Harpin, roi sarrasin de Nîmes occurs in a number of *chansons de geste*. – *W* 359,20

Harpîn a giant who has captured the six sons of Îwein's host and, having killed two, is to kill the remaining four if their sister is not delivered up to him; he is killed by Îwein and his lion. H. is called Harpin de la Montaingne in Chrestien's *Yvain*, and Harpyns in the ME poem *Ywain and Gawain*. – *I* m4463 n4500 a4916

Hartalas see Talas

Hartman 'von Ouwe', MHG poet, and author of *E* and *I*, among other works. – nm *I* 28; *Wigl* 6309; *P* 143,21; *Tn* 4619; *C* 2348; *A* 3126f.; *RW* 2176; *G* 22; *JT* 2352,1; *M* 106f.; *GM* 29

Harturam brother of Pandachîn and *ami* of Bonafeide. H. is a knight and is overcome by Gayol (2) as the latter is on his way to succour Sêkurîe. – *Crane* a2700 n2806

Hartzier 'herzoge von Nordin', also called 'von Vordein', *ami* of Pioles, whom he leaves in his castle whilst he attends a tourney. The castle is burnt down, but Pioles is safely brought by Wigamur to the house of Lygronite. Later, when Wigamur is searching for the abducted Dulcefluor, he meets H. and brings him and Pioles together again. – *Wigm* m897 a5581 n5660

Hastê 'künec von Alligues', one of the group of 15 Saracen kings who attack Willehalm (1) at the end of the first battle at Alischanz. H. is wounded or killed by Willehalm in that encounter. [See Appendix (9).] In the existing MSS of *Aliscans*, none of which was used by Wolfram, he is called Aristés, but it could hardly be fortuitous that Hastes is a common OF name and is, moreover, the name of one of the twelve peers of Charlemagne. – *W* m71,22 a72,17f. n74,21 [†]

Haterel 'herzoge', father of Equinot. This name does not occur in Chrestien's *Erec*. – *E* nm1669

Haukauus 'künec von Nûbîâ', one of the group of 15 Saracen kings who attack Willehalm (1) at the end of the first battle at Alischanz. H. is wounded or killed by Willehalm in that encounter. [See Appendix (9).] H. probably corresponds to Ahuré in *Aliscans*. – *W* m71,22 a72,17f. n74,11 [†]

Havelîn see Jovelîn

---

2   Schulz, 'Eigennamen', p. 404.
3   Martin (1), p. 73, to 65,5.
4   Singer (1), p. 58.

Hêgâtêus a warrior who is compelled by Amintas (1) to join Alexander. So also in *Expeditio Alexandri* and Curtius Rufus, where he is called Hecataeus. – *A* nm20145

Hegelôch (1) a warrior in Alexander's army. With Amfotêr he attacks Kîun and completely defeats the Persians. So also in *Expeditio Alexandri* and Curtius Rufus. – *A* 5073

Hegelôch (2) formerly a warrior in Dârîus's army, he suggests the conspiracy to Parmênîôn (q.v.). So also in Curtius Rufus. – *A* nm20004

Heylanna, Heylena, Heylenna see Elena

Heilman 'grâve von Hollant', a knight who fights for the Christian army against the heathens under Gêrfridolt. – *Loh* 5115

Heimereis see Ehmereiz

Heimerich see Heimrîch (1)

Heimet a knight who attends the tourney held by Leigamar. – *C* 18138

Heimrîch (1) 'cuns von Naribôn', husband of Irmschart, and father of Willehalm (1), Bertrams (1), Buovun, Arnalt, Heimrîch (2), Bernart (2), and Gîbert (2). In *W*, he sends his sons into the world to seek their own fortune and adopts, as his heir, the son of one of the men who had died in his service. This is also the case in the OF *Guibert d'Andernas*, whilst in *Les Narbonnais* he makes Gîbert, as his youngest son, his heir.[5] H. fights for Willehalm in the second battle at Alischanz. In *UW*, where he fights for Lôis against Terramêr, Heimrîch (2) does not appear as one of his sons, his place being taken by Witschart. In the OF *chansons de geste* he is called Aymeri; the story of his youth is told in *Girard de Vienne*,[6] whilst his death is recounted in *La Mort Aymeri*.[7] He occurs in the *Chancun de Willame* and has been identified, not very conclusively, with Hadhemarus, who fought under Louis d'Aquitaine at Catalonia.[8] – *W* 5,16; *UW* m4,13 an7,6

Heimrîch (2) son of Heimrîch (1). H. comes with his friend Schilbert and a ragged and battle-worn army to Oransche to assist Willehalm (1) in the second battle against Terramêr. They had been fighting for the Venetians when the news of Willehalm's peril reached them. He does not occur in *UW*, where he is replaced by Witschart. In *W* he is called 'der schêtîs' (= the poor), from the OF Aïmers li caitis, a title he acquires because of the raggedness of his followers. H. is never present at the reunions of the brothers, but whenever there is trouble he always appears in the nick of time with his ragged army with rusty arms, and disappears after the fight.[9] There is no extant poem in which H. is the hero, but it is almost certain that with so picturesque a character one existed at one time. – *W* a5,16f. n6,25

Heimrîs see Heimrîch (1)

Heinrîch (1) 'kaiser', German emperor (Heinrich I). H., who is the husband of Mehtilt and the father of Otte (1), Prûn (1), and Heinrich (6), is present at the fight between Lohengrîn and Friderîch (2). He obtains the assistance of Lohengrîn in repelling an invasion by the Hungarians, and later, at the request of Johan (4), he joins Lohengrîn in the battle against the heathens under Gêrfridolt. In *Ll* he plays no part beyond that of acting as a spectator at the fight between Lohengrîn and Friderîch. – *Loh* m346 a1890 n2598; *Ll* a11,6 [†]

Heinrîch (2) 'kaiser', Emperor of Germany (Heinrich II), son of Heinrich (6). His wife is named Kunegunt, and his sister Gysel. – *Loh* m7521 [n7533]

Heinrîch (3) 'kaiser', Emperor of Germany (Heinrich VI). – *L* nm9335

---

5 Bédier, I, pp. 60ff.
6 Bédier, I, pp. 26ff.
7 Bédier, I, pp. 62f.
8 Bédier, I, p. 360.
9 Bédier, I, pp. 55ff.

Heinrîch (4) 'grâve', sent the MS of *Ed* to Thüringen (brother of Ludwig der Eiserne, Heinrich Raspe?). – *Ed* nm13458ff.

Heinrîch (5) clerk to Friderîch (4), he found the dead body of Friderîch at the battle of Leitha. – *FD* 1667,7f.

Heinrîch (6) 'herzoge von Bayern' (Heinrich I), third son of Heinrîch (1). – *Loh* nm7314 [†]

Heinrîch (7) 'der Breuzel', brother of Wernhart, he welcomes Ulrich von Liechtenstein to Neustadt during his *Artusfahrt*. – *FD* 1470,1ff.

Heinrîch (8) 'bischof von Brihsen', he is present at the tourney held at Friesach. – *FD* 239,2

Heinrîch (9) 'von Buseke', a knight who rode out against Ulrich von Liechtenstein during the latter's *Artusfahrt*. He was met, however, by Heinrîch (28), who jousted with him in the place of Ulrich. – *FD* 1446,1

Heinrîch (10) 'von Grâvenstein', a knight who jousts with Ulrich von Liechtenstein during the latter's *Venusfahrt*. – *FD* 629,4

Heinrîch (11) 'von Grîffenvels', a knight who jousts with Ulrich von Liechtenstein during the latter's *Venusfahrt*. – *FD* 628,6f.

Heinrîch (12) 'schenke von Habechspach', brother of Uolrich (4), a knight who welcomes Ulrich von Liechtenstein to Neustadt during his *Artusfahrt*. – *FD* 1467,1

Heinrîch (13) 'von Hakenberc', a knight who jousts with Ulrich von Liechtenstein during the latter's *Venusfahrt*. – *FD* 888,1.

Heinrîch (14) 'margâve von Ysterich', a knight whose quarrel with Bernhart (3) gave rise to the tourney at Friesach. – *FD* 177,3

Heinrîch (15) 'von Kempten', tutor to the young son of the herzoge von Swâben. H.'s charge is beaten by the chancellor to Otte (4), and H. in his anger accidentally kills the chancellor. For this he is sentenced to death, but he saves himself by taking hold of Otte's beard and threatening his life unless he annuls the sentence. He later springs naked from his bath to defend Otte against some assassins and is received back into favour. – *HK* [93ff.]

Heinrîch (16) 'von Kîowe', a knight who is present at the tourney held at Friesach, jousts with Ulrich von Liechtenstein during the latter's *Venusfahrt*, and takes part in the tourney at Kornneuburg. – *FD* 198,7

Heinrîch (17) 'von Küenringe', brother of Hadmâr (1), a knight who is present at the tourney at Kornneuburg. – *FD* 1056,7

Heinrîch (18) 'von Liehtenstein', cousin of Ulrich von Liechtenstein, whom he welcomes at Neustadt during the latter's *Artusfahrt*. – *FD* 1474,2f.

Heinrîch (19) 'von Linouwe', MHG poet, author of a poem called *Der Wallære*, of which the hero is Ekken. This poem and its author are known only through Rudolf's references.[10] – nm *A* 3254ff.; *RW* 2226ff.

Heinrîch (20) 'von Lüenze', a knight who is present at the tourney held at Friesach and who jousts with Ulrich von Liechtenstein during the latter's *Venusfahrt*. During Ulrich's *Artusfahrt*, he acts the part of Parzivâl and fights on Ulrich's side. – *FD* 286,2

Heinrîch (21) 'Marschant', helped Konrad with the translation of *PM* from the French. – *PM* 202

Heinrîch (22) 'margrâve von Oesterreich'. Ulrich von Liechtenstein was in his service as squire. The identity of H., whom some scholars have thought to be identical with Heinrîch

---

10 *Verfasserlexikon*, II, col. 296.

(14), and some to be Heinrich von Oesterreich-Mödling,[11] has not been satisfactorily explained. – *FD* 29,3ff.

Heinrîch (23) 'von Ofterdingen', a legendary (?) MHG poet, who is first mentioned in the *Wartburgkrieg*, from which the reference in *Loh* is taken. – *Loh* nm221

Heinrîch (24) 'von Püten', a knight who is present at the tourney held at Friesach and who jousts with Ulrich von Liechtenstein during the latter's *Venusfahrt*. This is not the same character as Heinrîch (25). – *FD* 194,7

Heinrîch (25) 'von Püten', a knight who is present at the tourney held at Friesach. This is not the same character as Heinrîch (24). – *FD* 194,7

Heinrîch (26) 'von Rîspach', presumably an official at the Bavarian court. Reisbach is a town on the Vils in the neighbourhood of Landshut.[12] – *P* nm297,29

Heinrîch (27) 'von Rücke', a MHG poet. – *C* nm2442

Heinrîch (28) 'von Spiegelberc', a knight who jousts under the name of Lanzelet with Ulrich von Liechtenstein during the latter's *Artusfahrt*. – *FD* nm1430,2ff.

Heinrîch (29) 'von Triwanswinkel', a knight who is present at the tourney held at Friesach. – *FD* 287,6ff.

Heinrîch (30) 'von Truhsen', a knight who is present at the tourney held at Friesach. – *FD* 195,1

Heinrîch (31) 'von dem Türlîn', MHG poet, and author of *C* and *Mtl.* – nm *C* 246f.; *A* 3222f.

Heinrîch (32) 'von Veldeke', MHG poet, and author of *Ed.* – nm *Ed* 13433; *P* 292,18; *Tn* 4724; *LT* 17381; *W* 76,25; *A* 3113ff.; *RW* 2173; *MC* 1160; *JT* 4831,1; *GT* 8891

Heinrîch (33) 'Vigân', a knight who is present at the tourney held at Friesach. – *FD* 273,4

Heinrîch (34) 'von Vrîberc', MHG poet, and author of *HT*. – *HT* nm82

Heinrîch (35) 'von Wazzerberc', a knight who is married to the sister of Ulrich von Liechtenstein and who is present at the tourney held at Kornneuburg. – *FD* 1033,2

Hecktor see Hector (1)

Hector (1) son of Priam and the most valiant of all the Trojan warriors in the war against the Greeks. In *TK* he is present at the wedding of Thetis and Pêleus, and there fights the latter in single combat for the possession of Paris and wins. His death follows the account in Homer, where he is slain by Achilles, who drags his body behind his chariot ('rossewagen'). Achilles cedes his body to Priam when the latter comes to the Greek camp at night to beg for it. In *LT*, H. is left dead on the battlefield and carried into Troy at the end of the fight like all the other dead. In *GT* he is the hero of innumerable minor encounters, but it is interesting to note that in this version it is H. who suggests the abduction of Helen. Achilles slays him in single combat after he has twice put the former to flight. In *Ed* H. is seen by Ênêâs in Hades. – *Ed* 3325; *LT* nm1664ff. a1910; *MC* nm20; *FB* nm1630; *Wigm* nm3424; *TK* 1093ff.; *RB* nm20165; *GT* 116ff.; *GM* nm3561

Hector (2) son of Parmênîôn, one of the bravest of Alexander's warriors. In *A*, as in Curtius Rufus, he is drowned whilst boating at Alexandria. According to *UA* (18569f.), he was slain in battle, but no account of his death is given. – *A* 10642; *UA* 3191ff.

Hecuba see Ecubâ (3)

Helên, Helena (1) see Elena

Helena (2) mother of Constantine the Great. – *RB* nm18147

Helêne (1) see Elena

---

11 Ulrich von Liechtenstein, *Frauendienst*, ed. by R. Bechstein, I, p. 11, note.
12 Martin (1), p. 259, to 297,29.

Helene (2) see Elene

Heleus 'von Kypre', a warrior in the Greek army against the Trojans. H. does not occur in any of the sources to *LT*. – *LT* 3399f.

Hêlî (1) see Ely

Helye (2), **Helîas** see Elîas

Helizêô see Êlisêus

Hellanna see Elena

Helpherîch 'künec von Nasserân', an ally of Ehkunat in the war against Arthur. He is wounded by Klârîs (1) in the battle between Gârel and Ehkunat, and is captured by Gerhart (2). – *G* m371 n11794 a12498

*Hemereis see Ehmereiz

Heneyda a warrior in the Trojan army against the Greeks. – *GT* 22714

Henec 'suctellois fil Gawîn', a knight at Arthur's court when Êrec returns with Ênîte. H. does not appear in the corresponding list in Chrestien's *Erec*. – *E* 1671

Hênete a knight who is unhorsed by Meljaganz when the latter is abducting Ginovêr. H. does not occur in the *Yvain* of Chrestien, who does not give a list of the knights unhorsed by Meljaganz. – *I* nm4703

Herbort 'von Fritslar', MHG poet, and author of *LT*. – *LT* nm18450

Herek see Êrec

Heres see Ares

Hercolas *amie* of Pictagines. – *GT* nm10386

Hercûles the well-known Greek hero. In *LT* he goes with Jason to fetch the Golden Fleece, and fights for the Greeks in the first war against the Trojans. This is the same account as in Benoît and Dares, and substantially the same as in *TK*, where he slays Laomedon. In the latter version Filothêtes relates to the Greeks how H. abducted Dîanîra, and how she was the innocent cause of his death by sending to him the poisoned shirt of Nessus, exactly as the story is told in Ovid's *Metamorphoses* IX. In *GT* he is the brother of Medea and Ajax (1), whom he accompanies to Troy. He is one of those who go in search of Achilles, and on his return to Troy, he challenges a Trojan to single combat. Hector accepts and kills him. – *Ed* nm5047; *LT* 213; *C* nm11582; *Port* nm22; *JT* nm99,6; *TK* 6868; *Loh* nm215; *UA* nm9937; *GT* m14678 n14685 a14756f.; *RB* nm21896; *SA* nm6015; *WA* nm3909

Herlinde a lady on whose account Vridebrant (q.v.) killed Hernant. – *P* nm25,5; *JT* 1528,6 [†]

Herman (1) a knight who captures Partonopier and imprisons him. The latter persuades H.'s wife to let him go to Meliûr's tourney, on the condition that he returns after the tourney has finished. There he unhorses H., who tries to take his revenge by attacking Partonopier simultaneously with a number of other knights, but he is killed by Partonopier. When H.'s wife hears that her husband is dead, she releases her prisoner. – *PM* 12746ff.

Herman (2) 'der Palenzgrâve', afterwards 'lantgrâve von Thüringen', a famous patron of the MHG poets. – nm *Ed* 13475; *P* 297,16; *LT* 92; *W* 3,8; *JT* 3757,6f.; *WW* 4369

Herman (3) 'von Kranperc', a knight who is present at the tourney held at Friesach. – *FD* 194,5

Herman (4) 'von Krotendorf', a knight who jousts with Ulrich von Liechtenstein during the latter's *Artusfahrt*. – *FD* 1427,3

Herman (5) 'grâve von Ortenburg', a knight who is present at the tourney held at Friesach. – *FD* 189,8

Herman (6) 'schenke von Osterwitz', a knight who is present at the tourney held at Friesach and who later jousts with Ulrich von Liechtenstein during the latter's *Venusfahrt*. – *FD* 300,1

Herman (7) 'von Plintenpach', a knight who jousts with Ulrich von Liechtenstein during the latter's *Venusfahrt*. – *FD* 549,6

Hermiones see Ermiona

Hermogenes a warrior in Alexander's army who is killed by Negûsar during the battle at Issôn. So also in Gualterus. – *UA* 8239

Hermolaus 'de Therbund', counsellor to Agâmennon. – *GT* 14988

Hernant 'künec', slain by Vridebrant because of Herlinde. H.'s relatives attack Vridebrant, compelling him to leave Zazamanc and return to Scotland. – nm *P* 25,4; *JT* 1528,5

Herôd biblical, king of the Jews at the time of the birth of Christ. – *RB* nm18013

Hertnît (1) 'von Ort', a knight who is present at the tourney held at Friesach. – *FD* 192,4f.

Hertnît (2) 'künec von Riuzen', leader of the army in which Engelhart fights at the tourney at Normandie. – *Eng* 2690

Hertnît (3) 'von Wildonie', a knight who is present at the tourney held at Friesach. – *FD* 192,7

Herzeclius 'von Focidis', a warrior in the Greek army against the Trojans. H. does not occur in any other version of the Trojan legend. (Identical with Cedius (1) or Celidis?) – *LT* 3324ff.

Herzelaude see Herzeloide

Herzeloide (Already Schulz pointed out that, owing to the consistent spelling of the ending *oy* in *P* and *ou, eu* in *JT*, it is impossible for this name to be derived from *Leid*, as would seem at first sight the most obvious etymology.[13] Schulz suggested < Welsh *erch*, 'dismal', and *llued* or *lluydd*, 'warfare'.[14] Bartsch suggested that the ending *oyde* is derived from the German name-ending *hilt*, through *haut, l* in conjunction with *hilt* being common in names (cf. Godalhildis beside Godahildis).[15] *Herze-* he would derive from *hardo*, 'hard'. Alternatively Bartsch suggests that the original form of the name might be Harchelildis (*harc-* < OHG *haruc, fanum*) for Harchehildis, the former giving OF Herceleude. Gaston Paris disagrees entirely with the suggestions made by Bartsch, and asserts that H. is a form of the OF name Herselot,[16] a view which is held also by Golther and Bruce.[17] Martin agrees with Bartsch that the second half of the name seems to contain the German *hilde* (cf. Rischoide and Mahaute), and he therefore doubts the etymology suggested by Gaston Paris. Martin has no explanation for the former half of the name, *Herzel-*.[18])

H. is the daughter of Frimutel and sister of Amfortas. She marries Kastis, who is killed on the day of their wedding, leaving her a virgin. She holds a tourney at which the prize is her hand, which is won by Gahmuret. The latter is killed in battle shortly before the birth of their son, Parzivâl, with whom H. retires into solitude, in an endeavour to bring him up without any knowledge of knighthood. He insists on leaving her to become a knight, however, and H., dressing him up in fool's garb, lets him go, but dies of a broken heart

---

[13] Schulz, 'Eigennamen', p. 392.
[14] Schulz, 'Eigennamen', p. 392.
[15] Bartsch (2), p. 143.
[16] Paris (2), p. 149.
[17] Golther (1), p. 193; Bruce (1), I, p. 314, note 2.
[18] Martin (1), p. 89f. to 84,9.

almost before he is out of sight. H. is not named in Chrestien's *Perceval*, and all references to her by name can be traced to *P*. – *P* a61,3 n84,9; *Wigl* m6330; *T* nm10,3 [a26,2]; *UW* nm200,12; *JT* nm619,5 a622,1f.; *Loh* nm7103; *UA* nm3392; *RB* nm9240; *RP* m394,36

Herzeloude, Herzelöude   see Herzeloide

Hesse   'von Strasburg', 'der schreiber', a contemporary MHG poet mentioned by Rudolf but otherwise unknown. – *RW* nm2280

Hester   biblical, the Jewess who became the wife of Xerses (1). – *UA* nm11800

Hidarnes   a warrior who was placed by Dârîus to garrison Milête. He was driven out by Balacrus. So also in *Expeditio Alexandri* and Curtius Rufus. – *A* 9494ff.

Hierobal   'künec', to whom Romulus surrendered his land for money. Koppitz, in his Index to *GT*, is of the opinion that this is probably intended to be Heliogabalus. – *GT* nm24944

Hilde   mother of Kudrun in the MHG epic *Kudrun*. – *Loh* nm299

Hildebrand   'meister', the Gothic warrior and right-hand man of Dietrich von Bern. – nm *ET* 5976; *W* 439,16

Hylyon   a knight who is charged by Ecubâ (3) to kill the newly-born Paris. He leaves the babe in a forest. – *GT* 1328ff.

Hiltebort   'von Ascalîe', a warrior who is slain whilst fighting for the Trojans against the Greeks. This character was invented by Konrad. – *TK* 36308

Hippopotitikûn   'künec von' (*W*), see Josweiz

Hystroyss   wife of Ysachor, for whose life she pleads with Paris. – *GT* 7737ff.

Hiutegêr   'herzoge', 'der Schotte'. (Martin and Singer are of the opinion that this name is derived from the OF Audigier, which is the name of a knight who appears in the continuation to *Perceval* by Gerbert (4416).[19]   Brugger, on the other hand, thinks that the name is a distorted form of some German name, probably Liudeger.[20]) H. is the first of Gahmuret's victims among the besiegers of Patelamunt. In *JT*, where he is called 'Hutteger, künec von Navarre', he is married to Margatine and is present at a tourney held by Arthur. – *P* nm25,8f. a37,12; *JT* 1713,5 [†]

Hohenloch   'ein Franken', a knight on the side of the Christians in the final battle against the heathens. – *WO* 16745ff.

Hoygier (1)   'grâve von Bêamunt', an ally of Lôîs against Terramêr. (See also Hoygier (2).) – *UW* 39,3

Hoygier (2)   'von Lianit', a knight in Lôîs's army against Terramêr. This is the only mention of H., and it would seem to rest on a confusion of Hoygier (1) and the land of Ritschart (1). – *UW* nm43,20

Hojir   'von Mannesvelt', a knight who robs Êlamîe of her horse. The wrong is righted by Wigalois, who forces H. to return the horse to its owner and to repair as captive to Arthur's court. – *Wigl* m2577 a2755 n2861f.

Holofernes   the captain of Nebuchadrezzar's army who was slain by Judith. – nm *JT* 2927,2; *UA* 11814; *RB* 15928

Homerus   the Greek poet. – nm *A* 4868; *JT* 3496,2; *UA* 4810

Hônestus   a king who befriends Dânus and Boizlabe and gives them high positions at his court. They leave him, however, to go in search of their parents. – *WW* a5120 n5148

Horant   the singing warrior who abducts Hilde in the MHG epic *Kudrun*. – *Loh* nm299

Horestes   see Orestes (1)

Horchan   a knight (?). See Aschos

---

19   Martin (1), p. 36 to 25,9; Singer (1), p. 52.
20   Brugger (1), p. 62.

Hostras son of Anthisass, with whom he fights for Gamorett against the Greeks. – *GT* 5671

Houpt a wandering minstrel. He and his comrade, Plôt, were used in a trick by Îsolt (2) to gain time for the escape of Tristan after the failure of his disguise as a fool. The fact that this name is certainly German seems to Golther to provide grounds for the assumption that Eilhart invented this episode in imitation of the gleeman's poems.[21] – *ET* 8368ff.

Hûbert 'ein Anglois', a warrior who is killed by Mathêus (1) at Issôn, whilst fighting for Alexander against Dârîus. – *UA* 4747

Hudos see Isdex

Hûes see Hûwes

Hûg 'von Salzâ', MHG poet mentioned by Heinrich. – *C* nm2445

Hûc (1) 'bischof'. H. makes peace between Meie and his men, who are indignant over the loss of Bêaflôr. – *MB* 161,2

Hûc (2) 'von Lunzel', father of Anshelm (2). Both are killed by Purrel in the second battle against Terramêr at Alischanz. Singer is of the opinion that this name stood in the MS of *Aliscans* which was used by Wolfram.[22] – *W* 428,29

Hûc (3) 'von Morville', a knight who, as a hostage in the place of Richard the Lionheart, is said by Ulrich to have brought the story of *L* with him to Germany. – *L* nm9338 [†]

Hûc (4) 'von Tûfers', a knight who jousts with Ulrich von Liechtenstein during the tourney held at Friesach. – *FD* 190,5

Humildîs brother of Gener, he was imprisoned by Rahîn for the sake of his inheritance. It appears that he afterwards slew his captor. – *C* m14545 n14558f.

Hûnas 'von Sanctes', a knight who is captured by Halzebier whilst fighting for Willehalm (1) at Alischanz. He is later released by Rennewart but is killed by Halzebier (419,6) in the second battle. H. occurs in *Li Covenans Vivien* and in *Aliscans* as Hunaus de Saintes. – *W* 15,4

Hunes a warrior in the Greek army against the Trojans. He is slain by Hector. H. is called Nerius on his first appearance, and later (4889f.) Hunes, both forms deriving from Benoît, where he is called Hunerius (var. Huniers, Nerius). – *LT* 3343

Hûpolt see Hupos

Hupos a warrior in the Trojan army against the Greeks. In *TK* he is called Hûpolt von Colabiâ, whilst he appears in Benoît as Hupoz. – *LT* 3999; *TK* 24824f.

Hupus see Hupos

Hûsinet 'künec von Kanar', an ally of Lôîs against Terramêr. – *UW* 38,7

Hutteger see Hiutegêr

Hûwes 'von Meilanz', a knight who is captured whilst fighting for Willehalm (1) at Alischanz. H. does not occur among the eight knights whose capture in the first battle is related (*W* 47,2ff.), but he is mentioned as a captive by Willehalm (151,22) and by Gîburc (258,24). He occurs among the names of the eight, to the exclusion of Gaudîers, when they are released by Rennewart (416,10). In *UW* he assists Lôîs against Terramêr. Of the OF *chansons de geste*, H. occurs for certain only in *Aliscans*, where he is called Huës de Melans, but he is probably identical with Huges, who appears in the *Chancun de Willame*. – *W* 14,26; *UW* 46,3 [†]

---

21 Golther (2), p. 79.
22 Singer (2), p. 122.

I (Y)

(see also under J)

Iban see Îwein (1)

Iberne 'der von' (*JT*), see Vridebrant

Ibert in some editions of *P*, the form in which Gîbert (1) (q.v.) appears.

Ibilis, Ible see Iblis (1)

Iblet 'von Tesariole', nephew of Teanglis, *ami* of Laudelie. I. is unhorsed by Schîonatulander. – *JT* 1309,1

Iblis (1) daughter of Iweret. She falls in love with Lanzelet, who has come to fight her father, and tries to prevent the contest. It takes place nevertheless, and Iweret is killed, I. then becoming Lanzelet's wife. She is really the heroine of the romance, as she alone of the ladies of Arthur's court is able to make the cloak of chastity fit perfectly, and she is the only one of Lanzelet's wives who becomes queen of Genewîs (see also Îblis (2)). – *L* m3878f. a4016ff. n4060; *G* nm20200f.; *JT* 1611,4

Îblis (2) 'küneginne von Sizilje', wife of Gîbert (1). Her misconduct with Klinschor caused her husband to have the latter rendered impotent. Bartsch thought that this name had some connection with the town of Hybla in Sicily.[1] Golther is of the opinion that it was taken over from *L*,[2] whilst Singer thinks that I. and Iblis (1) are one and the same person.[3] – *P* nm656,27

Ybrot a warrior in Gamorett's army against the Greeks. Y. and Zirus (2) slay each other during the battle. – *GT* 5929

Idaspis a former king of Persia (Hystaspes). – *A* nm15711

Iddippe a warrior who is wounded whilst fighting for the Greeks against the Trojans. His opponent is Hector. This character appears to have been invented by the continuator of *TK*. – *TKf* 40460

Idele see Do

Yden sister of Kahendin. She is present at the tourney between Ris and Cadoalans, and there she sees and falls in love with Kardors, whom she afterwards marries. In Pseudo-Gautier she is called Ydein and is the cousin of Îwein (1). – *RP* a85,5 n85,29

Îdêr 'fil Niut', a knight who first appears in MHG literature in *E*, where he challenges all comers for a sparrow-hawk which is presented yearly by Îmâin to the most beautiful lady present. Êrec accepts the challenge on behalf of Ênîte and defeats I. whom he compels to go to Arthur's court and place himself at the mercy of Ginovêr. I.'s dwarf, Maledicur, is flogged for his insulting treatment of Êrec and one of Ginovêr's maidens. In *I* we learn that I. was one of the knights who unsuccessfully pursued Meljaganz when the latter was abducting Ginovêr (see below). An unnamed son of his attends Arthur's tourney in *C*, whilst he himself fights for Arthur against Bruns (1) in *RP*, and later, as 'Ydierz der lantfarer', takes part in the tourney between Ris and Cadoalans. I. first occurs in William of Malmesbury's *De Antiquitate Glastoniensis Ecclesiae*, where he dies of wounds after killing three giants. Gaston Paris says that this reference bears all the features of an early

---

[1] Bartsch (2), p. 155.

[2] Golther (1), p. 186.

[3] Singer (1), pp. 116f.

127

Anglo-Norman poem, although there is a possibility that it is a later interpolation.[4] He is the hero of the OF romance *Yder*, in which he is considered by Ginovêr to be the next best knight in the kingdom to Arthur, a confession which arouses the latter's jealousy. It seems to be quite evident that I. was originally connected with Ginovêr's infidelity to Arthur; in an OF poem on *Tristan*, considered by Gaston Paris to be of the 12th century,[5] Tristan reminds Îsolt of I.: 'Onques Yders, cil qu'ocist l'ors/ N'ot tant ne poines ne dolors/ Por Guenievre la fame Arthur'. On the bas-relief of the Modena Cathedral, however, I., who is called Isdernus, is not the abductor of Ginovêr, but one of the rescue party. There is not the slightest reason for supposing, however, that the appearance of I. in the light of rescuer in *I* and in the bas-relief is anything more than a coincidence, since Chrestien's *Yvain* does not specify the names of any of Ginovêr's would-be rescuers, and Hartmann undoubtedly chose the names of a few knights at random. – *E* a7ff. n465; *I* nm4706ff.; *P* nm178,12; [C nm587]; *RP* 22,8

Ideus the Trojan messenger who is sent by Ecubâ (3) to Achilles, inviting him to come to the temple in which he is slain. So also in Dictys, where he is called Idaeus. I. occurs in Homer as Idaios. – *TKf* 43778ff.

*Ydier (1) see Îdêr

Ydier (2) 'von Lis', father of Brandelis (q.v.). Y. is slain by Gawein when he tries to avenge the latter's disgrace of his daughter, Gylorette. Y. is called, in Pseudo-Gautier (Potvin's edition), Nores de Lis and Morre de Lis, but never Yder. Bran says of him (17457) that Y. is his brother, whilst he calls Meljanz his father, but this has been brought into line with the earlier story by the translators of *RP*. It is interesting to note that, in *L'Estoire de Merlin*,[6] an Yder de la Terre as Morois (var. Norois) is said to have achieved the adventure of the five rings (i.e. avenged Raguidel). It would seem therefore that Yder stood in the MS of Pseudo-Gautier used by the authors of *RP*, whilst in some MSS the name of the person became displaced by the territorial name. – *RP* m36,14f. a37,39 n205,27

Idiers (1) see Îdêr

Ydiers (2) 'der schöne', a knight who extends hospitality to Arthur and his knights as they are on their way to rescue Gifles. He knocks Keiî down with a roasted fowl when he ill-treats Y.'s dwarf. In Pseudo-Gautier Y. is called Yder li biaus. – *RP* a182,18 n186,9

*Ydiers (3), **Ydierz** see Îdêr

Idîoxenes one of the conspirators with Dimnus against the life of Alexander. I. occurs in Curtius Rufus as Theoxenus (MS C: idioxenum (accusative case)). – *A* nm18890

Idirs see Îdêr

Îdœl, Idol see Do

Ydomeneus 'künec von Krete', a warrior in the Greek army against the Trojans. In *LT*, where he is also called Domerius and Idomeus, he looks after the education of the young Orestes. So also in Dictys, whereas in Dares he is slain by Hector. Y. occurs in *TKf*, where he wounds Hector, in Benoît, where he is called Idomeneus (var. Domerius), and in Homer. – *LT* 3353; *TKf* 40478

Idomeus see Ydomeneus

Idoneus one of the sons of Helen, who murders them in order to ingratiate herself with Menelaus. I. occurs in Dictys as Idaeus. – *TKf* a47165ff. n47179

Ydroges a knight who brings the challenge of Ascalaphus to Paris. – *GT* 18255ff.

---

4   Paris (3), pp. 199ff.
5   Paris (3), pp. 200f.
6   *Vulgate Version of the Arthurian Romances*, II, p. 218.

Îger a knight who is present at the tourney held by Leigamar. – *C* 18045

Îgerne (Schulz derived Wolfram's form of this name (viz. Arnîve) from Celtic *arnwyf*, 'spirit, vigour'; but in *Brut Tysylio* she is called Eigr, 'virgin', and Schulz thought that *Eigr arnwyf* probably became OF Igraine.[7] Martin points out that *Perceval* (10111) reads: 'Ugierne i vint', and suggests that Arnîve was misread from '-erne i v-'.[8] Brugger seeks to explain the change from Îgerne to Arnîve by metathesis (Iguerne > *Iverne > *Ernive > Arnîve).[9] Golther thinks the change was made arbitrarily by Wolfram,[10] whilst Singer is of the opinion that Kîôt made the change to provide alliteration between the names of Arthur and his mother.[11]) I. occurs already in Geoffrey of Monmouth (VIII,19), where as Igerna, the wife of Gorlois (see Urlois), she arouses the admiration of Utepandragûn, who is transformed by Merlin into the likeness of Gorlois and lies with I., begetting Arthur on her. It is afterwards learned that Gorlois has been killed some few hours previously in battle, and as Utepandragûn marries I. long before the birth of Arthur, the regularity of the latter's parentage is not open to question. Chrestien, in his *Perceval*, introduces the story of I.'s voluntary retirement from the world into a magic castle, built for her by 'Uns clers sages d'astrenomie, / Que la reine i amena' (7548f.). It seems to be quite certain, as Golther points out,[12] that 'Que' was misread, probably by Wolfram, as 'Qui', and thus grew up the story of the abduction of Arnîve by Klinschor (q.v.), whilst in *C*, where Heinrich did not misread the original, the character of Gansguoter (q.v.) is quite different from that of Klinschor. (Singer, however, holds that the abduction story is the original, and Chrestien's version the innovation.[13]) *P* is the first extant poem in which I. is called Arnîve, and it is followed by *JT*. *C*, on the other hand, has the French name, Îgern, whilst in *Mer* she is named only in a chapter-heading (before verse 175,1) which reads: 'Ygrena, die man in frantzois nennt Arnifa'. – *P* m66,2 n334,16ff. a565,21; *C* m8310 n13179f. a20804ff.; *JT* m2407,5 n4595,1; *Mer* chapter heading before 175,1

Iglâ niece of the Emperor of Rome. I. falls in love with Anshelm (1), but through the machinations of Phâres (1) the latter is forced to flee the country. – *PM* nm17970ff.

Ignodeloch a famous knight whose death is mentioned by Terramêr. – *R* nm Eing. I,25

Ygrena see Îgerne

Îhêr, Icher see Îthêr

Icolach 'der von' (*JT*), see Ympries

Yconie see Itonjê

Îlamert sister of Laamorz, for whom she makes a magic ball of thread, which Gawein takes from Laamorz to enable him to find the court of vrou Sælde. – *C* nm15346

Ylar a knight who is killed by Paltriot whilst fighting for Atroclas. – *Wigm* 3758

Ilâtrûn a warrior in the Trojan army who is slain by Ulixes and Dyomedes whilst fighting against the Greeks. This character was invented by Konrad. – *TK* 33456f.

Île 'vrouwe', one of the ladies at Arthur's court who spill Priure's cup of chastity. – *C* 1607

Îlet 'künec', 'a dure mains', a knight who attends the tourney held by Arthur. (For the epithet, cf. Agravains.) – *C* 598

---

7   Schulz, 'Eigennamen', p. 395.
8   Martin (1), p. 278, to 334,21.
9   Brugger (1), p. 63, note 5.
10 Golther (1), p. 186.
11 Singer (1), p. 56.
12 Golther (1), p. 186.
13 Singer (1), p. 117.

Ylie see Elye

Ilinôt see Lohût

Ilîôn (1) son of Artâbâzus, a young Persian who is captured by Alexander at the same time as he captures Roxane and the other ladies of Dârîus's household. I. occurs in MS A of Curtius Rufus, but appears in all the other MSS as Hystanes. – *A* 7613

Îlîôn (2) 'von Rôîdôn', *truhsæze* to Meie, whom he accompanies to Rome. – *MB* 208,39

Ylion (3) a Trojan who joins Ênêâs in the conspiracy to betray Troy. – *GT* 19212ff.

Ilioneus son of Priam, he is slain by Ajax (1) whilst fighting for the Trojans against the Greeks. So also in Dictys. – *TKf* 43160ff.

Ylionix 'der wîse', the chief of a band of warriors which Ênêâs sends out to reconnoitre when he reaches Libia. Y. is called Ilioneus in the OF *Eneas* and in Virgil. – *Ed* 270

*****Ylmot** see Lohût

Ilsunc 'von Scheuflich', called 'Schwendenwalt', because of the large number of lance shafts he destroys. I. jousts with Ulrich von Liechtenstein during the latter's *Venusfahrt*. – *FD* 653,5

Ylus founder of Ilion. – *LT* nm15606

Îmâin 'herzoge von Tulmein', a nobleman who institutes the contest for the sparrow-hawk, which is won from Îdêr by Êrec. I. is not named in Chrestien's *Erec*, but Bartsch[14] explains Hartmann's form from a misreading of Chrestien (1347f.):[15] 'et sa cosine estoit germaine / et niece le conte domaine', I. being derived from *'d'Omain-e'. I. is uncle to Ênîte and brother of Karsinefîte. – *E* 176

Imâne 'von der Bêâfontâne', a maiden who had been abducted from Karnahkarnanz by Meljaganz. The girl is not named in Chrestien's *Perceval*, and Golther thinks that the name was invented by Wolfram as a feminine counterpart to Îmâin.[16] There was, however, an OF name Ysmaine, and, in point of fact, two maidens of this name occur in Gerbert's continuation to *Perceval*. – *P* m121,18f. n125,15f.

Imilôt 'vürste', an old knight in whose charge Gârel (1) leaves Laudamîe when he goes to fight for Arthur. – *G* a10699 n10730

Ympries 'von Ycolat', a warrior in Schîonatulander's army against Ipomidôn. – *JT* a4074,4 n4076,1ff.

Ingram 'herzoge', a knight who is present at the tourney held by Arthur. – *JT* 2011,6

Ingûse 'de Bahtarliez', (Schulz derived this name from OF *iniaus*, 'courageous'.[17]) I. is mentioned by Wolfram as having saved Gawein's life when the latter was defeated by Lehelîn. Golther believes that this is a reference to an adventure current at the time, and not invented by Wolfram.[18] Bartsch tentatively connects the story with the fragments of *S*,[19] but *Meraugis de Portlesguez*, on which *S* appears to be based, relates no such incident. – *P* nm301,13ff.

Inmerna see Minervâ

Inpripalenôt one of the knights present at Arthur's court when Êrec returns with Ênîte. This name appears to be based on a misunderstanding of Chrestien's *Erec* (1743): 'Ne Letrons de Prepelesant'. The passage in which this line occurs is thought by Foerster to be

---

14 Bartsch (1), p. 183.
15 This is ll. 1357f. in Foerster's editions of *Erec*.
16 Golther (1), p. 148.
17 Schulz, 'Eigennamen', p. 391.
18 Golther (1), p. 160.
19 Bartsch (2), p. 127.

a later interpolation,[20] but some form of it would appear to have stood in the MS used by the author of *C* (see Neletons). Golther identifies I. with Plipalinot, the knight of the ferry to whom Gawein gives his defeated opponents as prisoners in *P*.[21] Plipalinot is the father of Bêne (2) and acts as host to Gawein on the night before he enters the Schastel Marveile (cf. Karadas (1)). Brugger, basing his suggestion on the similarity of Estravagaot, who occurs in the same line of *E* as I., thinks that I. may be an orthographical distortion of Guingaso(a)ins (see Gasosîn).[22] – *E* 1686; *P* a535,25 n564,4

Ypadens 'von Agremontine', a warrior in Ipomidôn's army against Akarîn. – *JT* 3220,5

Ypodomia daughter of Brises. She is taken by Achilles. So also in Dictys and Homer, and also Benoît. – *LT* nm16664f.

Ypocrate the Greek physician (Hippocrates). – *JT* nm1755,1

Ipolitus son of Theseus (Hippolytus) in Greek legend. He was slain by a sea-monster sent by Poseidon at the instigation of I.'s step-mother. – *C* nm11599

Ypomêdon (1) seen by Êneas during the latter's visit to Hades. He is mentioned in *UA* as being one of those killed in the battle between Ethiocles and Polinices. – *Ed* 3315; *UA* nm3166

Ypomedôn (2) see Ipomidôn

Ipomenes a warrior in the Greek army against the Trojans. This character appears to have been invented by Benoît. – *TK* 30634ff.

Ipomidôn brother of Pompêjus. He and his brother twice fight Akarîn, who has taken from them Ninivê, and on the second occasion Gahmuret meets his death. A third battle takes place in *JT*, and this time the two brothers are decisively beaten, and I., who had slain Gahmuret, is himself slain by Schîonatulander. It is generally agreed that I. is the same character as appears in the *Roman de Thebes*, but whether it is taken direct from the OF, as Singer thinks,[23] or whether it came to Wolfram through the OF *Eneas* and Veldeke's *Ed*,[24] is open to doubt, and the answer depends on the existence or non-existence of Kîot. – *P* 14,3; *T* nm73,4; *UW* nm200,8; *JT* 712,6; *TF* nm2083; *RB* nm16592

Ipothamîe *amie* of Achilles. She is in the camp after his death and meets Pirrus there. This character appears to have been invented by the continuator of *TK*. – *TKf* 44761

Ippote 'von Larîs', a warrior in the Trojan army who is captured by the Greeks and slain. This character appears to have been invented by the continuator of *TK*. – *TKf* 40504f.

Irekel sister of Meliûr. She pleads with her sister for Partonopier, who has lost her favour. She finds Partonopier in a wood, restores him to health and gives him new hope of winning Meliûr, whom she eventually persuades to take Partonopier back into favour. – *PM* 8606ff.

Îrîac 'von Litze', *marschalc* to Meie; he rides on before Meie to announce the latter's arrival in Rome. – *MB* 209,26ff.

Yrkâne daughter of Fontânâgrîs and wife of Reinfrit. – *RB* m192f. n206 a774f.

Irlande 'der von' (*JT*), see Môrolt

Yrlande 'künec von' (*RP*), see Cadoalans

Irmenschart, Irmentschart, Irmetschart see Irmschart

Irmingart baptismal name of Rudolf's *amie*, the daughter of Halap. – *GR* aE,4 nK,27

---

20 Chrestien de Troyes, *Erec und Enide*, ed. by W. Foerster, p. 311.
21 Golther (1), p. 184.
22 Brugger (2), p. 70, note 131.
23 Singer (1), p. 53.
24 For this view, see Martin (1), p. 27, to 14,4.

Irmschart wife of Heimrîch (1) and mother of Willehalm (1). I. is the sister of the king of the Lombards in the OF *chansons de geste*, where she is called Ermenjart; the story of Heimrîch's wooing is told in *Aymeri de Narbonne*.[25] – *W* nm121,20 a142,24; *UW* nm12,8ff. a15,22

Îrôt 'künec', father of Gramoflanz. He gave Klinschor the rock on which the latter built the Schastel Marveile. I. was killed by Lôt (1) and was thus the cause of the feud between Gramoflanz and Gawein. – *P* nm604,19 [†]

Isaâc biblical, son of Abraham. – *A* nm17210; *JT* m2099,4; *UA* nm11301

Ysabon the father of one of the knights at Arthur's court when Êrec returns with Ênîte. Y. does not appear in the corresponding list in Chrestien's *Erec*. – *E* nm1677

Isâias biblical (Isaiah), the OT prophet. – *UA* nm15

Isâjes father of Maurîn and a former marshal of Utepandragûn. – *P* nm662,16

Isachâ daughter of Saraballâ and wife of Manasses (1). – *A* a9915f. n9934; *UA* 17809ff.

Ysachor husband of Hystroyss. Paris and Cornoysse arrive at Y.'s castle on their way to India. Paris has to fight Y., whom he defeats but spares at the pleading of his wife. – *GT* 7590ff.

Îsalde see Îsolt (2) and (3)

Isalt see Îsolt (2)

Isannes 'künec von Agrimontin', a warrior who is killed by Parmênîôn whilst fighting for Dârîus at Issôn. This character appears to have been invented by Ulrich. – *UA* 8101

Isazanz a maiden who is rescued by Gawein when she is being abducted by Anfroihin. – *C* nm9013

Isdex 'von muns dolerous', a knight who is present at Arthur's court when Êrec returns with Ênîte. In Chrestien's *Erec* (1724) he is called Yders del Mont Dolereus, which is corrupted in *C* to Hudos von Mondoil, one of the knights who spill Priure's cup of chastity. – *E* 1657; *C* 2314

Ysdor natural son of Priam, he fights for the Trojans against the Greeks. Y. occurs in Benoît as Ydors (var. Hisdoz), and it is thought by Greif that the name may have originated in Hipposidus, one of the names in Hyginus.[26] – *LT* a4808 n4827

Isel 'von Clâmeroi', sister of Branîe, and one of the ladies at Arthur's court who spill Priure's cup of chastity. – *C* 1617

Îsenhart Belakâne's first lover. She commands him to prove his love, and he complies, going out in search of adventure without his armour. He is met and killed by Protizilas, a knight in the service of Belakâne. I.'s cousin, Vridebrant, does not believe in Belakâne's innocence and collects an army to avenge I.'s death, but is frustrated by the arrival of Gahmuret. This name is, of course, a Germanic one, and Martin is of the opinion that it probably crept into the story in place of the OF name Isambard,[27] but Golther thinks that Wolfram deliberately introduced all German names for Belakâne's enemies.[28] – *P* nm16,4f.; *UW* nm74,18; *JT* nm2550,1

Îseret a warrior in Terramêr's army who defends the ships with Ehmereiz in the second battle at Alischanz. So also in *Aliscans*, where he is called Isorés. – *W* 438,29

Iserterre 'der von' (*JT*), see Klâmidê

---

25 Bédier, I, p. 32.
26 Greif, pp. 26ff.
27 Martin (1), p. 29, to 16,5.
28 Golther (1), p. 141.

Iseve 'von Karoes', niece of Arthur, wife of Karode, and lover of Elyafres (q.v.), by whom she has Karadot. So also in Pseudo-Gautier, where she is called Isaune de Carahais. – *RP* 45,39ff.

Ysyas a prince to whom Alexander, on his deathbed, promised his child, if it should prove to be a girl. Y. does not occur in any other history of Alexander. – *WA* nm6214

Isilia see Elyze

Isilie see Elsam

Iscandus see Liscandes

Ismahêl biblical (Ishmael), son of Abraham and Agar. – *A* nm17220f.

Ismane 'vrouwe', relative of Lore (q.v.). In Pseudo-Gautier she is called Ysaune. – *RP* 25,43ff.

Isolaus the illegitimate son of Hercules. I. fights for the Greeks against the Trojans. This character is almost certainly Iolaüs, the half-brother of Hercules, who occurs in Ovid's *Metamorphoses* IX. – *TK* 37916ff.

Îsolt (1) wife of Gurmûn and mother of Îsolt (2). I. is not named in *ET*, whilst in *Tn* it is she who heals the wound which Tristan has received from her brother, Môrolt. – *ET* m358f. a2264; *Tn* m5937 n6950 a7169

Îsolt (2) (Bruce weighs the evidence of the various etymologies suggested for this name, and arrives at the conclusion that it is of Celtic origin, Welsh Essylt, Cornish Eselt, giving OF Iselt.[29] According to Zimmer, Essylt is not a Kymric name, but comes from the OE Ethyld, Ethelhild.[30] Golther is of the opinion that the OF form is the original one and that this was replaced in the Celtic versions by Essylt, a name with which the Celts were familiar, in the same way that Perceval was replaced by Peredur.[31] Ranke considers that the question still awaits a satisfactory answer.[32] The name appears in two forms in the OF: Iselt (> MHG Îsalde, Îsalde, Îsolt), and Iseut (> MHG Îsôt).) I. is the daughter of Gurmûn and Îsolt (1) (in *Tn*) and lover of Tristan (q.v.). In *ET* she is skilled in medicine, but in *Tn* it is her mother who has this skill. The name became very popular in Germany during the Middle Ages, numerous instances of its occurrence being recorded by Panzer and Zingerle.[33]

I. appears also in *C*, where she is one of the ladies at Arthur's court who spill Priure's cup of chastity, and she is present at Arthur's court in *JT* (1777,2ff.). In this latter poem 'Isalde von Legrois' is mentioned as being at Arthur's court (1606,5), and it seems probable that the two characters are identical.

– *ET* nm42f. a944f.; *L* nm8093; *P* nm187,19; *Tn* [nm130] a7172; *C* 1598; *UT* nm44 a1012f.; *RW* nm2187; *FD* nmXII,12; *JT* 1606,5; *Eng* nm2991; *TK* nm2312; *MB* nm28,37; *HT* nm49 a2534; *RB* nm15288; *RP* nm852,7

Îsolt (3) 'als blansche mains', daughter of Jovelîn and wife of Tristan (q.v.). In *ET* the name occurs as Îsalde, Wolfram's form, Îsalde, in *P* being derived from this, whilst in *Tn* she appears as Îsôt and Îsolde, the former being followed by *UT* and by *HT*, which adds the epithet 'Blanschemanîs'. – *ET* m5544f. an5687ff.; *P* nm187,19; *Tn* nm18704ff. a18960; *UT* nm56ff. a172f.; *HT* nm96f. a384

---

29   Bruce (1), I, p. 183.
30   See Golther (2), p. 32.
31   Golther (2), p. 32.
32   Ranke, p. 3.
33   Panzer (2), p. 218; I.V. Zingerle, p. 294.

Ysope 'küneginne von Holdrafluosz'. She is being oppressed by Marroch and sends to Arthur for help. The latter brings an army and succours her. – *Wigm* m2638 an2677

Ysopey see Ysope

Îsôt see Îsolt (1), (2), and (3)

Yspani 'künec von' (*UW*), see Liliander

Istâmenes a warrior whom Alexander leaves in charge of Kapadocia, whilst he himself goes off to fight Dârîus. This character does not occur in any of the other histories of Alexander. – *A* 5598ff.

Îthêr (Schulz derived this name from the Welsh Edeyren,[34] an etymology with which Bartsch agreed, tracing it through the OF Ider.[35] Singer also believes it to be identical with the OF Ider, and identifies I. with the hero of the OF romance *Yder*, who is, in *P*, distinguished from Îdêr the son of Noit.[36] Martin denies the connection with the OF Yder, and asserts that it occurs as Itier.[37]) I., who is called both 'von Gaheviez' and 'künec von Kukumerlant', is the husband or lover of Parzival's aunt Lamîre. He is slain by Parzival in contravention to the rules of chivalry with a javelin, because Parzivâl coveted his red armour. I. is not named in Chrestien, where he is always referred to as 'li Vermauz Chevaliers'. Golther identifies him with 'Îhêr', a knight who is present at Arthur's court when Êrec returns with Ênîte.[38] *E* (1658) reads: 'Îhêr Gaherîez', and it is thought that the latter word (in reality the name of Gawein's brother) was taken by Wolfram to be the territorial name of I. and became in *P* 'von Gaheviez'. This seems to be supported by the form 'Icher', which appears in *JT*, but the names in the only edition of this epic are in too chaotic a state to carry any authority. – *E* 1658; *P* 145,7ff.; *Wigm* 4777; *FD* nm1546,3; *JT* m1344,1 a1937,1 n2132,7; *WO* nm17095; *UA* nm1709 [†]

Ithinorat see Itinorat

Itinorat a warrior in the heathen army in the final battle against the Christians. He is always referred to as 'der I.', usually with a qualifying adjective, but on one occasion (17443) without. – *WO* 16317

Ytis see Dictys

Itonî see Itonjê

Itonjê (It is generally agreed that this name is derived from OF *idoine*, 'capable', < Latin *idonea*, with the same meaning.[39]) I. is the daughter of Sangîve and sister of Gawein. She is one of the women whom he releases by achieving the adventure of the Schastel Marveile, and after her release she marries Gramoflanz, whom she loves although they have never seen one another. In Chrestien's *Perceval* she is called Clarissanz, and is therefore identical with Clarisanz, who plays the same part in *C*. In *JT*, where she is called Yconie, she is present at Arthur's court when Schîonatulander is there, whilst in *RP* she is the mother of Gyngenor. – *P* nm334,16ff. a565,21; *C* 20966ff.; *JT* 1612,2; *M* nm153; *Sey* m6,1; *RP* nm77,41

Yttra brother of Utepandragûn. Y. entertains Wigamur and makes him a knight. He had also been the tutor of the young Arthur (cf. Antor). This character, who seems to have

---

34 Schulz, 'Eigennamen', p. 397.
35 Bartsch (2), p. 145.
36 Singer (1), pp. 74f.
37 Martin (1), p. 147, to 145,15.
38 Golther (1), p. 151.
39 This etymology was first suggested in Schulz, 'Eigennamen', p. 396 and is accepted in Bartsch (2), p. 146, Singer (1) p. 112, and Martin (1), p. 278, to 334,19.

been invented by the author of *Wigm*, apparently figured in the part of MS W which is now missing. – *Wigm* a1261 n4124

Yven see Îwein (1)

Iphigenie daughter of Agâmennon. She is about to be sacrificed to appease the wrath of Diana, when the latter takes pity on her and snatches her away in a cloud. Konrad got the story from Dictys, where it is also related. – *TK* nm24340 a24548

Ivreins 'von Brandigân', uncle of Mabonagrîn. He entertains Ênîte, Guivreiz, and Êrec on the night before the last-named undertakes the adventure of Schoidelakurt. In Chrestien's *Erec* he is called Evrains. – *E* m8018 a8175 n8605

Îwân see Îwein (1), (2), (5), (6), and (7)

Îwânet a squire who befriends Parzivâl when the latter first arrives at Arthur's court. He is also present at the feast at Arthur's court in *RP*, when the decision is made to rescue Gifles. A knight of the same name is captured by Tandareis during the latter's battle with Arthur in *TF*. In Chrestien's *Perceval* he is called Yonet, a name which Miss Weston derives from the Breton Yonec.[40] – *P* 147,16; *TF* 2205f.; *RP* 173,4

Iwaret see Iweret

Îwein (1) (Schulz took this name to be identical with the Welsh Owain,[41] but Rhys derived it from the name of the Welsh god of War, Esus, through Esugenus, 'offspring of Esus' > Euein and Ywein, the colloquial form of which was Owein.[42] Zimmer shows this etymology to be false and derives the name from the Greek-Latin name Eugenius.[43] Like Arthur, the name is a relic of the Roman occupation of Britain. Bruce also gives this etymology.[44]) I., who is the son of Urjên and who first occurs in Geoffrey of Monmouth (XI, 1) as Eventus, is one of the most popular of the knights of the Round Table. He occurs in most of the romances, and is the hero of Chrestien's poem *Yvain*, which was translated into ME as *Ywain and Gawain*, and into MHG by Hartmann. In this poem, *I*, he defeats and kills a knight, Ascalôn, who issues forth to defend a magic spring, from which I. has poured water on to a stone. With the aid of a maiden, Lûnete, I., who has been entrapped in Ascalôn's castle, avoids death at the hands of the latter's irate knights and marries Laudîne, the widow of the knight he had killed. She grants him permission to go to Arthur's court for a year, but he overstays his leave, and Laudîne dismisses him, sending Lûnete to retrieve the ring she gave him. I., who goes mad at the thought of losing his wife, is cured by a lady for whom he defeats Aliers (1). A lion which he rescues from a serpent accompanies him everywhere, and thenceforth he is known as the Knight of the Lion. Numerous other adventures, such as the slaying of Harpîn, the rescue of Lûnete from her accusers, an undecided fight with Gawein, whom he does not recognize, are achieved before the final reconciliation with Laudîne is brought about by Lûnete. In the other MHG romances his appearances are episodic only. His character as one of the three bravest knights in Britain in *GM* (a poem in which I.'s lion and Gauriel's buck are both killed in a fight between their masters) has no significance, since another of the three bravest knights is the otherwise unknown Walwân (2). I. is called Iban in *Ll*, where a reference is made to the number of saddles which he had emptied at Turnau in der auen. He is also said to have

40 Weston (2), p. 95.
41 Schulz, 'Eigennamen', p. 387.
42 Sir John Rhys, *Lectures on the origin and growth of religion as illustrated by Celtic heathendom* (London, 1888), p. 63, quoted in Zimmer, p. 818, note 1.
43 Zimmer, p. 818, note 1.
44 Bruce (1), I, p. 3, note 1.

killed a king, whose horse carried his dead body back to his castle. According to Steinmeyer,[45] these two adventures are otherwise unknown, but the second is surely a reference to Ascalôn. – *E* 1641; *I* 88; *Wigl* m6397 an9567ff.; *P* nm583,29; *DB* 254f.; *C* 795; *FD* nm1436,7; *G* m36 an17682; *JT* nm1611,3 a1976,5; *TF* 1692; *RB* nm8931; *GM* nm634 a1288; *RP* 17,17; *FS* nm4818; *Ll* 40,1 [†]

Îwein (2) 'von Lafultêre', a knight who is present at Arthur's court when Êrec returns with Ênîte. In Chrestien's *Erec* [1708] he is called Yvains li avoutre (i.e. the Bastard; he is an illegitimate son of Urjên in the OF romances). In *E* he is called Îwân, and in *RP* he appears as 'Ywon der andere', the result of a mistranslation of Gautier, in which he was called Yuvains li Aoutres (a form of *avoutre*); in this poem he takes part in the tourney held by Arthur at Orgelus. – *E* 1645; *RP* 472,34 [†]

Îwein (3) 'mit den wissen henden', a knight who is present at the tourney held by Arthur before Orgelus. In *RP* he is called Ywen, and later (526,18) 'der dritte Ywon'. Yvain aux blansches Mains occurs in the romances of the Vulgate Cycle and in the prose *Tristan* (Löseth's analysis). – *RP* 472,32 [†]

Îwein (4) 'von Canabuz', a knight who spills Priure's cup of chastity at Arthur's court in *C*. In *E* he is called Onam von Galiot, the origin of both appearances being Chrestien's *Erec* (1709), where he is called Yvain de Cavaliot (var. Caneliot). – *E* 1646; *C* 2301

Îwein (5) 'von Lônel', a knight who is present at Arthur's court when Êrec returns with Ênîte. In *E* he is called Îwân. In *L*, where he takes part in Lôt's tourney, he is called Iwân de Nônel. In *P*, where he is called 'cuns Îwân von Nônel', he is the father of one of the Graal maidens who carry the silver knives. He appears as Yvain de Loenel in Chrestien's *Erec* (1707) (see Lohencis). – *E* 1643; [*L* 2936]; *P* nm234,12 [†]

Îwein (6) 'von Penelôî', a knight who preceded Lanzelet to Genewîz in order to announce his coming. The name appears in *L* in the form Iwân. – *L* [8155] [†]

Îwein (7) 'von Roems ûz Normandî', a knight who fights for Willehalm (1) in the second battle against Terramêr at Alischanz. This name, which appears in *W* in the form Îwân, does not occur in *Aliscans* and was no doubt taken by Wolfram from *P* (cf. Iwein (5)). – *W* 424,24 [†]

Ywen see Îwein (1) and (3)

Iweret 'von Dôdône', a knight who issues forth to fight when Lanzelet strikes a cymbal at the side of a well (cf. Ascalôn). I.'s daughter, Iblis (1), tries to avert the fight, but in vain, and I. is slain. – *L* nm328ff. a4408

Ywin see Îwein (1)

Ywon see Îwein (1), (2) and (3)

---

45 *Lorengel*, ed. by E. Steinmeyer, p. 235. The text reads as though these two adventures took place on one and the same occasion, which is no doubt the reason for Steinmeyer's verdict, but the parallel with the Ascalôn episode is too close to be mere coincidence.

J (I, Y)

Iadamus see Liddamus

Jadand see Jaddus

Jaddus chief priest in Jerusalem. Alexander demands duty (in *WA*), soldiers (in *SA*), or both (in *A*) from the Jews. These requirements being refused, he is determined to wipe them out, but at the sight of J., who wears on his head the image of a god whom Alexander has seen in a dream, the latter prostrates himself before J. and gives the Jews their freedom. In *UA* there is no demand made for help, and the entrance of Alexander into Jerusalem is peaceful, but the inevitable prostration before J. takes place. The story is related in the *Historia Scholastica (Liber Esther* IV). – *A* 8786f.; *UA* a2293 n17784f; *SA* 1687ff.; *WA* a856f. n927

*****Jadus, Jadüs** see Jaddus

Jâcob (1) 'sant'. – *FB* nm429

Jâcob (2) biblical, son of Isaac. – nm *A* 16234; *UW* (MSS B and D) 111,114; *UA* 11304; *WW* 2933

Jâcob (3) 'von dem Berge', a knight who jousts with Ulrich von Liechtenstein during the latter's *Venusfahrt*. – *FD* 627,5

Jacobin marshal to Melchinor (see Persit), whom he accompanies in his campaign against Walwan (3). – *WO* 6316ff.

Jâkop (1) 'der zwelfte bote, der wont in Galîzjâ'. Saint James of Compostela. – *W* nm275,24ff. [†]

Jâkop (2) see Jâcob (2)

Jaldus see Jaddus

Jambrî 'vürste', one of the defenders of Gaza, which was being besieged by Alexander. J. was killed in a sortie carried out by the defenders. J. is not named in Gualterus, and is called Betis in Curtius Rufus. Toischer attributes the discrepancy to the marginal annotations in Ulrich's MS of Gualterus.[1] – [*UA* 9719]

Jambruz a knight who attends Leigamar's tourney in the service of Aram. – *C* 18166

Jamêne brother of Ascalaphus, a warrior in the Greek army against the Trojans. J. does not occur in any other version of the Trojan legend, but the name is very similar to a variant form of Almenus (see Alinus), which occurs in Dares. – *TKf* 42399f.

Jâmor Alexander bequeathed to him the lordship over the Pardôs. This name does not occur in any of the other histories of Alexander. – *UA* nm27034

Jandûz 'vrouwe von Lann', a lady present at Arthur's court, where she is one of those who spill Priure's cup of chastity. – *C* 1595

Janphîe *amie* of Lanzelet. She fails in the test of the glove of chastity sent to Arthur's court by Giramphiel. – *C* 20475ff.

Janfûse 'küneginne von', 'diu heidenîn von' (*P*), see Ekubâ (2)

Jâpis a physician who heals Ênêâs when the latter has been wounded in battle. So also in the OF *Eneas*, where he is called Iapis, and in Virgil, where he is called Iapyx. – *Ed* 11895

Iaran 'künec von Syrie', a knight who is present at a tourney held by Arthur. – *JT* 2162,4ff.

Jarant see Jôrant (2)

Jâre 'mit dem guldînen hâre'. Her sister is the *amie* of a giant, and both J. and her sister are among the ladies at Arthur's court who spill Priure's cup of chastity. – *C* 1609f.

---

1 Toischer, pp. 346f.

Jarêt biblical (Jared), father of Enoch. – *A* nm17038

Jascaphîn 'von Orcanîe', father of Mancipicelle. – *C* nm20429f.

Jason the Greek hero, whose quest for the Golden Fleece is described in *LT* and *TK*. He and his party are refused hospitality by Laomedon on the way, and the subsequent wars with Troy are an effort to avenge this insult. In *TK* it is related how Medea sends J.'s lover, Grêûsâ, a poisoned dress which bursts into flames, killing her and Jason. In *GT*, J. is one of the besiegers of Troy, which he leaves to go and fight the Minotaurus, returning, after he has been successful, with Minos's two daughters, Meierra and Fedra, whom he abandons on the way. Their uncle, Gamylle, has his revenge by killing J. at Troy. – *LT* 117ff.; *TK* 6498ff.; *RB* nm24556; *GT* 21661ff.

Iaspideis 'von Fardinzidole', a warrior in Ipomidôn's army against Akarîn. – *JT* 3263,5

Japhêt biblical, son of Noah. – nm *A* 17113; *UA* 11285

Japhîen 'vrouwe', a maiden who had been defended by Gawein against her sister's claim on her inheritance. – *C* nm9001f.

Îaphîne a knight who slays the *ami* of Andeclis, who is avenged by Gawein. – *C* nm9007ff.

Japhîte wife of Rôaz and sister of Panschavar and Zaradech. She watches the fight between Wigalois and Rôaz and dies of grief when the latter is killed. – *Wigl* m7043 an7395

Jechônîas biblical, last but one of the kings of Judah. – *A* nm16322

Jelakîn a maiden in the service of Gîburc. She accompanies her mistress and Willehalm (1) on their flight from Tîbalt. – *UW* 132,25

Yels 'künec von Gâlôes', a knight who is present at Arthur's court when Êrec returns with Ênîte. – *E* 1514

Iemon 'von Suntarise', a warrior in Ipomidôn's army against Akarîn. – *JT* 3261,1

Jenator 'von Taffar', called 'der starke', a warrior in Akarîn's army against Ipomidôn. – *JT* nm3091,6

Jenephus 'herzoge von Angûs', a knight who attends a tourney held by Arthur. – *C* 591f.

Ienilegars 'künec von Ligernuntze', a knight who attends a tourney held by Arthur. – *JT* 2019,1f.

Jenôver (1) 'von Bêumont', a knight who attends a tourney held by Arthur. – *C* 588

Jenovêr (2), **Jenower** see Ginovêr

Ieolarz a knight who attends a tourney held by Arthur. – *JT* 1982,4

Jêômetras see Geometras

Ieori see Georg

Ierant 'von Arsidole', a warrior in Akarîn's army who is killed whilst fighting against Ipomidôn. His slayer is Secureis. – *JT* nm3925,1ff.

Ierasabel 'von Kanfoleise', *amie* of Lesurant. – *JT* nm3165,5f.

Jeremias 'sante', whose bones were brought by Alexander to Egypt to dispel a plague of serpents. This character is evidently the OT prophet Jeremiah. – nm *A* 10603; *UA* 17; *SA* 1549

Jerichô 'künec von' (*Loh*), see Gesparis

Iermidantz 'vürste von Gergidole', a knight who attends the tourney held by Arthur. – *JT* 2042,3f.

Iermidol son of Pardrigun and grandson of Akarîn. He is the father of Bâligân and Kanabeus. – *JT* nm2835,6

Jerneganz 'herzoge von Jeroplîs', a knight who is overcome by Parzivâl. – *P* nm772,11

Jernîs see Lernîs

Jerôboam (1) biblical, king of Israel, 937–915 BC. – nm *A* 16147; *UA* 11640

Jerôboam (2) biblical, 13th king of Israel. – *A* nm16694

Jerome a dwarf queen who compels Fridrich (3) to enter her mountain and offers him her love, which he returns outwardly, and they have a child, Ziproner. Fridrich eventually contrives to escape, but returns to J. after the death of Angelburg, and marries her. – *FS* a2428 n2964

Jerônimus 'der heilige' (St. Jerome). – *A* nm16069

Jeroparg a magician, lover of Flanea, for whom he turns Angelburg into a hart. When Fridrich's army has defeated that of Mompolier, J. fights Fridrich in single combat on three different days and, being eventually defeated, confesses the conspiracy against Angelburg and is burnt to death. – *FS* m179 a1031ff. n5426

Ieruchubar 'von Todierne', a warrior in Akarîn's army against Ipomidôn. – *JT* nm3168,1

Jerusalem 'künec von' (*WO*), see Koradin

Jesabel biblical, according to *UA*, the wife of Nabôt. Although the part which she plays in the story of Naboth's vineyard is told correctly in *UA*, she was historically the wife of Ahab (see Achap). – *UA* nm11661

Jesebon 'künec von Brizia', a warrior on the side of the heathens in the final battle against the Christians. – *WO* 16437ff.

Iesibudantze 'von Valveste', a warrior in Akarîn's army against Ipomidôn. – *JT* nm3137,1

Iesipont 'von Siglimisse', a warrior in Akarîn's army against Ipomidôn. – *JT* nm3625,1

Jeschûte 'von Karnant'. (Bartsch thinks that this name is the result of a misunderstanding of Chrestien's *Perceval* (670f.): 'El lit tote sole gisoit / Une dameisele andormie'.[2] The mistake of supposing 'gisoit' to be the name of the maiden could not possibly have been made by a Provençal poet, however, such as the Kîôt in whom Bartsch firmly believes.) J. is the sister of Êrec, and is found by Parzivâl asleep in a tent. Parzivâl, who has only just left his mother, takes her advice too literally and robs J. of some kisses and some jewelry. Orilus, realising that someone has been with his wife, thinks she has been unfaithful to him, and dressing her in miserable rags, he makes her ride behind him as he goes about looking for adventures. He is eventually overcome by Parzivâl, who then explains the true position, and makes Orilus take his wife back into favour. There is no suggestion in Chrestien's poem that J. is the sister of Êrec, and the relation may have been suggested to Wolfram by the similarity in the treatment of J. and Ênîte by their respective husbands. – *P* 129,28ff.; *Wigl* nm6325; *JT* 1432,1; *RB* nm2194 [†]

Jescuse, Jescute see Jeschûte

Iesoral a knight who is present at a tourney held by Arthur. – *JT* 2042,6f.

Jesse biblical, father of David. – *UA* nm11498

Iessurel 'von Grassudie', a warrior in Akarîn's army against Ipomidôn. I. is the brother of Senebor. – *JT* nm3111,1f. a3896,3f.

Jesfurel see Iessurel

Jetakranc 'künec von Gamfassâsche'. (The territorial part of this name has been identified as identical with Gamphasantes, the name of a tribe mentioned in Solinus. Jetakranc was derived by Bartsch from Provençal *Jeta-gram-s*, 'he who repels the foe'.[3] Hagen tried to find a connection between *grams* and OF *estrange*, because Solinus says of the tribe (137,10): 'nulli se extero misceri sinunt'.[4] It is noteworthy that, apart from Archeinor, this is the only name in this list which is not derived from Solinus.) J. is a knight who is defeated by Feirefiz. – *P* nm770,28

---

2   Bartsch (2), p. 133.
3   Bartsch (2), p. 150.
4   Martin (1), p. 505, to 770,28.

Ietrassin 'von Olmidende', a warrior in Akarîn's army against Ipomidôn. – *JT* nm3137,4

Jêû biblical (Jehu), 10th king of Israel. – *A* nm16621

Jewin see Îwein (1)

Jhêsus son of Jûdas (3). J. is killed by his brother, Johannes (3), because Vagôsus had promised to make him chief priest. – *UA* nm17747ff.

Jôab biblical, brother of Abner. – *UA* nm11559

Joachas biblical, king of Israel. – *A* nm16660

Joachim (1) father of the Virgin Mary and husband of Anna (2). J. was driven out of the temple because of the barrenness of his wife. – *RB* nm13001

Joachim (2) counsellor of Evilmôradac. It is related in *Historia Scholastica* (*Liber Danielis* V) how J. was taken out of prison by Evilmôradac and raised to a position next to the throne. – *UA* nm7703

Joachim (3) biblical (Jehoiakim), king of Judah (Jeremiah 22). – *UA* nm11757

Joachim (4) king of India, defeated by Nâbuchodônosor. – *RB* nm26732

Jôas (1) biblical (Joash), king of Israel. – *A* nm16664f.

Jôas (2) biblical (Joash), king of Judah. – *A* nm16297

Jôathan biblical (Jotham), king of Judah. – *A* nm16313

Job biblical, the hero of the Book of Job in the OT. – nm *W* 307,5; *Eng* 6087; *Mer* 21,6

Jôbal biblical, descendant of Cain. This name could be intended either for Jabel or Jubal, both of whom were sons of Lamech. Since Tubal is here called Tobal, it would seem probable that Jubal is intended here. The name occurs as Jobel in Pseudo-Methodius. – *A* nm17041

Jobas son of Antipater, chamberlain to Alexander, whom he poisons. In *SA* he kills himself after Alexander's death. (See Pâtrôn (2).) In *Expeditio Alexandri* and Curtius Rufus he is called Jollas, whilst in Leo he is called Jolus. He is said to be the brother of Antipater in *WA*. – *SA* 8206ff.; *WA* nm6026

Jôbusêus a king who is captured by Eresdes. J. does not occur in the passage from Pseudo-Methodius in which this part of *A* originated. – *A* nm17163

Jôhan (1) elder son of Lohengrîn and Elsam. – *P* m826,9; *Loh* 3825

Jôhan (2) 'Priester', son of Feirefîz and Repanse de Schoie, and, in *JT*, the eventual guardian of the Graal. Prester John, as he is called in English, was first heard of in Europe from the Chronicle of Bishop Otto of Freising (Chapter 33, for the year 1145), who heard about him from the Bishop of Gabula.[5] He has been identified by Zarncke as a Chinaman, Ku-Khan (i.e. the all-highest king), whose real name is Yeliutasche.[6] According to Golther, J. wrote a letter to the emperor at Byzantium, describing the wonders of his kingdom.[7] This letter, which filled the Christians with the hope of an ally at the rear of the Saracens, was, in Golther's opinion, known to Wolfram, who utilized it in *P*. – *P* nm822,23ff.; *JT* nm307,7 a6031,1ff.; *Loh* nm3826; *RB* nm21932

Johan (3) 'sante'. – nm *E* 8652; *I* 901; *Wigl* 10274; *UW* 288,23; *Mer* 244,4; *UA* 43; *WW* 3532; *RB* 10892; *WO* 199; *RP* 229,34; *KT* 1430; *Ll* 171,8

Jôhan (4) 'bâbest'. He is attacked by Gêrfridolt and an army of heathens. He raises an army under the leadership of Heinrîch (1) and Lohengrîn and defeats them. – *Loh* nm3503f. a4111

---

5   Zarncke, p. 847.
6   Zarncke, pp. 863ff.
7   Golther (1), pp. 191f.

Jôhan (5) 'von Brûnswîch'. Berthold says that J. told him the story of *Crane*. This would be the son of Otto das Kind; he was Herzog von Braunschweig-Lüneburg AD 1252–77. – *Crane* nm27ff.

Jôhan (6) 'bâbest' (Pope John XV). – *Loh* nm7461

Johan (7) 'herzoge von Brabant', a knight who fights on the side of the Christians in the final battle. – *WO* 16869ff.

Jôhan (8) 'grâve von Lützelburc'. J. pleads for Friderîch (2) before Heinrîch (1), and later fights for the latter against Gêrfridolt. – *Loh* 2229

Johan (9) 'ûz Pavermunde', a knight who is present at a tourney held by Arthur. – *JT* 2040,1

Johan (10) son of Wide, a knight who is captured by Avenis during the tourney at Poys and who is also present at the tourney held near Kurnoy. – *RW* 7259ff.

Johanet 'von Lacrika', a knight who is present at the tourney held by Crispin. – *WO* 14674

Johannes (1) 'sante' (St. John the Baptist). – nm *JT* 6036,6; *RB* 13061

Jôhannes (2) a judge who was left in Rome by Constantine. – *A* nm12981

Johannes (3) son of Jûdas (3) and father of Jaddus. J. murdered his brother Jhêsus (q.v.). – *UA* nm17747f.

Johannes (4) chamberlain of Alexander. He is sent to fetch Simeôn (2) to the latter's deathbed. J. does not appear in any of the other histories of Alexander. – *SA* 8421

Johannes (5) 'von Würzburg', MHG poet and author of *WO*. – *WO* nm13228ff.

Johannes (6) 'mit der sunne', biblical (John of the *Book of Revelation*?). – *JT* nm272,1

Johannes (7) 'lebtzelter gegenschriber am zoll zuo Geiszlingen'. The writer of the Straßburg MS of *FS*. The name appears at the end of a short rimed appendix to *FS*.

Johannes (8) 'von Ravensburg', who brought the story of *RW* to Germany from France. – *RW* nm15601ff.

Johenis a warrior who fights on the side of the heathens in the final battle against the Christians. – *WO* 16346

Iohiote 'herzoge', husband of Ligronite and father of Flogrifite. I. is slain by Lespurant. – *Wigm* (MS M) nm109929

Johfrit 'de Liez', a knight who meets Lanzelet and teaches him how to bear and use his armour. – *L* a466 n487

Jocundille the name assumed by Achilles whilst he is masquerading as a woman at the court of Lycomedes. This name appears to have been invented by Konrad. – *TK* nm15295

Jokfrid see Jofrit (1)

Îolê daughter of Euritus. I. was loved by Hercules (q.v.), and it was through the jealousy thus aroused in Dîanîra that Hercules met his death. So also in Ovid's *Metamorphoses* IX. – nm *C* 11585; *Port* 22; *TK* 38186ff.

Jollas (1) 'grâve', a warrior in Alexander's army. He is slain (8009ff.) by Mâzêus (2) at Issôn. So also in Gualterus. – *UA* nm4607 a8009f.

Jollas (2) a warrior in Alexander's army at Issôn. He is slain by Negûsar. J. does not appear in any of the other histories of Alexander. – *UA* 8280

Jonant see Jûdas (2)

Jonas biblical (Jonah), the OT prophet who was swallowed by a whale. – *FS* nm2899

Jonatham biblical (Jonathan, here in the accusative case), son of Saul and friend of David. – *UA* nm11545

Ionatris 'von Sermiel', also called Lonatris von Sarviele, a warrior who is slain by Môrolt whilst fighting for Ipomidôn against Akarîn. – *JT* nm3235,3 a3675,1

Jônitus biblical, son of Noah (identical with Japhêt?); he occurs as Jonithus in Pseudo-Methodius. – *A* nm17091

Jôram (1) a prince who was married by Alexander to the widowed queen of Thebes. J. does not occur in any of the other histories of Alexander. – *UA* 3836

Jôram (2) a knight who arrives at Arthur's court and offers Ginovêr a magic girdle, which she refuses, whereupon J. challenges all the knights at the court to fight for its possession. He defeats them all, including Gawein, whom he takes back to his land as a prisoner. Gawein marries his niece, Flôrîe (2). – *Wigl* a260 n5818; *TF* nm2551

Jôram (3) biblical (II Kings 8, 29), king of Israel. – *A* nm16613

Jôram (4) biblical (II Kings 8, 21), king of Judah. – *A* nm16264

Joram (5) a poet who takes part in the singing contest with Wolfram and Klinschor. – *Ll* nm2,9

Joram (6) see Jorant (2)

Jôrân (1) 'grâve von Provenz', a warrior in Alexander's army. This character appears to have been invented by Ulrich. – *UA* 4729

Jôrân (2) see Lerân

Iorande a knight who is present at a tourney held by Arthur. – *JT* 2042,6

Jorans 'herzoge von Iorapfise', a knight who swears allegiance to Parzivâl after the latter's victory over Agors (see Strangedorz). – *JT* 5659,1

Jôrant (1) 'künec von Galicî', an ally of Lôis against Terramêr. – *UW* 36,14

Jôrant (2) a young knight who offers himself as champion for Elsam, when the Graal message is read. In *Ll* he is called Joram, whilst in MS K he is Jarant. – *Loh* 572; *Ll* 46,1 (MS K) 32,3

Jorant (3) 'Paide', a knight who abducts the daughter of the grâve von Asteriân. He is captured by Gauriel. – *GM* m3203f. n3425 a3510

Joranz 'von Belrapeire', a knight who attends a tourney held by Arthur. – *C* 605

Joraffin a knight who is lord of a fire-mountain. J. is defeated by Wildhalm and takes the latter through a ring of fire, which cannot burn anyone, to his fiery palace, where he gives Wildhalm a wonderful helmet. – *WO* 3652ff.

Iorbideis 'von Iorde', a warrior in Akarîn's army against Ipomidôn. – *JT* 3637,1

Jordanich 'kaiser von Kriechen', who, together with Jôhan (4), is attacked by Gêrfridolt and his heathen army. J. fights in the ensuing battle under Heinrîch (1). He is also called (6035) Andrêas. – *Loh* m3511 a4704f. n4855

Jorêl see Lâr

Joret 'künec', a knight who is present at a tourney held by Arthur and who also fights for Orilus against Schîonatulander. – *JT* 1997,1

Jörg see Georg

Jorye 'künec', an ally of Agrant against Melchinor. He is captured by Wildomis at Firmin. – *WO* 7726

Joryol 'von Mofetyol', a knight who takes part in the tourney held by Arthur for the crown of Deleprosat. – *Wigm* 2125

Iosafat (1) 'von Lurgande', a warrior in Akarîn's army against Ipomidôn. – *JT* nm3140,1

Jôsafât (2) one of the protagonists in the poem *Barlaam und Josaphat* by Rudolf von Ems. – nm *A* 3283; *RW* 15639

Josêp (1) interpreted Solomon's dreams for him. This seems to be confused in the mind of the author with Joseph (1). – *RB* nm13691

Yosep (2) see Joseph (2)

Josepus see Jôsephus

Joseranns father of Albazona, with whom he is rescued from two giants by Seyfrid and Waldin. – *Sey* a335,4 n344,5

Joseph (1) biblical, the son of Jacob who became governor of Egypt. – nm *UA* 11353f.; *WW* 2803

Joseph (2) 'von Aramate' (i.e. of Arimathea), a secret disciple of Christ who procured the latter's dead body from the cross, in order to give it a decent burial. J. appears in an uncanonical writing of early Christianity, called *Vindicta Salvatoris*, in which he tells Vespasian of his former imprisonment and of his release by Christ. The earliest medieval romance in which J. appears is the *Joseph* of Robert de Boron, written between AD 1180 and 1199, in which the author utilizes the *Vindicta Salvatoris* and the apocryphal book, *Evangelium Nicodemi*.[8] In *Joseph*, J. is the first to learn of the existence of the Graal, which he eventually brings to England. – nm *JT* 6176,1; *Mer* 149,5; *RB* 181,28; *RP* 612,44

Jôsephus a Jewish historian (Josephus Flavius), who wrote in Greek and lived AD 37–*c*.100. – nm *A* 12884; *SA* 48

Jôsîas biblical, king of Judah (Josiah). – nm *A* 16321; *UA* 11710

Iosimor 'von Kante', a warrior in Akarîn's army against Ipomidôn. – *JT* nm3638,1ff.

Josofat see Jôsafât (2)

Jôsuê biblical (Joshua), the Israelite leader. – nm *UA* 11460; *RB* 15834

Josuêle 'von Agricolanz', a warrior who is slain by Hector whilst fighting for the Greeks against the Trojans. This character was invented by Konrad. – *TK* 31316

Joswê 'künec von Alahôz', one of the group of 15 Saracen kings who attack Willehalm (1) at the end of the first battle at Alischanz. J. is wounded or killed by Willehalm in that encounter. [See Appendix (9).] J. appears in *Aliscans* as Josués, who is taken by Langlois to be identical with the Josuez who is the OF original of Josweiz (q.v.).[9] Wolfram evidently thought them separate persons and gave them different lands. – *W* m71,22 a72,17f. n74,25 [†]

Josweiz 'künec von Amatiste', son of Matûsales, and nephew of Terramêr, for whom he fights at Alischanz. J. is probably identical with the 'künec von Hippopotitikûn', who assists in arming Terramêr, since the men of Hippopotitikûn are said (349,12ff.) to be under his command, and it is stated (386,8ff.) that his father sent him from that country. (See also Joswê.) – *W* 28,30

Jovedast 'von Arle, ein Provenzâl'. (Bartsch considered -*dast* a corruption of *dats* < Latin *datus*, i.e. *Jove datus*.[10]) J. is included in the list of knights whom Parzivâl states that he has overcome. – *P* nm772,22

Jovelîn (< Kymric Hoel or Howell, a popular name for Kymric princes, which means, according to Zeuss, 'visible from afar', or 'gazing into the distance'.[11]) J. is the father of Îsolt (3) and Kâedîn. *HT* follows the spelling of *Tn*, Jovelîn, whilst in *ET* he is called Havelîn. In the OF prose *Tristan* (Löseth's analysis) he is called Hovel, and in Malory, Howell. – *ET* nm5532 a5592; *Tn* m18694 n18715 a18727; *UT* m94 a115f.; *HT* nm89 a380ff.

Jovis the heathen god. – nm *R* Forts. I,103; *UA* 672; *RB* 16398; *GT* 12213

Jôfreit (1) 'von Sâlîs', a knight who fights for Willehalm in the second battle at Alischanz. J. does not occur in any of the OF versions. – *W* 437,12

---

8 Bruce (1), I, pp. 238f.
9 Langlois, p. 383.
10 Bartsch (2), p. 151.
11 Gottfried von Straßburg, *Tristan und Isolde*, transl. by W. Hertz, p. 627.

Jofreit (2)   see Gifles

*Iofret   see Gifles

Jofrit (1)   'herzoge von Brabant', husband of Elise and foster-father of Willehalm (4), whom he makes his heir. – *RW* 253ff.; *FS* nm7445

Jofrit (2)   second son of Willehalm (4) and Amely. He marries the daughter of Robert (2) and has a son, Jofrit (3). – *RW* 15266ff.

Jofrit (3)   son of Jofrit (2). J. frees the Holy Sepulchre at Jerusalem. – *RW* 15586f.

Jofrit (4), **Ioffreit, Joffreitte**   see Gifles

Joffrit   see Jofrit (1)

Jozeranz   a knight who is slain whilst fighting for Willehalm (1) at Alischanz. In *UW* he is an ally of Lôîs against Terramêr. J. appears once, as Joserans, in both *Aliscans* and *Les Narbonnais*. – *W* 14,25; *UW* 46,8

Jôzêus   one of the conspirators with Dimnus in the plot to murder Alexander. J. appears in Curtius Rufus as Iolaus (MS A: ioceum, in the accusative case), and is probably identical with Lotilâus (q.v.). – *A* nm18891

Jubel   a warrior in the Trojan army against the Greeks. – *GT* nm22767

Jûdas (1)   biblical, name-father of the tribe of Judah. – *A* nm8795

Jûdas (2)   brought a costly cloth 'ûz dem Pelibronne', in which they clothe the Graal maidens. In *Ll* (MS K) he is called Jonant. – *Loh* nm465f.; *Ll* (MS K) nm18,6

Jûdas (3)   son of Elyasip. J. becomes chief priest on the death of his father. He has two sons, Johannes (3) and Jhêsus. – *UA* nm17744

Jûdas (4)   'Iscariot', the betrayer of Christ. – nm *P* 219,25; *JT* 93,5; *MB* 152,35; *SA* 6089

Judas (5)   'Machabeus', the leader of the Jewish rebels against Antiochus Epiphanes (see Antiochus (3)). – *RP* nm603,6

Jûdith   the slayer of Holofernes. – nm *UA* 11815; *RB* 15930f.

Juliander   a warrior in Terramêr's army who is overcome by Zukander in the battle against Lôîs. J. appears only in MS G. – *UW* (MS G) 43,18

Juliens   a knight who fights for Athis against Bilas. He is slain by Aimon. J. is also called Iulion, but appears as Juliens in the OF version. – *AP* A*,101

Iulion   see Juliens

Iulius (1)   a knight who fights for Athis against Bilas. In the OF version he is called Jules. – *AP* A*,101

Jûljus (2)   'Cêsar', the Roman general. – *Ed* 13381ff.; *P* 102,3; *LT* 14190f; *MC* 116; *FB* 1563; *UA* 14676

Julkôn   a warrior who is slain by Alexander whilst fighting for Porrus. In Gualterus, where he appears for the first time, he is called Enachides Hiulcon, but because the patronymic did not immediately precede the name, they were taken to be two separate persons by Ulrich (see Enachus). – *UA* 19654

Jûlus   see Ascânjus

Junalet   a knight who is overcome by Prinel. – *UW* nm255,20

Junamûr   castellan in the castle of Senebalŷn. – *UW* a154,28 n172,4

Jûne, Junno   see Jûnô

Jûnô   one of the three goddesses among whom Paris has to decide which is the most beautiful. In *TK* she is said to be the step-mother of Hercules, whom she tried to murder; he was saved by being dressed in women's clothes by his mother, Alcmêne. Although the facts are obviously confused, this is certainly a reference to one of the numerous attempts made to injure him by Hera, who was identified by the Romans with Juno. – *Ed* nm156; *P* nm748,17; *LT* nm2194f.; *C* nm8289; *FB* 1587ff.; *UW* nm90,19; *TK* 1027; *Loh* nm232; *UA* nm4881ff.; *RB* nm16415; *GT* m1926ff. n1939ff. a2009; *GM* (MS I) nm3760ff. (MS D) nm353[168]

Jupiter the Roman god. On the occasion of the wedding of his sister Thetis to Pêleus, J. gave a great feast, to which Discordia, the only deity uninvited, brought (or in some versions sent) her apple of discord. – *P* nm748,19; *LT* nm963; *A* nm5056; *R* nm Bl. I,24; *G* nm14678; *JT* nm3692,5; *TK* 813; *Loh* nm4237; *UA* nm688; *WW* nm290; *RB* nm16399; *GT* nm20185; *WO* nm5363; *SA* nm4945; *WA* nm5917

Iuppite, Juppitter see Jupiter

Jurân a dwarf who oppresses vrou vom Trüeben Berge and is slain by Daniel (1). J. has a magic sword which can bite through anything. Daniel gets him to fight with an ordinary sword, and after his death, takes possession of the magic one. – *DB* m1226 n1290 a1513

Jûrâns 'cuns von Blemunzîn'. (Bartsch derived this name from OF *jurans*, 'der Schwörende'.[12]) J. is one of the knights whom Feirefîz states he has defeated. – *P* nm770,29

Jurie see Georg

Justînus (1) 'künec'. The emperor of the eastern Roman Empire; J. became emperor in AD 518. – *UA* m27839 n27889

Justînus (2) 'vürste', one of those who, with Thedalûn, are left in charge of Alexander's peoples whilst the emperor is campaigning. J. does not appear in any of the other histories of Alexander. – *UA* a2361 n2400

---

[12] Bartsch (2), p. 150.

K (C)

Kabellitor see Kalebitor

Cabcaflir 'künec', father of Batewain. This name does not appear in Chrestien's *Erec*. –
E nm1675

Cabrians 'von Sinagorie', a warrior who fights for Ipomidôn against Akarîn. – *JT* nm3241,1

Cadoalans 'künec von Yrlande'. (Foerster quotes Zimmer as deriving this name from Old
Breton Catwallon, Middle Breton Cadwallen.[1] Cadwallo is a king who occurs in Geoffrey
of Monmouth.) C., who in Pseudo-Gautier is called Cordovalan, Cadoalant, is one of the
protagonists in a tourney, at which his side, assisted by Karadot, defeats Ris. – *RP* nm72,42
a86,39

Kadoalant see Cadoalans

Cadoc a knight who is rescued by Êrec from two giants. He is called 'von Tabriol'. So also
in Chrestien's *Erec*. – *E* m5349ff. a5297ff. n5644f.

Cadolt (1) a knight who welcomes Ulrich von Liechtenstein at Feldsberg during his
Venusfahrt. – *FD* 906,8ff.

Kadolt (2) 'der Weise', a knight who jousts with Ulrich von Liechtenstein at Neustadt and
who fights on his side in the subsequent tourney against Friderîch (4). – *FD* m1496,1ff.
an1500,2

Kador see Kardors

Kaedens a knight who is present at the tourney between Ris and Cadoalans. This name is
not mentioned in Pseudo-Gautier. (Identical with Kâedîn?) – *RP* 81,29

Kâedîn brother of Îsolt (3). He accompanies Tristan to Cornwall to see Îsolt (2) and there
falls in love with Gymêle (q.v.), who, however, cheats him with a magic pillow. K.'s ill-
fated love for Gariôle is the cause of the death of both Tristan and himself. He is called
Kehenis in *ET*, and Kahenîs in *P*, but *HT* and *UT* follow the form Kâedîn in *Tn*, *UT* also
showing the variant Kahendin. In Thomas he is called Kaherdin, which Villemarqué, as
quoted by Hertz,[2] derives from the Kymric Kaerden, 'handsome man'. – *ET* nm5568f.
a5660; *P* nm573,14ff.; *Tn* nm18704ff. a18742; *UT* a66 n115; *HT* nm91 a332

Kahedin see Kâedîn

Kahendin brother of Îdêr. – *RP* nm85,26

Kahenîs (1) see Kâedîn

***Kahenîs** (2) see Gabenîs

Kaheret a knight who fights for Arthur against Tandareis. (Identical with Gaherîez?) –
TK 1697

Kâhûn a heathen deity, also called Kâun. – nm *W* 358,13; *R* Bl. I,85; *JT* 4137,4; *Loh* 4237;
UA 385

Kay, Kaii see Keiî

Kailet (Schulz derived this name from the Welsh *caled*, 'hardy'.[3] Bartsch thought Wolfram
probably took it from *L*, and considered the possibility of its being a diminutive of the
German name Gailo (< OHG *gail*, 'happy').[4] Golther agrees that it might have been taken
by Wolfram from *L*, but also considers it possible that it is a distorted form of Gahillet, who

---

[1] Chrestien de Troyes, *Karrenritter*, ed. by W. Foerster, p. xxxviii.
[2] Gottfried von Straßburg, *Tristan und Isolde*, transl. by W. Hertz, p. 626.
[3] Schulz, 'Eigennamen', p. 404.
[4] Bartsch (2), p. 136.

occurs in E.[5]) K., who is called 'von Hoskurast', is 'künec von Spâne, Spânôl, Spangen, Spaniol', and is cousin to Gahmuret. He is one of the army besieging Belakâne in Patelamunt, and is later one of the protagonists at the tourney held by Herzeloide. He has incurred the enmity of Hardîs through his treatment of the latter's sister, Alîze (1), whose love he has enjoyed, but whom he refuses to marry. In *JT* he is the son of Laeo and marries, as in *P*, Rischoide. K. occurs also in *WO*, where he is called Gaylet, and rescues Wildhalm from the fire into which Merlin (2) in his death throes has cast him. He is the chief noble in Crispin's land and eventually marries her. – *L* 6032; *P* nm25,16f. a39,11; *JT* 440,1f.; *WO* a12188ff. n12239 [†]

Kaym see Kâîn (1) [†]

Kâîn (1) son of Adam and murderer of Abel. – nm *P* 464,16; *A* 17008; *PM* 952; *UA* 11222; *GT* 23006; *RP* 637,39 [†]

Câin (2) see Kâîn (1) and Câm [†]

Kaiver 'künec von Schotten', a knight who is present at the tourney held at Kurnoy. – *RW* nm8408f. a8788ff.

Cacharet see Talkaret

Cacudeiz 'grâve von Geinte', a warrior who is slain by Cardes whilst fighting for the Greek army against the Trojans. This character was invented by Konrad. – *TK* 32718

Calabrus a giant, husband of Ruell. C. is slain by Paris as the latter is returning with Marcus (1) to the court of Agâmennon. – *GT* a6649ff. n6668

Calaidâ see Galaidâ

Kalaminde see Klâmidê

Kâlas 'vürste', a warrior who is placed by Alexander over Paflagonîe. K. occurs as Calas in Curtius Rufus, *Expeditio Alexandri*, and the *Historia Successorum Alexandri*. – *A* 5107

Kalafrê see Galafrê

Calaphus see Ascalaphus

Kalebitor 'von Ackraton', a warrior who is slain by Môrolt whilst fighting for Ipomidôn against Akarîn. He is the brother of Serut. K. is also called Kabellitor, Frabellitor, and Frabilitaltz. – *JT* 3363,1 [†]

Calebrant a burgher who is the first person to witness the arrival of Lohengrîn and the swan and notifies Waldemar. – *Ll* a59,7 n67,10

Kaleopacia see Cleôpatra

Kâles see Galez

Calestenâ see Calistenes

Calesce see Galesche

Calides see Arides

Caliopatra see Cleôpatra

Calipsa a lady who captured Ulixes and won his love during his voyage back from Troy. So also in Benoît, Dictys, and the *Odyssey*. – *LT* nm17685

Calistenes tutor to Alexander when he was seven years old. In *UA* he is the tutor of Ermolâus (q.v.), and is slain at the command of Alexander because of the advice which he gives his charge. – *A* 1354; *UA* 18925

Calistrida see Tâlistrîâ

Kalif 'bâbest zu Baldac' (obviously the Caliph of Bagdad). Melchinor consults him as to whether he should slay Wildhalm. K. advises him not to do so, and thus saves Wildhalm's life. – *WO* m5514 an5544

---

5   Golther (1), p. 141.

Kalcas a Trojan who is sent by Paris to consult the oracle at Delfos before the siege of Troy. Learning that Troy is doomed, he changes sides and joins the Greeks, where he is later joined by Brîsêîdâ. This version is derived by *LT* from Benoît and Dares, but in *TK*, as in Homer, K. is a Greek from the commencement, and in Homer he is the soothsayer who demands the return of Chryseis to her father. – *LT* 3512; *TK* 24208; *RB* nm22586

Callebrant see Calebrant

Callicrates a warrior who is left by Alexander as tribute-collector with Abûlites. So also in Curtius Rufus. – *A* 13501

Kallikrâtides a warrior who is captured by Alexander after the defeat of Dârîus. So also in *Expeditio Alexandri* and Curtius Rufus. – *A* 7640

Calmanan daughter of Eve. This name occurs in Pseudo-Methodius as Chalmanan. – *A* nm17008

Kalo a warrior in the service of Achilles, at whose command he drags Troilus round the walls of Troy behind his horse. K. is slain by Mennon (2). This character was invented by Herbort. – *LT* 13219

Kâlôes see Gâlôes (1)

Kalogreant a knight of the Round Table and cousin of Îwein (1). K. is the first knight to undertake the adventure of the spring, but unlike Îwein, K.'s attempt ends in disgrace. In *C* he accompanies Gawein in search of the Graal, but he sleeps whilst Gawein is being granted a view of its wonders. In *TF* he is captured by Tandareis when fighting for Arthur, whilst in *RP* it is related how he is slain by Lyonel when he tries to prevent the latter from killing Boort. This story is told also in *Les Aventures del Saint Graal* (Vulgate Cycle). K. is called Colgrevance in the ME *Ywain and Gawain*, and as such plays a prominent part in Malory. – *I* 92; *C* 2195; *FD* nm1416,5; *JT* nm1747,4 a2353,2; *TF* 2205f.; *RB* nm20161; *GM* nm634 a(MS I only) 3861; *RP* nm627,16 a806,13

Kalogrians, Kalogriant see Kalogreant

Kaloys counsellor to Agâmennon, who consults him as to a suitable reward for Paris. – *GT* 3725

Kalokrêant, Kalocrîant see Kalogreant

Kalopeiz 'künec von Tûsî', a warrior who fights for Terramêr in the second battle against Willehalm (1). According to *W*, fanfares were invented in his land. No satisfactory explanation of this name has yet been found. – *W* 360,8f.

Calopin a warrior in the Trojan army against the Greeks. – *GT* nm22767

Kaltzedanc 'von Atrimonie', a warrior in Akarîn's army against Ipomidôn. – *JT* nm3112,1

Kalubîn 'grâve', a knight who is seen by Tandareis to strike Claudîn, who had scorned his love. K. is challenged and defeated by Tandareis. – *TF* a10271f. n10396

Calcidius a soothsayer at Troy. When told of Ecubâ's dream regarding the unborn Paris, he ascertains that only Samlon can interpret it. – *GT* 55

Câm biblical (Ham), son of Noah. – *A* nm17105; *UA* m11250 n11283

Kamân 'der valsche', a knight who recommends a concerted attack by forty knights on Dêmantîn, when the latter has stolen Sirgamôte. K. is surely identical with Kêmân, a knight who is slain by Firganant during the siege of Antrîûn. The index to *Dem* does not connect the two characters, but it is said of Kêmân (9268): 'der phlag valscher sete'. – *Dem* 4240f.

Cambîses son of Cyrus (1), historically called Cambyses. – *A* nm15705

Kamele, Kamelîn see Gymêle

Kamille (1) the leader of a band of woman warriors. She is slain by Arras after fighting valiantly for Turnus against Ênêâs before Laurente, and is buried in a magnificent temple

148

built especially for her tomb. K., who is called 'küneginne von Volcâne', occurs in the OF *Eneas* and Virgil. – *Ed* 5142ff.; *P* nm504,25; *W* nm229,29; *A* nm17776

Camille (2) 'mit der wîzen keln', one of the ladies at Arthur's court who spill Priure's cup of chastity. A lady of the name of Camille occurs in the *Estoire del Saint Graal* as the daughter of King Orcant, whilst Arthur has an *amie* of this name in the Vulgate *Lancelot*. – *C* 1614

Camille (3) one of the parents of Turpin, who is referred to as 'Camillen sun'. – *GT* nm24371

Campîes a knight who is overcome by Gawein. – *C* nm9037

Kanaân 'künec von Frigiâ', nephew of Dârîus (3). K. is slain by Philôtas whilst fighting for Dârîus at Erbela. So also in Gualterus, where he is called Caynan. – *UA* 12047

Kanabêus father of Terramêr and brother of Bâligân. This name occurs elsewhere only in Konrad's *Rolandslied*. In *JT* he is said to be the son of Jermidol. – nm *W* 320,4; *JT* 2835,7f.; *UW* (MS x2) 35,5

Kanadic 'der ûz' (*JT*), see Ehkunat

Kanar 'künec von' (*UW*), see Hûsinet

Kanâze in Greek mythology the sister and wife of Macareus. – *Tn* nm17194

Kandalîon see Kandaljôn

Kandaljôn 'herzoge', a knight who compels all knights who are accompanied by maidens to fight with him and his knights. Tandareis has to fight to protect Claudîn and slays many of the fifty knights who attack him at once, before he submits on the condition that Claudîn is permitted to go unmolested. Tandareis is thrown into prison, where he is left by K. to starve to death. He is released, however, by Antonîe (q.v.). – *TF* 10737f.

Kandanûr 'herzoge von Roynal', an ally of Lôîs against Terramêr. – *UW* 37,6f.

Kandarîs the mariner on whose ship Willehalm (1) and Gîburc escape from Tîbalt. – *UW* a138,30 n139,13

Candaulus son of Candacis and brother of Karator. C. fights for his father-in-law, Porrus, against Alexander. His wife, Agyris, is abducted by Schoieranz but is rescued by Alexander. In Valerius and Pseudo-Callisthenes, C. takes Alexander to Candacis, but there is no mention of the abduction of his wife, which is related only in Leo, *WA*, and *UA*. – *UA* 19434ff.; *WA* nm4891 a4981

Candacis mother of Candaulus, Karâtor, and (in *WA*) Masippus. C. possesses a painting of Alexander, and when the latter is brought to her court by Candaulus and pretends to be his own messenger, she recognizes him and grants him her love. Later the griffons deposit Alexander at her palace, when they again spend some time together. C., who is the widow of Fizcator, occurs in Pseudo-Callisthenes, Valerius, and Leo. – *UA* a14503 n14521; *WA* 4889ff.

Candëlo, Candeolo, Candeolus, Canderlus see Candaulus

Candiacis see Candacis

Kandimant see Candimôn

Candimôn 'grâve', father of Pfandimoi (q.v.). He entertains Dêmantîn and later fights for him against Eghart, when he is slain by Tervagâmîs. – *Dem* 2309ff.

Candis a person who is apparently present at the castle in which Gawein is held prisoner. This is the only mention of this name in the extant fragments of *S*. – *S* Ib,13

Candicis see Candacis

Candolus see Candaulus

Kandor 'von Seline', a knight who fights for Arthur against Bruns (1). He is called Conder in Pseudo-Gautier. – *RP* 22,11

Kandus 'von Lirivine', a warrior in Ipomidôn's army against Akarîn. – *JT* nm3233,2

Kanebras 'von Kare', a warrior in Akarîn's army against Ipomidôn. – *JT* nm3101,2

Kanêl, Kanêlengres see Riwalîn (1)

Kanerel one of the knights of the Round Table. – *FS* nm4820

Kanias 'der von' (*JT*), see Rodoltzen

Kankor a skilful and cunning man. According to Golther this is intended to be the Arabian physician Kenkeh al Kendi.[6] – *P* nm643,17

Kanlîûn 'künec von Lanzesardîn', eldest son of Terramêr by his first wife. He is slain by Rennewart whilst fighting in the second battle at Alischanz. This name does not occur in *Aliscans* but appears to be derived from Caneliu, the name of a people in the *Rolandslied*. – *W* 358,14

Canopus Menelaus's mariner. In *LT*, as in Benoît and Dictys, he is killed by a serpent during the return from Troy. In the *Odyssey* the steersman is Phrontis, who dies a natural death during the return voyage. – *LT* nm17473f.

Kansordibes a warrior in Akarîn's army against Ipomidôn. – *JT* nm3094,5

Cantipus (1) 'grâve von Calzedonie', uncle of Philithoas, a warrior who is slain by Hector whilst fighting for the Greeks against the Trojans. In *TK* he is called Santippus, whilst he appears in Benoît as Antipus (var. Zantipus) de Caledoine. – *LT* 3347; *TK* 23832

Cantipus (2) see Antipus (1)

Cantola see Contulo

Kanphyant a knight, the *ami* of a *Meerweib*. K. had captured many knights and kept them prisoner. They are released when Dêmantîn fights and kills K. – *Dem* m2403 a2593 n2827

Kanfinôn wife of Bondonîl and mother of the queen of Tussangulê, who is the widow of Tûzamanz. – *UW* nm83,4f.

Capador 'von Capadie', a warrior in the Greek army against the Trojans. In *TK* he is called Cappadon, and in Benoît, Agapanor (var. Capedor). – *LT* 4934f.; *TK* 30694f.

Capanêus one of those killed in the battle between Ethiocles and Polinices. In *Ed* he is seen by Ênêâs in Hades. – *Ed* 3316; *UA* nm3166

Cappadon see Capador

Karabîn the son (or nephew) of Malserôn. K. is sent by Ehkunat to Arthur's court with the declaration of war. – *G* a220ff. n286

Karadas (1) a knight who plays the same part in *C* as does Plipalinot (see Inpripalenôt) in *P*. – *C* 20270ff.

Karadas (2) see Karadot

Caradin 'vürste von Lindin', a knight in Paltriot's army against Atroclas. – *Wigm* 3805

Karadog a knight who fights for Arthur against Bruns (1). K. is called Caridoc in Pseudo-Gautier. – *RP* 22,8

Karadors, Karados see Karadot

Karadot 'Briebras', the illegitimate son of Elyafres (q.v.) and Iseve. As a young knight K. rescues Gyngeniers, with whom he falls in love, from Alardins. He unhorses Keiî at the tourney held between Ris and Cadoalans, where he carries off the prize. When he learns of his illegitimate parentage, he tells his putative father, Karode, and later finds his mother together with her lover. In revenge they make a serpent fasten itself round K.'s arm. K. flees and lives as a hermit until he is eventually found by Kardors. The latter finds out from Iseve the only way that K. can be cured, and Gyngeniers sits naked in a tub of milk, whilst K. is placed in a tub of acid. The serpent springs from K.'s arm to Gyngeniers' breast but

---

6   Golther (1), p. 202.

is cut in two in the air by Kardors, who, however, wounds Gyngeniers in the breast as he kills it. K. and Gyngeniers are then married, and the former is the only knight who is able to drink cleanly out of the horn of chastity which is brought to Arthur's court shortly after their marriage. One of K.'s arms was, however, permanently shorter than the other, hence the epithet Briebras (= short-armed). The epithet is really a corruption of the Celtic Breichbras (*breich*, 'arm', *bras*, 'strong'), the OF poets being misled by the similarity of the words with the OF.[7] The story of K. is a popular one in Celtic literature, where it originated.[8] He occurs already in Chrestien's *Erec* (1719), where he is called Karadues Briébraz, a name which appears in *E* as Garedeas von Brebas, one of the knights at Arthur's court when Êrec returns with Ênîte, and as Caraduz von Caz, in *C*, where he spills Priure's cup of chastity. His *amie* is the only lady who can wear the cloak of chastity in the OF *La Vengeance de Raguidel*, and in the Dutch version of the same poem, the *Wrake van Ragisel* episode in the Dutch *Lancelot*. – *E* 1652; *C* 2309; *RP* m47,1 an47,27ff.

Karadus, Caraduz see Karadot

Karamphiet a dwarf in the service of Amurfinâ. – *C* a8030ff. n9093

Karânus a warrior in Alexander's army who fights for Erîgûus against Sâtibarzânes. So also in Curtius Rufus and *Expeditio Alexandri*. – *A* 20708

Caras a warrior in the Trojan army against the Greeks. This character appears to have been invented by Benoît. – *LT* 6843

Caratît one of the sons of Helen, who murders them in order to ingratiate herself with Menelaus at the fall of Troy. Their father, Paris, is already dead. In Dictys, C. is called Corythus. – *TKf* a47165ff. n47178

Karâtor son of Candacis and Fizcator. K. fights for Porrus against Alexander. So also in Leo. In Valerius he is called Charagos, a name that approaches the form Carexcis in *WA*. In Lampreht's *Alexanderlied* he is called Karacter. – *UA* 19434ff.; *WA* nm4893

Carafilîe wife of Dârîus (3). She is captured by Alexander after the battle at Issôn but dies of a broken heart before the battle at Erbela. This name appears to have been invented by Ulrich, as she is not named in any other history of Alexander. – *UA* a6215f. n10302

Carbison 'von Tollibete', a warrior who fights for Ipomidôn against Akarîn. – *JT* 3450,1

Karboissidole 'von Rasolde', a warrior who fights for Ipomidôn against Akarîn. – *JT* nm3235,5

Kardeiz (1) (Schulz thought this name to be derived from OF *car*, 'dear', and *dex*, 'God'.[9] Bartsch derived it from OF *cordeiz, cordez*, 'der Beherzte'.[10]) K. is the son of Tampenteire, whom he succeeds as 'künec von Brubarz', but he is killed at an early age in the service of a lady, leaving his sister, Kondwîrâmûrs, mistress of Pelrapeire. – *P* nm293,12; *T* 28,1; *JT* 644,5

Kardeiz (2) (Singer thinks that this name was Gardeiz in Kîôt, for the sake of the alliteration with li Loherain Garin (= Lohengrîn).[11] (Compare the form Gahardyz in *Loh*.) K. is one of the sons of Parzivâl and Kondwîrâmûrs and is obviously named after his uncle (see Kardeiz (1)). When Parzivâl becomes the Graal king he gives up his worldly kingdoms, which eventually fall to Kardeiz, who, according to *JT*, has to fight Lehelîn for them. – *P* nm743,16ff. a800,20; *JT* nm5869,1; *Loh* nm7107

---

7   Bruce (1), I, p. 91.
8   Bruce (1), I, p. 89.
9   Schulz, 'Eigennamen', p. 408.
10 Bartsch (2), p. 144.
11 Singer (1), p. 56.

Cardes 'ein Sarrazîn', a warrior in the Trojan army against the Greeks. This character was invented by Konrad. – *TK* 30120ff.

Kardêuz 'künec von Roconitâ', husband of Deselmiur and father of Lybials. – *M* m3481 n3776

Kardefablêt 'herzoge von Jâmor'. (Martin is of the opinion that this name looks very like a place-name, perhaps from Cardiff, which was conquered in 1091, and which would therefore have historical significance. If K. is the place-name, then Jâmor would be the original name of the character. He also draws attention to the similarity of Affibla (q.v.).[12]) K. is the brother-in-law of Lipaôt for whom he guards the four gates of Bêârosche. – *P* 376,15 [†]

Kardiant a knight who is present at Arthur's court. – *GM* (MS D only) 38574

Kardibadun see Kardibulunen

Kardibulunen 'von Kordeis', son of Akarîn, for whom he fights against Ipomidôn. – *JT* nm3131,3

Kardiesse see Kardeiz (1)

Kardiezen see Kardeiz (2)

Kardionese at first the wife of Athis (q.v.) and later the wife of Prophilias. She dies of a broken heart on hearing (incorrectly) that Prophilias had been slain in battle. So also in the OF version. – *AP* nmA^e,1ff. aA^e,43f.

Kardis see Kardeiz (1) and (2)

Kardiwalse a warrior in Ipomidôn's army against Akarîn. – *JT* 3978,1f.

Kardors 'von Kornvale', brother of Gyngeniers. K. is defeated by Alardins (q.v.) but is rescued by Karadot. He marries Yden, whom he meets at the tourney held between Ris and Cadoalans, and later seeks out and finds Karadot when the latter is hiding in the guise of a hermit. K. is called Cadors in the Mons MS of Pseudo-Gautier and would, therefore, appear to be unconnected with the Cardor who occurs as one of Arthur's barons in the *Estoire de Merlin* (Vulgate Cycle). – *RP* 58,45

Karduzal 'von Oreckune', a warrior in Akarîn's army against Ipomidôn. – *JT* nm3142,5

Karedôz a giant who has taken possession of the land of Mermîn and compelled all the knights there to become robbers. They waylay Tandareis on two occasions, but the intended victim kills large numbers of them. The wounded tell him all about K., and Tandareis goes to fight him. He succeeds in killing K. and, releasing all the knights and ladies that he holds captive, becomes king of Mermîn. – *TF* m4163 n5429 a6379f.

Karel (1) 'von Spolitte', a knight who is present at the tourney held by Arthur. – *JT* 1983,1

Karel (2) see Gârel (2)

Karel (3) see Karl (1)

Câres a commander in Dârîus's army. He is forced by Hegelôch and Amfôter to abandon Mitelêne. This character does not appear in any of the other histories of Alexander. – *A* 9641

Karet also called Claret, a knight who attends Leigamar's tourney in the service of Aram. – *C* 18171

Carexcis see Karâtor

Kargrilo son of Marguns. He is captured and slain by knights in the service of the maiden whom Gawein is aiding. So also in Manessier. – *RP* m690,22 n692,31

Karidant the second knight at Arthur's court to attack Gauriel, who unhorses him. – *GM* 752

---

12   Martin (1), p. 305, to 376,15.

Karidohrebaz a knight of the Round Table. – *C* 12547f.

Karis 'von Kartigale', a warrior in Ipomidôn's army against Akarîn. – *JT* 3367,1

Karisol 'ûz Valpinose' a warrior in Akarîn's army against Ipomidôn. – *JT* 3110,3

Carifegîs a knight who is defeated by Gayol (2). – *Crane* nm3209f. a3506

Carifeigîs see Carifegîs

Karifoltz 'von Rodekastel', a knight who is present at the festival celebrated by Arthur just before he holds his tourney. – *JT* 1713,7

Karjet a knight who jousts with Lanzelet at Lôt's tourney. K. accompanies Lanzelet when he goes to release Gawein and Êrec from Malduc (see Maldwîz), and also assists in the release of Lanzelet from Plûris. Since he is stated to be a relative of Gawein, it is probable that K. is identical with Gaherîez. – *L* 3188

Karl (1) 'der grôze' (Charlemagne). In *UW* he fights for Leo (2) and ensures the latter's security on the Papal Chair. In *FB* he is said to be the grandson of Flôre and Blanscheflûr (2). – *Wigl* nm9554; *Tn* nm275; *MC* nm240; *W* nm3,30; *FB* nm315; *UT* nm2269; *UW* nm11,23 a12,25; *Loh* nm1976; *HT* nm1677; *RB* nm16160; *FS* nm1513

Karl (2) king of France. K. ceded Lothringen to the German Emperor and also fought against Gêrfridolt. – *Loh* 3489ff.

Karl (3) 'herzoge', called 'der erste Karle'. – *JT* nm192,4 [†]

Karmedit a knight who is loved by a maiden who is able to work magic. She makes a bridge over the water, so that the army of which K. is a member can cross and storm the Schastel Orgelus. K. is killed, however, before the bridge is completed, and the maiden refuses to finish it. Several knights attempt to cross the bridge, but only Parzivâl succeeds in doing so. K. is called Karmadit in Gautier; a knight called Karmadan (various endings) occurs in the Vulgate *Lancelot*. – *RP* m466,31 n469,40

Carmelie daughter of Carpius. She is imprisoned by Melopar but released when the latter is slain by Paris and Hector. – *GT* m11452 an11522f.

Carmelus 'künec von Panphylia', father of Romûlus (1). – *GT* 24932ff.

Karmente a fairy who created a beautiful plain, full of singing birds, where lived Sirikirsan's wife. – *S* III, nm150

Karnahkarnanz 'leh cons Ulterlec', a knight from whom Imâne has been abducted. He is riding to recover her when he and his knights are seen by Parzivâl, who, never having seen knights before, takes them to be gods. K. explains to Parzivâl the meaning and use of his weapons. – *P* a121,13ff. n121,26; *W* nm271,18ff.

Karnant 'diu klare von' (*JT*), see Jeschûte

Kärndenlant 'der von' (*FD*), see Bernhart (3)

Karnisor 'grâve', a knight who is present at the tourney held by Arthur. – *JT* 1994,6

Carnîz 'künec von Schorces', one of the five young kings who attend the wedding of Êrec and Ênîte. In Chrestien's *Erec* he is called Garras de Corque, and he appears as Gartes von Nomeret in *C*, where he is one of the knights at Arthur's court who spill Priure's cup of chastity. – *E* 1971; *C* 2337

Carnoyse see Cornoysse

Karnoyt apparently someone who told Segremors and Nyobe that they would have to part. – *S* nmIII, 282

Cârô in Greek mythology the ferryman who rows the dead across the Styx to Hades (Charon). He ferries Ênêâs and Sibille across on their visit to Hades. – *Ed* 3004ff.

Karode 'von Nantes', a knight who marries Iseve, who, however, betrays him with her lover, Elyafres (q.v.). In Pseudo-Gautier he is called Caraduel. – *RP* 45,44f.

Caroes a knight who spills Priure's cup of chastity and who, as Gareles, is present at Arthur's court in *E*, when Êrec returns with Ênîte. In Chrestien's *Erec* he is called Carahés. – *E* 1660; *C* 2319

Carpeus see Carpius

Carpîde one of Kamille's maiden-warriors. She slays Arras at Laurente. This character is not named in the OF *Eneas*. – *Ed* 9020ff.; *W* nm229,27

Carpîte see Carpîde

Carpius husband of Orpfala and father of Carmelie. C. tells Paris and Hector how he had been captured by Melopar, who had burned down his castle. The two brothers slay Melopar and release C.'s wife and daughter. – *GT* 11424f.

Carpus see Carpius

Karrîax son of Terramêr, for whom he fights against Willehalm (1). In *Aliscans* he is called Quarraus, a character who occurs also in *Li Covenans Vivien*. – *W* a29,18f. n32,14

Karriôz a knight in the service of Rôaz. He is slain by Wigalois. – *Wigl* a6549 n6602

Karsidorus see Kassidorus

Karsîe wife of Jovelîn and mother of Kâedîn and Îsolt (3). – *ET* a6144f.; *Tn* m18704f. n18717 a19210ff.; *HT* nm90 a380ff.

Carsilôt a warrior who is slain by Hûpolt whilst fighting for the Greeks against the Trojans. This character was invented by Konrad. – *TK* 31814ff.

Karsinefîte wife of Coralus, mother of Ênîte, and sister of Îmâîn. In *JT* she is one of the ladies present at Arthur's court. She is called Carsenefide in Chrestien's *Erec*. – *E* m308ff. n430 a1456ff.; *P* nm143,30; *JT* 1610,3

Karsnafîte see Karsinefîte

Kartis see Karis

Kârub 'herzoge von Duskontemedôn', a knight whom Feirefiz claims to have defeated. In *JT*, where he is called 'herzoge von Duscanie', but is otherwise unnamed, he is one of the knights who take part in the tourney, won by Feirefiz, to decide which of her wooers shall marry Sekundille. – *P* nm770,18; *JT* a5280,1

Karfabalon a knight who takes part in the tourney held by Arthur for the crown of Deleprosat. – *Wigm* 2017

Karfidans 'von Virilasole', a warrior in Ipomidôn's army against Akarîn. – *JT* 3236,4

Karfidûn son of Lardentze and father of Aswerus (1). – *JT* nm2833,5

Karfite see Karsinefîte

Karfodjas 'herzoge von Triparun', a knight whom Parzivâl claims to have defeated. He occurs in *JT* as 'Karfolas von Treparune' and takes part in the tourney held by Arthur. – *P* nm772,23; *JT* 2135,5

Karfolas see Karfodjas

Karforas 'künec von Portigal', also called 'der geflorte', a knight who takes part in the tourney held by Arthur and later fights for Schîonatulander against Ipomidôn. – *JT* a1982,1 n2223,2

Karfunkel 'von Arabel', a warrior who fights on the side of the heathens against the Christians. – *WO* 16439ff.

Casandaria, Casandra see Cassandra

Casibilân, Casiliân see Kassibilaus

Caspar 'von Arabie', one of the three Magi who visit the Christ-child at Bethlehem. – nm *W* 307,8; *JT* 5475,1ff.

Caspus a warrior in the Greek army against the Trojans. This character does not appear in any other version of the Trojan legend. – *LT* 3344

Cassandaria see Cassandra

Cassander (1) son of Antipater and brother of Jobas. In *UA* Alexander dreams that he is killed by C., which first makes him suspect Antipater and his sons, but it is actually Pâtrôn (2) who does the deed. In *WA* he carries the poison from Antipater to Jobas, and in *SA*, although he is not implicated in the conspiracy, he flees on learning of the death of his brother. In *SA*, as in Valerius, he is remembered by Alexander in his will. C. occurs also in *Expeditio Alexandri*, Curtius Rufus, and Leo. – *UA* nm23597; *SA* 8206ff.; *WA* 6013

Cassander (2) to whom Alexander on his deathbed bequeaths the land of Carey. This character can hardly be identical with Cassander (1), as both are specifically provided for in Alexander's will. – *SA* nm8492

Cassander (3) see Cassandra

Cassandra daughter of Priam. In all versions she has the power of second sight and foretells the ultimate fall of Troy, but it is her curse never to be believed. In *GT* she kills herself at the sack of Troy. In the Middle Ages she acquired a reputation as a weaver, and a reference is made to her powers in this connection in *Tn*. – *Tn* nm4948; *LT* m1664 n1692 a2312; *MC* nm1136; *TK* nm1098 a19358; *GT* 678

Cassandre see Cassandra

Kassibilaus natural son of Priam. K. is slain (in *LT* by Thoas) whilst fighting for the Trojans against the Greeks. This character appears to have been invented by Benoît, who calls him Cassibilan. – *LT* a4768f. n4782; *TK* 30366

Kassidorus a knight who re-horses Peritheus in the battle at Athens. – *AP* nmE,14f. aE,24

Kassîe see Garîôle

Cassilian see Kassibilaus

***Castable** see Gastablê

Kastibier 'von Aribale', a warrior in Ipomidôn's army against Akarîn. – *JT* m3264,4ff. n3268,2f.

Kastipreise a knight who is unhorsed by Hiutegêr. – *JT* nm3308,6

Kastis (i.e. 'the chaste', because he died before his marriage was consummated[13]). K. married Herzeloide but died on the journey home from the wedding at Munsalvæsche, leaving his wife mistress over his kingdoms of Wâleis and Norgâls. – *P* nm494,15f.; *T* 26,1; *JT* 649,1f. [†]

Castor (1) brother of Helen and Pollux. C. fights with Jason in the first war against the Trojans, and in *LT*, as in Benoît and Dares, he takes part also in the siege of Troy. He is mentioned in Homer as the brother of Helen but takes no part in the war. – *LT* 1195; *TK* 11452ff.

Kastor (2) 'künec', a warrior in Ipomidôn's army against Akarîn. – *JT* 3978,1f.

Catênes one of those concerned in the conspiracy with Spitâmenes to deliver Bessus over to Alexander. So also in *Expeditio Alexandri* and Curtius Rufus. – *A* [21553ff.]

Kathelange 'diu ûz' (*JT*), see Sigûne

Katherine 'sante' (St. Catherine). – nm *RB* 26999; *KT* 8254

Cathmus the founder of the city of Thebes. C. is mentioned in Valerius, where he is called Cadmus. This is in accordance with Greek mythology, where he is the brother of Europa. – *UA* nm3819

Kathrin see Katherine

---

13 Golther (1), p. 181.

Kâtor father of Pînel. K. is slain by Rennewart whilst fighting for Terramêr against Willehalm (1). K. is mentioned in the OF *Aliscans*, where he is called Cadour, but he does not take part in the battle. – *W* nm21,1 a442,28

Catras 'künec von Resesse', brother of Cladas. C. attacks Arthur but is compelled to surrender. – *RP* nm574,12f. a580,17

Kaukasas 'der ûz' (*JT*), see Alexander (3)

Kâûn see Kâhûn

Cauterous see Gaueros

Cavaline 'künec von Iorfileise', a knight who is present at the tourney held by Arthur. – *JT* 2192,1ff.

Cavomet 'von Arâbîe', a knight who takes part in the tourney held by Leigamar. – *C* 18046

Ce- see under Z

Kege, Kegin see Keiî

Kehenis see Kâedîn

Keie, Keigin see Keiî

Keiî (This name is in all probability derived from the Latin Cajus.[14] In the OF poems he is called Keu, Keus and Kex, whilst the Welsh poems show forms nearer that used in the MHG poems, viz. Kai and Kei.)

K. is one of the most interesting of all the characters in the MHG Court Epics and the only one who is consistently characterized in almost all of the poems. He is seneschal to Arthur, and is a mixture of bravery, a legacy from Geoffrey of Monmouth, of discourtesy, a trait which first appears in Chrestien's *Erec*, and of maliciousness, a feature which does not appear in the *Conte de la Charrette* but is clearly delineated in *Yvain*. Zimmer uses this lower side of K.'s character to support his theory that the Round Table was artificially created on the model of Charlemagne and his twelve peers, K.'s character, he considers, being moulded on that of Ganelon.[15]

Of K.'s bravery there is never any question in the MHG epics. He is always the first knight to undertake any adventure or to joust with a stranger knight. If it is a constant test of the prowess of the hero of each poem that he shall fight an unfinished combat with Gawein, it is certainly the usual practice for the hero to fight and disgrace K. Such incidents occur in *P, E, I, DB, L, G, JT, TF, Sey, HT,* and *GM*.

Allusions to K.'s malicious tongue are frequent; he is called 'der kâtspreche' (slanderer) in *E* (4664), 'der zuhtlôse' in *I* (90), whilst the grimmest portrait of him is to be found in *Mtl*, where 'sie fluhen alle sînen nam/ wander manigem leider sprach' (*Mtl* 271f.), and a reference is made to his 'eitermeilige zunge' (*Mtl* 277); in *C* it is said of him (2130f.): 'Keiî, der vol nîdes/ Was und bitter galle'.

In this last poem, however, he appears in a more favourable light than usual. He is afraid, it is true, to cross the perilous bridge in his quest for Sgoidamûr's bridle, but his grief when Gawein is believed to be dead is very real, and he pays a fine and generous tribute to his fellow-knight (*C* 16860ff.). K. is also the only one who displays any common sense and suspects a trick when Giramphiel's knight comes to Arthur's court to steal the stone from the girdle of Fimbeus, which is in the possession of Gawein. K. insists on accompanying Gawein in his attempt to recover the stone, and on his search for the Graal. He is imprisoned in a chapel, from which he can only extricate himself by overcoming nine

---

[14] This etymology is supported by Zimmer, p. 818, note 1, Bruce (1), I, p. 3, note 1, and Martin (1), p. 152, to 150,13.

[15] Zimmer, pp. 829f.

knights, a feat which he eventually achieves, when he returns to Arthur's court amid general rejoicing. K. is not named in *Mer*, but this poem tells the story of how he sends his foster-brother, Arthur, to fetch his sword, and how Arthur pulls the sword from the stone in the churchyard, and K. pretends that he himself has drawn out the sword and is thus the predestined king of Britain. His failure to repeat the task proves the falseness of his claim. This story, is, of course, familiar from Malory. According to Panzer, Antor explains in MS P, that K.'s bad behaviour is the result of his having had to drink the milk of a woman of inferior birth, because Arthur had the milk of K.'s mother.[16] This explanation is, no doubt, of late invention, but it explains neatly Arthur's attachment to K. in spite of the latter's character.

K. appears in a really bad light in *RP*, where he and others hang Bagumades on a tree, and he kills Solimag. For this last act, he is challenged to single combat by Gawein, who defeats him. K. refuses to surrender and is saved from death only by the intervention of Arthur.

K.'s character has undergone a complete change in *Ll*, where a complete *Wandlung* appears to have been brought about by a period of dumbness.[17]

In the *Black Book of Carmarthen*, it is K. who is the original fighter of the wild cat, Cath Palug, and the adventure was later transferred to Arthur.

K. is identical with Gaîn, the father of Lernfras in *E* (1670), Chrestien's original (*Erec* 1739) reading: 'Ne li fiz Keu le seneschal'.

– *ET* 5213ff.; *L* 2890; *E* 1152f.; *I* 74; *Wigl* 451; *Mtl* 234; *P* 150,11ff.; *DB* 143ff.; *C* 490; *Wigm* 2200; *G* 600; *JT* 1350,1f.; *TF* 358; *Mer* a240,6; *Sey* 54,1f.; *HT* 2040; *Loh* 451; *GM* 435; *RP* 15,22ff.; *Ll* 23,2 (MS K) 11,5

Keilit 'von Galiz', a knight who fights for Lôîs against Terramêr. – *UW* 46,16

Keyn see Keiî

Kêmân see Kamân

Kêrubîn an archangel who appears to Vîvîans as he lies dying. This name is obviously a form of cherubin. – *W* 49,10f.

Châlamus 'künec von Agragente', a warrior who is captured when Alexander takes his land. He occurs in MS S of Leo.[18] – *UA* 22876

*Chanabeus see Kanabêus

Chandacor a warrior in Porrus's army. He is slain by Glaucus (2) whilst fighting for Porrus against Alexander. This character appears to have been invented by Ulrich. – *UA* 19684ff.

Cheiron the centaur who, as related in the *Achilleis* of Statius, acts as the tutor of Achilles and his companion, Patroclus. – *LT* nm6290; *TK* a5826 n5850; *GM* nm (MS D only) 375438; *RB* nm22574; *GT* nm14971f. a16487

Chemôn natural son of Priam. He is slain by Ulixes whilst fighting for the Trojans against the Greeks. – *TKf* 43154

Cherippus a warrior who is slain by Parmênîôn whilst fighting for Dârîus against Alexander at Issôn. This character appears to have been invented by Ulrich. – *UA* 8147

---

16 Albrecht von Scharfenberg, *Merlin und Seifrid de Ardemonte*, ed. by F. Panzer, p. li.
17 It is said of Keiî (*Ll* 23,3–6): 'der was ein stum und pot got wird und ere. / sein andacht da die glocken zwang/ die im erschrockenlich in seinen oren clang. / er ward reden und sprach . . .', and again (*Ll* 26,7–10): 'der engel hat den pösen geist mit kraft von dir getriben, / grosz wunder ist an dir geschehn. / kein wort hort nie kein mensch vor von dir ie gejehn. / die gnade gots ist ganz in dir bekliben.'
18 O. Zingerle, p. 64.

Chiona   see Esîonâ
Chyron   see Cheiron
Chomandîôn   a dwarf-king who entertains Firganant. – *Dem* a6944 m7146
Choralius   a warrior who is slain by Troilus whilst fighting for the Greeks against the Trojans. This character was invented by Konrad. – *TK* 31602
Chôres   a Trojan warrior who is slain by Kamille (1) whilst fighting for Ênêâs against Turnus. In the OF *Eneas* he is called Cloreüs (var. Chores), whilst in Virgil he is called Chloreus. – *Ed* 9064f.
Chrestien   'de Troyes', medieval French poet, and author of the first extant Arthurian romances. – nm *E* 4629¹²; *P* 827,1; *C* 16941; *RP* 845,25
Chummerlande   'der von' (*JT*), see Îthêr
Ci-   see under Z
Kibalîn   see Kibelîns
Kibelîns   'mit dem blanken hâr', a knight who is captured by Halzebier whilst trying to rescue Vîvîans at Alischanz. He is later (416,13) rescued by Rennewart. In *UW* he fights for Lôîs against Terramêr. K., who in *Aliscans* is called 'Guiëlin qui les cheveux ot blans', is the son of Buovun and appears in most of the OF *chansons de geste* of the Guillaume d'Orange cycle. A son of Boeve named Gui occurs in the *Chancun de Willame*, which contains also a Guibelin, as the youngest brother of Willehalm, and a Guiëlin, a Christian warrior who is taken prisoner. – *W* 15,2; *UW* 46,2
Kybert   see Gîbert (2)
Kyburg (1)   'küneginne von Arl', wife of Pirre. K. sponsors Gîburc at the latter's baptism. – *UW* a273,12 n275,1
Kyburg (2), Kiburc, Kyburck   see Gîburc
Kyir   'von Kummerlande', squire to Lohengrîn, whom he was to have accompanied to Brabant. The arrival of the swan, however, makes Lohengrîn decide to go alone. (See also Diether (2) and Neithart.) – *Loh* 604ff.
Kilikrates   'künec von Zentrîûn', a knight whom Feirefîz claims to have defeated. In *JT*, where he is the son of Killikrates (1), he is one of those who take part in the tourney held by Sekundille to decide which of her wooers she should marry. Martin points out that the name Callicrates occurs in Solinus (26,1).[19] – *P* nm687,6; *JT* nm3557,1ff. a5272,1
Kilimâr   'grâve', a knight who accompanies Tandareis from Antonîe to the tourney at Sabins. – *TF* 12284ff.
Killikratene   see Killikrates (1)
Killikrates (1)   father of Kilikrates. K. is slain whilst fighting as a commander in Ipomidôn's army. His slayer is Schîonatulander. – *JT* 2547,5
Killicrates (2)   see Kilikrates
Killicratres   see Killikrates (1)
Killirdeis   'von Parlordeise', a warrior in Akarîn's army against Ipomidôn. – *JT* nm3120,1f.
Killirjakac   (Schulz tried to derive this name from the Celtic *gwiliwr*, 'one who guards', and *jachâad*, 'a healing'.[20] Martin suggests that it may be an attempt to reproduce the name of the hero of an Old Norse saga, Kyrialax.[21] According to Golther, the name is still unexplained.[22]) K. is the nephew of Kailet and serves under Gaschier at the siege of

---

[19]   Martin (1), p. 503, to 770,12.
[20]   Schulz, 'Eigennamen', p. 404.
[21]   Martin (1), p. 56, to 46,25.
[22]   Golther (1), p. 141.

Patelamunt. He has been captured by Belakâne's men before the arrival of Gahmuret, who later effects his release. In *JT*, where he is called Kilrikaie von Schanipanie, he is present with Gaschier at the tourney held by Arthur. – *P* m31,20f. an46,16ff.; *JT* 1986,4

Kylloys (1) 'von Oreste', a knight who comes to welcome Willehalm (1) on his return with Gîburc from Tîbalt. – *UW* 212,15

Kyllois (2) see Willehalm (1)

Kilpert a knight who is slain by Gerhart (2) whilst trying to defend his sister, Sabîe (2). – *G* m1032 n1052

Kilrikaie see Killirjakac

Kymal 'von Lagdibore', a commander in Ipomidôn's army against Akarîn. – *JT* 3219,1

Kynabels 'künec', a knight who fights for Arthur against Bruns (1). In Pseudo-Gautier he is called Guinabel. – *RP* 22,24

Kingrimursel 'lantgrâve von Schamphanzûn', a relative of Vergulaht, for whom he brings to Arthur's court a challenge for Gawein. Having tacitly promised Gawein safety, he rescues him from the ugly situation which has been brought about by Gawein's advances to Antikonîe. In *RP*, where he is called Gynganbertil, he is about to start the arranged fight with Gawein, when Dinasdanres claims an equal right to fight Gawein, who agrees to fight them both together. The fight is prevented, however, by the timely arrival of Arthur, who marries Gawein's opponents to his two nieces, Tanete and Clarate. K. is called Guinganbresil in Chrestien's *Perceval*, and the story as told in *RP* occurs only in the Montpellier MS of Pseudo-Gautier. In *JT*, K. is one of the knights who take part in the tourney held by Arthur. – *P* a319,20f. n324,21; *JT* 1936,3; *RP* 11,43

Kingrisîn 'künec von Ascalûn', present at the tourney held by Herzeloide. K. is the father of Vergulaht (q.v.). He was slain by Ehkunat, but his death was imputed by Vergulaht to Gawein. In *JT* he is present, as 'künec von Ascalun', at the tourney held by Arthur. – *P* [m67,13] [a82,10] n420,7; *JT* 2013,1 [†]

Kyngron see Kingrûn

Kingrûn seneschal to Klâmîde. K. is overcome by Parzivâl, who sends him to Arthur's court. In *JT*, as 'Kyngron tschemschalte', he is present at the tourney held by Arthur. He is called Anguingueron in Chrestien's *Perceval* and occurs in *L'Estoire de Merlin* (Vulgate Cycle) as Aguinguernon. – *P* nm178,2f. a196,26; *JT* 1991,6; *RP* nm374,37

Kîôt (1) 'herzoge von Katelangen', husband of Schoisiâne and father of Sigûne. K. is the brother of Tampenteire and Manphiliôt. He acts as tutor to Kardeiz (2). Singer points out that in *Boeves de Hantonne*, the heroine is named Josiane, whilst her father-in-law is called Guiot.[23] – *P* 186,21; *T* 14,1; *JT* a626,3ff. n631,1 [†]

Kîôt (2) 'ein Provenzâl', a poet to whom Wolfram states that he is indebted for his account of *P*. The problem of the existence or non-existence of K. has never been satisfactorily solved, but most scholars are now of the opinion that he is an invention of Wolfram. The most ardent believers in his existence are Bartsch and Singer, but Golther, who identifies him with Chrestien's copyist, Guiot, gives the best explanation that has yet been attempted.[24] – *P* nm416,20; *JT* nm2942,4

Kiride see Tiridê

Kyrone see Cheiron

---

[23] Singer (1), p. 73.
[24] Golther (1), pp. 138f.

Kyrot 'zu Rosabinse', a knight who is present at the tourney held by Arthur. The territorial name of K. appears to be an attempt to reproduce Rosche Sabînes (*P* 610,26), Wolfram's form of Chrestien's Roche de Chanpguin. – *JT* 2046,1

Kîûn (1) 'burcgrâve von Bêâveis', a knight who is killed by Poidjus whilst fighting for Willehalm (1) at Alischanz. [See Appendix (8).] So also in *Aliscans*, where he is called Guion d'Auverne. – *W* 411,17

Kîûn (2) 'von Munlêûn', the smith who makes Rennewart's club. In *Aliscans* the smith is called Lionel. – *W* nm429,28

Kîûn (3) 'von Munsurel', a knight who is slain by Purrel whilst fighting for Willehalm (1) at Alischanz. In *Aliscans* he is called Guion de Montabel. – *W* 428,20f.

Kyfren uncle of Mabônagrîn. Pseudo-Gautier reads (16305f.): 'Et li biaus fius le roi Urain/ Que on apiéloit Mabounain'. – *RP* nm179,11

Klabûr 'künec', a relative of Tîbalt. He assists in the arming of Terramêr prior to the second battle at Alischanz. This name does not occur in *Aliscans*, but Singer is of the opinion that it appeared in the MS of *Aliscans* used by Wolfram.[25] – *W* 357,9f.

Cladas 'von der wueste', brother of Katras, whom he assists in his rebellion against Arthur. In the OF romances, C. is called Claudas de la deserte and is the traditional enemy of Ban (see Pant (1)), of whose death he is the indirect cause, and of Lanzelet. So also in Füetrer's *Lancelot*. C. is concerned in a revolt against Arthur in *Perlesvaus*, but this may be in imitation of Gautier. – *RP* nm579,27

Clamade see Klâmidê

Klâmidê (Bartsch derived the OF form of this name, Klamedex, from *clamer*, 'to shout' (so also Schulz[26]), and *dex*, 'God', i.e. 'cry to God'.[27]) K., who is 'künec von Brandigân', is the oppressor of Kondwîrâmûrs and is defeated in single combat by Parzivâl, who sends him to Arthur's court. K. is present at Arthur's tourney in *JT*, and he takes part in the tourney at Sabins in *TF*. In Chrestien's *Perceval* he is called Clamadeu des Isles, whilst in *Perlesvaus*, where he is named Clamadoz, he is the son of li Vermauz Chevaliers (= Îthêr) and, therefore, the mortal enemy of Parzivâl. – *P* nm178,2f. a203,12; *JT* nm1098,6 a1980,3; *TF* 11918; *RP* nm374,37

Clamorz a knight who attends Leigamar's tourney in the service of Lorez. – *C* 18149

Klangêla mother of Gîburc. This name was evidently invented by Ulrich, as Gîburc's mother is named only in the *Chancun de Willame*, where she is called Oriabel (see Arâbel). – *UW* m94,8 n270,1

Clarate niece of Arthur, who gives her and Tanete in marriage to Dinasdanres and Kingrimursel. – *RP* 19,30ff.

Clareanus natural son of Priam and a warrior in the Trojan army against the Greeks. Benoît, who appears to have invented this character, calls him Mondanz Clareax. – *LT* a4808 n4825

Clarencius 'von Pôre', a warrior in the Trojan army against the Greeks. This character was invented by Konrad. – *TK* 24932

Claret see Karet

Clarete *amie* of Monagris (q.v.). – *GT* nm8326ff.

Clarethe see Clarete

---

[25] Singer (2), pp. 107f.
[26] Schulz, 'Eigennamen', p. 407.
[27] Bartsch (2), p. 119.

Klâretschanze the lady for the love of whom Eskilabôn (q.v.) institutes his flower-garden. She is called 'von Portugal'. – *G* nm3847ff.

Clarette see Clarete

Clârîne (1) wife of Pant (1) and mother of Lanzelet, who is snatched from her arms by a *Meerweib*. She is sister to Arthur. In the OF romances Lanzelet's mother is named Elaine. – *L* 72ff.

Klârîne (2) wife of Amurât and mother of Duzabel (1). – *G* nm5888 a6945

Klârîne (3) wife of Elimâr, mother of Klârîs (1), and sister of Anfolê (1). She dies of grief when she hears of the death of her husband. – *G* nm6186

Clârins 'künec', one of the seven judges at the tourney held by Meliûr. – *PM* a13476 n13488

Klârîs (1) son of Klârîne (3) and Elimâr. K. is held in captivity by Purdân but is released by Gârel, for whom he fights against Ehkunat. He afterwards marries Duzabel (1). – *G* m5872ff a5990 n6187

Clârîs (2) friend of Blanscheflûr (2) during her captivity with the amiral. In *NRFB* she is called Cloyris (Cloris). – *NRFB* 158; *FB* nm4528ff. a5880f.

Clarisanz see Itonjê

Clarisidun 'von Marroch', a king who pays an unexpected visit to Arthur with a large following of knights and ladies. He arrives immediately after the close of the tourney which Arthur holds. – *JT* m2253,3 n2282,1 a2292,1

Klârischanze 'grævinne von Tenebroc', one of the maidens attendant on the Graal. Martin and Golther agree that this is an attempt by Wolfram to reproduce Clarissanz, the name of Gawein's sister (see Itonjê) in Chrestien's *Perceval*.[28] – *P* a232,11 n806,23f.

Clarisse wife of Frimutel. – *JT* 449,2

Klarissilie wife of Akarîn. – *JT* a2792,1 n2804,1

Clarit 'künec von Irlande', a knight who fights for the Christians in the final battle against the heathens. – *WO* 17122f.

Claudîânus the last of the Latin poets (fl. *circa* AD 400). – *RB* nm22488

Claudîn daughter of Moralde and Angnîe. Tandareis rescues her from Kalubîn, whose love she had scorned, and is taking her back to her father when they are attacked by Kandaljôn, who wants C. Tandareis kills many of Kandaljôn's men but finally surrenders when safe custody has been promised to his companion. When Tandareis has returned safely to Arthur's court, C. arrives with great ceremony and offers him her hand in marriage. Tandareis refuses, however, and she is married to Kalubîn. – *TF* a10271f. n10722

Klauditte (1) daughter of Scherules and playmate of Obilôt. – *P* a368,11f. n372,24

Klauditte (2) 'von Kanedic', *amie* of Ehkunat, to whom she sent the hound which was the cause of the death of Schîonatulander. She is the sister of Flôrîe (1). – *T* a146,2 n149,2; *G* nm16266f. a16612; *JT* m1144,6f. n1163,1ff. a1746,5 [†]

Klauditte (3) 'küneginne', a former *amie* of Feirefiz. – *P* nm771,15ff.; *JT* 5299,1f.

Claudius 'hêrre der Fabiâne', a warrior in the army of Turnus against Ênêâs. In the OF *Eneas* he is called Claudus, and in Virgil Clausus, a Sabine chief. – *Ed* 5119

Klêander 'herzoge', a warrior in Alexander's army who is sent to collect soldiers for the attack on Dârîus. At the command of Alexander he slays Parmênîôn. So also in *Expeditio Alexandri* and Curtius Rufus. – *A* 5017f.

Cleir 'von der Voie', a knight who takes part in the tourney held by Leigamar. – *C* 18143

---

28 Martin (1), p. 523, to 806,23; Golther (1), p. 158.

Cleôpatra a woman who is taken to wife by Philipp (1), who deposes Olimpias whilst Alexander is away fighting Nikolâus. On his return, Alexander persuades Philipp to resinstate Olimpias. So also in Pseudo-Callisthenes, Valerius, and Leo. – *A* 2579; *UA* 1789ff.; *SA* 931ff.; *WA* 476f.

Cleophas to whom Alexander bequeaths Persia. This name does not occur in any of the other histories of Alexander. – *WA* nm6225

Clerdenis a knight who attends Leigamar's tourney in the service of Aram. He is captured by Gawein. – *C* 18169

Clyades a prominent citizen of Thebes who tries to soften Alexander's wrath against the town. So also in Gualterus, where he is called Cleadas. – *UA* 3722

Clîan 'von Montforz', also called Elian von Moraforz, a knight who attends a tourney held by Arthur. – *C* 608

Klîas see Clyes

Klîboris 'künec von Tananarke', son of Haropîn. K. is slain by Bernart (2) whilst fighting for Terramêr in the second battle at Alischanz. K. occurs in the *Rolandslied*, where he is called Oliboris (var. Cliboris). – *W* 358,29 [†]

Clyes the hero, Cligés, of an Arthurian romance by Chrestien de Troyes. This was translated into MHG by Ulrich von Türheim, but his poem has been lost except for a small fragment, which is believed to be a part of it, published in *ZfdA*, 32 (1888), 123–28. He occurs in *P* as 'der Krieche Klîas' (not in Chrestien's *Perceval*), when he gives news to Arthur's court of the ladies captured and imprisoned in the Schastel Marveile. In *RP* he takes part in the tourney held between Ris and Cadoalans, but as he does not occur in Pseudo-Gautier, it is probable that his name was inserted by the authors in imitation of *P*. – *P* 334,11; *A* nm3247; *RW* nm2266; *RP* 87,17

Climant father of Asius and Ecubâ (3). So also in Dictys, where he is called Dymas. – *TKf* nm44032

Climestrâ see Clitemnestre

Clymona daughter of Ydomeneus. The text of Dictys is evidently corrupt at this point, as it reads as if C. were the daughter of Aethra (see Ethrâ (1)), whereas she is really identical with Dimena (q.v.), Ethra's companion. Ydomeneus is first mentioned as her father in Benoît, who appears to have misunderstood Dictys, where he is mentioned a few lines prior to C. – *LT* 17292

Klingezor, Klingsor, Clingzor see Klinschor

Klinschor (Schulz suggested < OF *clincher, cligner = cliner, inclinare*, i.e. 'der Lüsterne'.[29] Lucas derived the name from *clin-jour* (cf. *clin d'oeil*), i.e. 'Break of Day',[30] whilst Martin thinks that it may have originated in the OF *clenscheor < clenche*, 'Klinke', i.e. 'der Fessler', 'der Verschliesser'.[31] Singer, remembering Chrestien's gate-keeper to the Schastel Marveile, a man with one silver leg, suggests a derivation from OF *clencher*, 'to fall'.[32] Ersch and Gruber quote Simrock's derivation of the character in the *Wartburgkrieg* from Klingesäre, i.e. 'the Singer',[33] but this could not apply to Wolfram's Klinschor.) According to *P*, K. is a priest with a knowledge of magic, who has built for himself a castle, the Schastel Marveile, on land which was given to him by Îrôt, and in the

---

29 Schulz, 'Eigennamen', p. 408.
30 Lucas, p. 274.
31 Martin (1), p. 401, to 548,5.
32 Singer (1), p. 115.
33 Ersch and Gruber, pp. 125ff.

castle he has imprisoned Îgerne, Sangîve, Itonjê, and Kundrîe (2). As Golther has shown, this characterization of K. as abductor is the result of a misreading of Chrestien's *Perceval* (see Îgerne and Gansguoter). Wolfram invented an earlier history, which accords with the character he bears in *P*; he is a descendant of Virgîlîus and was discovered by Gîbert (1) in the arms of Îblis (2), the latter's wife, and was punished by being rendered impotent. In revenge K. studies magic and spends the rest of his life harassing the neighbouring lords. In *JT* the abduction of Îgerne is again told, and also the abduction of Pardiscale, who is rescued by Parzivâl when the latter defeats Agors (see Strangedorz). The Clingzor who appears in *Loh* claims to be a descendant of K., but since in the *Wartburgkrieg*, from which he is taken, he says that he has been studying magic for three years, there appears to be no doubt that they are one and same. K. was made one of the twelve *Meister* of the *Meistersinger*, possibly because of the part which he plays in the *Wartburgkrieg*, and possibly because the Paris MS of that poem is headed 'Klingesor von Ungerlant', which may have led the *Meistersinger* to believe that K. was the author.[34] – *P* m66,4 n548,5; *JT* nm2426,1; *Sey* nm27,6f.; *Loh* nm21; *Ll* nm2,10 [†]

Clinsor see Klinschor

Klîtemach 'von Têbê', a warrior who distinguishes himself in Alexander's army during the battle for Korintîn. In Pseudo-Callisthenes, Valerius, and Leo he is called Clitomachus. – [*A* 3539]

Clitemestre see Clitemnestre

Clitemnestre wife of Agâmennon, whom, with the assistance of her lover, Egistus, she slays on his return from Troy. She is herself killed by her son Orestes (1). This story is told in Benoît, Dictys, and the *Odyssesy*. – *LT* nm17213 a17252; *TKf* 49508

Klîtomedus a philosopher whose acquaintance Alexander makes at Troy. So in Leo, where he is called Clitomidis. – *A* 4865ff.

Clîtus a commander in Alexander's army. In *UA* he is slain by Alexander, who hears him boasting that he is braver than Alexander, whose life he had often saved. C. appears in *Expeditio Alexandri*, Curtius Rufus, and Gualterus. – *A* 11954; *UA* 2329

Clogiers 'künec', brother of Lucrête and uncle of Partonopier. He is killed whilst Partonopier is spending his first year with Meliûr. – *PM* 233f.

Cloyris see Clârîs (2)

Cloramatis see Gloramatis

Clore see Lore

Cloris see Clârîs (2)

Clôtô in Greek mythology, one of the Fates (Clotho). – nm *C* 286; *UA* 3737

Kloudite see Klauditte (2)

Kôbar 'künec von Marsiljis', the leader of the heathens who attack Meie's uncle in Spain. He is killed by Meie, and his army is defeated. – *MB* nm99,11f. a120,3

Cobares 'von Mediâ', a warrior who recommends to Bessus that he should surrender to Alexander. Bessus becomes extremely angry, and C. flees and joins Alexander. – *A* 20921f.

Côharz 'li bels' see Böse, 'der schöne'

Côîn one of the young kings who attend the wedding of Êrec. C. comes with his father, Angwisiez. So also in Chrestien's *Erec*. – *E* 1975

Kol (1) 'von Treven', a knight who jousts with Ulrich von Liechtenstein during the latter's *Venusfahrt*. – *FD* 616,4

Kol (2) 'von Truhsen', a knight who is present at the tourney held at Friesach. – *FD* 195,1

---

34 Ersch and Gruber, pp. 125ff..

Kol (3) 'von Vinkensteine', a knight who jousts with Ulrich von Liechtenstein during the latter's *Venusfahrt*. – *FD* 596,3

Kol (4) 'von Vrônhoven'. As a squire in the service of Otte (9), K. accompanies Ulrich von Liechtenstein on his disappearance after his *Venusfahrt*. He is later made a knight and is one of those (1495,1f.) to welcome Ulrich to Neustadt during his *Artusfahrt*. – *FD* 968,2ff.

Kolagrenans see Kalogreant

Kolatriande a knight who had been given a lance by Bol. – *JT* nm5010,5

Colebrant 'von Irlant', a warrior who fights for the Greek army against the Trojans. – *TK* 23936ff.

Kolibas a knight who fights for Bilas against Athis. This character does not occur in the OF version. – *AP* C,6

Colin 'Philippez', joint author with Wisze of *RP*. – *RP* nm846,21

Collas see Talas

Kollevâl 'von Leterbe', a knight whom Parzivâl claims to have defeated. In *JT* he is present at the tourney held by Arthur. – *P* nm772,21; *JT* 2022,5

Collevalle see Kollevâl

Kölner Fürst 'der', see Prûn

Comandîôn see Chomandîôn

Konderamus see Kondwîrâmûrs

Condiflor wife of Florendin, who is killed by Agraton, a heathen who loves C. She sends to Arthur's court for help, and Seyfrid, who comes as her champion, defeats Agraton. C. falls in love with Seyfrid and dies of a broken heart after he leaves. – *Sey* m81,5 n82,4 a162,4

Kondwîrâmûrs (Golther explains this name as an invention by Wolfram from an infinitive plus noun, put together in German style.[35] Bartsch, trying to avoid the infinitive plus noun construction, suggested < *coin de voire amors*, i.e. 'ideal of true love',[36] a suggestion which is ridiculed by Gaston Paris.[37] According to Singer, the name occurred in Kîôt, who had sometimes *Conduire amors*, 'Geleitung der Liebe', and sometimes *Conduire en amors*, 'Geleitung in die Liebe', thus accounting for the form 'Kondwîren âmûrs' in *P* 327,20.[38]) K., whose father, Tampenteire, and brother, Kardeiz (1), are both dead, is being besieged in Pelrapeire by Kingrûn and Klâmidê. She is rescued by Parzivâl and becomes his wife. He leaves her soon afterwards, in order to seek his mother, and she does not see him again until almost five years later, when she is summoned to accompany him as mistress of the Graal Castle. She is the mother of twins, Lohengrîn and Kardeiz (2). In Chrestien she does not marry Parzivâl, and thus the situation becomes a little confused in *RP*, where, in the translation of Gautier's continuation of Chrestien, she pays a nocturnal visit to Parzivâl's bed as his lover but not his wife. She is again rescued by Parzivâl in *RP*, when she is attacked by Aristes. In Chrestien she is called Blancheflor (so also in *C* – see Blanscheflûr (3)), and Golther thinks that Wolfram changed the name to avoid confusion with Blanscheflûr (1), who was well-known in Germany.[39] – *P* nm177,30 a186,17ff.; *T* 25,3; *JT* 643,5; *Loh* a591; *RB* nm15316; *RP* a374,15 n375,7; *Ll* a48,1 (MS K) a35,1

Kondwîren âmûrs see Kondwîrâmûrs

---

[35] Golther (1), p. 154. The actual meaning of the name is explained by Wolfram, when Parzivâl says (*P* 495,22f.): 'ir minne kondewierte/ mir vreude in daz herze mîn.'

[36] Bartsch (2), p. 144.

[37] Paris (2), p. 149.

[38] Singer (1), p. 81.

[39] Golther (1), p. 154.

Kongrefis 'cuns von Titulone', a knight who is present at the tourney held by Arthur. – *JT* 2021,3

*Conrât 'von Mîsne', a contemporary of Ulrich von Eschenbach who kept a wine-cellar in Lûtmeritz. – *UA* nm21492f.

Constanns brother of Moygines (1). C. is a God-fearing man who has two daughters, one of whom becomes a prostitute, causing C. to die of grief. The other daughter remains chaste but becomes the mother of Merlin. In Geoffrey of Monmouth Constans is the eldest son of Constantine and gives up his monk's habit to become king after the death of his father. In the OF prose versions of *Merlin*, he is king of Britain and father of Moygines, Uter, and Pandragon. – *Mer* 18,1f.

Constans see Constanns

Constantîn Constantine the Great, founder of Constantinople. – nm *A* 3965; *JT* 102,5; *RB* 18149; *GT* 23755

Constantinus see Constantîn

Contulo wife of Antinus (q.v.) and mother of Antonne. – *GT* 15586ff.

Koradin 'von Jerusalem', brother of Melchinor, for whom he fights against Walwan (3). K. also fights for the heathens in the final battle against the Christians. – *WO* nm5805 a6107 [†]

Koradinus see Koradin

Coradis 'künec von Kurnewal', father-in-law of Amelot, for whom he fights against Witechin. – *RW* nm10038ff. a10143

Coradiz see Coradis

Coralus 'grâve', an old knight who has been deprived of all his goods and possessions through war and now lives in poverty with his wife, Karsinefîte, and his daughter, Ênîte. He entertains Êrec as well as possible when the latter seeks lodging for the night, and when Êrec marries Ênîte, he sends C. to Lac with instructions that two lands, Montrevel and Rôadân are to be conferred on him. In Chrestien's *Erec* he is called Liconaus (var. Licoranz). – *E* a274f. n428 [†]

Kordeiz a warrior in Terramêr's army against Willehalm (1) at Alischanz. Bartsch thought that this name was taken over by Wolfram from *P* (Kardeiz),[40] but there can be little doubt that it is really the result of a misunderstanding of *Aliscans* (1779) where an Amis de Cordes (var. Cordres, i.e. Cordova) is in Terramêr's army. This name has become in *W* Âmîs *und* Kordeiz. – *W* 98,13

Korillaus a knight who fights for Bilas against Athis. So also in the OF version where he is called Corilaus. – *AP* C,8

Corinêis in Geoffrey of Monmouth, one of the fugitives from Troy (so also in Virgil). He accompanies Brutus to Britain and founds the duchy of Cornwall, which is named after him. In *Mer* he is called Kurnus. – nm *Tn* 16695; *Mer* 4,5

Cornayes see Cornoysse

Cornelius (1) 'bâbest', in office at the time of the conversion of Bohemia under Willehalm (2) and Bêne (1). – *WW* nm7831

Cornelius (2) a Latin author. – *LT* nm57

Kornêljus 'grâve', left by Meie in charge of his land when he goes to fight in Spain. With K. is Eufreide, and they prove exceedingly faithful to Bêaflôr, refusing to carry out the forged instructions to murder her and placing her and her baby in a boat. They lead the rebellion

---

[40] Bartsch (2), p. 131.

against Meie for his cruel act, and when he goes to Rome, they accompany him – *MB* 62,10ff.

Kornodas 'künec von Novoise', a knight who fights for Arthur against Bruns (1). In Pseudo-Gautier he is called Cormadan. – *RP* 22,4

Cornoysse a maiden who is sent by Penielle to Agâmennon's court for assistance against a giant who is oppressing her. Paris undertakes the adventure and returns with C. to Penielle. – *GT* a7224f. n7296

Cornosye see Cornoysse

Corodas 'der zühte wîse', a citizen of Trîtôniâ, who arranged the submission of the town with Alexander. This character appears to have been invented by Ulrich. – *UA* Anhang, 1695

Korodis see Coradis

Korradin see Koradin

Korsant see Korsâz

Korsâz 'künec', also (349,19) called 'künec von Jamfûse', and (97,19f) 'Korsant', a warrior in the service of Josweiz, under whom he fights for Terramêr against Willehalm (1). [See Appendix (3).] In *Aliscans* he is called Corsus, a variant reading of Corsuble (see Korsublê). – *W* 33,12ff.

Korsublê 'künec von Danjatâ', one of the group of 15 Saracen kings who attack Willehalm (1) at the end of the first battle at Alischanz. K. is wounded or killed by Willehalm in that encounter. [See Appendix (9).] K. occurs also in *Aliscans*. (See Korsâz.) – *W* m71,22 a72,17f. n74,16 [†]

Korsudê 'von Saigastin', one of the group of 15 Saracen kings who attack Willehalm (1) at the end of the first battle at Alischanz. K. is wounded or killed by Willehalm in that encounter. [See Appendix (9).] K. occurs also in *Aliscans*, where he is called Carboclés. – *W* m71,22 a72,17f. n74,17 [†]

Costriss a vassal of Gamorett, for whom he fights against Agâmennon. – *GT* 5669

Koxarî a vassal of Dârîus (3). Nostâdî reports to Dârîus that K. has barely escaped with his life from Alexander and that he is severely wounded. This name does not occur in any other history of Alexander. – *A* nm5933 [†]

Crane name given to Gayol (2) (q.v.). – *Crane* nm148

Crassandra see Cassandra

Krâterus a prominent warrior in Alexander's army. In *UA* he is captured by Candaulus in the battle against Porrus but is released on the condition that he does not fight against Porrus. K. occurs in all the Latin versions of the Alexander history. – *A* 7002; *UA* 4721

Crâthêrus see Krâterus

Crepeus nephew of Pretemisus, a warrior in the Trojan army against the Greeks. He occurs in Benoît as Steropeus (var. Crepeus). – *LT* 4016

Cressiâ 'von Îrone', one of the ladies at Arthur's court who spill Priure's cup of chastity. – *C* 1619f.

Krêsus a king who was defeated and killed by Cyrus (1). Historically Croesus, King of Lydia. – nm *A* 5610; *UA* 7051

Crescentius a Roman Senator who was hanged by the Emperor. – *Loh* nm7459

Krete 'künec von' (*LT*), see Ydomenêus

Creusa according to *LT*, a daughter of Priam. This name does not occur in Benoît or in any of the Latin versions of the Trojan legend and would appear to be the result of an imperfect recollection of Virgil by Herbort. In Virgil she is the wife of Ênêâs. – *LT* m1664 n1690

Kriechen 'kaiser von' (*Loh*), see Jordanich

Kriechenlant 'kameræ re über' (*UA*), see Mêtrôn

Kriemhilt the famous heroine of the *Nibelungenlied*. – *UW* nm103,5

Cricogelan a giant who tries to take Florand and Helen from Agâmennon. He is slain by Hector. – *GT* nm12034 a12071

Cricoglan see Cricogelan

Crîses a Greek who carries the statue of Pallas and who is the originator of the ruse of the wooden horse. This is his rôle in *LT*, and it corresponds to that in Benoît and Dictys, though in the latter version he quarrels with Agâmennon, who has taken his daughter, Chryseis, as in Homer. In *TKf*, however, he is represented as a Trojan priest, who is in charge of the temple in which Achilles is slain. – *LT* 15917; *TKf* 45125

Crîsôlâus 'der vreche', a warrior in Dârîus's army who had been captured by Hegelôch and Amfotêr at Kîun. Alexander gives orders that C. be put to death when he learns of the death of Andrômachus. – *A* nm10680

Crispin 'küneginne von Belgalgan', she is imprisoned in her kingdom, over which Merlin (2) stands guard, so that none can go in or out. Parklîse acts as a messenger for C. on her griffins and fetches Wildhalm, who slays Merlin. Crispin falls in love with Wildhalm, who points out that he is already in love with Agly, and C. resolves to help them to come together. A tourney is held, at which Wildhalm proves his valour, and a second one is held at Solia, when Agly and Agrant are present. Agly and Wildhalm are brought together, and they flee from Agrant. The latter collects a great army and attacks C. for her share in the ruse. After she has won the battle, C. becomes a Christian and marries Kailet. – *WO* nm10880f. a12413ff.

Crispus a messenger sent by Pirrus to obtain information about the movements of Acastus. This character appears to have been invented by Benoît. – *LT* 17833ff.

Cristân 'von Priks', a knight who jousts with Ulrich von Liechtenstein during the latter's *Artusfahrt*. – *FD* 1414,3f.

Cristiân see Chrestien

Cristôbolus the best of Alexander's physicians. C. occurs in *Expeditio Alexandri*, Curtius Rufus, and Gualterus. – *UA* 20711

Cristoffel 'sante' (St. Christopher). – *RB* nm18910

Critogelan, Critogoalan, Critogolan see Cricogelan

Krôhier 'von Oupatrîe', a king who fights for Terramêr against Willehalm (1) in the second battle at Alischanz. This name does not occur in the OF *Aliscans*. Singer, who identifies K. with Grôhier, uses the variation in the territorial name (cf. also Samirant and Oukidant) as proof of his theory that Wolfram improvised his work and recited it extempore.[41] [See Appendix (1).] – *W* 359,4

Kuene 'der schöne', the name given by Parzivâl to der schöne Böse. – *RP* nm820,16

Kuene 'der ungeschaffene', see Lays

Kukuber lande 'der von' (*JT*), see Îthêr

Culîanz 'der tôr', the jester at Arthur's court who plays the same rôle in *C* as does Antanôr (q.v.) in *P*. – *C* nm2225ff. a2577

Kummerlant 'künec von' (*JT*), see Îthêr

Kumuns see Bademagun

Kunal a knight who is sent by Willehalm (1) to announce his return with Gîburc to his father and mother. In MS C he is called Runal (196,17). – *UW* a196,15f. n197,20

Kundewiramors see Kondwîrâmûrs

---

41 Singer (2), p. 107.

Kundewiramurs see Kondwîrâmûrs

Kundrîe (1) (Schulz derived this name from the OF *contruit*, 'misshapen',[42] whilst Bartsch thought that the OF *conrée* 'die Lohfarbige', was the root,[43] a derivation with which Gaston Paris disagrees,[44] but which is supported by Martin, who translates *conrée* by the more usual 'die Geschmückte'.[45]) K. is the ugly messenger of the Graal. She had been sent to Amfortas by Sekundille, together with her brother, Malkrêâtiure. It is K. who denounces Parzivâl before the assembled Round Table for his failure to ask the sympathetic question of Amfortas, and it is she who brings him on the second occasion the glad news that his quest is ended and that he has been chosen Graal King. K. is not named in Chrestien's *Perceval* but occurs as Gondrée in Gerbert's continuation of that poem.[46] She is considered by Miss Weston to be originally identical with Kundrîe (2) (q.v.). – *P* a312,2 n312,26; *W* nm279,20; *C* 9027; *JT* 5105,6

Kundrîe (2) (This name Schulz derived from OF *cointerie*, 'gentillesse'.[47]) K. is the sister of Gawein and is one of the ladies imprisoned in the Schastel Marveile. After her release she is married to Lischois. In *JT* she is present at Arthur's court, whilst later (4587,1–5) she is confused with Bêne (2), when Lôt is said to be grieving over the loss of Sangîve, Itonjê, and Bêne. In *Sey* she is the mother of Seyfrid. This character appears to have been invented by Wolfram, but Miss Weston sees in K. a transformed Kundrîe (1) who corresponds to the more beautiful Graal messenger who appears in Gautier (and *RP*).[48] She draws attention also to the transformation of Gawein's wife in the ME poem, *Weddynge of Syr Gawene*, and sees a significance in the relationship of wife and sister. – *P* nm334,16ff. a565,21; *M* nm154; *JT* 1612,3; *Sey* 6,4f.

Kundwiramurs, Kundwiramus see Kondwîrâmûrs

Kûne see Kâhûn

Kunegunt wife of Heinrîch (2). – *Loh* nm7537

Künigîn 'diu' (*passim*), see Ginovêr

Kuniune 'Rois der', **Kuniuntze** (*JT*) see Bademagun

Kunnewâre 'de Lalant'. (Martin suggests that K. corresponds in Saxo Grammaticus to the sister of Frotho III, Gunvara, the Nordic form of the name being Gunnvör.[49] He suggests a connection with Ginovêr, an etymology which is adopted without comment by Singer.[50]) K. is the sister of Orilus and Lehelîn. She has never smiled at Arthur's court, but when she sees Parzivâl she smiles at him, for which she is soundly beaten by Keiî, who is made afterwards to regret his action by Parzivâl. (See Antanôr.) This character, called Lêde (q.v.) in *C*, obviously has its origins in folk-lore, and she occurs, unnamed, in Chretien's *Perceval*, the prose *Tristan* (Löseth's analysis), and the Vulgate *Lancelot*. – *P* nm135,14f. a151,11; *JT* 1778,3

Kuntikar 'künec von Belmunt', a knight who takes part in the tourney which Crispin holds at Solia. – *WO* 15705

---

42 Schulz, 'Eigennamen', p. 393.
43 Bartsch (2), p. 148.
44 Paris (2), p. 149.
45 Martin (1), p. 266, to 312,26.
46 Wolfram von Eschenbach, *Parzival*, transl. by W. Hertz, pp. 513f.
47 Schulz, 'Eigennamen', p. 396.
48 Weston (1), p. 50.
49 Martin (1), p. 135, to 135,15.
50 Singer (1), p. 77.

Kuone (1) 'von Guotrât', a knight whose name Ulrich gives as a guarantor that he has obtained the matter of *UA* from the bishop of Salzburg. – *UA* nm27621

Kuone (2) 'von Vrîberc', a knight who is present at the tourney held at Friesach and who also jousts with Ulrich von Liechtenstein during the latter's *Venusfahrt*. – *FD* 302,1

Cuonrat (1) son of Ruoprecht and brother of Fridrich (3). C. marries Osann and fights for Fridrich against Mompolier. – *FS* 5775f.

Kuonrât (2) 'von Heimesvurt', a MHG poet, of whom Rudolf says that he 'von Gote wol getihtet hât'. – *A* nm3189

Kuonrât (3) 'von Lebnach', a knight who jousts with Ulrich von Liechtenstein during the latter's *Venusfahrt*. – *FD* 626,6f.

Kuonrât (4) 'von Nîdekke', a knight who jousts with Ulrich von Liechtenstein during the latter's *Venusfahrt*. – *FD* 647,2

Cuonrat (5) 'grâve von Ötingen', whose recent death is lamented by Rudolf. – *RW* nm2085ff.

Cuonrât (6) 'von Souneke', a knight who jousts with Ulrich von Liechtenstein at Friesach. – *FD* 191,5

Cuonrat (7) 'von Stoffeln', MHG poet and author of *GM*. There is, however, some doubt as to whether the verse containing this reference is genuine. – *GM* nm41642

Kuonrât (8) 'von Stretwich', a knight who jousts with Ulrich von Liechtenstein during the latter's *Artusfahrt*. – *FD* 1408,2f.

Kuonrât (9) 'von Strîtwisen', a knight who jousts with Ulrich von Liechtenstein during the latter's *Venusfahrt*. – *FD* 864,3ff.

Kuonrât (10) 'von Sûrouwe', a knight who jousts with Ulrich von Liechtenstein during the latter's *Artusfahrt*. – *FD* a1410,2 n1412,2

Kuonrât (11) 'von Teinach', a knight who jousts with Ulrich von Liechtenstein during the latter's *Venusfahrt*. – *FD* 627,8

Cuonrat (12) 'her Vlec', MHG poet and author of *FB*. – nm *A* 3240; *RW* 2221

Cuonrat (13) 'der schenke von Winterstetten'. Rudolf states (*RW* 15649ff.) that C. commissioned him to translate *RW*. – nm *RW* 2319; *UT* 26

Kuonrât (14) 'von Wirzeburc', MHG poet and author of *PM*, *TK*, *Eng*, and *HK*. – nm *PM* 192; *TK* 266; *Eng* 208; *HK* 766

Cupesus 'von Arise', a warrior in the Trojan army against the Greeks. So also in Benoît and Dares. – *LT* 4000; *TK* 29800

Cupîde see Cupîdô

Cupîdô son of Venus and therefore, in *Ed*, brother of Ênêâs. – *Ed* nm48 a742f.; *ET* nm2467; *P* nm532,1f.; *C* nm4843; *TK* 964; *Mer* nm182,6; *FS* nm6748; *WO* nm2618

Kuprîân a giant, evidently identical with Kuperan, the giant in the *Lied vom Hürnen Seyfrid*. – *RB* nm25269

Kurâus 'von Gagunne', a knight who is found by Lanzelet, fighting with Orphilet. The three knights go to the house of Galagandreiz, where during the night they are all visited by the latter's daughter, who offers them her love. K. and Orphilet refuse her, as they fear the wrath of her father. Singer identifies K. with Hardîs.[51] – *L* 679ff.

Kuriôn the oppressor of Albiûn, whose lands he is trying to take. K. is overcome by Tandareis. – *TF* m8583f. n8629 a9075f.

Kurjôn see Kuriôn

Kurneval see Kurvenal

---

51 Singer (1), p. 58.

Kurnus see Corinêis

Cursabrê 'künec von Orchadîe', a warrior in the Greek army against the Trojans. This character was invented by Konrad, who probably copied the name from Cursabris in *PM* (cf. Margalîn). – *TK* 23932

Cursabris 'künec', one of the seven judges at the tourney held by Meliûr. – *PM* a13476 n13489

Cursalion 'künec von Ungerlant', a warrior who is slain by Pelagrîn whilst fighting for the Greeks against the Trojans. This character was invented by Konrad. – *TK* 23910

Kursamy 'künec', father of the *Meerweib* for whom Gauriel and his companions killed Geldipant. – *GM* nm (MS D) 375442

Cursanz 'künec', one of the seven judges at the tourney held by Meliûr. C. favoured Partonopier as the winner of the prize. – *PM* 13476ff.

Kursaus 'künec von Barberîe', one of the group of 15 Saracen kings who attack Willehalm (1) at the end of the first battle at Alischanz. K. is wounded by Willehalm in that encounter. He assists in arming Terramêr for the second battle. [See Appendix (9).] K. occurs in MS M only of the OF *Aliscans* (1017), where he is called Corsauç. – *W* m71,22 a72,17f. n74,13 [†]

Cursilabrê 'von Clarion', a warrior who is slain by Kassibilaus whilst fighting for the Greeks against the Trojans. – *TK* 33678

Kursîs one of the knights in the retinue of the Soldan at the tourney held by Meliûr. – *PM* 13596f.

Cursûn 'truhsæze' who guards the way to Godonas. He tends Meleranz after the latter has defeated Godonas and accompanies him on his campaign against Libers (1). – *M* m4550ff. a5074ff. n5233

Curtus 'Rûfus' (Curtius Rufus), the author of a Latin history of Alexander which Rudolf gives as one of his sources. – *A* nm13033

Curus see Cirrus

Kurvenâl (< OF Gorvenal, Governal, Guvernal = *gouverneur* < Latin *gubernare*, i.e. 'tutor'.[52] The form Kuneval, Kurnewal, which appears in *ET* and in the *Volksbuch*, is probably due to confusion with the name of the county, Cornwall.) K. is tutor to the young Tristan, whom he educates to perfection in every respect. Later at Marke's court he plays the same part of confidential accomplice to Tristan as does Brangêne to Îsolt (2). – *ET* 127ff.; *P* nm144,20; *Tn* 2256ff.; *UT* 700; *HT* 1166

Curvinal see Kurvenal

Cusdrô son of Eresdes. C. is mentioned in Pseudo-Methodius, where he is called Cosdri. – *A* nm17170

Cûsiresdes 'künec', a descendant of Nemrôt. So also in Pseudo-Methodius, where he is called Cusinisde. – *A* nm17157

---

[52] Gottfried von Straßburg, *Tristan und Isolde*, transl. by W. Hertz, p. 553.

L

Laamez 'von Babilôn', uncle of Aschalonê; he is one of the knights present at the tourney held by Leigamar. – *C* 18052

Laamorz (1) brother of Îlamert. L. is a knight who uses magic to fight and is unbeatable as he can fight for a year without tiring. Gawein, wearing magic armour and a magic girdle, succeeds in defeating L. He is called 'von Janfrüege'. – *C* nm15260 a15399

Laamorz (2) see Laamez

Lâbân biblical, father of Leah (see Lya) and Rachel, the wives of Jacob. – *UA* m11332 n11344

Lâbazar son of Êvilmôradac. L. is mentioned in the *Historia Scholastica* (*Liber Danielis* V), where he is called Labosardochus. – *UA* nm7709f.

Labigâdes a knight who spills Priure's cup of chastity at Arthur's court. L. is mentioned in Chretien's *Erec* (1741) as Labigodés but does not occur in the corresponding list in *E*. The passage in Chrestien's *Erec* is considered by Foerster to be the interpolation of a copyist.[1] – *C* 2324

Ladamus see Liddamus

Laeo father of Kailet. – *JT* nm440,1ff.

Lag 'künec von Panlannder', a knight who takes part in the battle between Atroclas and Paltriot. – *Wigm* 3781

Lahedumân (< 'leh cuns de Muntâne' (*P* 382,1)[2]). L. is a knight who is unhorsed by Gawein whilst fighting in the battle against Lipaôt. – *P* nm359,6 a382,1

Lahfilirost (Bartsch derives this name from *li fil li Rost*, 'the son of Rost',[3] but a really satisfactory explanation has not yet been found.[4]) L. is 'burcgrâve' of Patelamunt and marshal to Belakâne. He acts as host to Gahmuret at Patelamunt. He had seen Gahmuret fighting for Akarîn at Alexandria and is able to describe his prowess to Belakâne. – *P* a18,8 n43,16 [†]

Laiazze see Lîâze

Lays hardîz 'li', a knight who is present at Arthur's court when Êrec returns with Ênîte. In *C*, where he spills Priure's cup of chastity, he is called Lais von Lardis. The origin of both of these appearances is Chrestien's *Erec* (1697), where he is called li Lez Hardiz, 'the Ugly Brave'. He appears as 'der ungeschaffene Kuene' in *RP*, one of the knights who take part in the tourney between Ris and Cadoalans, and he occurs as a minor character in most of the OF romances of the Vulgate Cycle. – *E* 1634; *C* 2293; *RP* 81,26

Lâyus a former king of Thebes (Laius in Greek legend), the father of Oedippus. – *UA* nm2827

Lâîz 'cuns von Curnewâls', son of Tînas. L. is one of Gawein's pages. – *P* 429,18

Lac (1) 'künec von Karnant', father of Êrec and Jeschûte. In *E* his land is called Destregâles, of which Karnant is the capital. His death is reported to Êrec whilst the latter is at Arthur's court (9963ff.). In *P* he is unhorsed by Killirjakac at Herzeloide's tourney and is said to be called Lac from the spring Lac which is in his land and into which Parzivâl

---

1 Chrestien de Troyes, *Erec und Enide*, ed. by W. Foerster, p. 311.
2 Martin (1), p. 295, to 359,6.
3 Bartsch (2), p. 147; see also Martin (1), p. 54, to 43,16.
4 Golther (1), p. 141.

must dip his Graal sword when it breaks. – *E* nm2 a2884; *P* 73,22; *C* nm848; *L* nm2264; *Wigm* nm3139; *JT* nm2136,6; *GM* nm1398

Lac (2) 'künec von Sêlanden', a knight who attends the tourney held by Arthur. – *C* 609

Lacbuz 'marcgrâve', a knight who, with Losiôz, is besieged by Malloas. – *M* nm11697ff.

Lachesis 'vrouwe', in Greek mythology, one of the Fates. – nm *C* 291; *UA* 3739

Lack see Lac (1)

Lacridare 'der junge ûz' (*JT*), see Ediffrison

Lalander 'der ûz' (*JT*), see Orilus

*Lambekîn see Lembekîn

Lämbekin 'grâve von Leven', son of Lampert and standard-bearer to Jofrit (1), for whom he fights against Willehalm (3). – *RW* 964

Lambore wife of Garsidis, whom she follows, with a broken heart, into an early grave, leaving behind a young daughter, Tydomîe. – *M* nm7677

Lâmedôn see Laomedon

Lâmech biblical, in *A* correctly described as a descendant of Cain (Genesis 4. 17f.). In *UA* he is said to be the blind brother of Cain, whom he shot. – nm *A* 17041; *UA* 11227

Lamendragot a knight who is present at Arthur's court when Êrec returns with Ênîte. This name does not appear in the corresponding list in Chrestien's *Erec*. – *E* 1687

Lâmeôs to whom Alexander bequeathed Syria. This name does not occur in any of the other histories of Alexander. – *UA* nm27005

Lâmêr a knight who is slain by his brother, Brîen (2), for his fine armour. In *L'Estoire del Saint Graal* (Vulgate Cycle) this is the name received by Orcan on his baptism. – *Wigl* nm6069

Lamîre 'vrowe über Stîre', daughter of Gandîn (1) and aunt of Parzivâl. She is the wife or lover of Îthêr. – *P* nm499,3ff. [†]

Lammîre (1) wife of Meleranz and mother of Gârel (2). – *G* nm4192

*Lammîre (2) see Lamîre

Lampekine see Lembekîn

Lampert 'grâve von Loven', father of Lämbekin. L. is sent by Jofrit (1) on an embassy to Philipp (6). – *RW* 2351

Lamperten 'künec von' (*Crane*), see Ortamîn

Lampreht the author of the first MHG *Alexanderlied*. – *A* nm15785

Lamptekin see Lembekîn

Lampus 'vürste', a warrior in the Trojan army against the Greeks. So also in Dictys and Homer, in which latter he is called Lampos. – *TKf* 47330

Landô 'der hôchvertige', see Orilus

Landorye wife of Alpheolan, after whose death Ursyan comes to Agâmennon's court to claim her but is slain by L.'s brother, Ajax (4). – *GT* 4075ff.

Landrîs 'grâve', a knight who fights for Willehalm (1) at Alischanz and who, in *UW*, is present at the celebration to welcome Willehalm on his return with Gîburc from captivity. This name is a popular one in the OF *chansons de geste*, but it does not occur in any of the extant MSS of *Aliscans*, although it may well have appeared in the MS used by Wolfram. – *W* 329,10f.; *UW* 211,31

Landunal 'von Preduntze', a knight who attends the tourney held by Arthur. – *JT* 2019,3

Langalas 'emeral', a warrior whom Tîbalt leaves behind with Mamurtanit to look after Gîburc, whilst he goes to Terramêr. – *UW* nm90,24 a97,8ff.

Laniure 'von der Serre', father of Sgoidamûr and Amurfinâ. L. was a doughty knight but had almost been defeated by Gawein. – *C* m7910 n8864

Lanczilet, Lanczlin see Lanzelet

Lanois 'künec von Ziebe', a knight who attends the tourney held by Arthur. – *C* 584

Lansulet, Lanszeleht, Lanszelet see Lanzelet

Lanfal a knight who is present at Arthur's court when Êrec returns with Ênîte. He does not
appear in the corresponding list in Chrestien's *Erec*, but he does occur in the list in *C*,
where, as Lenval he is one of the knights who spill Priure's cup of chastity. (Cf.
Brantrivier.) He appears as Linvâl in *DB*, in which he is unhorsed by Daniel. L. is the hero
of a *lai* by Marie de France, *Lanval*, in which he wins the love of a fairy, whose existence
he must never reveal to mortal person (cf. Seyfrid and Gauriel). – *E* 1678; *C* 2292; *DB* 248

Lanverunz 'herzoge von' (*P*), see Astor (2)

Lanfie 'diu wilde', she had enchanted her *ami*, but the latter was freed from the enchantment
by Gawein. – *C* nm26573f.

Lanzelere see Lanzelet

Lanzelet the hero of the MHG poem (*L*) which bears his name. He is the son of Pant (1),
and as a baby he is stolen by a *Meerweib*, who brings him up and starts him out into the
world when he is fifteen years of age. He is not to know his name until he has slain Iweret,
and in the meantime he is called 'der ritter von dem Sê'. His first adventure is at the castle
of Galagandreiz, whom he kills and whose daughter he marries. He leaves the latter and
marries Ade, who accompanies him to the tourney held by Lôt (4), but who leaves him
when he is captured by Mâbûz. He escapes from the latter's castle by a ruse, defeats
Iweret, and then learns his name. He marries a third time, this time Iblis (1), the daughter
of Iweret, whom he takes to Arthur's court, where he defeats Valerîn, who is trying to
abduct Ginovêr. Afterwards he steals away to Plurîs, where a dwarf had thrashed him
when he first set out as a knight. At Plurîs he defeats 100 knights and is chosen by the
queen as her consort. He is carefully guarded and is unable to escape, but is eventually
rescued by Êrec, Gawein, Tristan, and Karjet. L. later leads the band of knights who
rescue Êrec and Gawein from Malduc (see Maldwîz), and releases Elidîâ from her
enchantment, before he finally returns to his father's land, Genewîs, with Iblis as his wife.
L. is first mentioned in Chrestien's *Erec*, where he is ranked third of the knights at Arthur's
court and is called (1694) Lanceloz del Lac. It is quite clear, therefore, that L.'s abduction
by a water-fairy, although not mentioned by Chrestien, is part of the earliest tradition
connected with his name.[5]

L has little or nothing in common with the *Conte de la Charrette* by Chrestien, in which L.
is the lover of Ginovêr, whom he rescues from her abductor, Meljaganz. The story of the
abduction is told briefly in *I*, but L. is not mentioned. Fuller particulars are given in *C*
(2098ff.), where L.'s ride in a cart, an important episode in the *Conte de la Charrette*, is
mentioned for the only time in MHG literature. Other references to the story are contained
in *P*, where the bridge consisting of a sword-blade, edge uppermost, is mentioned, and in
G. In *C* he is both priest and knight (the only reference to L. in the former of these
capacities), whilst (9016ff.) an adventure is mentioned in which L. is released by Gawein
from an enchantment. A feature which he seems to have borrowed from Gawein is that, in
C (2089ff.), his strength increases from midday until nightfall. His appearances in the
remainder of the MHG romances are of the usual episodic nature connected with minor
characters in these epics (see Wenzel).

L., whose character, according to Sommer,[6] was a purely French invention (only his fairy

---

5   Bruce (1), I, pp. 214ff.
6   *Vulgate Version of the Arthurian Romances*, I, p. viii.

upbringing being Celtic), displaced Gawein as the most brilliant knight at Arthur's court and is responsible for the blackening of Gawein's character which becomes so obvious in the later romances. Whilst this is true of the OF romances and, above all, of Malory, it is certainly not true of the MHG epics, in which Gawein retains his popularity to the end. Chrestien's form of the name ends in *-ot* (*-oz*), and this spelling is followed in *E*, *P*, and *GM*; all the other MHG epics follow Ulrich von Zatzikhoven's form in *-et*.
– *E* 1631; *L* a86f. n4706; *Wigl* 9567ff.; *P* nm387,2; *DB* 984; *C* 849; *RW* nm2199; *A* nm3203; *Wigm* 2056; *FD* nm1430,4; *G* 80f.; *TF* 1691; *Loh* nm458 a561; *RB* nm8931; *GM* (MS I) 3862; *RP* 22,31; *FS* nm4818; *Ll* (MS K) nm15,8 a26,1

Lanzelôt see Lanzelet

Lanzidant 'ûz Gruonlant'. (Bartsch derived this name from the Provençal *lanza dan*, 'der Verderbenschleuderer'.[7]) L. is one of the three young princes sent by Amphlîse (1) to Gahmuret whilst the latter is at Herzeloide's tourney. – *P* a76,2f. n87,19

Lanzilete, Lanzolet, Lanzulet see Lanzelet

Laomedon father of Priam. His suspicious treatment of Jason and Hercules during their quest for the Golden Fleece leads Jason to bring an army to Troy after his return, in order to avenge the insult. In the ensuing battle, L. is slain by Hercules. So also in Benoît and Dares. – *LT* nm347 a368; *TK* 4682; *UA* nm4807ff.

Laomedonta see Laudamanna

Lâr 'künec von Korntîn', father of Lârîe (1). L. is slain by Rôaz, but his spirit roams the land in the shape of a horse, which changes into the form of a man only in a certain meadow. Wigalois follows the horse and witnesses the transformation. L. tells him that he is destined to free Korntîn and to marry Lârîe. L. is also called Jorêl. – *Wigl* m3673f. a (as horse) 4486, (as man) 4625 n9880

Larabat 'von Ebron', a warrior in Akarîn's army against Ipomidôn. – *JT* 3124,6

Lardentze father of Karfidûn. – *JT* nm2833,6

Lardimes 'vrouwe', one of the ladies at Arthur's court. – *JT* 1797,5

Lare see Lore

Largeduntze 'künec von Garuntze' a knight who is present at the tourney held by Arthur. – *JT* 2023,1ff.

Lârîe (1) 'küneginne von Korntîn', daughter of Lâr and Amênâ. She is confined to one castle by Rôaz and sends to Arthur's court for help. She is rescued by Wigalois, whom she subsequently marries. She corresponds to la Blonde Esmerée in *Li Biaus Descouneus*. In *JT* she is called Lorie von Korntin and is one of the ladies at Arthur's court. – *Wigl* m1750 a4011 n4056; *JT* 1612,4; *UW* nm337,24

Larie (2) wife of Patroclus (q.v.). – *GT* m16540 an16570ff.

Larchidare 'der ûz' (*JT*), see Ediffrison

Larquines see Tarquines

Lasarus 'sante von Davalun' (identical with Lazarus?). – *RP* nm11,12

Laschoit see Laskoyt

Laskoyt son of Gurnemanz. L. was slain by Îdêr in the contest for the sparrow-hawk. – *P* m175,16 n178,11

Lâtin father of Lavînia, whom he gives to Ênêâs, although he had already promised her to Turnus. So also in the OF *Eneas* and in Virgil. – *Ed* nm3650f. a3908

Lâtînus (1) see Lâtin

---

7   Bartsch (2), p. 148.

Latinus (2) a knight who fights for Athis against Bilas. This name does not occur in the OF version but may be a variant of Palatines. – *AP* C,18

Latônâ a goddess worshipped by the people of Thebes. In Roman mythology she is the mother of Apollo and Diana and corresponds to the Greek goddess Leta. – *UA* nm2778

Latrisete 'der' (*W*), see Tesereiz

Laudamanna son of Hector. He is also called Laomedonta and, in *TKf*, Leodomant. Homer and Virgil know only one son of Hector, Astyanax, but L. appears in Dictys as Laodamas and in Benoît as Laudamanta. – *LT* nm9649 a18162f.; *TKf* 41001f.

Laudamîe daughter of Avenîs (1) and Anfolê (1). L., who is 'vrowe von Anferre', is oppressed by a centaur-like monster, Vulgân, from which she is rescued by Gârel (2), who marries her. – *G* 7343

Laudavine apparently a lady who was in love with Alexander. She does not occur in any of the more important histories of Alexander. – *RB* nm15157

Laudelie *amie* of Iblet. – *JT* nm1311,1

Laudet 'vrouwe', one of the ladies at Arthur's court who spill Priure's cup of chastity. – *C* 1606

Laudile see Laudîne

Laudîne wife of Ascalôn and, after the death of the latter, wife of Îwein (1) (q.v.). She appears in *C*, where she is one of the ladies who spill Priure's cup of chastity at Arthur's court, and she is also present at Arthur's court in *JT*, where she is called Laudine von Ascalon and Laudile von Berbester. She is called Laudine in Chrestien's *Yvain*, and Alundyne in the ME *Ywain and Gawain*. – *I* m1160f. a1307 n2421; *P* m253,12; *C* 1329; *JT* 1610,6

Laudunâl 'von Pleiedunze', a knight whom Parzivâl claims to have defeated. In *JT*, where he is called künec von Plenunde, he is one of the knights who swear allegiance to Parzivâl after the latter's victory over Agors (see Strangedorz). – *P* nm772,8; *JT* 5657,1

Lauernâtus a warrior who is slain by the burghers of Sûdrâcas, into which town he had penetrated in order to help Alexander. This character appears to have been invented by Ulrich. – *UA* 20651

Laumacors 'künec', a knight in the army of Thelamon. L. was slain in battle by Peritheus, who took his horse. This incident is related, but L. is not named, in the OF version. – *AP* nmE,50

Laumedôn see Laomedon

Launtzelet see Lanzelet

Laureine one of the woman-warriors under Kamille (1). L. is slain by Orilocus in the battle between Ênêas and Turnus. In the OF *Eneas* she is called Larine, whilst in Virgil she is called Larina. – *Ed* 8917f.

Laureliân 'künec', a warrior who is slain by Troilus whilst fighting for the Greeks against the Trojans. This character was invented by Konrad. – *LT* 40166

Laurengel see Lohengrîn

Lausus son of Mesentius. He is slain by Ênêas whilst fighting for Turnus. So also in the OF *Eneas* and Virgil. – *Ed* 5032

Lavîe, Lâvînâ, Lâvîne see Lavînia

Lavînia daughter of Lâtin. In spite of the warnings of her mother, who wants her to love Turnus, L. falls in love with Ênêas immediately she sees him. He returns her love, and they are eventually married. So also in the OF *Eneas* and in Virgil. – *Ed* nm3647 a9743; *E* nm7576; *C* nm533

175

Lazaliez (1) (Schulz derived this name from OF *las*, 'joyous', and *alis*, 'courteous', or *aliz*, 'firmly formed'.[8] Bartsch suggested < *lace-liez* < *lacer*, i.e. 'der Verbinder (der Mittelpunkt) der Frohen'.[9] Martin considers the possibility of its being a form of Tysylio, with *l* for *t* as in Luntaguel for Tintaguel (see Dâvît (2)).[10]) L. is the brother of Brickus and the son of Mazadân. He does not occur in any other romance. – *P* nm56,12ff.

Lazaliez (2) son of Meleranz and Tydomîe. – *M* 12801ff.

Lâzarus biblical, the New Testament character who was brought back to life by Christ. – nm *P* 796,2; *JT* 5123,5; *RB* 18075

Lazzarus see Lâzarus

Lazze see Lîâze

Lê a knight who is present at Arthur's court when Êrec returns with Ênîte. This name does not appear in the corresponding list in Chrestien's *Erec*. – *E* 1672

Leander in Greek legend the lover of Hero, to reach whom he swam across the Hellespont. – *C* nm11567

Lebant see Lewan

Leda daughter of Aurora and mother of Helen. – *Tn* m8270

Lêde a lady who is referred to by Keiî as having played the same rôle in *C* as does Cunnewâre in *P*. – *C* nm2229

Ledebrone see Leidebrôn

Ledibodantze see Ledibudantz

Ledibrot a knight who is present at the tourney held by Arthur. (Identical with Leidebrôn?) – *JT* 2132,5f.

Ledibudantz 'von Gredimonte', a commander in the army of Ipomidôn against Akarîn. L. carries on his shield the petrifying head of a basilisk. – *JT* 3232,1

Lehelein see Lehelîn

Lehelîn (Schulz was the first to identify this name with the Welsh name Llewelyn,[11] a derivation which is followed by Martin and Brugger.[12] Singer thinks that the name arose from the name Lohelin in Wace's *Brut* (5834), Loelin in Geoffrey of Monmouth (V, 8).[13]) L. is the brother of Orilus and Kunnewâre and is present at the tourney held by Herzeloide, at which he is unhorsed by Gahmuret. Herzeloide and Sigûne tell Parzivâl (128,3ff. and 141,7) that L. has taken two lands from him, whilst Trevrezent relates that L. killed a Graal Knight who barred his way to the Graal Castle, and took his horse. In *Wigm*, L. is present at the tourney held by Dymszogar, and in *JT* he attends the tourney held by Arthur. Brugger identifies L. with the historical Llewelyn ab Seisyll, who ruled over Wales, and died AD 1023.[14] (See also Ingûse.) – *P* nm67,18 a79,13; *Wigm* nm4744 a4957; *JT* nm1315,3 a1797,6 [†]

Leidebrôn 'von Redunzehte', a knight whom Parzivâl claims to have defeated. In *JT* he is present at the tourney held by Arthur. (Identical with Ledibrot?) – *P* nm772,20; *JT* 2021,6

Leidegast 'von Sahsen', a knight who welcomes Ulrich von Liechtenstein to Neustadt during his *Artusfahrt*. – *FD* 1486,1ff.

---

8   Schulz, 'Eigennamen', p. 397.
9   Bartsch (2), p. 134.
10   Martin (1), p. 64, to 56,15.
11   Schulz, 'Eigennamen', p. 387.
12   Martin (1), p. 75, to 67,18; Brugger (1), p. 76.
13   Singer (1), p. 49.
14   Brugger (1), p. 76.

Leigamar 'grâve von Ansgoi', a knight who gives a tourney for the hand of his elder daughter, Fursensephin. His younger daughter is named Quebeleplûs. L. corresponds to Lipaôt in *P*, and Tiebaut in Chrestien's *Perceval*. – *C* nm17577 a17856f.

Leigormon a maiden for whom Gawein is said to have plucked a flower, at great danger to himself, at Colurment. There seems to be no doubt that this is an attempt to represent Chrestien's l'Orguelleuse (see Orgelûse). – *C* nm6105

Leimas 'herzoginne von Sîandrîe', sister of Galaidâ. – *C* nm23895

Leyses see Linefles

Leifdet 'von Ispanien', a leader in Bêâmunt's army at Antrîûn. – *Dem* nm9780

Leiwart 'grâve', a knight who is present at the tourney held by Arthur. – *JT* 2028,1

Lechikrâtes 'vürste', a warrior who is captured by Alexander in the first battle against Dârîus (3). This character appears to have been invented by Rudolf. – *A* 7632

Lembekîn 'herzoge von Brabant'. (Singer thinks that this name is a diminutive, made by Wolfram, of Kîôt's Lambert, but he points out that there is a knight named Lambegues in the OF romance *Escanor* (14366).[15]) L. is present at the tourney held by Herzeloide, where he is unhorsed by Kailet. He is married to Alîze (1) (q.v.). He also takes part in the tourney held by Arthur in *JT*. – *P* m67,23 an73,29ff.; *JT* 2080,1f.

Lemberkin see Lämbekin

Lenial a knight who is present at Arthur's court. He occurs in MS D only. – *GM* (MS D) 38576

Lenomîe (1) 'von Alexandrîe', a queen who sends Arthur a magnificent cloth when he holds his tourney. – *C* 520ff.

Lenomîe (2) 'von Lêcester', sister of Ginovêr. – *C* 551ff.

Lenseyges see Linefles

Lenval see Lanfal

Lêô (1) 'bâbest' (Leo III). In fighting for L., Willehalm (1) sustained the wound to his nose, the scar of which is his distinguishing mark. In *UW* he baptizes Gîburc. – *W* nm92,1f.; *UW* a13,2f. n245,4 [†]

Lêô (2) 'ein meister ze Rôme'. The author of a Latin version of the history of Alexander which was one of Rudolf's sources. – *A* nm12986

Leodomant see Laudamanna

Leôn to whom Alexander bequeathed Ciria. This name does not occur in any of the other histories of Alexander. – *UA* nm27018

Lêônât, Lêônâtes see Leonatus

Leonatus a warrior who, in *A*, is sent by Alexander to watch Mitrênes (q.v.). In *SA* Alexander bequeaths Frigia to him. L. occurs as Leonnatus in *Expeditio Alexandri* and Curtius Rufus. (Identical with Leôn?) – *A* 7665; *SA* nm8503f.

Lêônidas a warrior who is appointed by Alexander to succeed Parmênîôn. So also in Curtius Rufus. – *A* 20526

Lêônides tutor to the young Alexander. So also in Pseudo-Callisthenes and Valerius. – *A* 1378

Leonzius a warrior who is slain by Hector whilst fighting for the Greeks against the Trojans. L. occurs as Leontius in Dictys, Leontins in Benoît, and Leonteus in Homer, but in none of these versions is his death mentioned. – *TKf* 40466f.

---

15 Singer (1), p. 59.

Leopolis 'künec von Thelaneis', a warrior in the Greek army against the Trojans. This character does not occur in any other version of the Trojan legend, but the name Leopolus occurs as a variant of Telopolus de Rhodes in Benoît. – *TK* 23864

Leofax standard-bearer in Ipomidôn's army against Akarîn. He is slain in the battle by Kailet. – *JT* nm3358,3f. a4179,1

Leofex see Leofax

Leprosi 'von Olmusate', a warrior in Ipomidôn's army against Akarîn. – *JT* 3259,3f.

Lerân 'von Berbester', also called Jôrân von Berbester (753), Jôrân von Wintsester (578), and Turnîs von Berbester (1529). L. is a knight who is present at the tourney at which Reinfrit wins the love of Yrkâne. – *RB* nm291 a578

Lerant 'künec von Schotten', a warrior who fights for the Greeks against the Trojans. This character was invented by Konrad. – *TK* 23920f.

Lermebion 'von Jarbes', a knight who is present at Arthur's court when Êrec returns with Ênîte. This character does not occur in the corresponding list in Chrestien's *Erec*. – *E* 1692

Lernîs 'künec von Riez', one of the five old kings who attend the wedding of Êrec. In Chrestien's *Erec* he is called (1985) Kerrins li viauz rois de Riël, and in *C* the territorial name has been confused with the personal name, with the result that he is called Darîel von Querquons. According to Golther, L. is identical with Jernîs von Rîle, the father of Amflîse (2) in *P*.[16] – *E* 2074; *P* nm234,13; *C* 2339

Lernfras 'fil Gaîn' (= Keiî), a knight who is present at Arthur's court when Êrec returns with Ênîte. L. is mentioned, but not named, in Chrestien's *Erec* (1739); in the next verse (1740) he is called Gronosis (q.v.). – *E* 1670

Lespia a *Meerweib* who steals Wigamur whilst Paltriot is at Arthur's court. She is later captured by Paltriot and confesses where Wigamur is, but when the king's men go to look for him, they find that he has been led away by a sea-monster. Paltriot slays L. when he learns this. – *Wigm* 111f.

Lespîn a knight who is present at Arthur's court when Êrec returns with Ênîte. This name does not occur in the corresponding list in Chrestien's *Erec*. A 'chastel de lespine' (= de l'Espine) and a 'Forest de lespine' occur in *L'Estoire de Merlin* (Vulgate Cycle). – *E* 1683

Lespurant a cruel knight who has defeated and killed the husband of Ligronite. Wigamur arrives at the castle and is told the story by a dwarf in the service of Ligronite. There is a gap here in MS W, as Wigamur later fetches Pioles from Ligronite, when he unites the former with her *ami*. He has evidently fought and defeated L. and brought Pioles to shelter in Ligronite's castle. – *Wigm* (MS M) nm10992⁴

Lespus a warrior in Alexander's army. This name rests on a misunderstanding by Rudolf of Curtius Rufus, III,I, where Lesbus, the land, was taken to be the name of the person. – *A* 5073

Lestugo brother of Cycrops (q.v.). So also in Benoît, where he is called Lestrigonain, and in Dictys, where he is called Laestrygon. In the *Odyssey*, Laestrygonia is the name of the land in which Antiphates lives. – *LT* nm17571

Lesular 'von Paneise', a warrior in Akarîn's army against Ipomidôn. – *JT* nm3127,1

Lesurant 'von Oriente', a warrior in Akarîn's army against Ipomidôn. He is the *ami* of Jerasabel. – *JT* 3165,1f.

Levenet a lady who extends hospitality to Gawein after his adventure with Aamanz. – *C* a17377ff. n17474

---

16 Golther (1), p. 158.

Leverzins 'von Larîse', a warrior in the Greek army against the Trojans. This name does not occur in any other version of the Trojan legend, but it seems possible that it may have been suggested by Leontine de Larise, who occurs in Benoît. – *TK* 23874

Lêvî biblical, name-father of the tribe of the Levites. – *A* nm16268

Lewan a young knight who offers himself at Arthur's court as a champion for Elsam. In MS K he is called Lebant. – *Ll* 39,1 (MS K) 30,1

*Lewen 'ritter mit dem' (*I*, *G*), see Îwein (1)

Lya biblical (Leah), Jacob's first wife. – *UA* nm11335

Lîahturteltart (Bartsch sees in '-turtelart', *turnel'dart*, 'der Pfeilendreher',[17] whilst 'liaht-' seems to Martin to be a form of Lîaz (Lîâze), as *st* > *ht* in East Franconian.[18]) L. is the son of Pansâmûrs and Bêâflûrs ('die wâren von der feien art' (*P* 87,29)) and is one of the three young princes who are sent by Amphlîse (1) to Gahmuret at Herzeloide's tourney. – *P* a76,2f. n87,30

Lîamêre a lady who dies of grief when she is abducted by Lîôn from her husband, Âmîre. Her death is avenged by Wigalois. – *Wigl* m9835 n9859 a9969

Liander 'von Testregeis', 'lantgrâve von Karneis', one of the knights held captive by Eskilabôn and released when Gârel defeats the latter. L. fights for Gârel against Ehkunat. – *G* 4830

Lyanit 'der von' (*UW*), see Ritschart (1)

Liasse see Lîâze

Lîâze daughter of Gurnemanz, who tries unsuccessfully to secure Parzivâl as her husband. Golther claims that, according to Wolfram's genealogy, L. is Parzivâl's great-aunt.[19] She is present at Arthur's court in *JT*, whilst in *Sey* she is one of the women imprisoned by Klinschor and released when Seyfrid slays Amphigulor. – *P* 175,12ff.; *JT* 1602,1; *Sey* m27,6f. a44,2 n65,5 [†]

Libaut 'von Winden', a knight who had been slain by Mabônagrîn whilst attempting the adventure of Schoidelakurt. This name rests on a misunderstanding of Chrestien's *Erec*, where Tiebauz (see Tîbalt) is mentioned (5777f.) as a very brave knight. – *E* nm8506ff.

Libêals 'von Prienlaschors', a Graal knight who is slain by Lehelîn when he attempts to bar the latter's way to the Graal Castle. L. does not occur in Chrestien's *Perceval*. – *P* m340,4 n473,24f.

Libers (1) 'künec von Lorgân', a knight whom Tydomîe's uncle is trying to compel her to marry. L. steals her meadow, in which her bathing pool is situated, but is forced to give it up by Meleranz. L. eventually marries Dulceflûr (1). – *M* m7692f. n7751 a9334f.

Libers (2) 'grâve von Treverîn', a knight who attends the wedding of Êrec. L. is not named in Chrestien's *Erec* (1941): 'De Treverain i vint li cuens'. It seems possible that Hartmann's MS of Chrestien may have read '. . . i vint li beals' (or 'li bauz'), but on the other hand Hartmann specifies L. as a 'grâve'. (See also Maheloas.) – *E* 1916

Lybials son of Kardeûz and Deselmiur, a knight who is sent by Sarîne to challenge the newly-made knight, Meleranz. The fight consists of one joust, in which neither combatant is unhorsed. – *M* m3209f. a3376 n3575

Libilûn 'künec von Rankulat', a cousin of Gîburc who is slain by Vîvîans whilst fighting against Willehalm (1) at Alischanz. This name rests on a misunderstanding by Wolfram of *Aliscans*, where he is called (346) 'un neveu Aerofle le blon'. – *W* 46,17 [†]

---

[17] Bartsch (2), p. 148.
[18] Martin (1), p. 92, to 87,30.
[19] Golther (1), p. 153.

Libiut see Lipaôt

Libute see Lipaôt

Lidamus 'vürste', a duke in the service of Vergulaht. In *JT* he is present at the tourney held by Arthur. – *P* 416,18ff.; *JT* 1936,6 [†]

Liddamus 'künec von Agrippe'. (Bartsch thought that this name was a form of the Greek name, Laodamus,[20] but Golther is of the opinion that its origin is Lygdamus Syracusanus, who occurs in Solinus.[21]) L. is one of the knights whom Feirefiz claims to have defeated. In *JT* he fights for Ipomidôn against Akarîn and also takes part in the tourney held by Sekundille to decide which of her wooers she shall marry; in this poem he is called Ladamus and Iadamus. – *P* nm770,4; *JT* 3220,1

Lidewant 'herzoge von Lida Bure', a knight who is present at the tourney held by Arthur. – *JT* 2032,5

Lîedarz (Bartsch derived this name from the Provençal *lia darz*, 'der Pfeilenbinder'.[22] Martin suggests < Liudhart or Liudhari.[23]) L., who is the son of Schîolarz, is one of the young princes sent by Amphlîse (1) to Gahmuret at Herzeloide's tourney. In *TF* he is called Liodarz and is rescued from robber-knights in a forest by Tandareis. – *P* a76,2f. n87,23; *TF* m4918f. a4928ff. n5129

Liechten Brunnen 'grâve von dem', a knight whose land is being laid waste by a monster, which petrifies its attackers by showing them a basilisk-like head. Daniel meets L.'s wife, vrouwe von dem Liechten Brunnen (a1792 n6302f), and kills the monster with the aid of a mirror. L. is so grateful that he accompanies Daniel on his adventures. He follows the grâve von der Grüenen Ouwe into the latter's castle, from which he is rescued by Daniel. – *DB* m1935 a2214 [n2316f.] [†]

Ligossomor 'von Iassolen', a warrior in Akarîn's army against Ipomidôn. – *JT* nm3128,2

Ligrison 'von Lirdibiessen', a warrior in Akarîn's army against Ipomidôn. – *JT* nm3113,4

Ligronite a lady who is oppressed by Lespurant, who is apparently killed by Wigamur. – *Wigm* nm (MS M) 10992[7] a (MS W) 5717

Lîcaon a warrior who is slain whilst fighting for the Trojans against the Greeks. So also in Benoît and Dares, where he is killed by Achilles, whilst in Homer, Lycaon, whose fate is not given, is a brother to Hector. – *TKf* 43611f.

Lîcas 'kamerære' to Dîanîrâ, for whom he carries the poisoned shirt to Hercules. Although L. is innocent of any knowledge of the poison, Hercules slays him in his death throes. So also in Ovid's *Metamorphoses* IX, where he is called Lichas. – *TK* nm38282ff.

Lîke see Lîcus

Lichmach to whom Alexander leaves Trana and Reussen. This name does not occur in any other history of Alexander. – *SA* nm8505f.

Licomedes 'künec von Scŷros', father of Deidamîe and later father-in-law to Achilles. So also in the *Achilleis* of Statius. In Homer, Lykomedes is a warrior in the Greek army, but there is no suggestion of a relationship with Achilles. In both *UA* and *GT* he is called Nicomedes. – *LT* m13847 n13861; *TK* m13887 n13932 a15150f.; *UA* nm18492; *RB* nm22579; *GT* nm15670ff. a16306ff.

---

20 Bartsch (2), p. 155.
21 Golther (1), p. 137.
22 Bartsch (2), p. 148.
23 Martin (1), p. 92, to 87,23.

Lîcomîde the leader of a band of knights which Ascanius sends out from Albanî to assist Ênêâs against Turnus. This character appears to have been invented by Heinrich. – *Ed* 7432f.

Lîcus a warrior in the Trojan army and a relative of Êlenor, with whom he guards the most vulnerable tower of Albanî. They are both killed. So also in the OF *Eneas* and Virgil. – *Ed* 6964ff.

Liliander 'künec von Yspani', an ally of Lôîs against Terramêr. – *UW* 36,12

Limacrîs 'herzoge', a warrior who is slain by Troilus whilst fighting for the Greeks against the Trojans. This character was invented by Konrad. – *TK* 40167

Lympondrigon 'von Gurgalet', a knight who had murdered the father of Dymszogar. At the tourney held by the latter, L. is Wigamur's chief rival for the prize but is defeated by Wigamur in single combat. He secretly leaves the tourney early in the morning, and meeting Dulcefluor, he abducts her. He is pursued by Wigamur and Atroclas, and the former severely wounds him and recovers Dulcefluor. – *Wigm* 4965f.

Lympontrogrön see Lympondrigon

Limual a knight who is unhorsed by Gauriel at Arthur's court. – *GM* 1240

Linefles 'künec von Franken', husband of Olimpîâ (1) and father of Meleranz. – *M* a142 n3776

Lînier 'von Lîmors', brother of Patricjus and uncle of Ade. He imprisons Lanzelet, who had followed Ade into his castle, and to regain his freedom, Lanzelet has to fight a giant, two lions, and finally L., all of whom he defeats and kills. – *L* nm1554 a1603

Linouwe 'der von' (*RW*), see Heinrich (19)

Linpondrigön see Lympondrigon

Linvâl see Lanfal

Liodarz see Lîedarz

Lyochin a warrior in the Greek army against the Trojans. This character appears to have been invented by Herbort. – *LT* 3385

Lîôn 'der ungehiure', a knight who slays Âmîre and abducts Lîamêre. Wigalois attacks L. with all his vassals and friends, and after a hard fight L. is slain by Gawein. – *Wigl* nm9820f. a10028

Lyonel brother of Boort, a knight of the Round Table. He is being led to his death when he is seen by his brother, who, however, leaves him to rescue a damsel. L. is rescued from the six knights by Gawein, and on meeting Boort, tries to compel him to fight for having left him to his fate. He kills Kalogreant, who endeavours to prevent the fight, which is, nevertheless, prevented by a cloud which envelops the brothers. (See Boort.) – *RP* nm794,13 a794,27

Lyones see Lyonel

Lypandrigän see Lympondrigon

Lipaôt father of Obîe and Obilôt, and guardian and tutor of Meljanz. Obîe scorns the love of Meljanz, who collects an army and attacks L., who, largely through the help of Gawein, wins the battle. He occurs as Libiut von Bearosch in *JT*, where he is present at the tourney held by Arthur. In Chrestien's *Perceval*, where he is called Tiebaut (on the interchange of *t* and *l*, see also Lazaliez), he holds a tourney to decide on a husband for his elder daughter; this is the case in *C*, where he is named Leigamar (q.v.). – *P* m345,1 n345,13 a354,12; *JT* 1998,5

Lyplagar a knight who is unhorsed at the tourney held by Dymszogar. (See Zingund.) – *Wigm* nm4782 a4844

Lippatreiz brother of Agulant, a warrior in the Greek army who is slain by Perseus (1) whilst fighting against the Trojans. This character was invented by Konrad. – *TK* 33546

*Lyppaut see Lipaôt

Lipperdisol 'von Perludesse', a warrior in Ipomidôn's army against Akarîn. – *JT* nm3239,1f.

Lippidîns 'von Agremuntîn'. (Martin suggests < Lepidis, a name in Solinus (19,21).[24]) L. is one of the knights whom Feirefîz claims to have defeated. In *JT*, where he is called Lippidius, he takes part in the tourney held by Sekundille to decide which of her wooers she shall marry. – *P* nm770,7; *JT* 5262,1

Lippidius see Lippidîns

Lirivone 'künec von' (*JT*), see Schirniel

Lis (1) a maiden attendant upon Agly. – *WO* 9216

Lis (2) see Quarcos

Lisaburdol 'von Radiffurbeise', a commander in Ipomidôn's army against Akarîn. – *JT* a3274,4 n3279,3f.

Lisande see Liscandes

Lisander see Lisavander (2)

Lisavander (1) 'schahteliur von Bêâveis', a knight who is unhorsed by Gawein in the battle between Meljanz and Lipaôt. L. corresponds to Chrestien's Traez d'Anet, a name which appears in widely varying forms in the different MSS. – *P* nm348,15ff. a349,17f.

Lisavander (2) 'von Ipopotitikôn', a knight whom Feirefîz claims to have defeated. In *JT* he is called Lisander and takes part in the tourney held by Sekundille to decide which of her wooers she shall marry. – *P* nm770,13; *JT* 5274,1

Lysian see Livian

Lysias (1) a giant who tells Philipp (1) that Cleôpatra will bear him a son and heir. Alexander, who hears him, strikes him down in rage and kills him. So also in Leo. In *WA* he is a son of Cleôpatra and says that he himself will be Philipp's heir. This story is also told in Pseudo-Callisthenes and Valerius, where he is only wounded by Alexander. – *A* 2622f.; *UA* 1769; *SA* 951; *WA* 483 [†]

Lisias (2) 'von Damascone', a warrior in Ipomidôn's army against Akarîn. – *JT* nm3600,5 a3610,1

Lîsias (3) 'von Macêt', a warrior who is slain by Alexander whilst fighting for Dârîus at Erbela. So also in Gualterus. – *UA* 10945ff.

Lysimâcus to whom Alexander left Trâces and Pontus. So also in Curtius Rufus and Gualterus. L. occurs also in *Expeditio Alexandri* and the *Successorum Alexandri*. – *UA* nm27019f.

Liscandes 'künec in Franken lande', a knight who is present at the tourney held by Arthur. – *JT* 1714,6f.

Lischeit son of Tînas, a knight who entertains Tandareis after the latter leaves Albiûn. – *TF* nm10157 a10177

Lischois Gwelljus 'herzoge von Gôwerzîn'. (Both Bartsch and Golther see in this name an attempt to represent l'Orguelleus (de la Roche a l'Estroite Voie), the name of one of Orgelûse's knights in Chrestien's *Perceval*.[25] Martin is convinced that the second half of the name is derived from OF *guilos*, 'cunning', and suggests Lischois < *li schois*, connected with the English 'scout'.[26] Singer follows Martin for the second half of the name, which he

---

24 Martin (1), p. 503, to 770,7.
25 Bartsch (2), p. 123; Golther (1), p. 192.
26 Martin (1), p. 382, to 507,2.

derives from Kîôt's *li joios guilos*, 'the joyous cunning'.[27]) L. is a knight in the service of Orgelûse and is defeated by Gawein, who gives him to Plipalinot (see Inpripalinôt), instead of the usual tribute, which is the loser's horse. L. is later released in exchange for a harp and marries Kundrîe (2). In *Sey* he is the father of Seyfrid, and in *JT*, where he is called Gewellis litschoie, he attends the tourney held by Arthur. – *P* nm507,2 a535,8f.; *JT* 2076,1; *Sey* 6,4 [†]

Liso   see Bessus

Litan 'der von' (*HT*), see Tînas

Litschois Gewellius   see Lischois Gwelljus

Littores   see Tors

Liupolt (1) 'von Heimenburg', a knight who welcomes Ulrich von Liechtenstein to Neustadt during his *Artusfahrt*. – *FD* 1484,1f.

Liupolt (2) 'von Lengenburc', a knight who is defeated by Ulrich von Liechtenstein at the tourney held at Friesach. – *FD* 227,8f.

Liupolt (3) 'von Medelic', a knight who welcomes Ulrich von Liechtenstein to Neustadt during his *Artusfahrt*. – *FD* 1483,6

Liupolt (4) 'von Oesterrîch', who holds a festival to celebrate the marriage of his daughter. Ulrich von Liechtenstein was made a knight at this festival. – *FD* 40,1

Liupolt (5) 'herzoge von Osterrich', who, concerned at having no heir, makes a pilgrimage to Ephesus. He is driven by a storm to Zyzya, where he makes the acquaintance of Agrant, who accompanies him on his pilgrimage. Some time after L.'s return, Wildhalm is born on the same day that Agrant's daughter, Agly, is born. L. fights for the Christians in the final battle against the heathens; later he is killed by the shock on hearing of the death of Wildhalm. – *WO* a173 n197

Liupolt (6) 'herzoge von Oesterrîch' (Leopold V), the captor of Richard Coeur de Lion (see Richart). – *L* nm9328

*Liupolt (7) 'von Österrich', brother of Fridrich (5); a contemporary of Johann von Würzburg. – *WO* nm18632

Liutolt (1) 'von Petach', a knight who jousts with Ulrich von Liechtenstein at the tourney held at Friesach. – *FD* 191,4

Liutolt (2) 'von Tobel', a knight who welcomes Ulrich von Liechtenstein to Neustadt during his *Artusfahrt*. – *FD* 1485,5

Liutfrit 'von Eppenstein', a knight who jousts with Ulrich von Liechtenstein during the latter's *Venusfahrt* and again, under the name of Kalogreant, during his *Artusfahrt*. – *FD* 503,4f.

Livian a knight who attacks and is killed by Eleander, as the latter is looking for the abducted Amalita. – *GT* 20461ff.

Liflanden 'künec von' (*RW*), see Gutschart

Lifort Gâwânides   see Gâwânides

Lifrenîs   see Kâedîn

Lifronîs 'grâve von Cesariâ', a warrior in the Trojan army against the Greeks. This character was invented by Konrad. – *TK* 24910

Lixa wife of Ribalin and foster-mother of Paris. – *GT* 1410

Lîz 'der von' (*G*), see Meljanz

Lodewîg 'lantgrâve von Doringen' (Ludwig III. von Thüringen). – *Ed* nm13474

Lôemêr 'künec von Norvegen', an ally of Sornagiur. – *PM* a3322 n4099f.

---

27   Singer (1), p. 112.

Loez see Lohût

Loga *ami* of the maiden who is sent to Persit by Darius (5) (q.v.). – *WO* nm4596

Logrois 'der ûz' (*JT*), see Zidegast

Lohein 'künec', at whose court Amely confessed her love to Willehalm (4), according to *FS*. This is apparently intended to be Rainher. – *FS* nm1561

Loheneis see Lohenis (2)

Lohengarîn see Lohengrîn (1) and (2)

Lohengrîn (1) (in *P*, Loherangrîn < (li) Loheren Gerin = Garin the Lorrainian[28]). Wolfram outlines the story of L., who is the son of Parzivâl and Kondwîrâmûrs, in a few words at the end of *P*. It is the story of the OF romance *Le Chevalier au Cygne*, which, according to Hertz,[29] Wolfram found without names, and so inserted the name of a popular hero, who has originally no connection with this legend. L., like the hero of the OF poem, is drawn by a swan to the court of the Duchess of Brabant (Duchess of Bouillon in the OF), where he rescues her from an oppressor and marries her. She must not, however, under any circumstances enquire about his parentage. For a time they live happily, but eventually his wife can restrain her curiosity no longer. The swan arrives, and L. is compelled to leave his wife and family. *JT* records how L. marries again after leaving Brabant, his second wife being Pelaie (q.v.), who is indirectly responsible for his death; this story is told also by Füetrer.[30] Wolfram's story serves as a basis for *Loh*, but a good deal of historical fact is woven into this version. L. fights for Heinrîch (1) against the Hungarians, and with him against the heathens under Gêrfridolt, whom he himself wounds and puts to flight. The legendary portion of *Loh* is the subject of a 15th-century poem, *Lorengel* (a name which identifies its bearer as *lur*, 'elf'[31]). L. is called Loherangrin in *P*; Lohengrin, Lorangrime, Lohrangrine in *JT*; Lohengrîn, Lohengarîn in *Loh*; Laurengel in *FS*; and Lorengel in *Ll*. – *P* nm743,16ff. a800,20; *JT* nm5882,6 a5918,3; *Loh* nm285 a581; *FS* nm4822; *Ll* nm43,5f. a47,1 (MS K) nm28,6 a34,1 [†]

Lohengrîn (2) younger son of Lohengrîn (1) and Elsam, brother of Jôhan (1). – *P* m826,9; *Loh* m7196 a7207 n7259

Lohenîs (1) 'von Rahaz', a knight who plays the same rôle in *C* as does Urjans in *P*. L. is surely identical with Lochneis, with whom Gawein compares Gasosîn when he sees the latter offering violence to Ginovêr (*C* 11767). – *C* a19351ff. [n19366]

Lohenis (2) 'von Zezily', a knight who is unhorsed by Seyfrid at the latter's *swertleite*. – *Sey* 74,6

Lohencis 'von Ouein', a knight who spills Priure's cup of chastity at Arthur's court. This name does not occur in Chrestien's *Erec*, but it may possibly be a distorted form of Yvains de Loenel (*Erec* 1707), in which the territorial name has become confused with the personal name. This name occupies an almost identical position in Chrestien's list as does L. in the list in *C*. – *C* 2302

Loherangrîn, Lohrangrime see Lohengrîn (1)

Lohût son of Arthur. He is present at Arthur's court when Êrec returns with Ênîte, and, as Loez, he is one of the knights who spill Priure's cup of chastity in *C*. In *P* he is said to have left Britain at an early age in order to serve his *amie*, Flôrîe (1), in whose service he was killed, and who, we learn from *T*, followed him to the grave with a broken heart. In *P*

---

28 Golther (1), p. 191.
29 Wolfram von Eschenbach, *Parzival*, transl. by W. Hertz, p. 549.
30 Hofstäter, II, pp. 174ff.
31 Albrecht von Scharfenberg, *Merlin und Seifrid de Ardemonte*, ed. by F. Panzer, p. cxii.

and *T* he is called Ilinôt, and in *G* Elinôt, whilst in *L* he appears as Lôût and in *JT* as Ylmot. According to the Vulgate *L'Estoire de Merlin*, L. is the son of Arthur, who begot him on Lisanor before he married Ginovêr. In *Perlesvaus* and the *Livre d'Artus* he is slain by Keiî, who wishes to take the credit for killing a giant which L. has just killed and over whose body he is lying exhausted. In the Vulgate *Lancelot*, L. dies of disease in prison. Bruce identifies L. with Llachau, the son of Arthur in the *Black Book of Carmarthen* and in the *Dream of Rhonabwy* in the *Mabinogion*, his subsequent adventures being the invention of the OF poets.[32] – *E* 1664; *L* a6875ff. n6891; *P* nm383,1ff.; *T* nm147,2; *C* 2322; *G* nm16745; *JT* nm1161,2f. [†]

Lôîs (1) 'künec von Rôme', husband of Willehalm's sister and father of Alîze (2). Willehalm (1) goes to him for assistance against Terramêr, and L. eventually promises him help. He collects an army, which he brings as far as Orleans, where he places it under Willehalm's command. In *UW*, L. is attacked by Terramêr, but with the help of Willehalm and his brothers, the invaders are driven back. It is at this battle that Willehalm, chasing the heathens too far, is surrounded and captured. L. is historically Louis the Pious, son of Charlemagne. – *W* m95,23 n103,13 a128,1; *UW* a33,1 n34,14; *RB* nm23367

Lôîs (2) king of France at the time of the death of Burchart. – *UA* nm18361

Lois (3) 'grâve', a Frenchman in the army of Alexander. This character appears to have been invented by Ulrich. – *UA* 4611

Loys (4) see Mamurtanit

Lôîs (5) see Schoiflôrîs

Loifilol a knight of the Round Table, who gets his *amie* to try on the cloak of chastity. – *L* 5972f.

Lok see Lôt (1)

Lochneis a knight mentioned by Gawein. Probably identical with Lohenîs (1) (q.v.). – *C* nm11767

Locridant 'von Parunte', a warrior in Akarîn's army against Ipomidôn. – *JT* nm3625,7

Locrin 'von Tusie', a warrior in Akarîn's army against Ipomidôn. – *JT* 3882,7

Lonatris see Ionatris

Longefiez 'cuns von Tutelêunz', a knight whom Parzivâl claims to have defeated. – *P* nm772,13

Longîmânus a former king of Persia. Historically this is the surname of Artâxerses (1), who is given in *A* as a separate person. – *A* nm15721

Longin see Longinus

Longinus (< λόγχη, a spear[33]). The name, invented in early Christian legend, of the Roman soldier who pierced the side of Christ as he hung on the cross. – nm *JT* 935,6; *PM* 19483; *Loh* 3879; *WO* 10431; *RP* 272,30

Lopidant 'von Anîe', a knight who pursues Firganant after the latter has defeated the *Vogt*. Firganant slays him. – *Dem* 6833ff.

Lorandin a dwarf-king who tends Seyfrid after the latter has slain Amphigulor. – *Sey* a21,1 n49,3

Lorandinol a knight who tries to compel Albazona to marry him. He is slain in single combat by her father, Joseranns. – *Sey* nm346,3

Lorangrime see Lohengrîn (1)

---

32 Bruce (2), pp. 179–84.
33 Bruce (1), I, p. 257.

Lore 'von Meilant', a maiden who, with her friend Ismane, bemoans the shortage of food in Meilant. Their cries are heard by Îwein (1), who reports the matter to Arthur, and the latter sends provisions into the town which he is besieging. L. is the daughter of Bruns (1) and is in love with Keiî. This story is told in the Montpellier MS of Pseudo-Gautier, but in the romances of the Vulgate Cycle, L. is the mistress of Branlant, and Bruns (1) (q.v.) is her seneschal. – *RP* 25,38ff.

Lorengel see Lohengrîn (1)

Lorez 'von Jassaidâ', a knight who brings an army to take part in the tourney held by Leigamar. – *C* 18146

Lorie see Lârîe

Lôrîs (1) 'künec von Schotten', a knight who takes part in the tourney at which Reinfrit wins the love of Yrkâne. – *RB* nm288 a575

Loris (2) see Gloris

Los see Lôt (1)

Losiôz 'marcgrâve', a knight who, with Lacbuz, is besieged by Malloas. – *M* nm11697ff.

Lôt (1) 'künec von Norwæge', father of Gawein. His wife is Sangîve, the sister of Arthur (but in *Mer*, as in *L'Estoire de Merlin*, she is the daughter of Arnîve (see Îgerne) by Urlois and is called (in *Mer*) Soye dy kewsch). L. appears already as king of Norway in Geoffrey of Monmouth, but in *RP*, as in Pseudo-Gautier and *L'Estoire de Merlin*, he is called 'künec von Orkanie'. He is called Los in *E* (Loz in Chrestien's *Erec* (1737)), where he is one of the knights present at Arthur's court when Êrec returns with Ênîte. In *L* he is unhorsed by Lanzelet at a tourney held by Lôt (4) (q.v.). He is present at Arthur's court and assists him against Bruns (1) in *RP*, where he is also apparently identical with Lok von Avenoys (22,15). – *E* 1667; *L* 3246f.; *P* nm39,25 a78,25; *G* nm74; *JT* 1416,2; *M* nm137; *Mer* nm236,7; *RP* nm16,19 a21,46

Lôt (2) biblical, brother of Abraham. – *RB* nm27078

Lôt (3) 'künec von Moabiten und Ammoniten', an ally of Agrant at Firmin. – *WO* 7756ff.

Lôt (4) 'von Johenîs', a knight who holds a tourney with Gurnemanz as his opponent. Lôt (1) is called king of Leonois in the Vulgate Cycle, and it seems possible that Johenîs may be a form of Leonois, and L. therefore identical with Lôt (1), a fact which appears to be assumed by Bruce.[34] – *L* nm2628

Loth see Lôt (1)

Lotier 'herzoge von Lorens', a knight who fights for Willehalm (3) against Jofrit (1). – *RW* 658f.

Lotilâus one of the conspirators with Dimnus in the plot to murder Alexander. This name is apparently a corruption of Iolaus, who appears in *A* as Jôzêus (q.v.). – *UA* 17978

Lôûmedon 'li granz', a knight who attends the tourney held by Arthur. – *C* 606

Lôût see Lohût

Lôcêdîan wife of Balifeit. – *Dar* 1

Lubîn 'von Klassenîe', a knight who is unhorsed by Anshelm whilst fighting for the Soldan against Partonopier. – *PM* 21170f.

Lûdân an ally of Soragiur. He is slain by Partonopier. – *PM* 3806f.

Ludesural 'von Irmiclube', a warrior in Ipomidôn's army against Akarîn. – *JT* 3230,2

Ludewîn 'herzoge von Ungerlant', a knight who is killed by Lohengrîn in the battle between Heinrîch (1) and the Hungarians. – *Loh* 2727ff.

Ludolf son of Otte (1). – *Loh* nm7361

---

[34] Bruce (1), I, pp. 208f.

Ludufis a knight who attends Leigamar's tourney in the service of Lorez. – *C* 18151

Ludwig son of Ruoprecht. He marries Pragnet and fights for Fridrich (3) against Mompolier. – *FS* 5775

Lugân a heathen knight who is unhorsed by Partonopier at the tourney held by Meliûr. – *PM* 13782

Lucâns the steward at Arthur's court. In *RP* he fights on the side of Cadoalans in the tourney against Ris. L. is first mentioned in Chrestien's *Erec* (1529), and although never outstanding, he appears in most of the OF romances. – *E* 1516; *C* 1793ff.; *RP* 81,13

Lûcânus (1) Latin author (Marcus Annaeus Lucanus), author of *Pharsalia*. – *E* nm5218

Lucanus (2) see Lucâns

Lûcanz see Lucâns

Lucas see Lucâns

Lucrête sister of Clogiers and mother of Partonopier, whose intercourse with Meliûr she does her best to stop. – *PM* m256 n268ff. a3166f.

Lumer a knight who attacks and is defeated by Hector, as the latter is on his way to Baldach. – *GT* a202ff. n243

Lûnete a maiden attendant on Laudîne. She rescues Îwein (1) from the predicament into which his pursuit of Ascalôn has led him, and then persuades her mistress to marry him. When Îwein fails to return to his wife at the end of the year which she has granted him at Arthur's court, L. is blamed for bringing about such a marriage and is just about to be burned when she is rescued by Îwein. She arranges later the final reconciliation of Îwein and Laudîne. L. is the real heroine of *I*, Laudîne being colourless beside the figure of her maid. In the *Livre d'Artus* she is the cousin of Niniane, Merlin's *amie*, and in both the French and German literatures she was famous for her beauty.[35] Panzer records that the name occurs once in the 14th century but was a popular one in the 15th century,[36] whilst Zahn also gives an example of its occurrence in the 15th century.[37] – *I* a1152f. n2717; *P* nm253,10; *Wigl* nm6396; *C* nm1346

Lütich 'der von' (*Loh*), see Wippreht

Lutringe 'der' (*Loh*), see Gyselbreht

Lutzelot see Lanzelet

Lûf 'von Anîs', a heathen knight who is unhorsed by Arnolt (4) whilst fighting for the Soldan against Partonopier. – *PM* 20526ff.

Lucegwie a knight who fights for Athis against Bilas. This name does not occur in the OF version. – *AP* C,17

Luciân a heathen knight who is slain by Partonopier whilst fighting for the Soldan. – *PM* 21614

Lucius 'kaiser von Rome'. He demands tribute of Arthur, and when this is refused, he commands Arthur to give up his kingdom, to which he is not entitled, owing to his illegitimate birth (see Utepandragûn). A battle ensues, in which L. is slain by Arthur. This story is first told in Geoffrey of Monmouth, where L. is called (IX, 15) 'procurator rei publicae'; Wace (*Brut* 10917) was the first to call him 'empereur' a title which he bears in *L'Estoire de Merlin*, where he is called Luces. (See also Arthur for a consideration of the importance of this episode in *JT*.) – *JT* nm4021,1ff. a4552,1

---

[35] See Vrowenlop (F. von der Hagen, *Minnesinger*, III, p. 397): 'schoene vrou Lunet'.

[36] Panzer (2), p. 209.

[37] J. von Zahn, p. 45.

Lûzifer the Devil. – nm *P* 463,4; *Tirol* H,5; *JT* 10,6; *Loh* 186; *UA* 1116; *WW* 5868; *WO* 17394; *Ll* 10,8

M

Mabônagrîn (Lot was the first to suggest the now generally accepted etymology of this name, viz., a combination of Mabon and Evrain (which Lot thinks is a mistake for Euuain, i.e. Îwein), two magicians who appear in *Li Biaus Descouneus*.[1]) M. is the knight who had run away with his *amie*, whom he promised that he would do anything she commanded. At her request he stays with her in Schoidelakurt, a garden belonging to his uncle Ivreins, until he is defeated by another knight. Here he has already slain a large number of knights, including (according to *P*) Gurzgrî, but he is defeated by Êrec, who spares his life. In *RP*, where he is called Mabungren (Mabounain in Pseudo-Gautier), he is one of the band of knights which Arthur leads to the rescue of Gifles. M. is first mentioned in Chrestien's *Erec*, where he is called Mabonagrains (6132), and he occurs also in the *Livre d'Artus* as Mabonagrains li nains. This romance contains also the enchanter Mabon, who appears also in the prose *Tristan* (Löseth's analysis, §290a, etc.). – *E* m8012 a8990ff. n9384; *P* nm178,23; *T* nm84,4; *JT* nm729,7; *GM* nm2250; *RP* 179,10

Mabones see Machtmes

Mabungren see Mabônagrîn

Mâbûz 'der blœde', son of the *Meerweib* who brings up Lanzelet. His mother, fearing his neighbour Iweret, gives M. the power of making anyone who enters the gates of his castle as great a coward as he himself is. In this way Lanzelet is captured, but, pretending to be more cowardly than the other captives, he is released for scouting work against Iweret and escapes. – *L* nm3542ff. a3618

Madaon biblical (Midian), enemy of Gideon. – *JT* nm3828,7

Mâdâtes 'künec von Uxîôren lant', a ruler who surrenders to Alexander. In *UA*, where he is called Medates, he refuses to surrender his castle to Alexander, but at the intervention of his liege-lady Sisîcâmis (see Rodone), peace is made. So also in Gualterus, where he is called Madates (probably Medates in the MS used by Ulrich), and in Curtius Rufus, where he is called Medates. – *A* 13552f.; *UA* 14922ff.

Mado a knight who takes part in the tourney held by Ris and Cadoalans. In Pseudo-Gautier he is called Madeu. – *RP* 90,3

Madrart counsellor to Agâmennon, who consults him as to a suitable reward for Paris. – *GT* 3728

Magnamus 'künec', a vassal of Agâmennon. – *GT* nm13905f.

Magog 'künec', biblical, one of the kings of the 10th tribe of Israel. In I Chronicles 6, he is one of the sons of Japheth. Magokck is the name of a people in *SA*. – *UA* nm20904

Magonogrin a knight who is slain by Eleander. His *amie* is Galantte (q.v.). – *GT* a20312 n20346

Mâhâmet see Mahmet

Mahardî brother of Behalim. When he learns of the unsuccessful efforts of his attendants to gather curative herbs for his wounds, he dies. – *C* m9547 a9572 n9709

Mahaute (According to Bartsch this name is the OF form of OHG Mehtilt,[2] which, however, does not appear in Chrestien's *Perceval*.) M. is the wife of Gurzgrî (q.v.) and the mother of Schîonatulander. – *P* nm178,16; *T* nm42,1; *JT* nm671,1

Mahede, **Mahedea** see Mahaute

---

1   Lot (3), p. 321; see also Bruce (1), I, p. 109, note 16.
2   Bartsch (2), p. 141.

Maheloas see Meljaganz

Mahmet the Arabian prophet Mohammed. – nm *Wigl* 6572; *W* 9,7; *R* Eing. I,86; *Tirol* F,7; *UW* 49,25; *JT* 2994,6; *PM* 3754; *MB* 118,14; *Loh* 4542; *UA* 389; *WW* 877; *RB* 16464; *WO* 4609

Mahode see Mahaute

Mahtines the mother of Doroschalcus by Priam. This character appears to have been invented by Benoît, who calls her Mahez. – *LT* nm4784

May (1) brother of Urlois. This character appears to have been invented by the author of *JT*. – *JT* nm4605,2

Mai (2) see Meie

Maymet see Mahmet

Macaon see Machaon

Machabeus the leader of the Jewish rebellion against Antiochus Epiphanes (see Antiochus (3)). – *JT* nm3075,5

Machaon 'von Tracia', son of Ascalofius, a warrior in the Trojan army against the Greeks. M. occurs in Benoît, Dares, Dictys, and Homer. – *LT* 3099; *TK* 23860

Machmerit a knight who is present at Arthur's court when Êrec returns with Ênîte. This character does not occur in Chrestien's *Erec*. – *E* 1684

Machmet see Mahmet

Machtmes mother of Hunes. She is also (4890) called Mabones; the form Machtmes occurs *LT* 5614. In Benoît she is called Mahont (var. Mabon); Huniers (= Hunes) is referred to as li fiz Mahont, and li fiz Mabon respectively, and Constans has taken this to indicate that M. was the father of Hunes.[3] – *LT* nm4890

Maculîn a knight in the service of Libers (1). M., who is 'herzoge von Optanus', fights with Cursûn (result not given). – *M* 9935ff.

Mal 'von Jellikrine', a warrior in Ipomidôn's army against Akarîn. – *JT* nm3263,3

Malabris 'von Exenise', a warrior in Akarîn's army against Ipomidôn. – *JT* nm3167,1

Malagriss a knight who is offering violence to Achanayss when Paris appears and kills him. – *GT* a7441 n7463

Malakîn a warrior who is slain by Rennewart whilst fighting for Terramêr against Willehalm (1) in the second battle at Alischanz. This name does not appear in any of the extant MSS of *Aliscans*, but it was a common name for a Saracen in the *chansons de geste* and may well have stood in the MS used by Wolfram. – *W* 442,27

Malakrons a heathen warrior who defends the ships with Ehmereiz during the second battle at Alischanz. M. appears to be identical with Malars, who defends the ships in *Aliscans* (CXXIb, 188). – *W* 438,30

Malapar see Melopar

Mâlarz a warrior who fights for his father, Terramêr, against Willehalm (1) at Alischanz. He occurs also in *Aliscans*. (See Marlanz.) – *W* a29,18f. n32,13 [†]

Malatons a warrior in Terramêr's army against Willehalm (1). M., who is called Malatars in *Aliscans*, is one of those defending the ships with Ehmereiz. – *W* 438,29

Malatras son of Terramêr, for whom he fights against Willehalm (1) at Alischanz. So also in *Aliscans*. M. occurs also in *Les Enfances Vivien*. – *W* a29,18f n32,13

Malatrîs a warrior who is slain by Cupesus whilst fighting for the Greeks against the Trojans. This character was invented by Konrad. – *TK* 31823

Maldis, Malduc, Malduz see Maldwîz

---

3 Benoît de Sainte-Maure, *Le Roman de Troie*, ed. by L. Constans, V, p. 63.

Maldwîz 'li sages', a knight who is present at Arthur's court when Êrec returns with Ênîte. In Chrestien's *Erec* he is called Mauduiz li sages, and occurs in *C* as Maldis der wîse, a knight who spills Priure's cup of chastity, and in *L* as Malduz der wîse, where he persuades his *amie* to try on the cloak of chastity. Cross and Nitze are of the opinion that M. is identical with the magician Malduc von dem Genibeleten Sê (*L* nm6990 a7221ff.) who is approached by Arthur in *L* to rescue Ginovêr from Valerîn.[4] He demands, as his reward, Êrec, who had slain his father, and Gawein, who had slain his brother. They are imprisoned by Malduc but are rescued by Lanzelet after the magician has killed Valerîn and recovered Ginovêr. According to Cross and Nitze, M. is also identical with Maduc le Noir in *La Vengeance de Raguidel* and the Mardoc who is depicted inside the fortress with Winlogee (= Ginovêr) in the bas-reliefs on the architrave of the cathedral at Modena.[5] – *E* 1636; *L* 6052; *C* 2295

Maledicur a dwarf attendant on Îdêr. M. carries a whip, with which he strikes the maiden sent by Ginovêr to learn the name of his master, and also Êrec, who goes with the same mission. After Êrec has defeated Îdêr, he has M. flogged. In *P* he is called Maliklischier. M. is not named in Chrestien's *Erec*, and Bartsch derived the name from a misunder-standing of Chrestien's *Erec* (1210): '(N'ai talant que nul) mal te quiere'.[6] Singer thinks that Wolfram's form is the correct one, and derives this from OF *mal eglisier*, 'bad churchgoer'.[7] – *E* a7ff. n1077; *P* nm401,14

Malêôn a commander in Alexander's army in the second battle against Dârîus. In Curtius Rufus, Malieon is the name of a people. – *A* 11991

Malgrim see Malgryn

Malgryn a dwarf who brought to Arthur's court the news of Gawein's imprisonment. The dwarf occurs, but is not named, in *Meraugis de Portlesguez*. – *S* II,4

Maliklischier see Maledicur

Malkrêâtiure (< OF *male creature*[8]). M. is the brother of Kundrîe (1) (q.v.) and is as ugly as his sister. As squire to Orgelûse he threatens Gawein, who unhorses him and takes his horse in place of his own, which has been stolen by Ûrjans. The same story is told, *mutatis mutandis*, in *C*, where, as in Chrestien's *Perceval*, M. is described but not named. – *P* 517,11ff.; *C* a19625

Malloas uncle of Tydomîe, whom he tries to compel to marry Libers (1), but when the latter is defeated by Meleranz he sets out to seize Tydomîe's lands. On learning of Meleranz's parentage, he becomes reconciled. He is called 'von Ibaritûn'. – *M* m7692 an11640

Malmelona one of the two maidens who are companions of Angelburg during her enchantment. M. marries Hainrich (1). – *FS* m350 a711ff. n1345

Maloans see Meljaganz

Malohat see Malolehat

Malolehat sister of Marguns, who rescues her after she has been abducted by Gogaris. In the Mons MS of Manessier she is called Damelehaut, and in the Montpellier MS she is la roïnne de Malohaut (cf. *RP* 701,14, where she is called von Malohat die künigin). La Dame de Malehaut occurs also in the Vulgate *Lancelot*, where she dies for love of Galehaut. – *RP* nm700,30 a701,13f.

---

4   Cross and Nitze, pp. 22ff.
5   Cross and Nitze, pp. 22ff.
6   Bartsch (1), p. 184.
7   Singer (1), p. 59.
8   Wolfram von Eschenbach, *Parzival*, transl. by W. Hertz, p. 531.

Malopar see Melopar

Malpardons a knight who attends Leigamar's tourney in the service of Aram. On his first appearance he is called Malpordenz. – *C* 18171

Malpordenz see Malpardons

*Malprimes see Palprimes (1) and (2)

Malserôn the chief of the giants, renowned for their courtesy, who guard the castle at the entrance to Ehkunat's land. With him are his brother, Zirijon, and their two sons, Karabîn and Zirdôs. M. fights Gârel, who defeats him. He surrenders for himself and the other giants, and they send their resignation in to Ehkunat and remain neutral throughout the war. – *G* nm11067ff. a11239

Malun 'künec von Maluna', to whom Parzivâl gives the land belonging to Agloval when the latter dies. – *RP* nm28 in the interpolated passage after *P* 823,10

Malupar see Melopar

Malfer son of Rennewart and Alîze (1). In *R* he captures Fansaserat and compels him to become a Christian. M. is at Terramêr's court, where his relationship to Terramêr is known. He is still at enmity with Tîbalt. The birth of M., who is so large that his mother dies in child-birth, is recounted in the *chanson de geste*, *La Bataille Loquifer*. He is called Malfer (in French, Maillefer) 'Por chou c'a fer de sa mere ostés' (*La Bataille Loquifer*, 493). He has a son, Renier, who is the hero of the *chanson de geste* of the same name. – *R* Eing. I, 4; *RB* nm23376; *FS* nm4824

Malfus 'von Filistine', a warrior in Ipomidôn's army against Akarîn. – *JT* nm3233,4

Mammo 'von Dassorien', a commander in Ipomidôn's army against Akarîn. – *JT* 3237,1

Mamoret a knight who attends Leigamar's tourney in the service of Lorez. – *C* 18149

Mamurtanit 'emeral', a warrior in the service of Tîbalt. He is on the ship which brings Willehalm and Gîburc to France, and he is at first faithful to Tîbalt but begs for mercy when Willehalm starts to slaughter the heathens on the ship. He is baptized on reaching France and assumes the name of Loys. – *UW* nm90,24 a123,15

Mamfiliôt see Manphiliôt

Manahê biblical, king of Israel. M. is mentioned in the *Historia Scholastica* (*Liber IV Regum* XXII). – *A* nm16708

Manalippus son of Acastus. He is slain by Pirrus because of his share in the imprisonment of Pêleus (1). So also in Benoît, where he is called Menalipus, and Dictys, where he is called Menalippus. – *LT* 17949

Mânâpin to whom Alexander bequeathed Irkânje. This name does not occur in any of the other histories of Alexander. – *A* 17604ff.

Manasses (1) brother of Jaddus. He marries Isachâ in *A* and leaves Judaea to found a colony of Jews, called the Samaritans. These are neither Jews nor heathens but call themselves whatever offers the greatest advantage. Alexander refuses them the freedom which he grants the Jews. M. occurs in the *Historia Scholastica* (*Liber Esther* IV). – *A* 9904ff.; *UA* 17788

Manasses (2) biblical (Manasseh), king of Judah. – *A* nm16318

Manbrî 'künec von Riuzen', a warrior in the Greek army against the Trojans. This character was invented by Konrad. – *TK* 23914

Manbur apparently the sister of Gansguoter. She is a fairy and entertains Gawein in her castle.[9] – *C* m28405 a28439 n28605

---

[9] Scholl (*Diu Crône*, to 28605) is uncertain whether this is a name or whether it should read: 'man bur' ('bor'?).

Mandagran father of Daniel (1). – *DB* nm343f.

Maneipicelle see Mancipicelle

Maneset 'von Hochturasch', a knight who is present at Arthur's court when Êrec returns with Ênîte. This name does not appear in the corresponding list in Chrestien's *Erec*. – *E* 1673

Maneschier the French poet who completed *Perceval*. Manessier wrote from l.34936 (*RP* 610,28) to the end. – *RP* nm845,33

Mangaris see Monagris

Mangins a knight of the Round Table who joins in the search for the missing Parzivâl. In Gautier he is called Amangins and appears as such in the *Vengeance de Raguidel*. – *RP* 526,2

Mansiluret a warrior who takes part in the battle between Akarîn and Ipomidôn. – *JT* 3000,3f.

Manuel a Greek prince whose wedding to Amande is the subject of the extant fragment of *MA*. After the wedding, which takes place at Arthur's court, M. takes his bride back to Greece. – *MA* 46

Manphiliôt (Martin believes this name to be an imitation of Marlivliôt in *E*.[10]) M. is the uncle of Kondwîrâmûrs and brother of Kîôt (1) and Tampenteire. In *P* and *T* he is called 'herzoge', and in *JT* 'herzoge von Arbusye'. – *P* 186,22; *T* 23,1; *JT* 640,1 [†]

Manphilot see Manphiliôt

Mancipicelle a maiden who plays the same part in *C* as does Orgelûse in *P*, except that she does not marry Gawein. Mention of Leigormon (q.v.) seems to indicate, however, that Heinrich himself did not realise that M. and Orgelûse were one and the same person. – *C* a20493ff. n20527

Marachîn a knight in Bêâmunt's army at Antrîûn. – *Dem* 10738

Marangliez 'herzoge von Brevigariez', brother of Lipaôt, for whom he fights at Bêârosche. We learn later (772,14) that he is unhorsed by Parzivâl in the battle. He is present at Arthur's tourney in *JT*. – *P* nm354,17f a384,11; *JT* 1998,6

Marases a knight who is slain by Partonopier whilst fighting for Sornagiur. – *PM* 3714ff.

Marbisine 'von Gralande', a knight who is present at the tourney held by Arthur. – *JT* 2060,1

Mardisibune 'von Schandimavia', a warrior in Akarîn's army against Ipomidôn. – *JT* nm3177,5

Mardochêi biblical (Mordecai), a Jew who disclosed to Aswerus (1) Haman's plot to exterminate the Jews; the story is told in the Book of Esther. – *UA* nm11803

Mareis a knight who had been raised from lowly origins to the rank of *grâve* by Sornagiur. During the latter's battle against Clogier's son, M. gives advice which displeases Sornagiur, and to get back into favour with his liege-lord, M. breaks the truce between the two armies during the duel between Sornagiur and Partonopier. He breaks in when Sornagiur is being defeated and captures Partonopier. – *PM* 4396ff.

Margalîn 'künec von Arâbe', a warrior in the Trojan army against the Greeks. This name was invented by Konrad, who took it from Margalîs in *PM* (cf. Cursabrê). – *TK* 24868

Margalîs 'künec von Sîre', a heathen knight who distinguishes himself at the tourney held by Meliûr. (See also Margalîn.) – *PM* 14476ff.

Margalius 'künec von Norwegen', a warrior in the Greek army against the Trojans. This character was invented by Konrad. – *TK* 23928

---

10 Martin (1), p. 182, to 186,22.

Margariton　natural son of Priam. M. is killed by Achilles whilst fighting for the Trojans against the Greeks. This character appears to have been invented by Benoît. – *LT* a4808 n4828; *TK* 29786ff.

Margatine　'ûz Patrigalde', one of the maidens abducted from Arthur's court, and recovered by Kailet. She marries Hiutegêr. She is probably identical with Margiton von Portigale, one of the ladies abducted by Klinschor in *Sey* and rescued by Seyfrid. – *JT* a1557,5 n1747,6ff.; *Sey* m27,6 a44,2 n64,7

Margiton　see Margatine

Margitt　see Marcus (1)

Margôn (1)　a giant who is slain by Tandareis as he is guarding the road to his lord, Karedoz. M. is the brother of Durkiôn and Uliân. – *TF* m5302 n5433 a6020 [†]

Margon (2)　see Margue Gormon

Margoriton　see Margariton

Margot　'künec von Pozzidant und Orkeise', a warrior who brings Gorhant to fight for Terramêr against Willehalm (1) at Alischanz. In *Aliscans*, where he is called Margot de Bocident, he is slain by his cousin Rennewart. – *W* 35,3

Margoz　'von Messine', a knight who is killed by Prophilias whilst fighting for Bilas against Athis In the OF version he is called Margoz de Meschine. – *AP* B,77

Margue Gormon　a knight who attends Êrec's wedding in *E*, where he is called 'marcgrâve Margôn von Glufiôn'. He appears at first in Chrestien's *Erec*, where he is called Menagormon (var. Margengomon) (1937). In *C* he spills Priure's cup of chastity. – *E* 1912; *C* 2329

Marguel　see Feimorgân

Marguns　'künec', a knight who tries to compel Solimag's sister to marry his son, Kargrilo. She calls Gawein to the rescue, and he defeats M. When the latter returns home, he finds that Gogaris has abducted his sister, Malolehat. He gives chase and rescues Malolehat. In *RP* he is identical with the King of a Hundred Knights, who, in the Vulgate *Lancelot*, is called Malaquin, Malaguin, the cousin of Malolehat, whilst his seneschal is called Marganor. In the prose *Tristan* (Löseth's analysis) the King of a Hundred Knights is called Heraut li aspres. – *RP* nm690,17 a693,40

Margwet　see Marques

Marholt　see Môrolt

Marîâ　the Virgin Mary. – *GR* mα,10; *P* m113,18; *W* m31,8f.; *A* nm8800; *UT* m2204; *R* m Bl. I,138 n Bl. III,198; *FD* nmIX,31; *G* m21105; *UW* nm111,11; *JT*m272,2 n275,1; *PM* nm1321; *Sey* m3,1 n4,1; *Mer* nm141,2; *Loh* m107 n150; *UA* m103 n4562; *HT* nm6804; *WW* nm710; *RB* m8524f. n13072; *PS* nm70; *WO* nm10462ff.; *RP* nm663,16; *FS* nm7502; *KT* nm336; *Ll* nm8,10 (MS K) nm13,7

Maribulus　see Matribulus

Marîe (1)　Magdalên, biblical.[11] – nm *JT* 5122,5; *RB* 18080

Marie (2)　see Marîâ

Maricus　see Marcus (1)

Marîne　granddaughter of Adan (1). M. dresses as a knight and fights for Wigalois against Liôn. She is slain in the battle by Galopêar. – *Wigl* m9150 n9165 a9355f.

Marînus　a judge who was left in Rome by Constantine the Great. – *A* nm12981

11　The reference in *JT* is to Mary, the sister of Lazarus, who was, historically, not Mary Magdalene, but Mary of Bethany.

Marjadox a heathen warrior who defended the ships with Ehmereiz in the second battle at Alischanz. In *Aliscans* he is called Meradus. – *W* 438,30

Marjodô 'truhsæze' to Marke (1). M. is Tristan's room-mate, and missing him one night, he follows Tristan's trail and sees him in bed with Îsolt (2). M. informs Marke, but the latter's suspicions are lulled. M. then gets into touch with Melôt, to whom he leaves the task of finding proof of the association of Tristan and Îsolt. M. is called Mariadoc in Thomas, and Meriadoc in the ME *Sir Tristrem*; he corresponds to Antrêt in *ET*. – *Tn* 13464ff.

Markabrê 'von Valdûne', a knight who tries to avenge the death of Turkîs. M. and his band of knights are attacked by Anshelm (1) (see Fursîn (2)) and Supplicius, the former unhorsing M., who pursues them, however, to the castle of Arnolt (4), where they are driven off by the latter's knights. Walther (1) pursues them and unhorses M. within sight of the Soldan's army. – *PM* 19070

Markalm see Sennes

Marke (1) 'künec von Kurnewal and Engelant', brother of Blanscheflûr and uncle of Tristan. He is the husband of Îsolt (2), in whose intrigue with Tristan he at first refuses to believe. When he is given irrefutable proof of its existence, he banishes them from his court. His grief, when he learns of the love potion after their death, is real and noble. Miss Weston suggests that M.'s character was deliberately blackened in order to make Tristan and Îsolt innocent;[12] whilst this is certainly true of Malory's version, it is not true of *ET*, where he is perhaps stupid but definitely not vicious, and the charge is certainly not true of *Tn*, in which he is altogether a kindlier and more noble character. The name is derived from the Celtic word *marc*, 'horse', and in Beroul he is represented as having horse's ears, which he tries to conceal; this would seem to be an old Celtic trait which has been preserved.[13] M. occurs, according to Ranke, in historical legend as early as the 6th century.[14] In *RP* he is called Mars (a form which occurs in *Li Biaus Descouneus*) and assists Arthur in the war against Bruns (1). – *ET* 54f.; *Tn* nm418ff. a478; *UT* nm53 a1012f.; *JT* nm1532,5 a1718,1; *TF* nm10156; *HT* nm270 a2480; *RP* 21,45 [†]

Marke (2) 'sante', biblical. – *W* nm241,6

Marke (3) 'von Ployss', a knight who is sent to woo Helen for Bevar. – *GT* 23313f.

Marke (4) see Marcus (2)

Marcholêr 'von Porigâle', a commander in Bêâmunt's army at Antrîûn. – *Dem* nm9785 a10819ff.

Marcus (1) a dwarf who rescues Paris from the tree to which Gamorett has tied him, and takes him home, where he is tended by M.'s wife, Artanna. M. then returns with Paris to Agâmennon's court. – *GT* a6227f. n6251

Marcus (2) a knight who is sent by Trifon (1) to woo Helen for him. M. is insulted by Paris, and in the combat which results, he is badly wounded by Paris. His suit is refused by Helen, and he is still lying wounded when Trifon attacks. M. tries to dissuade him but is mocked for being beaten by Paris, whom Trifon challenges to single combat. – *GT* a4930f. n4950

Marlanz 'künec von Jêrikop', a warrior in command of Terramêr's ninth army in the second battle at Alischanz. M. is probably identical with Mallars, who commands Terramêr's fourth army in *Aliscans* (5079ᵃ). (See Mâlarz.) – *W* 351,4f. [†]

---

12 Weston (1), p. 78.
13 Bruce (1), I, p. 182.
14 Ranke, p. 3.

Marlivliôt a knight who is present at Arthur's court when Êrec returns with Ênîte. This character does not appear in Chrestien's *Erec*. (See also Manphiliôt.) – *E* 1679

Marmisise a warrior in Akarîn's army against Ipomidôn. – *JT* nm3138,1

Marmorez see Mamoret

Maroltt brother of Barfartt. M. and his brother are two giants in the service of Melopar, and they attack any person who enters the country. They attack Hector and Paris, and M. is slain by Hector. It seems probable, in view of M.'s giant stature, that this name was suggested by Môrolt. – *GT* m11322 an11346

Marolf a warrior in Ipomidôn's army against Akarîn. – *JT* 3262,1

Maros a warrior in Akarîn's army against Ipomidôn. – *JT* nm3138,1

Marpigigal see Moabigal

Marques a knight who is killed by Absterne whilst fighting for Athis against Bilas. He is also called Margwet; in the OF version his name is Marques. – *AP* A*,101

Marroch 'künec von Saraczein'. M. tries to compel Ysope to marry him. She sends to Arthur for help, and he brings an army and defeats Marroch, who is captured by Wigamur. – *Wigm* m2755 an2861f.

Marroch 'künec von' (*WO*), see Persit (2)

Mars (1) the god of war. In *TK* he is present at the wedding of Thetis and Pêleus. – *Ed* nm5626; *LT* nm 989; *PM* nm4112; *TK* 954; *RB* nm16399; *GT* nm12225

Mars (2) see Marke (1)

Marsel 'von Marsidole', a warrior in Ipomidôn's army against Akarîn. – *JT* nm3236,2

Marsilî see Marsilje

Marsilje according to *W*, the uncle of Tîbalt who was slain by Ruolant. In *UW* he fights for Terramêr against Lôis. M. is the chief Saracen king in the OF *Chanson de Roland*. – *W* nm221,12; *UW* nm11,26ff. a31,1

Marsius a warrior in the Trojan army against the Greeks. So also in Benoît, where he is called Masius (var. Marsius). – *LT* 3985

Marsûn son of Arnolt (4). He fights for Partonopier against the Soldan. – *PM* 18802ff.

Marthe 'von Magdalene', biblical. This is an error for Martha of Bethany, who was the sister of Lazarus. – *JT* nm5122,5

Martin 'sante'. – *RP* nm231,41

Maruoc a mariner who leads Irekel to Partonopier when the latter is seeking death in the forest. – *PM* 10616f.

Marufin 'künec von Orchadie', an ally of Sornagiur. – *PM* a3323 n4253

Marfilius a disciple of Samlon, whom he accompanies to Troy. M. fights with great bravery against the robbers whom they meet on the journey. – *GT* 403ff.

Marfiluse a warrior in Ipomidôn's army against Akarîn. – *JT* 3262,1

Marx (1) 'künec von Ungern', a knight who fights on the side of the Christians against the heathens. – *WO* 16590

Marx (2) see Marke (1)

Marcius see Marcus (1)

Masippus son of Candacis. In Leo, Marpissa occurs as the name of the wife of Candaulis (see Agyris), but MS J of Leo omits all reference to Marpissa and includes Marsippus as the son of Candacis.[15] – *WA* nm4892

Masor 'von Pungratene', a warrior in Ipomidôn's army against Akarîn. – *JT* 3258,5

---

15 Leo, p. 117, l. 12, note.

Mathan natural son of Priam. M. fights for the Trojans against the Greeks. This character appears to have been invented by Benoît, who calls him Matan (var. Matham). – *LT* a4808 n4831

Mathathias biblical, the leader of the Maccabean revolt against Antiochus Epiphanes (see Antiochus (3)). – *RB* nm15902

Mathêus (1) 'von dem Vorste', brother of Medeamanz. M. is slain by Jôrân (1) whilst fighting for Dârîus against Alexander at Issôn. This character appears to have been invented by Ulrich. – *UA* 8599

Mathêus (2) biblical, the Evangelist. – *A* nm16300

Mathie a knight who jousts with Ulrich von Liechtenstein during the latter's *Venusfahrt*. – *FD* 563,6ff.

Matleide 'der wilde'. Gawein recalls how he fought with M. – *C* nm9011

Matreiz a son of Terramêr who is one of the warriors on the side of the Saracens against Willehalm (1) at Alischanz. M. appears to be identical with Malagrés (var. Marbrez), a son of Terramêr in *Aliscans*. – *W* a29,18f. n32,16

Matribais brother of Demetron, a commander in Ipomidôn's army against Akarîn. – *JT* a3274,4 n3279,5

Matribleiz 'künec von Skandinâvîâ', a warrior who is captured in the second battle between Terramêr and Willehalm (1) and is permitted to remove all the dead heathen kings from the battlefield and to transport them home for burial according to their own rites. In *Aliscans* he is called Mautriblé, and he occurs as such in *Li Covenans Vivien*, *Fierabras*, and *Aimeri de Narbonne*. – *W* [98,14] [†]

Matribulus 'von Tartarye', a knight who is killed whilst attacking Agâmennon in order to obtain Helen. – *GT* 3314

Mattahel 'künec von Tâfar', one of the group of 15 Saracen kings who attack Willehalm (1) at the end of the first battle at Alischanz. M. is wounded or killed by Willehalm in that encounter. [See Appendix (9).] M. occurs also in *Aliscans*, where he is called Matamars. Already in the *Chancun de Willame* are mentioned among the heathens (2060): 'Mathamar & uns reis Dauer' (Tyler's edition: 'Mathamar e uns reis d'Auer', the Auer being, according to the index, a Ural-Tartar people, defeated by Charlemagne in 796). – *W* m71,22 a72,17f. n74,4 [†]

Matûr 'künec von Cluse', a knight who declares war on Arthur because the latter refuses to take the oath of allegiance to him. Arthur marches with an army into Cluse and kills M. in single combat. – *DB* nm440 a2992f.

Matûsales 'künec von Hippopotitikûn', father of Josweiz. So also in *Aliscans*. – *W* nm33,9

Maunis see Aumagwîn

Maurîn (1) 'mit den liechten schenkeln', a knight who is captured by Lanzelet at the tourney held by Lôt (4). In *P* he is called 'mit den schœnen schenkeln Maurîn' and is the son of Îsâjes. (Identical with Maurin (2)?) – *L* 3048ff.; *P* nm662,19

Maurin (2) a wounded knight whom Segremors and Nyobe meet. (Identical with Maurîn (1)?) – *S* III,14

Mauricius (1) 'sante'. – nm *Mer* 17,6; *RB* 15945

Mauricius (2) Byzantine Emperor, who lived AD *c.*539–602. – *JT* nm3570,5

Mauricius (3) 'von Craun', a knight who holds a tourney in honour of his *amie*, grævinne von Beamunt. After the tourney he appears all bloody at her bed-side, and his appearance frightens away her husband, who is sleeping with her, and enables M. to take his place. – *MC* 263ff.

Maxencius a Roman Emperor who, according to Geoffrey of Monmouth, was defeated by Constantine, king of Britain. – *JT* nm4555,5

Mazadân (Schulz thought that this was an attempt to reproduce Maddan, a character in Geoffrey of Monmouth.[16] Martin accepts Bartsch's suggestion that the name is a form of Mac Adam, i.e. son of Adam (see Adanz),[17] although this etymology is denied by Gaston Paris.[18] Bruce also believes this etymology to be fanciful,[19] as also the suggestion made by Singer that the name is an attempt to reproduce Macedonian, i.e. Alexander (1), who, in medieval legend was supposed to have been united with a fairy.[20]) M. is the husband of Terdelaschoie (q.v.), who took him to the land of Feimorgân; through their sons, Lazaliez and Brickus, they are progenitors of the House of Anschouwe and the Arthurian line respectively. – *P* nm56,17; *G* nm4173 [†]

Mazazes a warrior who is placed in command of Pelûsium by Dârîus. He is slain by Amintas (1), and the remnants of his army are slain by Antigonus. So also in *Expeditio Alexandri* and Curtius Rufus, where he is called Mazaces. –*A* 8571ff.

Mazedân see Mazadân

Mazeus (1) a commander in Dârîus's army against Alexander. He surrenders Babylon to Alexander after the battle of Erbela. He occurs in *Expeditio Alexandri* and Curtius Rufus. – *A* 10796; *UA* 10925

Mâzêus (2) 'von Damascus', standard-bearer to Dârîus, who is his brother-in-law. M. is killed by Parmênîôn during the battle at Issôn. So also in Gualterus. – *UA* 7901f.

Meander nephew of Alexander, who bequeaths Libia to him. This name does not occur in any other history of Alexander. – *SA* nm8501f.

Mêdanz son of Meleranz and Tydomîe. – *M* 12801ff.

Medates see Mâdâtes

Medea daughter of Oertes. Both *LT* and *TK*, following Benoît (who took the story from Ovid's *Metamorphoses* – it is not told in Dares), relate the story of Jason's quest for the Golden Fleece and the assistance which M. gives him in obtaining it. *LT* stops at the return to Greece, but *TK* continues with the Greek legend, in which M. persuades the daughters of Pêleus to bleed him to death, pretending that this will rejuvenate him in the same way that she had rejuvenated Êson. As in the Greek legend, Jason later leaves her for Creusa (see Grêûsâ), and she sends him a poisoned shirt, which bursts into flames and kills Jason and Creusa. In *GT* she is the sister of Ajax (1) and Hercules. She is fetched by Ulixes to Troy, in order to cure Ajax's wound, and advises the Greeks to send for Achilles. – *LT* m543 n565 a585; *C* nm11568; *TK* 7417ff.; *RB* nm24556; *GT* m14620 n14636 a14721

Medeamanz 'künec von Samargône', a warrior in Dârîus's army. M., who is the brother of Mathêus (1) and husband of Dulcâmûr, is slain by Hûbert whilst fighting against Alexander at Issôn. This character appears to have been invented by Ulrich. – *UA* a3951 n4025

Media see Medea

Megara one of the Furies (Megaera – the jealous). – *LT* nm16404

Megulaz see Melygass

Mehtilt wife of Heinrîch (1). – *Loh* a1921 n2995

---

16 Schulz, 'Eigennamen', p. 394.
17 Martin (1), p. 64, to 56,17; Bartsch (2), p. 134.
18 Paris (2), p. 149.
19 Bruce (1), I, p. 316, note 7.
20 Singer (1), p. 49.

Meinhart 'grâve von Gorze', a knight who is present at the tourney held at Friesach and is the first knight to joust with Ulrich von Liechtenstein during the latter's *Venusfahrt*. M. procures the release of Ulrich from his imprisonment. – *FD* 188,7

Meiare see Meierra

Meie son of Elîacha (q.v.) and husband of Bêaflôr (q.v.). – *MB* nm52,8ff. a55,15f.

Meiera, Meierall see Meierra

Meierra daughter of Minos (q.v.) and Basiphe and sister of Fedra. M. holds the clue for Jason whilst he is in the labyrinth, and later she and Fedra persuade Jason to take them to Troy with him, so that they shall escape the anger of their mother. Jason abandons M. on an island during the journey, where she is found by Zacharia, and is eventually happily married to Emimor. – *GT* 21674

Meierun see Meierra

Meiones (Martin points out the similarity of this name with Maeonia, mentioned in Solinus (168,16).[21]) M., who is 'herzoge von Atrofagente', is one of the knights whom Feirefîz claims to have defeated. – *P* nm770,24

Meiora see Meierra

Mekka 'vogt von' (*JT*), see Essemerel

Melêager see Meljâger

Melegragram 'von Lunders', a knight who is present when the marriage is arranged between Wigamur and Dulcefluor. – *Wigm* 4206

Melehalin 'von Babylon', eldest son of Saffadin and brother of Melchinor (see Persit(2)), for whom he fights against Walwan (3). – *WO* nm5800 a6072ff.

Meleranz son of Olimpîâ (1) and Linefles, and nephew of Arthur. M. leaves home at an early age and falls in love with Tydomîe, whom he finds bathing under a linden tree. He goes on to Arthur's court, where he stays for a year before his identity is discovered, when he is made a knight and sets out to find Tydomîe. He defeats Godonas, becoming king of Terrandes in his place, and then defeats Verangoz for Dulceflûr (1), from whom he learns that Tydomîe is being oppressed by Malloas. He hastens to rescue her and defeats Libers (1); he is finally reconciled to Malloas and marries Tydomîe. In *G* he is the husband of Lammîre (1) and father of Gârel (2). He occurs also in MS D of *GM*, where he is one of the knights at Arthur's court. – *M* 161ff.; *G* nm4195; *GM* (MS D) 38578

Meliakanze, Meliachans, Meliachens see Meljaganz

Melîân husband of Modassîne and father of Sirgamôte. He refuses his daughter to Dêmantîn, because she is too young, but later gives her to Eghart. When Dêmantîn has abducted her, M. swears to recover her, and when he sees Dêmantîn fighting, although he would gladly have seen his daughter married to so valiant a knight, he is debarred by his oath from giving up the attempt to recover her. When, however, he is defeated, he is quite happy to consent to the wedding and abdicates in favour of Dêmantîn. – *Dem* a127f. n9435

Meliantz brother of Ginovêr. M. has grown out of all recognition, and arriving at Arthur's court, gives Arthur permission to give away his sister. Arthur promises her to Kardeiz (1), and M. then reveals that it is Ginovêr of whom he has just disposed. – *JT* 2448,5

Melyemodan 'künec von Asya', an ally of Melchinor (see Persit (2)) against Walwan (3) in the battle at Firmin. For M.'s possible involvement in the final battle between heathens and Christians, see *Sar. – WO* 6140f. [†]

Meliganz a knight who fights for Lôîs against Terramêr. – *UW* 46,9

---

21 Martin (1), p. 504, to 770,24.

Melygass a knight in the Greek army against the Trojans. He fights Paris in the first single combat of the siege and is killed. – *GT* 14093ff.

Melychpfat see Meluchpat

Melion see Mîlôn (2)

Melyoss a giant in the service of Hannor. M. is the companion of Gaball (q.v.) and arrives at the castle of Passirius, where Eleander is staying, and challenges the latter. Passirius fights and defeats him. – *GT* 21143ff.

Melysmaphat 'künec von Sar', a knight who fights for Melchinor (see Persit (2)) against Walwan (3) in the battle at Firmin. For M.'s possible involvement in the final battle between heathens and Christians, see *Sar. – *WO* 6150f. [†]

Meliûr 'küneginne von Scheifdeir', the daughter of the dead king of Constantinople. She is approached by her lords, who urge her to marry. She decides upon Partonopier, who is as yet still a boy, and by her arts she lures him to her castle. M. possesses a knowledge of magic and lies with Partonopier during the night, provided that he makes no attempt to see her face. When he disobeys her, she banishes him from her presence but is eventually brought round to love him again by her sister, Irekel. – *PM* a1227 n6552

Melyphat see Meluchpat

Mêlîz one of the leaders of the side opposed to Gawein in the tourney which is held to celebrate Êrec's wedding to Ênîte. So also in Chrestien's *Erec*. – *E* 2231ff.

Meljadoc one of the leaders of the side opposed to Gawein in the tourney held to celebrate Êrec's wedding to Ênite. So also in Chrestien's *Erec*. A knight called Meliaduc occurs in the *Estoire de Merlin* (Vulgate Cycle), whilst Meliadus occurs in Gerbert's continuation to *Perceval* (3986; Meliadas, 11926). – *E* 2231ff.

Meljaganz one of the protagonists of Chrestien's *Conte de la Charrette*, in which M., who is called Meleaganz, the son of Bademagun, abducts Ginovêr, who is eventually rescued by Lanzelet. The story is related in *I*, but her rescuer is not named. It is again referred to in *C*, where M. is called Milîanz (Milianz occurs in the Vulgate *Lancelot*[22] as a variant of Meliagant de Cardoil (not identical with M.)), and in this version Lanzelet's part, and his ride in the cart, are mentioned; the story is re-told in *G*. Wolfram introduces M. into *P* (no doubt from *I*), as Meljakanz, the abductor of Imâne. He is characterized as of evil disposition (*P* 343,24ff.) and fights for Meljanz against Lipaôt; his fight with Lanzelet is referred to also ([387,2ff.] and 583,8ff.). He is probably identical with Meliachens der grise, who takes part in the tourney held by Arthur in *JT*.

Lot mentions Rhys's derivation of this name from the Celtic Maelgwas < *mael*, 'prince', and *gwas*, 'young man'[23] (an etymology which is accepted by Foerster[24]), but Lot suggests < Malvasius (the form in Geoffrey of Monmouth) < *mael-vas* (*vas* = *bâs* in ancient Gaelic = 'death') i.e. 'Prince of Death', an etymology which is supported by his character, which appears to be rooted in that of the Genius of Death, who carries off people to the Other-world,[25] the supernatural nature of M.'s kingdom being stressed in the *Conte de la Charrette*.[26] M. is called Melwas in the *Vita Gildae*, written probably by Caradoc of Llancarvan, and as king of Somerset abducts Ginovêr, but is persuaded by Gildas and the Abbot of Glastonbury to return her. The author of the *Vita Gildae* derives Glastonbury

22 *Vulgate Version of the Arthurian Romances*, V, p. 344.
23 Lot (3), pp. 327f.
24 Chrestien de Troyes, *Karrenritter*, p. xxxviii.
25 Martin (1), p. 126, to 125,11.
26 Bruce (1), I, pp. 196ff.

from Town of Glass,[27] and M., in whose kingdom it lies, is therefore identical with Chrestien's Maheloas (var. Moloas), described as 'li sire de l'isle de Voirre' (*Erec* 1947), whose land is perfect, no snakes, no storms, not too hot and not too cold (i.e. Avalon). Maheloas appears in *E*, called 'von dem glesîn werde genant', as one of the knights who attend Êrec's wedding, and in *C*, where he is called Maloans de Treverim (see Libers (2)) and is one of the knights who spill Priure's cup of chastity.
– *E* 1919; *I* m4530f. n5680; *P* m121,18 an125,11; *C* nm2102ff. a2331; *G* a47 n17641; *JT* 1998,3; *TF* nm2538

Meljâger a warrior in Alexander's army. He is also called Melêager in *A*, the form in which the name occurs in *UA* and the Latin versions (*Expeditio Alexandri*, Curtius Rufus, Valerius, and Gualterus). – *A* 6994; *UA* 4719

Meljakanz see Meljaganz

Meljanz 'von Liz', a knight who is first mentioned in Chrestien's *Erec*, where, as in *E*, he is one of the knights present at Arthur's court when Êrec returns with Ênîte. He is the *ami* of Tiebaut's elder daughter in Chrestien's *Perceval*, but Wolfram has introduced complications into the story. M. is the son of Schôt, who dies when his son is still a child and leaves him in the care of Lipaôt, with whose daughter Obîe M. falls in love. She rejects him, however, and he collects an army which he leads against her father. Lipaôt is assisted by Gawein, who wounds and defeats M., and the latter becomes reconciled with Obîe. He is one of knights who spill Priure's cup of chastity at Arthur's court in *C* (2294), when he is called Milîanz de Lis. He may be identical with the Milianz li ros who attends the tourney held by Arthur (*C* 596), but it is to be noted that a Melians li Rus de la Marche d'Escoce occurs in the Vulgate *Lancelot*. A Miljanz jousts with and is unhorsed by Jôram (2) in *Wigl*, whilst in *G* he fights for Arthur against Ehkunat, is unhorsed by Gauriel in *GM*, and fights for Arthur against Tandareis in *TF*. When Gawein is telling Arthur the story of his adventure with Gylorette in *RP*, he says that M., who is the brother of Brandelis, is the first to catch him with Gylorette, and in the ensuing fight M. is killed. This is not related when the action takes place, when only Ydier (2) is killed, although the latter mentions his 'vetter' who had been killed by Gawein. In Gawein's version of this episode, M. corresponds to Gyamoure in the ME *Jeaste of Syr Gawayne*, Gyamoure being unhorsed, but not killed, by Gawein. – *E* 1635; *Wigl* 467; *P* nm344,15 a384,15; *C* 596; *G* 17686f.; *JT* nm5640,2; *TF* 1693; *GM* 1186; *RP* m198,21 n201,46

Melchinor see Persit (2)

Melchîor 'von Tharsis', one of the three Magi who go to worship the Christ-child. – nm *W* 307,9; *JT* 5475,1f.

Meloans see Meloantz (1)

Meloantz (1) a knight who had slain the father and wounded the mother, Syloys, of five maidens whom Paris finds naked in a wood, as he is returning from Penielle. Paris defeats M. and makes him ask the maidens for forgiveness. He is then sent to Helen. – *GT* nm9308 a9385ff.

Meloantz (2) a warrior in the Trojan army against the Greeks. M. is the brother of Anthonax. – *GT* nm22769

Mêlôn (1) a warrior in Dârîus's army against Alexander, to whom he reports the capture of Dârîus by Bessus. So also in Curtius Rufus. – *A* 14728f.

Melon (2) see Mîlôn (2)

---

27   Bruce (1), I, pp. 196ff.

Melopar a wicked king who keeps the giants Maroltt and Barfartt. Paris and Hector slay these giants, are told all about M. by his prisoner, Carpius, and slay M. and his men. – *GT* nm11319ff. a11485ff.

Melôt a dwarf whose services are enlisted by Marjodô in his endeavour to prove to Marke the guilt of Tristan and Îsolt (2). They are able to avoid most of his traps, but eventually M. strews flour between the beds of the two lovers, and their guilt is proved. M. comes in for a good deal of buffeting when Tristan returns to Marke's court in the guise of a jester. In *Tn* he is called M. von Aquitân, the name being copied in *UT* and *HT*, but in *ET* he is named only in MS D, where he is called Aquitain, a name which may possibly be due to the influence on the copyist of Gottfried's form. In Beroul he is called Frocis (in the oblique case, Frocin). – *ET* m3390f. a3403 n3931; *Tn* 14242ff.; *UT* 1498; *HT* 5279f.

Meluchpat 'künec von Gemelle', a knight who fights for Melchinor (see Persit (2)) against Walwan (3) in the battle at Firmin, where he is killed by the king of Alanya (8200ff.). (Cf. Firmonis.) – *WO* 6129 [†]

Memnôn see Mennôn (1)

Memrôt a giant. He is mentioned also in Gualterus, where he is called Nimrod (II,499), but there is no justification for identifying him with the biblical character (see Nemrôte). – *UA* nm7081

Menader 'von der tofeln' a knight who is unhorsed by Parzivâl, from whom he demands toll. In the Mons MS of Manessier he is called Menables de la Table, and in the Montpellier MS, Menandres. – *RP* a752,6f. n775,36

Menalus natural son of Priam, a warrior in the Trojan army against the Greeks. This character appears to have been invented by Benoît, who calls him Menelus. – *LT* a4808 n4821

Menassides son of Saladres, with whom M. and his brothers attack Parzivâl and are all defeated. In Manessier he is called Menastide. – *RP* a842,6 n844,43

Mendeus 'künec von Jerobin', to whom Antenor comes after leaving Troy. This name does not occur in any other version of the Trojan legend. – *LT* 17031

Menecles a tutor who taught Geometry to the young Alexander. So also in Pseudo-Callisthenes and Valerius. – *A* 1369f.

Menelaus husband of Helen and brother of Agâmennon. M. does not play a prominent part in the fighting before Troy; in *LT* he fetches Achilles from the court of Licomedes, whilst in *TK* it is Pirrus whom he fetches to Troy. In *GT* he is killed during the sack of Troy. He is one of the Greeks seen by Ênêâs in Hades in *Ed.* – *Ed* nm2 a3345; *LT* 2394f.; *FB* nm1611; *TK* nm19754f. a20367; *UA* nm18463; *GT* 3144f.

Menesteus 'herzoge von Athene', a warrior in the Greek army against the Trojans. So also in Benoît. In Dares, Dictys, and Homer, he is called Menestheus. – *LT* 4864; *TK* 30537f.

Mênêtas 'vürste', a warrior placed with Apollodôrus over the land around Babylon by Alexander. In *Expeditio Alexandri* he is called Menidas, and in Curtius Rufus he is named Menes (var. (in accusative case) Manetam). – *A* 13373

Mênidas a warrior in Alexander's army who is sent out scouting. He is afterwards slain on account of the severity of the wounds which he received. This character appears to have been invented by Rudolf (but see Mênêtas). – *A* 11605f.

Mennolauss see Menelaus

Mennôn (1) a warrior in Dârîus's army against Alexander. In *A* he is the first of the Persians to engage Alexander, and his army is routed, and he himself slain. He corresponds partly to Amontâ (q.v.) in *WA*. In *UA* he is the father of Fidias and is slain during the battle at Issôn. M. occurs in *Expeditio Alexandri*, Curtius Rufus, and Gaulterus. – *A* 4507; *UA* 5616

Mennon (2)   in *LT* he is 'künec von Persia' and nephew of Xerses (see Perseus (1)); in *TKf* he is 'künec von Môrlant (also 'von Êtiopiâ') und Indiâ' and is the son, as in Greek legend, of Tîton and Aurorâ. M. is a warrior in the Trojan army against the Greeks, and, as in Dares and Dictys, where he is called Memnon ex Aethiopia, he is slain by Achilles. In *TKf* (44088f.) he is erroneously mentioned as the slayer of Hector. M. occurs in Benoît and Homer also. – *LT* 3235; *TKf* 42611ff.

Mennon (3)   see Menon (2)

Menolass, Menolauss, Menoloss   see Menelaus

Mênôn (1)   a warrior who is made by Alexander 'herzoge von Arâcôsien lant'. So also in Curtius Rufus. – *A* 20740

Menon (2)   son of Agâmennon (from whom his name is obviously derived). He is attacked after the death of his father by Romulus and Ênêâs, but completely routs their combined armies. – *GT* 24995ff.

Mênze 'bischof von' (*Loh*), see Willekîn (2)

Merabjax   son of Terramêr, for whom he fights against Willehalm (1) at Alischanz. So also in *Aliscans*, where he is called Miradaus (var. Mirabias). – *W* a29,18f. n32,16

Merangin 'künec von Irlande', a knight who fights for Arthur against Bruns (1). – *RP* 22,6

Meranphit   a knight who attends Leigamar's tourney in the service of Aram. – *C* 18165

Merein 'von Biez', uncle of Helen. M. is a warrior in the Greek army against the Trojans and is slain by Polidamas. This character appears to have been invented by Konrad. – *TK* 32175ff.

Merian   a knight whom Parzivâl married to the daughter of Gouns Wueste. – *RP* nm11 in the interpolation after *P* 823,10

Merion   a warrior in the Greek army against the Trojans. He is wounded by Polidamas and later slain by Hector. In *TK* he is called M. von Cretenlant. He is slain by Hector in Benoît and Dares, where he is called Merion e Crete, but in Dictys he is wounded only, the name of his assailant not being given. He occurs also in Homer, but is neither wounded nor slain in this version. (Identical with Merius?) – *LT* 5882; *TK* 23838

Merius 'von Tygris', a warrior in the Greek army against the Trojans. This character does not appear in any other version of the Trojan legend. (Identical with Merion?) – *LT* 3358

Mercurio   see Mercurius

Mercurius   the messenger of the gods. In *TK* he is present at the wedding of Thetis and Pêleus. – *TK* 972; *GM* nm (MS D) 3531[69]

Merlin (1)   grandson of Constans, begotten on the latter's daughter by the Devil in a dream. He is brought up apart from his mother, and, as in Geoffrey of Monmouth and all the OF versions, he is brought to Vortigern (see Wertigier) in order that his blood may prevent the latter's castle from collapsing. M. constantly appears to Uter and Pandragon in different forms; he tells a knight that he will meet his death in three different ways. The knight, who has tried to prove that M.'s craft is false, meets his end in a combination of these three ways. As in Geoffrey and the OF versions, M. helps Utepandragûn to obtain access to Îgerne. – *Mer* nm4,6 a40,2ff.; *RP* nm592,25f.

Merlin (2)   'des tiuvels sun', a magician who stands on guard over Crispin's kingdom, so that none may enter or leave. He is slain by Wildhalm, who thus breaks the spell. M. is also called (12166) Gielewast (= *giel*, 'throat' and *waste*, 'vast'). – *WO* nm11063ff. a11920ff.

Mermidac 'grâve', a knight who is slain in the service of Kailet. – *JT* nm2824,6

Mertîn   a contemporary of Ulrich von Eschenbach, acquainted with the wine-cellar belonging to Conrât. – *UA* nm21500

Mesâpus son of Neptûnus, a knight in the army of Turnus against Ênêâs. So also in the OF *Eneas*. In Virgil he is called Messapus. – *Ed* 5085

Mesentius a warrior in Turnus's army against Ênêâs, by whom he is wounded. He attacks Ênêâs again to avenge the death of his son, Lausus, and is this time killed. In the OF *Eneas* he is called Mesencius, and in Virgil, Mezentius. – *Ed* 5026

Mêthâ 'von Dâmazôn', father of Sanga and Triphôn (2), a warrior who is slain by Clîtus whilst fighting for Dârîus against Alexander at Erbela. This character appears to have been invented by Ulrich. – *UA* 12113

Metôdîus 'der heilige', the supposed author of the *Revelationes Methodii*, a popular work in the Middle Ages, and one which contains a history of the life of Alexander. – *A* nm13042

Mêtrôn 'kameræe' to Alexander. He learns of the conspiracy to kill Alexander from Zêbalîn and tells Alexander. In *UA* Alexander bequeaths to him Pamphîlias and Siciôn. M. occurs in Curtius Rufus and Gualterus. – *A* 19008; *UA* 4691

Mezentio see Mesentius

Mîdâ (1) 'von Cênôs', a warrior who is slain by Antigonus whilst fighting for Dârîus against Alexander at Issôn. So also in Gualterus. – *UA* 8052

Mîdâ (2) 'von Sardîn', a relative of Mîdâ (1). He is not mentioned by Gualterus. – *UA* nm5898

Mydoras 'künec von Ypritz', a knight who, together with his men, is defeated and killed by Hector and Paris. – *GT* 13128

Migaz a Trojan who is the first to see Hector returning to Troy with Pictorye. – *GT* 13264

Myglares a maiden who is with Dulcefluor when the latter is abducted by Lympondrigon. M. is not abducted but is allowed to go free. A knight of the Round Table named Migloras appears in *L'Estoire de Merlin* (Vulgate Cycle). – *Wigm* 5320f.

Michaêle see Michahele

Michaell see Michahele

Michahele (St. Michael, the Archangel). He is guarding the gates of Paradise when Alexander makes his journey to Paradise in *SA*. – *ET* nm7087; *MC* nm932; *UT* nm3539; *JT* nm4307,1; *Sey* nm282,4; *RP* nm130,9; *SA* 6260ff.

Michêl (1) a priest who tells Tristan the story of Jovelîn when Tristan spends the night with him. – *ET* 5514f.

Michel (2) see Michahele

Myclares see Myglares

Mîle nephew of Willehalm (1), for whom he fights at Alischanz, where he is slain by Terramêr. In *UW* he is present at the celebrations held when Willehalm returns from Tîbalt with Gîburc. M. does not occur in *Aliscans*, although two knights called Milon appear, neither being a relative of Willehalm. The reference to M. in *W* occurs in the early part of the story, which does not occur in the OF. – *W* 14,21f.; *UW* 211,26; *RB* nm14860

Milête father of Persanîs. – *PM* nm11145

Mîlîag 'grâve', father of Galîag. – *ET* nm6472

Milîanz (1) see Meljanz

Milîanz (2) see Meljaganz

Miliun 'cuns', father of Fierliun. – *RW* nm526

Millemargot a knight of the Round Table who is unhorsed by Meljaganz when the latter is abducting Ginovêr. He is not mentioned in Chrestien's *Yvain*. – *I* nm4705

Mîlôn (1) 'grâve von Nivers', a knight who is killed by Terramêr whilst fighting for Willehalm (1) in the second battle at Alischanz. In *Aliscans*, Milon de Romorentin is slain by Baudus (see Poidjus). – *W* 413,18

Mîlôn (2) 'von Nomadjentesîn', a knight whom Feirefîz claims to have defeated. In *JT* he is
called Melion von Modientesine and fights for Ipomidôn against Akarîn, and Melon von
Modientisine when he takes part in the tourney held by Sekundille to decide which of her
wooers she shall marry. – *P* nm770,8; *JT* nm3220,6 a5264,1

Milceres see Misereiz

Minantas 'lantgrâve von Tandernas', 'veter barn' of Dulcemâr, for whom he fights against
Arthur. – *TF* 1997

Minervâ the goddess, identical with Pallas (q.v.). In *SA* she is called Inmerna. –
nm *TKf* 46197; *SA* 5172

Minos 'von Taurian', husband of Basiphe, who gives birth during his absence to the
Minotaurus, which he has placed in the Labyrinth. Jason slays the monster whilst M. is
absent from his kingdom, and then flees with M.'s two daughters, Meierra and Fedra,
whom he later abandons. When M. returns he slays Basiphe, who had been the ultimate
cause of the loss of his two daughters. He is present at the wedding of Meierra, and the
death of Fedra is avenged by M.'s brother, Gamille. M. is the father of the Minotaurus in
the Greek legend, where his wife is Pasiphaë, and his children Deucalion, Ariadne (=
Meierra? – see Adrîagnê), and Phaedra (= Fedra). The slayer of the Minotaurus is Theseus
in the Greek legend. – *Ed* nm3542; *GT* 21521

Minuss see Minos

Mîrabel (Bartsch states that this name is a Provençal place-name, meaning 'Blicke schön',
which, he argues could also be the name of a person.[28]) M., who is 'künec von Avendroin'
and brother of Schirniel, is captured by Parzivâl whilst fighting for Lipaôt against Meljanz.
In *JT* he is present at the tourney held by Arthur. – *P* m354,22 a384,9 n772,2; *JT* 2059,1

Miray a knight who takes part in the battle between Paltriot and Atroclas. – *Wigm* 3758

Mirangel a knight in Dulcemâr's army against Arthur. – *TF* 1993

Misahêl biblical, a comrade of Daniel during the captivity of the Jews in Babylon. Mishael is
referred to in *UA* by his Babylonian name, Mysach (= Meshach). – nm *A* 15442; *JT* 71,1ff.;
UA 1086

Mysach see Misahêl

Misereiz 'von Perse', a warrior who is slain by Menesteus whilst fighting for the Trojans
against the Greeks. In *LT* he is called Milceres (also: Miceres) von Frisce. He occurs in
Benoît as Misceres, a variant of Mercerès de Frise, who often fights, and is unhorsed by
Menesteus, but is killed by Dyomedes. – *LT* 4020; *TK* 29738

Misfrigall a knight who takes part in the tourney held by Arthur for the crown of
Deleprosat. – *Wigm* 2008

Mitarz 'von Ansgewen', a knight who unhorses Aschalonê at the tourney held by Leigamar.
– *C* 18143

Mitrâzênis a warrior who, with Orsines, reports to Alexander the treachery of Bessus. So
also in Curtius Rufus, where he is called Mithracenes. – *A* 14741ff.

Mitrênes 'vürste', a warrior who is sent by Alexander to comfort his prisoners regarding the
escape of Dârîus. After he has gone, Alexander is afraid that he may exult over the queen
and the other captives and sends Lêônâtes to ensure that M. states the position correctly.
M. occurs in *Expeditio Alexandri* and Curtius Rufus. – *A* 7546ff.

Miceres see Misereiz

Moabigal an ally of Nerorx, with whom he challenges Agâmennon. – *GT* nm12300f.

---

28   Bartsch (2), p. 150.

Moap   according to *UA*, the name of a Jew, the former husband of Ruth. Historically Moab is the name of the land of which Ruth was a native. – *UA* nm11484

Modassîne   mother of Sirgamôte. She is present at the battle between Eghart and Dêmantîn at Antrîûn, is favourably inclined towards the latter, and continually tries to get her husband, Meliân, to withdraw his opposition to the marriage of Dêmantîn and Sirgamôte. – *Dem* 5483ff.

Môdiâne   sister of Offiart. She accompanies Darifant and his companions to their resting place after the fight between Darifant and Offiart. – *Dar* 237

Modrens   see Mordelas

Mœrinne   'diu' (*P*), see Belakâne

Moygines (1)   brother of Constanns. M., who is king of Britain, is slain in battle and succeeded by his son, Moygines (2). M. appears to be the invention of Albrecht von Scharfenberg. – *Mer* a14,1 n15,1

Moygines (2)   son of Moygines (1), whom he succeeds as king of Britain. He is murdered by twelve traitors. M. appears as Moine, the eldest son of Constant, in the *Huth-Merlin* and the Vulgate *Estoire de Merlin*. In Geoffrey of Monmouth, Constantine has three sons: Constans (the eldest, who was at first a monk and later succeeded his father), Uther Pendragon, and Aurelius Ambrosius. Constans was murdered by the traitors in the service of Vortigern (see Wertigier). Wace translates the passage relating to Constantine's sons in *Brut* (6592ff.): 'Fist li rois apeler Constant; / A Guincestre le fist norir, / La le fist moine devenir', and, although he goes on to name the other two sons as in Geoffrey, it seems most probable that it is from this passage that the name Moine, Moygines originates. – *Mer* m16,5 a43,6 n45,2

Moyses   biblical (Moses). – nm *A* 9844; *JT* 287,7; *UA* 1130; *RB* 13106; *SA* 1954; *WA* 60

Molapar   see Melopar

Molîn   (< OF *molin*, 'mill'?) 'von Kynâ'. The king of Antîoch relates how M. slew the knight in the service of the queen of Pullêbin. – *Dem* nm4328

Mompolier   father of Angelburg (q.v.). M. is the victim of a deception on the part of his second wife, Flanea. He attacks Fridrich (3) (q.v.) when the latter returns to his land with Angelburg, and is captured, but pardoned. – *FS* m164 a5245 n5332

Monagaris   see Monagris

Monagris   'der schahteliur' who fights with and kills Zirell (q.v.). M.'s *amie*, Clarete, laughs with joy at the death of Zirell, and this so enrages Paris that he attacks and kills M. – *GT* nm8214f. a8289ff.

Mônîmus   a warrior who is captured by Alexander after the first defeat of Dârîus. This character does not occur in any other history of Alexander. – *A* 7638

Morachîn   a knight who pursues Firganant after the latter has slain the *Vogt* of Fandorich's castle. M. is killed by Firganant. – *Dem* 6816

Morâl   husband of Bêlêâre and brother of Bejolâre. M. is a knight who is rescued by Wigalois from a dragon and later fights for Wigalois against Liôn. – *Wigl* m4930ff. a5041ff. n5276

Moralde   'von dem schönen Walde', father of Claudîn (q.v.). – *TF* m10597f. n10725 a11681f.

Morande   wife of Licomedes. – *GT* a16334f. n16347

Môrant (1)   'herzoge' (*W* 27,9), 'künec' (*W* 46,21), a warrior who is slain by Vîvîans whilst fighting for Terramêr against Willehalm (1). M. occurs in *Aliscans*, where he is called Murgant (var. Morant) and is probably identical with Morans, who appears in the *Chancun de Willame*. – *W* 27,9

Morant (2) 'grâve', a knight who is in command of the town of Galverne when it is attacked by Witechin. He is sent by Amelot to Alan, calling the latter to account for his attack on Sävine, and is also sent to Rainher with the news of the marriage of Amely to Willehalm (4). – *RW* nm10805ff. a11052

Morax counsellor to Agâmennon, who consults him as to a suitable reward for Paris. – *GT* 3724

Morbonon Atgrine see Mabônagrîn

Mordelas the name assumed on baptism by Evaleth (q.v.). In *L 'Estoire del Saint Graal* (Vulgate Cycle) he is called Mordrains, which is almost identical with the form in *RP*, viz. Modrens. It is related in *L 'Estoire del Saint Graal* how the Graal company helps him to defeat Tholomer, after which M. becomes a Christian. He helps the Graal company to convert Britain but is blinded through an attempt to see the Graal. He retires to an abbey, where he awaits the arrival of Galahad (see Galaal), who alone can cure him. The sequel is told in *Les Aventures del Saint Graal* (Vulgate Cycle), when, four hundred years later, Galahad arrives at the abbey and cures M. of his blindness. M. then dies content. M. has a son, Nasiens, and a brother-in-law, Narpus. – *Mer* 165,6; *RP* nm614,38

Morderes, Morderet, Mordres see Mordret

Mordret (According to Brugger, the Kymric form of this name is Medrawt (see below), the form Modred being either Cornish or Breton.[29]) M. is one of the knights present at Arthur's court when der schöne Böse arrives to surrender himself. M. is the nephew of Arthur (in the OF prose versions of *Merlin*, Arthur's son by his own half-sister, the wife of Lôt (1)). The *Annales Cambriae*, a Welsh chronicle written in the second half of the tenth century, records for the year 537 the final battle between Arthur and Medraut,[30] whilst Geoffrey is the first to mention M.'s union with Ginovêr whilst Arthur is away fighting, and also M.'s usurpation of the throne during Arthur's absence. The story is the subject of the *Mort le Roi Artu* (Vulgate Cycle) and is related by Füetrer.[31] – *RP* 391,17

Môrende 'künec', a warrior who had come from 'jenhalp Katus Erkules' to assist Terramêr in the second battle against Willehalm (1). He is slain by Rennewart. So also in *Aliscans*, where he is called Morindes. – *W* 359,10 [†]

Môret 'diu mœrinne', one of the ladies at Arthur's court who spill Priure's cup of chastity. – *C* 1602

Morgan (a Celtic name meaning dweller by the sea.[32]) M. is Riwalin's liege-lord and is attacked by the latter and compelled to treat for peace. He attacks Riwalin's land whilst Riwalin is at Marke's court, and Riwalin is recalled and fights a battle against M. in which he is slain. Tristan later kills M. because he refuses to give him Riwalin's land, alleging that Tristan is of illegitimate birth. According to Golther, this character was introduced into the legend by Thomas, who may have taken the name from Geoffrey of Monmouth.[33] – *Tn* 329ff.; *HT* nm1892

Morgan 'diu fei', see Feimorgân

Morgowanz son of Terramêr, for whom he fights at Alischanz. In *Aliscans* he is called Morgans li faés. – *W* a29,18f. n32,17

Morholt see Môrolt

---

29 Brugger (2), p. 65, note 126.
30 Bruce (1), I, pp. 11f.
31 [Hofstäter, I, p. 252.]
32 Gottfried von Straßburg, *Tristan und Isolde*, transl. by W. Hertz. p. 545.
33 Golther (2), p. 145.

Mörlin see Merlin (1)

Morkadas a knight who is present at Arthur's court when Bagumades arrives to submit himself to Arthur. In Gautier he is called Marcadès. – *RP* 513,14

Morchades (1) a knight who is unhorsed by Anshelm (1) when the latter and Supplicius are rescuing Alîs from Markabrê. – *PM* 19429ff.

Morchades (2) according to *C*, the mother of Gawein, and one of the ladies in the Castle of Salîe. She is also (21034) called Orcades. Wolfram calls Gawein's mother Sangîve, but the form of the name in Malory, Margawse, is not altogether unlike that in *C*. – *C* 20966ff.

Morchartt counsellor to Agâmennon, who consults him as to a suitable reward for Paris. – *GT* 3727

Morlant 'künec von' (*LT*), see Perseus (1)

Mornandas a knight who is present at the tourney held by Arthur before the Schastel Orgelus. – *RP* 472,44

Môrolt (According to Golther, this name is Franconian, but possibly from Celtic origins (cf. Tristan).[34] Celtic *mor*, 'sea', or *môr*, 'large', is given as the root. Golther also quotes Gaston Paris, who correctly connects the black sail episode with the Theseus saga and sees in M. the Minotaurus, who demanded tribute from the Athenians, 'une sorte de monstre marin, plus tard anthropomorphisé'.[35] Hertz derives the name from the OHG Môrwalt, but quotes Gilbert as deriving it from the same root as the Irish Murragh.[36] Hertz also draws attention to the Welsh fairy story in which the Irish prince, Martholouch, the husband of Brangwen (see Brangêne), compels the Kymrians to pay tribute.) M. is the brother of Îsolt (1) and is sent by her husband to demand tribute from Marke. He is killed in single combat by Tristan. M. is shown in a consistently sympathetic light in all versions and tries to dissuade Tristan from undertaking a fight which he feels can only end in the death of the younger man. In *P* he is one of the besiegers of Patelamunt but leaves before the arrival of Gahmuret; he is present at the tourney held by Herzeloide. In *JT* he is present at Arthur's court and is unhorsed by Schîonatulander. – *ET* 351f.; *P* nm49,5 a73,18; *Tn* nm5876f. a6225; *JT* 1369,1; *HT* nm1639 [†]

Morfan counsellor to Agâmennon, who consults him as to a suitable reward for Paris. – *GT* 3727

Mubur 'grâve von Laseyn', a knight in Atroclas's army. – *Wigm* nm3616

Müelat 'marcgrâve von Raurzatel', a knight in Atroclas's army. – *Wigm* 3872

Mügelein 'herzoge', a knight of the Round Table who offers himself as a champion for Elsam. He had successfully fought Ortanne. – *Ll* 41,1

Mundiros see Mundirosa

Mundirosa wife of Seyfrid (q.v.). – *Sey* a304,1f. n317,1

Muntâne 'leh cuns de', see Lahedumân

Muntespîr 'der von' (*W*), see Terramêr

Murdres see Mordret

---

34 Golther (2), p. 17.
35 Golther (2), p 21.
36 Gottfried von Straßburg, *Tristan und Isolde*, transl. by W. Hertz, pp. 568f.

N

Nabarzânes see Narbâsones

Nabor 'von Dassarie', a warrior who takes part in the battle between Akarîn and Ipomidôn. – *JT* 3941,1

Nabôt biblical, a king who took Achap's vineyard. (See Achap). – *UA* nm11654ff.

Nâbuchodônosor biblical (Nebuchadnezzar). This form of the name, the only one which appears in the Court Epics, is that of the Vulgate Version of the Bible. In *P* he is said to be uncle to Pompêjus (1). – nm *P* 102,4; *A* 9961; *JT* 794,6; *UA* 912; *RB* 13694

Nâbuzar son of Êvilmôradac. N. is mentioned in the *Historia Scholastica* (*Liber Danielis* V), where he is called Nabar. – *UA* nm7709ff.

Nâbuzardas a man in the service of Nâbuchodônosor. He is mentioned in the *Historia Scholastica* (*Liber IV Regum* XLV). – *UA* nm7662f.

Nâdap biblical (Nadab), king of Israel. – *A* nm16356

Nachus a dwarf in the service of Waradach (q.v.). N. is slain by Hector. – *GT* a12368ff. n12498

Nactor son of Saladres, with whom he and his brothers attack Parzivâl, who defeats them all. In Manessier he is called Nastor. – *RP* a842,6 n844,44

Nampêtenis (< OF *li nains Bedenis*). N. is one of the knights attacking Jovelîn in *ET* (see Nautenîs). He keeps his wife locked in his castle, but Kâedîn, with Tristan's help, succeeds in effecting an entry. When N. returns, he realizes that someone has been with his wife, who is called Garîôle, and he pursues the two friends, killing Kâedîn and (in *ET*) mortally wounding Tristan. In *UT*, which is followed by *HT*, Tristan kills N., after the latter has slain Kâedîn, but is himself mortally wounded by one of N.'s knights. – *ET* 5986; *UT* nm2569ff. a3177; *HT* nm5744ff. a5805

Nampotanis, Nampotênis see Nampêtenis

Nanteis, Nantes 'der von' (*RP*), see Karode

Nârant 'grâve von Ukerlant', a knight in Klâmidê's army. He is the father of Bernout. Martin suggests that this name may have some connection with Neranden, the territorial name of Gangier (q.v.).[1] – *P* 205,13

Narbâsones a warrior in the army of Dârius, whom he assists Bessus (q.v.) to murder. N. is called Nabarzanes in *Expeditio Alexandri*, Curtius Rufus, and Gualterus, and this spelling is followed (approximately) by *A* and *UA*, whilst in Pseudo-Callisthenes, *Itinerarum Alexandri*, Valerius, and Leo, he is called Ariobarzanes, a form which corresponds to the Arbasones of *SA* and the Oriaber of *WA* (in Lampreht he is called Arbazân). – *A* 6913ff.; *UA* 6710f.; *SA* 3588ff.; *WA* a2705 n2718

Naribôn 'cuns von' (*W*), see Heimrîch (1)

Narilus a warrior in the Trojan army against the Greeks. He brings Hector the challenge from Hercules. – *GT* 17362

Narpus brother-in-law to Mordelas. He becomes one of the Graal brotherhood. In *L'Estoire del Saint Graal* he is the grandson of Nasciens and therefore great-nephew to Mordrains (= Mordelas). His story is told in *Les Aventures del Saint Graal*. – *Mer* nm168,1

Narcissus in Greek legend the youth who was loved by the nymph Echo and who became a flower through gazing at his own reflection in a pool. – *LT* nm11209f.

---

1 Martin (1), p. 195, to 205,13.

Nasiens son of Mordelas, according to *Mer*. N. is called Natigen in *RP*, where it is stated that this is the name assumed on baptism by Salafes. The story is told in full in the *Estoire del Saint Graal*, where Nasciens is the name assumed on baptism by Seraphe, the brother-in-law of Mordrain (= Mordelas). N. is blinded, when, out of curiosity, he uncovers the Graal, but he is healed by the blood which drips from the lance. After several adventures, he reaches Britain, which he assists the Graal company to convert. He is the founder of the line, of which Galahad is the last representative. The story is also told in brief in *Les Aventures del Saint Graal*. – nm *Mer* 167,6f.; *RP* 614,44

Nascur 'von Marbidille', a warrior in Ipomidôn's army against Akarîn. – *JT* nm3241,4

Nastano see Nastanüs

Nastanüs a vassal of Dârîus, to whom he sends a vivid account of Alexander's warlike army and power. This is the form of the name which occurs in *WA*; in *A* he is called Nostâdî. – *A* 5913; *WA* 2236

Natigen see Nasiens

Nationey 'von Spannyr', a knight who assists Paltriot against Atroclas. – *Wigm* 3648ff.

Nausica daughter of Alceon. She marries Thelemacus. So also in Dictys, Benoît, and the *Odyssey*. – *LT* 17786

Nautenîs 'von Hante', one of the leaders of the army attacking Jovelîn. He is captured by Tristan and Kâedîn. It seems highly probable that this name is a corruption of Nampêtenis (q.v.). – *Tn* 18843

Navarre 'künec von' (*JT*), see Hiutegêr

Naximeneâ see Anaximenes

Nazarus a name given to the devil. – *Loh* nm105

Nearchus to whom Alexander bequeaths Cylicia and Pamphilia. This name does not occur in any other history of Alexander. – *SA* 8499

Nebedons see Beduwiers

Negrasindt 'grâve', a knight in charge of Lydasar, a town in Deleferant. – *Wigm* nm3492

Negûsar 'von Ninivê', nephew of Nînus. He is slain by Philotas whilst fighting for Dârîus against Alexander at Issôn. This character appears to have been invented by Gualterus. – *UA* a8203ff. n8217

Neiliburz a knight who attends Leigamar's tourney in the service of Aram. – *C* 18170

Neini 'diu twerginne' (< OF *la naine*?), one of the ladies at Arthur's court who spill Priure's cup of chastity. – *C* 1603

Neithart 'ûz Ungerlant', squire to Lohengrîn. He is called Diether in MS K of *Ll* (see Diether (2)), whilst in *Loh* he is named Kyir (q.v.). – *Ll* 49,5f.

Nectanabus 'künec von Egipte', who flees to Macedonia when Egypt is attacked by Artâxerses (2). N., who is a magician, assumes the form of the god Amôn, lies with Olimpias, and on her begets Alexander. By his magic he contrives that Philipp (1) shall believe that Amôn is the father of the child. When Alexander is still a boy, he kills his father by pushing him over the battlements (into a pit in *SA*), and the dying N. tells Alexander the true history of his parentage. The story is told in Valerius and Leo, and is mentioned in the *Historia Scholastica*, but is denied by Lampreht. – *A* 108ff.; *UA* 234f.; *SA* 85; *WA* 101

Nectarius see Nectarus

Nectarus 'künec von Karnand', son of Palterius and Orgaloyse. N. spends some months at Agâmennon's court and later brings an army to assist the Greeks against Gamorett. – *GT* 4736

Nelotons a knight at Arthur's court who spills Priure's cup of chastity. This name originates in Chrestien's *Erec* (1743) in a passage which is considered by Foerster to be the interpolation of a copyist.[2] The line reads: 'Ne Letrons (MS A: litons) de Prepelesant' (see Inpripalenôt). – *C* 2327

Nemmoras, Nemoras see Nemores

Nemores an enemy of Turneas (q.v.), who is defeated by Friderich (3). – *FS* 3817

Nemrôte (Nimrod) a former king of Babylon. – *A* nm15663

Neptagente see Neptagint

Neptagint a commander in Ipomidôn's army against Akarîn. – *JT* 3245,6

Neptânabus (1) a young Trojan warrior who attacks Turnus after Ênêâs has been wounded, but is slain by the former. He is called Naptanabus (var. Neptanabus) in the OF *Eneas*, but does not occur in Virgil. – *Ed* 11976ff.

Neptanabus (2) see Nectanabus

Neptolomus 'künec', a warrior in the Greek army against the Trojans. This character was apparently invented by Benoît, who calls him Telopolon (var. Neptolemus). – *LT* 2842

Neptûnus the Roman god of the sea. In *TK* he is present at the wedding of Thetis and Pêleus. – *Ed* nm5086; *A* nm9350; *TK* 1001; *UA* nm4823ff.; *RB* nm16432

Nêre see Nero

Nêrejâ a maiden who fetches Wigalois from Arthur's court to Lârîe. N. corresponds to Helie in *Li Biaus Descouneus*, and to the unnamed maiden who is riding with Gingelens in *RP*. – *Wigl* a1720 n4069; *RP* a275,42

***Nerius** see Hunes

Nero the Roman Emperor. – nm *MC* 133ff.; *GT* 25085

Nerorx 'künec von Samari'. With Moabigal he sends a challenge to Agâmennon, which Hector leaves to accept on the latter's behalf. – *GT* nm12298

Nessus a centaur who tries to violate Dîanîra but is shot by Hercules. His poisoned shirt, which he gives to Dîanîra, is the cause of the death of Hercules. The story is told in *Metamorphoses* IX of Ovid. – *TK* nm37994ff.

Nesteus see Nestor (2)

Nestor (1) 'von Pîlon', a warrior who fights for Jason in the first war against the Trojans and who later takes part in the siege of Troy. N. occurs in all versions of the Trojan legend. – *LT* 1223; *TK* 11522ff.

Nestor (2) a warrior in the Trojan army against the Greeks. In *TK* is called 'herzoge von Agrimonîs', and in *LT* he is named Nesteus von Arpon. In *GT* he is the brother of Ênêâs and is actively concerned in the conspiracy to betray Troy to the Greeks. This character appears to have been invented by Benoît, who calls him Nestor (var. Nesteus). – *LT* 3986; *TK* 24908; *GT* 13265

Niarn a heathen god. – *R* nm Eing. I,86

Nibubais 'von Arabie', a warrior in Akarîn's army against Ipomidôn. – *JT* nm3178,6

Nigillubar 'von Narkilin', a warrior in Akarîn's army aginst Ipomidôn. – *JT* nm3178,6

Nicânor (1) brother of Philôtas, a commander in Alexander's army who is killed during the battle against Dârîus at Erbela. In *A* he dies just before Alexander's attack on Bessus. N. occurs in *Expeditio Alexandri* and Curtius Rufus, and also Gualterus. – *A* 6988; *UA* m3295f. an3525

---

2   Chrestien de Troyes, *Erec und Enide*, ed. by W. Foerster, 2nd edn, p. 311.

Nîkanor (2) a fellow conspirator in the plot with Dimnus to murder Alexander. This character appears to be a duplication of Nicânor (1), whose brother Philôtas is also concerned in the conspiracy. – *A* nm18889

Nicânor (3) a warrior in Alexander's army, who, with Symachus, makes a raid on Porrus's army and is killed. N. does not occur in any of the other histories of Alexander. – *UA* a19469 n19494

Nîcartides a warrior who is placed by Alexander in charge of Persipolis. In Curtius Rufus he is called Nicarchides. – *A* 14139f.

Nicauor a youth to whom Alexander bequeaths Parten lant. This character may be identical with a Nicanor, 'nobilis juvenis', who is mentioned by Curtius Rufus. – *SA* nm8525

Niclas see Nikolâus

Nycolâ 'von Lebenberc', a knight who rides with Ulrich von Liechtenstein to Neustadt and who bears the name 'Tristan' in the tourney which follows. – *FD* 1454,5

Nikolâus the first king to be overcome by the young Alexander. In all the MHG versions, except *UA*, he is killed by Alexander, but in the last-named, he submits and joins Alexander's army. N. occurs in Pseudo-Callisthenes, Valerius, and Leo. – *A* 2343ff.; *UA* 1725; *SA* nm835 a851; *WA* 415ff.

Nicômachus in *A* the brother of Zêbalîn. He hears of the conspiracy against the life of Alexander from Dimnus and reports the matter to his brother. In *UA* he is the brother of Dimnus and is referred to by both Alexander and Philôtas as having been instrumental in the betrayal of the conspiracy, but no indication is given of the part he plays. N. occurs also in Curtius Rufus and Gualterus. – *A* 18830ff.; *UA* 4670

Nicômacus see Nicômachus

Nicomedes see Licomedes

Nyntyn 'von Mantaltzein', a knight who takes part in the tourney held by Arthur for the crown of Deleprosat. – *Wigm* 2244

Nînus 'künec von Assirîâ', founder of the city of Ninivê. In *P* he is an ancestor of Pompêjus and Ipomidôn, whilst in *UA* he is uncle to Negûsar. – nm *P* 102,11; *A* 13183ff.; *UA* 8220

Nyobe *amie* of Segremors, whom she accompanies in his search for Gawein. She corresponds to Lidoine in *Meraugis de Portlesguez*. – *S* mIª,49 aIII,272ff. nIII,284

Niôbês wife of Amphiôn. N. incurs the wrath of the goddess Latônâ for refusing sacrifices to her. All N.'s children are slain by Phêbus (Apollo). – *UA* nm2774f.

Nîse see Nisus (1)

Nisus (1) a warrior in the Trojan army against the Greeks. He brings news of the approach of the Greek army under Atrides. In *Ed* he is killed by Volzân after a successful sortie with his friend Euriâlus (2) against the army of Turnus. So also in the OF *Eneas* and Virgil. – *Ed* 6540ff.; *GT* 17725ff.

Nisus (2) a warrior in the Greek army against the Trojans. – *TKf* 40961f.

Nîthart 'von Reuenthal', a well-known *Minnesinger*. – nm *W* 312,12; *JT* 889,6; *HT* 3780

Nitter (= Nîther?) a knight who is present at a tourney held by Arthur. – *JT* 2154,1

Niut see Noit

Nyfran a knight who fights with Paris against Matribulus. – *GT* 3447f.

Nyfrogar see Dymszogar

Nodengat 'künec von Deleprosat'. His death causes a tourney to be held by Arthur to decide on a successor. – *Wigm* nm3358

Nôê biblical (Noah). – nm *W* 178,14; *A* 17061; *JT* 2966,5; *UA* 1126; *RB* 19742; *WO* 10784

Noirs 'künec von Ethiopiâ', a knight who attends a tourney held by Arthur and who spills Priure's cup of chastity. Since the king of Ethiopia would certainly be black, it seems quite evident that this name is the result of a mistranslation from the OF, which probably read: 'li rois noirs d'ethiopia'. Taken in conjunction with the evidence offered by Êmenidis (q.v.), it seems most probable that the whole list of the knights who attend Arthur's court for the tourney is a translation from a list in a lost OF romance, just as the list of knights who spill Priure's cup of chastity is based closely on the list in Chrestien's *Erec*. – *C* 603

Noit father of Îdêr. N. is never mentioned apart from his son and first appears in Chrestien's *Erec*, where he is called Nut. – nm *E* 465; *P* 178,12; *RP* 87,20

Noradin cousin of Melchinor. – *WO* nm5790

Nôrant 'von Pimarge', an ally of Lôîs against Terramêr. – *UW* 39,17

Nordius 'von Lumilet', a warrior in Akarîn's army against Ipomidôn. – *JT* nm3625,6

Norwege 'künec von' (*JY*), see Lôt (1)

Norwege 'küneginne von' (*JT*), see Sangive

Nostâdî see Nastanüs

Noupatrîs 'künec von Ôraste Gentesîn', a warrior who is killed whilst wounding Vîvîans in the first battle between Terramêr and Willehalm (1) at Alischanz. This name rests on a misunderstanding of *Aliscans* (222), where he is called 'l'aupatris', an oriental title of distinction. As Singer points out, the MS used by Wolfram must have read 'un aupatris'.[3] – *W* 22,14ff.

Nûbjant 'künec von' (*W*), see Purrel

Nûnus biblical (Nun), father of Joshua. – *UA* nm11460

Nüs see Noit

Nutschier 'künec von Capadocia', the leader of an army composed of wild men and giants. He is slain by Melchinor. – *WO* 8010ff.

Nüwes see Noit

---

3 Singer (2), p. 13.

O

Obêth biblical, son of Ruth and grandfather of David (Obed). – *UA* nm11496

Obîe (Bartsch thinks this name is derived from *obier*, 'to move', i.e. the nimble,[1] whilst Martin suggests that it is a form of a name like Albîe, the diminutive form being Obilôt (q.v.).[2] Golther is of the opinion that both names still await a satisfactory explanation.[3]) O. is the elder daughter of Lipaôt and sister of Obilôt. Her refusal of the proffered love of Meljanz causes the latter to collect an army and attack her father. She is extremely scornful of Gawein, whom she takes to be a merchant. – *P* nm345,19ff. a352,9

Obilôt (Bartsch derived the name from *belot*, 'the pretty child', and suggests that the initial 'O' may either be a preposition misunderstood or for the sake of alliteration.[4] See also Obîe.) O. is the younger daughter of Lipaôt and the sister of Obîe. Although she is only a child, she recognizes Gawein's true worth and claims him for her knight. She persuades him to fight for her father, and during the battle he wears her sleeve as a favour. O. is one of the most delightful of the female characters in *P*. (Cf. Quebeleplûs.) – *P* nm345,19ff. a352,9

Odassîe 'küneginne', wife of Derafeit. (This name is incorrectly indexed in Bartsch's edition of *Dem*.) – *Dem* nm9899

Ôdere steward to Bêâmunt. (This name is incorrectly indexed in Bartsch's edition of *Dem*.) – *Dem* 10149

Odefîe the battle-cry of the burcgrâve von Angersper in his fight with Satrî. In Berthold almost all the battle-cries are the names of the *amies* of the respective knights, and it is therefore a reasonable assumption that O. is the *amie* of the burcgrâve von Angersper. – *Crane* nm4378

Odinas a knight who is found dead by Parzivâl during his search for the white hart's head. – *RP* a350,11f. n351,39

Odinias natural son of Priam and a warrior in the Trojan army against the Greeks. He occurs in *TK* as Odônje, and in Benoît as Odenel (var. Odoneax). Greif suggests that the origin of the name may be Iliona, who occurs in Hyginus.[5] – *LT* 4768ff.; *TK* 30372

Odônje see Odinias

Oedippus the hero of a Greek incest tragedy by Sophocles. The form of the name in *UA* is Edippus. – *UA* m2829 n2925 [†]

Oenônê a nymph who loved Paris when he was a herdsman, but he forgot her after he had been promised Helen. When he is lying mortally wounded, he sends for O., who is the only person who can cure him, but she at first refuses, and Paris dies on hearing of her refusal. She relents shortly afterwards, but arrives too late; she dies across his body. It has been thought that this story is the source of the final episode in *Tristan*.[6] The form of the name in *TK* is Egenoê. – *TK* 706ff.; *UA* nm4875 [†]

Oeônês see Oenônê

---

1 Bartsch (2), p. 149.
2 Martin (1), p. 288, to 345,24.
3 Golther (1), p. 170.
4 Bartsch (2), p. 149.
5 Greif, pp. 26ff.
6 Golther (2) pp. 20f.; Bruce (1), I, p. 188.

Oertes father of Medea. In Greek mythology he is called Aeëtes, whilst in *TK* he is called Oêtas, and in Benoît, Oëstès. – *LT* nm457 a521; *TK* nm7240 a7327

Oêtas see Oertes

Og 'künec von Basan', a warrior at the head of an army on the heathen side in the final battle against the Christians. – *WO* 16424f.

Oigeones standard-bearer on the side of Gârel (1) against Ammilôt. – *G* 13821ff.

Ochôzîas biblical (Ahaziah), king of Israel. – *A* nm16605

Ôchus (1) a warrior in Dârîus's army who is slain by Philôtas during the battle at Issôn. O. does not occur in any of the other histories of Alexander. – *UA* 8016ff.

Ochus (2) another name for Artâxerses (2). – *A* nm191ff.

Ocsiater see Oxîatres

Octavian the Roman soldier who afterwards became Augustus (1) (q.v.). – *JT* 4556,2; *RB* 21676

Octavîânus see Octavian

Olas 'von Tarbarie', a warrior in Akarîn's army against Ipomidôn. – *JT* nm3094,1

Olibantz 'von Molende', a warrior in Akarîn's army against Ipomidôn. – *JT* nm3137,2f.

Olibarise 'von Irmidele', a warrior in Akarîn's army against Ipomidôn. – *JT* nm3138,2f.

Olimpadis see Olimpias

Olimpîâ (1) sister of Arthur, wife of Linefles, and mother of Meleranz. – *M* 127ff.

Olimpîâ (2) daughter of Meleranz. – *M* 12801ff.

*Olympia (3) see Olimpias

Olimpiades see Olimpias

*Olimpiadis see Olimpias

Olimpias mother of Alexander (1) by Nectanabus (q.v.). O. is the wife of Philipp (1) and occurs in all the histories of Alexander. – *A* 427ff.; *UA* a193 n216; *SA* 227ff.; *WA* 163ff. [†]

Olimpjâ an oriental queen who had given her love to Feirefîz. – *P* nm771,15ff.

*Olymppias see Olimpias

Olifeus son (or nephew) of Cycrops, with whom he attacks Ulixes during the latter's return from Troy. In Benoît he is called Antiphat, whilst in the *Odyssey*, Antiphates is the name of a Laestrygonian (cf. Lestugo), a race of giants who attack Ulixes after his fight with Polyphemus. – *LT* nm17576ff.

Olivier (1) 'grâve' a knight who brings the news of Gârel's success against Ehkunat to Laudamîe. – *G* 17402f.

Olivier (2) 'grâve von Ploys', a knight who takes part in the tourney at Poys, where he is unhorsed by Diebalt. – *RW* nm7183 a7248

Olivier (3) one of the twelve peers of Charlemagne (see Karl (1)) and friend of Ruolant. – nm *W* [250,17]; *MC* 242; *UW* 31,1ff.

Olifrant 'herzoge', a warrior who is slain by Hector whilst fighting for the Greeks against the Trojans. This character was invented by Konrad. – *TK* 31298

Olifranz 'künec von Êthiopiâ', a warrior in the Trojan army against the Greeks. This character was invented by Konrad. – *TK* 24928

Omer, Ômerus see Homerus

Onam see Îwein (4)

Oniprîz 'künec von Itôlac'. (According to Martin this name is identical with Onuphrius, a well-known saint's name.[7]) O. is one of the knights whom Parzivâl claims to have overcome whilst he has been absent from Arthur's court. – *P* nm772,9

Onyphant a knight who is unhorsed by Phoriân. – *Dem* 1914

Onômastôrides a warrior who is captured by Alexander whilst fighting for Dârius. So also in Curtius Rufus. – *A* 7639

Onopel a warrior who is slain by Paris whilst fighting for the Greeks against the Trojans. – *GT* a17078f. n17100

Onorgûe see Feimorgan

Opinâus a knight who, according to *E*, has been slain by Mabônagrîn whilst attempting the adventure of Schoidelakurt. In Chrestian's *Erec* he is mentioned as being a conspicuously brave knight, but nothing is said of his death at the hands of Mabônagrîn. O., who is called Ospinel in the OF, was apparently the hero of a lost OF poem, and it seems reasonable to identify him with the 'herzoge Ospinel', who attends the tourney held by Arthur in *JT* and later fights against Orilus for Schîonatulander. – *E* nm8505; *JT* 1354,1

*Oquidant see Oukident. [See Appendix (5).]

Oralt 'von Arlatine', a warrior in Ipomidôn's army against Akarîn. – *JT* 3263,1

Oraste father of Zêrastes and grandfather of Pâusânîâ. – *A* nm3047

Orâtius (Horace) the famous Latin poet. – *UA* nm24425

Orbeis 'von Grikulanie', a warrior in Akarîn's army against Ipomidôn. – *JT* 3620,1

Ordabilies 'von Kartuzerculeise', a commander in Ipomidôn's army against Akarîn. – *JT* a3274,4 n3279,1

Ordegone 'künec von Affrisone', a warrior in Ipomidôn's army against Akarîn. – *JT* 3215,1ff.

Ordôphilôn a warrior who is killed by Clîtus whilst fighting for Dârius against Alexander at Issôn. This character appears to have been invented by Ulrich. – *UA* 7957

Ôreb 'künec von Madian'. O. is a Midianite chieftain who is mentioned in Pseudo-Methodius. – *A* nm17261

Orestes (1) son of Agâmennon. When he becomes a youth he learns of the death of his father and slays his mother, Clitemnestre, and Egistus, her lover. He marries Ermiona and slays Pirrus when the latter abducts her. The story is told in Dictys, but not in Dares. – *LT* 17276; *TKf* nm49313f. a49449

Orestes (2) a warrior in Alexander's army. This name rests on a misunderstanding of Curtius Rufus by Gualterus. The former has (IIII,13,28): 'post eum Orestae (a 'gens Macedoniae') Lyncestaeque sunt positi', and Gualterus took O. to be the name of a man, a mistake which was copied from him by the authors of *A* and *UA*. – *A* 11969; *UA* 3548

Orgaloyse wife of Palterius and mother of Nectarus. She is abducted by the giant Pligor, who is killed by Paris. – *GT* nm4453 a4526ff.

Orgaloysya, Orgaloysse see Orgaloyse

Orgelus founder of Castle Orgelus. It is related by Brios to Parzivâl that O. was defeated at a tourney held by Antipins Karadins. In Gautier he is called Li Orguellous, but there is no justification for identifying him with Orilus. – *RP* nm466,13

Orgelûse 'herzoginne von Lôgrois', widow of Zidegast, whose death she is determined to avenge on Gramoflanz. To this end she sets any knight who would win her love a series of difficult tasks to test his valour. Gawein, who is deeply in love with her, successfully undergoes these tests and is permitted to undertake the final task, the fight with

---

7   Martin (1), p. 505, to 772,9.

Gramoflanz, and, although the fight never actually takes place, he is rewarded with O.'s hand in marriage. O., who in Chrestien is called l'Orguelleuse de Logres, has, as her name implies, a certain symbolic significance. As the personification of worldly vanity, she is the cause of the suffering of Amfortas, who is smitten with an unchaste love for her. Her love is scorned by Parzivâl but is sought with exaggerated humility by the courteous, but worldly, Gawein. (Cf. Mancipicelle.) – *P* m478,17f. an508,18ff.; *W* nm279,13f.; *JT* 1728,1f.; *UA* nm14671; *RB* nm16667

Orgilus   see Orgelûse
Orgoillos, Orgolois   see Orilus (1)
Oriaber   see Narbâsones
Orilocus   a warrior in the Trojan army against Kamille (1). He slays one of the Amazons, Laureine. In Virgil he is called Orsilochus, whilst in the OF *Eneas* he appears as Orsileüs (var. Orsilocus). – *Ed* 8914
Orilus (1)   husband of Jeschûte. He first appears in Chrestien's *Erec* (2175) as li Orguelleus (= the proud) de la Lande, a knight who is unhorsed by Êrec at the tourney given to celebrate his marriage. In *E* (as far as it is possible to tell from the single extant MS of this romance) the name has become distorted to 'der hôchvertige Landô'. Wolfram translated the name, which appears also in Chrestien's *Perceval*, as Orilus de Lalander (Singer thinks that Kîôt was the first to make a proper name out of the epithet[8]), but he refers to the defeat of O. by Êrec, which would seem to point to an acquaintance with Chrestien's *Erec*, as he would hardly have recognized his Orilus in Hartmann's Landô.[9]
As his name implies, O. is arrogant and boastful. It has been said that he typifies the worst side of knighthood, fighting for the sake of fighting, and without the high ideals of the better type of knight.[10] O. makes Jeschûte, whom he suspects of unfaithfulness, ride behind him, poorly clad even in winter, whilst he goes in search of adventure. He is overcome by Parzivâl, who makes him receive his wife back into favour. A reference is made to this fight in *C* (5980), where he is called Orgolois de la lande. He is also present at a tourney held by Arthur in *C*, and on this occasion (595) he is called Orgoillos von der Lande. The part which O. plays in *JT* is determined by *P* (141,8f.), where Sigûne tells Parzivâl that Schîonatulander was slain by O. As the former is also said (*P* 141,16) to have met his death through a hound's leash, the two events are connected in *JT*. The hound, after escaping from Sigûne, comes into the possession of O., who gives it to Jeschûte; he refuses to give it up to Schîonatulander, and a fight is arranged for its possession. Before the fight takes place, he and his brother, Lehelîn, lead an army against Kanvoleiz (cf. *P* 141,6ff.) but are defeated by an army under Schîonatulander. The single combat between O. and Schîonatulander takes place, and O. is defeated. Shortly afterwards, he attacks the victor, who is riding with Sigûne, and kills him. In *JT* he is also referred to as Delabander, whilst he occurs in another hound incident in *Li Biaus Descouneus*, when he fights Guinglains (see Wigalois) for a hound which has been taken from him by the latter's companion, Helie (see Nêrejâ). In the ME version of the romance, *Libeaus Desconus*, he is called Otis de Lisle. – *E* 2576; *P* nm129,27 a132,28; *C* 595; *JT* 1265,5; *RB* nm20163; *FS* nm1460 [†]
Orilus (2)   see Orgelûse

---

8   Singer (1), p. 57.
9   Golther (1), p. 150.
10   Richey (3), p. 183.

Oringles 'von Limors', a knight who finds Ênîte mourning the apparently dead Êrec. He takes them both to Limors, where he tries to compel Ênîte to marry him. She refuses, and he strikes her, the sound of her cry waking the unconscious Êrec, who kills O., and scattering his retinue, makes his escape with Ênîte. So also in Chrestien's *Erec*. – *E* 6115ff.

Orîombates a commander in Dârîus's army against Alexander. In *Expeditio Alexandri* and Curtius Rufus, he is called Orontobates. – *A* 11656

Orise 'von Algoes', a warrior in Akarîn's army against Ipomidôn. – *JT* nm3093,1

Orcades see Morchades (2)

Orcamenis a warrior in the Greek army against the Trojans. In Dictys and Homer Orchomenius is the territorial name for Ialmenus, whilst it is the name of a person in Dares (Orchomenus) and Benoît (Orcomenis). In the last-named version, as in *LT*, he is slain by Hector. – *LT* 7442ff. [†]

Orkanîs 'von Griffûn', chamberlain to Meie, whom he accompanies to Rome. – *MB* 209,9

Orlendune 'der von' (*JT*), see Daries (1)

Ormaleis 'von Alamansura', a warrior in Akarîn's army against Ipomidôn. –*JT* nm3142,6

Orpries 'künec von Itolach', a knight who is present at a tourney held by Arthur. – *JT* 2023,4

Orsilôs see Orsines

Orsines a warrior in Dârîus's army against Alexander. He is later (14741ff.) called Orsilôs and reports to Alexander the treachery of Bessus. So also in *Expeditio Alexandri* and Curtius Rufus, where he is called Orsines. – *A* 11682ff.

Ortamîn 'künec von Lamperten', a knight who is unhorsed by Gayol (2) at the tourney for the hand of Acheloyde. In *Dem*, where he is called Ortanmîn von der Langbarten lant, he fights for Eghart against Dêmantîn and unhorses Ortân. – *Crane* a1416 n1509; *Dem* 5555

Ortân steward to Dêmantîn. He is unhorsed by Ortamîn in the battle between Dêmantîn and Eghart. – *Dem* 4780f.

Ortânes son of Achanes. This name does not appear in any of the known sources to *UA*. – *UA* nm6991

Ortanmîn see Ortamîn

Ortanne 'künec', a knight who is mentioned as having been defeated by Mügelein. – *Ll* nm41,7

Orte a giant. This name is probably intended to represent that of Orkise (var. Orco, Ocre), a giant who occurs in *Dietrichs erste Ausfahrt*. – *RB* nm25267

Ortolf (1) 'von Graetz', a knight who is present at the tourney held at Friesach and who jousts with Ulrich von Liechtenstein during the latter's *Venusfahrt*. – *FD* 195,4f.

Ortolf (2) 'von Kapfenberc', a knight who jousts with Ulrich von Liechtenstein during the latter's *Artusfahrt*. – *FD* 1434,3ff.

Ortolf (3) 'von Osterwizze', a knight who jousts with Ulrich von Liechtenstein during the latter's *Venusfahrt*. – *FD* 633,2f.

Oruogodelet a knight who is present at Arthur's court when Êrec returns with Ênîte. – *E* 1688

Orpfala wife of Carpius (q.v.). – *GT* m11451 an11519

Orphanus a goldsmith. – *FB* nm2029

Orphêe see Orfêus (1)

Orfêus (1) the famous musician of Greek mythology. – nm *Ed* 3107; *Tn* 4788; *PM* 1605; *RB* 22478

Orpheus (2)   a king who fights a brood of dragons in his land and dies of exhaustion. Paris and Hector, on their way to Greece, are just in time to save his three sons from another dragon. – *GT* nm11774ff.

Orphilet   a knight of the Round Table who fights with Kurâus (q.v.). Present at a tourney held by Arthur in *JT* is a knight called Orfilet, künec von Engellant. – *L* 679ff.; *JT* 1975,5

Osann   'von Prafant', a maiden whose father and mother are killed by Arminolt. She is championed by Fridrich (3) and brings an army to assist him against Mompolier. She afterwards marries Cuonrat (1). – *FS* a1852ff. n2193

Oseê   biblical (Hoshea), king of Israel. – *A* nm16782

Osias - biblical (Ahaziah, also called Jehoahaz), king of Judah. – *A* nm16309

Ospinel   see Opinâus

Otacker (1)   'von Wolkenstein', a knight who is present at the tourney held at Friesach. – *FD* 295,1

Otacker (2)   see Ottacker (1)

Ottacker (1)   'von Bêheim', father of Wenzelabe. – nm *UW* 8,24; *WW* 4346

Ottacker (2)   'Træge', a knight who jousts with Ulrich von Liechtenstein during the latter's *Venusfahrt*. – *FD* 698,2ff.

Otte (1)   'keiser', son of Heinrîch (1) (Otto I). In *Loh* he is left in charge of his father's country when the latter goes to fight against Gêrfridolt. – *JT* nm4005,5; *Loh* 3764f. [†]

Otte (2)   'der rote', 'keiser' (Otto II). – *Loh* m7382 n7401

Otte (3)   'keiser' (Otto III). – *Loh* nm7420f.

*Otte (3a)   'keiser' (Otto IV). – *W* nm 393,30

Otte (4)   'keiser', probably identical with Otte (1), (2) or (3). O. has a long beard, of which he is very proud, and by which he swears his most powerful oath. He sentences Heinrîch (15) to death on one occasion, but the latter, seizing O.'s beard, threatens to cut his throat unless he retracts his oath. Heinrîch is banished from the kingdom, but ten years later he is called upon by his overlord to serve in O.'s army. Here he witnesses a treacherous attempt by the burghers of a besieged town to murder O., and springing naked from his bath, he runs to the latter's assistance. For this service he receives a pardon. – *HK* 1

Otte (5)   'von Buches', a knight who is present at the tourney held at Friesach and who jousts with Ulrich von Liechtenstein during the latter's *Venusfahrt*. – *FD* 303,1

Otte (6)   'von Buochowe', a knight who dresses as a woman and jousts with Ulrich von Liechtenstein during the latter's *Venusfahrt*. – *FD* 685,2ff.

Otte (7)   'von Græze', a knight who is present at the tourney held at Friesach. – *FD* 195,3

Otte (8)   'von Haslowe', a knight who welcomes Ulrich von Liechtenstein to Neustadt during the latter's *Artusfahrt*. – *FD* 1489,1ff.

Otte (9)   'von Lengenbach', 'tuomvogt von Regensburg', a knight who is present at the tourney held at Friesach and who assists Ulrich von Liechtenstein in his disappearance after the close of his *Venusfahrt*. O. is also the last knight to joust with Ulrich at the tourney at Kornneuburg. – *FD* 191,3

Otte (10)   'von Meizen', a knight who is present at the tourney at Friesach. Karajan and Lachmann both considered O. identical with Otte (11).[11] – *FD* 299,1

Otte (11)   'von Mîssowe', a knight who welcomes Ulrich von Liechtenstein to Neustadt during his *Artusfahrt*. (See Otte (10).) – *FD* a1478,2f. n1527,1f.

Otte (12)   'von Ottenstein', a knight who jousts with Ulrich von Liechtenstein during the latter's *Venusfahrt* and is also present at the tourney held at Kornneuburg. – *FD* 887,3

---

11   Ulrich von Liechtenstein, *Frauendienst*, ed. by R. Bechstein, I, p. 107, to 299,1.

Otte (13) 'von Schœnkirchen', a knight who is present at the tourney held at Friesach. – *FD* 197,6

Otte (14) 'von Spengenberc', a knight who jousts with Ulrich von Liechtenstein during the latter's *Venusfahrt.* – *FD* 559,1

Otte (15) 'von dem Wasen', a knight who is present at the tourney held at Friesach. – *FD* 297,1

Ottêr 'von Brabant', a commander in Bêâmunt's army at Antrîûn. – *Dem* nm9836 a10902f.

Otzêr see Ottêr

Oukidant 'künec von Imanzîe', a warrior who assists in the arming of Terramêr. O. is slain by Rennewart in the second battle at Alischanz. O., who is also called (359,2) 'von Nôrûn', appears in the OF *Aliscans* as Malquidant. [See Appendix (5).] – *W* 356,10f.

Oukîn 'künec von Râbes', father of Poidwîz (1). In the second battle at Alischanz he sees his son's riderless horse, and he attacks Willehalm (1), by whom he is killed. On the first occasion he is mentioned he is called Ankî, but later (411,11 etc.) he appears as O. In the OF *Aliscans* he is called Aquin, and he occurs also in the *Enfances Vivien* and *Li Covenans Vivien.* [See Appendix (7).] – *W* nm36,24 a420,25

Ophantus a heathen god worshipped by Comandîon. – *Dem* nm7188

Ovid the Latin poet. – nm *Wigl* 991; *Port* 277; *JT* 99,6; *UA* 4899; *RB* 10772

Ôvîdîus see Ovid

Ofilart 'von Castilâ', a commander in Bêâmunt's army at Antrîûn. – *Dem* nm9799 a10827

Offe 'von Püten', brother of Heinrîch (24), a knight who is present at the tourney held at Friesach and who jousts with Ulrich von Liechtenstein during the latter's *Venusfahrt.* – *FD* 194,7

Offiart a knight who, at the commencement of the second fragment of *Dar*, is engaged in a fight with Darifant, which is won by the latter. – *Dar* a133 n193

Offosator 'von Zente', a warrior in Ipomidôn's army against Akarîn. – *JT* 3368,5

Offras 'von Pinte', a warrior in Ipomidôn's army against Akarîn. – *JT* nm3233,5

Offrat 'von Pardusibisse', a warrior in Ipomidôn's army against Akarîn. – *JT* 3263,4

Offratin 'herzoge zu Rutar', a knight who wounds Arthur whilst fighting in Marroch's army. – *Wigm* 3256

Oxîatres brother of Dârîus, for whom he fights against Alexander. In *UA*, where he is also called Exâtreus, O. is slain by Alexander during the battle at Erbela. O. occurs in all versions of the Alexander-history, except *SA* and *WA*. – *A* 4894; *UA* 1982 [†]

220

P

Pagrofitall a knight who takes part in the tourney held by Arthur for the crown of Deleprosat. – *Wigm* 2200

Palarei 'künec von Norwæge', a knight who is present at the tourney at which Reinfrit wins the love of Yrkâne. On one occasion (913) he is called 'künec von Engellant', but this appears to be a mistake, as everywhere else his land is given as Norwæge. – *RB* nm562ff. a912f.

Palatines uncle of Gayte, a knight who fights for Athis against Bilas. So also in the OF version, where he is slain by Bilas. – *AP* A*,118

Paldewein a knight of the Round Table who offers himself as a champion for Elsam. In MS K he is called 'markys von Purriel' but has no other name. The romances of the Vulgate Cycle give Bawdewyn as a variation of Banin, the godson of Ban (see Pant (1)), but there is no apparent connection between these two characters. – *Ll* 38,1 (MS K) a31,1

Paldriot, Paldryoth see Paltriot

Palestînus a king who is captured by Eresdes. This name does not occur in the passage in Pseudo-Methodius from which this part of *A* was taken. – *A* nm17165

Palidamas see Polidamus

Palietz 'von Mendisorie', a warrior in Ipomidôn's army against Akarîn. – *JT* nm3241,3

Paligan (1) accompanies Tristan and Kurvenal to Cornwall. – *UT* 782ff.

Paligân (2) see Bâligân

Palimedes a warrior in the Greek army against the Trojans. In *LT* he is chosen to succeed Agâmennon as leader of the Greek army, as the former commander had proved futile. P. is slain by Paris with arrows. This is the story as told in Dares and Benoît. In *TK* he himself suggests the alteration and is placed in command for the third battle, which the Greeks lose, and Agâmennon is reinstated. In Dictys, P. is slain by Ulixes and Dyomedes whilst he is still in command of the Greeks. He does not occur in Homer. – *LT* 3085; *TK* 30670f.

Palimenis 'von Iotharus', a warrior who is slain by Hector whilst fighting for the Greeks against the Trojans. This character is probably identical with the Polimenès who, in Benoît, is slain by Ampon (see Arpon). Iotharus is nowhere mentioned in Benoît. – *LT* 7474

Palimunder 'von Panfilje', a warrior in the Trojan army against the Greeks. This character was invented by Konrad. – *TK* 24854

Pallas (1) 'götinne', one of the three goddesses, amongst whom Paris has to decide which is the most beautiful. In *GT* she offers Paris an army of knights for the apple which Terius has given him, but her offer is refused. – *Ed* 1085; *E* nm8203; *LT* nm969; *C* nm8288; *FB* nm1587ff.; *JT* nm5298,5; *TK* 1038; *UA* nm3092; *RB* nm16408; *GT* nm1926ff. a2009; *GM* nm3566

Pallas (2) son of Êvander, who is made a knight so that he can accompany Ênêâs to Albani, where he is slain by Turnus. He is buried with great pomp, and his grave remains undiscovered until the day Fridrich (1) is crowned in Rome. P. occurs also in the OF *Eneas* and in Virgil. – *Ed* 6080f.

Palltinor a wild man, who is rescued by Seyfrid from a dragon. – *Sey* a151,6 n155,1

Palmsin 'marcgrâve', a knight who is present at a tourney held by Arthur. – *JT* 1988,6

Palomîdes see Palimedes

Palprimes (1) son of Bâligân. He and his father are both killed in the battle against Charlemagne (see Karl (1)). The story is told in the *Rolandslied*, where P. is called Malprimes. Malprimes occurs as a variant of P. in several MSS of *W*. – *W* nm441,12f. [†]

Palprimes (2) son of Purrel. P. is probably named by Wolfram after Palprimes (1), who is his uncle. In *Les Narbonnais* (3825) Palprimes (MS M: Malprimes) is mentioned together with Borrel (= Purrel). Malprimes occurs as a variant of P. in several MSS of *W.* – *W* a358,25 n428,14 [†]

Palterius 'von Pontte', husband of Orgaloyse and father of Nectarus. – *GT* a4432ff. n4696

Palteruss see Palterius

Paltriot 'künec von Lendrie', father of Wigamur. P. visits Arthur's court, and, whilst he is away, Wigamur is stolen by Lespia. P. is next seen fighting with Atroclas for the land of Amolot, P.'s cousin. Wigamur, who as the champion of Atroclas is just about to fight his father in single combat, discloses his upbringing, and his father recognizes him. The fight is abandoned, and P. and Atroclas are reconciled. – *Wigm* 4ff.

Paltryoth, Paltriotht see Paltriot

Palwîn standard-bearer for Meie, whilst the latter is fighting in Spain. – *MB* 114,17f.

Pamplus killed many of the Greeks on their return from Troy by toppling a rock over on to their ships. This character, who does not appear in any other version of the Trojan legend, appears to be one of the few characters invented by Herbort. – *LT* a17137 n17148

Pamphilias 'künec von Persiâ', a warrior in the Trojan army against the Greeks. This character was invented by Konrad. – *TK* 24840f.

Pamphilomîs a warrior who is slain by Troilus whilst fighting for the Greeks against the Trojans. His land is Alitrieht. This character was invented by Konrad. – *TK* 31596

Pandachîn 'künec', brother of Harturam. P., who is a heathen, tries to take Gayol's kingdom after the death of Dassir, but Assundîn, who is in charge of the kingdom, repels the attack and kills P. – *Crane* nm1472f.

Pandalus see Pandarus (2)

Pandaron a knight who fights for Bilas against Athis. P. does not appear in the OF version. – *AP* C,9

Pandarus (1) brother of Bêcias. They are two giants whom Ênêâs leaves in Albanî and who do great damage among the army of Turnus. In the OF *Eneas*, P. and his brother are ordinary Trojan warriors, and it is probable that P. is, therefore, identical with Pandarus (2). – *Ed* 7096ff.

Pandarus (2) 'von Sicilien', a warrior in the Trojan army against the Greeks. On the first occasion he is named in *LT*, P. is called Pyndarus, but later (6843, etc.) the correct form is used. P. occurs in all versions of the Trojan legend, and in *TKf* (43380), where he is called Pander von Celia, his death is lamented by the Trojans, although it has not been described. – *LT* 3979; *MC* nm50; *TK* 24858f.

Pander see Pandarus (2)

Pandragon elder brother of Uter (q.v.). He succeeds Wertigier as king of Britain and fights against Angurs, whom he defeats with the help of Uter, but he is slain in the battle. The story is told thus in the *Estoire de Merlin* (Vulgate Cycle). (See also Utepandragûn.) – *Mer* 67,4ff.

Pandragun see Utepandragûn

Pandulet husband of Pheradzoye (q.v.). P. is slain by Dêmantîn. – *Dem* m3020 n3092 a3320

Pannilius a Trojan who sees Hector returning to Troy with Pictorie. – *GT* 13264

Pannt 'künec', who had sold the land of Deleferant to Amolot. – *Wigm* nm3508

Panolope see Penelope

Panpor a warrior in the Trojan army against the Greeks. – *GT* nm22764

Pansâmûrs father of Lîahturteltart and husband of Bêâflûrs. They are said (*P* 87,29) to be 'von der feien art'. – *P* nm87,28

Panschavar 'künec von Asia', brother of Zaradech (q.v.) and Japhîte. He fights for Wigalois against Lîôn. – *Wigl* a9208ff. n9224

Pansor 'künec von Salanie', a knight who is present at a tourney held by Arthur. This name is first mentioned in 2862,3f. but it is probably identical with Pantschier, who is also present. P. later fights for Schîonatulander against Ipomidôn. – *JT* 1713,5

Pant (1) 'künec von Genewîs', husband of Clârîne (1) and father of Lanzelet. P. is a harsh ruler, and his people rebel, killing him during the revolt. It has been shown that Pant is a form of the OF name Banz (> Bant > Pant),[1] which Brugger identifies with the Gaelic word for white,[2] whilst Genewîs, Gomeret, and Benoic are forms of one and the same name,[3] the form Benewijc in the Dutch *Lancelot* apparently showing an intermediate form between Benoic and Genewîs. Banz is first mentioned in Chrestien's *Erec*, where he is called Bans de Gomoret (MS B: bauz). It is evident that the alternative form of *bauz*, viz. *beals*, stood in the MS used by Hartmann, who calls him 'künec Beâls von Gomoret', one of the five young kings who attend the wedding of Êrec (see also Quioques). The conception of P. as a tyrant is unusual; in the OF versions he is the victim of treachery after an unprovoked attack by Claudas (see Cladas). The story is told in full in the Vulgate *Lancelot* and in Füetrer's *Prosaroman von Lanzelot*. The relevant portion of the Dutch *Lancelot* is missing, but it is clear from a later reference (I, 14967ff.), where he is referred to as 'Die coninc Ban,/ die goede man,/ Die van rouwen starf', that this version follows the OF story. Gomoret has been thought by some scholars to be the origin of the name Gahmuret (q.v.). – *E* 1977; *L* 44

Pant (2) a warrior in the Trojan army against the Greeks. This character appears to have been invented by the author of *TKf*. – *TKf* 47447f.

Pantalêôn 'sant', his monastery in Cologne is mentioned. (St. Pantaleone, a popular Venetian saint.) – *Loh* nm7394

Pantanor the first owner of Arofel's sword, which he passed on to Salatrê. The name is mentioned as Plantamor only in a variant reading of *Aliscans*. – *W* nm77,24

Panthelamon 'künec von Barbarîe', a warrior in the Trojan army against the Greeks. This character was invented by Konrad. – *TK* 24902f.

Panthus a warrior in the Trojan army against the Greeks. He is one of the few Trojans who believe the tragic predictions of Elenus regarding the visit of Paris to Greece. P., who appears in all versions of the Trojan legend, is, in *TK*, the son of Euforbes (q.v.). – *LT* 2293; *TK* 19227

Pantimulus see Pantinmuls

Pantinmuls 'künec von Schotten', nephew of Agâmennon. He fights for the Greeks against the Trojans and challenges Hector, who kills him. – *GT* 18377f.

Pantschier see Pansor

Pantus see Panthus

Panfigâl 'ein barûn', a warrior who is slain by Hûpolt whilst fighting for the Greeks against the Trojans. This character was invented by Konrad. – *TK* 31804ff.

Panfileiz 'von Culmenîe', a warrior in the Trojan army against the Greeks. This character was invented by Konrad. – *TK* 24914

---

1   Bruce (1), I, p. 404, note 76.
2   Brugger (1), p. 84.
3   Bruce (1), I, p. 404, note 76.

Panfilias see Pamphilias

Panfilôt 'von Clerimûn', a Greek knight who lies wounded and lends Paris his sword. Paris afterwards carries him to safety. This character was invented by Konrad. – *TK* a35106 n35446

Panfilus one of the counsellors who are consulted by Agâmennon as to a reward for Paris. – *GT* 3723

Panfimeiz 'künec', a warrior in the Trojan army against the Greeks. This character was invented by Konrad. – *TK* 30224

Papires see Papirîs

Papirîs 'künec von Trogodjente'. (Martin identifies this name with Papirius, a name mentioned in Solinus (17,17 and 147,6), with the ending -*is* for Latin -*ius* apparently from the Low German form.[4]) P. is one of the knights whom Feirefîz states that he has overcome. In *JT* he takes part in the tourney held by Sekundille to decide which of the wooers shall win her hand. – *P* nm770,1; *JT* nm3215,6

Parabel 'von Brunswige', a knight who is present at a tourney held by Arthur. – *JT* 2083,5

Paranîs chamberlain to Îsolt (2), whom he accompanies to Cornwall. In *ET* he is called Perenîs, but *UT* and *HT* follow the form Paranîs in *Tn*. He appears as Peronis in the *Volksbuch* and Hans Sachs,[5] and it is interesting to note that the same form appears in Fragment III (41) of the very early MS of *ET*. – *ET* 1769; *Tn* 9322; *UT* 1505; *HT* 4756f.

Paranîsel 'der', see Paranîs

Parasidap 'der alte von Kananie', a warrior in Akarîn's army against Ipomidôn. – *JT* nm3141,5f.

Pardies 'von Partine', a warrior in Ipomidôn's army against Akarîn. – *JT* nm3217,1

Pardigrisun see Pardrigun

Pardiscale wife of Gloris, from whom she is abducted by Klinschor for Agors (see Strangedorz). She is rescued by Parzivâl. – *JT* m5538,5 n5548,6 a5577,1

Pardischal, Pardistal see Pardiscale

Pardrigun son of Akarîn and father of Jermidol. P. appears also as Bardigris and Pardigrisun. – *JT* nm2835,3ff.

Pargaltt a knight who, with six men, attacks Paris and Thedalus whilst they are out hunting. P. is killed by Paris, and his men are put to flight. – *GT* a2802ff. n2826

Parikoleis 'der riche von Tervilans', a warrior in Ipomidôn's army against Akarîn. – *JT* nm3235,1 a3674,1

Parilas a knight who takes part in the tourney held by Arthur for the crown of Deleprosat. (Identical with Parille (2)?) – *Wigm* 2448

Parille (1) son of Senebor (q.v.), also called Barille. P. occurs in *WO*, where he fights on the side of the heathens in the final battle against the Christians, whilst in *JT* he has become a Christian, and as father of Titurisone and grandfather of Titurel he is the founder of the Graal dynasty. The name was evidently taken from *JT* into *WO*. – *JT* nm90,1; *WO* nm 12280f. a16404f.

Parille (2) a knight who is present at Arthur's court. (Identical with Parilas?) – *GM* (MS I) 3862

Paris son of Priam. In *LT*, as in Benoît, there is no suggestion of anything unusual about P.'s childhood. He recounts how he was visited by the three goddesses whilst he was out hunting, and he decides Venus to be the most beautiful. She promises him the most

---

4   Martin (1), p. 502, to 770,1.
5   Gottfried von Straßburg, *Tristan und Isolde*, transl. by W. Hertz, p. 587.

beautiful woman on earth and tells him that she is in Greece. The Trojans make her abduction the pretext for their expedition against the Greeks, although they are really going to avenge Esîonâ and the insult to Antenor. The abduction story follows the usual lines. Later, at the request of his mother, he lays the trap for Achilles and slays him. He is himself slain shortly afterwards in battle by Ajax (1). In *TK* and *GT* his childhood is told as in the Greek legend. Ecubâ, warned by a dream of the trouble which her unborn son is to cause, commands a knight to kill him as soon as he is born. Touched by the baby's innocent laugh, he abandons it in a wood, where it is found and brought up by a shepherd. In *TK* the boy is made arbiter in all the petty quarrels of the other boys, who give him the name Paris 'dur sîn gelîchez reht' (i.e. Konrad derives the name from Latin *par*.) He falls in love with Oenônê, who returns his love. Jupiter calls him to the wedding of Thetis and Pêleus to decide to whom the apple from Discordia shall be given, and he awards it to Venus. A quarrel breaks out between Jupiter and Priam, both of whom wish to have Paris for their court. The question is decided by single combat between Hector and Pêleus, and, as the former wins, P. goes to Troy, where he is followed by his foster-father, who makes known the circumstances of P.'s childhood, and his true identity is discovered. He is slain in *TKf* by Pfiloctêtâ. In *GT* he is visited by the goddesses whilst he is minding his flock, and they tell him of his birth. He goes at once to Greece, where he distinguishes himself in the service of Agâmennon, who makes him a knight. After countless episodic adventures, he meets with Hector, who takes him to Troy. The two brothers then go back to Greece, where Hector advises P. to abduct Helen, which he does. P. is killed when Troy is taken. In *Ed* he is seen by Ênêâs in Hades. – *Ed* nm6 a3325; *LT* nm1664ff. a2164; *MC* nm20; *C* nm526; *FB* nm1587ff.; *Port* nm21; *M* nm589; *TK* m346f. a381 n662; *UA* nm4874; *RB* nm20166; *GT* m834f. a1318f. n1912; *GM* nm3561; *FS* nm4830

Parissulais 'von Lotte', a warrior in Akarîn's army against Ipomidôn. – *JT* 3633,1

Parkeis see Parkis

Parkîe one of the ladies who fail in the test of the glove of chastity which is sent to Arthur's court by Giramphiel. – *C* 24025

Parkis 'von Arobeise', also called 'von Arboleise' a warrior who is slain by Killikrates (1) whilst fighting for Akarîn against Ipomidôn. – *JT* 3122,5

Parkisudol 'von Sinoffale', a warrior in Akarîn's army against Ipomidôn. – *JT* nm3128,1

Parklise a beautiful sorceress in the service of Crispin. Riding on a griffin, she poses as a messenger from Mahmet and rescues Wildhalm, who has been condemned to die for slaying Wildomis. She brings Wildhalm to fight Merlin for Crispin. – *WO* a10868 n10909

Parlasîn an enemy of Tristan at the court of Marke. He informs Antrêt when Tristan is having a nocturnal meeting with Îsolt (2). This is the only mention of P. in all the Tristan romances. The MSS read: (D) parlagin, (B) barlasein, (H) parsalem. – *ET* 8268

Parludiezze 'künec von Damian', a warrior in Akarîn's army against Ipomidôn. – *JT* nm3092,1

Parlus 'von Wintsester', a knight who is present at the tourney at which Reinfrit wins the love of Yrkâne. On one occasion he is called (576) 'von Berbester' (see Leran), and once he is referred to (1057) as 'von Schotten'. – *RB* nm292f. a576

Parmelie *amie* of Prandidones. She appears after the latter has been slain by Hector. – *GT* a13045f. n13081

Parmenan, Parmeneis see Parmênîôn

Parmênîôn one of the chief princes in Alexander's army. He is jealous of Philipp (3) and warns Alexander against drinking the doctor's potion, which, he claims, is poisoned. Alexander drinks it notwithstanding and is cured. In *A*, where he is initially called

Parmênîus, and *SA*, where he is called Parmetrus, P. is beheaded for this, but in *UA*, where he is called Permêniô, he acts in good faith and no action is taken against him (so too in Curtius Rufus). Rudolf took this incident from Leo but did not realise that the Parmenion of Curtius Rufus and Leo's Parmetrus were one and the same person, and he introduces Parmênîôn later as the father of Nicânor (1), Philôtas, and Hector (2). As in *UA* and Curtius Rufus, P. is implicated in the plot to murder Alexander and is (justly in *A*, unjustly in *UA* and Curtius Rufus) slain at the command of Alexander. Leo does not mention the conspiracy against the life of Alexander, but even in this version P. appears again after he has been slain.[6] A similar confusion appears to exist in Valerius, where it is stated (85,20) that after the failure of his attempt to slander Philipp 'poenas capite dependit', whilst he appears constantly after this. – *A* 5774 (Parmênîus), 5886 (Parmênîôn); *UA* 2129; *SA* 1875; *WA* 983f. [†]

Parmênîus see Parmênîôn

Parmetra, Parmetrus see Parmênîôn

Parssap 'von Karlisibunse', a warrior in Akarîn's army against Ipomidôn. – *JT* 3194,1f.

Parthîe 'vrouwe', one of the ladies at Arthur's court who spill Priure's cup of chastity. – *C* 1398

Parthonopêjus see Partônopeus

Partigal 'der von' (*JT*), see Karforas

Partinias 'der unsinnige', nephew of Espinogres and slayer of Gouns Wueste. He is killed by Parzivâl with the sword with which he slew Gouns Wueste. In Manessier he is called Pertiniel. – *RP* m617,13f. n620,1 a831,20

Partiuir a knight who is present at Arthur's court. – *GM* (MS D) 38576

Partônopeus 'herzoge' a warrior who is slain during the battle between Polinices and Ethiocles. In *Ed* he is seen by Ênêâs in Hades. – *Ed* 3315; *UA* nm3157

Partonopier 'grâve von Bleis', son of Lucrête. He is brought up by his uncle, Clogiers, and, whilst still a youth, he loses himself one day at a hunt and is carried by a mysterious ship to a castle, where his wants are attended to by invisible hands. During the night he is visited in bed by Meliûr, and after a mutual declaration of love, she tells him that he must not see her face for three and a half years, after which time she will marry him, but in the meantime he must stay in that castle and its grounds, seeing nobody. Twice, however, P. gets permission to go home, and on the second occasion his mother persuades him to take back a light with him, so that he can see Meliûr's face during one of her nightly visits. He does this and discovers that she is marvellously beautiful, but Meliûr banishes him for ever from her sight. P. returns home but decides to seek death from the wild beasts in the forest of Ardenne. He manages to evade Fursîn (2), his companion, and lives on herbs in the forest until he is found by Irekel, who restores him to health. Meliûr holds a tourney to decide on a husband, and P. being the winner, they are reconciled. The poem breaks off during a battle with the Soldan of Persia, who was P.'s most conspicuous rival during the tourney for Meliûr's hand. – *PM* a256 n280

Partriban a knight who is present at Arthur's court. – *GM* (MS I) 3864

Partzefal, Partzifal see Parzivâl

Parfoias 'cuns von Lampregûn', a knight whom Parzivâl states that he has overcome. (Identical with Parfulas?) – *P* nm772,16

Parfulas 'grâve von Grede', a knight who is present at a tourney held by Arthur. (Identical with Parfoias?) – *JT* 2014,6

---

6   See. Leo, pp. 83 and 95.

Parcefâl see Parzivâl

Parcilôt 'von Campfelîe', a warrior who is slain by Paris whilst fighting for the Greeks against the Trojans. This character was invented by Konrad. – *TK* 31294

Parcinier a knight who is present at Arthur's court. – *GM* (MS I) 3864

Parzivâl (The OF form of this name is Perceval, which Schulz thought was an attempt to reproduce the Celtic Peredur, which he derived from *peredd*, 'sweetness', and *ur*, 'extreme'.[7] There is little doubt, however, that the OF form is the original one,[8] and Martin derives this from the OF *perce*, 'pierce', and *val*, which he finds inexplicable.[9] French poems assume that the meaning is 'pierce the valley' (an etymology which is accepted by Bruce;[10] in Godefroy *val* is not given with the meaning of valley.[11]) Wolfram (*P* 140,17) says: 'der name ist rehte mitten durch', whilst *C* (6390f.) states: 'Wan parce sprichet durch,/ Val ein tal oder ein vurch'.)

P. is first mentioned in Chrestien's *Erec*, but he is not included among the first ten knights at Arthur's court. In *Perceval* (*P* in MHG), he is, however, the best of the knights, better even than Gawein. In *P* he is the son of Gahmuret and is born after the death of his father. His mother, Herzeloide, tries to bring him up in ignorance of knighthood, but his father's blood stirs in the boy at an early age, and he goes to Arthur's court to be made a knight. His early actions are marked by his ignorance of the world, until he meets Gurnemanz, who instructs him in the rules of chivalry. He marries Kondwîrâmûrs, whom he frees from the oppression of Klâmidê but leaves to seek his mother. He arrives at the Graal Castle, where, owing to the lessons he has received from Gurnemanz, he suppresses the question of sympathy which springs to his lips. For this neglect he is blamed by Kundrîe (1) before the assembled Round Table, and his shame drives him forth, to wander for more than four and a half years, during which time he loses faith in God. Wolfram gives glimpses of P. during this time, tributes to his prowess and his character, as when he scornfully refuses the proffered hand of Orgelûse. His conversion is carried out by his uncle, Trevrezent, a hermit with whom he spends some days, and when next he joins the Round Table company, after an undecided fight with Gawein, he is ready for the change in his fortunes, which Kundrîe comes to announce. He is the predestined successor to Amfortas as the Graal King, and with Kondwîrâmûrs and Lohengrîn, he goes again to the Graal Castle, formally asks the question of sympathy, and is installed as Graal King.

Chrestien's poem, which was left unfinished, does not reach as far as P.'s return to Arthur's court, and three later OF poets provided continuations of the work, which were translated into MHG in *RP*, which the translators inserted between Books XIV and XV of *P*; in this interpolation, however, P. has lost all the individuality which he possesses in Chrestien and *P*, particularly the latter, and has become a typical knight, achieving innumerable meaningless adventures. He falls in love with a girl who owns a self-playing chess-board, but has to hunt for the head of a white hart before she will reward his love. In the course of this quest, he meets and defeats Abrioris and der schöne Böse, visits Kondwîrâmûrs, who is not his wife (so also in Chrestien), arrives at his home and meets his sister (*P* knows of no sister), and eventually recovers the hart's head, which he brings to the maiden. He leaves her to seek the Graal and meets a Graal maiden, who directs him over a glass bridge, giving

---

7   Schulz, 'Eigennamen', pp. 405ff.
8   Bruce (1), I, p. 252, note.
9   Martin (1), p. 141, to 140,17.
10 Bruce (1), I, p. 251, note 35.
11 Godefroy, *Dictionnaire de l'ancienne langue française*.

him a mule with a wonderful bridle and a ring with a magic stone to enable him to cross. On the other side he meets Brios and crosses Karmedit's bridge to a tourney which is being held by Arthur before the Castle Orgelus. He releases Bagumades, visits Blanschemor's chapel, and eventually reaches the Graal Castle, where he fits the two parts of the sword together. He then learns that he has to avenge the death of Gouns Wueste on Partinias, which he starts out to do. With Segremors he delivers a maiden from her persecutors, drives the evil spirit out of Blanschemor's chapel, and is visited by the devil, firstly in the guise of a knight, and then in the form of Kondwîrâmûrs, with whom P. is just about to lie, when he makes the sign of the cross, and the devil vanishes. P. is taken away in a boat by a priest, and on landing, fights with Menader, Gafyens, and Arides. Leaving Kondwîramûrs, he meets der schöne Böse, who is wounded in rescuing two maidens from being burned to death. He is unable to return to Arthur's court by Pentecost as arranged, and 25 knights go in search of him. After a successful visit to a tourney, P. and der schöne Böse part, the latter going to Arthur's court, and the former to find Partinias, whom he kills, taking his head back to Amfortas, who is cured when he catches sight of it. P. leaves after refusing the kingdom, and after defeating Saladres and his sons, arrives back at Arthur's court to take his place in Book XV of P.

The remainder of P.'s appearances in MHG literature are of the usual episodic nature associated with the minor characters in the Court Epics.

– E1512; *Wigl* nm6329; *P* m4,14ff. n39,26 a112,5ff.; *DB* 288; *W* nm4,20; *T* nm81,4; *C* nm1547 a2208; *RW* nm2181; *Blan* nmII,60; *FD* nmBüchlein I, 167; *G* nm4187; *Dem* nm1207; *JT* nm18,7 a1078,1f.; *TF* nm2540; *Sey* nm311,7; *Loh* nm457 a485; *UA* nm1708; *RB* nm8922ff.; *GM* (MS I) 3866 (MS D) 3857; *WO* nm12291; *RP* Prol. m261ff. n279 a22,31; *FS* nm4815; *Ll* nm23,7 a28,5 (MS K) 11,5 [†]

Pasilius, Pasirius see Passirius

Passacrius 'von Ituleise', a warrior in Ipomidôn's army against Akarîn. – *JT* 3230,5

Passigweiz (1) son of Terramêr, for whom he fights against Willehalm (1) at Alischanz. In *R* he is married to Bearosine. P. is called Persagués (var. Passeguez) in the OF *Aliscans*. – *W* a29,18f. n32,12; *R* Bl. II,35

Passigweiz (2) a warrior who, with Thedalûn, is left in charge of Alexander's people whilst the latter is on his campaigns. This character does not appear in any other version of the Alexander history. – *UA* a2361 n2381

Passirius a dwarf who is sent with eleven others by Acharon to assist Agâmennon at Troy. The latter scorns their offer, and they slay 5,000 Greeks and join the Trojan forces, for whom they do great deeds until they are recalled by Achanayss. Later (21307) P. receives Eleander and Amalita on their return from Hannor, and fights and defeats Melyoss for Eleander. – *GT* a14316f. n14335

Passirus see Passirius

Passural 'von Passurille', a warrior in Ipomidôn's army against Akarîn. – *JT* nm3241,2

Patoclus see Patroclus

Patryoth see Paltriot

Patris 'von dem Berge', a knight who is one of five who attack Gawein and Agravains. P. is overcome by the latter. In the Manessier continuation of *Perceval* he is called Patris de la Montagne tinte (MS Montpellier: mat) et morne. It seems possible that he is identical with Patricjus von den Bîgen, the father of Ade and brother of Lînier in *L.* – *L* nm1540; *RP* a718,1 n719,31

Patricjus see Patris

Patrokel, Patroclos see Patroclus

Patroclus a warrior in the Greek army against the Trojans. In *TK*, as in the *Achilleis* of Statius, he is brought up by Cheiron with Achilles, and the two are close friends. In all versions he is slain by Hector, and his death spurs Achilles on to greater deeds against the Trojans. In *GT* he is called 'von Thabal'. – *LT* 2839; *TK* 6472; *GT* 16522ff.

Pâtrôn (1) a warrior who leaves Alexander to join Dârîus. In *A* he remains faithful to Dârîus to the end, but in *UA* he leaves Dârîus and rejoins Alexander after trying in vain to convince Dârîus of the treachery planned by Bessus. P. occurs in Curtius Rufus and Gualterus. – *A* 14248ff.; *UA* 16097ff.

Pâtrôn (2) son of Antipater, at whose request he gives poison to Alexander. (See Jobas.) – *UA* m26644 an26857ff.

Pauls see Paulus

Paulus (St. Paul). (See also Saul (2).) – nm *MB* 66,40; *A* 17435; *Loh* 6350; *UA* 6291; *RB* 13438; *WO* 18170

Pâusânîâ 'künec von Bitînîâ', also called (in *SA*) 'von Britania'. P. attacks Greece and mortally wounds Philipp (1) whilst Alexander is away fighting Nikolâus. Alexander returns in time to kill P. and inform the dying Philipp. In *UA* he attacks and kills Philipp when the latter is alone with Olimpias before his palace. P. abducts Olimpias, who is rescued by Alexander, who slays P. He is called Pausônias in *UA*, a form which also occurs in Lampreht, whilst in Leo he is not a king but 'in Macedonia quidam homo nomine Pausania . . . subjectus Philippo'. Zingerle points out, however, that he is called king of Bythinia in MS S of Leo.[12] P. occurs also in Pseudo-Callisthenes and Valerius. – *A* 924f.; *UA* 2024; *SA* 1087f.; *WA* 576ff.

Pâusippus a warrior who is captured by Alexander whilst fighting for Dârîus. So also in Curtius Rufus, where he is called Pasippus. – *A* 7637

Pausônias see Pâusânîâ

Pavelun 'diu von dem', sister of Alardin, whom she accompanies to the tourney between Ris and Cadoalans. – *RP* 70,7ff.

Pafort a knight who attends Leigamar's tourney in the service of Aram. – *C* 18172

Pacîân see Pacîôn

Pacîôn a commander in Bêâmunt's army at Antrîûn. – *Dem* nm9819 a10894f.

Peatrise see Beatrise

Pehpimerôt a knight who is present at Arthur's court when Êrec returns with Ênîte. This name does not appear in Chrestien's *Erec*. – *E* 1687

Peilnetôsî the name assumed by Tristan whilst disguised as a fool at Marke's court. This word is obviously an invention of Heinrich, who made it by inverting 'Îsôten liep', the idea originating, no doubt, with the Tantris episode of the earlier writers. – *HT* nm5327

Pêkulâus one of the conspirators with Dimnus against the life of Alexander. So also in Gualterus, and Curtius Rufus, where he is called Peucolaus. – *A* nm18886

Pelagrîn 'künec von Marroch', a warrior in the Trojan army against the Greeks. This character was invented by Konrad. – *TK* 24898

Pelaie second wife of Lohengrîn. P. is afraid of losing her husband as Elsam lost him, and a waiting woman advises her to eat a piece of his flesh. She refuses to entertain the suggestion, but the woman arranges with P.'s relatives to cut a piece of flesh out of his side whilst he is asleep. Lohengrîn wakes up and is mortally wounded in the ensuing fight; he is followed to the grave by Pelaie, who dies of a broken heart. – *JT* 5921,2ff.

---

[12] O. Zingerle, p. 54.

Pêlân 'künec von Ungerlant', who leads his hordes against the Christians and is routed by Heinrîch (1). – *Loh* 2831

Pelde brother of Efroi, a knight at the tourney held by Leigamar. – *C* 18049

Peleas uncle of Jason and brother of Êson. P. is jealous of Jason's popularity and sends him to fetch the Golden Fleece in the hope that he will not return alive. In *TK* he is confused with Pêleus (1) (q.v.). P. occurs in Dares and Benoît, but is not mentioned in Dictys. – *LT* 100

Pêleus (1) father of Achilles and husband of Thetis. At his wedding he fights Hector in single combat for the possession of Paris and loses. He is confused with Peleas (the confusion is also to be found in Benoît (149ff.), but only in this one place, and not throughout as in *TK*), and is jealous of his nephew Jason, because the latter is the only rival to Achilles as the noblest of the Greeks. This enmity is the cause of his death, as Medea (q.v.), when she returns with Jason, gives incorrect instructions to his daughters, when they wish to rejuvenate P., and he bleeds to death. This is the story as it is told in *TK*. In *LT*, as in Benoît and Dictys, he is imprisoned by his father-in-law, Acastus, and released by his grandson, Pirrus. In Dares it is only recorded of him that he fought against the Trojans during the siege. – *LT* nm6289 a17914; *TK* nm850 a3618; *UA* nm4878

Peleus (2) see Peleas

Pelias see Peleas

Pelycân see Belakâne

Pelin see Belin

Peliot squire in the service of Îsolt (2), for whom he carries messages to Tristan. P. is probably identical with Pîloise (q.v.). – *UT* nm1840 a2467

Pelifrant a warrior who is slain whilst fighting for the Trojans against the Greeks. This character was invented by Konrad. – *TK* 36312

Pellêus 'Antoclar', a warrior in Dârîus's army. This character appears to have been invented by Ulrich. – *UA* nm3527f.

Pelliur 'der', a name under which Alexander is often referred to in *UA*. In Gualterus, Alexander is often referred to as Pellaeus, an adjective derived from Pella, Alexander's birthplace. – *UA* nm10706

Pelops mythical king of Phrygia, grandfather of Agâmennon. In Greek legend he was killed by his father and cut up and served to the gods for food, but was restored to life. P. was the father of Thyestes (see Thiesti). – *TKf* nm41291

Pelrapiere 'der junge ûz' (*JT*), see Kardeiz (1)

Penelêus a warrior who is slain by Euripilus (1) whilst fighting for the Greeks against the Trojans. So also in Dictys. This character is mentioned in Homer, but no reference is made to his death. – *TKf* 44982f.

Penelope the faithful wife of Ulixes. In *GT* she is said to have been slain by Eleander. – *LT* nm17764f.; *RB* nm24534; *GT* nm14746 a19934

Penielle 'küneginne von Indien', whom Paris succours from the oppression of Abigal. – *GT* m7300 n7317 a8648

Penile see Penielle

Penylle (1) daughter of Lanzelet. She reads the message of the Graal concerning the plight of Elsam. In *Ll* (MS K) she is called Benedige. – *Loh* nm458 a477; *Ll* (MS K) 15,8

Penille (2) see Penielle

Penitenze 'bischof', dedicated the temple of the Graal. – *JT* 415,1

Pentesileâ queen of the Amazons. In *LT*, as in Dares and Benoît, she joins the side of the Trojans against the Greeks when she hears of the death of Hector, Troilus, and Paris. She and her Amazons are valiant fighters, but P. is slain by Pirrus. In Dictys and *TKf* she arrives at Troy immediately after the death of Hector, of which she has not heard. She is slain in her first battle by Achilles, who wishes her to have a fitting burial, but Dyomedes commands her body to be thrown into the river. P. is not mentioned in Homer. – *LT* nm4794 a14374; *TKf* nm40588ff. a42183ff.

Penuell, Penuill, Penulle see Penielle

Perdica see Perdikkas

Perdikkas a warrior in Alexander's army. In *A* he is mortally wounded in the second battle with Dârîus, but in *WA* Alexander on his deathbed gives him Roxane and bequeaths Macedonia to him, whilst in *SA*, where he is said to be Alexander's uncle, he is elected emperor by the people after the death of Alexander. P. occurs in all versions of the Alexander history. – *A* 6993; *UA* 4711; *SA* 8630ff.; *WA* 6242ff.

Perenîs see Paranîs

Pereotestes to whom Alexander bequeathed Babylon. P. does not occur in any other history of Alexander. – *SA* nm8535f.

Pergalt 'herzoge von' (*JT*), see Retân

Perhtuleis 'von Silerete', a knight who is present at a tourney held by Arthur. – *JT* 2062,1

Periculeis see Parikoleis

Perilamor a knight who is present in the castle which Seyfrid frees from Rubel and Schruter. – *Sey* 135,6

Peringer 'künec' (Berengar, king of Lombardy). P. was defeated by Otte (1). – *Loh* nm7355

Peritheus son of Theseus (5). In Fragment F, P. is lying on his deathbed, but from the OF version of *AP* we learn that he is in love with Gayte and challenges Thelamon to a battle in order to prove his valour. He is mortally wounded in the second of the battles that result. In the OF romance he is called Pirithous. – *AP* E,1ff.

Permêniô see Parmênîon

*Peronis see Paranîs

Perre see Pirre

Perrin father of Dietherich. P. fights for Willehalm (3) against Jofrit (1) and is present at the *swertleite* of Willehalm (4). – *RW* 523

Persanîs daughter of Milête, a maiden who, with Irekel, nurses Partonopier back to health. – *PM* 11136ff.

Perseus (1) a warrior in the Trojan army against the Greeks. P. is identical with 'Xerses, künec von Morlant' in *LT*, and appears in Dares as Perses ex Aethiopia, and in Benoît as Sersès (var. Persès). P. does not appear in Homer. – *LT* 4049ff.; *TK* 30164

Perseus (2) in Greek mythology, the son of Danaë by Jupiter. – *UA* nm6985

Persevâus see Parzivâl

Persia 'der von' (*JT*), see Gloramatis

Persia 'künec von' (*LT*), see Mennon (2)

Persia 'künec von' (*W*), see Arofel

Persian 'herre über alles Kaukasas'. – *WO* nm2103f.

Persistas king of Egypt. This is apparently a biblical reference, but no king of this name is mentioned in the Bible. – *A* nm16789

Persît (1) a maiden attendant on Gîburc, whom she accompanies on her flight with Willehalm (1) from Tîbalt. – *UW* 132,23

Persit (2) 'künec von Marroch', father of Wildomis and Fel. P. makes a practice of killing all messengers who are sent to him. Knowing this, Walwan (3) sends Wildhalm to him, but

P. spares him, and, learning of the treachery of Walwan, leads a great army against him at Firmin. P. also fights on the side of the heathens in the final battle against the Christians. From 5100 onwards, P. is often called Melchinor. – *WO* nm3060 a4488

Pertholomeus, Pertolomeus see Ptolômêus (2)

Perfigal steward to Priam. P. is wounded by Agâmennon whilst fighting for the Trojans against the Greeks. This character was invented by Konrad. – *TK* 33792ff.

Peter (1) 'der Schaler', patron of Konrad von Würzburg. – *PM* nm180ff.

Peter (2) 'sante', biblical. – nm *W* 332,8; *Dem* 801; *JT* 102,4; *Loh* 5959; *RP* 149,44; *WA* 6294

Peterman 'von Stoufenberg, der Diemringer'. P. wins the love of a beautiful fairy, who appears to him whenever he wishes, but on the condition that he never takes a wife. He spends a long time enjoying her love and resists the attempts of his relatives to induce him to marry. Eventually the king induces him to marry his *muome*, a young girl of eighteen years. At the wedding feast a supernatural foot appears, and within three days P. is dead. – *PS* m33f. an47ff.

Petroculus see Patroclus

Peutêstes see Peucestes

Peucestes a warrior in Alexander's army. In *A* he is placed in charge of Egypt, whilst in *UA*, where he is called Peutêstes, he is severely wounded by the citizens of Sûdrâcas, into which he has penetrated to help Alexander. P. occurs in all the important histories of Alexander. – *A* 10624ff.; *UA* 20650 [†]

Pf– see under V

Ph– see under V

Piantze 'vürste', a knight who is present at a tourney held by Arthur. – *JT* 2104,2

Piblesûn 'künec von Lorneparz', a knight whom Parzivâl claims to have defeated. – *P* nm772,4

Pidras see Pidrol

Pidrol a squire at Agâmennon's court. P., who is a good runner, is the first to see Hector and Paris as they approach Agâmennon's court. – *GT* nm10602ff. a11893

Pidroll see Pidrol

Picorye see Pictorye

Pictagines 'künec von Kathan', a knight who arrives at Agâmennon's court, clad only in a silk shirt, and challenges any knight to fight for the honour of his lady, P.'s own *amie* being Hercolas. Paris accepts the challenge for the honour of Helen, and, clad also in a silk shirt, he fights and kills P. – *GT* a10361ff. n10373

Pyctagoras see Pytagoras (1) and (2)

Pictogimes see Pictagines

Pictoria see Pictorye

Pictorye *amie* of Tervian. Hector rescues her from the clutches of Waradach (q.v.) and falls in love with her. They spend the night together at the house of her brother, Amerillus. Later (19166) she accompanies Hector back to Troy. – *GT* a12368ff. n12529

Pilâtus 'von Poncia', biblical (Pontius Pilate), the Roman governor of Judah at the time of Christ. – nm *P* 219,24; *JT* 1603,6

Pilemenes 'künec der Paflagône', a warrior in the Trojan army against the Greeks. In *LT*, as in Benoît, he is badly wounded by Ulixes and secretly leaves Troy with the body of Pentesileâ, which he takes to her land to be buried. He is called in this version Philemenis, künec von Pafagoye and Fileminis, künec von Palatine. In *TKf*, which follows the account in Dictys, where he is called Pylaemenes, his death at the hands of Achilles is lamented but not described. – *LT* 4035ff.; *TKf* nm43392ff.

Pilêus 'von Larîs', a warrior in the Trojan army who is captured by the Greeks and slain. So also in Dictys, where he is called Pylaeus. – *TKf* 40504f.

Pilgerîn (1) 'von Capellen' a knight on the side of Friderîch (4) against Ulrich von Liechtenstein at Neustadt. P. is captured by Kadolt (2). – *FD* 1591,1

Pilgerîn (2) 'von Karsse', corrected by Bechstein to 'der Pilgerîn'.[13] P., who is in the service of Ulrich von Liechtenstein, probably an hereditary tenant,[14] imprisons Ulrich by force. – *FD* 1696,5ff.

Pillis *amie* of Demesticus. It seems quite certain that P. is identical with Phillis (q.v.), and Demesticus is, therefore, identical with Demophon (q.v.). – *RB* nm24552

Pillixenna see Pollixena

Pîloise a squire in the service of Îsolt (2). P. is probably identical with Peliot (q.v.). – *ET* 7127ff.

Pynal a squire in the service of Lôis, who sends him to fetch Alîze (2). – *UW* 334,18

Pyndarus see Pandarus (2)

Pine 'Sampson', a Jew who translated the OF continuations of *Perceval* for the authors of *RP*. – *RP* nm854,27

Pînel 'fiz Kâtor', a doughty Saracen who is killed by Willehalm (1) during the first battle at Alischanz. P. is called 'von Ahsim' and 'von Assim'. He is slain by Willehalm in the OF *Aliscans*, and occurs also in *Li Covenans Vivien*. – *W* 21,1

Pioles a maiden who is about to be married to Hartzier, when the latter leaves her to attend a tourney. The castle in which she is staying is burned down, and she is alone and helpless when Wigamur finds her and brings her into safety in the castle of Ligronite. – *Wigm* a857 n873

Pyoliys see Pioles

Piolplerin see Blîobleherîn

Pippîn father of Charlemagne (see Karl (1)). – *FB* nm313

Pîramus in Babylonian legend the youth whose attempted elopement with Thisbe (see Tispê) ended in a double tragedy. – nm *E* 7709; *C* 11575; *FB* 2435; *TK* 2315; *RB* 15274

Pirel 'von Mardussel', a warrior in Akarîn's army against Ipomidôn. – *JT* nm3625,4

Pirnas 'grâve', a knight who gives Fridrich (3) gold and silver when he leaves Turneas, who has refused him his due reward. P. successfully pleads for the life of Turneas, who is his overlord, when Fridrich has captured him in the battle against Mompolier. – *FS* a3715 n3731

Piros see Pirrus

Pirratus a pirate who is captured by Alexander's men. Alexander pardons him, and he joins the former's service, where he proves a model subject. As Toischer points out, this name was obviously based on the Latin *pirata*, 'pirate'.[15] – *UA* 24024ff.

Pirre 'künec von Arl', also called 'grâve von Ammanit' and 'Perre von Tungalit'. P. is the husband of Kyburg (1) and an ally of Lôis against Terramêr. – *UW* a38,22 n43,26f.

Pirrus son of Achilles and Deidamîa. After the death of his father, he is fetched by Menelaus and joins the Greeks against the Trojans, proving the deciding factor in the course of the war. He slays Pollixena over the grave of Achilles, and, in *LT* and *TK*, he then returns to

---

13 Ulrich von Liechtenstein, *Frauendienst*, ed. by R. Bechstein, II, p. 266, to 1696,7.
14 Ulrich von Liechtenstein, *Frauendienst*, ed. by R. Bechstein, II, p. 267, to 1697,2.
15 Toischer, p. 394.

Greece, where he hears of the imprisonment of his grandfather, Pêleus. He captures
Acastus, whose two sons he kills, and releases Pêleus. He later takes Ermiona from
Orestes, for which he is slain by the latter. In *GT* he is killed by Elyoss for strangling a
defenceless woman (Pollixena). P. is called Pyrrhus in the *Achilleis* of Statius, but is called
Neoptolemus in Dares and Dictys, a fact which is referred to by the author of *TKf*
(44184f.): 'er ist ouch Neoptolemus/ mit einem zuonamen genant'. – *LT* m13849 n13861
a14634; *TK* 28653ff.; *RB* nm22580f.; *GT* 17893

Pirus see Pirrus

Pîse natural son of Priam. P. is captured by Ajax (1) whilst fighting for the Trojans against
the Greeks. This character was invented by the author of *TKf*. – *TKf* 40520

Pistropleus 'künec von Ezenie', a warrior in the Trojan army against the Greeks. This
character appears to have been invented by Benoît. – *LT* 4073f.

Pystropus a centaur who fights for the Trojans against the Greeks, who kill him by a united
effort. This character seems to be the invention of Herbort. – *LT* 7677ff.

Pitagaras father of Aripuleis. – *JT* nm3196,5

Pytagoras (1) a warrior in the Trojan army against the Greeks. In *TK* he is a natural son of
Priam. P. first appears in Benoît. – *LT* 4711; *TK* 29982

Pitagoras (2) the Greek philosopher (Pythagoras). – nm *P* 773,25; *JT* 313,4

Pitipas a squire in attendance on Amely. He acts as messenger between Amely and
Willehalm (4) before the abduction. – *RW* nm5439 a6236

Pittipas see Pitipas

Planscheflûr see Blancheflûr (2)

Plansofeide wife of Acurteis and sister of Sêkurîe. – *Crane* m2077 n3901f. a3923

Plantzeflur see Blancheflûr (2)

Plastines son of Acastus. P. is slain by Pirrus, because of his share in the imprisonment of
Pêleus. In Dictys he is called Plisthenes, and in Benoît, Plistenès. – *LT* 17949

Plâtô the Greek philosopher. – nm *P* 465,21; *LT* 10670; *W* 218,13

Platôn 'vürste in Mêdîâ'. P. surrenders to Alexander. So also in Curtius Rufus. – *A* 14216

Plafigâne 'barûn von Protheis', a warrior who is slain whilst fighting for the Trojans against
the Greeks. The name does not occur in any other version of the Trojan legend, but in
Benoît, Plafagoine occurs as a variant of Paflagoine, a place-name (Paphlagonia in Dares
and Dictys). – *TK* 36318

Pleherîn an enemy of Tristan at Marke's court. He sees Tristan's squire fleeing from the
court and reports to Îsolt that it is Tristan who is fleeing. Îsolt, who believes him, scorns
Tristan, so that the latter, in his grief, takes Îsolt (3) to wife. This is the story as related in
ET. In *UT* he challenges Kurvenal, thinking that he is Tristan, and reports to Îsolt that
Tristan would not turn back to fight, even though challenged in her name. In both *UT* and
HT he realises who the fool is after Tristan has left Marke's court, and following him, he
challenges him in the name of Îsolt and is killed. – *ET* 6829ff.; *UT* nm1907 a1933; *HT* 5498

Plehirin see Pleherîn

Pleiære 'der', MHG poet, and author of *G*, *M*, and *TF*. – nm *G* 21303; *M* 102; *TF* 4081

Plîadêr a warrior who is slain by Deiphebus whilst fighting for the Greeks against the
Trojans. This character was invented by Konrad. – *TK* a32510 n32520

Pliamîn a knight who accompanies Êrec and Gârel (1) to the rescue of an abducted maiden.
– *GM* 3149ff.

Pligor (1) a giant who abducts Orgaloyse. She is rescued by Paris, who slays P. –
GT nm4463 a4505

Pligor (2) a warrior in the Trojan army against the Greeks. – *GT* 22714

*Plihopliherî see Blîobleherîn

Plimius the Latin historian (Plinius). – *WO* nm4008

Plinas see Plineschanz

Plineschanz 'cuns von Zambrôn', a knight whom Parzivâl claims to have overcome. In *JT*, where he is called Plinischartz, he is present at a tourney held by Arthur, whilst he appears later (5659,5f) as Plinas, herzoge von Zombrone, one of the knights who swear allegiance to Parzivâl after the latter's victory over Agors (see Strangedorz). – *P* nm772,12; *JT* 2021,1

Plînis expelled from Cîtîâ with Skôlôpêtus (q.v.). – *A* nm17917ff.

Plinischartz Plineschanz

Pliopleherîn, Plîopliherî, Plyopliris see Blîobleherîn

Plipalinot see Inpripalenôt

Pliporie see Blîobleherîn

Ploiborz a knight who attends Leigamar's tourney in the service of Lorez. – *C* 18151

Plôt a wandering minstrel, the comrade of Houpt (q.v.). In *UT* it is the name assumed by Tristan when he and Kurvenal visit Îsolt (2) in the guise of squires. – *ET* 8368ff.; *UT* 2358

Plurimanz a warrior who is slain by Kassibilaus whilst fighting for the Greeks against the Trojans. This character was invented by Konrad. – *TK* 33670f.

Plûto the Roman name for the god of the underworld. – nm *Ed* 2928; *LT* 13356; *RB* 16444

Pnîtagoras 'künec von Kipper', a warrior in Alexander's army. So also in *Expeditio Alexandri* and Curtius Rufus. – *A* 9163f.

Pôdius (1) 'künec von Assûr', a vassal of Rôisse, for whom he fights Alexander. P. is defeated and captured. He later marries Rôisse. This character appears to have been invented by Ulrich. – *UA* 23813

Pôdius (2) see Poidjus

Poestes 'künec von Tenebrî', a warrior who is slain by Hector whilst fighting for the Greeks against the Trojans. P. does not occur in any other version of the Trojan legend, but Benoît refers (15313) to Poëstez, the divine powers, the gods. The context, however, does not offer any excuse for Konrad's construing this as the name of a person. – *TK* 39808

Pohereiz 'künec von Etnîse', a warrior in the service of Josweiz, under whom he fights for Terramêr against Willehalm (1) at Alischanz. P. occurs in a variant reading of 1.490 of *Aliscans*, where he is called Buherez. – *W* 33,12ff.

Poidas 'der junge', a knight who attends the tourney held by Leigamar. – *C* 18090

Poidekunjunz see Bademagun

Poideusar 'von Palerne', a commander in Akarîn's army against Ipomidôn. He is slain in the battle. – *JT* nm3123,1

Poidikonjunz, Poidikuniuntze, Poidikunius see Bademagun

Poidiusar see Poideusar

Poidjus 'von Vrîende', also called 'künec' of Griffâne, Tasmê, Trîant and Kaukases. P. is the grandson of Terramêr and is identical with Poidwîz, son of Oukîn, both forms of the name originating in Baudus, fils d'Aquin, who occurs in *Aliscans* and *Li Covenans Vivien*. He fights for Terramêr against Willehalm (1) and kills Kiûn (1), but is himself slain by Heimrîch (2). [See Appendix (8).] In *UW* he is called Pôdius, künec von Frŷgende and assists Terramêr against Lôîs. – *W* 36,23f.; *UW* 42,12

Poidwîz (1) 'von Râbes', a commander in Terramêr's army against Willehalm (1) in the second battle at Alischanz. In *Aliscans* he is called Maudaus (var. Baudus) de Rames. [See Appendix (8).] – *W* 350,12

Poidwîz (2) see Poidjus. [See Appendix (8).]

Poytwîn (1) a warrior at Tîbalt's court when the latter returns with Willehalm (1) as prisoner. – *UW* 58,1

Poytwin (2) 'grâve von Potyeres', a knight who is present at the tourneys held at Komarzi, Poys, and near Kurnoy. – *RW* nm6206 a6641

Poitwîn (3) 'von Prienlaskors', a knight who is unhorsed by Gahmuret at the tourney held by Herzeloide. In *JT*, where he is called 'künec von Preciliorse', he is present at the tourney held by Arthur. – *P* 72,9f.; *JT* 1976,1

Poktziseiler a knight of the Round Table. He appears as Poytislier in Füetrer.[16] – *FS* nm4820

Pol 'von Miserande', a warrior in the army of Ipomidôn against Akarîn. – *JT* 3261,2

Polemôn brother of Amintas (1), a warrior in Alexander's army. P. is involved in the conspiracy to murder Alexander but is pardoned. So also in Curtius Rufus. – *A* 20042

Polibetes see Polipite

Polîdâmant a warrior in Alexander's army. He carries the command to Cleander that the latter is to kill Parmênîon. P. is called Polydamas in *Expeditio Alexandri*, Curtius Rufus, and Gualterus. – *A* 12329

Polidamas 'von Zizonie', a warrior in the Trojan army. He accompanies Paris on his journey to fetch Helen and is later one of the conspirators with Ênêâs to betray Troy to the Greeks. So also in Benoît and Dares. In Dictys he is slain by Ajax (1). – *LT* 2365ff.; *TK* 19427

Polidarius (1) 'von Tracia', son of Ascalofius, a warrior in the Greek army against the Trojans. So also in Benoît. In Dares and Dictys he is called Podalirius, and in Homer, Podaleirios. – *LT* 3091

Polidarius (2) a warrior in the Greek army against the Trojans. P. does not occur in any other version of the Trojan legend. – *LT* 3393

Polidius 'künec', a warrior in the Greek army against the Trojans. P. does not occur in any other version of the Trojan legend, but the name may well be a variant form of Polidarius. – *LT* 4912

Polimedes see Palimedes

Polimenne a warrior who is slain by Rubrîcus whilst fighting for Alexander against Porrus. This character was apparently invented by Ulrich. – *UA* nm19677f.

Polimides, Polimites see Polînices

Polimoda see Polidamas

Polîmones the commander of Alexander's fleet on the Nile. In *Expeditio Alexandri* and Curtius Rufus he is called Polemon. – *A* 10627

Polinîcus tutor to the young Alexander. So also in Pseudo-Callisthenes and Valerius. – *A* 1362f.

Polînices son of Oedippus and brother of Ethiocles. In *Ed* he is seen by Ênêâs in Hades. – *Ed* 3314; *C* nm15541ff.; *UA* nm3007ff.

Poliparcôn, Poliper see Polipercôn

Polipercôn a commander in Alexander's army. So also in Gualterus and Curtius Rufus, whilst in *Expeditio Alexandri* he is called Polysperchon. – *A* 11839; *UA* 12440

Polipêtes see Polipite

Polipite a warrior in the Greek army against the Trojans. He appears in Benoît as Polibetès, in Dares as Polypoetes, and in Homer as Polypoites. – *LT* 3385; *TK* 23874

Polipoetes see Polipite

---

16 *Friedrich von Schwaben*, ed. by M.H. Jellinek, p. 73, to l. 4820.

Polippus a shepherd who, according to *UA*, found and reared Oedippus. In the Greek legend, P. was the king of Corinth, to whom the shepherd who found Oedippus brought him. – *UA* m2893 n2923

Polisenar see Polixenus

Polistrâtus a warrior in Alexander's army who finds the wounded and abandoned Dârîus. So also in Curtius Rufus and Gualterus. – *A* 14844ff.; *UA* 16716

Politetes 'von Melibê', a warrior who is killed by Hector whilst fighting for the Greeks against the Trojans. Achilles, seeing him killed, attacks and kills Hector. This story is told in *LT*, and exactly the same story is told of Polypoetes (see Polipite) in Dares. In Benoît, P. is called Philotetès (var. Polithenès). – *LT* 3397; *TK* 23884

Politze 'von Alimet', a warrior in Akarîn's army against Ipomidôn. – *JT* nm3093,2 a3888,1

Polifemes son (or nephew) of Cycrops (q.v.). P. is mentioned in Dictys and Benoît, but in the *Odyssey* Polyphemus is the name of the Cyclops whom Ulixes and his companions blind. – *LT* nm17576ff.

Polixana, Polixanna, Polixena, Polixene, Polixenie, Polixenna see Pollixena

Polixenus a warrior in the Greek army against the Trojans. In *LT* he is slain by Pystropus, whilst in *TK* he is slain by Hector (35200ff.) and later by Dinodaron (36006ff.). In both Dares and Benoît, in which latter he is called Polixinart (var. Polixinus), he is slain by Hector. – *LT* 3335f.; *TK* 23812

Polixina see Pollixena

Pollidamas, Pollimades see Polidamas

Pollixena daughter of Priam and Ecubâ (3) and sister of Hector and Paris. Achilles falls in love with her and is lured into a trap by Ecubâ through this love. In *LT*, as in Benoît and Dares, she is beheaded by Pirrus on his father's grave at the fall of Troy. In *TKf* and Dictys she is not slain but given to Pirrus as his share in the spoils. In *GT* she sets the head of Achilles on a lance, and for this is strangled by Pirrus when Troy is taken. P. is not mentioned in Homer. – *LT* m1664 n1691 a7174f.; *TK* m13254 n13267 a39248; *GT* 743

Pollixene, Pollixinâ see Pollixena

Pollus see Pollux

Pollux brother of Castor (1) and Elena, a warrior in the Greek army under Jason in the first war against the Trojans. So also in Benoît and Dares. – *LT* 1195; *TK* a11452 n11463

Pomyzlâ 'herzoge von Pôlân', a knight who is killed whilst fighting for the Hungarians against the Christians. – *Loh* 2757

Pompeie see Pompêjus (2)

Pompêjus (1) the Roman colleague, and later enemy, of Julius Caesar. Terramêr claims descent from him and, therefore, a right to the Roman crown. – nm *W* 338,26; *UA* 14673

Pompêjus (2) brother of Ipomidôn (q.v.) and enemy of Akarîn. – *P* 14,3f.; *T* nm73,2; *JT* 712,4; *RB* nm16592

Pompeus a vassal of Gamorett, for whom he fights against the Greeks. P. is slain by Paris. – *GT* 5670

Ponolope see Penelope

Ponpeie see Pompêjus (2)

Ponpeus see Pompeus

Pontibus the founder of the land of Pontus. P. is mentioned in Pseudo-Methodius, where he is called Pontipus. – *A* nm17125

Pontimilus see Pantinmuls

Pontius Pilate see Pilâtus

Pontifier the third knight to attack Gauriel at Arthur's court. P., who is depicted as a very serious man who never laughs, is unhorsed by Gauriel. – *GM* 754

Ponturteise see Brandelidelîn

Pore 'künec von' (*JT*), see Bademagun

Porchtatus a warrior in the Greek army against the Trojans. P. is probably identical with Potarcus (var. Portarchus) who appears in Benoît. – *TK* 23850ff.

Porchthatus see Porchtatus

Porporius son of Thelemacus and Nausica. P. is not mentioned in Dares or Dictys but appears as Poliporbus in Benoît. – *LT* 17797

Porrus 'künec von Indiâ', a former vassal (in *A*, ally) of Dârîus and, after the latter's death, Alexander's most powerful enemy. In *A* he sends excuses to Dârîus for not helping him after his first defeat at the hands of Alexander, but he is not mentioned again before the poem breaks off. In *UA* he is defeated by Alexander in single combat, but the latter is so impressed by P.'s bravery that he spares his life. In *SA* and *WA*, P. is slain by Alexander. – *C* nm12281; *A* 8144ff.; *UA* 19347; *SA* nm2731ff. a4551ff.; *WA* nm2263ff. a2692; *RP* nm404,22

Porteneys a knight who takes part in the tourney held by Arthur for the crown of Deleprosat. – *Wigm* 2197

Portigal 'künec von' (*JT*), see Karforas

Portilagrîn 'barûn von Swâles', a knight who is slain by Hector whilst fighting for the Greek army against the Trojans. This character was invented by Konrad. – *TK* 31302

Portugal 'künec von' (*RW*), see Elymant

Portus a vassal of Gamorett, for whom he fights against the Greeks. – *GT* 5673

Portzifal see Parzivâl

Porus see Porrus

Porfilias see Prophilias

Posizônjus 'von Tilirastêr'. (Martin is of the opinion that this name is an attempt to reproduce Posidonius, a name which appears in Solinus (29,12 and 183,11), but he quotes Hagen, who thinks that it comes from Pusionem (var. Posionem), a giant who is also mentioned in Solinus (21,19).[17]) P. is one of the knights whom Feirefîz claims to have defeated. – *P* nm770,20

Possidamus a warrior in Alexander's army against Porrus. This character was invented by Ulrich. – *UA* 19668

Possitrius 'von Icolach', a warrior who is slain by Môrolt whilst fighting for Ipomidôn against Akarîn. – *JT* 3529,1ff.

Postefar 'von Laudundrehte', a knight whom Parzivâl claims to have defeated. – *P* nm772,19

Potschman 'von Potschâ', a knight who welcomes Ulrich von Liechtenstein to Neustadt during his *Artusfahrt*. – *FD* 1485,7

Potwin see Poitwîn (3)

Poufameiz 'künec von Ingulîe', a warrior who is slain by Willehalm (1) whilst fighting for Terramêr at Alischanz. P., who appears in most of the *chansons de geste* of the Guillaume d'Orange cycle, is called Baufumés in the OF versions. – *W* 28,29

Prabant 'der von' (*Loh*), see Lohengrîn

Pragnet 'von Persolon', the heroine of a *fier baiser* episode in *FS*. P., who is at first a hart, is transformed into a maiden by a kiss from Fridrich (3) and tells the latter the way to the

---

17 Martin (1), p. 504, to 770,20.

spring where he will find Angelburg. She later assists Fridrich with a large army against Mompolier and marries Ludwig. – *FS* a4282 n4353

Prandan see Brandân

Prandidones a knight who compels Hector to fight him just after the latter has left Amerillus with Pictorye. P. is defeated, to the sorrow of his *amie*, Parmelie. – *GT* a12959f. n13015

Prandin a knight in Dulcemâr's army against Arthur. – *TF* 1989ff.

Pranczopil 'ein getwerc', a cunning goldsmith. – *Wigm* nm2586

Prauerâûs a knight who is present at Arthur's court when Êrec returns with Ênîte. Bartsch thought that this name was a distortion of 'li desreez' (Chrestien's *Erec*, [1733]),[18] but there seems to be no doubt that it is an attempt to reproduce Bravaïns (MS B: Braauains), the name of a knight who appears in Chrestien's *Erec* (1737). This knight appears in *C* as Brainons, one of those who spill Priure's cup of chastity. – *E* 1665; *C* 2324

Pretemisus 'von Traze', uncle of Crepeus and a warrior in the Trojan army against the Greeks. This character appears to have been invented by Benoît. – *LT* 4013ff.; *TK* 29928ff.

Pretzel apparently a poet, contemporary with Füetrer. – *Mer* nm181,1f.

Priam king of Troy, husband of Ecubâ (3). In *TK* he is present at the wedding of Pêleus and Thetis and quarrels with Jupiter over the possession of Paris, who is gained for P. by Hector. By angering Ênêâs and his fellow-conspirators, P. is the immediate cause of the fall of Troy, as is also the case in Benoît, Dares, and Dictys. He is slain by Pirrus. In *GT* he is killed in a sortie made by the Trojans (18112) but is still alive at the fall of Troy, when he is again slain (23026). In *Ed* he is seen by Ênêâs in Hades. – *Ed* nm20 a3323; *LT* 1659ff.; *TK* a325 n336; *GT* 1ff.

Priamus, Priant see Priam

Pribandrôn a knight of the Round Table who is unhorsed by Daniel (1). – *DB* 250

Prienlaschors 'der von' (*P*), see Libêals

Priens see Briens

Primas 'von Chordubine', a warrior in Akarîn's army against Ipomidôn. – *JT* nm3094,2 a3887,1

Prymedes a knight who is slain by Patroclus whilst acting as standard-bearer for the Trojans against the Greeks. Since P. is a brother of Hector, it would seem that his name is a distortion of a patronymic formed from Priam. – *GT* 18064

Prîmus a vassal of Dârîus (3), who instructs him to capture Alexander with the aid of Antiochus (4). They write to Dârîus, giving him some idea of Alexander's real strength. So also in Leo. – *A* 4438ff.; *SA* 2206ff.

Prinel 'künec', *ami* of Amander (2). P., who is a knight, unhorses Junalet and Segremors. – *UW* nm255,6

Principene a warrior in Ipomidôn's army against Akarîn. – *JT* 3258,7

Prios see Brios

Pristalûn a Trojan who is slain by Ulixes and Dyomedes whilst fighting against the Greeks. This character was invented by Konrad. – *TK* 33456ff.

Priure 'künec', the sender of a cup of chastity to the court of Arthur. If the person attempting to drink out of this cup has been unfaithful to his or her love, or has done any unknightly deed, the cup spills over them, or else they are unable to drink at all. All the ladies of the court fail in this test, and of the knights only Arthur succeeds. – *C* 1012f.

Prô the name assumed by Tristan on his first visit to Ireland, when he goes to be healed from the wound he has received from Môrolt. – *ET* nm1182

---

18 Bartsch (1), p. 151.

Prohterewîz 'von Râbs', a heathen who is slain by Lohengrîn whilst fighting against the Christians. – *Loh* 4461

Proserpinâ see Proserpîne

Proserpîne the daughter of Demeter, whose rape by Pluto was, according to Greek legend, the origin of the seasons. – nm *Ed* 2931; *RB* 16442

Prothenor 'von Lenor', a warrior who is slain by Hector whilst fighting for the Greeks against the Trojans. So also in Dares and Benoît. P. appears in Dictys and Homer, but his fate is not given. – *LT* 3312ff.; *TK* 23794

Protheselaus, Prothesîlax see Prothesolaus

Prothesolaus a Greek who leads the first attack against Troy. He is slain by Hector. He is called 'künec von Prelarge' in *LT*, whilst in *TK* he bears the epithet 'von Notariâ'. In Dictys, where he is called Protesilaus ex Phylaea, he is killed by Ênêâs, but in Dares, where he is called Protesilaus e Phylaca, he is slain by Hector, as also in Benoît. In *Ed*, P. is seen by Ênêâs in Hades. – *Ed* 3348; *LT* 3069; *TK* 23856

Prôtheur see Prôtheus

Prôtheus a soothsayer who attends the wedding of Thetis and Pêleus and foretells the birth and probable death of Achilles. P. does not occur in any other version of the Trojan legend, but as the son of Poseidon he was famous as a soothsayer in Greek mythology. – *TK* a4496 n4548

Prothefilaus, Prothefilianus see Prothesolaus

Prothoilus a warrior in the Greek army against the Trojans. This name does not occur in any other version of the Trojan legend. – *LT* 4932

Protizilas a knight in the service of Belakâne. He jousts with Îsenhart, and they are both killed. It is generally agreed that this name is identical with the original Greek form of Prothesolaus, and Golther believes that it was taken over by Wolfram from *Ed*,[19] a view which is not accepted by Singer, who gives Benoît as the source.[20] Singer has no argument to support this opinion except his firm belief in the existence of Kîot. Martin mentions the *Roman de Protesilas* and suggests that this may be the origin of the name.[21] – *P* nm27,24

Profiliar a warrior in the Greek army against the Trojans. This character was invented by Konrad. – *TK* 34286

Prophilias friend of Athis (q.v.). So also in the OF version. – *AP* nA,52 aAb,10

Prûanz a warrior who is with Ehmereiz defending the ships in the battle between Terramêr and Willehalm (1). In the OF *Aliscans* he is called Bruians. – *W* 438,28

Prûn (1) son of Heinrîch (1), made bishop of Köln. P. fights for the Christian army against the heathens and slays Gesparis. – *Loh* 3212ff.

Prûn (2) 'neve' of Otte (3), who makes him Pope, with the name Gregorius (Gregory V) (7453ff.). P. is incorrectly called 'bischof' of Köln (cf. Prûn (1)). – *Loh* nm7422ff. [†]

Prunrîch 'von Toblîch', a knight who welcomes Ulrich von Liechtenstein to Neustadt during his *Artusfahrt*. – *FD* 1482,6

Prutus founder of Britain, brother of Silvius, who took all his inheritance, forcing him to leave and found a land of his own. His travels eventually bring him to Britain. In Geoffrey of Monmouth, where he first appears, P., who is called Brutus, is the son of Silvius and is the unwitting cause of the death of his father and mother, for which he is exiled from Italy.

---

19 Golther (1), p. 140.
20 Singer (1), p. 53.
21 Martin (1), p. 39, to 27,24.

P. is the titular hero of Wace's paraphrase of Geoffrey's history, the so-called *Brut*. – *Mer* nm1,3f.

Ptoloméus (1)   prince in Egypt at the time of Julius Caesar. This is historically Ptolemy XIV Philopator, who was king of Egypt 61–47 BC. – *UA* nm14684

Ptolôméus (2)   a warrior in Alexander's army. He slays Antipater in *UA* for his share in the death of Alexander. In Leo he pretends to be Alexander when receiving Candaulus at Alexander's command. He appears in all versions of the Alexander history. – *A* 6995; *UA* 4699; *SA* 8427; *WA* 4725ff.

Puhurat   'von Purelle', a warrior in Akarîn's army against Ipomidôn. – *JT* 3195,2

Pûlaz   a giant who extends hospitality to Meleranz for a night. P. and his friends had been driven out of their land into the forest by the künec von Gâzen, and they now lived by robbery. Meleranz overcomes P.'s lord and becomes king of the land. – *M* a4272ff. n4695

Punturteis   'künec von' (*P* and *JT*), see Brandelidelîn

Purdân   a giant who slays knights on the road. He is killed by Gârel, who releases his captives. P.'s wife is called Fidegart. – *G* a5484f. n5508

Purgunden   'künec von' (*Loh*), see Rulf

Purrel   'künec von Nubjant', a warrior who fights and does great deeds for Terramêr against the Christians under Willehalm (1). He is wounded in the second battle at Alischanz by Rennewart, who breaks his club on him. P. occurs in *Aliscans* as Borrel and is mentioned in other *chansons de geste* of the same cycle, including the *Chancun de Willame*. – *W* 358,23ff.

Purriel   'markys von' (*Ll*, MS K), see Paldewein

Putegân   'von Ormalereiz', a warrior who blows a horn when Terramêr is about to arm himself. P. appears in *Aliscans*, where he is called Puteçaingne. – *W* 353,24

Q

Quadoqueneis a knight at Arthur's court who spills Priure's cup of chastity. The name occurs in Chrestien's *Erec* (1742) as Cadorcaniois, but Foerster is of the opinion that this portion of *Erec* has been interpolated by a copyist.[1] – *C* 2325

Quarcos 'von Quine', a knight who is present at Arthur's court and spills Priure's cup of chastity. The origin of this name is to be found in Chrestien's *Erec* (1723): 'Et li vaslez de Quintareus' (the MSS differ widely however). This line appears in *E* as 'Lis von quinte carous', a knight who is at Arthur's court when Êrec returns with Ênîte. – *E* 1656; *C* 2313f.

Quebeleplûs younger daughter of Leigamar and sister of Fursensephin (q.v.). Q. plays a similar part in *C* to that played by Obilôt in *P*. – *C* a17678ff. n17994

Quenedinch the father of a knight who spills Priure's cup of chastity at Arthur's court. Chrestien's *Erec* (1722) reads: 'li fiz au roi Quenedic', which appears in *E* (1655) as 'des küneges sun von Ganedic'. – *C* nm2312

Quînas see Ginses

Quinotfiers 'de Bahanz', a knight who jousts with Joranz at a tourney held by Arthur. – *C* 781ff.

Quintiliens see Quintilion

Quintilion natural son of Priam, a warrior in the Trojan army against the Greeks. This character appears to have been invented by Benoît, who calls him Quintiliens, the form of the name which appears in *TK*. – *LT* a4768f. n4780; *TK* 30382

Quioques 'Gomeret', a knight who spills Priure's cup of chastity at Arthur's court. Gomeret is obviously the territorial name of Bans (see Pant (1)) de Gomeret, who appears in Chrestien's *Erec* (1975), but Quioques is inexplicable. – *C* 2338

Quoikos 'von Montichsdol', brother of Brun. Q. accompanies Gawein to Leigamar's tourney, where they fight side by side. – *C* a17522 n17597ff.

Quoitos see Quoikos

---

1 Chrestien de Troyes, *Erec und Enide*, ed. by W. Foerster, 2nd edn, p. 311.

R

Rabel a knight who is present at Arthur's court. – *Wigm* 2510

Rabellitor see Kalebitor

Râbs 'der von' (*Loh*), see Prohterewîz

Radamant see Râdamantus

Râdamantus according to *Ed*, the tormentor in Hades. In Greek mythology, Rhadamanthus was, on account of his upright life, made one of the judges in Hades. – *Ed* nm3402; *P* nm463,11

Rahîn 'de Gart', the captor of Humildîs (q.v.), who later slew R. – *C* nm14540ff.

Raimel 'von Louentel', a knight who spills Priure's cup of chastity at Arthur's court. This name does not occur in Chrestien's *Erec*, nor in *E*, unless it is an attempt to reproduce Rainduranz (see Boydurant). – *C* 2340

Rainher 'künec von Engellant', father of Amely. R. welcomes Willehalm (4), when the latter arrives at his court, and gives him Amely as a playmate. He betroths Amely to Avenis, without knowing of the love between her and Willehalm, but he has no hesitation in punishing the latter for the attempted abduction. When the two lovers have been brought together by Sävine, he considers that it is the will of God and submits gladly. – *RW* nm2880 a3468

Rains a knight who attends the tourney held by Leigamar. – *C* 18140

Rachel biblical, sister of Lya and second wife of Jâcob (2). – *UA* nm11345

Ramung 'von Sweden', a knight who attends the tourney held by Arthur in *JT* and who is also present at Arthur's court in *GM*. – *JT* 1975,7; *GM* (MS D) 385710

Rânes a warrior in the army of Turnus. He is one of those killed by Nîsus (q.v.), whilst they were lying in a drunken sleep. In the OF *Eneas* he is called Rannes, and in Virgil, Rhamnes. – *Ed* 6660

Rankulat 'der von' (*W*), see Libilûn

Râpot 'von Valkenberc', an unpopular knight who is one of those to welcome Ulrich von Liechtenstein to Neustadt during his *Artusfahrt*. – *FD* 1491,1f.

Râsim 'von Sûrîe', biblical (Rezin, king of Babylon). – *A* nm16719

Rassalie, Rassalic, Rassalit see Razalîc

Rassame see Razalîc

Rassilokant a warrior in Ipomidôn's army against Akarîn. – *JT* 3364,5

Raphael the archangel. – *JT* nm2506,3

Razalîc the leader of the Moorish army which is besieging Belakâne in Patelamunt. He is overcome by Gahmuret. In *JT* he marries Belakâne after the death of Gahmuret and is responsible for the education of Feirefîz. Bartsch thought that this name was an imperative formation from the Provençal *raissar*, 'to tear to pieces'; Razalîc < *raissa'nic* (*enic*), 'destroy the unjust'.[1] This etymology is denied by Gaston Paris,[2] as also by Singer, who derives the name from Ras Ali, Prince Ali,[3] but Golther considers the derivation still unexplained.[4] – *P* 41,9; *JT* nm1137,3 a2549,1

Razzalig see Razalîc

---

[1] Bartsch (2), p. 144.

[2] Paris (2), p. 149.

[3] Singer (1), p. 51.

[4] Golther (1), p. 141.

Rebedinch a knight who spills Priure's cup of chastity at Arthur's court. This name originated in Chrestien's *Erec* (1721): Caverons de Robendic (see Gaueros). – *C* 2311

Reimambram 'von Zadas', a giant who claims Behalim unless she can find a champion. Gawein defends her and defeats R., whom he gives to Behalim as a prisoner. – *C* nm9587f. [a9703ff.]

Reimbot (1) 'von Metters', a knight who is unhorsed by der von Lindeniz, who calls himself Ither, during Ulrich von Liechtenstein's *Artusfahrt*. – *FD* 1552,5f.

Reimbot (2) 'von Newalîn', a knight who is captured by Kadolt (2) (q.v.) at Neustadt. – *FD* 1591,2

Reinher 'von Eychelberc', a knight who is present at the tourney held at Friesach and who later jousts with Ulrich von Liechtenstein during the latter's *Venusfahrt*. – *FD* 301,1

Reinmâr 'von Hagenouwe', MHG poet. – nm *Tn* 4777; *C* 2416

Reinmunt 'von Liuchtenburc', the patron of Heinrich von Freiberg, the author of *HT*. – *HT* nm75ff.

Reinpreht 'von Muorekke', a knight who jousts with Ulrich von Liechtenstein during the latter's *Venusfahrt* and who is present at the tourney held at Friesach. – *FD* 193,3

Reinfrit 'von Brûneswîc', also called 'der von Sahsen', and 'der von Westevâl'. R. attends a tourney held by Fontânâgrîs, at which the prize is a kiss from Yrkâne. The two young people fall in love, and R. wins the prize. He is seen by a knight to enter Yrkâne's hut, and after he has left, the knight pesters her for her love and finally accuses her of misconduct with R. A day is appointed for the battle between Yrkâne's champion and her accuser, and R., appearing just in time, defeats the other knight, and snatching up Yrkâne, elopes with her. Fontânâgrîs pursues them but is captured and gives his consent to the marriage. It is a source of sorrow to R. and his wife that they have no child, and whilst they are praying, the Virgin Mary appears in a vision to R., telling him that he must first undertake a Crusade. He takes an army, defeats the king of Persia in single combat, and restores Jerusalem to the Christians. He then travels about the East, seeing the marvels and fighting for the king of Aschalun, until he is eventually recalled home by the news of the birth of a son. The poem breaks off during the homeward journey. – *RB* a65 n111

Remelus, Remolus see Romûlus (1)

Rêmôn 'barûn ûz Dânjû', a knight who is killed by Purrel whilst fighting for Willehalm (1) against Terramêr. In *Aliscans* he is called Renier d'Anjou. – *W* 428,22

Remulus see Romûlus (1)

Rêmus (1) brother of Romûlus (1). In *GT* he is a poor vassal in the service of Romûlus, who sends him with an offer of an alliance to Ênêâs. – *Ed* nm13365; *GT* 24950

Remus (2) 'künec von Zizonien' (also 'von Sytenenia', and (in *TK*) 'von Zeloniâ'), a warrior in the Trojan army against the Greeks. This character appears to have been invented by Benoît. – *LT* 4005; *TK* 24872

Rennewart son of Terramêr. R. was stolen from Terramêr's court whilst he was still a boy, and being very strong, he is made to act as kitchen scullion at the court of Lôîs. His true worth is recognized by Willehalm (1), when the latter comes to the court in search of assistance, and he is permitted to take R. back with him as his squire to Alischanz. During the second battle he is conspicuous for his strength and bravery, slaying many of the Saracens with his great club.[5] He chases some of Halzebier's army to the sea, and there he

---

[5] A similar, though not identical, transformation from scullion to knight is to be found in Malory, where Gareth (see Gârel (1)) spends, at his own request, a year at Arthur's court

finds and rescues the eight captive knights. After the victory has been won by the Christians, it is found that R. is missing and has possibly been taken prisoner. Wolfram's poem breaks off here, but in the OF *chansons de geste*, where R. is called Rainouart, he gradually displaces Willehalm as the central hero of the poems of the Guillaume d'Orange cycle. His robust vigour was far more likely to appeal to the imagination of the public than the stereotyped heroism of Willehalm, and gradually the comic side of his character comes more and more into prominence. R. marries Alîze (2) in *La Bataille Loquifer*, and they have a son Maillefer (see Malfer). In this poem and in *Gadifer*, R. fights the heathen champions in single combat, whilst in the *Moniage Rainouart* he becomes, in imitation of Willehalm, a monk. The story of his capture by Lôis at the age of eleven is told only in the prose *Enfances Rainouart*, whilst he appears, as Reneward, already in the *Chancun de Willame*. Panzer shows that the name Renwart occurs in the 14th and 15th centuries, but that a Renwardus is mentioned already *circa* 1180, though he considers that even in this case the origin may be the *chansons de geste*.[6] – *W* a187,30f. n189,1; *MB* nm118,3; *RB* nm23363; *FS* nm4824

Rennôn 'von Arâbiâ', a warrior who is slain by Nicânor (1) whilst fighting for Dârîus against Alexander at Erbela. In Gualterus he is called Rhemnon. – *UA* 13631

Reômitres 'herzoge', a warrior in Dârîus's army who is killed by Alexander. He appears in *Expeditio Alexandri* and Curtius Rufus, where he is called Rheomithres. – *A* 7488

Repanse de Schoie (Schulz thought that the form in *T*, 'Urrepanse', was the original, and he derived this from OF *ourer*, 'to pray', and *pens*, 'thought', i.e. 'sunk in reverence'.[7] Martin is more inclined to Lachmann's explanation that it is derived from OF *répenser*, 'to think again', i.e. 'remembrance of joy'.[8]) R. is the sister of Amfortas and guardian of the Graal, until she marries Feirefîz, by whom she has a son, Priester Jôhan. – *P* nm228,14 a235,15; *T* nm10,4 a13,1; *JT* nm619,6 a1765,1

Rêsus a warrior in the Trojan army whose death at the hands of the Greeks is lamented but not described. His death is described in Dictys, where he is called Rhesus, whilst in Homer he is one of those slain by Ulixes and Dyomedes when they make their night attack on the Trojans. – *TKf* nm43399

Retân brother-in-law of Gilân and father of Alexander (6) and Flôrîs (2). R. entertains Gârel (2) for the night just before his fight with Eskilabôn and later fights for Gârel against Ehkunat. – *G* m2485 a2804 n5463

Refrin 'von Iermiscande', a warrior in Ipomidôn's army against Akarîn. – *JT* nm3236,3

Refus 'von Aresse', a warrior who is slain by Deiphebus whilst fighting for the Greek army against the Trojans. In Benoît he is called Resa. – *LT* 11551ff.

Rial (1) the name under which Wildhalm passes when he is stranded on the shore of Azyzya. – *WO* nm1265

Riâl (2) 'künec von Jeraphîn', a knight who comes to take the oath of allegiance to Wigalois after the latter has defeated Rôaz and who later fights for Wigalois against Lîôn. – *Wigl* 9057

---

as scullion (VII,1ff.). He is christened Beaumayns by Keiî, who later learns to his discomfiture what a valiant knight the kitchen hand proves to be.

6   Panzer (2), pp. 216f.
7   Schulz, 'Eigennamen', pp. 391f.
8   Martin (1), p. 211, to 228,14.

Rîalt 'grâve', a relative of Gerhart (2), for whom he is fighting when he is captured by Gârel (2), who sends him captive to Sabîe (2). At Gârel's request, Sabîe afterwards releases R., who fights for Gârel against Ehkunat. – *G* 1355ff.

Ribal the leader of a band of knights whom Samlon and Hector meet on their way to Troy. R. is slain by Hector. – *GT* 439

Ribalin the shepherd who finds the infant Paris and rears him as his own son. He does not tell Paris that he is not his father until Paris has learned his true parentage from the goddesses. – *GT* 1372ff. [†]

Ribyan a squire at the court of Agâmennon. – *GT* 7242

Rienek 'ein Franken', a knight on the side of the Christians in the final battle against the heathens. – *WO* 16745ff.

Rigolîn 'von Nante'. (Bechstein in his index to *Tn* states that this is a Celtic name and quotes Golther as deriving it from Rigobilinus, from which also is derived Riwalîn.) R. is one of the leaders in the attack on Jovelîn and is captured by Tristan and Kâedîn. (Cf. Rîôle.) – *Tn* 18844

Rycart see Ritschart

Richart 'künec von Engellant', the historical Richard I, Cœur de Lion. In *WO* he fights on the side of the Christians in the final battle against the heathens. – *L* m9326; *WO* 16793

Richaude (1) 'von Ispanie', wife of Titurel and mother of Rischoide. – *JT* m418,6 n421,1 a423,6

Richaude (2) see Rischoide

Richoude see Rischoide

Rimal 'von Ladibor', a warrior who is slain by Fridebrant whilst fighting for Ipomidôn against Akarîn. – *JT* 3455,4

Rimalus a knight who is slain whilst fighting for Matribulus against Agâmennon – *GT* 3470

Rimolt 'von Arle', a knight who is present at a tourney held by Arthur. – *JT* 2029,1f.

Rymuluss see Romûlus (1)

Rinalt 'grâve', a knight who is sent as a messenger by Dulcemâr to try to calm Arthur, who is coming to attack him. – *TF* 1732ff.

Ryol 'künec von Spanniol', a knight who is present at the tourney held by Dymszogar. – *Wigm* 4959

Rîôle 'von Nantis', a knight who wishes to marry Îsolt (3) and is attacking Jovelîn. On two occasions he is beaten by Tristan. (Cf. Rigolîn.) – *ET* nm5542 a5734; *UT* nm142

Ris 'künec von Brescheliande', also called 'von Gales lant', one of the protagonists in a tourney held with Cadoalans for the maid Gyngenor (q.v.). The story of this tourney is not told in the Mons MS of Pseudo-Gautier but is related in the Montpellier MS, where he is called Ris de Volen. R. occurs in the OF romance *Li Chevaliers as Deus Espees*, where he demands Arthur's beard for his mantle, which is woven from the beards of conquered kings. The same incident occurs already in Geoffrey of Monmouth (X, 3), where he is a giant called Ritho. – *RP* nm72,43 a79,11

Risenburgære 'der edel' (*UA*), see Borse

Riscaude see Rischoide

Rischoide (According to Martin, this name is identical with the German Rîchhilt.[9]) R. is the wife of Kailet and, in *P*, aunt of Herzeloide. In *JT* she is the daughter of Titurel and Richaude (1). – *P* m49,8 n84,10; *JT* 435,6; *RB* nm2078 [†]

Ritschart (1) 'von Lyanite', an ally of Lôîs against Terramêr. – *UW* 39,19

---

9   Martin (1), p. 90, to 84,10.

Ritschart (2) 'von Nâvers', a knight who is captured by Arthur's knights during the brush with the men of Lôgrois whilst Arthur is on his way to witness the fight between Gawein and Gramoflanz. – *P* nm665,5ff.

Ritschart (3) 'grâve von Tumâne', a knight under whom Lanzelet fights at the tourney held by Lôt. – *L* 3130f.

Ritschier 'von Engellande', nephew of Fruot. R. is jealous of the popularity of Engelhart (q.v.), and when an escaped hawk leads him into the orchard in which the meeting of Engelhart and Engeltrût takes place, he loses no time in accusing the former in public. R. is defeated by Dieterich in the ordeal by combat. – *Eng* 1664ff.

Riuzen 'künec von' (*Eng*), see Hertnît (2)

Rivalîn see Riwalîn (1)

Riwachont a knight who is present at Arthur's tourney. (Identical with Riwalekunt?) – *JT* 1994,5

Riwalekunt a knight who is present at Arthur's tourney. Since R. is named just after Tristan, Marke, and Môrolt, it is possible that he is identical with Riwalîn (1). (Cf. also Riwachont.) – *JT* 2115,5

Riwalîn (1) 'von Lohnois'. (Bechstein in his index to *Tn* quotes Golther as deriving this name from the Celtic Rigobilinus (see Rigolîn). Hertz points out that Riwalus occurs as the name of a Breton leader in Geoffrey of Monmouth and was, in fact, a popular Breton name.[10] Bacmeister had suggested the derivation from the Gaelic Rigovellaunus < *rîx*, 'king', and *vellaunus*, 'hero'.[11] Bruce also accepts the Breton origin of the name.[12]) R. is the husband of Blanscheflûr (1) (q.v.) and the father of Tristan. In *ET*, the news of R's death is brought to Tristan after the latter has consummated his union with Îsolt (3). Gottfried denies in *Tn* that R.'s land was Lohnois and calls him 'von Parmenîe' and also Kanêlengres (and Kanêl), a byname which he got from Thomas. In *Tn*, R. is slain in a battle against his overlord, Morgân, before the birth of his son. He occurs in *P* as one of the knights present at the tourney held by Herzeloide, where he is called 'künec von Lohneis'. – *ET* 71ff.; *P* 73,14; *Tn* a243 n320; *TK* nm2311; *HT* nm250

Riwalîn (2) a knight who is compelled by Assiles to provide hospitality for knights errant, with a view to robbing them. Any knight who stays the night with R. has to fight four knights on the following morning, and R., who is chivalrous, tries to dissuade Gawein from spending the night there, but in vain. The outcome is, of course, favourable to Gawein. – *C* a5777 n5959

Riwalîn (3) 'grâve', a knight who announces a tourney against Glais. – *C* nm3212

Roax a king, of whose death the author of *GT* had read. Since this name is rimed with 'lasz', it seems possible that Rôaz is intended. – *GT* nm20417

Rôaz 'von Glois', a heathen magician, husband of Japhîte, and oppressor of Lârîe. R. drives out Lar, murders his companions, and confines Lârîe to one castle which he is unable to take. Wigalois kills him in single combat, and his body is spirited away by devils. – *Wigl* nm3652 a7316

Robert (1) 'Sir, von Tynasant', a knight who comes to welcome Willehalm (1) on his return from captivity with Gîburc. – *UW* 212,12

Robert (2) 'grâve von Flandern', a knight who fights for Jofrit (1) against Willehalm (3). His daughter marries Jofrit (2). – *RW* 475

---

10 Gottfried von Straßburg, *Tristan und Isolde*, transl. by W. Hertz, p. 544.
11 Gottfried von Straßburg, *Tristan und Isolde*, transl. by W. Hertz, p. 544.
12 Bruce (1), I, p. 186, note 60.

Robiel 'von Valpinose', a warrior in Akarîn's army against Ipomidôn. – *JT* nm3171,6 a3958,1

Rôbôâl a Roman Senator, in whose care Bêaflôr is placed on the death of Sâbîe (1). R. and his wife, Benignâ, bring her up and help her to escape from Teljôn. On her return to Rome, they find Bêaflôr and hide her until Meie arrives, when their meeting is arranged by R. – *MB* nm15,16 a16,26

Rôboam biblical (Rehoboam), son of Solomon and king of Judah. – nm *A* 16146; *UA* 11639

Rodago see Rodone

Rodegalte see Rogedâl

Rodois a warrior in the Greek army against the Trojans. This character was invented by Herbort. – *LT* 5822

Rodoltzen 'von Kanias', a warrior in Akarîn's army against Ipomidôn. It is said of R. that he produced children with horn skin by eating, and making his wife eat, certain herbs. – *JT* nm3313,1 a4118,1

Rodomalus see Rodomerius

Rodomerius natural son of Priam. R. fights for the Trojan army against the Greeks. This character appears to have been invented by Benoît, who calls him Rodomorus. – *LT* a4768f. n4778; *TK* 30376

Rodomolus see Rodomerius

Rodone mother of Dârîus (3). She is taken captive by Alexander after the first battle with Dârîus. In *A* and *UA*, as in Curtius Rufus and Gualterus, she is called Sisigambis, whilst in *SA* she is called Rodone and in *WA*, Rodago, these two forms deriving from Rodogoni, the name as it appears in Leo, which itself is derived from the Rogodune of Valerius and Pseudo-Callisthenes. – *A* a6820 n7575; *UA* a6215 n14938; *SA* a2918ff. n3719; *WA* a2043ff. n2283

Rogedâl 'cuns von Mirnetalle', a knight whom Parzivâl claims to have defeated. He occurs as 'grâve Rodegalte' in *JT*, where he is present at a tourney held by Arthur. – *P* nm772,7; *JT* 2017,2

Roibarbarke 'künec', a knight who fights for Orilus against Schîonatulander. – *JT* 4481,4

Royderodes a knight who is unhorsed by Êrec at the tourney held to celebrate the latter's wedding. This name appears to be a distorted form of Le roi de la Roge Cité, who is likewise unhorsed in Chrestien's *Erec* (2192). – *E* 2770f.

Roides a knight who attends the tourney held by Leigamar. R. is in the service of Aram. – *C* 18165

Roidurant a knight who brings to Arthur's court the first news of Elidîâ. – *L* nm7844

Roygier 'grâve von Tŷnant', who reports to Willehalm (1) the willingness of Lêô (1) to baptize Gîburc. – *UW* 244,13

Roynal 'herzoge von' (*UW*), see Kandanûr

Roisabins 'der ûz' (*JT*), see Kyrot

Roisilator a warrior in Akarîn's army against Ipomidôn. – *JT* 3624,1

Rôisse daughter of Zalancus. Alexander arrives at her land after the death of her father and defeats her army. She marries Pôdius (1). This character appears to have been invented by Ulrich. – *UA* a23728 n23805

Rocke 'der mit dem übelen gesnittenen', also called 'der mit dem ungesnitten R.', a knight who takes part in the tourney held by Arthur at Orgelus and who later joins in the search for the missing Parzivâl. In Gautier he is called cil à le Cote Mautaillie. – *RP* 472,41

Romûlus (1) the founder of Rome. In *GT* he is said to have surrendered his land to Hierobal for money, and to have sent his vassal, Remus, with the offer of an alliance to Ênêâs after the latter had left Troy. Together they attack Menon, who completely defeats them, and they retire to Rome, of which R. lays the first stone. He is the son of Carmelus in *GT*, whilst in Roman legend he is the son of Mars by Rhea Silvia. – *Ed* nm3674; *GT* 24935

Rômulus (2)   brother-in-law of Turnus. R. is slain by Ascânjus during the battle at Laurente. In the OF *Eneas* he is called Remullus, and in Virgil, Remelus. – *Ed* 7051f.

Rösane, Rosanne   see Roxane

Rosela 'küneginne von Kanadit', *amie* of Wildichon. – *WO* nm14698

Roscalcus   see Doroschalcus

Roxa   see Roxane

Roxane   daughter of Dârîus (3). She is captured by Alexander, who makes her his wife after the death of Dârîus. In Pseudo-Callisthenes, Valerius, and Leo, she is the daughter of Dârîus, but in *Expeditio Alexandri* and Curtius Rufus she is the daughter of Oxîatres. – *A* m5792f. a7586 n7599; *UA* m16828 a16977 n17208; *SA* 2921; *WA* a2043ff. n2065

Rûal 'li foitenant', husband of Floræte and marshal to Riwalîn. R. acts as foster-father to the boy Tristan and is deeply grieved when the latter is abducted. He searches for years through Europe and at last finds him at Marke's court, when he makes known the boy's true identity. Golther is of the opinion that this character was invented by Thomas,[13] who calls him Rohault (Roald), a name derived from the German Hrodowalt, Hruodwalt.[14] – *Tn* 463ff.; *HT* m5484 n6422

Rüall   see Ruell

Rûalt   see Rûal

Rubal   wife of Schrutor. R. is a giantess and is slain by Seyfrid. – *Sey* 94,4ff.

Rubel 'der schwartze', fetched by Hannor's sister to fight Eleander, who defeats him. – *GT* 20903ff.

Rubell   see Rubel

Ruben   biblical, brother of Jâcob (2). – *A* nm16239

Rubert (1)   ally of Ehkunat against Arthur. R., who is called 'künec von Gandîn', slays Elimâr (2) in the battle between Gârel and Ehkunat. – *G* m377 n11796 a12699

Rubert (2)   see Robert (2)

Rubin 'grâve von Sungalit', an ally of Lôîs against Terramêr. – *UW* 39,15

Rubiol   see Robiel

Rûbîûn   a warrior who is slain by Vivîans whilst fighting for Terramêr against Willehalm (1). So also in the OF *Aliscans*, where he is called Rubion. – *W* [27,12]

Rubrîcus   a warrior who is slain by Aristôn whilst fighting for Porrus against Alexander. So also in Gualterus. – *UA* 19669

Rûbûâl 'künec von Nourîente', a warrior in the service of Josweiz against Willehalm (1). Singer is unable to identify this character and suggests that there may have been an additional line in the MS of *Aliscans* used by Wolfram, which contained the name Roboant, a common name for Saracens.[15] – *W* 33,12ff.

Rudolf 'grâve von Arraz', the hero of a fragmentary 12th-century poem. R. fights for the Christians against the Saracens at Jerusalem, but then he apparently quarrels with the king of Jerusalem and goes over to the Sultan Halap, with whose daughter he falls in love. He fights for Halap against the Christians but uses only the flat of his sword. He later elopes with Halap's daughter, who is christened and receives the name Irmingart. – *GR* βb,2ff.

---

13   Golther (2), p. 145.
14   Gottfried von Straßburg, *Tristan und Isolde*, transl. by W. Hertz, p. 546.
15   Singer (2), p. 15.

Rüedegêr 'bischof von Passau'. R. is present at the tourney held at Friesach. Lachmann states that in 1224 Gebehart was bishop of Passau;[16] the mistake was probably due to a lapse of memory on the part of Ulrich. – *FD* 239,3

Rüedgêr 'von Antschowe', a knight who is present at the tourney held at Friesach and who also jousts with Ulrich von Liechtenstein during the latter's *Venusfahrt*. – *FD* 197,8

Ruel (1) 'der Sarasin', a giant who attacks Hector after the latter has just taken Samlon back to Baldach. R. is slain in the fight. – *GT* a1127 n1149

Rûel (2) wife of Ferôz. R. is a monstrous woman who captures Wigalois, as the latter will not deign to fight with a woman. Wigalois is saved by the neigh of his horse, which R. takes to be the roar of a dragon and flees. – *Wigl* a6285ff. n6353

Rüel (3) see Ruell

Ruell wife of Calabrus. R., who is a giantess, is slain by Paris as he returns with Marcus (1) to the court of Agâmennon. – *GT* a6654ff. n6670

Rugier 'von Doleise', one of the leaders in the army attacking Jovelîn. R. is captured by Tristan and Kâedîn. – *Tn* 18842

Rulf 'künec von Purgunden', a knight who is slain whilst fighting for the Christians against Gêrfridolt. – *Loh* nm3877 a3901

Rumalus see Romûlus (1)

Rûmolt the master of the royal kitchen at Worms in the *Nibelungenlied*. – *P* nm420,26 [†]

Rumolus, Rumuloss see Romûlus (1)

Runal see Kunal

Ruodelîn 'von Nuzperc', a knight who jousts with Ulrich von Liechtenstein during the latter's *Venusfahrt*. – *FD* 628,1

Ruodolf (1) 'von Ems', MHG poet, author of *RW* and *A*, among other works. – *RW* nm12241

Ruodolf (2) 'von Ras', a knight who is present at the tourney held at Friesach and who jousts with Ulrich von Liechtenstein during the latter's *Venusfahrt*. – *FD* 193,5

Ruolant the famous warrior in OF literature, one of the twelve peers of Charlemagne (see Karl (1)) and friend of Olivier (3). – nm *MC* 242; *W* 221,13; *UW* 31,1ff.; *RB* 16161; *FS* 1515

Ruopreht (1) 'grâve', a contemporary of Johann von Würzburg. – *WO* nm16921

Ruopreht (2) 'grâve von Nazzou', standard-bearer for the Christians in the battle against Gêrfridolt. – *Loh* 5107

Ruopreht (3) 'von Orbênt', the author of a poem which served as the original for *FB*. – *FB* nm142

Ruopreht (4) 'von Purstendorf', a knight who jousts with Ulrich von Liechtenstein during the latter's *Venusfahrt*. – *FD* 927,2f.

Ruoprecht son of Hainrich (5) and brother of Fridrich (3), for whom he fights against Mompolier. – *FS* m16 a31 n5040

Ruother 'künec', the hero of the MHG gleeman's poem which bears his name. – *RB* nm25280f.

Rûth biblical, the daughter-in-law of Naomi. – *UA* nm11485f.

---

16 Ulrich von Liechtenstein, *Frauendienst*, ed. by R. Bechstein, I, p. 89, to 239,3.

S

Sabaa 'der von' (*JT*), see Sabelle

Sabelle 'von Sabadale', also called 'von Sabaa' and Sabellus, a warrior who is unhorsed by Ehkunat whilst fighting for Ipomidôn against Akarîn. – *JT* m3264,4ff. n3268,1f. a3977,1

Sabellus see Sabelle

Sâbîe (1) wife of Teljôn and mother of Bêaflôr (q.v.). S. dies when her daughter is ten years old. – *MB* a4,32f. n5,5

Sabîe (2) a maiden who is being persecuted by Gerhart (2), who fights her father and has killed her brother Kilpert. Gârel (2) fights and defeats Gerhart for her but refuses her proffered hand and lands. She marries Flôrîs (2). – *G* a834 n901

Sabilor brother of Parille (1). – *JT* m104,1 n105,5

Sabrinuntze 'grâve', a knight who takes part in the tourney held by Arthur. – *JT* 2050,1f.

Sadoch (1) a heathen king who distinguishes himself at the tourney held by Meliûr. Saduc occurs as a variant of Sardup, a Saxon against whom Arthur and his knights fight in *L'Estoire de Merlin* (Vulgate Cycle). (See also Sadoch (2).) – *PM* 14476ff.

Sadoch (2) the king for whom the helmet was made which Wildhelm chooses from the treasure of Joraffin. (Identical with Sadoch (1)?) – *WO* nm3918

Sadolech a king who had built a temple in Baldac (Bagdad). – *WO* nm5534

Sagar a vassal in the service of Gamorett, for whom he fights against Agâmennon. – *GT* 5673

Sagarz a knight who attends Leigamar's tourney in the service of Aram. – *C* 18169

Sagoss 'amiral von Tamys', a knight who challenges Segromans after the latter has killed Avenor. S. is also killed. – *GT* 24217ff.

Sagramamors see Segremors

Sagramans see Segromans

Sagremors see Segremors

Sahsen 'der von' (*RB*), see Reinfrit

Sakur 'de Laloe', the owner of a castle past which Parzivâl travels. In Manessier he is called Sacus de la Loy. – *RP* nm750,45f.

Saladres 'von den Inseln', father of Dinisodres, Menassides, Nactor, Aristes, and Gorgone. They all attack Parzivâl and are defeated by him. In Manessier he is called Salandres. – *RP* a842,6 n844,37

Salamôn see Salomôn

Salander 'von Iparat', a warrior in Ipomidôn's army against Akarîn. – *JT* 3230,1

Salatel (1) 'künec', a knight who fights on the side of the heathens in the final battle against the Christians. – *WO* 16347

Salatel (2) 'von Antioche', a warrior in Akarîn's army against Ipomidôn. – *JT* nm3140,6f.

Salatiele 'künec von Leunnigrunse', a warrior who is killed whilst fighting for Akarîn against Ipomidôn. – *JT* nm3091,1

Salatin 'von Setzeleise', a warrior who is killed (3913,1) whilst fighting for Akarîn against Ipomidôn. – *JT* 3122,6f.

Salatrê a former owner of Arofel's sword. He passes it on to Antikôte. In *Aliscans* he is called Salatrez. – *W* nm77,24f.

Salatrias 'künec von Kaldê', a heathen ally of Ehkunat against Arthur. He is killed by Eskilabôn during the battle between Gârel (2) and Ehkunat. – *G* m368 a12512f. n12692

251

Salaphat 'künec', brother of Melchinor (see Persit), for whom he fights against Walwan (3). He is slain by Wildhalm in the final battle between the Christians and the heathens. – *WO* nm6155 a7948

Salafes the pre-baptismal name of Nasiens (q.v.). – *RP* nm614,42

Salîn 'vürste', a knight who wounds Gawein whilst fighting for Lîôn against Wigalois. – *Wigl* 11070f.

Salistria see Tâlistrîâ

Salmanâ 'künec von Madiân', biblical (Zalmunna, the Midianite chieftain). In Pseudo-Methodius he is called Salmana. – *A* nm17263

Salmânasar 'künec von Assîrîâ', biblical (Shalmaneser). According to *SA*, he was 'künec von Nyniphe'. – nm *A* 16784; *SA* 4228

Salmanîde a knight who, together with his brother, Ansgavîn, attacks any knight who sounds the horn in the castle of Blandukors. S. is killed by Gawein. – *C* m7395 a7434ff. n7463ff.

Salme one of Angelburg's companions in her enchantment. On regaining permanently her human shape, S. marries Uolrich (1). – *FS* m350 a711ff. n1347

Salmurte 'herzoge von Zwäge', uncle of Diether (1), a knight who takes part in the tourney held by Arthur for the crown of Deleprosat and who also accompanies Arthur to the relief of Isope. – *Wigm* 2195

Saloman see Salomôn

Salomôn biblical, son of David. He is mentioned in *P* (453,26) as an ancestor of Flegetanîs: 'ûz israhêlscher sippe'. Golther points out that one of the ancestors of Thabit (see Têbit) was named Salaman or Solomon and sees in this reference a mixture of the Arabian and the biblical.[1] Bruce and Martin, on the other hand think that the reference is purely biblical.[2] – nm *E* 2816; *L* 4761; *P* 289,17; *LT* 8519; *MC* 1162; *DB* 1586; *W* 448,13; *C* 8452; *A* 9963; *Wigm* 2697; *FD* Büchlein III,42; *JT* 199,5; *PM* 8892; *TK* 1990; *MB* 130,2; *UA* 21; *RB* 13691; *SA* 1928

Salustine wife of Evas and mother of Gayte and Prophilias. – *AP* aA*,62 nC*,17

Salvidantze 'vürste von Ipodone', also 'von Permidone', a knight who takes part in the tourney held by Arthur. – *JT* 2047,1

Samaidîe the name given by a knight, who challenges Gawein, to a maiden who is riding at Gawein's side. S. strengthens Gawein when he appears to be giving way to the temptation to joust with this knight, as he has been warned by Aanzim to ride straight ahead and to ignore all challenges. It transpires that S. is Aanzim's sister and a messenger from Vrou Sælde. – *C* a16352ff. n16449ff.

Sambron a knight who takes part in the tourney held by Arthur. – *JT* 2132,5

Samias see Sanias

Samiledech 'von Baldac, der heiden bâbest', present in the Trojan army against the Greeks. This character was invented by Konrad. – *TK* 24820

Samirant (1) 'von Boitendroit', a warrior who assists in arming Terramêr prior to the second battle at Alischanz. He is also (359,1) called 'von Bêâterre' (see Krohier) and is slain by Rennewart. In *Aliscans* he is called Salmuant (var. Samiant – all MSS are different). [See Appendix (6).] – *W* 356,18f.

Samirant (2) see Samirat

---

1   Golther (1), p. 202.
2   Bruce (1), I, p. 316; Martin (1), p. 350, to 453,26.

Samirat 'von Falfunde', also called 'Samirant ûz Valgun', a warrior in Akarîn's army against Ipomidôn. There seems to be no doubt that the source of this name is Samirant (1), who is mentioned in *W* 413,27, whilst 414,7 there occurs: 'des hers ûz Falfundê'. – *JT* nm3140,5 a3946,6

Samlon a wise man who lives in Baldach and who alone can interpret the dream of Ecubâ (3). He is fetched to Troy by Hector and foretells the fall of the city. – *GT* nm99 a311f.

Sampson biblical. – nm *E* 2818; *LT* 11227; *DB* 1579; *JT* 1726,5; *PM* 8888; *TK* 2182; *UA* 11478f.; *RB* 15167; *Ll* 70,4

Samsab biblical, 'künec von Êôthâ'. S. is mentioned in Pseudo-Methodius. – *A* nm17191

Samsôn (1) 'von Blavî', a knight who is captured by Halzebier whilst endeavouring to rescue Vîvîans. He is later (416,11) rescued by Rennewart. In *UW* he fights for Lôis against Terramêr. S. occurs in *Aliscans*, where he is called Sanson. – *W* 25,10; *UW* 46,3

Samsôn (2) see Sampson

Sâmûêl (1) 'künec', a warrior who is slain by Rennewart whilst fighting for Terramêr in the second battle at Alischanz. So also in *Aliscans*. – *W* 359,8

Samuêl (2) biblical, the prophet. – nm *A* 16086; *UA* 11517; *RB* 13146f.

Sandarap see Bandarap

Sandinôse daughter of grâve von der Grüenen Ouwe (q.v.). S. captures Daniel in an invisible net but releases him, and he frees her father's land. Later she marries Beladigant. – *DB* a4161ff. n8283ff.

Sanga son of Mêthâ, a warrior who is slain by Clîtus whilst fighting for Dârîus against Alexander at Erbela. This character appears to have been invented by Ulrich. – *UA* nm12115ff.

Sangîve (The MSS vary widely with the reproduction of this name, Sagive, Sayve and Seifê (see below) appearing. Bartsch and Martin take Sayve to be the correct form < OF *saive*, 'wise', as also did Schulz.[3] Martin thinks, however, that the more correct MS variants are the work of later copyists, who realised what Wolfram's form came from.[4]) S. is the wife of Lôt (1) and mother of Gawein. In *P* she is imprisoned by Klinschor with her two daughters, Itonjê and Kundrîe (2), and her mother, Arnive (see Îgerne); S. is also the sister of Arthur. On her release by Gawein she marries Flôrant. She is not named in *C*, where her retirement, like that of Îgerne, is voluntary, but in *Meleranz* she is called Seifê, and in *JT*, Savie. In Geoffrey of Monmouth she is called Anna; she is identical with Morchades (2) (q.v.) and Soye (1) (q.v.). – *P* m66,4 n334,16ff. a565,21; *L* m2495; *C* m13588; *M* nm127ff.; *JT* 1774,1; *RP* m9,28

Sanias a warrior in the Trojan army against the Greeks. S. is also called Samias, and the name appears in both these forms in Benoît. – *LT* 4026

Saniel 'herzoge von Tulangar', an ally of Lôîs against Terramêr. – *UW* 36,29

Sannabâlâch see Saraballâ

Sannoriz a knight who attends Leigamar's tourney in the service of Aram. – *C* 18167

***Sansôn** see Samsôn

Santippus see Cantipus (1)

Sanfalê a heathen king who is slain by Willehalm (1) whilst fighting for Terramêr against Lôîs. – *UW* 50,28f.

---

3 Bartsch (2), pp. 145f.; Martin (1), pp. 278f., to 334,22; Schulz, 'Eigennamen', p. 395.
4 Wolfram von Eschenbach, *Parzival und Titurel*, ed. by E. Martin, vol. I, p. xxxiii.

Sanze the subject of some songs sung in French by Îsolt (2). The index to Bechstein's edition of *Tn* quotes San Marte's suggestion that this name is < San Dde (the father of St. David) > Sandde, which would be spoken with a soft *z* sound, and > Sanze. – *Tn* nm8066

Saptesî a warrior whom Alexander turns out of his army and who joins Dârîus. S. occurs only in the S group of MSS of Leo, where he is called Stapsy.[5] – *A* 6003ff.

Sar 'künec von' (*WO*), see Melysmaphat

*Sar 'künec von Asya', a knight who fights on the side of the heathens in the final battle against the Christians. The death of the 'künec von Asya' is reported in line 17815. (Identical with Melysmaphat, 'künec von Sar', or with Melyemodan, 'künec von Asya'?) – *WO* nm16365f. a17757ff.

Sârâ biblical, wife of Abraham. – nm *A* 17210; *UA* 11300

Saraballâ a judge appointed by Dârîus over Judah. In *A* he is the father-in-law of Manasses (1), whilst in *UA* he is called Sannabâlâch. – *A* 9900f.; *UA* 17793f.

Sarant (1) the weaver of a fine cloth worn by Gawein. This name seems quite certainly an invention of Wolfram, who took the name of the cloth, *sârantasmê*, which, as Martin points out,[6] occurs already in *Ed* (9310), and divided it into Sarant, the name of the maker, and Tasme, the town, which he places in Sekundille's land, in which it was made (629,21). – *P* nm629,17

Sarant (2) 'der Vâlant', whom Gawein recalls having defeated. – *C* nm9031

Saras a warrior in the Trojan army against the Greeks. This character does not appear in any other version of the Trojan legend. – *LT* 3985

Sardineas see Sardineus

Sardineus natural son of Priam, a warrior in the Trojan army against the Greeks. This character appears to have been invented by Benoît, who calls him Sarde. – *LT* a4808 n4826

Sareht 'soldan von Babylônje', a warrior in the Trojan army against the Greeks. This character appears to have been invented by Konrad. – *TK* 24805ff.

Sâret nephew of Sornagiur, for whom he is fighting when he is slain by Partonopier. – *PM* 3714ff.

Sargidun 'von Waledeise', a warrior in Akarîn's army against Ipomidôn. – *JT* 3191,1

Saridên a Greek warrior whom Alexander turns out from his army. S. goes to Dârîus. He tells Dârîus that his army is not strong enough to fight Alexander, and Dârîus kills him in rage. This character appears to have been invented by Rudolf. – *A* 5207

Sarîne *amie* of Lybials, whom she sends to challenge Meleranz. – *M* m3470f. n3582

Sarpedon 'von Lize', a warrior in the Trojan army against the Greeks. S. is the brother of Glaucon, and in *LT* he is slain by Palimedes. So also in Benoît and Dares. In *TK* he is called 'künec von Laucônje', but he is correctly described as 'künec von Liciâ' in *TKf* when his death (not described) is lamented, as in Dictys. In Dictys, as in Homer, S. is slain by Patroclus. – *LT* 3990; *TK* 24808f.

Sarsencius 'grâve', a warrior in the Greek army against the Trojans. This character was invented by Konrad. – *TK* 26134f.

Sârtibarzânes a warrior, formerly in the service of Dârîus, who surrenders to Alexander but becomes unfaithful and flees to Bessus. He offers single combat to Alexander's army, and this is accepted by the commander, Erîgûus, who kills him. S. is also called (20701) Sâtibarzânes, the form in which his name appears in *Expeditio Alexandri* and Curtius Rufus. – *A* 18544f.

---

5   O. Zingerle, p. 58.
6   Martin (1), p. 439, to 629,17 and 629,27.

Saruz a knight who attends Leigamar's tourney in the service of Aram. – *C* 18167

Sarfrasatam wife of one of Noah's sons. (See Farsatam.) – *UA* nm11251

Sassine see Saffein

Satam wife of one of Noah's sons. (See Farsatam.) – *UA* nm11252

Satanâs (Satan). – nm *ET* 3400f.; *LT* 3499; *MB* 20,39; *Mer* 20,5; *Sey* 3,7; *UA* 17955; *WO* 3614

Satâzes 'von Egiptô', a warrior who is killed by Alexander whilst fighting for Dârîus. This character appears to have been invented by Rudolf. – *A* 7489

Sathan, Sathanas see Satanâs

Sâtibarzânes see Sârtibarzânes

Satrî 'von Angorant', a knight who has to fight a duel for his fief. If he wins, he can choose any lady of the court for his wife. He has to fight the burcgrâve von Angersper, whom he defeats, and he chooses and marries Achûte. – *Crane* 4282ff.

Satrôpates a warrior who leads the first attack in the second battle against Alexander. He is defeated and killed by Aristonâ. S. occurs also in Curtius Rufus. – *A* 10788f.

Saturnus the Roman god of agriculture. In *TK* he is said to be the father of Jupiter. – nm *TK* 14456; *GT* 12213

Saul (1) biblical, the OT king. – nm *A* 16091; *UA* 11531; *RB* 13153

Saul (2) biblical (St. Paul). – *UA* nm6292

Sapfadin a heathen king who has fifteen wives and sixteen sons, one of whom is Melchinor (see Persit). – *WO* nm5785

Saphatine 'von Montanie', a warrior in Akarîn's army against Ipomidôn. – *JT* 3124,3ff.

Savie see Sangîve

Savilôn a magician born in Athens who imprisoned the devil in a glass and prophesied the birth of Christ 1200 years before the event. He is mentioned in *Wartburgkrieg* (Manesse MS, CXXXII): 'Wer gab dir Zabulones buoch sage fürwert wiser man/ das Virgilius uf den agetsteine mit grossen nöten gewan'.[7] Virgil's acquisition of S.'s secrets is related also in *RB*.[8] – *RB* nm21028

Sävine sister of Rainher and abbess on the Isle of Desylvoys. She is attacked by Alan, but Amelot, to whom she appeals, routs the latter's army. S. goes to Rainher to report the matter and finds that Amely is very ill. She learns that the reason is Amely's love for Willehalm (4), whom she recognizes from Amely's description. She takes Amely back to Norway with her and unites the two lovers. – *RW* 11795ff.

Saffadin see Sapfadin

Saffein daughter of Saffian, a maiden who is rescued by Êrec from the persecution of the grâve von dem Wizen berg. – *GM* nm (MS I) 13552 a2137f.

Saffian father of Saffein. – *GM* (MS I) nm13553

Sê 'ritter von dem' (*L*), see Lanzelet

Sebin see Sibille (1)

Sedechîa see Sedechîê

Sedechîê biblical (Zedekiah), the last king of Judah, who reigned at the time of Jeremiah. He is called Sedecia in the *Historia Scholastica*. – *UA* nm7651

Segramans, Segramansz see Segromans

Segramurs see Segremors

---

7   *Wartburgkrieg*, p. 88.

8   An estimation of the position occupied by Savilôn in the medieval legends about Virgil is to be found in Comparetti, pp. 316f.

Segremans see Segromans

Segremors (Schulz derived this name from Celtic *segr*, 'apart', and *mawr*, 'mighty'.[9] It is one of the few names which are always met in MHG with the OF nominative *s* as a part of the word.) S. is first mentioned in Chrestien's *Erec* (1733), where he is called Sagremors li desreez, i.e., 'the uncontrollable', a characteristic which is well brought out by Wolfram (*P* 285,2), where S. rushes into Arthur's tent to obtain permission to fight the unknown knight (Parzivâl), in spite of Arthur's orders that no fighting is to take place in that vicinity. Wolfram adds (285,3ff.): 'swâ der vehten wânde vinden,/ dâ muoste man in binden/ oder er wolde dâ mite sîn'. He is evidently visualized by Wolfram, as Schulz puts it, as a 'ritterlicher Berserker'.[10] S. is called (*P* 286,25) 'Segremors rois', and since this particular combination of words does not occur in Chrestien, Singer argues that Wolfram must have had another French poem from which he was translating, i.e. Kîot.[11] In *Wigm* this has become S. von Roy (cf. Seckmur). The adventures of S. in the MHG epics are the customary adventures of a minor character, his usual fate being that he is unhorsed by the hero (so in *P*, *JT*, *GM*, and *Sey*). (See also Editons.) S. is the hero of a fragmentary poem (*S*) which bears his name and which seems to be a very free rendering in MHG of the OF *Meraugis de Portlesguez*; it is possible to fit the existing fragments of *S* into the framework of *Meraugis*, but every name has been altered, with the exception of Gawein, who is virtually a prisoner with a lady who compels any knight who defeats her champion to stay with her until he is himself defeated and killed. S. escapes with Gawein by a trick, and then the two knights have to rescue S.'s *amie*, Nyobe, who had accompanied him on his quest for Gawein, but who had in the meantime been made a prisoner.[12] – *E* 1665; *I* 88; *P* 285,2; *Wigl* 463; *C* 2323; *S* Iᵃ,3; *Wigm* 2005; *FD* nm1439,2; *UW* nm256,1ff.; *JT* 1349,3; *Sey* 56,4; *RB* nm20162; *GM* 696; *RP* 81,23

Segrimors see Segremors

Segromans 'Conuz, künec von Persia, künec von Saba', son of Agboys. A knight who comes to Agâmennon's court to woo Helen after her return from Troy and after the unsuccessful attempt of Bevar. He kills many of Agâmennon's knights in battle and leads Helen away to Persia, where he marries her. Agâmennon follows with a large army, and S. offers him wide lands to avoid war. He refuses, and a battle is fought, in which Agâmennon is slain. – *GT* 24038ff.

Segudaris a young knight who fights for the Trojans in the first war against the Greeks. In Benoît he is called Seguradon. – *LT* 1446f.

Segufar entertains Firganant in Fandorîch's castle. – *Dem* a6561f. n10646f.

Seigremors see Segremors

Seimeret a maiden who plays the same part in *C* as does Antikonîe in *P*. When Gawein is relating the story to Arthur he calls her (22750) Soreidôz. – *C* a18797ff. n18881

***Seimoret** see Seimeret

Seifê see Sangîve

Seyfrid (1) son of Kundrîe (2) and Lischois Gwelljus. At an early age S. leaves home to go to Arthur's court. On the way he frees four ladies from Klinschor's clutches by killing the giant Amphigulor, and when he arrives at Arthur's court, he is met by many knights, all of

---

9 Schulz, 'Eigennamen', p. 396.
10 Schulz, 'Eigennamen', p. 396.
11 Singer (1), pp. 97f.
12 In *UW* the name of Segremors's *amie* is given as Dulcicors, and an adventure is mentioned in which he is unhorsed by a knight named Prinel.

whom he unhorses. He undertakes the rescue of Condiflor, in which, after numerous adventures, he succeeds, and then makes the acquaintance of a fairy, Mundirosa, with whom he falls in love and who loves him. She warns him to be constant and to return in a year but in the meantime to let no-one know of their love. S. wins Duzisamor in a tourney but will not marry her, as he confesses that he knows a lady far more beautiful, thus breaking his promise to Mundirosa. The latter arrives just in time to save S. from death, the penalty for not marrying Duzisamor, but tells him that he will never see her again, since he has broken his promise. By sewing himself inside a horse's hide (cf. *Herzog Ernst*), he gets a griffin to carry him to Ardemonte, where he arrives just in time to rescue Mundirosa from the attentions of Girot, whom he kills. S. marries Mundirosa, and they have a son, Flormund. (Cf. Gauriel.) – *Sey* m2,6 a7,6 n8,6

Seyfrid (2) the author of *SA*. The name is given only in some of the MSS. – *SA* nm9067

Seifrit see Sîvrit (7)

Seckmur 'von Rois', a knight who is at Arthur's court when Êrec returns with Ênîte. This name does not appear in Chrestien's *Erec* in the corresponding list of knights, and Singer is of the opinion that it is a later interpolation in imitation of Segremors[13] (taken from *P* or *Wigm*?). – *E* 1685

Secoraisse see Secureis

Secundare see Sekundille

Sekundille (It is generally agreed that this name is taken from Solinus, who mentions a Secundilla who was buried in Rome.[14]) S. is a heathen queen who sends to Amfortas Malkrêâtiure and Kundrîe (1). She is mentioned later (740,10) as the *amie* of Feirefîz, and news of her death is brought just before Feirefîz marries Repanse de Schoie. In *JT* she is the daughter of Secureis and Arabadille, names obviously invented from Sekundille, and she holds a tourney to decide which of her many wooers she shall marry. The winner is Feirefîz. – *P* nm519,2; *W* nm55,1; *R* nm Forts. II,28; *JT* nm2935,2 a4812,3f.; *RB* nm15284

Secureis 'ûz Tabrunit', husband of Arabadille and father of Sekundille (q.v.). S. is a brave and courteous knight, and it is agreed before the battle between Akarîn and Ipomidôn, in whose service S. stands, that he and Schîonatulander shall avoid each other. During the battle, however, S. loses his distinguishing sign and is unwittingly slain by Schîonatulander, to the great grief of both sides. – *JT* nm2933,1f. a2980,1; *RB* nm16648

Sêkurîe a maiden whose kingdom is usurped by Acurteis. She comes to the court of the kaiser for a champion and chooses Gayol. On their way to fight Acurteis they are joined by Agorlîn, who falls in love with S., who is only twelve years old. After Gayol has slain Acurteis, Agorlîn takes S. back with him to Austria, where he marries her. – *Crane* a2067f. n3814

Seleucus Nicânor a prince who took Pontus and Asîâ after the death of Alexander. In *SA* he is called Seleutus and is a nephew of Alexander, who makes him marshal on his deathbed. Historically S. is Seleucus Nicator, who became ruler of Syria and Asia Minor on the death of Alexander. He is mentioned in Valerius and Leo. – *UA* 27643ff.; *SA* nm8507

Seleutus see Seleucus Nicânor

Sellum biblical, king of Israel. S. is mentioned in the *Historia Scholastica* (*Liber IV Regum* XXII). – *A* nm16702

Selrogier a knight who brings the news of Arthur's help to Ysope. – *Wigm* 3105

Sem biblical (Shem), son of Noah. – nm *A* 17103; *UA* 11285

---

13 Singer (1), p. 60.
14 Martin (1), p. 387, to 519,2.

Sembrant a commander in Bêâmunt's army at Antrîûn. – *Dem* nm9934 a11023

Semeî biblical, an enemy of David. He is mentioned in the *Historia Scholastica* (*Liber II Regum* XV). – *UA* nm11620

Semilidac 'von Atropiezze', a warrior in Ipomidôn's army against Akarîn. – *JT* 3231,5

Semligors see Senilgorz

Semöss a knight who is killed whilst fighting for Matribulus against Agâmennon. – *GT* 3469

Sempitebruns see Brun

Senabor (1) 'von Valturnie', a warrior in Akarîn's army against Ipomidôn. – *JT* 3623,1

***Senabor** (2) see Senebor

Senator 'von Ponte', a warrior in Akarîn's army against Ipomidôn. – *JT* 3195,1

Senebalŷn an ally of Lôîs against Terramêr. Willehalm (1) and Gîburc later shelter at his castle during their flight from Tîbalt. – *UW* 36,28

Senebor father of Parille and ancestor of Titurel. S. is the first of the family to become a Christian. In *WO* he is called 'künec von Capadocia' and comes to the assistance of his grandson, Agrant, with giants and 'snabelohte liute'. He fights on the side of the heathens against the Christians in the final battle and is captured. It is then that his conversion takes place. S. is called Senabor in *JT*. – *JT* nm89,1f.; *WO* 7766f. [†]

Seneca the Roman philosopher and dramatist. – nm *MA* 250; *UA* Anhang,1268; *SA* 46

Senibalin see Senebalŷn

Senilgorz 'künec von Sirnegunz', a knight whom Parzivâl claims to have defeated. In *JT* the scene of this defeat is where S. is attacking Teanglis, who is rescued by Parzivâl. – *P* nm772,5; *JT* a5522,3f. n5524,4

Sennes 'herzoge von Narjoklîn'. (Martin quotes Hagen as deriving this name from Solinus, who mentions (50,14) Campus Hennensis; Narjoklîn, he says, looks like Narici, another fertile district mentioned by Solinus, thus causing it to be linked by Wolfram with Campus Hennensis, which is the fertile Sicilian district of Enna.[15]) S. is one of the knights whom Feirefîz claims to have defeated. The author of *JT*, misreading *P*, calls him Markalm von Semolonie; in this poem he is one of the knights who take part in the tourney held by Sekundille to decide which of her wooers she shall marry. – *P* nm770,21; *JT* 5280,3f.

Sennor one of a band of robbers who attack Paris and Marcus (1) as they are returning to Agâmennon's court. S. is killed by Paris. – *GT* a6491ff. n6528

Senpitebrun see Brun

Senuligoz see Senilgorz

Serabel see Serabil

Serabil 'künec von Rozokarz', a knight whom Parzival claims to have defeated. He is present at Arthur's tourney in *JT*, where he is called Serabel von Katekarte. He occurs again later (5514,3f.), when he takes Parzivâl to be Îthêr, who had slain his brother. He attacks Parzivâl, and it is now that the defeat recorded in *P* takes place. – *P* nm772,3; *JT* 1986,1

Serapis the Egyptian god. In all versions he tells the Egyptians of the finality of the flight of Nectanabus. – *A* 398; *SA* 157; *WA* 115f.

Serapheis, Seraphin see Serapis

Sêren 'von Trîbalibôt', a warrior in Dârîus's army. This character appears to have been invented by Ulrich. – *UA* 10951

Sermiduns 'von Irdibol', a warrior who is killed by Ehkunat whilst fighting for Ipomidôn against Akarîn. – *JT* 3230,6

---

15 Martin (1), p. 504, to 770,21.

Serpentariax 'von Pante', a warrior in Ipomidôn's army against Akarîn. – *JT* 3366,1

Serre 'künec von der' (*C*), see Laniure

Seruk 'von Firmidise', also called Serut, brother of Kalebitor. S. is a warrior in Ipomidôn's army against Akarîn. – *JT* 3370,1

Serut see Seruk

Set biblical, son of Adam. He is called Sheth in I Chronicles 1. – *A* nm17015

Sgaipegaz daughter of Blandukors. She falls in love with Gawein during his short stay at her father's castle. – *C* 6943

Sgoidamûr sister of Amurfinâ (q.v.) and daughter of Laniure. She eventually marries Gasosîn. – *C* m7914 n7926 a12640ff.

Siamerac 'von Lembîl', a lady to whose house Gawein comes after he has defeated the dragon to which Giramphiel sent him. S. gives him a magic suit of armour. – *C* 15220ff.

Sibeche counsellor to Ermenrîch in MHG heroic literature. – *P* nm421,23

Sibene 'von Melibete', a warrior in the Greek army against the Trojans. This character does not occur in any other version of the Trojan legend. – *LT* 3398

Sibillâ see Sibille (1)

Sibille (1) in classical legend there were ten Sibyls, but in the Middle Ages the word came to be used as the name of one, the Cunaean Sibyl who shows Ênêâs round Hades in Virgil and also in the OF *Eneas* and *Ed*. She was popularly supposed to have foretold the birth of Christ, and she constantly appeared with Virgil in the Mystery Plays.[16] – *Ed* nm2600 a2687f; *L* nm8866; *E* nm5216; *P* nm465,23; *W* nm218,13; *JT* nm2433,3; *Loh* nm231; *Ll* (MS K) nm19,9

Sŷbille (2) wife of Gûrâz and sister-in-law of Fênix (2), who sends Flôre to her to be educated. Whilst Flôre is with S., Blanscheflûr is sold into captivity. – *FB* nm958f. a1387

Sîbot 'von Richenvels', a knight who jousts with Ulrich von Liechtenstein during the latter's *Venusfahrt*. – *FD* 700,4ff.

Sydaras daughter of Amerillus. – *GT* 12854ff.

Sydrach see Ananîas

Sygan see Sigûne

Sygelint daughter of Gawein, one of the maidens who read the Graal message concerning Elsam. – *Loh* nm459 a477

Sigenant see Signant

Sigeram 'burcgrâve', killed in battle (for Tirol and Vridebrant?) against the heathens. – *Tirol* nmF,15

Signant 'grâve von Haspingo', a knight who fights for Jofrit (1) against Willehalm (3) by whom he is killed. – *RW* 481ff.

Sigris a knight who carries the challenge of Nerorx and Moabigal to Agâmennon. – *GT* a12238f. n12311

Sigûne (Schulz suggested a derivation of this name from *cygne*, 'swan',[17] whilst Bartsch sees in it the feminine of the OF name Seguin < OHG Siguwin,[18] a view which Singer shares.[19] Martin compares S. with Signý, the faithful wife of Loki.[20]) S. is the daughter of Kîot (1) and Schoisiâne. Her early history is told in *T*, where her mother dies in child-birth,

---

16 Comparetti, pp. 309ff.
17 Schulz, 'Eigennamen', p. 391.
18 Bartsch (2), p. 14.
19 Singer (1), pp. 72f.
20 Martin (1), p. 139, to 138,17.

and S., at an early age, goes to live with Herzeloide. She and Gahmuret's young squire, Schîonatulander, fall in love with each other but are separated when Gahmuret returns to Bagdad. The second fragment of *T* shows the two lovers together in a wood. Schîonatulander captures an escaped hound, and whilst S. reads the inscription on the collar and leash, Schîonatulander goes fishing. The hound escapes, and S. insists on Schîonatulander's finding it and bringing it back for her to finish reading the inscription. In *P*, Parzivâl meets her immediately after his encounter with Jeschûte. S. has the embalmed body of Schîonatulander in her arms. She tells Parzivâl that she is his cousin, informs him of his parentage, and tells him that the hound's leash had caused the death of Schîonatulander at the hands of Orilus. Parzivâl meets her again after his first visit to the Graal Castle (249,11), and a third time in a hermit's cell (435,13). Always she has the body of her dead lover with her. Once more Parzivâl sees her, this time dead in a posture of prayer by the body of Schîonatulander (804,21ff.), as he is on his way to take up his position as Graal King. In Chrestien, S. is not named and occurs only once, whereas Wolfram, who no doubt invented the story in *T*, deepens her character out of all measure, and introduces her immediately prior to each turning point in Parzivâl's career. *JT* combines the stories of *T* and *P* but adds little new matter. That the story of S. and Schîonatulander enjoyed considerable popularity in Germany during the Middle Ages, is clear from the numerous instances in which historical persons bore the name of Sigûne, Panzer recording many instances from 1330 onwards,[21] and Zingerle quoting it as the most popular feminine name from the Court Epics from 1286 onwards.[22] – *P* 138,13ff.; *T* a18,1 n24,1; *C* a13980ff.; *JT* a635,1 n642,1; *WO* nm14531; *FS* nm1457 [†]

Sicamor a Moor who is wounded by Palimedes whilst fighting for the Trojans against the Greeks. So also in Benoît. – *LT* 4527f.

Sichêus a former husband of Dîdô. S. was slain by Dîdô's brother. So also in the OF *Eneas*; in Virgil he is called Sychaeus. – *Ed* nm298

Sicrass a vassal of Gamorett, for whom he fights against Agâmennon. – *GT* 5670

Silâres see Ares

Silarin a lady who was loved, according to medieval legend, by Aristôtiles, whom she persuaded to wear a saddle so that she could ride on his back, to the amusement of the court. The story is told in the MHG poem *Aristoteles und Phyllis*,[23] in which she is called Fillis, and also in a *Fastnachtsspiel* by Hans Sachs, *Persones, die königin reit den philosophum Aristotelem*. F. von der Hagen gives a list of other versions of this story,[24] but in none of them is the lady called Silarin. – *RB* nm15182

Sylilous natural son of Priam, a warrior in the Trojan army against the Greeks. This character appears to have been invented by Benoît, who calls him Sisilens. He occurs as Sysileus also in *LT*, whilst in *TK* he is called Sinfiliens and Simfiliens. – *LT* a4768f. n4781; *TK* 30380f.

Syloys the wounded mother of the five maidens whom Paris finds naked in a wood. Paris defeats their oppressor, Meloantz (1). – *GT* m9315 a9546 n9621

Silvester 'sante'. – *P* nm795,30

Silviâne daughter of Tŷrus (1) (q.v.). In the OF *Eneas* and Virgil she is called Sylvia. – *Ed* 4582ff.

---

21   Panzer (2), p. 215.
22   I.V. Zingerle, p. 294.
23   F. von der Hagen, *Gesammtabenteuer*, I, pp. 17ff.
24   F. von der Hagen, *Gesammtabenteuer*, I, pp. lxxvff.

Silvius brother of Prutus, whose lands S. usurps. According to Geoffrey of Monmouth, S. is the son of Ascanius (cf. Silvjus). – *Mer* nm1,5

Silvjas Ênjas see Silvjus Ênêâs

Silvjus son of Ênêâs and Lavinîa. He is called thus because he is born (13332f.) in a wood. (See also Silvius.) S. is called Silvius in the OF *Eneas* and in Virgil. – *Ed* nm3652

Silvjus Ênêâs son of Silvjus, so called because he is the exact image of Ênêâs. He occurs in the OF *Eneas* and in Virgil. – *Ed* nm3659

Symachus a warrior who is killed whilst making a raid with Nicânor (3) on Porrus's army. This character does not occur in any other history of Alexander. – *UA* a19469 n19494

Sîmam one of the fellow-conspirators of Dimnus in the plot to murder Alexander. In Curtius Rufus and *Expeditio Alexandri* he is called Simias. – *A* 20041

Symeôn (1) Alexander's scribe. Alexander bequeaths to him Capadocia and Paphlagonia. S. occurs in Leo. – *UA* 26987; *SA* 8422f.; *WA* 6169f.

Simeôn (2) biblical, the priest in Jerusalem to whom the Christ-child was brought. (Luke 2. 25). – *RB* nm18003

Symo see Symeôn (1)

Simfiliens see Sylilous

Sînagûn 'künec von Bailîe', a warrior who fights for Terramêr against Willehalm (1) at Alischanz. He flees with Terramêr when the heathens are defeated in the second battle. The story of the capture of Willehalm by S., told briefly in *W* (220,15ff.), is related in *UW*, where S. fights for Terramêr against Lôis. S. is called Sinagon in *Aliscans* and occurs also in *Les Enfances Vivien* and *Anseïs de Cartage*. – *W* 27,13; *UA* 42,3

Sinagune 'von Eropisune', a warrior in Akarîn's army against Ipomidôn. A Saxon king named Synagons occurs in *L'Estoire de Merlin* (Vulgate Cycle) and the *Livre d'Artus*, but the name in *JT* is almost certainly taken from *W*. – *JT* nm3172,1ff.

Siniur 'grâve', standard-bearer for Melchinor (see Persit) in the battle at Firmin. The standard is torn from S.'s grasp. – *WO* 8724

Synon according to *LT*, a warrior in command of the Greeks inside the wooden horse. In *TKf* he holds the key to the trap door in the horse. The story as told by Virgil is related in *Ed*: how S. pretends to be a fugitive from the Greeks and persuades the Trojans to draw the horse into the city. He is not mentioned in Homer. – *Ed* m996f. n1033; *LT* 16161f.; *TKf* 48106

Sinofel 'grâve', husband of Delofin and father of Syrodamen. S. comes to court with his wife after Syrodamen has been pardoned. – *FS* nm3233 a7838ff.

Sinoffel see Sinofel

Sinthys a god whom Alexander sees during his campaigns. This name does not occur in any other history of Alexander. – *WA* 5397ff.

Sinfiliens see Sylilous

Syrene the name of a syren whom Reinfrit passes, bound to the mast like Ulixes in the *Odyssey*. – *RB* 22370

Sirgamôte daughter of Melîân and Modassîne, later the wife of Dêmantîn (q.v.). S. provides an absolutely colourless picture on the few occasions that she appears. – *Dem* a98 n449

Sirgamût see Sirgamôte

Syrie 'künec von' (*JT*), see Iaran

Sirikirsan 'von Bonkovereye', a knight who holds a festival at which Segremors hears news of Gawein. S. corresponds to Amargons in *Meraugis de Portlesguez*. – *S* III,30ff.

Syrodamen daughter of Sinofel and Delofin. Fridrich (3) finds S. chained to the rock in the dwarf-mountain. She had possession of a stone by which the mountain could be opened and had enabled Tytrian to enter and attack Jerome. Fridrich finds her stone and is thus able to escape from the mountain. When he returns later as Jerome's husband, he uses his influence to secure the release of S. – *FS* a3081ff. n3232

Syrus 'von Nepson', a warrior in Ipomidôn's army against Akarîn. – *JT* nm3235,5

Sisenes a warrior in Alexander's army. He receives a letter from Dârîus asking for particulars of Alexander's strength. S., who is faithful to Alexander, is going to show him the letter, when it is stolen by jealous colleagues, who give it to Alexander, with the result that S. is suspected of treachery and put to death. So also in Curtius Rufus, where he is called Sisines (MS A: Sisenes), and Gualterus. – *UA* 6710ff.

Sisigambis, Sisîcâmis see Rodone

Sysileus see Sylilous

Sitalces one of the men who were commanded by Alexander to kill Parmênîôn. So also in *Expeditio Alexandri* and Curtius Rufus. – *A* 20327

Syteus to whom Alexander left the lordship over the Sardimôs. This name does not occur in any other version of the Alexander history. – *UA* nm27033

Sîflois 'vrouwe', one of the ladies at Arthur's court who spill Priure's cup of chastity. – *C* 1605

Sîfrit (1) 'von Medelic', a knight who welcomes Ulrich von Liechtenstein to Neustadt during his *Artusfahrt*. – *FD* 1483,6

Sîfrit (2) 'der Rebestoc', a knight who welcomes Ulrich von Liechtenstein to Neustadt during his *Artusfahrt*. – *FD* 1485,1

Sîfrit (3) 'der Sahse', a knight who jousts with Ulrich von Liechtenstein during his *Venusfahrt*. – *FD* 635,4f.

Sîfrit (4) 'von Torsiul', a knight who jousts with Ulrich von Liechtenstein during his *Venusfahrt*. – *FD* 667,1

Sîfrit (5) 'von Tozenpach', a knight who is present at the tourney held at Friesach and who later (867,2f.) jousts with Ulrich von Liechtenstein during the latter's *Venusfahrt*. S. is the cousin of Gotfrit (4). – *FD* 272,1

Sîfrit (6) 'Weise', a knight who jousts with Ulrich von Liechtenstein during the latter's *Venusfahrt*. – *FD* 919,1ff.

Sîvrit (7) the hero of the first half of the *Nibelungenlied*. In *JT* he is called 'der hürnin Seifrit'. – nm *P* 421,10; *JT* 3312,2

Skaarez a knight who attends Leigamar's tourney in the service of Aram. – *C* 18168

Skandinâvîâ 'künec von' (*W*), see Matribleiz

Scare see Stare

Schaitîs a knight of the Round Table who is unhorsed by Daniel. – *DB* 249

Schampfanzune 'burcgrâve von' (*JT*), see Kingrimursel

Schandalec a squire in the service of Larîe, whom he accompanies when she goes to meet Wigalois after the latter has defeated Rôaz. – *Wigl* 8860

Schandamur 'des hertz nur mords und grosses mains pfliget', a knight who oppresses all around him and has imprisoned Anziflor. He is killed by Seyfrid. – *Sey* nm216,6 a239,1ff.

Schanndamur see Schandamur

Scharlotte 'künec von Effraym', a knight who is unhorsed by Gahmuret at Bagdad. – *JT* 898,3ff.

***Schaut** see Schôt

Schafillôr 'künec von Arragûn', a knight who unhorses Utepandragûn at Herzeloide's tourney but is himself unhorsed by Gahmuret. In *JT* he takes part in the tourney held by Arthur. – *P* m67,14 a74,5 n79,2; *JT* a1932,1 n1980,1

Schaffilûn 'künec von Medârîe und Belakûn', a knight whose vassals come to take the oath of allegiance to Wigalois. He is probably the knight whom Wigalois defeats and kills (3329ff.). – *Wigl* nm9086ff.

Scheifdeir 'diu küneginne von' (*PM*), see Meliûr

Schelopfîs 'künec von Fotiliâ', a warrior in the Greek army against the Trojans. This character appears to have been invented by Konrad. – *TK* 30590

Schenteflûrs (Golther is of the opinion that this name was taken by Wolfram from *E* (see Genteflûr);[25] Singer thinks that it is only a coincidence that the name appears in both poems, and denies any connection.[26]) S. is the son of Gurnemanz and is killed by Kingrûn and Klamidê whilst trying to succour Kondwîrâmûrs. He is called 'der ûz Gentrilurs' in *JT*, where he attends Schîonatulander's *swertleite*. In Chrestien's *Perceval* an unnamed brother of Gurnemanz is said to have been slain by Kingrûn. – *P* m175,16 n177,29; *JT* 1098,5

Scheorise see Tôarîs

Schêrins 'von Pantali', a knight who accompanies Buovun and Alîze (2) to Lôîs's wife in their attempt to persuade her to assist Willehalm (1). In *UW* he fights for Lôîs against Terramêr. S. is called Garins de Pontarlie in *Aliscans*. – *W* 160,9f.; *UW* 46,11

Scherules 'burcgrâve von Bêârosche', father of Klauditte (1). S. fights for Lipaôt against Meljanz. In Chrestien he is called Garin le fil Berte, and Bartsch thinks that the name comes from 'Gerin le';[27] Singer, on the other hand, thinks it comes from OF Gerouls (German: Gerolt).[28] – *P* nm361,1ff. a361,17

Schêtîs 'der' (*W*), see Heimrîch (2)

Schîanatulander see Schîonatulander

Schilbert (1) 'von Tandarnas', a knight who is brought by Heimrîch (2) to fight for Willehalm (1) against Terramêr in the second battle at Alischanz. In the OF *Aliscans* Guibert d'Andernas is the brother of Willehalm (1); this character is called Gîbert (see Gîbert (2)) in *W*. That Wolfram considered them as two separate characters is clear from 249,28ff., when Heimrîch (1), who has brought S. to be kissed by Gîburc, says that neither he nor his sons shall kiss Gîburc until all the stranger-knights have done so. [See Appendix (4).] – *W* 240,26

Schilbert (2) see Gîbert (2) [See Appendix (4).]

Schiltung see Schiltunc

Schiltunc uncle of Kailet and father-in-law of Vridebrant. S. is present at the tourney held by Arthur in *JT*. – *P* nm48,18; *JT* 2031,5 [†]

Schinahtelander, Schinachtulander see Schîonatulander

Schîolarz (Bartsch derived this name from Provençal *guialarcs*, 'the leader of the generous',[29] but Martin is inclined to see a form of the German name Gîselhart, possibly through an OF form Gielarz.[30]) S., who is called 'von Poitouwe', is the father of Liedarz and opens the *vesperîe* at Herzeloide's tourney with a joust against Gurnemanz. He is called Teschelarz in *TF* and is lord of the town in which Tandareis is healed by Todilâ. – *P* 68,21; *TF* nm4390ff. a5512

Schionalander see Schîonatulander

---

25 Golther (1), p. 153.
26 Singer (1), p. 59.
27 Bartsch (2), p. 120.
28 Singer (1), p. 103.
29 Bartsch (2), p. 147.
30 Martin (1), p. 76, to 68,21.

Schîonatulander (Schulz derived this name from *joiant*, 'joyeux', or *jointoiant*, 'avoir une tournure'.[31] Bartsch suggested < OF *(li) joenet ù l'alant*, 'der Jüngling mit dem Hunde'; he concludes that the reference in *E* is a later interpolation. Grâswaldâne Bartsch represents as the little-known county of Graisivodan, and as Wolfram could scarcely have known of the existence of this county, he places Kîôt in this district and uses this as an argument for the existence of Kîôt.[32] Gaston Paris challenges Bartsch's etymology on the grounds that *joenet* should be *jonez*, an adjective which was never used absolutely, whilst *alant*, which should be *alan*, is of Spanish origin and did not exist in medieval French.[33] Martin suggests a derivation from *(le) joenet de la lande*;[34] Golther thinks that Wolfram took the name from *E*.[35]) S. is first mentioned in *E*, where he is called Ganatulander, one of the knights at Arthur's court when Êrec returns with Ênîte. He does not occur in the corresponding list in Chrestien's *Erec*, nor in *C*, so that the name here may well be, as has been supposed (see above), a later interpolation. In *P* he occurs as the dead lover of Sigûne (q.v.), a character who appears, but is not named, in Chrestien's *Perceval*. In *T*, which was to have been the story of Sigûne and S., the latter is called 'vürste ûz Grâswaldîse' and is given by Amphlîse (1) to Gahmuret as a page; he accompanies Gahmuret when he first goes to take service with Akarîn. S. returns with Gahmuret to Wales, and there he falls in love with Sigûne, but they are parted when S. accompanies Gahmuret on his second journey to the East. A second fragment of *T* describes how S. sets out to recover Ehkunat's hound for Sigûne, a quest which is to prove his death. The continuation of the fragment is given in *JT*: Orilus has, in the meantime, gained possession of the hound and refuses to give it up. A combat is arranged for six weeks later, and in the meantime S. takes an army to Baldac, where he fights for Akarîn against Ipomidôn, avenging on the latter the death of Gahmuret. On his return he leads an army against Orilus and Lehelîn, who are invading Herzeloîde's land. The fight between S. and Orilus eventually takes place, and the former, who wins, spares the life of his opponent. He is shortly afterwards challenged by Orilus again, and this time S.'s spear, a temporary one, breaks, and he is slain. In *JT* he is called der Grahardois and der Talfin. He is the son of Gurzgrî and Mahaute. – *E* 1691; *P* 138,21; *T* a38,1 n42,3; *C* a13980ff.; *JT* a665,1f. n671,5; *RB* nm15244; *WO* nm12293; *FS* nm1459 [†]

Schiosiane see Schoisiâne

Schirniel (Bartsch suggested < OF *irnel*, a variant of *isnel*, 'der Schnelle', with initial *i* or *j* added, as in Lischois Gwelljus.[36]) S., who is also (772,1) called Schirnîel, is the 'künec von Lirivoin' and is captured by Parzivâl whilst fighting for Lipaôt against Meljanz. He is the brother of Mirabel. In *JT* he takes part in the tourney held by Arthur. – *P* nm354,19f. a384,8; *JT* a1943,3 n2058,1

Schirnvel see Schirniel

Schyro see Cheiron

Schyromelans see Gramoflanz

Schŷrôn, Schirow, Schirro see Cheiron

---

31 Schulz, 'Eigennamen', p. 391.
32 Bartsch (2), p. 142.
33 Paris (2), p. 150.
34 Martin (1), p. 139, to 138,21.
35 Golther (1), p. 159.
36 Bartsch (2), p. 149.

Schôette (Schulz derived this name from OF *joiette*, 'jouissance', or *jouete*, 'jeunesse', 'petite joue'.[37] Bartsch thought it came from the OHG name Gauda, with a diminutive ending > Provençal Gaudeta > OF *joette*,[38] whilst Martin points out that the name occurs as Joetha (presumably = Latin Juditha) in a document of 1188.[39]) S. is the wife of Gandîn (1) (q.v.) and the mother of Gahmuret; she dies of a broken heart when she hears of the death of Galôês. – *P* a10,13 n92,24; *T* nm126,4

Schoieranz 'von Berikôn', the abductor of Agyris. He is captured by Alexander's men, who recover Agyris. S. is not named in any other history of Alexander. – *UA* 23308

Schoyr falconer to Persit, whom he accompanies in his campaign against Walwan (3). – *WO* 7280

Schoisiâne (Schulz derived this name from OF *joiax*, 'plaisir',[40] whilst Bartsch derived it from the Provençal Jauziana, Gauziana (< *gauzir*), 'die Freudespendende', or from OHG Gauda (see Schôette).[41] Martin and Singer point to the name Josiane (the heroine of *Boeves de Hantonne*) as the origin,[42] and Singer stresses the relation of Josiane to Guiot (see Kîot (1)), who, in *Boeves de Hantonne*, is her father-in-law.) S. is the mother of Sigûne, at whose birth she dies, and the wife of Kîot (1). – *P* nm477,2; *T* nm10,1 a13,1; *JT* nm594,5 a622,1f.

Schoit son of Trebuchet and the maker of Terramêr's helmet. – *W* nm356,20

Schoiflôrîs son of Meie and Bêaflôr. He is brought up by Rôbôâl, who pretends that S. is his own son. From 212,15 onwards he is called Lôîs. – *MB* m97,14 a128,1 n190,36

Schonebâr a knight who is present at Arthur's court when Êrec returns with Ênîte. This name does not appear in the corresponding list in Chrestien's *Erec*. – *E* 1677

Schôt father of Meljanz. In *JT* he is called Schute and takes part in the tourney held by Arthur. – *P* m344,21 n345,14; *JT* 1719,1f.

Schotten 'künec der' (*JT*), see Vridebrant

Schoufe 'der von', **Schoufer** 'der', see Acurteis

Schrutor husband of Rubal, a giant who has seized a castle and imprisons all maidens who pass. He is killed by Seyfrid. – *Sey* 94,4ff.

Schute see Schôt

Skôlôpêtus expelled with Plînis from Cîtîâ. From their descendants came the Amazons under Tâlistrîâ. This name does not occur in any other history of Alexander. – *A* nm17917ff.

Scos brother of Gangier, a knight who is present at Arthur's court when Êrec returns with Ênîte. This name does not appear in the corresponding list in Chrestien's *Erec*. – *E* 1682

Sodiân 'von Averne', a commander in Bêâmunt's army at Antrîun. – *Dem* nm9794f. a10027

Sodines a knight who is present at Arthur's court. He is probably identical with Dodines (q.v.). – *GM* (MS D) 38574

Sogdîânus a former king of Persia. He is mentioned in *Expeditio Alexandri* and Curtius Rufus. – *A* nm15722

Soye (1) 'dy kewsch', wife of Lôt (1) and daughter of Îgerne by her first husband (see Urlois). (See Soye (2) and Sangîve.) – *Mer* 236,1ff.

---

37 Schulz, 'Eigennamen', p. 397.
38 Bartsch (2), p. 136.
39 Martin (1), p. 95, to 92,24.
40 Schulz, 'Eigennamen', p. 391.
41 Bartsch (2), p. 140.
42 Martin (1), p. 365, to 477,2; Singer (1), p. 73.

Soye (2) sister of Gawein. She marries Turkoit (q.v.). S. seems to be confused with Soye (1), as in *P* it is Sangîve (i.e. Soye (1)) who marries Florant der turkoit. – *Sey* nm253,7

Sôcrates 'ein wîser degen', placed by Alexander in command of Sicily. So also in *Expeditio Alexandri* and Curtius Rufus. Although it is chronologically impossible, S. was no doubt intended to be the philosopher and is therefore identical with the Socrates referred to in *WO*. – *A* 9469; *WO* nm11949

Soladin brother of Crispin. He is already dead at the time of the story. – *WO* m11247 n13325

Soldener 'der Riche', a knight who is present at the tourney between Ris and Cadoalans. He later imprisons Gifles in the Schastel Orgelus but is compelled by Gawein to release him. In Pseudo-Gautier he is called li Riches Soudoiers (i.e. the rich mercenary). – *RP* 81,29

Solenus a knight in the Greek army. This name does not occur in any other history of Alexander. – *SA* 8663ff.

Solimag a knight who is seen by Ginovêr passing Arthur's court. She sends Keiî to fetch him, but Keiî's challenge is too crude, and S. unhorses him. Gawein persuades S. by kindness to come to the court and later leaves with him in order to help him against Marguns (q.v.). S. is killed by an arrow just as they leave the court, and it afterwards transpires that the murderer is Keiî. In Pseudo-Gautier, where the story is told, the character is not named, but Manessier names him Silimac. The first part of the episode is, of course, directly copied from the similar episode in *Perceval*, where Parzivâl is gazing at the blood-stains in the snow. – *RP* a256,6 n704,30

Sondelban a vassal of Elsam. Steinmeyer, in his annotation to this name, suggests that it is a corruption of Sand Alban (see Albîân, who occurs in the corresponding stanza of *Loh* and *Ll* (MS K)). – *Ll* 12,4f.

Soreidôz see Seimeret

Sorgarit a knight who is present at the tourney held by Leigamar. S. and his brother, Bigamê, are unhorsed at the tourney by Gawein and Quoikos. – *C* 18135

Sornagiur 'künec von Agisors', a heathen of noble character who attacks Clogier's son, a mere boy. Partonopier comes to his assistance, and a single combat is fought, S. being defeated. The truce is broken by Mareis (q.v.), and Partonopier is captured. S. returns, however, and surrenders in order to prove that he had no hand in the breaking of the truce. A mutual release of the two prisoners is arranged. A Sornigres (many variants) occurs in *L'Estoire de Merlin* (Vulgate Cycle) and in the *Livre d'Artus* as the name of a Saxon king (a heathen) who is slain by the King of a Hundred Knights. – *PM* a3318 n3332

Sot see Lôt (1)

Spân 'der', a knight who welcomes Ulrich von Liechtenstein to Neustadt during his *Artusfahrt*. – *FD* 1484,7

Spâne 'künec von' (*P*), see Kailet

Spangen, Spaniol 'der vogt ûz' (*JT*), see Kailet

Spichêr 'vürste', a warrior who is expelled from Alexander's army and joins Dârîus. He occurs in MS S of Leo, where he is called Spchichir.[43] – *A* 6003ff.

Spitâmenes a former friend of Bessus. S., who is shocked by the treachery of Bessus towards Dârîus, conspires to capture him and hand him over to Alexander. The poem breaks off at this point. S. occurs also in *Expeditio Alexandri* and Curtius Rufus. – *A* 21529ff.

Stare the name given by Acheloyde to Agorlôt (q.v.). – *Crane* 148

---

[43] O. Zingerle, p. 58.

Stelenus see Stenelus

Stelophîs a warrior in the Greek army against the Trojans. This name does not occur in any other version of the Trojan legend, but it may be an attempt to reproduce the form of Stenelus (q.v.) which appears in Benoît. – *TK* 31616

Stenelus 'herzoge', a warrior in the Greek army against the Trojans. In *TKf* he is wounded by Hector. S. is called Stelenus in *LT*, Sthelenus in Benoît (see Stelophîs), Stenelus in *TKf*, and Sthenelus (-os) in Dares, Dictys, and Homer. – *LT* 3389; *TKf* 40468f.

Stesichêr 'vürste', a warrior in Alexander's army. S. occurs in Leo, where he is called Stisichorus. – *A* 3479

Stephan (1) a bishop who baptizes Bearosine. – *R* Bl. III,221

Stefan (2) a vassal of Avenis. S. wounds and captures Willehalm (4). – *RW* 9274ff.

Steven (1) chaplain to Willehalm (1) at Oransche. In *W* he is depicted as very old. He is called Estievenes in *Aliscans*. – *W* 89,4; *UW* 332,6ff.

Steven (2) see Stefan (2)

Steffan 'künec von Ungern'. In *Loh* he marries Gysel. – nm *JT* 3570,4; *Loh* 7543f.

Stier 'von Lahssendorf', a knight who welcomes Ulrich von Liechtenstein to Neustadt during his *Artusfahrt*. – *FD* nm1482,4

Stiport a knight who attends Leigamar's tourney in the service of Aram. – *C* 18173

Strandagaro, Strandagoras see Strâsagoras

Strangedorz 'von Villegarunz'. (Bartsch derived this name from the Provençal *estreignedor*, 'der Dränger'.[44] Brugger thinks that it is identical with the place-name Estrangor(t), and the name of the person is therefore Villegarunz, which he derives from Gasouain (see Gasosîn).[45]) S. is one of the knights whom Parzivâl claims to have defeated. In *JT* he is called Agors von Vilgaruntz and is the champion of Klinschor, who has stolen Pardiscale from Gloris. S. is a valiant knight who can defeat six knights at once, but he is overcome by Parzivâl, who thus rescues Pardiscale. – *P* nm772,6; *JT* m5543,1 n5551,5 a5565,1f.

Strâsagoras 'von Platêâ', a warrior who is expelled from the army by Alexander and goes to Athens, where he is given shelter. He is reconciled with Alexander when Athens is taken. So also in Leo. In *WA* he is called Strandagoras von Planthea. – *A* 3582ff.; *WA* 1594

Strâtô 'künec von Aradus', from which he is driven out by Parmênîôn. He is later called 'künec von Sîdônje (8349f.). In Curtius Rufus, Strato rex Aradi and Strato rex Sidonis are two separate persons. They occur also in *Expeditio Alexandri*. – *A* 8237

Strennolas 'herzoge von Piktakôn', a knight whom Parzivâl claims to have defeated. – *P* nm772,15

Strikaere 'der', MHG poet, and author of *DB*, among other works. – nm *DB* 16; *RW* 2230; *A* 3257

Stubenberc 'der von' (*FD*), see Wülfinc (3)

Sundifâr a knight who is unhorsed by Firganant during the siege of Antrîûn. – *Dem* 9266

Sunom son of Helen and Paris. S. and his two brothers, Caratît and Idoneus, are slain by Helen when she hears of the plot to betray Troy, in order to ingratiate herself with Menelaus. In Dictys he is called Bunomus. – *TKf* a47165ff. n47178

Sunsch see Factor

Supacias a warrior in the Greek army against the Trojans. This character appears to have been invented by Konrad's continuator. – *TKf* 43583

---

44 Bartsch (2), p. 151.
45 Brugger (2), p. 46.

Supplicius son of Arnolt (4) with whom he fights for Partonopier against the Soldan. S. and Anshelm (1) are sent by Partonopier as messengers to the Soldan. On the journey they assist Alîs, whom they bring back with them. – *PM* 18802ff.

Sûrdâmûr sister of Gawein and wife of Alexander (4). S. is the mother of Cligés and the heroine of the first part of Chrestien's poem of that name. – *P* nm586,26f.

Susanne the apocryphal Susanna, whose story was very popular in the Middle Ages. – nm *UA* 795; *RB* 8458

Susavant a knight who attends Leigamar's tourney in the service of Aram. – *C* 18173

Suzzît a maiden in the service of Senebalŷn's wife. – *UW* 207,16

Swarzen Dorne 'grâve von dem', a knight who dies leaving his property to his two daughters. They quarrel about the division, the elder one wishing to take everything, and they both seek champions at Arthur's court. The quarrel culminates in the fight between Gawein and Îwein (1). In *JT* he is one of the knights who take part in the tourney held by Arthur. Chrestien calls him Li sire de la Noire Espine in *Yvain*. – *I* 5625ff.; *JT* 2025,1

Swikkêr 'von Vrowenstein', a knight who jousts with Ulrich von Liechtenstein during the latter's *Venusfahrt*. – *FD* 607,1

T

Tabrôn *amie* of Aristômenes. This name does not occur in any other history of Alexander, and Toischer thinks that Ulrich derived it from Wolfram's Tabronit.[1] *– UA* nm13099

Tabrunit 'der ûz' (*JT*), see Secureis

Talabius see Taltibius

Talas 'von Rotenberg', a knight of the Round Table. He is first mentioned in Chrestien's *Erec* (1729), where he is called Taulas, and appears in *E* as Baulas, one of the knights at Arthur's court when Êrec returns with Ênîte. He is called Collas in *C* (MS V of *C* has Tallas, a form which appears in MS H of Chrestien's *Erec*) and is one of the knights who spill Priure's cup of chastity. In *RP*, as in Pseudo-Gautier, T. is one of the party of knights who accompany Arthur to the rescue of Gifles, being referred to on one occasion (185,10) as Hartalas (= her Talas?).[2] He is later (*RP* 348,16) called T. 'von Rüschimunt', and (*RP* 472,36) 'von Rusimunt' in the translation of Gautier, in which he takes part in the tourney held by Arthur before Orgelus. A Talac occurs in the OF romance *Yder*; Freymond, who mentions this, does not commit himself as to their identity but draws attention also to Palach, whom Arthur slays in the *Black Book of Carmarthen* (31).[3] *– E* 1653; *C* 2321; *RP* 179,24

Tali son of Ptolômêus (2). Alexander bequeathed Persia to him. The form of the name here is in the dative case (nominative: Talis?), but no name of this nature appears in any other history of Alexander. *– UA* nm27039

Talides 'von der marke', a knight who is oppressing the Castle of Maidens. He is defeated by Segremors. In Manessier he is called Calidès de la Marche. *– RP* m649,41 n650,13 a653,30

Talimôn (1) 'künec von Boctân', a warrior who is slain by Willehalm (1) whilst fighting for Terramêr at Alischanz So also in *Aliscans*, where he is called Telamon. Singer is of the opinion that T. is identical with Talimôn (2).[4] [See Appendix (2).] *– W* 56,18

Talimôn (2) 'künec von Valpinôse', a vassal of Josweiz, under whom he fights for Terramêr at Alischanz. Singer assumes that T. is identical with Talimôn (1), but this is impossible, since T. is still alive when the second battle takes place,[5] whilst the men of Boktâne are said (*W* 363,15ff.) to fight hard to avenge the death of Talimôn; moreover, they fight under Halzebier, not under Josweiz. [See Appendix (2).] A Talimôn von Samargôn, who is presumably identical with Talimôn (1) or (2), fights for Terramêr against Lôîs in *UW*. *– W* 33,12ff.; *UW* 47,18

Talimore 'künec von' (*JT*), see Teanglis

Tâlistrîâ an Amazon queen whom Alexander meets during his campaigns. In *UA*, as in Curtius Rufus, Alexander lies with her at her request. In Gualterus she is called Thalestris, the form of the name which occurs in *UA* and Curtius Rufus. *– A* 17780ff.; *UA* a17407ff. n17457; *SA* m4902 n4994 a5027; *WA* 3332ff.

---

1   Toischer, pp. 354f.
2   The corresponding passage in Pseudo-Gautier (Potvin's edition: l.16567f.) reads: 'Li rois a regardé Talas/ et dist . . .'
3   Freymond (2), p. 331.
4   Singer (2), p. 15.
5   Terramêr refers to Talimôn (2) as still alive (*W* 349,27ff.), and the künec von Valpinôse appears in the battle (*W* 387,16).

Talkaret 'künec', a heathen who is baptized with Bearosine. In the Munich MS he is called Cacharet. – *R* Bl. III,268

Taltibius 'künec', a warrior in the Greek army who is sent to Troy with the conspirators. In *LT*, as in Dictys (but not in *TKf*), he takes Orestes to Ydomeneus on the death of Agâmennon. In *TKf* he is called Talabius, and in Dictys, Talthybius. – *LT* 15337ff.; *TKf* 46201

Talfialte, Talfin 'der' (*JT*), see Schîonatulander

Tamberfal 'künec', from whom Dodinas (see Wigalois) won his shield. In the Mons MS of Pseudo-Gautier he is called d'Abernal, in the Montpellier MS Brandeval, and in the prose edition of 1530, Dambreval. – *RP* nm280,20

Tamiris an Amazon queen who captured and killed Cyrus. T. is historically Tomyris, queen of the Massagetae, against whom Cyrus, according to Herodotus, waged a war, in the course of which he was killed. – *UA* nm7763f.

Tampanîs the chief of Gahmuret's squires who brings the news of his death to Herzeloide. – *P* 105,1; *JT* 985,1ff.

Tampastê (1) 'künec von Naroclyn', a warrior who is slain by Vîvîans whilst fighting for Terramêr at Alischanz. T., who is the father of Tampestê (2), does not occur in *Aliscans*.[6] – *W* 27,8 [†]

Tampastê (2) 'künec von Tabrastên', one of the group of 15 Saracen kings who attack Willehalm (1) at the end of the first battle at Alischanz. T. is wounded by Willehalm in that encounter and is later killed by Rennewart (442,29). [See Appendix (9).] In the OF *Aliscans* he is slain by Willehalm, but in MS M (6800) Tanpeste is mentioned as one of those who escape. T. is the son of Tampastê (1). – *W* m71,22 a72,17f. n74,8 [†]

Tampenîse see Tampanîs

Tampenteire (Schulz derived this name from OF *tempesté*, *temps*, and *tempesteis*, 'tempest'.[7] Bartsch supposed it to be composed of *tamp* (imperative of *tampir*, the Provençal verb, 'to enclose') and *en-taire*, i.e. 'to enclose in silence';[8] this etymology is not admitted by Gaston Paris.[9] Martin suggests that the initial *T*- may be an old *d'*- which has become attached to the name.[10]) T. is the father of Kondwîrâmûrs, who inherits Pelrapeire from him. – *P* nm180,26; *T* 15,2; *JT* 632,3

Tampunteire, Tampuntiere see Tampenteire

Tandareis son of Antikonîe and Dulcemâr. He is brought up at Arthur's court, where he falls in love with Flordibel, and together they flee from Arthur's court to Dulcemâr. Arthur, who is bound by his oath to Flordibel, attacks Dulcemâr, and in the battle T., who has just been made a knight, distinguishes himself. Flordibel points out to Arthur that she is still a virgin, so that their only crime has been to run away from Arthur. T. is sentenced to go out on knight-errantry until Arthur gives him leave to return. He has numerous adventures, culminating in his imprisonment at the hands of Kandaljôn and Antonîe (q.v.). He is eventually brought back to Arthur's court, where he is claimed as husband by

---

6   Tampastê (1) does not occur in the list of knights who are slain by Vîvîans in *Aliscans*, but at the end of this list (*Al.* 350ᵃ) the line occurs: 'Turs ni Persans n'a vers lui garison.' It seems possible that in the MS of *Aliscans* used by Wolfram, which differs considerably from any extant MS, 'Turs ni Persans' may have been corrupted to Tampaste.

7   Schulz, 'Eigennamen', p. 393.

8   Bartsch (2), p. 144.

9   Paris (2), p. 149.

10 Martin (1), p. 177, to 180,26.

Claudîn, Antonîe, and Flordibel. Arthur sits in judgment, and, as an afterthought, permits T. to decide which he shall have. He chooses Flordibel, and they are married. – *TF* m172 a198f. n231

Tandarnas 'künec von' (*TF*), see Dulcemâr

Tandernas 'der von' (*UW*), see Schilbert (1)

Tandreas 'künec', a knight who takes part in the tourney held by Arthur. – *JT* 2077,5

Tane 'vrouwe', one of the ladies at Arthur's court who spill Priure's cup of chastity. – *C* 1605

Tanete niece of Arthur. T. and Clarate are given in marriage to Dinasdanres and Kingrimursel. So also in the Montpellier MS of Pseudo-Gautier. – *RP* 19,30ff.

Tangulor a warrior who is slain by Daries whilst fighting for Akarîn against Ipomidôn. The passage reads (3465,6): 'Aloguries und Tangulor', but previously (3113,1) 'Alogries ûz Tangulor' has been referred to. – *JT* 3465,6

Tankanîs father of Îsenhart and uncle of Vridebrant. – *P* nm26,23

Tanchrête 'von Agrippe', a warrior who is slain by Ênêâs whilst fighting for the Greeks against the Trojans. This character was invented by Konrad. – *TK* 32734

Tanna see Theanus

Tanreie sister of Guivreiz in *RP*. She entertains Gawein when the latter is in search of Parzivâl, and they fall in love with each other. In Gautier she is called Tanrée. – *RP* a531,22 n542,25

Tantalus in Greek mythology, the son of Zeus who was condemned to perpetual torment for betraying the secrets of his father. – nm *Ed* 3484; *FD* Büchlein III,113

Tantris the name assumed by Tristan when he goes to Ireland. – *ET* nm1585; *Tn* 7791

Tantrîsel (diminutive of Tantris) a child, relative of Tristan, who facilitates considerably the meetings between Tristan and Îsolt (2). – *HT* 2691ff.

Tarbigant 'von Talle', a warrior in Akarîn's army against Ipomidôn. – *JT* 3637,2

Tares see Dares

Tarcôn uncle of Elemîn, a warrior in the Trojan army under Ênêâs. He is slain by Kamille (1) in the battle against Turnus. He is called Tarcon in the OF *Eneas*, and Tarchon in Virgil. – *Ed* 8966

Tarlunt 'der lantgrâve ûz Komerzie', a knight who is present at the tourney held by Arthur. – *JT* 2029,5

Tarquines a knight who fights for Athis against Bilas. So also in the OF version. – *AP* A*,99

Tartanôs to whom Alexander bequeathed Archôs and Trancerôs. This character does not occur in any other history of Alexander. – *UA* nm27031

Tarfilas 'herzoge von Clarifonte', a knight who attends the tourney held by Arthur. – *JT* 2025,5

Tarffian a heathen god (= Tervigant?). – *WO* nm3564

Taurîan brother of Dodines, a knight whose lance Parzival takes from outside Trevrezent's hermitage after defeating Orilus and reconciling him with Jeschûte. – *P* nm271,12

Tavernas to whom Alexander bequeathed Armenia. This name does not occur in any other history of Alexander. – *SA* nm8528

Taxilles to whom Alexander bequeathed the district around the Cancasus (= Caucasus). This name does not occur in any other history of Alexander. – *SA* nm8519

Taxillîs brother of Porrus. He flees at the critical point in the battle against Alexander. T. occurs in *Expeditio Alexandri* and Curtius Rufus, where he is an Indian king but no relation to Porrus. In Gualterus he is the brother of Porrus. – *UA* 19753

Têâdetus one of the former soldiers of Alexander who had been mutilated by Dârîus whilst his prisoner. (See Euctêmôn.) T. is called Theseus in Gualterus, and Theaetetus in Curtius Rufus. – *A* 14035ff.

Teanglis 'künec von Talimone', also called 'künec von Teseac', a knight who is defeated by Orilus in a fight for Ehkunat's hound. He is also defeated by Schîonatulander. – *JT* a1263,1 n1264,7

Têbit the Arabian astonomer Thabit ben Qorah, AD 826–901.[11] (See Flegetanîs.) – *P* nm643,17

Tedalûn 'burcgrâve von Tasmê', 'vorstmeister' of 'walt Lignâlôê', and standard-bearer to Poidjus. T. is slain by Rennewart whilst fighting for Terramêr against Willehalm (1) in the second battle at Alischanz. He does not occur in the OF *Aliscans*, and Singer thinks that his name originates in Dedalus, who occurs in Albrecht von Halberstadt.[12] – *W* 375,22

Telamon see Thelamon

Telepolemus a warrior in the Greek army against the Trojans. He wins the prize for jumping in the games which are held. T. does not occur in Dictys, but occurs in Benoît as Telopolon (var. Telepolemus). – *TKf* 40948

Telestes a warrior who is slain by Dyomedes whilst fighting for the Trojans against the Greeks. So also in Dictys. – *TKf* 43201ff.

Telêfus father of Euripilus (1). So in Dictys. – *TKf* nm44662

Teljôn Emperor of Rome. After the death of his wife, Sâbîe (1), he evinces incestuous designs on his daughter, Bêaflôr. She manages to put him off with promises of acquiescence and makes her escape from the land. When she is later discovered by Rôbôâl, T. confesses his guilt and abdicates, passing his crown on to Meie. – *MB* a4,19ff. n5,3

Tenebreiz brother of Bargis and son of Purrel. T. flees with Terramêr from the second battle at Alischanz. He occurs as Tenebrez in MS D of *Aliscans* (6800), but here he is probably identical with Tenebré, the son of Terramêr. – *W* a358,25 n443,19

Tenebroc a knight who is one of the leaders of the side opposed to Gawein in the tourney held to celebrate the wedding of Êrec. This name rests on a misunderstanding by Hartmann of Chrestien's *Erec*, where the venue of the tourney is given as 'Antre Evroïc et Tenebroc' (see Entreferich). Hartmann appears to have realised his mistake, as he gives the venue (2241) as 'zwischen Tarebron und Ebrurin'. Tenebroc is stated by Walshe to be Edinburgh,[13] but its derivation from Pembroke has also been suggested.[14] Teneborc occurs frequently as a place-name in the romances of the Vulgate Cycle. – *E* 2231ff.

Tenebroc 'grævinne von' (*P*), see Klârischanze

Tenebruns 'künec von Liwes Nûgruns', a warrior who is killed by Willehalm (1) whilst fighting for Terramêr at Alischanz. In *Aliscans* he is called Danebur (var. Danebrons). – *W* 76,2ff.

Tenedon 'von Frisca', a warrior in the Greek army against the Trojans. This name occurs only as a place-name in Benoît, but Tenedeus occurs as a variant of Crenus. – *LT* 3403

Têôdêtus a commander in Alexander's army. So also in Curtius Rufus, where he is called Theodotus. – [*A* 13417]

Teoral see Theoris

Ter'amer see Terramêr

---

11 Golther (1), p. 202.
12 Singer (2), p. 110.
13 Walshe, p. 15.
14 Richey (3), p. 81, note 1.

Terdelaschoie (= Terre de la Joi), according to *P*, a fairy whom Mazadân married and who took him to the land of Feimorgân (q.v.). Wolfram has obviously confused here the place-name with the name of the person, and Bartsch uses this fact to support his theory that Kîôt actually existed.[15] – *P* nm56,19 [†]

Terêus a warrior who is slain by Euripilus whilst fighting for the Greek army against the Trojans. So also in Dictys, where he is called Nireus (var. Nereus); Nireus is mentioned in Homer, but his fate is not given. – *TKf* 44992

Terius a goddess who appears with Discordia to Paris in a wood. She tells him of the coming visit of the three goddesses and gives him the golden apple which is to be the prize. She also tells Paris the secret of his parentage. – *GT* 1787ff.

Terramêr 'künec von Muntespîr', 'vogt von Baldac', also called 'von Suntîn', and 'von Tenabrî'. T., who is the son of Kanabêus, is the leader of the heathen army which comes to Oransche to recover Gîburc for Tîbalt. The first battle at Alischanz results in a victory for T., but in the second, owing largely to his unrecognized son, Rennewart, the Christians are successful, and T. is badly wounded by Willehalm (1) as he is fleeing to the ships. T. is called Desramé in the OF *chansons de geste* and appears in all of the *chansons* of the Guillaume d'Orange cycle, including the *Chancun de Willame*, in which he is called Deramé. T. is the father of Gîburc, and the manner in which the latter becomes converted to Christianity is told in *UW*, where T. brings a huge army to attack Lôîs. He is defeated, but Willehalm is captured and kept in prison by Tîbalt, T.'s son-in-law. The latter is called by T. to attend a conference, and whilst he is away, Gîburc and Willehalm make their escape. – *W* 8,30; *UW* 35,17; *JT* nm2836,3ff.; *RB* nm16157; *WO* nm7724; *FS* nm1386

Terredelaschoie see Terdelaschoie

Terribilis 'der ferge ûz Grandimonte', a knight who is present at the tourney held by Arthur. – *JT* 2025,6f.

Terrimant a knight who is present at the tourney held by Arthur. – *JT* 2149,5

Tersippe a commander in Alexander's army. He takes the town of Biblô. In *Expeditio Alexandri* and Curtius Rufus he is called Thersippus. – *A* 8345f.

Tervagâmîs a knight who is captured by Dêmantîn whilst fighting for Eghart at Antrîûn. He is called 'T. von Iberne'. – *Dem* a5658 n5669

Tervan see Tervian

Tervian a knight who is slain by Waradach whilst he is lying asleep with his *amie*, Picorye. – *GT* nm12505ff.

Tervigant a heathen god (see Tarffian). – *W* nm11,16; *R* nm Bl. I,24; *Tirol* nmF,8; *UW* nm90,8 a261,1; *JT* nm115,6; *MB* nm118,15; *Loh* nm4236; *UA* nm387; *WW* nm2448; *RB* nm16391

Terwigant see Tervigant

Teseac 'der von' (*JT*), see Teanglis

Tesereiz 'künec von Kollône', called 'der Latrisete', and 'der rîche Sezîljas'; he leads the Arabeise, Sezîljeise, die von Grikulâne, Sôtiers, and die Latriseten. T. is a warrior who is slain by Willehalm (1) whilst fighting for Terramêr in the first battle at Alischanz. In *Aliscans* he is called Desreé d'Argolaigne. – *W* 36,11f.; *TF* nm2077; *RB* nm18438

Têseus a warrior in the Greek army against the Trojans. This name occurs in Benoît as a variant of Heseus. – *TK* 35772

Têsiphône one of the furies (Tisiphone, the avenger). In the OF *Eneas* she is called Thesiphone. – nm *Ed* 3465; *LT* 16406

---

15 Bartsch (2), p. 134.

Teschelarz see Schîolarz

Tetis, Tettis see Thetis

Teucer a warrior in the Greek army against the Trojans. He is the brother of Ajax (1), and after the death of the latter he takes charge (in *LT*) of Antides and Eustates. He attacks Dyomedes and drives him away after the latter had been exiled by Egyal. T., who is also called Theucrus in *LT*, is called Teucer in Dares, and Teucrus in Dictys, neither of whom mention his attack on Dyomedes. Benoît calls him Teücer (var. Theucrus), and in Homer he is called Teukros. – *LT* 3335ff.; *TKf* 42385

Tefilant a knight in the service of Fandorîch. After being unhorsed by Berichel, he takes the latter to Fandorîch. – *Dem* a10260 n10315

Têcius one of the prisoners maimed by Dârîus and released by Alexander. T. speaks against the advice of Euctêmôn and advises his comrades not to accept the land offered by Alexander, but to return to Greece. This character appears to have been invented by Ulrich. – *UA* 15636

Thalêstris see Tâlistrîâ

Thare natural son of Priam, a warrior in the Trojan army against the Greeks. In Benoît he is called Tharé. – *LT* a4808 n4837

Thaurôn a warrior in Alexander's army. He is the leader of the party which storms the castle of Mâdâtes. This character seems to have been invented by Ulrich. – *UA* 14951

Theanus the woman guardian of the Palladium, which she surrenders to Antenor in *LT*, and to the Greeks in *TKf*, where she is called Tannâ. She occurs as Theano, the wife of Antenor, in Benoît, Dictys, and Homer, and in the first two she is also the guardian of the Palladium. – *LT* nm15645; *TKf* 47597f.

Theas see Thoas

Thebires a vassal of Gamorett, for whom he fights against Agâmennon. – *GT* 5675

Thebrant the leader of a band of knights who pursue Dêmantîn and Sirgamôte as they flee from Eghart. T. is unhorsed by Dêmantîn. – *Dem* 4151

Thedalius see Thedalus

Thedalûn 'vürste von Gâzôn', 'burcgrâve von Korinthiâ'. He is left with Passigweiz (2), Philodant, and Justînus (2) in charge of Alexander's people whilst the latter is away on his campaigns. All these names appear to have been introduced into the narrative by Ulrich, as none is to be found in any other history of Alexander. – *UA* a2361 n2380

Thedalus 'von Arlas', a knight who entertains Paris at his castle when the latter first arrives in Greece. Paris kills Gariell, T.'s oppressor, and stays with T. and his wife, Aloysse, for a year. T. takes Paris to the tourney held by Agâmennon and is later rescued by Paris from death at the hands of Aschos. T. hides the Trojan army which accompanies Paris on his journey to abduct Helen. – *GT* 2411f.

Thedis see Thetis

Thelamon a warrior who fights for Jason in the first war against the Trojans. T. plays an important part in the Greek victory and receives Esîonâ as his reward. Their son is Ajax (1). In *TKf* he is called 'von Salafîn'. This story is told in Benoît and Dares; T. is mentioned as the father of Ajax (1) in Homer, but there is, of course, no mention of the first war or of Esîonâ. – *LT* 1212; *TK* 11484f.

Thelafus son of Hercules, a warrior in the Greek army against the Trojans. So also in Dictys, Dares, and Benoît. – *LT* 3917

Thelemacus son of Ulixes and Penelope. T. marries Nausica, and they have a son, Porporius. T. occurs in Benoît, Dictys, and the *Odyssey*. – *LT* 17786f.

Thelefus see Thelafus

Thelogonus son of Ulixes and Circe, who, as foretold in a prophecy, slays his own father. So also in Benoît and Dictys. T. does not occur in Homer's *Odyssey*, but appears in a cyclic poem attributed to Eugammon of Cyrene.[16] – *LT* 18281ff.

Themisa mother of Eustates by Ajax (1). In Benoît and Dictys she is called Tecmissa. – *LT* nm16903

Theoborus 'von Prandigan', a knight who fights with Nectarus against Gamorett. – *GT* 5750

Theodosîus (surnamed 'the Great'), a Roman Emperor, AD 346–395. – *UA* nm14885

Theoris 'ûz Valpinos', a warrior who is killed whilst fighting for Akarîn against Ipomidôn. – *JT* nm3110,1 a3901,1f.

Theophilus 'künec von Tosdon', a warrior in the Greek army against the Trojans. This character appears to have been invented by Herbort. – *LT* 3371

Therefeus a warrior in the Trojan army against the Greeks. This name does not occur in any other version of the Trojan legend, but Terepex occurs in Benoît as a variant of Sterepeus. – *LT* 5402

Thesaris wife of Ydomeneus. This character is not mentioned in any other version of the Trojan legend. – *LT* 17290ff.

Thesereyse see Tesereiz

Theseus (1) a warrior in the Greek army against the Trojans. So also in Benoît. In *TK* he is slain by Hector. – *LT* 3335ff.; *TK* 23815

Theseus (2) 'künec von Thesidas', who supplies the Greek army besieging Troy with food. This character does not occur in any other version of the Trojan legend. – *LT* 11113

Theseus (3) a king who had abducted Helen but returned her unharmed. This character appears to have been invented by Konrad. – *TK* nm21110

Theseus (4) 'von Therasche', father of Archilogus, a warrior in the Trojan army against the Greeks. In Benoît he is called Heseüs, a name doubled with Resa (see Refus) from Rhesus, king of Thrace, in Dares. – *LT* 4063

Theseus (5) 'künec', father of Peritheus. T. is not named in the extant fragments of *AP* but is so called in the OF version. – *AP* aF,1

Thêseus (6) in Greek legend, the former lover of Ariadne (see Adrîagnê) and husband of Hippolyte. He was slain by Licomedes. – *C* nm11576

Thesifone see Têsiphône

Thetis sister of Jupiter, wife of Pêleus (1), and mother of Achilles. She places Achilles in the care of Cheiron, but learning of the warlike way in which he is being brought up and remembering the prophecy made concerning him on her wedding day, she tries to hide him, disguised as a woman, at the court of Licomedes. In *LT*, as in Benoît and Dictys, she pleads with Pirrus for mercy to Acastus. – *LT* nm17854 a18085; *JT* nm2433,3; *TK* m821 n838 a1007; *UA* m4878f.; *RB* nm16418; *GT* m14943f. n14954f. a17875; *GM* nm375438 (MS D)

Thetisz see Thetis

Theucrus see Teucer

Theucer 'künec von Messin', a warrior who is slain by Achilles when the Greeks are foraging in his land. In Benoît he is called Teütrans. – *LT* 3906

Thydeus see Tydeus

Thiesti in Greek mythology, T., who is the father of Aegysthus (see Egistus) by his own daughter, unwittingly eats his own son, who is set before him by T.'s brother, Atreus. – *C* nm11596

---

16 Homer, *Odyssey*, ed. by A. T. Murray, I, p. 395, note.

Thymodes a warrior in charge of the mercenaries in Dârîus's army. In *UA* he leaves Alexander to join Dârîus. So also in *Expeditio Alexandri* and Curtius Rufus, where he is called Thymondes (var. Thimodes). – *A* 5312; *UA* 6767

Thynas see Tînas

Thindarîus see Tindarîus

Thytorison, Thytoryzon see Titurisone

Thoas a warrior who is captured whilst fighting for the Greeks against the Trojans. In *TK* he is called Dôas (*TKf* 47800: Tôas) von Tholîe. T. appears in Benoît, Dares, Dictys, and Homer. – *LT* 3341; *TK* 23822

Thobîas see Tobîas

Tholomer a heathen who is defeated by Evaleth. In *Mer* he is said to be the king of Gaul, whilst in *L'Estoire del Saint Graal* (Vulgate Cycle) he is called Tholomers (= Ptolemy), king of Egypt, and in *Les Aventures del Saint Graal* (Vulgate Cycle) he is referred to as li rois d'Orient. – nm *Mer* 157,4; *RP* 614,30

Tholomêus see Ptolômêus (2)

Thomas (1) 'sante'. – nm *JT* 6139,5; *UW* 6,27

Thômas (2) 'von Britanje', the author of an Anglo-Norman poem on Tristan which was used as a source of *Tn* by Gottfried von Straßburg. – nm *Tn* 150; *HT* 6842

Thulomedes see Tholomer

Thurbund see Thuribund

Thuribund a squire in the service of Segromans. He announces the arrival of Agâmennon's army and is sent to offer them terms of peace. – *GT* 24599

Thuribuntt see Thuribund

Tybalis counsellor to Agâmennon, who consults him as to a suitable reward for Paris. – *GT* 3726

Tîbalt (1) 'von Kler', also called 'von Arabî', and 'von Todjerne'. T. is the first husband of Gîburc, who runs away from him with his prisoner Willehalm (1) and becomes a Christian. T. joins his father-in-law with a large army, and together they attack Willehalm at Alischanz. In *R* he is still at enmity with Malfer, although Terramêr is now a Christian and friendly to Malfer. T. is called Tiebaut in *Aliscans* and occurs in all of the *chansons de geste* of the Guillaume d'Orange cycle, including the *Chancun de Willame*, in which he is called Tedbalt. (See Libaut.) – *W* [nm8,2] a28,25; *R* nm Eing. II,59f.; *UW* nm5,1, a42,4

Tybalt (2) son of the king of Portimunt. He sends love-letters by a talking bird to his *amie*, who is separated from him. – *Port* m2 n62

Tyberie 'kaiser'. This is the OF form (as in the romances of the Vulgate Cycle) of the name of the Emperor Tiberius of Rome. – *JT* nm125,1

Tibullus Latin author, 53–18 BC. – *Port* nm278

Tŷde see Dîden

Tydeus father of Dyomedes. So also in Benoît and Homer. In *Ed* he is seen by Ênêâs in Hades, whilst, according to *UA*, he is one of the warriors slain in the battle between Polinices and Ethiocles. – *Ed* 3314; *LT* nm8546; *UA* nm3154

Tydomîe 'küneginne von Kamerîe'. She is bathing when Meleranz comes riding across the plain. T., who has been warned of his approach, sends her maidens away and makes Meleranz wait on her. They fall in love, but Meleranz rides off the following day to Arthur's court. T.'s uncle, Malloas, tries to compel her to marry Libers (1), but Meleranz arrives in time to restore justice and marries T. himself. – *M* 508ff.

Tiebalt see Tîbalt (1)

Tierrich see Dietherich

Tiestes a warrior who is slain whilst fighting for the Trojans against the Greeks. His slayer is Dyomedes. So also in Dictys, where he is called Thyestes. – *TKf* 43201ff.

Tîmant 'der von' (*L*), see Aspjol

Tîmodes see Thymodes

Tymôteus a warrior who is killed by the burghers of Sûdrâcas, into which he had penetrated in order to help Alexander. – *UA* 20670f.

Tinal 'ein meister von Senibalin'. He made the clothes for Gîburc and Willehalm. – *UW* 188,7

Tînas 'von Lîtân'. (Lot has pointed out that in Beroul he is called Dinas de Lidan;[17] *Dinas lidan* means in Welsh and Cornish 'large fortress', so that it would seem that the original Celtic name has fallen out, and Dinas has been taken to be the name of the person. So also Bruce.[18]) T. is placed in charge of Tristan at Marke's court and is later very helpful to him in his attempts to see Îsolt (2). In *P* he is said to be the father of Lâîz, and in *TF* the father of Lischeit. – *ET* a300ff. n328; *P* nm429,18; *UT* nm931 a942; *HT* 3110f.; *TF* nm10157

Tindarîus 'künec', father of Helen and grandfather of Ermiona. So also in Dictys; in the *Aeneid* (II,569) Helen is referred to as Tyndarida, i.e. daughter of Tyndareus. (Cf. Elena.) – *TKf* 49234f. [†]

Tyntayol 'herzoge von' (*Mer*), see Urlois

Tintayol 'herzoginne von', (*Mer*) see Îgerne

*Tintarides see Elena

Tîrîdates chancellor to Dârîus. He tells Alexander the amount of Dârîus's treasure at Persîpolis. This character appears to have been invented by Rudolf. – *A* 14144

Tiridê (Martin thinks that this name originated in Solinus (68,10), where Tirida, a town, is mentioned.[19]) T., who is called 'von Elixodjôn', is one of the knights whom Feirefîz claims to have defeated. In *JT* he is called Kiride von Eliavdione and takes part in the tourney held by Sekundille to decide which of her wooers she shall marry. – *P* nm770,14; *JT* 5275,1

Tîriotes 'kameræere' of Dârîus, to whom he brings the news of the death of his wife, who was captive in the hands of Alexander. T. occurs in Gualterus and Curtius Rufus. – *A* a11209ff. n11253

Tirol father of Vridebrant. Hero of a MHG epic which bears his name and of which only a small fragment is extant. In the epic he is apparently engaged in battle with the heathens. He occurs in a didactic poem published by F. von der Hagen,[20] in which he gives advice to his son, but this poem shows obvious traces of the influence of *P*. Boppe makes a reference in one of his poems to 'des küniges Tirols buch'.[21] – *Tirol* A,20

Tirosiente 'künec', a warrior in Ipomidôn's army against Akarîn. – *JT* 3216,3

Tyrric see Dietherich

Tŷrus (1) father of Silviâne. T. is an old man who lives near the place where Ênêâs builds his new town, Albanî. Ascanjus is out hunting one day, when he kills a hart, which, although he did not know it, was tame and belonged to Silviâne. T.'s men are very angry and slay one of the Trojans, whereupon a pitched battle takes place, in the course of which T.'s house is burned down. In the OF *Eneas* he is called Tirus, and in Virgil, Tyrrhus. – *Ed* 4566f.

---

17 Lot (3), pp. 337f.
18 Bruce (1), I, pp. 182f.
19 Martin (1), p. 503, to 770,14.
20 F. von der Hagen, *Minnesinger*, I, pp. 5ff.
21 F. von der Hagen, *Minnesinger*, II, p. 385.

Tirus (2)   see Cyrus (1)

Tysabê, Tisbê   see Tispê

Tismas   the repentant thief who was crucified at the same time as Jesus and whose soul was saved. – *W* nm68,26 [†]

Tispê   lover of Pîramus (q.v.) (Thisbe). – nm *E* 7709; *Tn* 3612ff.; *C* 11574; *FB* 2435; *TK* 2317; *RB* 15268; *WO* 3604

Titegast   Zidegast

Tyterel   see Titurel

Tŷtides   a Greek warrior who is seen by Ênêâs in Hades. So also in the OF *Eneas*. This is evidently Dyomedes, the son of Tydeus (i.e. Tydides). – *Ed* 3345

Tytomîe   see Tydomîe

Tîton   husband of Aurorâ and father of Mennon (2). So also in Dictys, where he is called Tithonus. In Greek mythology T. is the son of Laomedon. – *TKf* nm42614

Tytorison   see Titurisone

Tytrian   a king who had bribed Syrodamen to open the mountain in which lived Jerome and her people, so that he could capture Jerome. His army was defeated, and he himself captured. – *FS* m3127 n3140

Titurel   (Bartsch derived this name from the OHG name, Tiether, with the suffix *-el*.[22] Golther believes that it was taken from *E*, which took it from the Breton *lai*, *Tydorel*.[23] According to Martin, however, this *lai* was not written until after 1200 and could hardly have been the source of the reference in *P*, and certainly not of that in *E*.[24] The reference in *E* may be the interpolation of a later copyist who took it from *P*, since the name does not occur in the corresponding list in Chrestien's *Erec*, and, moreover, it is rimed with Gârel (1), which also does not appear in Chrestien's list but does appear in *P*.) T. is the grandfather of Amfortas and the founder of the Graal dynasty. Parzivâl catches a glimpse of him on his first visit to the Graal Castle and is struck by his great beauty and age. T. is kept alive only by sight of the Graal. T. appears, but is not named, in *C*, where he is fed by the blood brought by the Graal maidens. In *JT* he is the son of Titurisone and is the builder of the Graal temple. When he is 400 years old (the Graal makes him appear and feel 50), he marries, at the command of the Graal, Richaude (1). An attempt to explain his name is made in *JT*, when it is derived from Titur-(isone), his father, and El-(yzab)-el, his mother, but of course the parents' names were in point of fact derived from that of T. A knight Tydorïans (4047: Tydoriaus, of which the oblique case would by Tydorel) appears in Gerbert's continuation of *Perceval* (3959), but this may have been taken from the Breton *lai* or even from *P* (cf. Kundrîe (1)). – *E* 1651; *P* a240,24ff. n251,5; *T* 1,1; *C* a14620ff.; *JT* nm80,6 a149,1f.; *RB* nm143; *WO* nm12285; *FS* nm4821 [†]

Titurell   see Titurel

Titurisone   son of Parille (1), husband of Elyzabel, and father of Titurel. – nm *JT* 91,1ff; *WO* 12284

Titus   Emperor of Rome. T. was the son of Vespasian and lived AD 40–81. – *RB* nm18140

Tîcius   in Greek mythology called Tityos. He tried to offer violence to Diana and was slain by Apollo. T., who was a giant, covered nine acres of ground with his body and had two vultures perpetually tearing his liver. – *Ed* nm3516ff.

---

22   Bartsch (2), p. 140.
23   Golther (1), p. 179.
24   Martin (1), p. 229, to 251,5.

Tjofabier a commander in Gârel's army against Ehkunat. T. is in the service of the father of Sabîe (2). – *G* a9599 n9871f.

Tjofrit a knight who is sent by Gârel to announce his approach as an enemy to Ehkunat. – *G* 12066ff.

Tôarîs (Bartsch was inclined to think that this name was a form of the Greek name Thoas,[25] but Martin points to the name Toranius (var. Thoranius) mentioned by Solinus (21,3,7) as the source.[26]) T., who is 'künec von Oraste Gentesîn', is one of the knights whom Feirefîz claims to have defeated. In *JT*, where he is called Scheorise, he takes part in the tourney held by Sekundille to decide which of her wooers she shall marry. – *P* nm770,15; *JT* 5277,1

Tôas see Thoas

Tôbal biblical, a descendant of Cain (Tubal-cain, son of Lamech). – *A* nm17042

Tobîas biblical, the chief character in the apocryphal *Book of Tobit*. – nm *A* 16821; *MB* 92,7; *JT* 2506,5; *UA* 11809

Todan 'von Ardonte', also called 'der von Ardente', a warrior in Ipomidôn's army against Akarîn. – *JT* 3220,2

Todilâ a merchant trading in Poytowê who tends Tandareis and nurses him back to health after an encounter with a band of robbers. – *TF* m4407ff. an4424f.

Todines see Dodines

Tolr see Tolrr

Tolrr 'grâve von Rotenburch', a knight who fights on the side of the Christians in the final battle against the heathens. T. is an ancestor of Albreht (3). – *WO* 16647

Toranus to whom Alexander bequeathed Pania. This name does not occur in any other history of Alexander. – *SA* nm8523

Tores Tors

Torgalis a warrior who is slain whilst fighting for Ipomidôn against Akarîn. – *JT* 4120,5f.

Torkuleis 'der künec mit dem Korne', a warrior who is slain whilst fighting for Ipomidôn against Akarîn. – *JT* nm3319,1 a4120,5

Tors the putative son of Ares (q.v.). T. is first mentioned in Chrestien's *Erec* (1728) and appears in *E* as Estorz (the Ambraser MS reads 'Torsuilroi ares'), a knight who is present at Arthur's court when Êrec returns with Ênîte. In *L*, where he is called Torfilaret (Tor fil Ares), he assists Lanzelet to recover Genewîs. He appears in *RP*, when Arthur gives him the castle of Langerde, and he is also present at the tourney held by Arthur before the Schastel Orgelus. It is somewhat doubtful whether T. is identical with Littores von Baradigan (*RP* 525,46), a knight who joins in the search for Parzivâl, or Tores von Baradigan, a relative of Orgelus who was at the tourney held by Antipins Karadins (nm *RP* 466,17), since in the first instance the Mons MS of Gautier has Li Tournis de Baradigan, and in the second instance, li Sires de Baradugan. Brugger is of the opinion that T. is identical with Estor (q.v.).[27] – *E* 1515; *L* 8070; *RP* 45,3

Torfilaret see Tors

Totan apparently a figure out of classical mythology.[28] – *C* nm8449

Tradas see Trîdanz

Trackune see Trakunt

---

25 Bartsch (2), p. 155.
26 Martin (1), p. 504, to 770,15.
27 Brugger (1), pp. 84f.
28 *C* 11572f.: 'Und dô Totan under betten/ Durch liebe erdructen diu wîp'.

Trakunt 'von Yspanie', a knight who unhorses a number of knights of the Round Table (see Durans). T. is probably identical with Trackune, a knight who takes part in the tourney held by Arthur (*JT* 2704,6). A knight named Trahant appears in the Vulgate *Lancelot* and the *Livre d'Artus*, where the young Lanzelet pulls two pieces of lance from his body and vows to avenge his injury. – *JT* 1324,5

Translapîns (Bartsch thought that this word was a corrupt form of Transalpins, 'living on the other side of the Alps',[29] whilst Martin points out that Solinus mentions (21,4) transalpina Gallia.[30]) T., who is 'künec von Rivigitas', is one of the knights whom Feirefîz claims to have defeated. In *JT* he is called Eralapins von Nigitas and takes part in the tourney held by Sekundille to decide which of her wooers she shall marry. – *P* nm770,10; *JT* 5267,1

Tranzes see Drances

Trebasîn see Trebassîn

Trebassîn a commander in Bêâmunt's army at Antrîûn. – *Dem* nm9681 a11027

Trebuket see Trebuchet

Trebuchet (< OF *trebuchet*, 'sling'[31]). T. is a famous smith in OF legends and is the maker of the Graal sword which Amfortas gives to Parzivâl. He also makes the two knives which cut the glassy frost from Amfortas's wound off the Graal lance. In *RP* he is called Tribuet (so also in the Mons MS of Manessier), but it is clear that T. is intended, as he is said to have repaired Parzivâl's sword (769,19). In *W* he has a son called Schoit. – *P* nm253,29; *W* nm356,21; *JT* nm3698,5; *Sey* nm158,5; *RP* m764,37 a765,17 n765,30

Trebuchnet see Trebuchet

Trenolas 'künec von Badacone', a knight who attends the tourney held by Arthur. He is later (5658,1) called 'künec von Pilakone' and is one of the kings who take the oath of allegiance to Parzivâl after the latter's victory over Agors (see Strangedorz). – *JT* 2010,1f.

Trefiezent, Trefiezzent, Trefizent, Trevressent, Trefrescent see Trevrezent

Trevrezent (Schulz thought that this name was derived from OF *treve recéant* = 'trêve établi', 'peace established'.[32] Bartsch derived it from *trev* < Provençal *treu* = 'peace';[33] this etymology is contested by Gaston Paris.[34] Martin also sees in the first half of the name OF *tref*, 'peace' (modern French *trêve* (Martin has, incorrectly, *trève*) < OHG *triuwa*) and suggests that the second half of the name might be a corruption of *recevant*, i.e. 'receiving peace'.[35]) T. is the brother of Amfortas and uncle of Parzivâl. He was formerly a knight noted for his bravery (he is referred to as 'der snelle' in *T*), but he renounces knighthood after his brother receives his wound, and becomes a hermit, devoting his life to God in the hope of mitigating his brother's pain. He brings Parzivâl back to the path of Christianity after he has been wandering about for four and a half years despairing of the existence of justice and mercy. T. appears as a young knight in *JT*, where he is present at Schîonatulander's *swertleite*. – *P* nm251,13ff. a452,15; *T* nm9,3; *JT* nm618,5 a1141,5 [†]

Treffrezzent see Trevrezent

---

29 Bartsch (2), p. 154.
30 Martin (1), p. 503, to 770,10.
31 Schulz, 'Eigennamen', p. 392.
32 Schulz, 'Eigennamen', p. 391.
33 Bartsch (2), p. 140.
34 Paris (2), pp. 149f.
35 Martin (1), p. 229, to 251,15.

Tryachta   a knight who takes part in the tourney held by Arthur for the crown of Deleprosat.
– *Wigm* 2017

Tribol   'von Tribalgidise', a warrior in Ipomidôn's army against Akarîn. – *JT* 3369,1

Tribuet   Trebuchet

Trîdanz   (Martin suggests < Tritannum, the name of a gladiator in Solinus (19,3), but points
out that the form of the name which appears here would seem to have come from a
Provençal original.[36]) T., who is 'künec von Tinodonte', is one of the knights whom
Feirefiz claims to have defeated. In *JT*, where he is called Tradas von Tinotente, he takes
part in the tourney held by Sekundille to decide which of her wooers she shall marry. –
P nm770,5; *JT* 5257,1

Triptolomeus   to whom Alexander bequeathed Persia. This character does not appear in any
other version of the Alexander history. – *SA* nm8529

Trischans   a maiden who calls upon her *ami*, Garsalas, to fight Parzivâl, who has cut down
the head of a hart which she had tied to a tree. In the Mons MS of Gautier she is called
Riseut, and in the Montpellier MS, Iseut la bloie (i.e. Îsolt (2)). – *RP* a423,40 n430,15

Tristam   see Tristan

Tristan   (Hertz quotes Owen and Spurrell as deriving this name from *trystio*, 'resound',
'thunder', i.e. 'the Thunderer'.[37] The generally accepted etymology is from the Pictish
king's name, Drost, Drostan, then as Drest, Drestan (Kymric Drystan) taken over by the
Celts as a personal name.[38]) The earliest MHG poem dealing with T. is *ET*, in which he is
born by being cut out of his mother's dead body. When a young man he leaves his father's
court and goes to Marke, where he conceals his identity. He defeats Môrolt for Marke but
is badly wounded in the fight and is placed in an open boat which drifts to Ireland. Here he
meets and is healed by Îsolt (2). T. pays a second visit to Ireland shortly afterwards, in
search of Marke's bride with the golden hair, and after killing a dragon which is devastating
the countryside, he is recognized as the slayer of Môrolt but succeeds in bringing Îsolt (2)
back to Marke. On the journey T. and Îsolt unwittingly share a love potion destined for
Marke which compels them to seek opportunities to be together even after Îsolt is married
to Marke. When their association is discovered, T. is banned, but he is later permitted to
return; they are again discovered, and T. is condemned to be broken on the wheel, but he
escapes and rescues Îsolt who is about to be handed over to a leper colony. They hide
together in a wood, and after four years, when the effect of the potion has worn off, Îsolt
returns to Marke, whilst T. goes to Arthur's court, where a hunt gives him an opportunity
to spend a night with Îsolt, and then to Jovelîn, whom he assists against Rîol and whose
daughter, Îsolt (3), he marries. He visits Îsolt (2) four times after this, the last time
disguised as a fool, and is mortally wounded whilst fighting with Kâedîn against
Nampêtenis. T. sends for Îsolt (2), who alone can heal him; the ship which is sent for her is
to carry a black sail if she refuses to come, a white one if she is on board. Îsolt (3) tells T.
that the sail is black, and he dies instantly, whilst Îsolt (2), when she arrives and finds T.
dead, falls across his body and dies also.

Substantially the same story is told by Gottfried in *Tn*. Gottfried used the Anglo-Norman
version of the story by Thomas, whereas Eilhart, in *ET*, had used the OF version of Beroul.
Minor variations are introduced into Thomas and *Tn* to soften the harsh outlines of the
story as it appears in *ET*, and it is clear from the extant fragments of Thomas that the

---

36   Martin (1), p. 503, to 770,5.
37   Gottfried von Straßburg, *Tristan und Isolde*, transl. by W. Hertz, p. 550.
38   Ranke, p. 3.

ending of *Tn* would have differed considerably from that of *ET*, but Gottfried only brought his poem to the point where T. is contemplating marriage with Îsolt (3). Two continuations of *Tn* – *UT* and *HT* – were written, but both were based entirely on *ET*. The OF forms of this name are:[39] Beroul: Tristran (and Tristrant); Chrestien: Tristran (some MSS Tristanz) (Tristran also in Gerbert's continuation to *Perceval*); Chardri (an Anglo-Norman poet) and Marie de France: Tristram; the Provençal poets use the form Tristan. The ME poem *Sir Tristrem* shows the reverse form (see below) as Tramtris.

In *ET*, T. is called Tristrant, but when he is hiding his identity during his first visit to Ireland, he calls himself Tantris, so that Tristan is obviously the original form of the name. The form Tristrant occurs in *L*, *RB*, *GM*, and *FS*. The form Tristram appears in *E*, *C*, *FD*, *JT* (see below), and *RW*. F. von der Hagen publishes two anonymous poems giving this form.[40] *G* has Tristran, and *MB* has Tristam. All other poems show the form Tristan as in *Tn*. Panzer, who records the historical appearance of this name in documents of the 14th, 15th, and 16th centuries,[41] points out that the presence of *r* in the termination is not proof that the name was taken from *ET*, since T. is spelt Tristrant in the Munich MS of *Tn*, whilst in *JT* he is called Tristram von Parmanie, a name which could only have come from *Tn*.[42] In *E*, T. is called Tristram, but Chrestien (*Erec* 1713) has 'Tristanz (MS V: Tristrans) qui onques ne rist'. Foerster differentiates between this Tristan and T., but there seems to be no justification for this, The epithet 'who never laughed' appears to be the result of the popular medieval derivation of this name from *triste*.[43] 'Tristans qui onques ne rist' appears also in the *Livre d'Artus*.

– *ET* nm36 a99f.; *E* 1650; *L* 6234; *Tn* nm125ff. a1746ff.; *C* nm11562; *MB* nm28,39; *A* nm3159; *RW* nm2187; *UT* 40f.; *FD* nmXII,12; *G* nm2456; *JT* 1993,1; *TK* nm2313; *HT* nm49 a111; *RB* nm15291; *GM* (MS I) 3860 (MS D) 38573; *FS* nm4818 [†]

Tristant, Tristram, Tristran, Tristrant see Tristan

Tritunel 'herzoge von Tangelant', an ally of Lôîs against Terramêr. – *UW* 37,4

Trifon (1) 'von Araby', a knight who sends Marcus (2) to woo Helen for him. His suit is refused, and he attacks Agâmennon, against the advice of Marcus. T. is killed by Paris in single combat, but his army attacks Paris, who, with the help of Marcus, succeeds in routing them. T.'s brother, Gamorett, comes to avenge his death. – *GT* nm4988ff. a5215

Triphôn (2) son of Mêthâ, a warrior who is slain by Clîtus whilst fighting for Dârîus at Erbela. This character appears to have been invented by Ulrich. – *UA* nm12115ff.

Triphone 'von Plurente', a warrior in Ipomidôn's army against Akarîn. – *JT* 3258,1f.

Trôas son of Dardanus; Troy was named after him. He is called Tros in the OF *Eneas*. – *Ed* nm11687

Trogrey 'von Fuszes', a knight who takes part in the tourney held by Dymszogar. – *Wigm* nm4764

---

39 Eilhart von Oberge, *Tristrant*, pp. cxliif.
40 F. von der Hagen, *Minnesinger*, III, pp. 427 and 441.
41 Panzer (2), p. 218.
42 See Gottfried's refutation of *ET* (*Tn* 322ff.): 'genuoge jehent und wænent des:/ der selbe hêrre er wære/ ein Lohnoisære,/ künec über daz lant ze Lohnois:/ nu tuot uns aber Thômas gewis,/ der es an den âventiuren las,/ daz er von Parmenîe was.'
43 Cf. *Tn* (1997ff.): 'Nu heizet triste triure/ und von der âventiure/ sô wart daz kint Tristan genant.'

Trohazzabê 'von Karkasûn', standard-bearer to Ehmereiz in the second battle at Alischanz. He flees when he sees his son, Ektor (2), slain. This character does not occur in *Aliscans* and appears to have been invented by Wolfram. – *W* 365,8

Troilus son of Priam, a warrior in the Trojan army against the Greeks. He is compelled by the Trojans to give up Briseida (q.v.), who is sent to join her father with the Greeks. T. is slain by Achilles, whom he had badly wounded and who orders his servant to drag T. round the walls of Troy behind his horse, just as Achilles himself does to Hector in Homer. This is the story as told in *LT* and Benoît, whilst Dares also states that he had wounded Achilles, but neither in Dares nor in Dictys, in which, as in *TKf*, his death is reported without any unusual incidents, is Briseida mentioned in connection with T., nor is there any mention of his being dragged round Troy behind a horse. In *Ed*, Ênêâs sees T. in Hades. – *Ed* 3324; *LT* nm1664ff. a2253; *MC* nm22; *TK* nm13254ff. a19110

Troymar 'lo mechschin' (< OF *li meschins*, 'the youth'), one of the knights at Arthur's court when Êrec returns with Ênîte. This name does not appear in the corresponding list of knights in Chrestien's *Erec*. – *E* 1667

Trôstelîn a knight who welcomes Ulrich von Liechtenstein to Neustadt during his *Artusfahrt*. – *FD* 1481,1

Trotula a celebrated woman physician in Rome at the time of Augustus. – *Mer* nm36,7

Trüeben Berge 'vrouwe von dem', a maiden who meets Daniel as he is following the messenger from Matûr and who tells him how her father, herzoge von dem T. B. (nm1224f.), had been slain by Jurân, who was now trying to make T. marry him. Daniel slays Jurân and frees T.'s land. T. is present at Daniel's wedding and marries Belamîs. – *DB* a1115 n[1498f.]

Tschaflore see Schafillôr

Tscherines see Schêrins

Tschinovere see Ginovêr

Tschyonatulander see Schîonatulander

Tschirnivel see Schirniel

Tschoisiane, Tschosian see Schoisiâne

Tschoveranz a knight of the Round Table who is present at the banquet held in honour of Gârel's victory over Ehkunat. – *G* 20047

Tschute, Tschutte see Schôt

Tugat 'von Barbarie', a knight who is present at the tourney held by Arthur for the crown of Deleprosat. – *Wigm* 2086f.

Tugrisol a warrior in Ipomidôn's army against Akarîn. – *JT* 3320,5

Tulant apparently an ally on the side of Etzel in a fight which he had with Parzivâl. The story of this battle is told to Lorengel (see Lohengrîn) by Waldemar. – *Ll* nm78,7

Tulius see Tullius

Tullius Latin author. He is probably identical with Tulius, one of Alexander's learned advisors in *UA*; the name does not occur in any of the other histories of Alexander and was probably added by Ulrich. – *MA* nm244; *UA* 24341

Tulmein 'herzoge von' (*E*), see Îmâin

Tumbe 'der klâre' (*JT*), see Parzivâl

Tuntanîs advisor to Tîbalt. T. is in the army which pursues Willehalm (1) and Gîburc when they escape from Tîbalt. – *UW* 164,20

Tuorhaimare 'der', see Uolrîch (14)

Türantt see Turian

Turbalitus 'von Aquilon', a warrior in Ipomidôn's army against Akarîn. – *JT* 3258,6

Turbar see Turbart

Turbart a scout in Marroch's army against Arthur. He is defeated by Wigamur. – *Wigm* a2880ff. n2894

Turbuleis 'von Ragulie', a warrior in Akarîn's army against Ipomidôn. – *JT* nm3177,1

Turian a knight who challenges Paris at the tourney held by Agâmennon and is defeated. – *GT* 2956

Türiantt see Turian

Turkant 'künec von Turkânîe', a warrior who is slain by Willehalm (1) whilst fighting for Terramêr in the first battle at Alischanz. So also in *Aliscans* (471ª), where he is called Turbant d'Urconie. – *W* 29,2

Turkecals, Turkeltals, Turkeltas see Turkentâls

Turkentâls a prince who is mentioned by Herzeloide as having been slain by Lehelîn. In *JT* he is present at the tourney held by Arthur, and his death is reported when Lehelîn is attacking Kanvoleise. – *P* nm128,8; *JT* 2006,1

Turkîs a heathen who is slain by Alîs. Markabrê attempts, unsuccessfully, to avenge his death. – *PM* 19046ff.

Turkoit brother of Anziflor; T. is a knight and marries Soye (2), Gawein's sister. This character is obviously taken from *P* or *JT*, where Florant, the turkoit, marries Sangîve, Gawein's mother, who, in *Mer*, is called Soye (1) and appears to have become confused with Soye (2). – *Sey* nm253,5f. [†]

Turkuleis see Torkuleis

Turneas a king whose service Fridrich (3) enters. Fridrich routs T.'s foe, Nemoras, who, however, returns after six years, when he is defeated by Fridrich in single combat. T. refuses to give Fridrich his reward unless he serves for a further period of eight years, which he declines to do. He is given only a hart, which it transpires is Pragnet. T. is a friend of Flanea, and at her request he brings an army to fight for Mompolier against Fridrich. T. is captured, and his life is saved only by the intercession of Pirnas. He is deprived of his kingdom and made a *grâve*. – *FS* a3709 n3890

Turnîs see Lerân

Turnûs 'herzoge', a warrior to whom Lâtin had formerly promised his kingdom and his daughter, Lavînia. When the promise is revoked, T. attacks Ênêas with an army, and after a fierce battle, T. jumps into a boat to kill a bowman and is carried away by the wind to the shores of his father Daunus's land. He does not accept the peace which his army has made with Ênêas, and a duel is arranged. News is brought of an attack by the Trojans, and a pitched battle takes place before Laurente. A further battle is also fought before the duel eventually takes place, and T. is killed by Ênêas. So also in the OF *Eneas* and Virgil. – *Ed* nm3982 a4356; *P* nm419,12; *C* nm17269

Turpîn (1) the fighting bishop of Reims. He is mentioned in most of the *chansons de geste* as one of Charlemagne's companions; he was slain at Roncevaux. – nm *W* 455,9; *UW* 31,19

Turpin (2) 'künec von Kadess', a knight who is slain by Segromans whilst fighting for his uncle, Agâmennon. – *GT* 24330

Turpiûn 'künec von Falturmîê', a warrior who is killed whilst fighting for Terramêr against Willehalm (1) at the first battle of Alischanz. T. occurs only in certain MSS of *Aliscans* (471), where he is called Harpin de Valturquie. – *W* 28,26

*Tûzamanz 'künec von Tussangulân', husband of Kanfinôn, slain in combat by Willehalm (1). – *UW* 73,20ff.

Twimant see Gwimant

U

Ûgrîm a hermit to whom Tristan goes whilst he is living in the wood with Îsolt (2). U. refuses Tristan absolution until Îsolt is sent back to Marke. She does not go back, however, until the effects of the love-potion have worn off. Then Tristan returns to the hermit. In Beroul he is called Ogrin. – *ET* 4702ff. [†]

Ucalegon one of the conspirators with Ênêâs to betray Troy to the Greeks. U., who is called Encalegon in *LT*, does not occur in Dares or Dictys, but he is mentioned by Virgil (*Aeneid*, II, 311f.) and is included by Benoît among the number of the conspirators. – *LT* 15190; *TKf* nm46831

Ulexes see Ulixes

Uliân a giant who is slain by Tandareis whilst guarding the road to his master, Karedôz. U. is the brother of Durkiôn and Margôn (1). – *TF* m5302 n5432 a6180

Ulixes 'der wîse', one of the leaders of the Greek army against the Trojans. In *LT* he does little to justify the epithet, except to ask an occasional question. His journey home from Troy is related in a similar way to the story in the *Odyssey*, the account reaching Herbort through Dictys and Benoît, whilst his death at the hands of his son by Circe, Thelogonus, also related by Dictys and Benoît, follows the story in the cyclic poem *Telegony*, which is attributed to Eugammon of Cyrene. In *TK*, as in the *Achilleis* of Statius, he accompanies Dyomedes to fetch Achilles to Troy and shows himself to be a master of cunning persuasion. He is suspected of being responsible for the death of Ajax (1) and leaves Troy in a hurry after the sack of the city. In *GT* he is the constant advisor of Agâmennon, who consults him whenever he is in difficulty. U. fetches Medea to Ajax (1) and accompanies the latter and Hercules when they go to fetch Achilles. A good deal of rough humour of the gleeman's type is provided by the attempts of U. to avoid getting drawn into a fight – he is an incorrigible coward in this version. After the fall of Troy he quarrels with Ajax (1) for the possession of the shield of Achilles. It is awarded to U., and Ajax kills himself, and U. is banished. He sails away from Troy with his army and is followed by Eleander, who kills him, together with his wife, Penelope. According to *Ed* and Virgil, it was U. who first conceived the idea of the wooden horse. – *Ed* nm960; *LT* 3021; *TK* 23842f.; *UA* nm18453; *RB* nm22570; *GT* 3729

Ullixes see Ulixes

Ulrîch bishop, defeated in Augsburg, which he was holding for Heinrîch (1) against the unbelievers. – *Loh* nm2547f.; *RP* nm60,32

Ülsenbrant a giant who is slain by Dietrich von Bern in *Virginal* (751). – *RB* nm25269

Ulsin also called Ülsin, a trusty knight in the service of Utepandragûn, whom he accompanies, together with Merlin, to the castle of Îgerne on the night that Arthur is begotten. In Geoffrey of Monmouth he is called Ulfin, whilst in the OF romances he is usually called Urfin. – *Mer* 203,6ff.

Umbrîz the most skilful of all saddlers. U. made the harness for the horse given to Ênîte by Guivreiz. The maker is not named in Chrestien's *Erec*. – *E* 7462ff.

Unargk see Unarck

Unarck a knight who is unhorsed by Wigamur at the tourney held by Arthur for the crown of Deleprosat. He later acts as a scout for Arthur's army against Marroch and unhorses Grymuas. – *Wigm* 1999

Unbekante, Unerkante 'der schön' (*RP*), see Wigalois

Unfassôn 'von Arragûn', a commander in Bêâmunt's army at Antrîûn. – *Dem* nm9789 a10823

Uolrich (1) son of Ruoprecht. U. marries Salme and fights for Fridrich (3) against Mompolier. – *FS* 5775f.

Uolrîch (2) 'von Eschenbach', MHG poet, and author of *UA* and *WW*. – nm *UA* 122f.; *WW* 4363

Uolrîch (3) 'von Guotenburc', a MHG poet. – *C* nm2444

Uolrîch (4) 'von Habechspach', brother of Heinrîch (12), a knight who welcomes Ulrich von Liechtenstein to Neustadt during his *Artusfahrt*. – *FD* nm1467,5ff.

Uolrîch (5) 'von Hasendorf', who, at the request of Ulrich von Liechtenstein, cuts off the latter's finger. – *FD* 437,2ff.

Uolrîch (6) 'von Hutensdorf', a knight who welcomes Ulrich von Liechtenstein to Neustadt during his *Artusfahrt*. – *FD* nm1481,3f.

Uolrich (7) 'von Liehtenstein', the hero of an autobiography which, whilst showing the absurd lengths to which knights were prepared to go in the service of *Minne*, gives, nevertheless, a very clear picture of the state of knighthood at the commencement of the 13th century. In spite of constant discouragement from his lady, U. continues to perform deeds in her honour, and he even has his finger cut off and sent to her in order to prove his love. On another occasion he joins a company of lepers at her gate but never receives a tangible reward for his devotion. He takes part in a great tourney held at Friesach, and he undertakes a *Venusfahrt* in honour of ladies in general, and his lady in particular, that is to say, he dresses up as Venus, concealing his identity, and travels round jousting with any knights who care to accept his challenge. His lady offends him, however, with some unnamed deed, and for a while he is inconsolable; soon, however, he chooses another, and in her honour he undertakes an *Artusfahrt*, jousting once again with any knights who accept the challenge, but on this occasion he collects six knights to whom he gives Arthurian names. A great tourney is held at Neustadt, Friderîch (4) eventually leading a side against U. in an undecided encounter. Finally U. is imprisoned by two of his own men, who keep him there until he is released by Meinhart. – *FD* n44,5

Uolrîch (8) 'von Mûrberc', a knight who takes part in the tourney held at Friesach. – *FD* 294,1

Uolrich (9) 'von Rapolzstein', the patron of the authors of *RP*. – *RP* nm849,28

Uolrîch (10) 'von Sahsendorf', a knight who welcomes Ulrich von Liechtenstein to Neustadt during his *Artusfahrt*. – *FD* 1482,1

Uolrîch (11) 'von Stouz' a knight who jousts with Ulrich von Liechtenstein during the tourney at Friesach, and again during Ulrich's *Venusfahrt*. He is also present at the tourney held at Kornneuburg. – *FD* 198,1

Uolrîch (12) 'von Torsewel', a knight who jousts with Ulrich von Liechtenstein during the latter's *Venusfahrt*. – *FD* 704,7ff.

Uolrîch (13) 'von Treven', a knight who jousts with Ulrich von Liechtenstein during the latter's *Venusfahrt*. – *FD* 616,5

Uolrîch (14) 'von Türheim', MHG poet, and author of *UT*, *R*, and a lost poem *Clîes*. – nm *UT* 3593; *A* 3262; *RW* 2257 (in full, 4390f.)

Uolrîch (15) 'von dem Türlîn', MHG poet, and author of *UW*. – nm *UW* 3,26; *UA* 16225

Uolrîch (16) 'grâve von Pfannenberc', a knight who is present at the tourney held at Friesach. – *FD* 190,1f.

Uolrîch (17) 'von Zezichoven' (in *L*: 'von Zatzikhoven'), MHG poet, and author of *L*. – nm *L* 9344; *A* 3199; *RW* 2198

Uolrîch (18) 'sante', see Ulrîch

Uolschalch 'von Pôtzen', a knight who wounds Ulrich von Liechtenstein at Brihsen, where he almost strikes off a finger. – *FD* [342,3]

Uote the wife of Hildebrand. – *W* nm439,16 [†]

Uranîas the passage of *Loh* in which this name occurs is taken from the *Wartburgkrieg*, and in this poem the name appears as Origines (l. 1000), one of the fathers of the church. – *Loh* nm117

*Urebalise see Vrebalise

Urgân 'li vilus', a giant who is oppressing Gilân. Tristan slays U. and obtains Gilân's dog, Petitcriu, as a reward. – *Tn* nm15921ff. a15973; *G* m2459; *HT* nm1906

Urgenius (1) 'künec von Spangen', a warrior who is slain by Lifronîs whilst fighting for the Greeks against the Trojans. This character was invented by Konrad. – *TK* 23940f.

Urgenius (2) 'von Trâse', a warrior who is slain by Priam whilst fighting for the Greek army against the Trojans. This character was invented by Konrad. – *TK* 34278f.

Urîâ biblical, husband of Bersabê (Uriah). U. was sent to his death by David, who coveted his wife. – *UA* nm11568

Urian (1) 'von Navarre', a warrior in the Greek army against the Trojans. This character was invented by Konrad. – *TK* 23952

Uryan (2) 'künec von Schotten', overlord of Marcus (1). – *GT* nm6456

Urielus 'künec', see Eurialus

Urîen 'künec von Love', a knight who attends the tourney held by Arthur. He appears later (2300) as one of the knights who spill Priure's cup of chastity. This second reference corresponds to Chrestien's *Erec* (1706): 'Yvains li fiz Uriien'. – *C* 586

Urigiens see Urjên

Urîolus see Eurialus

Ûrjans 'vürste ûz Punturtois'. (Bartsch preferred the form Vrians, which the MHG orthography might equally well represent, and derives the name from OF *frians*, 'der Lecker',[1] an etymology which is denied by Gaston Paris.[2] Singer thinks the name was taken from Wace's *Brut*, where it is the name of the son of Androgeus.[3] Martin points out that Geoffrey of Monmouth mentions Urianus, which Zimmer derives from Urbgen < Urbigenus.[4]) U. has a grudge against Gawein because the latter had punished him for assaulting a maiden. Gawein finds him wounded but fails to recognize him and cures him of his wounds. U. then steals Gawein's horse, at the same time taunting him with his stupidity. In Chrestien's *Perceval*, this character is called Greoreas (var. Grigoras), whilst in the Dutch *Lancelot* he is named Gregorias. The same story is told of Lohenîs (1) (q.v.) in *C*. In *G* he is again represented as an untrustworthy character, and although he is defeated by Eskilabôn, he does not fulfil his vow to surrender to Klârischanze, thus causing the latter to reject Eskilabôn. In this version he is called Frîans von Ponterteis. – *P* a505,12 n524,19; *G* nm3945ff.; *JT* nm1558,5 [†]

Urjên (In Geoffrey of Monmouth this name appears as Urianus, which Zimmer derives from Urbgen (Nennius, §63) < Latin Urbigenus.[5] This etymology is accepted by Bruce.[6]) U. is

---

1   Bartsch (2), pp. 149f.
2   Paris (2), p. 149.
3   Singer (1), p. 112.
4   Martin (1), p. 390, to 524,19.
5   Zimmer, p. 818, note 1.
6   Bruce (1), I, p. 3, note 1.

the father of Îwein (1) and is mentioned in Geoffrey already as such. He appears, however, only in one MHG epic, *RP*, where he assists Arthur against Bruns (1). He is not one of those present in the corresponding portion of the Montpellier MS of Pseudo-Gautier. – *E* nm1641; *I* nm1199f.; *JT* nm2104,1; *RP* 22,23

Urlois the former husband of Îgerne, who is killed in a war started by Utepandragûn, who covets his wife. In Geoffrey of Monmouth he is called Gorlois, but in the OF romances of the Vulgate Cycle he is called Hoel. In *Mer* he is referred to as 'herzoge von Tyntayol' (= Tintagel). – *JT* nm4596,6; *Mer* 194,4ff.

Urrepans der Tschoien, Urrepanse de Schoie see Repanse de Schoie

Ursyan brother-in-law of Landorye (q.v.). He is slain by Ajax (1). – *GT* nm4110 a4214f.

Ursîn 'grâve von Sâlîe', a knight who fights for Wigalois againt Lîon – *Wigl* 10115

Ursyon see Ursyan

Usurap 'von Fabulare', a warrior in Akarîn's army against Ipomidôn. – *JT* nm3127,2

Utepandragûn (In Geoffrey of Monmouth he is called Uther Pendragon, Uther being, according to Martin,[7] the name proper, whilst Pendragon (= dragon's head) is an epithet. Hertz sees in this epithet a symbol of war-like power derived from the *draco*, the emblem of the old Roman cohorts.[8]) U., king of Britain, falls in love with Îgerne, the wife of Gorlois (see Urlois), against whom he declares war. With the assistance of Merlin he effects an entry to Îgerne's bedchamber in the guise of Gorlois and begets on her Arthur. In Geoffrey, where this story is first told, U. dies whilst Arthur is still a boy, but in MHG literature (with the exception of *C*), the fashion being set by *P*, he is usually represented as being alive when Arthur is a grown knight, and as king of Britain. In *C* he dies when Arthur is six years old, but in *P* he is present at the tourney held by Herzeloide, and in *JT* he takes part in a tourney held by Arthur. (See also Uter and Pandragon.) – *E* nm1786f.; *I* nm893ff.; *L* nm6734; *P* nm56,12 a74,5f.; *DB* m3247; *C* m315f. n361; *Wigm* m1405; *G* m187 n735; *TF* nm12919; *JT* 1703,1; *RP* nm167,21f.

Utepantragûn see Utepandragûn

Uter brother of Pandragon, whom he succeeds as king of Britain. His wooing of Îgerne is related in accordance with the account in Geoffrey of Monmouth for Utepandragûn (q.v.). U. appears as the brother of Pandragon in the OF prose romances, both the Vulgate *Merlin* and the *Huth-Merlin* giving the names of the two brothers thus. – *Mer* 67,4ff.

Utereis see Utreiz

Uterpandagrun, Uterpandragôn, Uterpandragrun, Uterpandragûn, Utpandagron see Utepandragûn

Utreiz son of Terramêr, a warrior who fights for the heathens against Willehalm (1) at Alischanz. In the *chansons de geste*, U., who is called Outrés, occurs in *Aliscans* and *Les Enfances Vivien*. He is probably identical with Utereis, künec von Gruenlanden, whose valour is praised by Akarîn in *JT*. – *W* a29,18f. n32,15; *JT* nm3200,6f.

---

7   Martin (1), p. 64, to 56,12.
8   Wolfram von Eschenbach, *Parzival*, transl. by W. Hertz, p. 478.

V (F, Pf, Ph)

Fâbors 'von Meckâ', son of Terramêr, for whom he fights against Willehalm (1) at Alischanz. Miss Bacon considers F. identical with Fâbûr, which name occurs, as she points out, only once in *Aliscans*, whilst Faburs plays a prominent part in the *Moniage Guillaume*.[1] It seems far more likely, however, that F. is not the Faburs of *Aliscans*, but is identical with Jambus (MS M of *Aliscans*: Saburs), who appears three times in *Aliscans*, each time (4392, 5844, and 6363) together with Persagués (cf. *W* 32,12: 'Fâbors und Passigweiz'). – *W* a29,18f. n32,12

Fabruin see Falbruîn

Fâbûr a warrior who fights for Terramêr against Willehalm (1). So also in *Aliscans*. In *W* he is slain by Rennewart. (See Fâbors.) – *W* 359,17

Vagôsus a warrior who is left in command of Jerusalem by Dârîus (3). He lays waste the city owing to the death of Jhêsus at the hands of Johannes (3) (q.v.). This character does not occur in any of the known sources to *UA*. – *UA* nm17739f.

Vagroficall 'von Portynys', a knight who takes part in the tourney held by Arthur for the crown of Deleprosat. (Cf. Pagrofitall.) – *Wigm* 2013

Factor 'künec', father of Welf. On the occasion of his first appearance (9312), when he is sent to fetch Agly for her marriage to Wildomis, he is called Sunsch. – *WO* nm6216 a9312

Phala a commander in the army of Mennon (2) against the Greeks at Troy. This character appears to have been invented by the author of *TKf*. – *TKf* 42647ff.

Falbruîn 'von Gruonlant', an ally of Sornagiur. – *PM* a3327 n4190f.

Valdone 'der schwarze ritter von', a knight who is bound by a promise to his *amie* to live in a cell until he is overcome by another knight. Parzivâl defeats him and thus releases him from his vow. V., who is the brother of Garsalas, is called li Noirs Chevaliers de Valdoune in Gautier; a knight by the name of quens de Valdun is mentioned in the Vulgate *Lancelot*. – *RP* m331,5ff. a331,40 n435,38

Valeria wife of Zacheria (q.v.). – *GT* m22285 an22295ff.

Valerian see Valeria

Valerîn 'künec von dem Verworrenen tan', a knight who comes to Arthur's court and demands a boon. This being granted, he, like Meljakanz, asks for Ginovêr, for the possession of whom he is prepared to fight. Lanzelet severely wounds him, but later he returns and abducts Ginovêr. He is killed and his castle is destroyed by Malduc (see Maldwîz). Brugger makes a tentative suggestion that this name is a corruption of either Maheloas or Gasenin (= Gasoain, see Gasosîn).[2] – *L* nm4980 a5164

Valgaruntz a knight who is unhorsed by Teanglis. – *JT* 2133,5

Phaligrus Balacricôs a commander in Alexander's army. This name is the result of a misunderstanding of Curtius Rufus, where Phaligrus is the son of Balacrus (q.v.). – *A* 11976ff.

Falissân 'von Barbarîe', a commander in Bêâmunt's army against Eghart at Antrîun. – *Dem* nm9687f. a10966f.

Valke the name given by Acheloyde to Agorlîn (q.v.). – *Crane* nm148

Vallerîn see Valerîn

Vallordine 'von Adramatute', a warrior in Akarîn's army against Ipomidôn. – *JT* 3622,1f.

---

1. Bacon, p. 74.
2. Brugger (2), p. 70, note 131.

Valpidun 'von Valpidande', a warrior in Ipomidôn's army against Akarîn. – *JT* nm3236,1

Valpinôse 'künec von' (*W*), see Talimôn (2)

Valtzone see Vulkân

Vamgainziers a knight who attends Leigamar's tourney in the service of Aram. – *C* 18172

Fâmurgân see Feimorgan

Fandalîs a knight who takes the place of Dêmantîn when the latter leaves Pheradzoye. A Saxon named Vandalis is slain by Gawein in *L'Estoire de Merlin*, but there is no justification for identifying the two characters. – *Dem* 3488ff.

Pfandimoi daughter of Kandymant. She tells Dêmantîn of the capture of her *ami*, Arisaim, five years previously by Kanphyant. Dêmantîn accompanies her to the place where Arisaim was captured and kills Kanphyant, uniting Arisaim and his *amie*. – *Dem* a2336f. n2695

Fandorîch 'marcgrâve', a knight whose land is taken from him by the *Vogt* (see Firganant), who demands toll from all passers-by. F. assists Bêâmunt, who recovers his town for him, in the fight for Dêmantîn and Firganant at Antrîûn. – *Dem* nm6484ff. a10324f.

Fandrât a knight who breaks the news of Sirgamôte's flight to her father. – *Dem* 5003

Fanianus natural son of Priam, a warrior in the Trojan army against the Greeks. In Benoît he is called Fanoël, a name which, it is thought by Greif, may have originated in the Pammon (var. Palemon) of Hyginus.[3] – *LT* a4808 n4829

Fanisôr 'von Britanien', a commander in Bêâmunt's army at Antrîûn. – *Dem* nm9920f. a10720f.

Fanissôr see Fanisôr

Fansaserat 'künec von Marocco', father of Gamelarot and Bearosine. F. is captured by Malfer and becomes a Christian at his command. – *R* Eing. I nm2ff. a49

Fantur 'von Furmuleise', a warrior in Ipomidôn's army against Akarîn. – *JT* 3262,2

Pfantzune 'der von' (*JT*), see Kingrimursel

Phâraô (1) father of Eliphat. – *UA* nm11990

Phâraô (2) king of Egypt, for whom Joseph was governor. – *UA* nm11359

Pharâô (3) king of Egypt at the time when Moses led the Israelites out of bondage. – nm *JT* 69,5; *RB* 15806ff.; *WA* 56

Phâres (1) a knight who is slain by Partonopier in the battle against Sornagiur. – *PM* 3714ff.

Phâres (2) a man whom the Roman Emperor had raised from a humble position to that of favourite at his court. P. is jealous of Iglâ's love for Anshelm (1) and contrives to turn the Emperor against the latter. – *PM* m17900 n18525

Pharîôn the first knight to be unhorsed by Phorîân. P. marries Phorasîe. Pharien occurs as the name of a faithful vassal of Bohort the elder in the Vulgate *Lancelot*. – *Dem* 1661

Farjelastis 'herzoge von Africke'. (Bartsch derived this name from the Greek Perjelastes, 'der Umhergetriebene';[4] Martin quotes Hagen as deriving it from Agelastus, the surname of a Roman, Crassus, which in the Engelberg MS of Solinus is corrupted to Faregelastus.[5]) F. is one of the knights whom Feirefîz claims to have defeated. As Foriastes, he takes part in *JT* in the tourney held by Sekundille to decide which of her wooers she shall marry. – *P* nm770,3; *JT* 5252,1ff.

Farmîôn 'grâve', a knight who is unhorsed by Dêmantîn at the tourney held by Bêâmunt. – *Dem* 821

---

3   Greif, pp. 26ff.
4   Bartsch (2), p. 155.
5   Martin (1), p. 503, to 770,3.

Farnâbâzus a warrior who was formerly in command of the foreign troops in Dârîus's army. He is sent to recruit a new army after the first defeat of Dârîus and settles at Kîun, where he is captured by Hegelôch (1). F. occurs in *Expeditio Alexandri* and Curtius Rufus. – *A* 5305

Varnande see Vernande (1)

Pharo see Pharâô (3)

Pharos 'von Cyriâ', son of Archanî, a warrior in Dârîus's army at Erbela, where he is slain by Alexander. So also in Gualterus. – *UA* 12007

Farsatam the wife of one of Noah's sons. According to *UA*, the other two wives are Sarfrasatam and Satam. In the *Historia Scholastica* these wives are called Pharphia (Toischer has Parsia[6]), Cathaflua, and Fliva (*Liber Genesis* XXXIII). – *UA* nm11252

Färtes with Fyses (see Bessus) and Oriaber (see Narbâsones) one of the murderers of Dârîus. This is the only version in which a third murderer is involved. – *WA* a2705 n2719

Vâruch a knight who is unhorsed by Gawein at Leigamar's tourney. V. is a relative of Aschalonê and is called (18058) 'ein jüngelinc von Syriâ', this last fact being used by Brugger to derive V.'s name from Beirout in Syria, although the word itself is, he contends, the same as Baruch (see Akarîn (1)).[7] – *C* 18058ff.

Vasolt 'der merkære', an otherwise unknown friend of Rudolf von Ems. – *RW* nm2290

Vastie biblical (Vashti), the former wife of Aswerus (1). – *UA* nm11801f.

Faunet 'von Prîanit', a knight who fights for Lôis against Terramêr . – *UW* 46,15

Fausabrê see Faussabrê

Faussabrê 'von Alamansurâ', a warrior who fights for Terramêr at Alischanz. According to Terramêr (*W* 255,8), he was slain in the first battle. F. appears in *Aliscans* as Fauseberc (var. Faussabre). – *W* 27,7 [†]

Phâceê king of Israel. He is mentioned in the *Historia Scholastica* (*Liber IV Regum* XXII). – *A* nm16712

Phâceiâ king of Israel. He is mentioned in the *Historia Scholastica* (*Liber IV Regum* XXII). – *A* nm16710

Phêax a warrior who is killed by Antigonus whilst fightir.g for Dârîus against Alexander at Issôn. This character appears to have been invented by Ulrich. – *UA* 8049f.

Febrefluior 'von Tubys', a knight who takes part in the tourney held by Arthur for the crown of Deleprosat. – *Wigm* 2012

Phêbus in Greek mythology (Phoebus) the name given to Apollo as the sun-god. – nm *Ed* 1800; *LT* 10736; *UA* 2803

Fedakîne see Fiacrôde

Fedra daughter of Minos and sister of Meierra (q.v.). She accompanies Jason to Troy but is abandoned by him on the way and dies of grief. – *GT* 21674

Phedrias a knight who fights for Athis against Bilas and Thelamon at Athens. So also in the OF version. – *AP* E,69

Feimorgân sister of Arthur, famous as a healer of wounds (*E* 5156; *L* 7185). Chrestien, who calls her Morgain la fee in *Erec* (1957), identifies her with the fairy *amie* of Guingomars (see Gwinganiers), and she is therefore identical with Marguel in *E* (1934). As 'Onorgûe, ein rîchiu fei' (MS V: Morgue), she is one of the ladies at Arthur's court who spill Priure's cup of chastity in *C*. Wolfram obviously confuses the name of the person with the name of the place and makes Mazadan's wife Terdelaschoie, and the place where they live Feimorgan. The earliest extant reference to F. is in Geoffrey of Monmouth's *Vita*

---

6   Toischer, p. 402.
7   Brugger (1), p. 59, note 1.

Merlini, where she is the person who is to heal Arthur in Avalon.[8] Her relationship to Arthur appears to have been invented by Chrestien, as she is called Arthur's sister for the first time in *Erec*. In the romances of the Vulgate Cycle she becomes Arthur's declared enemy and the enemy of all the best knights of the Round Table. The OF forms of her name are Morgue in the nominative, and Morgain, Morgan in the oblique cases. – *E* 1934; *L* nm7185; *P* nm[56,18]; *C* 1601; *RP* nm498,45

Feirefîz (Schulz derived this name from OF *feie*, 'fairy', and *fiz*, 'son',[9] but Bartsch was the first to suggest the etymology which is now generally accepted, viz. < OF *vairs fiz*, 'particoloured son',[10] which Bruce suggests was invented by Wolfram by analogy with Chrestien's 'biax fiz', the manner in which Parzivâl is always addressed by his mother in *Perceval*.[11]) F. is the son of Gahmuret and Belakâne, and his mixed blood is manifested in his complexion, which is half black and half white. He is the *ami* of Sekundille (whom, in *JT*, he wins in a tourney), and he comes to the West to seek his father. He meets Parzivâl, and the two knights engage in a great combat, in the course of which Parzivâl's sword breaks. F. will not take an unfair advantage and throws his own sword away. The two brothers parley and discover each other's identity. Parzivâl takes F. to Arthur's court, where he is welcomed and made a knight of the Round Table. He accompanies Parzivâl to the Graal Castle, where he sees and falls in love with Repanse de Schoie, for whose sake he is baptized and whom he marries. They have a son, Prester John (see Jôhan (2)). There is such a close resemblance between F. and Agloval's son Moriaen in the Dutch *Lancelot* that there can be no reasonable doubt that either the latter is based on the former or the two characters emanate from a common source; but there are no other signs of MHG influence in the Dutch *Lancelot*, which is, however, admittedly a collection of individual romances and might, therefore, have included one of MHG origin, whilst the rest were drawn from the OF romances. F. is certainly the prototype of Garamant in *Apollonius von Tyrland*. – *P* m55,14f. an57,15ff.; *W* nm45,15; *Blan* nmII,59; *Dem* m1206; *FD* nm1410,5; *JT* nm524,1 a5238,1ff.; *TF* nm15271; *UA* nm9887ff.; *RB* nm8922ff. [†]

Phectetes to whom Alexander bequeathed the lordship over the Babilônes. This name does not appear in any other history of Alexander. – *UA* nm27037f.

Vectigâl placed over the Jews by Vagôsus. This name appears to have been invented by Ulrich. – *UA* nm17779f.

Fel daughter of Melchinor. She falls in love with Wildhalm. – *WO* a5863ff. n5888

Pfelerîn see Pleherîn

Felicîâ daughter of Sibille (1). So also in the *Wartburgkrieg*. – *Loh* nm231 a481; *Ll* (MS K) 19,9ff.

Velle a giant, who occurs in the MHG epic, *Wolfdietrich*, where he is called Helle (MS D: Velle). He brings the young dragons to Ortnît's land and is slain by Ortnît. – *RB* nm25267

Phemiflor 'von Ascalon', a knight who is killed by Merlin (2). He was the owner of a marvellous horse, which Crispin gives to Wildhalm. – *WO* nm13604ff.

Venegus a knight who has been slain by Mabônagrîn in attempting the adventure of Schoidelakurt. In Chrestien's *Erec* a reference is made to Fernaguz, a heathen giant, who, in the *chansons de geste*, is slain by Roland in single combat. – *E* nm8502

---

8   Bruce (1), I, p. 79, note 85.
9   Schulz, 'Eigennamen', pp. 404f.
10   Bartsch (2), p.138.
11   Bruce (1), I, p. 314, note 2.

Fenesteus a warrior in the Greek army against the Trojans. This character does not occur in any other version of the Trojan legend. – *LT* 3405

Veniss see Vênus

Fênix (1) a warrior who fights under Achilles for the Greek army against the Trojans. So also in Dictys, where he is called Phoenix. – *TKf* 41240

Fênix (2) 'künec von Hispanje', father of Flôre. Whilst F. is on a raiding expedition he meets a band of Christians, all of whom are killed except the mother of Blanscheflûr (2), whom F. gives as a slave to his wife. In order to break off the attachment between Flôre and Blanscheflûr, F. wants to kill the latter, but he is persuaded by his wife to sell her into slavery. He dies whilst Flôre is at the court of the amiral. – *NRFB* m349; *FB* a359 n370

Phennene biblical (Peninnah), one of the wives of Elchanâ. – *RB* nm13096

Fennus see Vênus

Phenstis apparently a person who related to Alacîe the story of the Titans' revolt against Jove.[12] – *RB* nm25292

Vênus the goddess of love. In *Ed*, as in Virgil, she is the mother of Ênêâs, whilst in *LT*, *TK*, and *GT* she is awarded the golden apple by Paris, who deems her the most beautiful of the goddesses. – *Ed* nm45 a742; *P* nm532,3; *LT* nm874; *MC* nm1164; *DB* nm6532; *AP* nmC*,101ff.; *C* nm8291; *FB* nm1587ff.; *FD* nm(B),1; *UW* nm73,25; *Dem* nm6161; *JT* nm5298,5; *M* nm662; *TK* a1184ff. n1202; *Mer* nm182,6; *UA* nm393; *RB* nm3578; *GT* m1926ff. n1943ff. a2009; *WO* nm662; *FS* nm2398

Venusz see Vênus

Pheradzoye a fairy queen who taunts Dêmantîn with being afraid to undertake the adventure which awaits him in a neighbouring castle. Dêmantîn goes there and is attacked by Pandulet, whom he kills. He then has to become P.'s consort, but he is her husband in name only (cf. Laudîne; Gawein in *S*; and Lanzelet at Plûris). After six months Fandalîs arrives, and P. permits Dêmantîn to depart. – *Dem* nm2991ff. a3158

Verangôz 'von Fortsoborest', a knight who slays Gediens, the father of Dulceflûr (1), whom he tries to compel to marry him. – *M* m4852ff. n4867f. a7967ff.

Ferafis, Fêravîz see Feirefiz

Ferducorz a knight who attends Leigamar's tourney in the service of Lorez. – *C* 18150

Ferefen a knight of the Round Table. (Identical with Feirefiz?) – *FS* nm4815

Ferefis see Feirefiz

Vergolaht see Vergulaht

Vergulaht (Schulz suggested a derivation from the Celtic *ffer*, 'dense, fixed, strong', and *gwlâd*, 'country', or *gwladwr*, 'countryman, patriot'.[13] Bartsch thought that it was the result of a misunderstanding of Chrestien's *Perceval* (6029) '(li sire qui) herbergié l'ot',[14] a mistake which surely could never have been made by a Provençal poet (cf. Bêne (2) and Jeschûte). Brugger thinks that the name comes from Alain Fergant de Camelon, who, he states, became confused with the historical Alain, Graf von Vannes, to give Alain de Gomeret, whom in turn he identifies with Alain li gros, father of Parzivâl in Robert de Boron and *Perlesvaus*.[15] Singer offers no suggestion beyond expressing the opinion that

---

12 The story of the Titans' revolt is told, and *RB* (25292ff.) then continues: 'als Phenstis fabellîchen sprach,/ gên der wandels frîen/ juncfrowen Alacîen'.

13 Schulz, 'Eigennamen', pp. 399f.

14 Bartsch (2), p. 133.

15 Brugger (1), pp. 78ff.

the name appears Celtic.[16]) V. is 'künec von Ascalûn'. He thinks that Gawein is responsible for the death of his father, Kingrisîn, and he sends Kingrimursel to challenge Gawein to single combat. V. is defeated by Parzivâl, who compels him to search for the Graal, and V. releases Gawein, whose treatment of Antikonîe (q.v.) has placed him in his hands, on the condition that Gawein undertakes the search. (Cf. Angaras.) In *TF* he takes part in the tourney held by Arthur at Sabins. – *P* m[321,19] an400,5; *TF* nm227 a11880 [†]

Fermisolt 'von Parlikonte', a warrior in Ipomidôn's army against Akarîn. – *JT* nm3221,3

Vernande (1) wife of Amerillus (q.v.). – *GT* 12787ff.

Vernande (2) a maiden attendant on Amalita. – *GT* 20131f.

Fernes to whom Alexander left the lordship over the Armenôs. This name does not occur in any other version of the Alexander history. – *UA* nm27036

Ferol 'von Ivrisale', a warrior in Akarîn's army against Ipomidôn. – *JT* nm3179,1

Ferôz husband of Rûel (2). He is slain by Flojir but kills the latter at the same time. – *Wigl* nm6356

Verses see Xerses (1)

Verworren Tan 'der ûz' (*L*), see Valerîn

Vespesianus Roman Emperor (Vespasianus) at the time of the destruction of Jerusalem. – nm *JT* 100,5; *RP* 612,45

Vespesion see Vespesianus

Fessidral 'von Massolen', a warrior in Akarîn's army against Ipomidôn. – *JT* nm3127,5

Fetoron a knight who takes part in the tourney held by Arthur for the crown of Deleprosat. – *Wigm* 2016

Feures 'von Râmide', 'der gerner streit, dan er het vride', a knight who spills Priure's cup of chastity at Arthur's court. This name rests on a mis-reading of Chrestien's *Erec* (1717), where he is Li Fevres d'Armes, the armourer. – *C* 2307

Fiacrôde 'küneginne', present with Offiart when the latter is defeated by Darifant. Her intervention saves Offiart's life. – *Dar* nm138f. a172f.

Fidegart a giantess who tries to avenge the death of her husband, Purdân, on Gârel, but is likewise slain by him. – *G* nm5492ff. a5666

Fidelaz a knight who attends Leigamar's tourney in the service of Aram. – *C* 18166

Fidias son of Mennôn (1), a warrior who is slain by Eufêstiô whilst fighting for Dârîus against Alexander at Erbela. In Gualterus he is called Phidias. – *UA* 13842f.

Fierlieun see Fierliun

Fierliun 'von Ansowe', a knight who is killed by Willegin whilst fighting for Willehalm (3) against Jofrit (1). – *RW* 525

Fierlun see Fierliun

Fiers 'von Arramîs', *ami* of Fursensephin, a knight who is captured by Gawein at the tourney held by Leigamar. F. corresponds approximately to Meljanz in *P*. – *C* nm17831ff. a18312

Figras a merchant whom Paris and Marcus (1) meet on their return to the court of Agâmennon. – *GT* a6606f. n6885f.

Philemenis, Fileminis see Pilemenes

Pfilenor a warrior in the Trojan army against the Greeks. He is a son of Priam and is slain by Ajax (1). So also in Dictys, where he is called Philenor. – *TKf* 43160ff.

Philetas to whom Alexander bequeathed Illyria. This name does not occur in any other version of the Alexander history. – *SA* nm8491

---

16   Singer (1), p. 103.

Philip   see Philipp (1)

Philipp (1) 'künec von Mâzedônje', putative (according to Lampreht, the genuine) father of Alexander (1). He is slain by Pâusânîâ. – *A* 425; *JT* nm3076,2; *UA* 173f.; *RB* nm26775; *SA* 217ff.; *WA* 127ff.

Philipp (2) brother of Alexander (3) (q.v.). – *JT* a4677,6 n4778,1f.

Philipp (3) Alexander's physician. Parmênîôn, who is jealous of P., warns Alexander against drinking a potion which P. has prepared for him and which Parmênîôn declares to be poisoned. Alexander demonstrates his trust in P. by drinking the potion, which cures him of his illness. P. occurs in all versions of the Alexander history, except *WA*. – *A* 5753ff.; *UA* 6515; *SA* 2781f.

Philipp (4) a commander in Alexander's army against Dârîus. So also in Curtius Rufus. In *SA*, Alexander bequeaths to him Hircanya. – *A* 12000; *SA* nm8527

Philipp (5) 'von Utilimare', a warrior in Ipomidôn's army against Akarîn. – *JT* nm3233,3

Philipp (6) 'künec von Francrîche', father of Gillelm and nephew of Willehalm (3). P. attends the *swertleite* of Willehalm (4). – *RW* nm157 a2359ff.

Philippus   see Philipp (1) and (3)

Phylips 'künec von Francrîche', he fights on the side of the Christians in the final battle against the heathens. – *WO* 17910f.

Filison   see Filones

Philithoas 'von Calcidon', a warrior who (in *LT*) is slain by Hector whilst fighting for the Greeks against the Trojans. P. occurs in Benoît, who appears to have derived the name from Philippus Thoas, a warrior who appears in MS G of Dares. In Homer, Thoas leads the men from, amongst other places, Kalydon. – *LT* 3347; *TK* 23832

Filitoas   see Philithoas

Filledâmûr   sister of Guivreiz. She nurses Êrec back to health after his encounter with Oringles. She is not named in Chrestien's *Erec*. – *E* a7207ff. n7786

Filleduoch   *amie* of Galez. She attempts unsuccessfully to wear the glove of chastity which Giramphiel sends to Arthur's court. – *C* 24249ff.

Phillip (1) 'sante'. – *FD* nm180,4

Phillip (2), **Villippe**   see Philipp (6)

Phillis   the ruler of Thrace, who was transformed into an almond tree when she pined away for love of Demophon, who failed to keep his promise to return to her. The story is told by Ovid in the *Heroides*. (See also Pillis.) – nm *Tn* 17194; *C* 11590; *TK* 2318f.

Philodant   one of those left with Thedalûn in charge of Alexander's people whilst the Emperor is away campaigning. This character appears to have been invented by Ulrich. – *UA* a2361 n2389

Pfiloctêtâ   'von Muten', a warrior in the Greek army against the Trojans. He slays Paris by wounding him with a poisoned arrow. So also in Dictys. – *TKf* 40934

Filomenis   see Pilemenes

Filones 'cuns von Hiberbortikôn'. (Bartsch took this name to be the Greek Philon,[17] but Martin points out that Philomides (var. Pilonis) occurs in Solinus (25,12).[18]) F. is one of the knights whom Feirefîz claims to have defeated. In *JT* he is called Filison and is one of the combatants in the tourney held by Sekundille to decide which of her wooers she shall marry. – *P* nm 770,11; *JT* 5271,1

---

17   Bartsch (2), p. 155.
18   Martin (1), p. 503, to 770,11.

Philôs to whom Alexander bequeathed Assirîe. This name does not occur in any other history of Alexander. – *UA* 27006

Philôtas son of Parmênîôn, a commander in Alexander's army. He is concerned in the conspiracy of Dimnus to kill Alexander and himself become king. In *A* he confesses under torture, but he is pardoned and becomes a model vassal thereafter. In *UA* he tries to protest his innocence and is slain. P. occurs in *Expeditio Alexandri*, Curtius Rufus, and Gualterus. – *A* 9473; *UA* 3288

Pfilotetâ see Pfiloctêtâ

Filothêtes a warrior in the Greek army who relates to the besiegers of Troy the death of Hercules (as told in Ovid's *Metamorphoses* IX), at which he was present. No person of this name is mentioned in Ovid or in any other version of the Trojan legend. – *TK* nm37933f. a37951ff.

Phimacus a warrior in the Trojan army against the Greeks. So also in Benoît, where it is most probably a corrupted form of Amphimachus (1) or (2). – *LT* 3986

Fimbeus 'von Karlin', a knight from whom Gawein takes a magic girdle at the command of Ginovêr. The girdle had been made for F. by his *amie*, Giramphiel (q.v.). – *C* nm4885ff. a27717f.

Finbeus see Fimbeus

Finc 'von Seminis', a knight who attends Leigamar's tourney in the service of Aram. – *C* 18174

Fiolêde *amie* of Darifant. – *Dar* nm115

Vîolet 'diu snelle', one of the ladies at Arthur's court who spill Priure's cup of chastity. – *C* 1612

Fion 'von Greste', son of Glaucon, a warrior in the Trojan army against the Greeks. So also in Benoît. – *LT* 4069f.

Phyoplerin see Blîobleherîn

Firamîe *amie* of Florandâmîs. She begs him to spare Deyrant, but he refuses. – *Dem* nm7869 a8077

Firganant son of Assuntîn, a knight who wins Bêâmunt (3) at a tourney and becomes king of England. He learns the peril in which Dêmantîn stands, and he starts off to join him, leaving Bêâmunt to collect an army and follow. F. stays the night at Fandorîch's castle and leaves without paying the toll. He is pursued by the *Vogt*, whom he kills, treating a number of other knights who pursue him in the same way. He arrives eventually at Antrîûn, where he meets and fights with Dêmantîn, until F.'s battle-cry 'Bêâmunt' betrays his identity. In the battle against Eghart, F. distinguishes himself. – *Dem* nm320ff. a1097

Virgily see Virgîlîus

Virgîlîus the Latin author of the *Aeneid*. In the Middle Ages V. acquired a reputation as a magician, and he is mentioned as such in *P*, where he is the uncle of Klinschor, in *WO*, where he manufactures a golden chair with magic properties, in which Wildhalm spends his first night at the court of Persit, and in *RB*, which tells of his escape from the magnetic island in the *Lebermeer* (see Athanatâ). V. is mentioned as a writer in *Ed* and *SA*. – nm *Ed* 41; *P* 656,15ff.; *RB* 21023; *WO* 4904ff.; *SA* 45

Virgîljus see Virgîlîus

Virgunt a knight who is worsted by Edolanz before Arthur and his court for a sparrow-hawk, which is given to Grysalet. – *Edol* B, a130 n180

Firliun see Fierliun

Firmolis 'künec', a knight who fights for the heathens in the final battle against the Christians. (Identical with Firmonis?) – *WO* 16345 [†]

Firmonis 'künec von Gemelle', a knight who is killed whilst fighting for the heathens in the final battle against the Christians. (Identical with Firmolis?) (Cf. Meluchpat.) – *WO* 17817f. [†]

Firmutel see Frimutel

Phirrus see Pirrus

Virtas 'von Tralapinse', a warrior in Ipomidôn's army against Akarîn. – *JT* nm3221,2

Fîrus 'Bahandîn', a knight who is mentioned by Gawein as having been present at a tourney held some years before by Arthur. – *C* nm22647

Fyses see Bessus

Vischære 'der arme' (*C*), see Amfortas

Vischer 'der riche', 'der arme', 'der' (*RP*), see Amfortas

Phiton to whom Alexander bequeathed Susamaria. This name does not occur in any of the other histories of Alexander. – *SA* nm8494

Vîtus 'sante'. – *FD* nm1661,4

Phiun see Fion

Viversîn a maiden attendant on Gîburc, whom she accompanies with Willehalm (1) on her flight from Tîbalt. – *UW* 263,20

Vivîans the young nephew of Willehalm (1), for whom he fights at Alischanz. He is badly wounded by Noupatrîs, whom he kills, but he returns to the fray. He fights valiantly but receives a mortal wound from Halzebier. In answer to his prayer, Willehalm is with him at his death. V. is the hero of a number of *chansons de geste* of the Guillaume d'Orange cycle; in *Les Enfances Vivien* he is sent to the Saracens as a ransom for his father but escapes immediately. In *La Chevalerie Vivien* and its continuation *Aliscans*, he is fighting against the Saracens when Willehalm arrives, too late, to help him. In the *Chancun de Willame*, he is the son of Willehalm's sister, as in *W*, but not in the remainder of the *chansons de geste*. – *W* 13,15ff.; *UW* 211,10; *RB* nm14860; *FS* nm1508

Viviantz (1) a knight who fights for Fridrich (3) against Mompolier. – *FS* 5777ff.

Viviantz (2), **Vîvîanz** see Vivîans

Fizcâtor husband of Candacis and father of Candaulas and Karâtor. This name appears to have been invented by Ulrich. – *UA* nm19445

Flandismer apparently a person in the castle in which Gawein is imprisoned. If the *S* fragments follow *Meraugis de Portlesguez* closely, he would probably be in the castle in which Segremors is fighting for Nyobe's captors against Arthur and his knights. – *S* Ib,48

Flanea step-mother to Angelburg (q.v.). When Jeroparg confesses to the conspiracy against Angelburg, F. is condemned to be burned with him. – *FS* nm179 a1031

Flegetanîs a heathen who, according to Wolfram, had read the history of the Graal in the stars. Bartsch derived this name from the Greek Flegetôn; *phlegedonios* would be 'der Brennende', which would also provide a suitable name for a heathen.[19] Martin sees a corruption of *Felek thâni*, a book by the Arabian astronomer, Thabit ben Qorah,[20] a theory with which Golther is inclined to agree.[21] Flegetine is also the name of a sister of Evalac-Mordrain (see Evaleth) in *L'Estoire del Saint Graal* (Vulgate Cycle) and is thus intimately connected with the early history of the Graal. – *P* nm453,23; *JT* nm77,2

Flogrifite daughter of Iohiote and Ligronite. – *Wigm* nm (MS M) 109928

Floyres see Flôre

---

19 Bartsch (2), p. 154.
20 Martin (1), p. 350, to 453,23.
21 Golther (1), pp. 202f.

Flôis 'künec von dem grüenen wert', a knight who attends the tourney held by Arthur. He is later (5579) oppressed by Assiles and sends a squire, Giwanet (q.v.), to Arthur's court for assistance. – *C* 599

Flojîr a knight who slays Ferôz but loses his life at the same time. – *Wigl* nm6357

Floræte wife of Rûal and foster-mother of Tristan. F. occurs only in *Tn*,[22] but Golther is of the opinion that the character was invented by Thomas.[23] – *Tn* a1821 n1904

Floragune 'herzoge von Karifole', a knight who is present at the tourney held by Arthur. – *JT* 1994,1f.

Floramie daughter of Flordibintze and Albaflore. She was the cause of the death of Frimutel, who was in love with her. – *JT* 5704,5

Florand mother of Helen and wife of Agâmennon in *GT*. – *GT* 3669

Floranda see Florand

Flôrandâmîs 'herzoge', a knight who had defeated Deyrant and was letting him bleed to death. At the request of Deyrant's *amie*, Firganant fights and overcomes F., then compels him to tend and cure Deyrant. – *Dem* nm7695ff. a7897f.

Flôrant 'vürste von Îtolac', 'der turkoite', a knight in the service of Orgelûse. Gawein fights and defeats F. after having successfully achieved the adventure of the Schastel Marveile. F. is present at the tourney held by Arthur in *JT*, where he is called 'der florant turkoie'. (See also Turkoit.) – *P* m334,14 a593,10ff. n624,2f.; [*JT* 2076,3] [†]

Floranz 'von Portigâl', a warrior in the Greek army against the Trojans. This character was invented by Konrad. – *TK* 23944ff.

Flordawins see Flordibintze

Flordiâne sister of Eskilabôn. She is promised to the knight who defeats Eskilabôn. Gârel achieves this but refuses the prize. She marries Alexander (6). – *G* a3442 n3455

Flordibel a young girl who comes to Arthur's court and makes him promise to kill anyone who makes love to her and makes her his wife. She falls in love with Tandareis and is largely responsible for their elopement. After Tandareis has been banished, she returns to Arthur's court to await his return, when she marries him. – *TF* m172 a354 n614

Flordibintze 'künec von Flordibale', husband of Albaflore and father of Floramie. F. compels all the wooers of his daughter to joust with him and in this way is responsible for the death of Frimutel. In *Sey*, where he is the father of Albaflore, he is called Flordawins. – *JT* 5704,1; *Sey* nm65,2 a68,3

Flordigan a warrior who is slain by Hector whilst fighting for the Greeks against the Trojans. This character was invented by Konrad. – *TK* 29305

Flordimander 'künec von Egyptenlant', a warrior in the Trojan army against the Greeks. This character was invented by Konrad. – *TK* 24830

Flordipintze see Flordibintze

Flôre son of Fênix (2). F. is born on the same day as Blanscheflûr (2), and the pair, brought up together, become child-lovers. This is noticed by Fênix, who separates them, sending F. to Gûraz and selling Blanscheflûr into captivity at the court of the amiral. F. follows her there and, by winning a wager on a game of chess, he secures the help of the *pfortenære* of the tower in which Blanscheflûr is imprisoned. F. effects an entry, concealed in a basket of flowers, but his presence is eventually discovered when Blanscheflûr oversleeps on two occasions. They are condemned to be burned, but both refuse to take advantage of a magic ring which will ensure safety to one of them. The amiral is so touched by the unselfishness

---

22 Gottfried von Straßburg, *Tristan und Isolde*, transl. by W. Hertz, p. 548.
23 Golther (2), p. 145.

of their love that he pardons them both and makes F. a knight. News is brought of the death of Fênix, and they both return to Hispanje, where F. is baptized and marries Blanscheflûr. They have a daughter, Berhte (q.v.). In *NRFB* F. is called Floyres. – *NRFB* a1 n120; *FB* m120ff. n298 a584; *A* nm3243; *RW* nm2222; *FS* nm1519

Floreys   see Flôre

Florendel   see Florendin

Florendin   'von Kerlingen', a knight who was slain by a heathen who loved F.'s wife, Condiflor (q.v.). – *Sey* nm82,4f.

Florentinus   a knight who fights for Athis against Bilas. So also in the OF version. – *AP* C,17

Flôrete   the son of a vassal of Heimrîch (1). Heimrîch makes F. his heir to the exclusion of his own children. The name appears to have been invented by Ulrich. – *W* a5,22; *UW* 16,26ff.

Florefadêne   *amie* of Watsêr. – *Dem* nm10900f.

Flôriân   'ein Aliman', a warrior in Alexander's army. This character appears to have been invented by Ulrich. – *UA* 4756ff.

Floridîs   'künec von Libîâ', a knight who is slain by Partonopier whilst fighting for the Soldan. – *PM* 21752ff.

Flôrîe (1)   'von Kanedic', sister of Klauditte (2) and *amie* of Lohût (q.v.), in whose service the latter met his death; F. died subsequently of a broken heart. According to Martin, F. is identical with Florie de Syrie, who has a son (probably Wigalois) by Gawein in the *Livre d'Artus*;[24] she would therefore by identical with Flôrîe (2) and Florine (q.v.). – *P* nm586,4; *T* nm147,1; *G* m16744 n17196; *JT* nm1161,2f. [†]

Flôrîe (2)   niece of Jôram (2) and mother, by Gawein, of Wigalois. She dies of a broken heart when she hears nothing of her son or her husband for a long time. Her land can only be found by a mortal if the latter is wearing a certain magic girdle (i.e. she is a fairy). In *C* she is one of the ladies at Arthur's court who spill Priure's cup of chastity. The mother of Wigalois is called Florie de Syrie in the *Livre d'Artus*, Blancemal in *Li Biaus Descouneus*, and Gloriète in Pseudo-Gautier. (See Flôrîe (1), Florine, and Gylorette.) – *Wigl* a723 n1317; *C* 1294

Flôrîe (3)   'von Lûnel', daughter of Îwein (5), one of the maidens who tend the Graal. – *P* a234,12ff. n806,15

Florien, Florîn (1)   see Flôrîe (1)

Flôrîn (2)   see Flôrîs (1)

Florine   'von Syrie', a lady present at Arthur's court. A Florie de Syrie (see Flôrîe (1)) occurs in the *Livre d'Artus*, and her presence here would seem to indicate a knowledge of that romance by the author of *JT*. F. may be identical with Florione. – *JT* 1612,1

Florione   a lady who is present at Arthur's court. F. may be identical with Florine (q.v.). – *JT* 1775,2

Flôrîs (1)   'künec von Engellant', a knight who takes part in the tourney at which Reinfrit wins the love of Yrkâne. – *RB* 744ff.

Flôrîs (2)   son of Rêtân, nephew of Gilân. F. tries to rescue his brother, Alexander (6), from Eskilabôn but is himself captured. He is released when Gârel defeats Eskilabôn, and he fights for the former against Ehkunat. He marries Sabîe (2). – *G* nm2489ff. a3532

Floris (3)   see Flôre

---

24   Martin (1), pp. 421f., to 586,4.

Florminius 'künec von Schaldeie', a warrior in the Trojan army against the Greeks. This character was invented by Konrad. – *TK* 24886f.

Flormund son of Seyfrid and Mundirosa. – *Sey* 517,4f.

Florose a lady who is present at Arthur's court. – *JT* 1797,6f.

Florszgeniten see Flogrifite

Flûrdâmûrs daughter of Gandîn (1) and Schôette, sister of Gahmuret, wife of Kingrisîn, and mother of Vergulaht and Antikonîe. – *P* nm420,6 [†]

Flursensephîn see Fursensephin

*Vogelweide 'her' (*W*), the MHG *Minnesinger* Walther von der Vogelweide (see Walther (4)). – *Tn* 4799; *W* 286,19

Foitenant 'li' (*Tn*), see Rûal

Fôle 'küneginne' (*P*), see Anfolê (2) and Annôr [†]

Volka, Volcân, Volcanus see Vulkân

Foltze 'von Rodekal', a knight who takes part in the tourney held by Arthur. – *JT* 1987,2

Volzân 'grâve', a warrior who is bringing an army to join Turnus, when he notices Euriâlus and Nisus (1) (q.v.). He gives chase and kills them both. V. is called Volcens in the OF *Eneas* and Virgil. – *Ed* 6694

Fontânâgrîs 'künec von Tennemark', father of Yrkâne (see Reinfrit). – *RB* m192f. n287 a560

Vorangôz see Verangôz

Phorasîe daughter of Phoriân (q.v.). She marries Phariôn. – *Dem* nm1754ff. a1760

Forbante 'künec', slain by Achilles, who took his daughter, Diomedea. The story is told in Benoît, Dictys, and Homer. The nominative form of the name is Phorbas, but the oblique form Phorbanta is the only one which appears in Dictys, and therefore also in Benoît. – *LT* nm16643

Forduchorz see Forducorz

Forducorz a knight who attends Leigamar's tourney in the service of Lorez. – *C* 18150

Forenses the father of a girl whom Egistus leaves for Clitemnestre. He joins Orestes in avenging the death of Agâmennon. So also in Benoît, where he is called Focensis. – *LT* 17400

Phoriân a knight who arrives at the court of the king of England during the wedding celebrations of Firganant and Bêâmunt. His wife pretends that he is a stranger-knight who has slain her husband, that she does not know his name, and that he has taken away her daughter, Phorasîe. P. unhorses many knights but is finally overthrown by Dêmantîn, to whom he gives Phorasîe. Dêmantîn gives her to Phariôn. – *Dem* nm1634f. a1760

Foriastes see Farjelastis

Formîant 'grâve', a knight who is unhorsed by Dêmantîn at the tourney held by Bêâmunt. – *Dem* 848f.

Fortasîn a knight who is unhorsed by Phoriân. – *Dem* 1709

Fortinus a warrior in the Trojan army against the Greeks. F. is probably identical with Fortis in Benoît, who appears in Dares as Phoreys (var. Phortus). – *LT* 4026

Forumar 'von Berole', a commander in the army of Lucius against Arthur. He surrenders when Lucius is slain. – *JT* nm4627,1ff.

Fossaborat see Fossoborat

Fossarune mentioned by Ipomidôn, without any indication as to his identity. A Saxon king Fausaron occurs in the *Estoire de Merlin* (Vulgate cycle). – *JT* nm3210,3

Fossoborat 'von Oroste gente', a commander in Akarîn's army against Ipomidôn. This name looks like a corruption of Faussabrê. – *JT* 3126,1f.

Frâbel 'künec von Korâsen', one of the group of 15 Saracen kings who attack Willehalm (1) at the end of the first battle at Alischanz. V. is wounded or killed by Willehalm in that encounter. [See Appendix (9).] V. occurs in *Aliscans*, where he is called Oribles. – *W* m71,22 a72,17f. n74,19 [†]

Frabellitor, Frabilitaltz see Kalebitor

Frâdâtes a commmander in Dârîus's army against Alexander, to whom he surrenders after the death of Dârîus. F. occurs in *Expeditio Alexandri* and Curtius Rufus. – *A* 11686

Franzoiser 'küneginne der' (*P*), see Amphlîse (1)

Franzoisinne 'diu' (*T*), see Amphlîse (1)

Fraort 'von Absan', a knight in Marroch's army. – *Wigm* 3245

Frâtafernes a ruler who surrenders to Alexander. So also in *Expeditio Alexandri* and Curtius Rufus. – *A* 17592f.

Vrebalise (or Urebalise) 'vürste von Bona Vinalterre', a knight who is present at the tourney held by Arthur. – *JT* 2048,1

Frederîch see Fridrich (1)

Frîam 'herzoge von Vermendois', a knight who is captured by the knights of the Round Table during the brush which takes place with the men in the service of Orgelûse as Arthur is on his way to witness the fight between Gawein and Gramoflanz. – *P* nm665,6f.

Frîâns see Ûrjans

Frîdanc MHG poet, author of the *Bescheidenheit*. – nm *A* 3235; *RW* 2206

Fridebant see Vridebrant

Vridebrant 'von Schotten' (< Frideschotten, a land in *Kudrun*.[25]) V. is the son-in-law of Schiltunc and comes to avenge the death of his kinsman, Îsenhart, on Belakâne. He leaves before the arrival of Gahmuret, in order to defend his own land against the relatives of Hernant, whom he had slain on account of Herlinde. In *JT* he is called 'der Schotten künec zu Yberne' and 'der von Iberne', and he is present at the tourney held by Arthur. A fragment exists of an apparently lengthy epic (*Tirol*), in which V. and his father, Tirol, are engaged in battle against the heathens. A didactic poem, containing the advice given by Tirol to his son, is published by F. von der Hagen.[26] – *P* nm16,15f.; *Tirol* C,19; *JT* 1527,4ff. [†]

Friderich (1) see Fridrich (1)

Friderîch (2) 'von Telramunt', a knight who is left by the Duke of Brabant in charge of Elsam. He tries to compel her to marry him, but Lohengrîn arrives in time to champion her and defeats F., who is beheaded by Heinrîch (1). – *Loh* 331ff.; *Ll* 5,1ff. (MS K) 1,1f.

Friderîch (3) 'der Mîhsner vürste', also called 'lantgrâve von Düringen', a knight who fights for the Christians against Gêrfridolt. This is not an historical figure. – *Loh* 4169

Friderîch (4) 'von Oesterreich' (Friedrich der Streitbare). F. sends his household out to welcome Ulrich von Liechtenstein to Neustadt during Ulrich's *Artusfahrt* and leads the side opposed to Ulrich during the subsequent tourney at Neustadt. He is slain in battle against Bela of Hungary. (See Fridrich (2).) – *FD* m1456,2f. a1461,4 n1464,1

Friderîch (5) 'von Witeginsdorf', a knight who welcomes Ulrich von Liechtenstein to Neustadt during his *Artusfahrt*. – *FD* 1483,4

Fridrich (1) 'kaiser' (Friedrich Barbarossa), father of Fridrich (4), whom he accompanies in *WO* to take part in the final battle between the Christians and the heathens. He is drowned, however, in the course of the journey (historically accurate). In *RW*, Rudolf says that he is

---

25   J. Grimm, 'Tyrol und Fridebrant', p. 8.

26   F. von der Hagen, *Minnesinger*, I, pp. 5ff.

the subject of a lost poem by Absolôn. – *Ed* nm8378; *RW* nm2212; *RB* nm17973; *WO* 16615

Fridrich (2) son of Agly and Wildhalm. After the death of his father, he becomes lord over Austria. (Identical with Friderîch (4)?) – *WO* nm18667ff.

Fridrich (3) 'von Swaben', youngest son of Hainrich (5). F. falls in love with Angelburg (q.v.) but loses her through his eagerness to see her face. He sets out in search of her and meets with a number of adventures, including imprisonment by the dwarf-queen Jerome, with whom he has a daughter, Ziproner. Eventually he finds Angelburg and breaks the spell under which she has the form of a dove. They return to the land of Mompolier, who is still under the influence of Flanea and who collects a large army to attack them. F. is victorious in the ensuing battle, but then has to fight Jeroparg in single combat on three successive days and defeat him on each occasion. When Mompolier learns of the deception practised on him by Flanea, he becomes reconciled with F. and Angelburg. After nine years of married life, Angelburg dies, and at her request F. marries Jerome. – *FS* m16 a31 n146

Fridrich (4) 'herzoge von Swaben', son of Fridrich (1). F. fights on the side of the Christians in the final battle against the heathens. – *WO* 16614f.

Fridrich (5) 'herzoge von Österrich' (Friedrich der Schöne), a contemporary of Johann von Würzburg. – *WO* nm18630f.

Friederîch 'von Hûsen', a famous MHG *Minnesinger*. – *C* nm2443

Frien see Urjên

Frŷgende 'künec von' (*W*), see Poidjus

Frigene a knight of the Round Table who is present at the banquet held to celebrate Gârel's victory over Ehkunat. – *G* 20050f.

Frigureis see Frístines

Frimutel (1) 'von Spanien', father of Richaude (1) and father-in-law of Titurel. – *JT* nm420,1

Frimutel (2) son of Titurel and father of Amfortas, Trevrezent, Schoisiâne, Repanse de Schoie, and Herzeloide. He is already dead when the action of *P* takes place, although his father is still alive. In *JT* it is related that he fell in love with Floramie and had to joust with her father, Flordibintze, who slew him. In *T* he is represented as still alive. – *P* nm230,4; *T* nm7,2; *JT* 449,1

Frístines 'cuns von Jamfûse', a knight whom Feirefîz claims to have defeated. F. appears, in *JT*, to be identical with Frigureis von Ianfuse, brother of Ecubâ (2), who fights for Akarîn against Ipomidôn. – *P* nm770,23; *JT* nm3152,1

Fruot 'künec von Tenemark', father of Engeltrût. Engelhart and Dieterich come to F.'s court as young men, and both fall in love with Engeltrût, who eventually marries Engelhart. The latter succeeds F. as king of Denmark on his death. – *Eng* nm309ff. a640

Füetrer 'Uolrich', a poet who wrote, about 1430, a rimed compendium of Arthurian romances, called *Das Buch der Abenteuer*, the sole extant version of *Mer* and *Sey*, and a prose *Lanzelot*, which follows closely the Vulgate *Lancelot*. – nm *Mer* 10,4; *Sey* 313,1

Phûl 'künec von Assûr'. This name does not appear to occur in any of the known sources to *A*. – *A* nm16747

Vulkân in Roman mythology, the god of fire and the working of metals (identical with Hephaestus in Greek mythology). He is the maker of the armour of Ênêâs in *Ed*, of the weapons of Achilles in *LT*, of Schîonatulander's sword in *JT*, where he is called Valtzone, and of the weapons of Pêleus (1) in *TK*. – *Ed* 5602; *LT* nm2987; *Tn* nm4930; *FB* nm1580; *JT* nm3482,2; *TK* nm3802; *GT* nm19608

Fulcanus see Vulkân

Fûlsîn 'von Valbrûl', an ally of Sornagiur. He is slain by Partonopier. – *PM* 3810ff.

Funas 'von Philistea', a warrior in the Trojan army against the Greeks. This name does not occur in any other version of the Trojan legend, but Philisteas occurs in Benoît as a variant of Filitoas. – *LT* 4023

Fursensephin daughter of Leigamar, elder sister of Quebeleplûs. Leigamar holds a tourney, at which Gawein, whom F. takes to be a merchant, is present. Her sister recognizes him for a valiant knight and wagers that he will defeat F.'s *ami*, Fiers, which he does do. F. corresponds to Obîe in *P.* – *C* a17678ff. n17894

Fursilyon 'der Mêden vogt', a warrior in the Trojan army against the Greeks. This character was invented by Konrad. – *TK* 24846

Fursîn (1) 'künec von Irlant', an ally of Sornagiur. – *PM* 4327ff.

Fursîn (2) nephew of Sornagiur, son of Fabruîn. He is sent by Sornagiur to Partonopier to learn to become a knight. He accompanies Partonopier, when the latter seeks death in the forest after his break with Meliûr, and he is there baptized, receiving the name Anshelm, after which Partonopier manages to escape from his care. They meet again after Partonopier has married Meliûr, and F. tells him of his unhappy love for Iglâ (q.v.). He fights for Partonopier against the Soldan and accompanies Supplicius on his embassy. – *PM* a6508 n6524

Furtimar see Forumar

W

Wahsmuot 'künec von Schotten', the leader of the side opposed to that on which Engelhart is fighting at the tourney at Normandie. – *Eng* 2680

Walbân see Walwân (2)

Walberun 'markîs', a knight who takes part in the tourney held by Arthur. – *JT* 2027,1

Waldein see Waldin

Waldemar a knight who looks after Lohengrîn when the latter arrives at Brabant. Two knights of this name are mentioned together, but only one of them does the talking. – *Ll* m31,8 n66,7 a69,1

Waldin 'grâve', a young knight who accompanies Seyfrid on some of his adventures. He is a brave fighter, and Seyfrid makes him king of Igerlant when he himself gives up the crown of that land. – *Sey* 199,5ff.

Waldinn see Waldin

Wâleis 'küneginne von' (*P*), see Herzeloide

Waleys 'der' (*Loh*), see Lohengrîn

Walman see Walwân (2)

Walther (1) son of Arnolt (4), a knight who fights for Partonopier against the Soldan. Egged on by a charge of timidity by his brother, he pursues Markabrê into the Soldan's army and unhorses him. W. is nearly captured by Aspatrîs, who, however, scorns to make use of the thousand of his men who come to assist him and permits W. to escape. – *PM* 18802ff.

Walther (2) (M. Philippus Gualterus) the French author of a Latin *Alexandreis*. – *UA* nm155

Walther (3) 'von Dunsin' (Gautier, or Wauchier, de Denain), one of the continuators of Chrestien's *Perceval*, who carried the poem from line 21916 (*RP* 314,13) to line 34935 (*RP* 610,27). – *RP* nm582,20

Walther (4) 'von der Vogelwaide', the most famous of all the MHG *Minnesinger*. (See also Vogelweide.) – nm *P* 297,24; *RW* 4468f.; *JT* 578,4; *Loh* 226 [†]

Walthesar see Balthasar (1)

Walfaram a knight who fights for Bilas against Athis (q.v.). This character does not appear in the OF version. – *AP* C,8

Walwân (1) see Gawein

Walwân (2) a knight of the Round Table. This knight was originally identical with Gawein, and such is the case in *ET* and *E*, but in *Loh*, *Ll*, and *GM* he appears in addition to Gawein. Vrowenlop also includes Waliban in addition to Gawein in a list of famous knights,[1] though this may possibly have been taken from *GM*, where he is called Walbân. – *Loh* 541; *GM* 668; *Ll* 43,1 (MS K) 28,1

Walwan (3) 'künec von Frigia', a knight who hears of the beauty of Agly, and who woos her and obtains permission to marry her. On the wedding day news is brought that the people of Marroch have invaded Frigia. The festivity is broken off. Later Agrant takes Agly to Firmin, so that the marriage can take place in Walwan's land, and they are here surprised by Wildhalm and Melchinor. In the battle which follows, W. is slain by Wildhalm. – *WO* 2144f.

Wâlwein see Gawein

---

[1] F. von der Hagen, *Minnesinger*, III, p. 150.

Waradach a knight who attacks and kills Tervian, as he lies sleeping beside Pictorye, whom W. then tries to violate. Failing in this, he orders his dwarfs, Nachus and Arpfenan, to flog her, which Hector sees them doing. He slays them both, and also W., who attempts to come to their rescue. – *GT* 12411ff.

Warrast a squire in the service of Wildhalm. W. fights in the battle against Walwan (3). – *WO* 6670f.

Warridach the Sultan, husband of the daughter of Gêrfridolt. W. is slain by Lohengrîn in the battle against the Christians. – *Loh* nm4227 a5677

Waschuni 'künec von' (*RW*), see Belin

Watsêr 'von Frankreich', a knight who is unhorsed before and during the tourney for Bêâmunt by Dêmantîn. W., whose *amie* is called Florefadêne, is a commander in Bêâmunt's army at Antrîûn. – *Dem* 521

Weatreyse 'vrouwe von Schampania', a lady who is captured by Klinschor but released when Seyfrid slays Amphigulor. – *Sey* m27,6 a44,2 n65,6f.

Weygamur see Wigamur

Weinolt a man in the service of Ulrich von Liechtenstein whom he conspires with Pilgerîn (2) to imprison. – *FD* a1696,5 n1698,1

Welf 'künec von India', son of Factor, a warrior who fights on the side of Melchinor (see Persit (2)) and Wildhalm against Walwan (3) in the battle at Firmin. He fights for the heathens in the final battle against the Christians and is killed by the men of Wildhalm. – *WO* nm5816 a6216ff. [†]

Wenzel a knight of the Round Table who offers himself as a champion for Elsam. This name corresponds in *Loh* to Lanzelet, and Elster considers that, the latter not being a well-known knight, W., a better known knight (*sic!*), was substituted.[2] The change seems to be more reasonably explained by purely orthographical corruption. – *Ll* 45,1

Wenzelâ 'von Bêheimlant', defeated and forced to conversion by Heinrîch (1). – *Loh* nm2568

Wenzelabe son of Ottacker (1). – *WW* nm4344

Wenzelaus 'von Beheim'. There is no indication as to which king is referred to. – *JT* nm3570,6

Wenzeslaw a king for whom Ulrich von Eschenbach wrote *UA*. – *UA* nm27633ff.

Werhthain 'ein Francken', a knight who fights on the side of the Christians in the final battle against the heathens. – *WO* 16745ff.

Wernhart 'der Breuzel', brother of Heinrîch (7), a knight who welcomes Ulrich von Liechtenstein to Neustadt during his *Artusfahrt*. – *FD* 1470,1ff.

Wertigier becomes king of Britain on the death of Moygines (2). W. kills the murderers of the latter, but he is attacked by their relatives and flees from the subsequent battle. He tries to build a castle, but it always falls down at night. His wise men tell him that Merlin's blood is needed, but the latter shows that it is two dragons who are the cause of the collapse. W. is later slain in battle with Uter and Pandragon, as foretold by Merlin. This is the story as it is told in *Mer*, and it is substantially the same as in Geoffrey of Monmouth, where he is called Vortigern, and in the OF versions (Vulgate *Merlin* and *Huth-Merlin*), where he is called Vertigier. – *Mer* a44,1 n45,4

Wetzel (1) a MHG poet who wrote a life of St. Margaret. He was a friend of Rudolf von Ems. – *A* nm3261

---

2   Elster, pp. 139f.

Wetzel (2)   right-hand man of Ernst in the MHG gleeman's poem, *Herzog Ernst*. – *RB* nm21059

Wide 'grâve von sant Gylien lant', relative of Willehalm (3), for whom he fights against Jofrit (1). – *RW* 511ff.

Widehelmus   see Wildhalm

Wigalais   see Wigalois

Wigalois   the hero of the MHG poem, *Wigl*, in which he is usually called Gwîgâlois, but on one occasion (1574) Gwî von Gâlois. W. is the son of Gawein and Flôrîe (2), and he leaves his mother whilst he is still a young man in order to find his father. He arrives at Arthur's court, where he is found sitting on a stone of chastity, which only Arthur is usually able to approach. Nerejâ comes to the court in search of a champion, and W. accompanies her to the rescue of Larîe, whom, after a series of adventures, they eventually reach. He slays her oppressor, Rôaz, and marries Larîe, becoming king of Korntîn, and learns that Gawein is his father. He has a number of further adventures to achieve, including a pitched battle with Lîôn, before he hears of the death of his mother and returns to Arthur's court with his wife. Their son is called Gâwânides Lifort. Whilst there is considerable divergence in detail, there is plenty of evidence to admit of the identification of W. with the hero of the OF romance *Li Biaus Descouneus*, Guinglains. He occurs in the ME *Libeaus Desconus*, again as the hero and unknown son of Gawein, whilst in the ME poem *Weddynge of Syr Gawene*, where he is called Gyngolyn, he is the legitimate son of Gawein and Dame Ragnell. The story of *Li Biaus Descouneus* was worked into the Pseudo-Gautier continuation of Chrestien's *Perceval*, where he is called Guiglains and is the son of Gawein and Gloriète (see Gylorette). In *RP* he is called 'der schön Unbekante', 'der schön Unerkante', and finally his name is given: Gingelens. Pseudo-Gautier and *RP* have one interesting feature in common with *Libeaus Desconus*, which reads (l.7f.): 'Beyete he was of syr Gaweyn / Be a forest syde'. Judging from the popularity of this name in documents, the story must have been a favourite one in Germany. Panzer records numerous examples of its occurrence from *circa* 1350 down to the end of the 18th century,[3] whilst J. Grimm and Zingerle give instances of its occurrence in the 15th and 14th centuries respectively.[4] – *Wigl* a1023 n1574; *RW* nm2204; *UW* nm337,26; *RB* nm8930; *GM* (MS I) 3860 (MS D) 3857[3]; *RP* m43,31 a215,25 n573,40; *FS* nm4821

Wigamuor   see Wigamur

Wigamur   son of Paltriot, from whom he is stolen by Lespia. W. enters the world in order to seek his father, without any knowledge of knighthood. He succours Pioles and champions Eydes against her *muome*, Affrosydones. Although he wins the prize at the tourney, W. refuses the crown of Deleprosat. He plays a prominent part in the relief of Isopey and is about to fight for Atroclas against his own father when his identity is discovered. He marries Dulcefluor and wins the prize in the tourney held by Dymszogar, but then he has to fight and defeat Lympondrigon, who has abducted Dulcefluor. Their son is called Dulciweygar. At one point W. rescues an eagle which is fighting a vulture and which, we are told, follows W. constantly after that, but it is never mentioned, nor plays any part other than that of providing W. with an epithet, 'ritter mit dem arn', as padding for the versification. W. occurs also in *JT*, where he is unhorsed by Schîonatulander at Arthur's court. W. appears to be identical in name with the hero of the *lai* of Marie de France,

---

3   Panzer (2), p. 210.
4   J. Grimm, 'Über eine Urkunde des XII. Jahrhunderts', p. 358; I.V. Zingerle, p. 294.

Guingamor (see Gwinganiers), but there is only the faintest resemblance in the story. – *Wigm* a23 n618; *JT* 1356,1; *FS* nm4818 [†]

Wigolais, Wigoleis see Wigalois

Wigrich 'der marschalk', a knight who rescues Wildhalm from the tree in which he has been towed across the sea by a whale. Agrant, surrounded by Melchinor's army, later sends to W. for help, and the latter raises a huge army and proceeds to Firmin. He is slain in battle by Welf. – *WO* 1116

Wîchart (1) 'von Karlesperc', a knight who jousts with Ulrich von Liechtenstein during the latter's *Venusfahrt*. – *FD* 634,1

Wîchart (2) 'von Spitze', a knight who welcomes Ulrich von Liechtenstein to Neustadt during his *Artusfahrt*. – *FD* 1481,8

Wilde der Blumen, Wilde von Blumental 'der' (*JT*), see Ehkunat

Wildehelm see Wildhalm

Wildekin 'grâve von Hollant', a knight who fights on the side of the Christians in the final battle against the heathens. – *WO* 16876f.

Wildhalm 'herzoge von Osterrich', the son of Liupolt (5). W. falls in love with an unknown maiden and sets out to find her. He climbs a tree, to which a whale is tied, and when the whale dives into the sea, uprooting the tree as it does so, W. is carried across the water in its foliage. He arrives at the land of Zyzya, where, under the name of 'Rial', he sees and loves Agly, who, however, is betrothed to Walwan (3). The latter sends W. with a message to Persit (q.v.) in the hope that he will be killed, but his life is spared, and Persit attacks Walwan at Firmin. During the battle W. kills Walwan and Alyant and captures Agrant. It is arranged that Agly shall marry Wildomis, but in a tourney on the day of the wedding he is slain by W., who is sentenced to death for this. He is rescued by Parklise, who takes him to fight Merlin (2) for Crispin, after which he does, at last, marry Agly. After the final battle between the heathens, led by Agrant, and the Christians, in which W. distinguishes himself, he returns to Austria with his father to visit his mother. He then rejoins Agly in Zyzya after the birth of his son, Fridrich (2), and is there murdered by Graveas whilst he is out hunting the unicorn. – *WO* a542 n560f.; *FS* nm4827 [†]

Wildhelm see Wildhalm

Wildichon 'künec von Rosamunt', a knight who is present at the tourney held by Crispin. – *WO* 14683ff.

Wildikon see Wildichon

Wildomis son of Melchinor. He captures Jorye during the battle at Firmin, and it is arranged that he is to marry Agly, but on the wedding day he is killed in a tourney by Wildhalm. – *WO* nm5834 a6231

Wilhalm (1) 'herzoge', 'der haiden'. – *FS* nm4828

Wilhalm (2) see Wildhalm

Wilhalm (3) see Willehalm (1) and (4)

Wilhelm see Willehalm (1), (3), and (5)

Wilheln see Willehalm (4)

Wilis see Bîlêî

Willalm see Willehalm (2)

Willegin 'margrâve von Brandenburg', a knight who fights for Jofrit (1) against Willehalm (3). – *RW* 478f.

Willehalm (1) 'cuns von Orangis', son of Heimrîch (1). Before *W* opens, W. has escaped from the hands of the Saracens, bringing with him Gîburc, whom he has married. The latter's father, Terramêr, and her former husband, Tîbalt, come with a huge army to

Oransche to recover her, and a great battle is fought at Alischanz, in which the Christians under W. are defeated. Leaving Gîburc to guard the castle, W. goes to Lôîs's court at Munlêûn to obtain help. He is coldly received, but his father and brothers promise assistance, and Lôîs is at last prevailed upon to send an army. W. returns with Rennewart as his squire, and a second great battle is fought, the Christians this time being the victors. The brief summary given in *W* of the events leading up to the battles at Alischanz serves as a basis for the story of *UW*, in which W.'s capture at the hands of Sînagûn is related. He is fighting for Lôîs against Terramêr but pursues the fleeing Saracens too far and is surrounded and captured. He is imprisoned by Tîbalt, with whose wife, Arâbel (afterwards Gîburc), he falls in love. Tîbalt is called away to attend a conference, and W. takes the opportunity of expounding the doctrines of Christianity to Arâbel. The two escape together and make for Christian territory; they are pursued by Tîbalt but manage to beat him off at an island governed by Senebalŷn. They eventually reach France, where Arâbel is baptized, assuming the name of Gîburc, and the poem closes with the arrival of Terramêr's avenging army.

This version of W.'s captivity is entirely different from that related in the OF *chanson de geste*, *Prise d'Orange*, which tells how he visits Orange, where Tîbalt lives in unconsummated marriage with Arâbel, is recognized and thrown into prison, but is rescued by his army. The earliest extant poem dealing with W. is the *Chancun de Willame*, an Anglo-Norman poem of the early 12th century. After the death of Gîburc, W. retires to a monastery in *Le Moniage Guillaume*.

This legend arose around an historical figure in Charlemagne's army who retired to a monastery in his old age and who was canonized. The first historical reference to him is made in the *Vita Hludovici*, where he is created comte de Toulouse in 790.[5] According to the *Chronique d'Aniane*,[6] he became a monk in 806.

– *W* m2,25f. n3,11 a5,16f.; *RW* nm2183; *UW* m4,14f. a21,1 n21,14; *JT* nm3570,6; *UA* nm8748; *RB* nm14854; *FS* nm1392

Willehalm (2) 'von Wenden', a heathen who hears of Christ and determines to leave his wife, Bêne (1), and go and seek Him. Bêne learns of his intention and compels him to take her with him. In a wood she gives birth to twins, Boizlabe and Dânus, but W., fearing that their burden will prove too much for her, sells them to some passing merchants. He then takes Bêne to the nearest town, and leaving her in the care of a widow, he steals away to the Holy City, where he becomes a Christian and covers himself with glory in a battle against the Saracens. He returns to Bohemia, where Bêne has in the meantime become *herzoginne*, but they do not recognize each other. W. hears of two robbers and suggests to Bêne that they be forgiven. He recognizes them as his two sons and confesses the fact to Bêne, who then realises who he is. Together they carry out the conversion of Bohemia, and later return to Wenden, which they also convert to Christianity. At the age of 60 they both retire to monasteries. – *WW* 6ff.

Willehalm (3) 'von Orlens', father of Willehalm (4). W. has a quarrel with Jofrit (1), whom he defeats in battle. He pursues Jofrit with 10 knights into the town of Nivel, where the gates are shut behind him, and he and nearly all his men are killed. Jofrit does his best to save them but is himself severely wounded. On the day of W.'s death his son is born. – *RW* a133 n147

---

5   Bédier, I, p. 154.
6   Bédier, I, p. 158.

Willehalm (4) 'von Orlens', son of Willehalm (3). W. is born on the day of his father's death, and his mother, Elye, dies shortly afterwards of a broken heart. W. is brought up by Jofrit (1), who makes him his heir when he is 13 years of age. He goes to Rainher's court, where he falls in love with Amely, and is later made a knight at Brabant. He attends with great honour tournaments which are held at Komarzi, Poys, and near Kurnoy, and then elopes with Amely, who is betrothed to Avenis. In the fight which follows, W. is wounded and captured by Stefan (2). He is condemned to give up all his inheritance, never to set foot in England, and always to carry the point of the lance with which he was wounded in his shoulder, unless it should be drawn out by a princess. He leaves the court and comes upon Corodis and Amelot, and the latter's daughter, Duzabel, withdraws the splinter. W., who pretends to be dumb, returns to Norway and helps Amelot in his battles. When Sävine learns the true reason for Amely's illness, she recognizes Willehalm from Amely's description and takes her to Amelot's court, where they are united. They are forgiven by Rainher, and W. rules as duke of Brabant for fifteen years, after which he is succeeded by his son, Willehalm (5). – *RW* m69 a1632ff. n2055f.; *FS* nm1531

Willehalm (5) eldest son of Willehalm (4) and Amely. W. is brought up by Rainher and succeeds his father as duke of Brabant. He marries the daughter of Avenis and is chosen to be king of England, i.e. he is identified with William the Conqueror. – *RW* 15259ff.

Willehalm (6) see Willikys

Willekîn (1) 'grâve von Gerunde', an ally of Lôîs against Terramêr. – *UW* 39,7

Willekîn (2) 'bischof von Mênze', sent a message from Heinrîch (1) to Lohengrîn. This name appears to have been invented by analogy with Willikys (q.v.). – *Loh* 3914

Willhalm see Willehalm (1)

Willibrot 'herzoge', a knight who is present at the tourney held by Arthur. – *JT* 2026,6

Willigruns 'von Wilgurose', a warrior in Akarîn's army against Ipomidôn. – *JT* nm3625,5

Willikys 'bischof von Mênze', son of Otte (1) and brother of Otte (2). In *Loh* he is also called Willehalm. – *Loh* nm7445f.

Willoys the leader of a band of knights who come from Holland to attend Bêâmunt's tourney. – *Dem* nm290f.

Wîmâr (1) a friendly merchant who offers Willehalm (1) hospitality at Munlêûn. In *Aliscans* he is called Guimar. – *W* a130,17 n130,30

Wîmar (2) patron of der Pleiære, for whom the latter wrote *M*. – *M* nm12775

Wintsester 'der von' (*RB*), see Parlus

Wippreht 'bischof', also called 'der von Lütich', present at the fight between Lohengrîn and Friderîch (2). – *Loh* a729 n2031

Wîpreht see Wippreht

Wirnde see Wirnt

Wirnt 'von Grâvenberc', MHG poet and author of *Wigl*. – nm *Wigl* 141; *C* 2942; *A* 3192; *RW* 2201

Wis 'von Irlant', son of Brangelis. W. is captured by Îwein (1) at the Castle Orgelus when Arthur is trying to rescue Gifles. – *RP* a239,46 n240,27

Wise 'der' (*LT*), see Ulixes

Wisze 'Clawez', joint author with Colin of *RP*. – *RP* nm854,7

Witege a famous warrior in the MHG heroic poems of the Dietrich von Bern cycle. – nm *W* 384,23; *JT* 3355,6f.

Witechin 'künec von Tenemarke'. He attacks Amelot and surrounds Galverne. His allies are put out of action by the capture of their kings, Gutschier and Gierrart, and on the arrival of Coradis, W. is himself captured. He falls in love with Duzabel (2), whom he marries. – *RW* 10525ff.

Witekin see Witechin

Witolt a famous giant who appears in the MHG gleeman's epic, *König Rother*. In *GM* he is called Witolf, a form of the name which occurs throughout the Ermlitzer fragments of *König Rother*,[7] whilst in the Osantrix episode in the *Þiðriks saga* he is called Viðolf mittumstangen.[8] – nm *RB* 25266; *GM* 3465

Witolf see Witolt

Witschart a knight who fights for Willehalm (1) against Terramêr. He is captured by Halzebier whilst attempting the rescue of Vîvîans and is released by Rennewart in the second battle. In *UW* he is one of the sons of Heimrîch (1) to the exclusion of Heimrîch (2); in this poem he fights for Lôis against Terramêr. In *Aliscans*, where he is called Guichars li aidans, he is the brother of Vîvîans. – *W* 13,15f.; *UW* m4,14f. a21,1 n25,1

Wittechin see Witechin

Wittich 'vom Jordan', a prince who, according to *FS*, suffered for the sake of his *amie*. – *FS* nm4830

Witze an old lady attendant on the queen of Zyzya, the mother of Agly. – *WO* 9442

Wîzen Sê 'herzoge von dem' (*L*), see Buroîn

Wîzen Steine 'grâve von dem', a knight who is oppressing a duchess. Erec fights and kills his champion. – *GM* nm1359f. a2228

Woldickin (pet-name form for Waldemar) a contemporary of Johann von Würzburg, i.e. Waldemar der Große, 'margrâve von Brandenburg'. – *WO* nm16838ff.

Wölfelîn see Wolfgêr

Wolferan see Wolfram

Wolfgêr 'von Gors', a knight who jousts with Ulrich von Liechtenstein during the tourney at Friesach and who is also present at the tourney at Kornneuburg. – *FD* 197,3

Wolfhart a famous warrior in MHG epic, vassal to Dietrich von Bern, and noted for his impetuosity, which is the subject of this reference in *P*. – *P* nm420,22

Wölfinc see Wülfinc (3)

Wolfkêr see Wolfgêr

Wolfram 'von Eschenbach', MHG poet, and author of *P*, *T*, and *W*. – nm *P* 114,12; *Wigl* 6343f.; *W* 4,19; *C* 6380; *A* 3134; *RW* 2179; *UW* 4,7; *Dem* 4834; *JT* 231,6; *M* 109; *Loh* 37ff.; *UA* 124; *WW* 4364; *RB* 10421; *GT* 169; *GM* 30; *WO* 14517f.; *RP* 845,18; *SA* 2673; *Ll* 2,8

Wolfran see Wolfram

Worholt see Môrolt

Wülfinc (1) 'von Gurnetz', a knight who jousts with Ulrich von Liechtenstein during the latter's *Venusfahrt*. – *FD* 629,1

Wülfinc (2) 'von Horschendorf', a knight who jousts with Ulrich von Liechtenstein during the latter's *Venusfahrt*. He is unhorsed on two occasions. – *FD* 725,4f.

Wülfinc (3) 'von Stubenberc', a knight who is present at the tourney held at Friesach and also jousts with Ulrich von Liechtenstein during the latter's *Venusfahrt*. – *FD* a193,1 n253,7

Wuote the Norse god (Odin). – *RB* nm479

---

7   *Rother*, pp. 80ff.
8   *Þiðriks saga af Bern*, I, p. 56, l.2.

X

Xênôphilus a warrior in Alexander's army. So also in Curtius Rufus. – *A* 13496ff.

Xerses (1) Emperor of Persia (Xerxes I). X. is thought to be identical with Aswerus (1) (q.v.). In *SA*, X. is called Exersus, Xcerses, and Verses. – nm *A* 3676ff.; *UA* 5803; *SA* 2597; *WA* 2498ff. [†]

Xerses (2) Emperor of Persia (Xerxes II), son of Artaxerses I. – *A* nm15722

Xerses (3) 'künec von Morlant' (*LT*), see Perseus (1) [†]

Xcerses see Xerses (1)

Y

(see under I or J)

Z (C)

Zage 'der schöne', see Böse, der schöne

Zacharîas (1) biblical, father of John the Baptist (see Johannes (1)). – *RB* nm13056

Zacharîas (2) biblical (Zechariah), king of Israel. – *A* nm16698

Zacharîas (3) biblical, son of Achas. Historically the son of Ahaz was called Hezekiah. – *A* nm16731

Zacheria a dwarf who finds the abandoned Meierra. He and his wife, Valeria, care for her until she is married to Z.'s overlord, Emimor. – *GT* a22238 n22296

Zacheus 'von Himelberc', a knight who jousts with Ulrich von Liechtenstein during the latter's *Venusfahrt*. Ulrich says of him that he was a well-known poet, but none of his songs has come down to us. – *FD* 616,6f.

Zalancus father of Roisse, a knight who is slain whilst attempting to rescue an abducted maiden. This character appears to have been invented by Ulrich. – *UA* m23727 n23741

Zambrî biblical (Zimri), 7th king of Israel. – *A* nm16359

Zaradech 'künec von Asîâ', brother of Panschavar, with whom he comes to Wigalois to fetch their sister, Japhîte. Z. is slain whilst fighting for Wigalois against Lîôn. – *Wigl* a9208ff. n9224

Zazamanc 'künec von' (*P*), see Gahmuret

Zazamanc 'küneginne von' (*P*), see Belakâne

Zazant a knight who was being carried to a cave by a dragon, when he was rescued by Gawein. – *C* nm9009

Zeb a Midianite (Zeeb). This name occurs in Pseudo-Methodius. – *A* nm17262

Zêbalîn brother of Nicômachus, from whom he hears of the conspiracy against the life of Alexander. In *UA* he hears Dimnus sighing in the temple of Pallas, and inquiring about the cause of his grief, Z. learns of the conspiracy. In both cases, as in Curtius Rufus and Gualterus, he reports the matter to Alexander. – *A* 18955f.; *UA* 4685

Cebalînus see Zebalîn

Zebeê biblical (Zebah), a Midianite. This name occurs in Pseudo-Methodius as Zebeae. – *A* nm17263

Cedar a young warrior who fights for the Trojans in the first battle against the Greeks. In *TK* he captures Castor. This character appears to have been invented by Benoît. – *LT* 1420ff.; *TK* 12006

Cedius (1) 'von Focidis', brother of Epistropus (2). C. is slain by Hector whilst fighting for the Greeks against the Trojans. So also in Homer, where he is called Schedios, in Dares and Dictys, and in Benoît, where he is called Scedius (var. Cedius). – *LT* a7485f. n7499; *TK* 23798

Cedius (2) natural son of Priam, a warrior who fights for the Trojans against the Greeks. This is the only mention of a son of Priam with this name. – *LT* 5788

Zedoêch a knight who tries to rescue Gîgamec from Aamanz (q.v.) but is defeated by the latter. – *C* a16540ff. n16558

Zehattell a knight who is present at the tourney held by Arthur for the crown of Deleprosat. Z. is almost certainly identical with Zeyhatat (q.v.). – *Wigm* 2016

Zeyhatat a knight who acts as a scout for Atroclas in the battle against Paltriot. This character is almost certainly identical with Zehattell. – *Wigm* 3694f.

Celidis 'künec von Focidis', a warrior who is slain by Polidamas whilst fighting for the Greeks against the Trojans. Chelidus occurs in Benoît as a variant of both Cedius (1) and Almenus (see Alinus), both of whom are, however, slain by Hector. – *LT* 5254f.

Celidomas see Celidonias

Celidonias natural son of Priam, a warrior in the Trojan army against the Greeks. So also in Benoît, who, according to Greif, probably derived the name from the Chirodamas of the *Fabulae* of Hyginus.[1] – *LT* a4808 n4823

Cênôs a warrior in Alexander's army. He appears also in the *Anhang* to *UA* (763). C. is called Coenos in Curtius Rufus and Gualterus. – *A* 6993; *UA* 4719

Centipus 'von Frisce', a warrior in the Trojan army against the Greeks. This name does not occur in any other version of the Trojan legend, but Cantipus may have stood in the MS of Benoît used by Herbort, as a variant of Antipus (2), in the same way as it appears in some of the extant MSS as a variant of Antipus (1). – *LT* 4019

Zentrun 'künec von' (*Loh*), see Avarôz

Zêrastes father of Pâusânîâ. So also in Leo MS S.[2] – *A* nm3043

Ceres mother of Proserpîne. In *TK* she is present at the wedding of Thetis and Pêleus. – *TK* 1046; *RB* nm16438

Zernubilê 'von Amîrafel', a warrior who is slain by Heimrîch (1) whilst fighting for Terramêr against Willehalm (1). According to Singer, Wolfram took this name from the *Rolandslied*.[3] – *W* 360,1ff.

Cêsar see Julîus (2)

Zesarius an author who is mentioned by Füetrer as his source. – *Mer* nm6,3

Cêfalus son of Jupiter and father of Bêlûn. A Cephalus occurs in Greek mythology as the son of Mercury (some accounts ascribe a different father to him), but there is no suggestion of a son named Bêlûn. – *UA* nm6970

Cephilus a warrior in Alexander's army who finds a spring when they are all parched. He is able to bring a little water in his helmet to Alexander, but the latter will not enjoy what is denied his men and pours the water away. This story is told in the *Epistola Alexandri ad Aristotelem*, and is recounted in Leo (MSS B and S). In both of the Latin versions he is called Zephyrus. – *UA* 21468ff.; *WA* 3526ff.

Zephûs 'her', a name invoked by Keiî.[4] – *C* nm1378

Zidegast (Bartsch suggested a derivation from *Ziti-* (connected with 'Zeit'?) and *gast*, 'stranger'.[5] Brugger sees in this name a distorted form of the German name Liudegast.[6]) Z., who is called 'von Lôgrois', is the husband of Orgelûse, his marriage to whom is related in *JT*. He is slain by Gramoflanz, who is in love with Orgelûse, and the latter, to avenge the death of her husband, places a treasure before the Schastel Marveile and proclaims that she will marry any knight who will brave the perils of the castle. Gramoflanz cannot be

---

1 Greif, pp. 26ff.
2 O. Zingerle, p. 23.
3 Singer (2), p. 108.
4 This name occurs in the middle of a reference to the return of Êrec to Arthur's court with Ênîte, which reads (*C* 1376ff.): 'Ouch mohte wol von rehte gezemen/ Mînem herren, künec Artûs,/ Dô sie kâmen, her Zephûs,/ Daz er sînes küssens reht/ An ir stætem lîbe speht.' The doubtful verse in MS V reads: 'do si kam hern hus', but it seems possible that the original may have been: 'Dô sie kâmen her ze hûs'.
5 Bartsch (2), p. 146.
6 Brugger (1), p. 62.

tempted, however, to undertake the adventure. Z. is not named in Chrestien's *Perceval*. – *P* nm67,15; *JT* nm1733,4 a2074,3

Cignus a warrior whose death, whilst fighting for the Trojans against the Greeks, is lamented but not described. In Dictys, where he is called Cycnus, he is slain by Achilles. – *TKf* nm43400

Cycrops brother of Lestugo. The two brothers, with their two sons, Olifeus and Polifemes, attack Ulixes and his companions during their voyage back from Troy. So also in Benoît and Dictys, where he is called Cyclops. In the *Odyssey*, the Cyclops are a race of one-eyed giants, one of whom, Polyphemus, is blinded by Ulixes. – *LT* nm17571

Cileus 'von Demonîe', a warrior in the Greek army against the Trojans. This character appears to have been invented by Konrad. – *TK* 23826

Cyneras a messenger from Acastus. He is slain by Pirrus. So also in Benoît and Dictys. – *LT* 17995f.

Cyneus a warrior in the Greek army against the Trojans. He is slain by Hector. In Dictys he is called Guneus (MSS G and B: Cyneus) rex Cyphius (see Cîfen). – *TKf* 40475ff.

Zingund a knight who is present at the tourney held by Dymszogar.[7] – *Wigm* nm4782

Zippar counsellor to Agâmennon, who consults him as to a suitable reward for Paris. – *GT* 3725

Zipproner see Ziproner

Ziproner daughter of Jerome and Fridrich (3). She comes to live with Fridrich and Angelburg after they are married, and she is the means of Fridrich's reconciliation with Jerome after Angelburg's death. – *FS* a2920ff. n3003

Zirdôs a giant, son (or nephew) of Malserôn (q.v.). – *G* nm11067ff. a12132f.

Zirell a knight who, with his *amie*, entertains Paris and Cornoysse on their way to India. Z. has to fight Monagris, who kills him but is himself slain by Paris. – *GT* 8138ff.

Zirelld, Zirheddus see Zirell

Zirijôn a giant, brother of Malserôn (q.v.). – *G* nm11067ff. a12132f.

Zirilon see Zîrolân

Zirius see Zirell

Zirculanc see Circulant

Circulant 'von Ciglodonie', a warrior who is slain whilst fighting for Akarîn against Ipomidôn. – *JT* nm3112,3 a3901,3

Zîrolân 'künec von Semblidac', a knight whom Parzivâl claims to have defeated. In *JT*, Zironale von Seimdalke appears as one of the knights at Arthur's tourney, whilst as Zirilon von Samilidacke he fights for Akarîn against Ipomidôn. – *P* nm772,10; *JT* 2142,6f.

Ciron see Cheiron

Zironale see Zîrolân

Ziropol counsellor to Agâmennon, who consults him as to a suitable reward for Paris. – *GT* 3728

Cirrus natural son of Priam. C. fights for the Trojans against the Greeks. In Benoît he is called Chirrus, a name which, according to Greif, is probably derived from Ce(b)riones, which occurs in Hyginus.[8] – *LT* a4808 n4822

Cyrus (1) the Great, the first king of Persia. – nm *A* 5609; *UA* 974ff.; *SA* 3229; *WA* 2768

---

[7] The text at this point in *Wigm* is obviously corrupt, 4782f. reading: 'Zingund und Lyplagar / Hat da manigen ritter schnell.' This is possibly a corruption of Zingund von Lyplagar, but the latter name (q.v.) occurs elsewhere in the poem.

[8] Greif, pp. 26ff.

Zirus (2) 'der margriss', a knight who is slain by Ybrot whilst fighting for Agâmennon against Gamorett. – *GT* 5751

Zirusz see Zirus (2)

Circe the famous sorceress with whom Ulixes spends a long time during his return voyage from Troy. – *LT* nm16222ff.

Cis 'grâve von Arragus', a knight who attends the tourney held by Arthur. – *C* 611

Zitegast see Zidegast

Ziphar a squire in the service of Samlon, to whom he takes Hector. – *GT* a292 n306

Cîfen a warrior who is slain by Hector whilst fighting for the Greeks against the Trojans. This character rests on a misunderstanding of Dictys, where it is stated: 'Guneus (see Cyneus) interfectus rex Cyphius', i.e. Guneus king of Cyphius was killed. – *TKf* 40480f.

Cicillanor natural son of Priam. C. fights for the Trojan army against the Greeks. So also in Benoît. – *LT* 4661f.

Zlâwat 'von Valkenstein', a knight who welcomes Ulrich von Liechtenstein to Neustadt during his *Artusfahrt*. – *FD* 1484,5

Zloidas a knight who attends the tourney held by Leigamar. – *C* 18045

Zôlus a warrior who joins Alexander with an army of Greeks just before the attack on Bessus. In Curtius Rufus he is called Zoilus. – *A* 18719

Zorcas 'vürste von Êgyptô', a warrior who wounds Alexander at the battle of Issôn and is himself wounded by Meleâger. He is trampled to death by the armies. – *UA* 8352f.

Zôrôastêr 'künec von Arâbîe', a knight whom Feirefîz claims to have defeated. In *JT*, where he is referred to by his title only, he is one of the knights who take part in the tourney which is held by Sekundille to decide which of her wooers she shall marry. Martin points out that this name occurs in Solinus (18,6 etc.).[9] – *P* nm770,19; *JT* a5280,2

Zorobabêl biblical (Zerubbabel), the re-builder of the Temple at Jerusalem. – nm *A* 9959; *UA* 11795

Zot see Lôt (1)

Zukander 'von Genalî', called 'der Raspær', brother-in-law to Bêonet. Z. fights for Lôis against Terramêr. – *UW* 37,12f.

---

9 Martin (1), p. 504, to 770,19.

APPENDIX

This appendix provides notes on a number of names of particular difficulty and interest. Their purpose is to clarify and correct entries in the catalogue in cases where this could not be done without a radical revision of the original text. The names treated are, in the main, ones which are known to be in some way problematical and which have been the subject of discussion by commentators; for this reason, too, it seemed appropriate to give them separate consideration.

It will come as no surprise to anyone with an interest in medieval German literary names that these notes refer to names in the works of Wolfram von Eschenbach. Wolfram's practice with names, not least his penchant for creating doublets, deriving two names for distinct persons from one name (usually that of one person) present in his source, has been a cause of considerable confusion both for medieval scribes and modern scholars. All but the last of the notes concern names in *Willehalm*, for which text Chandler takes as his principal authority the study by Samuel Singer, *Wolframs 'Willehalm'* (Bern, 1918). As Chandler observes in his entry for Krôhier, Singer's comments on specific instances are at times coloured by the conception of Wolfram's relationship to his source which he wished to promote. More objective accounts of the names in *Willehalm* are available today in the studies by Werner Schröder and Charles E. Passage, with which the information in the catalogue has been compared. In the following notes, these studies are indicated in abbreviated form, 'Schröder' referring to *Wolfram von Eschenbach: 'Willehalm'*, ed. by Werner Schröder (Berlin/New York, 1978), pp. 617–63: Register B. Die Namen, and 'Passage' to *The Middle High German Poem of Willehalm by Wolfram of Eschenbach*, transl. by Charles E. Passage (New York, 1977), pp. 318–404: List of 434 Proper Names in *Willehalm*.

(1)   **Grôhier von Nomadjentesîn** and **Krôhier von Oupatrîe**. These names have correctly been taken by Chandler, in opposition to Singer, to refer to two distinct persons (cf. Schröder, p. 627 (Crohir), p. 633; Passage, p. 335 (Crohier), p. 347, pp. 371–72 (Oupatrie)).

(2)   **Talimôn (1), künec von Boctân,** and **Talimôn (2), künec von Valpinôse.** It is argued by Chandler, again explicitly in opposition to Singer, that two persons named Talimôn must be distinguished. This accords with the findings of Schröder (p. 655 (Talimon/ Thalimon), p. 658 (Thalimon)) and Passage (p. 390), but Chandler differs from these scholars in taking the Talimôn of *W* 33,15, who is not associated with any kingdom at that point, to be Talimôn von Valpinôse rather than Talimôn von Boctân (whom he therefore regards as being first named in *W* 56,18). The reason for this identification is not stated, but it may be presumed that the case rests on the observation that the Talimôn of *W* 33,15 occurs in company with three other kings, Pohereiz, Korsâz, and Rûbûâl, all of whom are under the command of Josweiz, and that these kings (for the possible identification of Korsâz and Korsant, see the following note) are named again with Talimôn, now called 'der künec von Valpinôse', in *W* 349,19–30, and with 'der künec von Valpinôse' in *W* 387,16–24, all four kings being under the command of Josweiz in both these instances as well.

(3)   **Korsant** and **Korsâz**. Chandler regards the first of these forms as a variant of the second, both therefore signifying one person. The form Korsâz is chosen as the headword, although it is attested only once (*W* 33,14) against the three occurrences of Korsant (*W* 97,20; 349,19; 387,19). Schröder registers two distinct persons here (p. 627 (Corsaz) and p. 633 (Gorsant)), whereas Passage (p. 357) agrees with Chandler in regarding them as one person but uses the form Korsant as the headword. The identification of the names can be entertained on similar grounds to those considered in the preceding note, in so far as the 'same' quartet of

kings appears in three of the four passages where the name Korsant/Korsâz occurs, while in the remaining passage (*W* 97,20) Korsant is coupled with one of the four, Pohereiz. For a possible explanation of Korsant as a variant of Korsâz, see Fritz Peter Knapp, 'Der Lautstand der Eigennamen im *Willehalm* und das Problem von Wolframs "Schriftlosigkeit"' (*Wolfram-Studien*, 2 (1974), 193–218): 'Sollte Wolfram etwa *Corsant* als Obliquus zu *Corsas* (in falscher Analogie zu Fällen wie *enfes-enfant*) gebildet haben?' (p. 202, n. 44).

(4) **Gîbert (2), Schilbert (1),** and **Schilbert (2)**. Schröder (pp. 633–34 (Gybert)) documents the confusion which exists in the manuscripts between the forms Gîbert and Schilbert. Both names are derived from Guibert (d'Andernas), which is the basis for Chandler's observation that Gîbert (2) is 'identical with Schilbert (1)'; as Chandler clearly demonstrates in the entry for Schilbert (1), the names refer to separate characters (cf. Passage, pp. 344 and 385). The entry for Schilbert (2), with cross-reference to Gîbert (2), arises from *W* 146,19, where Schilbert (the reading overwhelmingly supported by the manuscripts) erroneously stands for Gîbert. (See Gunda Dittrich, '"Gybert" und "Schilbert" im *Willehalm*', *Wolfram-Studien*, 2 (1974), 185–92.)

(5) **Oukidant** and **Oquidant**. It is evident from Wolfram's account of the disposition of Terramêr's forces for the second battle at Alischanz that the King of Imanzîe and the King of Nôrûn are separate persons (see Schröder, p. 646 (Oquidant, Oukidant); Passage, p. 371). Chandler's conflation of the two characters no doubt arose from the fact that Leitzmann in his edition of *Willehalm* gives both these kings the same name, viz. Oukidant, whereas the Lachmann and Schröder editions, reflecting the manuscript evidence, distinguish between Oquidant of Imanzîe (*W* 356, 10f.) and Oukidant of Nôrûn (*W* 359,2). It is Oquidant of Imanzîe who assists in the arming of Terramêr, while Oukidant of Nôrûn is slain by Rennewart. Both names are derived from OF Malquidant.

(6) **Samirant (1)**. As in the preceding instance, it is clear that there are two kings of this name, distinguished by their kingdoms and the place which they are assigned in Terramêr's army in the second battle at Alischanz. Samirant, King of Boitendroit (*W* 356,19), assists in the arming of Terramêr, presenting him with his helmet, and is positioned to his right, while Samirant, King of Beâterre (*W* 359,1), is positioned to Terramêr's left and is killed in the course of the battle by Rennewart. (See Schröder, pp. 652–53; Passage, p. 384.)

(7) **Ankî** and **Oukîn**. Chandler's entry for Oukîn is correct except for the identification of this figure with Ankî. Ankî, who makes no appearance in the work and is mentioned and named on only two occasions (*W* 36,24 and 351,12), is a heathen king and father of a Poidwîz but not of the Poidwîz, king of Râbes, who is the son of Oukîn (see next note). Oukîn is first mentioned and named in *W* 411,11 and first appears in *W* 420,25. (See Schröder, p. 620 (Anchi) and pp. 646–47; Passage, pp. 322 and 371.)

(8) **Poidjus, Poidwîz (1),** and **Poidwîz (2)**. The confusions concerning these three names are prodigious and notorious. They arise in part from the derivation of all three names from the same OF name, Baudus, which is used of several persons in *Aliscans*, and in part from uncertainty in the manuscripts of *W*; they are compounded by the conflation of Ankî and Oukîn noted above. Passage (pp. 375–77) gives a full account of the difficulties (cf. Schröder, pp. 648–49). It must suffice here to summarize the consensual view of the modern commentators, which is that three persons are to be distinguished:

    (a) Poidjus, heathen king of five lands, a kinsman of Terramêr; he participates in the first battle at Alischanz; in the second battle he commands the fifth Saracen battalion; he appears and is named for the first time in *W* 36,8.

(b) Poidwîz (1), king of Râbes, son of Oukîn, commander of the eighth Saracen battalion in the second battle at Alischanz; he slays Kîûn (1) and is slain by Heimrîch (2); he appears and is named for the first time in *W* 350,12.

(c) Poidwîz (2), son of Ankî, he participates in the first battle at Alischanz; in the second battle he fights in the ninth Saracen battalion under the command of Marlanz; he appears and is named for the first time in *W* 36,24.

(9)   **The fifteen Saracen kings who attack Willehalm.** The fifteen Saracen kings (*W* 71,21f.; 72,17f.) who attack Willehalm as he makes his way from the battlefield at Alischanz to Orange are named in *W* 73,17–74,25. Chandler correctly noted that Willehalm inflicts bloody wounds on each of his adversaries in this incident apart from **Ehmereiz**, with whom he refuses to engage in combat on account of his being Gîburc's son (W 74,26–75,2). However, the further information provided by Wolfram – that while eight of the kings were able to flee from the scene of the encounter, seven remained there dead (*W* 75,30–76,2) – appears to have escaped Chandler's attention. All his original entries for these persons recorded that they were wounded by Willehalm, with the exception of that for **Ehmereiz** (correctly) and that for **Akarîn (2)** (which, presumably by an oversight, omitted specific mention of the incident altogether). The question as to which of the fourteen kings with whom Willehalm engages in combat (**Ehmereiz** is excluded) were killed and which only wounded is answered in three instances – **Akarîn (2)**, **Kursaus**, and **Tampastê (2)** – by their later appearance in the work, and the amended entries for these names include information which justifies the conclusion that they were wounded and fled. In the remaining instances, certainty eludes us. Werner Schröder addresses this problem, along with others of a similar nature, in his important essay 'Der Markgraf und die gefallenen Heidenkönige in Wolframs *Willehalm*' (in *Festschrift für Konstantin Reichardt*, ed. by Christian Gellinek (Bern/Munich, 1969), pp. 135–67, here pp. 146–48), and he tentatively suggests, on the basis of a comparison with *Aliscans*, that the kings who are slain may be identified as **Mattahel, Gastablê, Korsudê, Frâbel, Hastê, Embrons**, and **Joswê**. In the list of names appended to his edition, however, Schröder is less tentative, stating in all seven cases that the king is killed by Willehalm in this encounter. Since the evidence is inconclusive, the amended entries in the catalogue for these seven kings and for the remaining four whose fate is not clear – **Gôrîax, Haukauus, Bûr**, and **Korsublê** – describe them as having been 'wounded or killed by Willehalm'.

(10)   **Ehkunat and Ehkunaver.** There is little room for doubt that Chandler was mistaken in identifying the Ehkunat of *P* and *T* 42,1, who is the brother of Mahaute and the slayer of Kingrisîn, with the Ehkunat of *T* 151,1, who is the *ami* of Klauditte (2). It is the latter figure alone – 'Ehkunat de Salvâsche Flôrîen' – who is referred to in the 'German' form of 'Ehkunaver von Bluomederwilde'. The position is clearly set out in Werner Schröder, *Die Namen im 'Parzival' und im 'Titurel' Wolframs von Eschenbach* (Berlin/New York, 1982), pp. 29–30, with references to discussions of this question. That misgivings about the separation of the two figures have not, however, been entirely removed is demonstrated by the comments of Charles E. Passage, *Titurel: Wolfram of Eschenbach. Translation and Studies* (New York, 1984), pp. 80–83 and 168–70.

319